Girdler

WHAT OTHERS ARE SAYING ABOUT
SOUL PHYSICIANS

"*Soul Physicians* is a great and unique book: deeply shaped by Scripture; promoting of a personal engagement with biblical teaching and with Christ; challenging and focused against sin; but practical, gentle in spirit, and discerning in method and counseling skill. The book itself exemplifies what a biblical counselor should be like. Its use of a redemptive-historical structure (creation-fall-redemption-consummation) alone is worth the price of the book, since the value of this framework has not yet been fully realized in Christian counseling. It should be widely used in counseling programs and local churches that value the Bible."

Eric Johnson, *Ph.D., Professor of Pastoral Theology and Biblical Psychology*
The Southern Baptist Theological Seminary

"Dr. Kellemen's book came as a great refreshment to me. It was both clear and comprehensive, elucidating a theological foundation for counseling ministry based on a solid biblical hermeneutic. This book is beneficial for a multitude of audiences: from the lay counselor, to the pastor, to the licensed clinician. Its impact is to clarify the need, mandate, and roots of personal ministry taken from the Word of the One who created all.

"*Soul Physicians* addresses all the imperative issues of our fallen and redeemed state without trying to simplify the complexities of sanctification. It should not be considered merely a textbook contribution to the literature on biblical counseling, but instead a foundation for a curriculum. I require it for all my biblical counseling students."

Lynelle Buchanan, *Professor of Counseling,* Baptist Bible College

"*Soul Physicians* is an excellent resource for counselors, pastors and students who believe that knowing and loving people in our world begins with knowing and loving God and His Word. The confluence of Dr. Kellemen's comprehensive grasp of the story of redemption in Scripture and his practical wisdom about people with problems makes this book a unique and important contribution for those that want to counsel from a distinctively Christian perspective."

Sam R. Williams, *Ph.D., Professor of Counseling*
Southeastern Baptist Theological Seminary

"In *Soul Physicians*, Robert W. Kellemen explores seven key biblical categories for developing a theology of soul care and spiritual direction. The result is a thoroughly biblical systematic theology written with the insights and illustrations of a mental health professional—appropriately constructed against the backdrop of a relational emphasis. I highly recommend this book as an important reference for evangelical pastors, counselors (both professional and lay), and other soul care providers."

Gary W. Moon, *M.Div., Ph.D., Vice President and Chair of Integration,*
Psychological Studies Institute, *Author of* Falling for God

"*Soul Physicians* is no naïve verse-to-issue, sin-to-solution, mix-and-match biblical counseling reference. This is rich theology relayed in readable terms for grace-based care as shared by a stellar scholar-teacher. Soul care worthy of the title 'Christian' must address the core of *shalom*, the cancer of *shame*, and the destiny of the *sacred*. *Soul Physicians* passionately brings that holistic biblical redemptive story line to bear on the everyday life stories common in the practice of discipleship, Christian counseling, and spiritual formation."

Stephen P. Greggo, *PhD., Professor of Counseling,*
Trinity Evangelical Divinity School

"*Soul Physicians* offers theological depth leading to personal maturity. It unlocks a systematic, exhilarating understanding of how God created us to relate, think, choose, and feel in an imperfect world as redeemed Christians. Providing a myriad of scriptural tools, *Soul Physicians* equipped me to understand suffering and sin, enabling me to connect with people who are impacted by the evils of suffering and with those who are dealing with personal sin issues. In *Soul Physicians*, Dr. Kellemen shares his years of experience, diligent research, and dependence on the Spirit to endow counselors, pastors, students, and lay people with a scriptural blueprint to become more soul aware and, in turn, empower others with God's profound grace."

Robin Shell, *Graduate Counseling Student*

"In *Soul Physicians*, Dr. Kellemen captures the essence of delivering practical ministry in the real world. His teachings are applicable to the 'every member a minister' approach to caring for others, as well as being foundational for the professional Christian counselor. This material has enabled me to incorporate solid biblical principles into my counseling practice."

Melvin Pride, *Director of Strategic Planning,*
Southern Baptist Convention of Maryland and Delaware

"The tremendous issues that people face today call for a work that skillfully guides those who labor in helping Christians reach maturity in Christ. *Soul Physicians* meets that need and will be of great value to pastors, professional Christian counselors, students, and lay people. Dr. Kellemen's credentials both in the theological world and the world of counseling make him uniquely qualified to produce a work like *Soul Physicians*. His work will prove to be invaluable in the field of Christian counseling."

Dr. Homer Heater, Jr., *President Emeritus,* Washington Bible College

"Personally, I can attest to the challenge of facing deep hurts and overcoming them through the use and application of *Soul Physicians'* principles. Professionally, as a biblical counselor, pastor's wife, and teacher, God has allowed me to use *Soul Physicians* as an equipping tool to mentor women. My classes using these concepts have now included over 400 women who testify that *Soul Physicians* deepened their personal maturity and equipped them to more powerfully minister to others."

—Sister Ellen Barney, *Women's Ministry Director,*
New Antioch Baptist Church

"*Soul Physicians* is a 'theological breath of fresh air.' This comprehensive guide offers a wealth of knowledge that translates theology into everyday human relationships. It catapults the reader into confidently connecting with people soul-to-soul. My life and ministry will never be the same after reading *Soul Physicians*."

Pastor Dwayne Bond, *Counseling Pastor,* Woodstream Church

"*Soul Physicians* captures the essence of Christian soul care and spiritual direction. A unique balance of biblical theology and compassionate spiritual friendship makes *Soul Physicians* vital for the pastor, Christian counselor, or student of counseling. *Soul Physicians* will revolutionize the study of counseling at higher learning institutions that embrace the Christian worldview in their counseling programs."

Douglas McCracken, *Professional Christian Counselor,*
Safe Harbor Counseling

"*Soul Physicians* revives the timeless tradition of soul care in the Christian community. If you are longing for a deeper relationship with the Lord and others, read on. If you desire to see others as God sees them, keep reading. If you want to relate God's Word to suffering and sinning as you interact with image bearers, *Soul Physicians* is for you. If you're willing to allow God to pierce your heart with His holiness and grace, then *Soul Physicians* will transform you and those you encounter."

Susan Ellis, *Author of* Sacred Friendships

"*Soul Physicians* swaps shop-worn theology for biblically sound, compassionate soul care. Dr. Bob Kellemen skillfully invites readers into the huddle where academic theology is spelled out and onto the field where practical theology is lived out. It's a privilege to endorse such a fine work."

Tammy Schultz, *Ph.D., LMHC; Department Chair,*
Graduate School in Counseling, Grace College

"The information in *Soul Physicians*, the perspective it gives on life, and the passion with which it is written has been the catalyst for my walk with Christ soaring to an entirely new level. The framework for life it presents has deepened my understanding of who Jesus is and provided me a clearer picture of God's plan for my personal life and pastoral ministry. It has greatly enhanced my understanding of people and equipped me to powerfully minister to them."

Pastor John Heater, *Youth Pastor,* Forcey Memorial Church

"Not only is *Soul Physicians* based upon solid exegesis and deep theological convictions, it is also presented creatively and insightfully. God will use these truths to transform readers into greater lovers of God and better lovers of God's people. Personally, I 'understood' truth before I was introduced to these concepts, but now God is giving me His heart through *Soul Physicians*. Undoubtedly, I am more like Jesus and better equipped to minister for Jesus because of *Soul Physicians*."

Chris Boucher, *Counseling Professor,* Capital Bible Seminary

"As a pastor and a church planter, I resonate with the major theme found in *Soul Physicians*—how to change lives with God's changeless truth. The principles found in *Soul Physicians* are so practical and life-giving that I am using them in the foundation of our church plant. Solidly biblical and refreshingly relational, Bob combines his wealth of experience as a pastor, shepherd, coach, and counselor with his strong exegetical skills to outline an easily understandable theology of counseling that masterfully addresses the human soul's need for healing from both suffering and sin."

Pastor Tom Gill, *Church Planter,* Life in the Balance Ministries

"I read *Soul Physicians* expecting to learn many facts that I would need to become an excellent Christian counselor. God's plans were that and so much more. He used *Soul Physicians* to speak truth into the deepest regions of my heart. It is naïve of us to plan to make an impact on those who are hurting, and hurting others, without first dealing with those parts of ourselves. *Soul Physicians* gave me a thorough knowledge of the subject, an increased self-awareness, and a realization of the many sensitive areas I face as I minister to God's people. *Soul Physicians* is an apt title for a work that so eloquently presents the application of the Word of God to human suffering and sin."

Terri Polm, *Lay Counselor*

SOUL
PHYSICIANS

SOUL PHYSICIANS

A Theology of
Soul Care and Spiritual Direction

ROBERT W. KELLEMEN, PH.D.

BMH BOOKS
WINONA LAKE, IN
www.bmhbooks.com

Soul Physicians
Revised Edition Copyright © 2007 by Robert W. Kellemen
ISBN: 978-0-88469-255-3

Published by BMH Books
P.O. Box 544, Winona Lake, IN 46590
www.bmhbooks.com

The personal identities of the individuals described in this book
have been disguised in order to protect their privacy.

Kellemen, Robert W.
Soul physicians: a theology of soul care and spiritual direction / Robert W. Kellemen.
Includes bibliographic references and index.

ISBN: 978-0-88469-255-3
Library of Congress Control Number: 2005900658

1. Pastoral counseling—Biblical teaching. 2. Spiritual life—Christianity.
3. Bible—Psychology.
253.5—dc 22

Printed in the United States of America

CONTENTS

FOREWORD

As today's generation searches wildly for meaning, purpose, and value, many are experiencing a pervasive sense of emptiness and loneliness. Dazed by a life that is "not the way it is supposed to be," the persistent cry of the soul is for *relief* from the pain and press of our day. The truth is that as a society we will stop at nothing to find peace. Untold millions are needlessly taking prescription medication, and we are flooded with escapism through drugs, alcohol, consumerism, sexual promiscuity, violence, and even suicide.

Tranquilized by the trivial, we are still empty. I agree with Dallas Willard, "…obviously the problem is spiritual and so must be the cure."

While it seems to be the worst of times, something seems to be happening across America—people are searching for God. According to a recent Gallup poll, 82 percent of Americans desire a more intimate relationship with God. That's the good news. The bad news is that so much of what is being offered in the modern-day church is a message that we can trust God for salvation *but not for everyday life*.

What I have loved since a child was the unwavering affection my Baptist preacher father had for God and His Word. He meditated in it both day and night, yearning to divide rightly the "Word of Truth" to anyone who would lend an ear. Like the many parishioners he served, it took me awhile (I'm still learning) to understand that "the word of God is quick, and powerful, and sharper than any twoedged sword, piercing even to the dividing asunder of soul and spirit, and of the joints and marrow, and is a discerner of the thoughts and intents of the heart" (Hebrews 4:12, KJV). Even more, what I have loved about my dad is that he is an *everyday theologian*. He trusts God for everyday life—that God is the great Physician and from Him flow the words of life, "our guide even unto death" (Psalm 48:14, KJV).

As president of the 50,000-member American Association of Christian Counselors, I have noticed a growing hunger among counselors, pastors, and lay people for the deeper things of God. There is a strong movement to bring Him alive in the counseling office, the pastor's study, and in everyday spiritual friendship.

That's why I am so pleased that Dr. Bob Kellemen, like my father, has a passion for nourishing the hungry soul with the Word of God. While wonderful directions are taking place in and through Christian counseling, we have been guilty, at times, of running far ahead of our biblical and theological roots. Bob writes with a confidence that our peace, freedom, victory, and wholeness in life are to be found in and grounded upon our Master and *His truth applied to everyday life*.

What scares me about counseling and pastoral care is that when we read and uncritically accept the writings and teaching on personality and counseling from a non-Christian perspective, we are often tainted and influenced to pull together assumptions, values, and techniques that are inconsistent with our faith. Such unbiblical teachings and even hostile writings can lead us to promote or tolerate ideas in opposition to Scripture. Hence we enable people to live lives devoid of God. Even more, we often don't recognize the assumptions that underlie much of the contemporary writings in counseling and psychology. That's why we desperately need a work like *Soul Physicians*. May God use it to carefully guide us in our quest to know and apply His truth.

My prayer is that you will be refreshed by *Soul Physicians*. Through Bob's work, may you more fully learn to think theologically, serve faithfully, and live more authentically as you offer Christ's changeless truth to broken lives.

> *O the depth of the riches both of the wisdom and knowledge of God! How unsearchable are his judgments, and his ways past finding out! For who hath known the mind of the Lord? Or who hath been his counselor? Or who hath first given to him, and it shall be recompensed unto him again? For of him, and through him, and to him, are all things: to whom be glory for ever. Amen* (Romans 11:33-36, KJV).

Blessings,
Dr. Tim Clinton, President,
American Association of Christian Counselors

Acknowledgments

Partners on My Journey

My wife, Shirley, has been my life partner for more than a quarter-century. If any human being embodies unconditional love, she does. Shirley has artfully sustained, healed, reconciled, and guided my faith in ways beyond description and in times beyond numbering. No one I have ever met depicts and dispenses grace like Shirley. Thank you, Shirley, for living out your faith with compassion and sensitivity.

My son, Josh, has demonstrated wisdom from God far beyond his years. If any human being embodies a hunger for truth, he does. Josh has valiantly entered life's grand adventure, his tenacity empowering me to fight the good fight of faith. Thank you, Josh, for living out your faith with insight and courage.

My daughter, Marie, has enveloped my life with the joy of Jesus. If any human being embodies gentleness and kindness in relationships, she does. Marie has jubilantly entered life's passionate love story, her sweetness encouraging me to learn to love well. Thank you, Marie, for living out your faith with tenderness and selflessness.

Lay leaders at four churches (Church of the Open Door, Uniontown Bible Church, Fredericktowne Baptist Church, and Westminster Bible Church) have been my thinking and training companions over the past twenty-five years. Thank you for grappling with me concerning how to ponder and practice soul care and spiritual direction in the local church.

Graduate students at Capital Bible Seminary have stimulated my thinking and sharpened my saw for more than a decade. Thank you for stretching me and for helping me to think through the most powerful ways to present these practical truths.

The following graduate students at Capital Bible Seminary have sacrificed their time and energy to shape *Soul Physicians*: Bobby Baden, Carole Boucher, Tracy Bumgarner, Karen L. Curry, Susan Ellis, Kirstin Kimmel, Josephine Lee, Leighera Leffin, Daniel P. Miller, Olivia Scruggs Pilson, Jane Putnam, Tom and Susanne Rose, and Patrick Walker. My incredible editor, Lynn Vernon, examined the manuscript with diligence and excellence. Though any lingering faults are mine alone, without these individuals *Soul Physicians* would have been impossible. Thank you for using your specialized talents and precious time to assist in the development of this project.

Most importantly, I thank the Lord of the journey. We've had a few titanic wrestling matches over the years. *You've done a "Jacob on my hip" leaving me lame, limping, and eventually surrendered to your Lordship. In my weakness, you have shown yourself not only strong, but also restful. I can't wait for the day when I fall before you in worship, leap onto your lap for an eternal embrace, and jump into your arms for a longed for high-five.*

INTRODUCTION

CHANGING LIVES WITH CHRIST'S CHANGELESS TRUTH

"A lot of Christian psychology is theologically bankrupt. We haven't struggled with the great themes of the Christian gospel. We've been pragmatic. We try to help people with their emotions, but we don't have a theology of emotions" (Archibald Hart, quoted in Tim Stafford, "The Therapeutic Revolution: How Christian Counseling Is Changing the Church," *Christianity Today,* May 13, 1993, p. 26).

"From the beginning, God's Word was a necessary factor in human existence; that need did not begin with the fall. Man does not (and did not) live by bread alone; life requires a Word from the mouth of God" (Jay Adams, *More Than Redemption: A Theology of Christian Counseling*, p. 2).

"Releasing the energy of Christ is enhanced by thinking through biblical categories for understanding people, their problems, and what can be done to help" (Larry Crabb, *Connecting*, p. 182).

Their Story

Christians once knew how to relate God's truth to human relationships. Then, as if an evil spell had been cast on the church, Christians abdicated their calling, allowing it to be abducted by aliens. These aliens, separated from the life of God, claiming the mantle of relevancy, built great soulless soul physician schools and proceeded to prescribe cures for soul sickness. Meanwhile, vanquished Christians erected academies that dissected God's truth, but ignored human relationships.

Soul Physicians returns us to our heritage as students both of the *Scriptures* and of the *soul*. Its purpose is to infuse biblical counseling with Christian theology to equip the body of Christ to change lives with Christ's changeless truth.

This call is not new. As long ago as 1964, William Clebsch and Charles Jaekle recognized the history of Christian soul care and identified a modern shift away from theologically informed spiritual direction.

The Christian ministry of the cure of souls, or pastoral care, has been exercised on innumerable occasions and in every conceivable human circumstance, as it has aimed to relieve a plethora of perplexities besetting persons of every class and condition and mentality. Pastors rude and barely plucked from paganism, pastors sophisticated in the theory and practice of their profession, and pastors at every stage of adeptness between these extremes, have sought and wrought to help troubled people overcome their troubles. To view pastoral care in historical perspective is to survey a vast endeavor, to appreciate a noble profession, and to receive a grand tradition (Clebsch and Jaekle, *Pastoral Care in Historical Perspective*, p. 1).

The church has always ministered to hurting and hardened people. Recently, however, we've experienced a radical shift. We've lost our confidence in the relevancy and potency of Christ's gospel of grace.

Faced with an urgency for some system by which to conceptualize the human condition and to deal with the modern grandeurs and terrors of the human spirit, theoreticians of the cure of souls have too readily adopted the leading academic psychologies. Having no pastoral theology to inform our psychology or even to identify the cure of souls as a mode of human helping, we have allowed psychoanalytic thought, for example, to dominate the vocabulary of the spirit (Clebsch and Jaekle, p. xii).

Past generations crafted their counseling models from pastoral theology—a biblical theology that produced practical methods to relate God's truth to human life. Today we tend to borrow counseling models from our secular society.

As a result, we've lost the trail of those who journeyed before us. They blazed their trail with the words "truth" and "love." Our predecessors followed a thoughtful biblical theology and a loving pastoral methodology. We tend to wander off on one path or the other. Some of us are very loving; we relate well to people, but we don't adequately relate God's truth to people's lives. Others of us are quite truth-oriented; we know a lot about God, but we don't know how to relate His Word to our world adequately. It's time for us to rediscover our way.

My Story

As chairman of a seminary Christian counseling and discipleship program, I interview prospective counseling faculty. I'm saddened by how few think theologically. When asked to share the essence of their approach to soul care and spiritual direction, they are unable to explain how their theology supports their counseling. Some describe secular models and sprinkle in Scripture. Others discuss how a specific biblical passage might apply to a specific issue. The second response might seem theologically informed, but it tends to maintain a "one-verse-one-problem" mindset, rather than grappling with how to formulate a biblical approach to Christian counseling.

Some may be thinking, *Great, another academician/theologian who thinks he can tell practitioners how to practice!* Or, *Theology—that dry as dust, cold, sterile exploration of truth—doesn't help when yet another depressed person sits in front of me. It doesn't help when I counsel someone trapped in the web of pornography.*

A quarter-century ago I was forced to wrestle with the relationship between theology and counseling. As a Bible college graduate and seminary student, I accepted a job as a mental health counselor on a psychiatric inpatient unit. From day one I realized that I did not understand how to relate the Greek, Hebrew, Bible, and theology that I was learning to the struggles these folks were facing. I was convinced then, as I am now, that the problem was not with the Bible, but with my inability to understand how to relate the Bible to people's lives. How do we change lives with God's changeless truth? How do we relate God's truth to human relationships? What is the bridge between the Scriptures and the soul or society?

The book that you hold in your hands is the 25-year culmination of my quest to address these questions. I have doggedly pursued the fundamental question: *What would a model of biblical counseling and discipleship that was built solely upon Christ's gospel of grace look like?* What does the gospel offer? What difference does the gospel make in how we live, how we relate, and how we offer help? *Soul Physicians* is my presentation of a theology of counseling—a gospel-centered, grace-focused model of soul care and spiritual direction.

God's Story

Theology has laryngitis. "The Bible seems to have lost its voice not only in the wider society but, more significantly, even in the community of Christ" (Stanley Grenz and John Franke, *Beyond Foundationalism*, p. 58). This is true of modern Christian counseling that has effectively relegated theology to the sidelines. We are "people of the Book" who need to learn how to read the Book with confidence that theology is God's story that gives meaning to our individual and group stories.

We must relate God's truth to human relationships by infusing biblical counseling with four types of Christian theology: academic, historical, spiritual, and practical. By investigating and integrating these four theologies, we learn how to use God's changeless Word to change lives. Box I:1 outlines that method. My hope in following this procedure is to present in *Soul Physicians*:

- ◆ An *academic* theology that provides us with a way of thinking about life God's way—His perspective on our daily lives and personal relationships. I want us to develop the conviction that biblical counseling is the intersection of God's old, old story and our very post-modern story.
- ◆ An *historical* theology that gives a voice and vote to past perspectives and practices in caring for souls. I want us to reclaim the forgotten art of ancient soul care and spiritual direction.
- ◆ A *spiritual* theology of life that re-ignites our first love for Christ and equips us to become soul physicians who dispense Christ's grace to heal people's disgrace. I want us to relate God's truth to human relationships.
- ◆ A *practical* theology of biblical counseling that equips us to deal with suffering and sin as Christ would. I want us to be able to sustain, heal, reconcile, and guide people's faith in a biblically faithful and personally fruitful manner.

Box I:1

Relating God's Truth to Human Relationships:
Infusing Biblical Counseling with Christian Theology

Academic Theology: **Foundation—Information/Meaning**
What? **—Content and Conviction from God's Perspective**
    Systematic Theology
    Biblical Theology
    Exegetical Theology
    Lexical Theology
    Contextual Theology

Historical Theology: **Forebears—Validation/Humility**
What Then? **—Church History and Contribution of Our Predecessors**
    Historical Perspective
    Historical Practice

Spiritual Theology: **Formation—Transformation/Wisdom**
So What? **—Categories and Constructs for Personal Relevance**
    Personal Implications
    Life Applications

Practical Theology: **Friendship—Ministry Application/Love**
What Now? **—Care and Cure through Personal Relationship**
    Soul Care: Sustaining and Healing
    Spiritual Direction: Reconciling and Guiding

Your Story

You would not be reading *Soul Physicians* unless you embraced my passion to speak God's truth in love. We share the conviction that the Scriptures are our guidebook for spiritual growth and spiritual friendship. My prayer for you is the same as the Apostle Paul's prayer for his friends in Philippi.

And this is my prayer: that your love may abound more and more in knowledge and depth of insight, so that you may be able to discern what is best and may be pure and blameless until the day of Christ, filled with the fruit of righteousness that comes through Jesus Christ—to the glory and praise of God (Philippians 1:9-11)

Love is not enough. Truth is not enough. *Love and truth must kiss.* When our love abounds in depth of insight, we are able to discern what is best so our lives are pure, our ministries are fruitful, and our worship is delightful.

Paul is excited. It is as if he says, "I'm praying that your love very much exceedingly spills over!" The word he uses for "abound" (*perisseuē*) relates to the word used for the abundance remaining after Christ fed the 5,000. It speaks of liberality, lavishness, overabundance, and spoiling. Don't you want to spoil others with Christ's love?

You can if you do it in full knowledge and depth of insight. "Full knowledge" (*epignō sei*) pictures noticing attentively, discerning, fully perceiving, observing, and discovering. That's what God calls soul physicians to do: diligently dig to uncover the buried treasure of truth—the *academic theology*—contained in God's Word.

"Depth of insight" (*aisthēsei*) suggests the experiential use of wisdom—knowledge applied to life. *Spiritual theology* allows us to *spend* our theological treasure wisely. Don't you long to share Christ's changeless truth to change people's lives?

You can. Paul says that love that abounds in knowledge and insight enlightens us to discern what is best and pure. This is *practical theology*—the ability to look at situations with spiritual eyes, to cut to the heart of issues, and to help others scrutinize the will of God in the particulars of their complex, crazy world. Paul says we can learn to do this in a way that is pure and blameless or sincere and unoffending. Don't you want to be able to share truth in a courageous, yet non-offensive way that empowers people to race after God's will?

It takes work, the kind of work we read about in Hebrews 10:24. "And let us consider how we may spur one another on toward love and good deeds." To "consider" (*katanoōmen*) implies studying, pondering, and directing one's mind toward a topic. It encompasses thinking, understanding, grasping, deliberating, and conceptualizing. The author of Hebrews selects an intensifying form of the word picturing immersion into a topic. In classical Greek, the word spoke of the apprehension of a topic through thorough study and scrutiny.

"Wait!" we protest. "This must be for scholars. Not me!" Read on. "Let us not give up meeting together, as some are in the habit of doing, but let us encourage one another" (Hebrews 10:25a). The context is the local church—small house churches meeting together for one anothering. God calls average, ordinary Christians to take seriously the responsibility of pondering thoughtfully how to spur one another on toward maturity.

Why study a theology of biblical counseling? To incite love. God is calling each of us to invigorate, arouse, stir up, fan into flame, intensify, and energize others to love. Isn't that what you long to do?

My purpose is to offer you a way of thinking about life—the gospel way, the grace way, God's way. I want to provide you with a way of relating Christ's gospel of grace to the lives of people filled with disgrace. I want to provide you with a way of thinking about relationships that equips people to be better lovers.

I know that you long for this. You long to know what makes counseling truly Christian. You want to practice uncompromising Christian counseling that relates God's truth to people's daily lives. So join me in a biblical exploration of the art and science of soul care and spiritual direction.

Where We've Been and Where We're Heading

If you are going to read *Soul Physicians*, then you deserve to know my purpose, and now you know.

I also want you to know how personally involved *you* were in the development of my purpose. I pictured you and thousands of people like you as I wrote.

- Committed lay people wanting desperately to know how to help friends and family members.
- Loving pastors longing for training in the *personal* ministry of the Word.
- Competent professional Christian counselors wanting more than anything to practice truly Christian counseling.
- Bible college, Christian liberal arts college, graduate school, and seminary students needing a text that helps them grapple with God's Text and people's context.

Box I:2 offers you my personal *MVP-C Statement* summarizing *Soul Physicians*. It gives you my *M*ission, *V*ision, *P*assion, and *C*ommission statements that drove every word I penned as I prayed for every future reader of *Soul Physicians*.

As you read *Soul Physicians*, you will also need to know where I am headed. You will discover my path in Chapter One, *The Soul Physician's Desk Reference Manual*. Here you will view the core truths that you will learn in "soul school."

At the end of this Introduction, you will encounter two sections that follow each chapter. There is *Caring for Your Soul: Personal Applications*. You can use this section either as an individual or a group study guide, encouraging you to consider how each chapter relates to your life. This is crucial since God's Word must impact us if we are to use it to minister to others.

You will also find *Caring for Others: Ministry Implications*. This volume is theological in nature, but theology is eminently practical. Thus every chapter concludes with implications to help you integrate biblical theology into your biblical counseling.

Box I:2

Soul Physicians' MVP-C Statement

Mission Statement

My mission is to equip you to think biblically
about soul care and spiritual direction
by developing a comprehensive and comprehendible
way of viewing life from God's perspective:
His story of love offered, rejected, and restored,
His story of lovers designed by God, depraved by sin, and dignified by Christ,
His grace-story of our ultimate spiritual friend, Jesus Christ,
who became like us, died for us, and was resurrected
to sustain, heal, reconcile, and guide our faith.

Vision Statement

It is my dream to present passionately a spiritual theology of life
that re-ignites your first love for Christ,
empowers you to relate God's truth to human relationships, and
equips you to become soul physicians who dispense Christ's grace.

Passion Statement

My passion is to infuse biblical counseling with Christian theology to
change lives with Christ's changeless truth.

Commission Statement

You will be enlightened to the four acts in the drama of redemption,
encouraged to become Romancers, Dreamers, Creators, and Singers,
and equipped to sustain, heal, reconcile, and guide,
as you enjoy and dispense Christ's grace.

Caring for Your Soul: Personal Applications

1. Regarding your personal confidence in God's Word:

    a. To what degree do you have confidence in the relevancy and power of God's Word in your life?

    b. How do you demonstrate your confidence in God's Word to help you when you are suffering?

    c. How do you demonstrate your confidence in God's Word to help you to have victory over sin and to grow in sanctification?

2. Concerning Paul's prayer from Philippians 1:9-11:

    And this is my prayer: that your love may abound more and more in knowledge and depth of insight, so that you may be able to discern what is best and may be pure and blameless until the day of Christ, filled with the fruit of righteousness that comes through Jesus Christ—to the glory and praise of God.

    a. What difference would it make in your personal life if you prayed this prayer daily?

    b. What difference would it make in your people-helping ministry if you prayed this prayer daily?

    c. Love and truth must kiss. Which do you tend to emphasize more, love or truth? How? Why?

    d. What does it look like when you spoil others with Christ's love?

    e. What does it look like when you share Christ's changeless truth to change people's lives?

    f. What does it look like when you share truth in a courageous, yet non-offensive way so others are empowered to race after God's will?

Caring for Others: Ministry Implications

♦ **Evaluate Modern Christian Counseling and Spiritual Friendship:** Do you agree or disagree that modern Christian counseling lost its confidence in the relevancy and power of God's Word? How will your answer impact your ministry as a soul physician?

♦ **Evaluate Your Own Counseling and Spiritual Friendship:** To what degree is your counseling theologically informed? What could you do to infuse your soul care and spiritual direction with Christian theology?

♦ **Assess Christian Counseling and Spiritual Friendship:** What makes biblical counseling biblical? What makes soul care and spiritual direction Christian?

♦ **Assess Your Own TQ—Theology Quotient:** What type of theology do you tend toward: academic, historical, spiritual, practical, all of the above, or none of the above? How could you sharpen those theological areas that you tend to minimize?

PROLOGUE:
LOVE'S STORY—NARRATIVE

NOURISHING THE HUNGER OF THE SOUL:
PREVENTATIVE MEDICINE—GOD'S WORD

DIRECTOR'S NOTES

Watching the Broadway musical *Les Misérables* was a moving experience. My wife was familiar with the story from having read Victor Hugo's novel while in high school. I knew little about the plot. So I devoured the *Director's Notes* in the program. They described the background, characters, story line, and plot development scene by scene. From prologue to epilogue, the director sketched the action.

Similarly, I can sketch the action in *Soul Physicians* with four acts sandwiched between a prologue and an epilogue:

PROLOGUE: LOVE'S STORY—NARRATIVE
Nourishing the Hunger of the Soul: Preventative Medicine—God's Word

ACT ONE: LOVE'S ETERNALITY—COMMUNITY
Knowing the Creator of the Soul: The Great Physician—The Trinity

ACT TWO: LOVE'S HONEYMOON—THE ROMANCE
Examining the Spiritual Anatomy of the Soul: People—Creation

ACT THREE: LOVE'S BETRAYAL—THE ADULTERY
Diagnosing the Fallen Condition of the Soul: Problems—Fall

ACT FOUR: LOVE'S TENACITY—THE RECONCILIATION
Prescribing God's Cure for the Soul: Solutions—Redemption

EPILOGUE: LOVE'S DESTINY—THE RESTORATION
Envisioning the Final Healing of the Soul: Home—Glorification

Readers of a certain age may recall television's *The FBI*. Each episode contained a prologue that laid the groundwork for the rest of the story. If you missed it, you were lost. The same is true of the prologue you now read—skip it and you will miss foundational answers to core biblical counseling questions.

- What makes biblical counseling biblical? Chapter 1 overviews the training regimen in the soul physician's education.
- What makes the Bible totally sufficient for life and godliness? Chapter 2 demonstrates that the Bible is God's heroic adventure narrative. Chapter 3 illustrates how the Bible is God's passionate romance novel.

CHAPTER ONE

THE SOUL PHYSICIAN'S DESK REFERENCE MANUAL

"Pastoral care is defective unless it can deal thoroughly with the evils we have suffered as well as with the sins we have committed" (Frank Lake, *Clinical Theology*, p. 21).

"The task of theological anthropology is to set forth the Christian understanding of what it means to be human" (Stanley Grenz, *The Social God and the Relational Self*, p. 23).

The Tale of Two Counselors

Several years ago, Jim shared his story with me. His uncle had repeatedly sexually abused him while he was in elementary school. Jim never told anyone about the damage in his soul until he finally found the courage to tell a pastoral counselor. Hear Jim's words.

> Bob, it was incredibly hard. I felt so ashamed, but I got the words out—sobbing as I shared. The second I finished, my counselor whipped out his Bible, turned to Genesis 3, and preached a thirty-minute message on sin. Bob, it wasn't even a good sermon! But worse than that, I knew that I was a sinner. I'm clueless as to how my pastoral counselor intended to relate that passage to my situation. At that second, did I need a sermon on my personal sin?

Jim did not return for his second session with his pastoral counselor. Instead, he arranged an appointment with a professional Christian counselor. Here is Jim's rendition of his second counseling experience.

> Bob, at first things went well. My counselor seemed to be able to relate to me, seemed to have compassion for what I went through. But after two months of counseling I was ready to have him help me move beyond sympathy and empathy. I knew that I wasn't loving my wife and kids like Christ wanted me to. But my counselor kept telling me that I was too hard on myself and that I was too damaged to love the way I wanted to love.

The tale of two counselors. One hears a sordid story of sexual abuse and immediately responds to his sobbing counselee with a sermon on sin. The second hears his counselee's longing to move beyond damage to dignity, from victim to victory, and informs him that he's too disabled to function fully. These two diverse approaches illustrate the ongoing divide concerning what makes Christian counseling Christian. What biblical perspectives guided the thinking of Jim's pastoral counselor? What biblical premises did Jim's professional Christian counselor follow? Just what is biblical counseling? What is its focus? Its foundation?

The SPDR

Two books are standard in any physician's office: *The Physician's Desk Reference* (*PDR*) and *The Merck Manual of Diagnosis and Therapy* (*Merck*). Both are considered "the bibles of medical knowledge and practice." With its 3,223 pages of prescription drugs, the annually updated *PDR* is the most comprehensive, widely used drug reference available. It details the usage, warnings, and precautions for more than 4,000 prescription drugs. *Merck* is the most widely used medical text in the world. It provides the latest information on the vast expanse of human diseases, disorders, and injuries, as well as their symptoms and treatments. Intended for physicians, it is still useful for the layperson. As one sage has commented, "[It is] a must for everyone in a human body."

As the *PDR* and *Merck* are the Old Testament and New Testament for physicians treating the body, so the Bible is God's final, authoritative word for physicians treating the soul. It is the soul physician's desk reference manual for dispensing grace. It's "a must for anyone who is a soul." God's Word provides not only the latest, but also the eternal, enduring information on the soul's design and disease, as well as its care and cure.

What do we discover as we read the pages of the *Soul Physician's Desk Reference* (*SPDR*)? We learn what makes Christian counseling Christian. We learn our Great Physician's authoritative truth about:

- Nourishing the Hunger of the Soul: Preventative Medicine—God's Word
- Knowing the Creator of the Soul: The Great Physician—The Trinity
- Examining the Spiritual Anatomy of the Soul: People—Creation
- Diagnosing the Fallen Condition of the Soul: Problems—Fall
- Prescribing God's Cure for the Soul: Solutions—Redemption
- Envisioning the Final Healing of the Soul: Home—Glorification
- Dispensing God's Care for the Soul: Spiritual Friends—Sanctification

These seven biblical categories are essential for developing a theology of soul care and spiritual direction. We will examine them meticulously, as a physician would the skeletal structure of the human body.

Nourishing the Hunger of the Soul: Preventative Medicine—God's Word

Doctoring the body does not begin with the treatment of illness, but with preventative maintenance. Knowing how to keep the body healthy requires that we understand what the body needs. What diet? What nutrients?

So it is with doctoring the soul. What does the soul need? What nutrients? We nourish the hunger of our soul by living *coram Deo sola scriptura*: face-to-face with God by Scripture alone. *Deo* is Latin for God; *coram* is Latin for in the presence of, face-to-face with. Martin Luther used *coram Deo* to illustrate that we live with reference to God every second in every situation. Luther taught that all existence finds its final meaning and ultimate object in God and that all emotions, actions, volitions, cognitions, and relations have God as their circumference. He perceived all of life as a story of personal encounter with God and that the deepest questions in the human soul are God questions. Luther used the term *sola scriptura* to emphasize his conviction that we do not live by bread alone, but by every word that comes from the mouth of God.

If we are to use the Bible to nourish hungry souls, we must hear the Bible's story the way God tells it. And God tells it like it is. The message of the Bible teaches us that *life is a war and a wedding*.

Life is a *war*—a grand adventure in which God calls us to die daily. Life is a battleground—an epic quest to join God in the ultimate defeat of His archenemy—Satan.

Life is a *wedding*—a passionate romance in which Christ calls us to love intimately. Life is a battle for our love—the ageless question of who captures our heart—Christ or Satan.

We win the war and wed our Worthy Groom through the power of God's Word. But what does that mean? Does dispensing God's Word mean we tell our counselees and parishioners to "take two Scriptures and call us in the morning"? Does it mean that life is so simple that it consists of a one-problem-one-verse-one-solution formula? No. Not if life is a war and a wedding.

Dispensing truth demands that we derive our understanding of earthly life from heaven's viewpoint. We intersect Christ's eternal story and our temporal story; we connect His heavenly perspective and our earthly perspective; we look at life not with eyeballs only, but with spiritual eyes; we live under the *Son*, not just under the *sun*.

Soul physicians master at least three core counselor competencies for using God's truth: trialogues, spiritual conversations, and scriptural explorations. In a monologue, I talk to you, teach you, or preach to you. In a dialogue, the two of us converse back and forth. However, in a trialogue, you and I engage a third party in our interaction—the Holy Spirit by way of His inspired Word. "For where two or three are gathered together in my name, there am I in the midst of them" (Matthew 18:20, KJV). Counseling is a powerful trialogue interaction about God's Word between three people—a counselor, a counselee, and the Wonderful Counselor.

In spiritual conversations, the counselor and counselee explore together how *biblical principles* relate to daily life—how God's larger story relates to our smaller stories. In scriptural explorations, the counselor and counselee explore together what relevance and application a *specific passage* may have to the counselee's life story.

How do you handle a hungry soul? With truth—God's truth about life as a war and a wedding—dispensed with wisdom and love.

Knowing the Creator of the Soul: The Great Physician—The Trinity

Some Christian counseling models begin with salvation, others with sin; still others begin with the beginning. We start earlier. Exploring eternity, or before the beginning, helps us to address the question, "What is the nature of reality?" Knowing the Trinitarian Creator of our soul helps us to answer that question: "Reality is relational." Before time began, God existed in community—the sacred community of the holy Trinity. Reality is relational because God is social, communal, never once alone, but forever in intimate personal interaction within the Trinity. Created in the image of our Triune God, we are relational. This central awareness shapes every aspect of our soul care model.

Knowing the Great Physician also helps us to know His creation. To understand image bearers, we must first understand the One whose image we bear.

Additionally, beginning before the beginning enables us to understand what went wrong. By probing the fall of Satan, who once led the angelic hosts in worshiping the Trinity, we expose the hidden spiritual warfare at work behind every temptation to sin. We learn not only about the onset of the evil disease that infects image bearers, but also how Satan attempts to spread the virus of sin.

Examining the Spiritual Anatomy of the Soul: People—Creation

Three categories typically form the core of biblical counseling: people, problems, and solutions. Everyone involved in the personal ministry of the Word must ponder these three constructs.

- Creation: How to understand *people* biblically—the nature of human nature.
- Fall: How to diagnose *problems* theologically—the root causes of sin and suffering.
- Redemption: How to prescribe *solutions* scripturally—the pathway to growth in grace.

I remember the day I was introduced to this way of thinking about life. It was the first day of my first Bible college class. More than a hundred intimidated freshmen awaited the arrival of Dr. Lawler. The bespectacled, diminutive Old Testament scholar's reputation preceded him. When he entered, all chatter ceased. Staring us down, he said, "Repeat after me. Creation. Fall. Redemption."

"Creation. Fall. Redemption," we mimicked in unison.

"Never, ever forget those three words," he instructed us. "They summarize the entire story of the Bible."

I label them the *CFR Narrative* which condenses God's story of life through the lenses of Creation, our Fall, and our Redemption in Christ. Box 1:1 illustrates and explains God's Creation, Fall, Redemption story.

Box 1:1

The CFR Narrative: Creation, Fall, Redemption

The Bible tells one story in three stages: Creation, Fall, Redemption. These stages condense the story of life into its three grand themes. To understand how to help hurting and hardened people, we must comprehend the nature of God's CFR Narrative.

- ◆ **Creation** describes how life was meant to be lived. It gives us a glimpse into what healthy living looks like from God's perspective, according to His intentions.
- ◆ **Fall** explains how life became the distorted mess that it is today. It demonstrates why things are not the way they are supposed to be.
- ◆ **Redemption** shows us how we can live life as we find it through Christ's resurrection power. It explains the way back to health—to shalom, to wholeness.

Creation, Fall, and Redemption are theological terms that summarize the message of the Bible. However, they are not the only terms we can use. Notice other compelling descriptions.

Creation	Fall	Redemption
People	Problems	Solutions
Psychology	Psychopathology	Psychotherapy
God's Design	Human Sin	God's Salvation
Design	Depravity	Dignity
Soul Study	Soul Sickness	Soul Healing
Soul Order	Soul Disorder	Soul Reorder
Anthropology	Hamartiology	Soteriology
Genius	Madness	Reawakening
Genius	Grief	Grace
Generation	Degeneration	Regeneration
Paradise	Paradise Lost	Paradise Restored
Paradise	Cistern	Spring
Health	Sickness	Healing
Ideal	Ordeal	Real
Connection	Alienation	Reconciliation
Integrated Self	Scattered Self	Gathered Self
Capacity	Incapacity	Competency

As I have noted, some models of biblical counseling do not begin at the beginning, but at the Fall. They act as if the way things are now is the way things were meant to be. Life as we now find it, however, is not the way it was supposed to be.

In the film *Grand Canyon*, an attorney attempts to bypass a traffic jam. His route takes him along streets that are progressively darker and more deserted. His expensive car stalls on a secluded street patrolled by a local gang. The attorney manages to phone for a tow truck, but before it arrives three young thugs surround his disabled car and threaten his life. Then, just in the nick of time, the tow truck driver arrives. Savvy enough to understand what is about to go down, the driver takes the leader of the group aside to introduce him to metaphysics.

"Man," he says, "the world ain't supposed to work like this. Maybe you don't know that, but this ain't the way it's supposed to be. I'm supposed to be able to do my job without askin' you if I can. And that dude is supposed to be able to wait with his car without you rippin' him off. Everything's supposed to be different than what it is here." (Cornelius Plantinga, Jr., *Not the Way It's Supposed to Be*, p. 7, introduced me to this outlook).

The Creation narrative teaches us how we were meant to live life with God and with each other. It also teaches us God's original design for the soul—the nature of human nature as bearers of God's image (the *imago Dei*). It enables us to answer the questions, "What is health? What does a healthy image bearer look like?"

My wife still talks about her *Anatomy 101* college course. "Shudders" might be a better description. Her "favorite" memory was her dissection of a mink. The purpose was not to end up with a mink coat, but to gain an understanding of the inner physical structure of mammals.

In *Soul Physicians*, we will examine the anatomy of the soul. We will gain an understanding of the inner psychological structure of human beings as generated by God (Creation), degenerated by sin (Fall), and regenerated by grace (Redemption).

Our examination of biblical psychology will reveal that each human being has certain capacities of personhood. We are:

- ◆ Relational Beings: Romancers—Affections (Longing)
- ◆ Rational Beings: Dreamers—Mindsets (Thinking)
- ◆ Volitional Beings: Creators—Purposes (Choosing)
- ◆ Emotional Beings: Singers—Mood States (Feeling)
- ◆ Physical Beings: Actors—Habituated Tendencies (Acting)

Various models of Christian counseling emphasize one or another of these capacities of personhood. Truly biblical counseling understands and addresses all of them.

Various models of Christian counseling emphasize our original personality structure (Creation), our fallen personality structure (Fall), or our saved personality structure (Redemption). Once again, truly biblical counseling understands and addresses all of these.

Box 1:2 (Soul Anatomy 101) portrays the fundamental nature of human nature as created, fallen, and redeemed. We will flesh out God's anatomy of our soul throughout this book.

Box 1:2

Soul Anatomy 101

Created Personality Structure

1. Relational Beings: Romancers Loving Passionately—Affections
   a. Spiritual Beings: Communion
   b. Social Beings: Community/Connected
   c. Self-Aware Beings: Conscience

2. Rational Beings: Dreamers Thinking Wisely—Mindsets
   a. Images
   b. Beliefs

3. Volitional Beings: Creators Choosing Courageously—Purposes
   a. Intentions/Goals
   b. Actions/Behaviors

4. Emotional Beings: Singers Experiencing Deeply—Mood States
   a. Responding to Our Inner World
   b. Responding to Our Outer World

5. Physical Beings: Actors Living Fully—Habituated Tendencies

Fallen Personality Structure

1. Fallen Relational Beings: Adulterers—Impure Affections
2. Fallen Rational Beings: Fools—Fleshly Mindsets
3. Fallen Volitional Beings: Destroyers—Self-Centered Purposes
4. Fallen Emotional Beings: Addicts—Ungoverned Mood States
5. Fallen Physical Beings: Traitors—Disconnected Habituated Tendencies

Redeemed Personality Structure

1. Redeemed Relational Beings: Virgin Brides—Purified Affections
2. Redeemed Rational Beings: Penetrating Sages—Renewed Mindsets
3. Redeemed Volitional Beings: Empowering Shepherds—Other-Centered Purposes
4. Redeemed Emotional Beings: Soulful Poets—Managed Mood States
5. Redeemed Physical Beings: Connected Characters—Reconnected Habituated Tendencies

Diagnosing the Fallen Condition of the Soul: Problems—Fall

As important as it is to return to Creation, we would be naïve to end our journey there. God didn't. The true story of life must include the sad story of our descent into the abyss of sin.

Though sad and tragic, without this story we could never make sense of life. People all around us are asking, "How do you explain life as we now find it?" They may not word it quite like that. Perhaps it sounds more like, "How could a good God allow such evil and suffering?" "Would a loving God really send people to hell?" "If God is so good, why did He allow my daughter to be accidentally run over and killed by my husband right in our driveway?"

Life as it now exists is inexplicable apart from understanding the Fall. The narrative of the Fall teaches us that our present condition neither corresponds to our original state nor to God's ultimate design for us.

By dissecting the fallen soul, we are able to diagnose the impact of sin on the human personality and predicament. Throughout *Soul Physicians*, we will learn about sin's deep impact upon our fallen motivational structure—why we do what we do. We will come to understand and apply issues such as false lovers of the soul, idols of the heart, self-centered purposes/pathways, and ungoverned mood states. We will also learn about suffering in a fallen world and our response to it. Specifically, we will contrast and compare the world's method of grieving with a biblical model of healing—sufferology.

Prescribing God's Cure for the Soul: Solutions—Redemption

If the Bible ended with the Fall, life would be hopeless and we would despair. Thankfully, God's story moves to Redemption.

The Bible is comedy, not tragedy. No, not comedy as in modern-day situation comedies that wrap up every problem in twenty-three minutes, but comedy in the classic sense of that word in literature.

The Bible would follow the literary form of tragedy if it stopped at the Fall. Tragedy moves from a wonderful beginning to a horrible ending without any resolution.

The second episode in the original *Star Wars Trilogy* was tragedy. *The Empire Strikes Back* told a tale that began with the victory of the Republic (the "good guys"), but ended with their defeat at the hands of Darth Vader and the Empire (the "bad guys"). To this day, that film is the least watched and liked of all the *Star War* movies. No one enjoys tragedy. Yet we all experience it.

The Bible, though not denying the tragedy of the Fall, is comedic in scope. Like all classic comedy, it begins on a high note, moves to a note of despair, but ends triumphantly. Thus we have Redemption. We learn how to live life as we now find it. More than that, we are rescued from our old life and empowered to live the new life.

The award-winning movie *A Beautiful Mind* is classic comedy. It's the story of the mystery of the human mind in three acts: genius, madness, and reawakening.

John Nash enters Princeton as one of the top two mathematical scholars in the United States. Here we find genius—Creation—life as God intended it. Nash has the uncanny ability to see the big picture. The eyes of his mind have perfect 20/20 vision.

As we follow John's life, however, we move to madness—the insanity of the schizophrenia that engulfs his once beautiful mind. In his paranoia, he imagines roommates, little girls, government agents, and a plot not only to take his life, but to bomb vital American cities. This is the Fall; it is not the way things were supposed to be for John.

Through perseverance, medication, treatment, family and community support, John fights back. He has at least a partial reawakening. His "redemption" comes when he receives the Nobel Prize for his totally new mathematical theory of economics. Although his reawakening is a pale reflection of the Redemption offered by Christ, it does give us a glimpse of our final hope.

Nash's life is a microcosm of all human existence. We have fallen from our God-created state of *shalom*—health and wholeness, to a Satan-inspired state of shame—sickness and dis-integration, and we're invited to enter a Christ-initiated state of grace—healing and restoration.

At times we mistakenly counsel Christians as if they were non-Christians. We view our clients or parishioners only through the lens of depravity. This is like a heart surgeon transplanting a perfectly healthy new heart into her patient, but then treating the patient as if he still has the old heart in his chest.

We are new creations with a new *nature*: regeneration and redemption. God has implanted a new heart into the core of our being with new power to live godly lives. We have a new *nurture*: reconciliation and justification. Christ provides a new relationship of complete acceptance with God and freedom from condemnation. We are cleansed and forgiven.

In *Soul Physicians*, we will explore how these truths about who we are *in* Christ and *to* Christ dramatically alter the way we counsel and disciple one another. We are people who have rejected false idols for the true God; people who have rejected filthy cisterns for God, the Spring of Living Water; people who are no longer disordered, but reordered. These realities about our newness in Christ guide every interaction and intervention when counseling fellow Christians.

We will learn about the power of Christ's gospel of grace, not only to save us, but also to sanctify us. To grow spiritually we must live *coram Deo sola gratia*: face-to-face with God by grace alone. We are in-relationship-to-Deity beings designed with a fundamental nature which must worship. God designed humans to trust, to place faith in, and to display loyalty to Someone who transcends the self. When healthy and sane, we orient ourselves with our faces to God. When unhealthy and senseless, we orient ourselves with our backs to God. Sane or senseless, we are God-oriented people—*coram Deo* people.

We can translate the Latin phrase *sola gratia* as "by grace alone"—*gratia* being grace and *sola* being alone or solely. Our soul's necessary nutrient is grace. Even prior to the entrance of sin into the universe, man's existence was by grace. God never needed us, so His creation of us was a gift. Since man sinned, God's grace became all the more evident and indispensable. Christ died for us while we were sinners, while we were yet His enemies, while we were still ungodly (Romans 5:1-11).

Every non-biological problem is a grace-deficiency problem. Our souls starve, shrink, and struggle either because we have never received God's gracious acceptance in Christ or because, having received His grace, we are now bewitched by Satan to live by works and blinded by Satan to reject our acceptance.

For biological deficiencies we need physical nutrients and medicinal cures. Thus, most doctors spend much of their time as dispensers of medicine. Soul physicians are dispensers of grace. We spend most of our time either bringing others into a grace relationship with Christ or helping them to accept their acceptance in Christ. In *suffering*, people need grace to help in their time of need and pain, doubt and confusion. In *sinning*, people need grace to experience forgiveness in times of defeat and besetting sin, idolatrous attitudes and false loves. In *sanctification*, people need grace to equip them for power, love, and wisdom.

The heart of *Soul Physicians* revolves around understanding how to help new creations with new hearts to live healthy lives. Step by step, we'll build an in-depth, practical theology of sanctification (*sancticology*). We'll equip you to empower others to put off the "flesh" and to put on the new person they already are in Christ.

Envisioning the Final Healing of the Soul: Home—Glorification

Creation, Fall, and Redemption summarize life on planet Earth. However, we are everlasting beings. Just as we began our diagnosis with a look into eternity past, so we end our prognosis with a peek into eternity future. What is our destiny? Does our future destiny make any difference during our present suffering? Does our future destiny make any difference to our current sinfulness?

Our future destiny is home—sacred communion within God's holy and happy family. Our present sufferings, the apostle Paul reminds us in Romans 8, are not worthy to be compared with our future glory. Paul also reminds us in Romans 8 that we groan with hope for the coming day when we will be glorified—renewed into the image of Jesus Christ. In counseling, we fan into flame hope, resilience, longsuffering, patience, power, love, and wisdom by reminding our spiritual friends that we've read the end of the story.

Dispensing God's Care for the Soul: Spiritual Friends—Sanctification

We will explore sequentially the first six biblical categories (preventative medicine, the Great Physician, people, problems, solutions, and home). The seventh area—spiritual friends—we will integrate into every aspect of *Soul Physicians*. In fact, I've devoted an entire book to it (*Spiritual Friends: A Methodology of Soul Care and Spiritual Direction*). Since I integrate dispensing God's care for the soul into *Soul Physicians*, it's vital that I introduce it to you now. Do the Bible and church history provide us with an approach to soul care and spiritual direction that is powerful and practical, biblical and relevant, comprehensive and comprehendible? I am convinced that they do. In the pages to come, I will introduce you to soul care through sustaining and healing and to spiritual direction through reconciling and guiding. (*Spiritual Friends* walks you through a detailed training process that equips you to develop twenty-two relational competencies necessary to practice the art of spiritual friendship.) Box 1:3 pictures this biblical approach to Christian counseling, outlining the following process (see page 23).

Box 1:3

Soul Care and Spiritual Direction
Sustaining, Healing, Reconciling, and Guiding

Soul Care: The Evils We Have Suffered
"God Is Good Even When Life Is Bad"

Soul caregivers compassionately identify with people in pain
and redirect them to Christ and the Body of Christ
to sustain and heal their faith so they experience
communion with Christ and conformity to Christ
as they love God (exalt God by enjoying and trusting Him) and love others.

Sustaining: *"It's Normal to Hurt"*
Sense Your Spiritual Friend's Story of Despair
Empathize with and Embrace Your Spiritual Friend

Healing: *"It's Possible to Hope"*
Stretch Your Spiritual Friend to God's Story of Hope
Encourage Your Spiritual Friend to Embrace God

Spiritual Direction: The Sins We Have Committed
"God Is Gracious Even When I Am Sinful"

Spiritual directors understand spiritual dynamics
and discern root causes of spiritual conflicts,
providing loving wisdom that reconciles and guides people so they experience
communion with Christ and conformity to Christ
as they love God (exalt God by enjoying and trusting Him) and love others.

Reconciling: *"It's Horrible to Sin, but Wonderful to Be Forgiven"*
Strip Your Spiritual Friend's Enslaving Story of Death
Expose Your Spiritual Friend's Sin and God's Grace

Guiding: *"It's Supernatural to Mature"*
Strengthen Your Spiritual Friend with Christ's Empowering Story of Life
Equip and Empower Your Spiritual Friend to Love

- ◆ Soul Care: The Evils We Have Suffered
  - • Sustaining: "It's Normal to Hurt"
  - • Healing: "It's Possible to Hope"

- ◆ Spiritual Direction: The Sins We Have Committed
  - • Reconciling: "It's Horrible to Sin, but Wonderful to Be Forgiven"
  - • Guiding: "It's Supernatural to Mature"

Soul Care and Spiritual Direction

The tale of Jim's two counselors exposed a common problem in modern Christian counseling. We have a tendency to focus *either* on suffering *or* on sinning. We see our counselee *either* as a victim to be comforted, *or* as a sinner to be confronted. Biblical counseling is not either/or. It is both/and. "Soul care" is the term I use to describe the biblical and historical role of coming alongside people to comfort them in their *suffering*. "Spiritual direction" refers to the role of confronting people about their *sin* and challenging them to grow in grace.

How does growth occur and for what purpose? Growth happens as we love God and others. We want to grow not simply or primarily so we feel better. Instead, *God's glory is the goal of Christian counseling*. God's glory is the reason we sustain, heal, reconcile and guide, and the purpose of growth. We grow in love for God, which exalts Him as the onlooking universe sees how enjoyable He is and how worthy of our trust.

Soul Care: The Evils We Have Suffered

Offering soul care, we focus on the evils suffered by our spiritual friend. Certainly, Jim suffered despicable evil at the hands of his uncle. In counseling Jim, we want to identify with his pain compassionately and redirect him to Christ and the Body of Christ to sustain and heal his faith so he can experience communion with Christ and conformity in Christ.

The counselor acts as a conduit. Counselors build bridges from the counselee to Christ and to other Christians. Too often we view counseling as *the* answer rather than seeing counseling as a subset of discipleship—one aspect of what God uses in the sanctification process. Too often we see the counselor as *the final* hope, rather than seeing the counselor as the one who points to the Wonderful Counselor who is our hope and to the wonderful counseling that takes place as believers connect to one another in the Body of Christ.

Sustaining: "It's Normal to Hurt"

Soul care for suffering begins with sustaining. While sustaining Jim, I wanted to help him to know "It's normal to hurt." Living in a fallen world, it's natural to grieve. That's why the psalmists cry out to God in complaint; it's why Jeremiah pens his laments; and why Job rues the day he was born.

In talking with Jim, I sensed his story of suffering. Before I rushed in where angels fear to tread to shower him with biblical clichés, I chose to hear his story. Before interjecting

God's story, I embraced his. Before insisting that God is good, I agreed with Jim that life is bad—life in our fallen world is out of joint.

I call this process *climbing in the casket*. I intend this rather macabre image to shock us into realizing the nature of sustaining. When Paul wrote his second letter to his friends in Corinth, he told them he did not want them to be ignorant of his hardship and suffering. He wanted them to know he was under great pressure far beyond his ability to endure, so much so that he despaired even of life. Indeed, in his heart he felt the sentence of death (2 Corinthians 1:3-9). Jim, too, felt like he had been handed a death sentence. His soul felt dead, disintegrated, shamed, and crushed. I joined him on death row. I climbed in Jim's casket, entering his despair.

Healing: "It's Possible to Hope"

I did not intend to leave Jim there. A casket is an appropriate place to visit, but it's no place to live. While it's certainly true that life is bad, it's eternally certain that God is good. Because He is good, healing says, "It's possible to hope." Yes, we grieve, but not as those who have no hope. So while listening to Jim's sordid story of suffering with one ear, with my other ear I was listening to God's beautiful narrative of healing. He always offers beauty for ashes, gladness for mourning, and a garment of praise for our rags of despair.

It is not enough that *I* heard God. Jim needed to hear God. My role was to trialogue with Jim, using spiritual conversations and scriptural explorations to stretch him to God's perspective. I wanted to encourage Jim to embrace God even as Paul had. Paul indicates that God allowed his suffering so that he might not rely on himself, but on God who raises the dead (2 Corinthians 1:9). I not only climbed in the casket with Jim, I also *celebrated the resurrection* with him. We raised the roof over the resurrection. Jim began to find healing when he embraced his pain, expressed his pain to God, experienced God's embrace of his pain, and found God's healing partnership, perspective, and purposes in his pain.

Spiritual Direction: The Sins We Have Committed

Some of you may be wondering, *Are we going to talk about suffering only? What about responsibility? Whatever happened to sin?* Jim and I did talk about sin. We engaged in spiritual direction: reconciling and guiding Jim in relationship to God and others.

Reconciling: "It's Horrible to Sin, but Wonderful to Be Forgiven"

While assuring Jim that he was blameless with regard to the abuse he suffered, I took Jim at his word when he admitted he wasn't loving his wife and kids the way he should. Jim needed to face the sins he had committed, knowing that God is gracious even when men are sinful. As a spiritual director, I needed to understand the spiritual dynamics and discern the root causes of Jim's failure to love so I could offer loving wisdom that could reconcile and guide Jim.

Reconciling Jim included helping him to know in a very personal way that "It's horrible to sin, but wonderful to be forgiven." The Puritans spoke of "loading the conscience with guilt" and "lightening the conscience with grace." I loaded Jim's conscience with biblical conviction about the damage his sin was doing to God's reputation, his family's health, and his own soul. Coming to see the depth of his sin and taking personal responsibility for it, Jim repented of his failure to love his family.

While exposing his sin, I also exposed God's grace, because wherever sin abounds, grace superabounds. We trialogued about God as Jim's forgiving Father and Christ as his forever Friend. We pictured the Father running to Jim, throwing His arms around him, kissing him impetuously, and throwing a wild party because His son had returned home. We lightened Jim's conscience with grace.

Guiding: "It's Supernatural to Mature"

Some soul physicians are content to stop at this point, believing the work of repentance and forgiveness completes the spiritual direction process. But Jim still had to walk into his home, face his past failures, tackle his fears, and offer his family courageous love. My task was to empower Jim to experience the truth of who he was *to* and *in* Christ so he could realize that through Christ's supernatural power he was capable of mature love. He could be a shepherd in a jungle.

We did not enter the "Twilight Zone" of confusion, but the arena of spiritual guidance. We talked about what love would look like in his home, what risks Jim would need to take, and how he could continue to find strength in Christ. Over time, Jim began to exercise power, love, and wisdom as a husband and father. He was not too damaged to love. In Jim's weakness, Christ showed His strength. Jim applied the truth that in Christ, "It's supernatural to mature."

Where We've Been and Where We're Heading

There are certain facts that every medical school student must know by heart. So too, soul physicians must graft into their minds the seven biblical categories of:

- ◆ Nourishing the hunger of the soul
- ◆ Knowing the Creator of the soul
- ◆ Examining the spiritual anatomy of the soul
- ◆ Diagnosing the fallen condition of the soul
- ◆ Prescribing God's cure for the soul
- ◆ Envisioning the final healing of the soul
- ◆ Dispensing God's care for the soul.

With these seven categories, your orientation to *my* book is complete. Now it is time to crack *the Book*—the Bible. What type of book is the Book of books? How did the Author of authors compose it and why? How are we to read it and use it in soul care and spiritual direction?

Soul physicians understand the nature of the Great Physician's Book. Join me in our next two chapters as we view the old, old story from the Author's perspective. We'll learn that the Word of God is our soul physician's manual written in the form of a heroic adventure narrative ("life is a *war*") and a passionate romance novel ("life is a *wedding*").

Caring for Your Soul: Personal Applications

1. Reread the "Tale of Two Counselors" from the beginning of the chapter.

   a. Which counselor/spiritual friend do you tend to be more like? Why?

   b. Has anyone interacted with you like either of Jim's counselors? What did it feel like? What were the results?

2. Of nourishing the hunger of the soul, knowing the Creator of the soul, examining the spiritual anatomy of the soul, diagnosing the fallen condition of the soul, prescribing God's cure for the soul, envisioning the final healing of the soul, and dispensing God's care for the soul:

   a. Which category seems most important for you to learn more about? Why?

   b. Which concepts could you apply to your own life now? How?

3. How might your daily life change if you lived *coram Deo sola scriptura* (face-to-face with God by Scripture alone)?

4. How might your daily life be different if you lived *coram Deo sola gratia* (face-to-face with God by grace alone)?

Caring for Others: Ministry Implications

♦ **Develop Your Understanding of People Biblically:** Dissect my theory. Be a Berean. Examine the Word to see what God teaches about the nature of human nature. Do you have a biblical personality theory? If so, how does it guide your counseling interactions? To what degree do you think your personality theory has been impacted by secular theory? In what ways?

♦ **Diagnose Problems Theologically:** Commit to developing your own understanding of the fallen personality structure. Probe what constitutes relational (spiritual, social, and self-aware) rational, volitional, and emotional sickness. Why do we do what we do? What is the fallen motivational structure of the human personality?

♦ **Prescribe Solutions Scripturally:** What are the marks of the relationally (spiritually, socially, and self-consciously), rationally, volitionally, and emotionally maturing believer? How can our inner lives increasingly reflect the inner life of Christ? What difference should our newness in Christ make in how we counsel and disciple one another? What is a biblical process of growth in grace?

♦ **Provide Spiritual Friendship with Grace and Truth:** Truth without grace leads to pharisaical, legalistic, rigid, self-righteous, law-based counseling. Grace without truth leads to humanistic, lawless, self-serving, feel-good counseling. Biblical counselors integrate truth and grace by sharing the Scripture and their own souls. They explore grace narratives that highlight God's truth perspective, and they offer grace relationships that emulate Christ's style of relating. Which do you tend toward most: grace or truth? Why? How could you better balance and better integrate these two essential counseling components?

♦ **Follow a Biblical Treatment Plan:** Whether it is "sustaining, healing, reconciling, and guiding," or some other model/approach, we all need some map or guide for interacting with people. What is yours? Are you consciously aware of it? Where did you learn it? How does it assist you? Is it biblical? Historical?

CHAPTER TWO

GOD'S HEROIC ADVENTURE NARRATIVE

"God made people because He loves stories" (Ancient Rabbinic Saying).

*"The one thing the Bible is *not* is what it is so often thought to be—a theological outline with proof texts attached"* (Leland Ryken, *How to Read the Bible as Literature*, p. 9).

"We live in narrative, we live in story. . . . Existence has a story shape to it. We have a beginning and an end, we have a plot, we have characters. . . . Story is the language of the heart" (Eugene Peterson, interviewed by Michael Cusick in *Mars Hill Review*).

A New View of the Old, Old Story

The Bible is the greatest adventure story ever imagined, the greatest love story ever told. From cover to cover, God's Word narrates a vision quest that towers over *The Lord of the Rings*. God spins a tale that makes any *Matrix* movie boring by comparison. From front to back, and everywhere in between, the Bible recounts a love story far greater than any *Harlequin Romance*. God describes a romance that makes *Romeo and Juliet* seem altogether dull.

Don't misunderstand. The Bible is a true story—*the* true story. It's simply not the dry-as-dust academic treatise that we've been led to believe. The Bible is a true love story set amidst a grand adventure. Because it is, it relates to you and me. Because it is, we're able to relate God's truth to human relationships. Because it is, we're able to learn and apply a biblical theology for soul care and spiritual direction.

The book that we share as spiritual friends, soul caregivers, spiritual directors, pastors, and counselors is the grandest adventure ever undertaken. When people come to us with defeated lives, we share the story that they are more than conquerors. When they tell us of their losses, we tell them of their final victory. When they tell us they feel powerless, we share that they are armed with God's power.

For the Bible to make a difference in our lives and in the lives of those we love, we must read it as the story of the greatest love ever displayed. Not Romeo for Juliet, nor

Anthony for Cleopatra, nor the Prince for Cinderella, but the Prince of Peace for those smitten by the Wicked Witch, the Worthy Groom for His undeserving bride, the Father for the prodigal, and God for you and me.

The Bible as Story

But why story? Why is more than 75 percent of the Bible narrative? Why is much of the remaining 25 percent poetry (the cry of the soul set to music) and epistles (real letters to real people with real struggles)? Because God is the God who creates and relates in history. He is the God who stands and stays, acts and speaks in relationships. Leland Ryken, biblical literature specialist, explains this truth well.

> As Amos Wilder has written, "The narrative mode is uniquely important in Christianity." One of the most pervasive human impulses can be summed in the four words "Tell me a story." The prominence of narrative as a biblical form arises from the Bible's view of God. The God of the Bible is, above all, the God who acts. . . . By bringing human characters into interaction with God and with each other, biblical narrative is able to explore the dynamics of relationship that is so central to the biblical view of man. By presenting a double plot in which spiritual and earthly levels of action occur simultaneously, biblical narrative illuminates the spiritual reality that is always the context for human experience. Because narrative is a progression of events moving toward a goal, it is uniquely suited to depicting the dynamic, growing nature of religious experience (Ryken, *The Literature of the Bible*, p. 77).

Didactic outlines simply would not have sufficed. Such outlines would not have been able to communicate the reality of Christ's heroic love for us, nor to express the nature of spiritual life as the drama of the competition for our souls. The Bible is theology, but it is more, it is *theo-drama*. The Bible is theology for reality—theology for real life. As Dr. Reginald Grant notes:

> A right understanding of God's Word includes a right understanding of the Divine artistry that informs God's revelation to us. He could have communicated His Word to us in the form of a rather dry epistle. Instead, the Bible as a whole is an artistic expression of a story of God and His relationship to us (Grant, *Dallas Theological Seminary Newsletter*, p. 4).

Our role as soul physicians is quite simple. *We listen well to our spiritual friends' earthly stories, and then we assist them to see their stories from the perspective of God's eternal story.* This is the final uniqueness of Christian counseling. We have the meta-narrative—the one overriding true story that explains all the confusing themes of our own life stories.

The Bible is the truest of true stories because it provides the rest of the story by pulling back the curtain to expose the charade of the Wizard of Oz—Satan. It rips off the blinders to show life as it really is. The Word presents God's way of looking at life from His eternal perspective. It provides us with the spiritual eyes to see life with 20/20 vision.

The Bible: God's Heroic Adventure Narrative—Life Is a War

The Bible is a love story plopped down in the middle of a grand adventure. So is life.

When we are young we dream of the victories we'll win, the challenges we'll surmount, the accolades we'll accumulate, the children we'll raise, the damsels we'll rescue, or the princes we'll attract. But life has a way of killing our dreams.

As children, neighborhood bullies, detached dads, latchkey homes, sexual abuse, or parental divorce—these shattered our dreams . . . During our teen years, our dreams were crushed by not making the team, losing the big game, never being asked to the dance, too few friends, school failure, sex before marriage, college rejection, drugs, gangs . . . By our young adult years, if we are brave enough still to be dreaming, our dreams are turned to nightmares by broken proposals, a crisis pregnancy, a string of meaningless jobs, a degree that we never use, confusion about our purpose, church splits, shallow relationships, money problems . . . Some brave middle-aged adults dare to dream again, only to be slapped down by divorce, downsizing, prodigal children, "Dilbert-like bosses," dead-end jobs, distant spouses, cancer, death of parents . . . The few proud senior citizens still dreaming face death on the horizon, immobilizing sickness, the tedium of retirement, adult children who never call, loneliness, regrets, churches that have forgotten them . . .

Solomon was right. Hope deferred makes the heart sick. Dashed dreams squash our zest for life. We review our life story and it reads more like a depressing soap opera than any heroic epic. So we wonder, "Is this all there is?" Then we decide to live for the cheap thrill. Or we decide, "This is too hard for me." Instead of thriving, we merely survive. But neither cheap thrills nor mere survival are the way life was supposed to be.

At least not life as God designed it. From cover to cover, the Bible is a startling revelation about life as the grandest adventure. Open the front cover. Genesis 1—"The planet is yours! Subdue it! Rule it! Craft it! Go for it!" Genesis 2—"The Garden is yours. Protect it. Guard it. Shape it. Expand it. Beautify it. Have a ball!" Genesis 3—Warfare. Enemies. Tension. Decisions. Combat. Seduction. Genesis 3:15—The first-ever Bible prophecy which predicts the ongoing battle between the forces of good and evil, of God and the Devil.

Flip to the other cover—Revelation. The end of our story was the grandest of grand adventures long before LaHaye and Jenkins novelized it into the best-selling *Left Behind* series. Epic battles. Heroic martyrs. Monstrous evil. Gigantic armies. Wars to end all wars. The return of the King. The defeat of the great dragon.

The epicenter of the book of God—the Gospels—is nothing less than a victory narrative. Gospels were a common literary form in the ancient Near East during the time of Christ. Whenever a great king won a major victory, he commissioned the writing of a gospel—a vivid retelling of the good news of the vanquished enemy and the victorious king. This glorious good news was told again and again, often from multiple points of views, to exalt the king and encourage His people.

The four Gospels are nothing less than the retelling of Christ's grand adventure from multiple perspectives. The Gospels are the universal announcement of the joyous victory of our Worthy Groom over the False Seducer (Colossians 1:12-14; 2:13-15).

Genesis, Revelation, the four Gospels, and the other sixty books of the Bible show soul physicians that life makes sense. History is moving toward a God-ordained purpose. More than that, the stories of our lives have purpose. God is directing all of history toward our wedding. Toward the final defeat of our enemies—every enemy. Toward happily ever after.

When our current dreams are dashed, we must remind ourselves that we've read the end of the story. We've listened to Paul Harvey's *The Rest of the Story*. In the end, we marry the Prince. In the end, we join the Prince in subduing the Evil One. In the end, we rule.

Many sports fans, if they can't watch the big game live, tape it. Then they swear all their friends to secrecy. "Don't you dare spoil it for me! Don't tell me who won. I want to watch it and enjoy the thrill of the whole game without knowing the end."

I guess I'm odd. When I can't watch the big game live, I tape it, but I watch the end first! Especially if the big game involves one of my beloved teams. I'm a major fan of the Chicago Bulls. Back when Michael Jordan was leading them to six NBA titles, I taped one of the championship games between the Bulls and the Phoenix Suns. First, I watched the end. The Bulls won! Then I rewound the tape and watched the entire game. When the Bulls were behind by 17 points, I never panicked. I never threw bricks at the TV. Normally I would have left the room if they were behind by that much. I would have told my son to call me only if the Bulls tied the game. I couldn't take watching them struggle. But not this time. I knew the end of the story. So I could handle the ups and downs of the game, knowing the grand result.

Whether or not you agree with my sports-watching philosophy, you can see the benefits we gain from knowing the end of God's story—the end of *our* story. These truths not only guide our own lives, we also use them to enlighten and empower our spiritual friends when they crash their souls on life's pothole-filled highways. We engage them in spiritual conversations encouraging them to ponder: "Why give up when you lose one battle, since you know we have won the war?" "Why sweat the small stuff?" "Why choose mere survival, when we are more than conquerors?" "Why choose cheap thrills when in the end we rule the universe forever?"

Interpreting Our Grand Adventure Narrative

Some of us do indeed choose cheap thrills or mere survival. Why? What separates the survivors and thrill seekers from the thrivers?

In *The Sacred Romance*, Brent Curtis and John Eldredge explain that the individual events of our life story seldom seem like a grand adventure narrative. Our role in God's story rarely causes us to feel like heroes. Hope deferred—dashed dreams—can make our heart sick, weak, discouraged, ready to quit because *when life stinks, our perspective shrinks*.

What we need are *CliffsNotes*—an instruction manual on how *not* to read our grand adventure and on how *to* read our heroic narrative. No one in the Bible is a better reading tutor than Job. Join me as we read Job's grand adventure narrative and learn that God and Satan use the same material—the stories of our lives. Whose interpretation of our life stories will we believe? Satan's or God's?

To interpret accurately Job's story and ours, we need to understand that God tells it on two levels. We find the smaller story—the earthly, temporal perspective—and the larger story—the heavenly, eternal perspective. Satan desires that we focus only on the smaller story and conclude that "Life is bad, and so is God." God urges us to focus upon the larger story and realize that "Life is bad, but God is good." One of the keys to our spiritual life and to soul care and spiritual direction is to move people from Satan's view of life toward God's perspective on this life and the next.

The Smaller Story: The Earthly Perspective—Life Is Bad

Though the plot of Job's smaller story is familiar, I wonder how many of us can put ourselves in his place. Consider his losses and crosses all coming at once. He loses his life's savings; his business is bankrupt. What would that be like for us? Then he loses not one, but ten children. How would we respond? Later Job loses his health. Sickness, on top of death and grieving, on top of bankruptcy. What would our perspective be like? Then he loses the support of his wife and dearest friends. His wife tells him to give up on God and on life. His friends accuse him of gross sinfulness. Truly, for Job, life was bad.

While Job retains his integrity, his wife loses hers. "Curse God and die!" she demands. Her words suggest that Job should view God with dishonor and disrespect, that he should see God as a lightweight. For Job's wife, God was either too weak to stop their suffering or too cruel to care. "Life is bad, and so is God." When life stinks, our God perspective shrinks. So, curse God *and die*. That is, give up hope.

Job's "friends," his so-called "comforters," are hardly any better. They were more effective counselors when silent than when speaking. They concluded that God was judging Job because of his sinfulness. Like the Jews in Jesus' day, they wanted to know who sinned, the blind man or his parents? Jesus taught that in the case of the man born blind, the cause was neither the personal sin of the blind man nor of his parents, but that higher purposes (the glory of God) were at work (John 9:1-3).

God informs us that the counsel of Job's friends was not only poor, but sinful. God's wrath is kindled against Job's three counselors because they did not speak what was "right" (*kun*) about God (Job 42:7-9). When used of God, "right" highlights what a generous Provider He is, what a Rewarder God is, what a Blesser. It always has royal overtones, picturing God as the Divine King who accomplishes His works through wisdom. The great test of God's kingship is the problem of sin. To say that God is "right" reflects the conviction that God always overcomes evil with good. Those who view God as "right" fix their hearts confidently on God, trusting His affectionate sovereignty even during tempestuous times (John Oswalt, *Theological Wordbook of the Old Testament*, Vol. I, pp. 433-434).

Job's counselors failed to see God's trustworthy heart. Specifically, they succumbed to the culture of their day that believed that God was a tit-for-tat God. "If you are good, then God will be good to you. If you are bad, then God will treat you poorly. Life is bad because God is bad." Their God was like the gods on *Star Trek*—cruel gods who took rather than gave. Gods who demanded to be fed by the populace because they would starve without their sustenance.

Together, this rather motley crew sees only the smaller story—the earthly perspective. They accept Satan's interpretation of Job's life story. "God is a Hoarder, not a Rewarder. Job is a zero, not a hero."

The vast majority of men and women live in the middle of such a story. Dark sentences cloud their thinking. "Life is bad and so is God." "Life is bad because God is mad." "God's a Hoarder, not a Rewarder." "I'm a loser, not a hero." "Forget thriving, I'm barely surviving."

The Larger Story: The Universal Perspective—Life Is a Battleground

What can change such interpretations? How did Job maintain his heroic integrity? How can we help our spiritual friends to keep trusting through tragedy? We must open the pages to the larger story, the eternal perspective, God's universal viewpoint.

As later readers of Job's story, we see what the original characters, including Job, never saw. God unveils for us the rest of the story. He pulls back the curtain to expose the heroic narrative that Job and you and I are engaged in every second of our lives. This larger story demonstrates that "Life is bad, but God is good." It teaches that we are leading characters in God's drama of redemption, that we have a special, heroic role to play.

Step behind the curtain to gain a spiritual perspective on everyday life (Job 1:6-12; 2:1-6). God is bragging about Job. God brags about you, too. Satan, the accuser of the brethren, slanders us before God. But God says, "Did you see Betty? How she trusts me! What a godly life she's living! She's showing the entire universe that I have a trustworthy heart. I'm so proud of her! She's a real heroine."

Satan responds, "But would Betty trust your so-called good heart if her life were bad? Would she demonstrate to the entire universe that you are a good God, if her life were a mess? Or would she curse you, seeing you as a lightweight God, a Hoarder, a tit-for-tat Deity?"

The scene is set. God announces the real theme of the drama of Job's life, of Betty's life, of your life, and of your spiritual friend's life. Life is a battleground between two views of God—God as a lightweight Hoarder who cannot be trusted, or God as our affectionate Sovereign whom we can always trust to be a grace Rewarder.

We are not bit players in an off-Broadway play. We have leading roles on Broadway. God, the great Director, hands us the script. Act after act, He orchestrates everything so our lives can be testimonies to His trustworthiness.

We say to God, our Director, "Uh, let me see if I understand Your script. I have a lead role. There's no stunt double. You have me not getting the girl, losing the big game, getting fired, going through two church splits, my son getting cancer, and my daughter getting divorced. All the while I'm shouting, 'God is good! Trust His heart!' Do I have it about right?"

God says, "Yes."

To Job, and to us, God seems more like the director of a *Matrix* movie than a *Leave It to Beaver* television episode. And why not, since life is a battleground, a grand adventure, a love story in the middle of Armageddon?

Trace Yahweh's relationship to Job and you'll discover that Yahweh is always ready for some new, outrageous self-disclosure meant to subvert Job's dominant earth-bound reality. As Walter Brueggemann notes, the Old Testament is the constant retelling of life with Yahweh—our Wild Lover (Brueggemann, *Theology of the Old Testament*, pp. 359-372).

Our Wild Lover, our Loving Sovereign, uses life's battlegrounds to reveal Himself more fully to us. With Job, God discloses His nature by discussing nature (Job 38-41). "Job, you think you're pretty smart. You consider yourself strong. Could you set the constellations in space? Do you understand the ways of the sea and the stars?" God offers Job a new view of the old stars he had seen every day of his rural existence. More than that, Job receives a new view of his place in God's grand universe.

God's character is astonishing and Job's role amazing. Job's script requires him to play the part of an epic hero who demonstrates to the entire universe that God's heart can and should be trusted through tragedy. He tenaciously clings to the conviction that even when life is ugly, God is beautiful. God's hero sees comedy where others see only tragedy.

Few people believed it would be possible to make a comedy set in the Nazi concentration camps of World War II. However, in *Life is Beautiful*, Roberto Benigni had a vision of one possible way to tell this tale of horror without dehumanizing the lead characters.

There are two distinct stages in the film. The first half concentrates on Guido Orefice's efforts to woo his chosen lady. He is funny, courageous, and irrepressible in his attempts to win the heart and hand of the lovely Dora. He uses cunning strategies that take advantage of all the quirks of Florence and its people to impress the woman he constantly greets with, "Buono giorno Principessa" (Good day, Princess).

Soon they are married and joined by a precocious son, Giosué. He clearly takes after his father and is the apple of his parents' eyes. It would take a hard-hearted person to avoid loving this little angel, an angel who will go to any extreme to avoid his bath time. His other main concern seems to be getting enough time to play with his toy tank.

However, love and optimism are unable to dam the tide of history. Italy aligns with Germany and begins persecuting their Jewish population. On Giosué's fourth birthday, while Dora is out, soldiers seize him and his father, stacking them like cattle into a train headed for the concentration camps. As soon as Dora realizes what has happened, she follows them into the depths of hell.

Although Guido doesn't know exactly what's going to happen, he knows enough to want to shield his son in the only way he can. While they're in the train, he concocts a story to convince Giosué that they're taking a surprise trip to celebrate his birthday. As their situation worsens, the fiction becomes more convoluted. Guido controls every aspect of his son's perception to persuade him they're participating in a most challenging competition, with a full-sized tank as the prize!

Despite the horrors of the situation—death all around, brutal labor, starvation, and dehumanizing barracks—Guido focuses all his efforts on his son's perception of reality. In the riveting final scene, the war is ending. The Italian soldiers realize they must destroy all evidence of their atrocities. Desperate, Guido hides his son in a metal container with peepholes. Later that day the guards force Guido on a death march. Realizing that his son can see him, he whistles, smiles, and winks. Gunshots signal his death, out of sight of his son.

The next morning, all is quiet. Giosué finally leaves his tiny cage. Thunderous rumbling noises in the distance announce the coming of tanks. The huge barrel rounds the corner first. Rather than being terrified, Giosué shouts, "We won! We won!" He's sure the tank is his personal prize for winning the grand competition.

Like Giosué, Job evidences a childlike faith in God's greatness and goodness, along with a humble trust that His Father's version of reality is the only one that truly matters. Some may read the final chapters of Job and simply see God the Bully, pulling rank on Job. That's not how Job saw it. He recognized God's affectionate sovereignty. He perceived the holy love of God. He understood the intimacy of God's presence. Yes, God is big, but He is also good.

Job testifies to God's good heart by naming his first daughter Jemimah. Her name means "dove, affectionate one." In Job's day, a child's name reflected the spiritual beliefs of her parents. Job tells us, "I've looked at life from both sides now. From up and down and all around. I've seen it from my perspective and from God's, from the earth and from the heavens. And I can tell you from personal experience that God is good. He is loving. He is an affectionate Dove."

Thousands of years later, the biblical author James reminds us of Job's God-perspective. "You have heard of Job's perseverance and have seen what the Lord finally brought about. The Lord is full of compassion and mercy" (James 5:11). In the face of suffering, Job saw the face of his compassionate and merciful God.

And God testifies to Satan. "Do you see my heroic servant Job? Though his life was horrible, he says I am beautiful!"

And we trialogue with our spiritual friends. "What do you think God's up to in this?" "Tell me how you've been able to keep clinging to Christ." "How have you been cooperating with Christ to bring God glory even in your suffering?"

The Intersection of God's Story and Ours

Job's role is ours also. Watch as Paul draws back the curtains for the church.

Although I am less than the least of all God's people, this grace was given me: to preach to the Gentiles *the unsearchable riches of Christ*, and to make plain to everyone the administration of this mystery, which for ages past was kept hidden in God, who created all things. His *intent* was that now, *through the church*, the manifold wisdom of God *should be made known to the rulers and authorities in the heavenly realms*, according to *his eternal purpose* which he accomplished in Christ Jesus our Lord (Ephesians 3:8-11, emphasis added).

Our Father's eternal intent and our earthly purpose mingle when our lives testify "God is good even when life is bad!"

Eugene Peterson's paraphrase of Paul's words captures the essence of our plan:

And so here I am, preaching and writing about things that are way over my head, *the inexhaustible riches and generosity of Christ*. My task is to bring out into the open and make plain what God, who created all this in the first place, *has been doing in secret and behind the scenes all along. Through Christians like yourselves* gathered in churches, *this extraordinary plan of God is becoming known and talked about even among the angels!* (Peterson, *The Message*, p. 2129, Ephesians 3:8-11, emphasis added).

Angelic forces stand on tiptoe to gain a glimpse of the church. There's an unseen world just as real as our present existence. It's a world of heavenly powers—the realm of angels and demons. As God accomplishes His eternal plan of redemption, the entire universe watches. We—the church—are the main actors and actresses in His drama of redemption. We have the privilege and responsibility to reveal our Lover's good and gracious heart to all creation. We are the guardians of the sacred truth (1 Timothy 3:15).

When the final curtain draws back on all of history we will declare the truth of Christ's victory narrative.

And when he had taken it, the four living creatures and the twenty-four elders fell down before the Lamb. Each one had a harp and they were holding golden bowls full of incense, which are the prayers of the saints. And they sang a new song: "*You are worthy* to take the scroll and to open its seals, *because you were slain, and with your blood you purchased men for God* from every tribe and language and people and nation. You have made them to be a kingdom and priests *to serve our God*, and *they will reign* on the earth." Then I looked and heard the voice of many angels, numbering thousands upon thousands, and ten thousand times ten thousand. They encircled the throne and the living creatures and the elders. In a loud voice they sang: "*Worthy is the Lamb, who was slain*, to receive power and wealth and wisdom and strength and honor and glory and praise!" Then I heard every creature in heaven and on earth and under the earth and on the sea, and all that is in them, singing: "To him who sits on the throne and to the Lamb *be praise and honor and glory and power, for ever and ever!*" The four living Creatures said "Amen," and the elders fell down and worshiped (Revelation 5:8-14, emphasis added).

What is the plot of God's larger story? What is the nature of our leading part in His grand adventure? What is the point of life? The point always revolves around reveling in our Worthy Groom (enjoying Him), revealing how lovely our Worthy Groom is (exalting Him), and reflecting our Worthy Groom (emulating Him).

Nothing can thwart our purpose. *Every experience of suffering is an opportunity to glorify God.* Our lives are on display. We are on a universal stage. Not only is the whole world watching, the entire universe is gripped by the drama of our lives. All want to know whether we will display God's glory by trusting His good heart even when life stinks.

Knowing our role is both frightening and freeing. In *Black Hawk Down*, the retelling of the 1993 incident in which fewer than one hundred Army Rangers and Delta Forces were swarmed upon by more than one thousand Somali fighters, we witness fear and freedom. "Grimes" is known not for his courage in battle but for his expertise in coffee making. When an injury to a fellow soldier forces him into combat, his fears surface. Trained to fight, part of him prefers the safety far from the frontlines. Making coffee seems a preferable role to making war.

Grimes was not only trained for combat, he was called to combat. Little by little, as the planned one-hour mission erupts into a thirty-six-hour life-and-death dogfight, Grimes finds his true calling and accepts his larger role in the story. At a pivotal point when a fellow soldier is shot, bleeding, and pinned down under heavy enemy fire, it is Grimes who volunteers to risk his life. Rescuing a friend seems preferable to making coffee. Grimes discovers the freedom to be all he can be, all that God created him to be.

His friend's wounds are critical. Despite frantic calls for evacuation, help will not arrive in time. The medic, with little experience and less equipment, does all he can, first to save his life, later to minimize his pain. Bleeding to death and knowing the end is near, the wounded soldier expresses his last request to his sergeant. While the sergeant grips his bleeding body and strains to hear his fading voice, the dying soldier asks that a message be conveyed to his parents. "Tell them that I fought like a hero." He, too, has identified and accepted his role in the larger story. He dies free, without regrets of battles avoided or roles refused.

Paul reminds us that we can't have the glory without the suffering. ". . . indeed we share in his sufferings in order that we may also share in his glory" (Romans 8:17b). When we are in Christ, we're in Him for the whole experience. More than that, Paul reminds us that we can handle both suffering and glory because we are heroes. ". . . we are more than conquerors . . ." (Romans 8:37b). Between these two reminders, we find a third point to remember—the future. "I consider that our present sufferings are not worth comparing with the glory that will be revealed in us" (Romans 8:18).

Soul physicians say to their spiritual friends, "Remember the future." "Read the end of the story." "Discover the intersection between God's eternal, universal story and your temporal, earthly story."

We are heroes and heroines in God's grand adventure narrative. At times fear tempts us to prefer the coffee-making roles. But eternity calls us to accept the death-to-self roles. We'll do anything to hear our Father's, "Well done, Son." "I'm so proud of you, my daughter."

We're called to brag on God during battle. We refuse to curse the general who sends us into combat. We refuse to request a lesser role. Instead, bullets flying around, disasters sweeping over us, we bless our affectionate Sovereign.

Where We've Been and Where We're Heading

The Bible that forms our model of counseling and guides our methods in counseling tells the story of the war to end all wars. The war is not fought in some far away galaxy by soulless clones guided by an impersonal force fighting for territorial control. No. Our war is fought in our hearts between two lovers in competition for our souls. No more personal conflict has ever been waged. No outcome ever more momentous.

Our grand adventure of Chapter 2 melds into our romantic encounter of Chapter 3. Take your seat. The lights are dimming. Characters embroiled in a love triangle enter the next scene.

Caring for Your Soul: Personal Applications

1.　How does God's Word touch you?

　　a.　Do you dissect it? Doubt it? Are you bored by it? Captivated by it? Surrendered to it? Amazed by it?

　　b.　After reading Chapter 2, what are you prompted to do to change how you approach and respond to God's heroic adventure narrative?

2.　Ponder a difficult situation you have recently experienced, or are now enduring. Fast forward to the "end of the story."

　　a.　What differences can your ultimate victory in Christ make in how you handle your situation?

　　b.　How will you think and what will you do differently because you know the end of the story?

3.　Are you ever astonished by God?

　　a.　By what?

　　b.　When you are, what do you do with your astonishment?

4.　Still thinking of that difficult situation, honestly evaluate it through the grid of, "Life is bad, but God is good."

　　a.　What are the bad, painful, hurtful aspects of your situation? Perhaps you could write them to God in the form of a Psalm of Lament like Psalm 13 or 88.

　　b.　Where can you see God's goodness, even in this situation? How is your situation driving you to dependence? Perhaps you could write a Psalm of Thanks and Trust to God like Psalm 23 or 27.

5.　What grand adventure is God calling you to?

　　a.　What amazing role has He cast you to play? Is it like Job? Like Guido? Like Grimes? Like Ruth? Like Daniel? Like Lois and Eunice (2 Timothy 1:5)? Like whom?

　　b.　As angelic forces stand on tiptoe, what message about God are you showing them? Do you want to keep showing the same message? If not, specifically what could you do to begin to demonstrate that you trust God's good heart?

Caring for Others: Ministry Implications

♦ **Read and Share the Bible as Story:** The next conversation you have with a fellow struggler, remember these four words: "Tell me a story." Engage your spiritual friend in an exploration of God's grand adventure. Ask yourself, "How can the biblical theo-drama encourage my friend?"

♦ **See Life with 20/20 Spiritual Vision:** Help your spiritual friend to ponder, "What is God up to in this?" "Where is God in this?" "How could His eternal perspective offer me wisdom to face my temporal situation?"

♦ **Listen with Both Ears:** As your friend shares his or her earthly story of suffering and sin, listen well. Remember, however, there is another story, a larger story. Listen well to God's story. Be wondering, "How do God's story and my friend's story collide? How can we relate the two, intersect the two, integrate both stories?"

♦ **Picture the Big Picture:** Every experience of suffering is an opportunity to glorify God. Nothing can thwart our purpose. Help your spiritual friends to see how they can revel in their Worthy Groom (enjoy Him), reveal how lovely their Worthy Groom is (exalt Him), and reflect their Worthy Groom (emulate Him).

CHAPTER THREE

GOD'S PASSIONATE ROMANCE NOVEL

"Every man who knocks on the door of a brothel is looking for God" (G. K. Chesterton, *Collected Works*, Vol. I).

"There is only one being who can satisfy the last aching abyss of the human heart, and that is the Lord Jesus Christ" (Oswald Chambers, *My Utmost for His Highest*, July 30).

"There is a God-shaped vacuum in the heart of every person" (Commonly attributed to the seventeenth-century French philosopher, Blaise Pascal).

Looking for Love in All the Wrong Places

Presentation papers for my counseling seminar filled the empty plane seat beside me. The gentleman behind me poked his nose through the space between the two seats asking, "You a pastor or something?"

"Something like that, yeah." I replied.

"Think I could come up there and talk with you for a while? I've got a moral dilemma that I'm really confused about."

Joe proceeded to tell me that he was returning from a rendezvous with a woman he had first met through an Internet chat room. "She's married, but unhappy. I'm unmarried and unfulfilled. What's your take on this, am I wrong to be involved with a married woman?"

"I'm curious," I responded. "Why would you want to ask a pastor-type about this? Surely you know the answer I'm going to give you."

"Yeah, you're right. I know what I'm doing is wrong. I know that in my heart. I guess I'm looking for more than just an answer. I want to figure out why I'm doing this. I know better."

"You mentioned that you're unfulfilled. What do you mean by that?"

"Well, I'm a vice-president of a *Fortune 500* company. But, like lots of corporations lately, we've had tons of layoffs, even in management. To tell you the truth, the past year my number one goal has been to be invisible. I figure if they don't see me, they can't fire

41

me. This is so unlike me. For my entire adult life I've been driven, successful, a risk-taker. Now I just want to survive."

"So the thrill is gone at work, and you're trying to find it in an affair?"

"I never thought of it that way. I guess I've never really linked the two before, but I think you're onto something."

"Joe, that's so beneath you."

"What!"

"What you're doing is wrong. It's sinful in God's eyes. *And* it's beneath you. God designed you to make a difference in life—a difference for Him that helps others. Imagine Bill Gates finding himself in an epic litigation with the United States government. He becomes so overwhelmed that he hides away in his office. Every once in a while he sneaks out to a Seattle street corner to pick up a cheap prostitute. I'd say that's a little bit beneath Bill Gates, wouldn't you?"

"Yeah, when you put it that way, I see what you mean. So what should I do?"

"One decision is obvious, Joe. You need to end your affair. Another decision is less obvious, but equally important. You need to get back in the game at work. Additionally, you're facing a third decision that's even harder and much more vital."

"What's that, Bob?"

"You need to decide if you're going to join Christ in His grand plan for your life, or if you're going to continue to play games with your life . . ."

As I noted earlier, life is a love story plopped down smack dab in the middle of a grand adventure. Joe was missing the mark on both accounts. C. S. Lewis pictures how Joe, and many of us, have traded our birthright for a mess of oatmeal.

> We are half-hearted creatures, fooling about with drink and sex and ambition, when infinite joy is offered to us, like an ignorant child who wants to go on making mud pies in a slum because he cannot imagine what is meant by the offer of a holiday at the sea. We are far too easily pleased (Lewis, *The Weight of Glory*, p. 20).

When we merely survive, or like Joe, attempt to become invisible, we fail to live God's role for our lives—heroes and heroines. When we seek cheap thrills, we refuse to accept God's desire for our relationship—adult sons loved by God and beautiful brides cherished by Christ.

In addition to being a heroic adventure narrative, God's Word is a passionate romance novel. In fact, it is His love letter to you. Just imagine how your perspective could change should you begin to understand that God is moving all of history toward your marriage to His Son. Ponder how your thinking about life would be reshaped if you began to read God's Word as the letter you always wished your earthly father had sent you—a letter filled with fatherly love, intimacy, respect, pride, and counsel.

Love Is the Point—Life Is a Wedding

Perhaps what holds some of us back is a cloudy view of the nature of Scripture. *Of course the Bible is true. Certainly much of it comes in narrative form. But, a love story?* we wonder.

We fail to realize that even the Pharisees—those grim, grumpy old men with their harsh view of reality as rituals, rules, and regulations—saw the Bible as a love story. In the most famous of many attempts by the Scribes, Sadducees, and Pharisees to trip Jesus, they quiz Him about the greatest commandment in the Old Testament (Matthew 22:35-40).

Greek scholar Dr. Daniel Wallace portrays the incident as the ultimate WWE (World Wrestling Entertainment) tag-team match. On one side of the ring rage those who insist that the essence of the Old Testament consists of loving your neighbor as yourself. Ready to rumble on the opposite side of the ring are those who contend that the basic nature of the Law and Prophets should be summed up with the words of Deuteronomy 6:5, "Love the LORD your God with all your heart and with all your soul and with all your strength." Standing between them, in the presence of the raucous, mocking crowd—Jesus. Certainly, they all conclude, He's trapped. Down for the count. No matter how He answers, He will lose half His followers.

Taking on His first opponent, Jesus forcefully declares that the greatest commandment is to love God. "Ahh! We've got Him," they anticipate. Until His verbal pause ends with His statement directed toward His second adversary, "And the second is like unto it. Love your neighbor as yourself."

"Like unto it," they wonder. A phrase they know well to mean, "of equal weight, validity, and importance."

"The whole Old Testament, all of God's revelation, the law and the prophets," Jesus informs them, "hang on these two commands as a door hangs on its hinges. You can't separate them. You cannot claim to love God whom you have not seen, and not love one another, whom you see everyday."

We know the story, but do we understand the implications? Even the Pharisees understood that love is the point. They never questioned whether the battle was between truth and love, or doctrine and application. They made no such dichotomy. Reality, for the Pharisees, was relational. As biblical scholars, they could not deny that.

What they could not deny, Jesus explains. The law is about love—loving God and each other. Old Testament professor and author, Dr. Ray Ortland, Jr., illustrates:

> Pastorally, the biblical story lifts up before us a vision of God as our Lover. The gospel is not an imperialistic human philosophy making overrated universal claims; the gospel sounds the voice of our Husband who has proven his love for us and who calls for our undivided love in return. The gospel reveals that, as we look out into the universe, ultimate reality is not cold, dark, bland space; ultimate reality is romance. There is a God above with love in his eyes for us and infinite joy to offer us, and he has set himself upon winning our hearts for himself alone. The gospel tells the story of God's pursuing, faithful, wounded, angry, overruling, transforming, triumphant love. And it calls us to answer him with a love that cleanses our lives of all spiritual whoredom (Ortland, *Whoredom*, p. 173).

Jack Miles disagrees. Miles is the Pulitzer Prize winning author of the national bestseller *God: A Biography*. Miles' God does not love in Genesis, knows not love throughout the Pentateuch, cannot love during the historical books, and only stumbles upon love in the Prophets. What a frightening profile! What a sinfully warped account of God's character.

Love is the point because God is love. Reality is relational because God is romantic. Christianity is an invitation to a love story, a drama of reconciliation because God is the forgiving Father, Christ the pursuing Groom, and the Spirit the wooing best Man.

For the Bible to make a difference in our lives, we need to understand the difference the Bible intends to make. The Bible is God's love letter designed to melt our adulterous hearts.

Love changes everything. So sings Sarah Brightman in "Love Changes Everything" from Andrew Lloyd Webber's Broadway musical *Aspects of Love*.

> Love, Love changes everything: Days are longer, Words mean more.
> Love, Love changes everything: Pain is deeper Than before.
> Yes, love, Love changes everything: Brings you glory, Brings you shame.
> Nothing in the World will ever Be the same.*

Brightman sings of secular love, of romantic love between a man and a woman. If such love is so powerful, how omnipotent must God's love be? If love between a man and a woman changes everything, then what difference does God's love for us make? It changes how we live and how we die. In fact, it leads us to live by dying—by dying to self and living for God and others. As Henry Scougal describes:

> The love of God is a delightful and affectionate sense of the divine perfections which makes the soul resign and sacrifice itself wholly unto him, desiring above all things to please him, and delighting in nothing so much as in fellowship and communion with him, and being ready to do or suffer anything for his sake or at his pleasure (Scougal, *The Life of God in the Soul of Man*, p. 38).

Imagine how Scougal's mind-set might change the mind of a wife bent on leaving her husband who is less than attentive to her. Think how it could change the thinking of a disrespectful teenager who feels neglected by his parents.

A Grace Love Story

What type of love completely changes us? Grace love. *Soul Physicians* presupposes something unique about the Christian solution to the problems of relationships, attitudes, behaviors, and emotions. That something is *GRACE*. This book addresses the fundamental question: "What would a model of counseling and discipleship look like that was built solely upon Christ's gospel of grace?"

Richard Lovelace in *The Dynamics of the Spiritual Life* rightly calls Luther's rediscovery of grace the "Copernican Spiritual Revolution" (p. 83). As Copernicus' discovery that the Earth revolves around the sun revolutionized our understanding of the physical universe, so Luther's discovery that our spiritual existence revolves around the Son (and His grace)

Box 3:1
The Bible as God's Love Story

The following passages help us appreciate God's Word as His love letter. Those with an asterisk are clear biblical summaries of the nature of God's revelation.

♦ Leviticus 19:18*—Love your neighbor as yourself.
♦ Deuteronomy 6:4-5*—Love the Lord your God with all your being.
♦ Matthew 7:12—Do unto others as you would have them do unto you, summarizes the Law and the Prophets.
♦ Matthew 22:35-40*—The two greatest commandments: love God and one another.
♦ Mark 12:28-34—No commandments are greater than these: loving God and loving others.
♦ Luke 6:27-36—Love your enemies.
♦ Luke 10:25-37*—We read the Law correctly when we summarize it as loving God wholeheartedly and loving our neighbor as ourselves.
♦ John 3:16—"God so loved the world that he gave his only begotten Son."
♦ John 13:34-35*—Christ's new commandment: "Love one another."
♦ John 15:9-17*—Christ's commandment: "Love each other as I have loved you."
♦ Romans 13:8-10*—When we love one another, we fulfill the Law. "Love your neighbor as yourself" summarizes God's holy standard.
♦ 1 Corinthians 8:1—Knowledge puffs up, but love builds up.
♦ 1 Corinthians 13:1-13*—Three things remain: "Faith, hope, and love. But the greatest of these is love."
♦ Galatians 5:14*—We summarize the entire Law in a single command: "Love your neighbor as yourself."
♦ Galatians 5:22-23—The fruit of the Spirit is love.
♦ Ephesians 4:15-16—Speak the truth in love.
♦ Ephesians 5:22-33—Love as Christ loves.
♦ Philippians 1:9—Our love is to abound more and more in depth of insight.
♦ Colossians 3:14*—Over all virtues put on love, which binds them all together.
♦ 1 Timothy 1:5—The goal of our instruction is love.
♦ James 2:8*—The royal law found in Scripture: "Love your neighbor as yourself."
♦ 1 John 2:9-10—Living in God's light means loving one another.
♦ 1 John 3:14—We know we have passed from death to life when we love one another.
♦ 1 John 4:7-21—God is love. Whoever does not love, does not know God. Since God so loved us, we also ought to love one another.

revolutionizes our understanding of the spiritual universe. Grace is the pivot and center of Christianity. Christ's gospel of grace is the center point of all history, of all reality.

Only two things have ever changed the human soul: sin and grace. Sin altered our original, God-dependent nature. The moment Adam and Eve sinned, they chose self-righteousness and self-sufficiency by attempting to deal with their shame apart from God. "Then the eyes of both of them were opened, and they realized they were naked; *so they sewed fig leaves together and made coverings for themselves*" (Genesis 3:7, emphasis added). Ever since then, each of us has perfected the spiritual seamstress art. Rather than turn to God, we attempt to beautify ourselves. As Emil Brunner explains:

> All other forms of religion—not to mention philosophy—deal with the problem of guilt apart from the intervention of God, and therefore they come to a "cheap" conclusion. In them man is spared the final humiliation of knowing that the Mediator must bear the punishment instead of him. To this yoke he need not submit. He is stripped absolutely naked (Brunner, *The Mediator*, p. 474).

Author and theologian John R. Stott pictures how works—the opposite of grace—reveal the depraved nature of our self-sufficient souls.

> The proud human heart is there revealed. We insist on paying for what we have done. We cannot stand the humiliation of acknowledging our bankruptcy and allowing somebody else to pay for us. The notion that this somebody else should be God himself is just too much to take. We would rather perish than repent, rather lose ourselves than humble ourselves. . . . But we cannot escape the embarrassment of standing stark naked before God. It is no use our trying to cover up like Adam and Eve in the garden. Our attempts at self-justification are as ineffectual as their fig leaves. We have to acknowledge our nakedness, see the divine substitute wearing our filthy rags instead of us, and allow him to clothe us with his own righteousness (Stott, *The Cross of Christ*, pp. 162-163).

Grace changes everything, including how we counsel. Every other model of people-helping helps people help themselves. Christianity alone helps people receive help—grace. True soul physicians dispense grace—Christ's grace.

Augustus Toplady's *Rock of Ages* reminds us that grace returns us to our God-dependent, God-sufficient original design. "Nothing in my hand I bring, Simply to Thy Cross I cling; Naked, come to Thee for dress, Helpless, look to Thee for grace; Foul, I to the mountain fly, Wash me Saviour, or I die!"

The Bible is our Worthy Groom's grace love letter to us in which He whispers, "Come home. I forgive you. I love you. Trust my good heart." Will we?

Two Love Stories: The Eternal Love Triangle

Life is not only a love story; it is two love stories.

The story of life is the drama of two loves, the old story of the "eternal triangle": Whom will I marry? God, my true beloved? Or some idol, and thus ultimately myself? This is the fundamental option, the fundamental question of every human life (Peter Kreeft, *The God Who Loves You*, pp. 50-51).

Relationship is the ultimate reality in the universe and the drama of two loves is the ultimate reality in life. Life is a battle for our love. Which lover captures my soul: Christ my Worthy Groom, or Satan the False Seducer? Whose version of the love story captivates my mind?

Adam and Eve confronted this competition for their souls. Walking with God in the cool of the day, they experienced His lavish goodness. Everything He made was theirs to enjoy fully. Everything except one tree.

The False Seducer pounced upon the Father's one prohibition, twisting it to imply that God was a Hoarder. "Why is God holding back from you? If His heart is so good, why is He keeping His best from you?" Since God's love story is a grace love story, it makes sense that Satan would call into question the generosity of God's good heart. Thus, Satan seduces us away from grace and toward works, away from Christ-sufficiency and toward self-sufficiency. "If you can't trust God, then who can you trust? Well, yourself, of course!"

Thousands of years later, the author of Hebrews identifies trust in God's goodness as the essence of faith. "And without faith it is impossible to please God, because anyone who comes to him must believe that he exists and that he rewards those who earnestly seek him" (Hebrews 11:6). The Greek word for "rewards" (*misthapodotēs*) emphasizes that God rewards as a Father, not as a Judge. His reward far exceeds what is deserved; thus it is a matter of divine generosity, not human merit. As linguist H. Preisker notes:

> Reward, then, is a term for God's gracious generosity. It is the loving gift of the Father toward which believers may move with confident and childlike trust in the love that will perfect their calling in glory (Preisker, *Theological Dictionary of the New Testament*, p. 605).

So which is it? Who's telling the truth about God's heart toward us, Satan or Christ? Is God a Rewarder or a Hoarder? A Blesser or a Bully? A Lover or a Tyrant? Does God have a good heart, or doesn't He? Is Christ our Worthy Groom, or is He unworthy of our trust and love? Whose interpretation of my life story will I believe? These questions echo down the halls of history, reverberating in the soul of every person we will ever counsel.

The Two Competing Love Stories in Abraham's Life

Abraham was such a person. His journey jolts back and forth between trust and mistrust of God. In his first encounter with God (Genesis 12), Abraham displays an almost unbelievable faith. God says, "Leave everything. Your father. Your people. Your country. Go to a land I will show you. And I will bless you and bless others through you."

Genesis 12:4 records Abraham's response in such a quaint manner that we almost ignore the magnitude. "So Abram left, as the LORD had told him." God says, "Go." Abraham goes! How many of us would have left everything simply because we believed God when He told us that He was a Blesser?

Abraham's Human Reasoning

As is often the case in our lives, however, trust flows quickly to mistrust. Twice Abraham fails to trust God enough to protect his own wife. In Genesis 12, he tells Sarah to pretend that she is his sister so the Egyptians will not kill him. Years later, when Abraham and Sarah enter Gerar (Genesis 20), he does it again. Abraham risks his wife, not his life. Why? Why would Abraham trust God enough to leave everything he knew, but not trust God enough to keep His promise to bless all nations through Abraham and Sarah?

Interestingly enough, Abimelech, the secular king, helps us answer our spiritual question. Abimelech asks Abraham, "What was your *reason* for doing this?" (Genesis 20:10, emphasis added). The King James version translates his question, "What *sawest* thou, that thou hast done this thing?" "Reason" and "sawest" are two accurate translations of one Hebrew word. The word, *rāāh*, means "perception of reality." The Old Testament often uses it for a person's image of God. Abimelech is asking, "What mistaken view of reality, what faulty image of God, could possibly lead you to lie to me and risk your wife?"

Abraham replies, "I said to myself" (Genesis 20:11). His first mistake is that he speaks to himself, rather than to God. He bases his decision upon human reasoning, reasoning that fails to take God at His word. "There is surely no fear of God in this place," Abraham continues, "and they will kill me because of my wife" (20:11). God had promised to bless Abraham and Sarah with offspring as plentiful as the sands of the sea, yet Abraham doubts that God will keep him alive.

Abraham is guilty of non-*coram Deo* reasoning. Abraham reasons apart from God. More than that, he reasons that God would treat him like a *Star Trek* red shirt. As any true fan knows, on the original *Star Trek* series it was a sure invitation to death to be a red-shirted security guard beaming down to some hostile planet. Captain Kirk, Mr. Spock, Dr. McCoy, or Engineer Scotty could not be killed. But someone had to die to maintain the building tension. It was always the red-shirted, no-name security guard.

It is as if Abraham says to himself, in his human reasoning, "This is a hostile planet God has beamed me down to. I've seen this episode before. If I don't put my shields up, if I don't take matters into my own hands, then I'm as good as dead." From a non-*coram Deo* perspective, such self-protective logic makes sense.

Abraham's Reason Redeemed by Faith

God does exist, however, and He is a Rewarder, not a Hoarder. The author of Hebrews 11:17-19 chooses Abraham as a classic example of reason redeemed by faith. When God told Abraham to offer his son Isaac as a sacrifice, all the blessings of the covenant were at risk in Isaac's death. All Abraham's hopes and dreams were wrapped up in Isaac, the son of the covenant. "He who had received the promises was about to sacrifice his one and only son, even though God had said to him, 'It is through Isaac that your offspring will be reckoned'" (Hebrews 11:17-18).

What decision might we make? God is demanding that we give Him a blank check. More than that, God insists that we hand over our entire life's savings. "Give Me your relationships. Give Me your career. Trust Me with your health, with your children, with your future. Completely trust My heart."

Somehow Abraham, the man who could not trust God to keep Him alive, trusts God to keep his hopes and dreams alive. He trusts that God is a Blesser, not a Bully, a Rewarder, not a Hoarder. How?

"Abraham *reasoned* that God could raise the dead, and figuratively speaking, he did receive Isaac back from death" (Hebrews 11:19, emphasis added). The Greek word for "reasoned," (*logizomai*) means "to calculate, to add up." Various New Testament authors use it in a relational context for adding things up spiritually and factoring God into the equation. Abraham does some spiritual mathematics and figures that *zero times God equals infinity*. Abraham's reason is redeemed by faith. He does not simply accept the smaller, earthly story. He refuses to buy the lie of Satan that God is a Hoarder.

Instead, Abraham believes that God will provide. Abraham and Isaac trek up a mountain for three days.

> As the two of them went on together, Isaac spoke up and said to his father Abraham, "Father?" "Yes, my son?" Abraham replied. "The fire and the wood are here," Isaac said, "but where is the lamb for the burnt offering?" Abraham answered, "God himself will provide the lamb . . ." (Genesis 22:6b-8a).

Later, his faith vindicated, Abraham names the place, "The Lord will provide" (Hebrew, "Jehovah Jireh"—"Yahweh Provider," Genesis 22:14). He accepts God-reality, not Satan-reality.

But what changed Abraham who so recently had doubted God's ability to save him and mistrusted God's promise to bless him? What occurred between Genesis 12-20 and Genesis 22 that alters the story Abraham chooses to believe?

Abraham encounters God. "Abraham planted a tamarisk tree in Beersheba, and there he called upon the name of the LORD, the Eternal God" (Genesis 21:33). Abraham calls upon God—he knows Him *coram Deo*—face-to-face. He knows God as the Everlasting God—the God who is from perpetuity, from eternity, the God of the everlasting love story. Abraham's intimate encounter with God's good heart enlightens his mind to the conviction that God is a God who always provides exactly what is best for us—from His eternal perspective, not from our temporal vantage point.

The Two Competing Love Stories in "Pastor Bill's" Life

As I write, my mind recalls the pastor I counseled who was terminated by two churches. No moral indiscretion, doctrinal heresy, family failures, insubordination, nor lackadaisical approach to ministry—not in either church. As he said to me, "Bob, what am I doing wrong? What is it about me that causes people to hate me? Why does God keep letting this happen to me? I don't think I can go through this again."

If you were working with "Pastor Bill," how might you relate God's truth to his situation? How could you help Bill find answers to his questions?

To begin to address Bill's questions, we must first recall that Satan is all too willing to help Pastor Bill decipher the meaning behind his life story. But Christ longs to help Bill view life from God's perspective. So the deeper question becomes, "Whose interpretation of Bill's life story will he believe?"

False Seducer implanted and imprinted questions in Pastor Bill's mind about God's heart. When Bill and I explored his question, "Why does God keep letting this happen to me?" we peeled off layer after layer of doubts about whether God even cared. "Oh, theologically I know all the answers," Bill assured me. "But personally, in my heart, emotionally, I just don't see it. I don't get it. I can't accept it. How could God do this to me *again*, if He really loved me?"

In his state of mind, Pastor Bill was ripe for Satan's follow-up blow. "Since God has betrayed your trust, trust yourself." Indeed, Bill was tempted. "I'm not letting anyone in again. Whenever I open up to people, it all comes back to haunt me. I'm better off doing this alone."

Perhaps Melville was peering into Bill's heart when he wrote, "the reason the mass of men fear God and at bottom dislike him is because they rather distrust his heart, and fancy him all brain, like a watch." Before we jump on the Bill-bashing bandwagon, we might admit that we have fallen prey to such insidious thoughts at various points along our journey. "With eyeballs only" we do a little spiritual calculation. "Let's see, when my life is unfair, when I suffer unjustly, when the wicked prosper, the options are: God doesn't care or God is not in control. He's either not strong enough or not loving enough."

We would not be the first to be so brutally honest. "As flies to wanton boys, are we to the gods," the pagan King Lear was warned, "they kill us for their sport." "The world in which we live can be understood as a result of muddle and accident," Bertrand Russell wrote, "but if it is the outcome of a deliberate purpose, the purpose must have been that of a fiend" (Russell, *Why I Am Not a Christian*, p. 93).

Satan delights in these interpretations for they all lead down the same blind alley. "Doubt God/Trust Yourself."

Once headed this direction, Satan altered Pastor Bill's terrain and said, "Doubt God/ Hate Yourself." Thirty-four times the Bible calls Satan the Devil: *Diabolos*, the slanderer, the one who hurls abusive arrows our way. In Revelation 12:10 he's the "accuser of our brothers." In New Testament times, an accuser was a legal prosecutor who brought charges against people.

Martin Luther, the great Reformer and skilled spiritual warrior, saw through Satan's schemes.

> By the temptation of faith is meant that the evil conscience drives out of a person his confidence in the pardoning grace of God, and leads him to imagine that God is angry and wishes the death of the sinner, or that, in other words, the conscience places Moses upon the judgment-seat, and casts down the Savior of sinners from the throne of grace. He says, "God is the enemy of sinners, you are a sinner, therefore, God is your enemy" (A. Nebe, *Luther as Spiritual Advisor*, pp. 189-190).

When Satan assaulted Luther's parishioners, he urged them to cling to the gospel of grace.

> It is the supreme art of the Devil that he can make the law out of the gospel. If I can hold on to the distinction between law and gospel, I can say to him any and every

time that he should kiss my backside. Even if I sinned, I would say, "Should I deny the gospel on this account?" (Luther, *Works*, Vol. 54, p. 106).

Satan weaves his schemes into a web of deceit. First he tempted Pastor Bill to sin, and then he condemned Bill for sinning. "How stupid to trust God!" he shouted. "How wicked you are for not trusting God," he hissed.

Detect the condemning narrative that Pastor Bill swallowed. "What am I doing wrong? What is it about me that causes people to hate me? Why does God keep letting this happen to me?" Satan snared Bill in his trap marked, "Doubt God/Hate Yourself."

False Seducer, however, wasn't satisfied. Next he said to Pastor Bill, "Doubt God/Beautify Yourself." If we're wicked, then we'd better beautify ourselves before we dare step into God's presence. So says Satan, the Anti-Groom who is pro works. He appeals to our vanity, telling us, "You'll be wanted if you beautify yourself." Paul was furious when he learned that the Galatians had succumbed to Satan's ploy.

You foolish Galatians! Who has bewitched you? Before your very eyes Jesus Christ was clearly portrayed as crucified. I would like to learn just one thing from you: Did you receive the Spirit by observing the law, or by believing what you heard? Are you so foolish? After beginning with the Spirit, are you now trying to attain your goal by human effort? (Galatians 3:1-3).

To "bewitch" (*ebaskanen*) means to mislead with an evil eye, with the false eyesight of an evil spirit. Pastor Bill was battling evil spiritual eyesight. "Maybe if I earned a second doctoral degree. Maybe if I changed how I preach." He was grasping at straws, works-straws. He was desperate to find some strategy that could somehow guarantee he would be acceptable to others, and to God.

What Bill needed was spiritual eyesight. He needed Christ's 20/20 spiritual vision. The Worthy Groom is pro grace and faith. Before the Fall, Christ addressed us as free beings; "I want you because I want you. You are beautiful by gift. You are loved by gift. Be free in my love." After the Fall, Christ addresses us saying, "I want you even though you can never of yourself reclaim the beauty you once had. I beautify you by grace." Bill, and you and I, need our Worthy Groom's grace meta-narrative.

Faith is Christ's antidote to counteract Satan's mistrust poison. Pastor Bill needed spiritual eyes to see his life from God's perspective. In Ecclesiastes, Solomon views life "under the sun." He looks at life from a temporal, earthly vantage point. Consequently, all seems "meaningless." Occasionally a glimmer of true Son light breaks through the clouds, allowing Solomon to view life under the Son. He looks at life from an eternal, heavenly vantage point.

Bill and I explored his life from the Son's perspective. We wondered together, "What is God up to in this? How is Christ orchestrating something grand and glorious out of this seeming mess?" With the Pastor Bills of your life, always seek to go "behind the curtain." Probe the good purposes of a good God. Luther explains the difference that can make.

If only a man could see his God in such a light of love. How happy, how calm, how safe he would be! He would then truly have a God from whom he would know with certainty that all his fortunes—whatever they might be—had come to him and were still coming to him under the guidance of God's most gracious will (Luther, *Works*, Vol. 43, p. 154).

After paraphrasing Luther's quote, I asked Pastor Bill to start listing, in two categories, all his thoughts about his situation. He chose the titles for the categories. Category One: *Foolish Interpretations that God's Out to Get Me.* Category Two: *Wise Interpretations that God Guides Me with His Most Gracious Will.* Gradually Bill began to counter Satan's mistrust poison with Christ's faith antidote. Slowly he began to experience how happy, how calm, how safe he was in Christ regardless of his circumstances.

Hope was Christ's antidote to counteract Satan's condemnation poison in Bill's life. He needed eternal eyes to understand that justification is his current standing before the Father, that sanctification is his ongoing promise by the Spirit, and that glorification is his future guarantee in Christ. Bill and I scrutinized Romans 8, applying those truths to his relationship with Christ. He needed to internalize the truth that God was for him and not against him. He needed to apply the truth that "Therefore, there is now no condemnation to those who are in Christ Jesus" (Romans 8:1). Luther understood the necessity of such reminders.

He who does not believe that he is forgiven by the inexhaustible riches of Christ's righteousness is like *a deaf man hearing a story*. If we considered it properly and with an attentive heart, this one image—even if there were no other—would suffice to fill us with such comfort that we should not only grieve over our evils, but should also glory in our tribulations, scarcely feeling them for the joy that we have in Christ (Luther, *Works*, Vol. 42, p. 165, emphasis added).

Apart from accepting our acceptance in Christ, we are deaf to Christ's grace narrative. When deaf to Christ, we are vulnerable to the whispers and the shouts of Satan's story.

As Bill began to live according to the truth that God was for him, he still wondered what God was doing in him *currently*. So we examined 2 Corinthians 4:16. "Therefore we do not lose heart. Though outwardly we are wasting away, yet inwardly we are being renewed day by day." Bill began to understand, deeper than ever before, that whatever was happening around him, in his situation, God was at work inside him—in his soul. He came to understand that there is not only an *eternal* story, but also an *internal* story.

His past settled by justification, his present assured by sanctification, Bill still needed hope concerning his future glorification. It's easy for us to think, "But he's a pastor. He knows this stuff!" Let's be honest. When life comes crashing down around us, we're tempted to believe our ultimate destiny is at stake. We believe that somehow what is most precious to our soul and most central to our being—who we are in relationship to God and what we will be for all eternity—is on the line. So Bill and I explored Romans 8:28-39. He had counseled others with these verses many times. Now he required counsel. Bill rejoiced in the reminders that God guaranteed his ultimate glorification and that nothing could ever separate him from the love of God in Christ Jesus.

Luther believed that the consciousness of being loved by the Father through the Son was the only power capable of changing us. He was simply paraphrasing a prayer of the apostle Paul from Ephesians 3:14-21. Paul's ultimate prayer concern for Christians is simple yet profound. "And I pray that you, being rooted and established in love, may have power, together with all the saints, to grasp how wide and long and high and deep is the love of Christ, and to know this love that surpasses knowledge" (Ephesians 3:17b-19a).

That's what Bill wanted. It's what I desire. It's what you long for. We crave the assurance at a personal, relational level that God loves us beyond our wildest imagination.

As Bill and I were talking, an odd memory struck me. It was September, so I can think of no earthly reason why my mind would move to *Rudolph the Red-Nosed Reindeer*. But suddenly I pictured the scene where Rudolph, feeling like a misfit, feeling unloved even by his own father, is struggling as he competes in the Reindeer Games. Then the sweet, beautiful little doe, Clarice, whispers in his ear, "I think you're cute." Rudolph swells with pride, leaps for joy, shattering all records as he screams, "She thinks I'm cute! She thinks I'm cute!"

I decided to share the image with Pastor Bill. It clicked. No, he didn't want to be seen as cute. Nevertheless, he longed to know that God thought the world of him. He wanted, more than life itself, to grasp together with all the saints how high and deep and wide and long Christ's love was to him. So I said, "Okay, He doesn't say, 'I think you're cute.' But what is Christ saying to you?"

Bill stopped. Thought. Reflected. "I sense Him saying to me through His Spirit and His Word and through you that I'm His son and He loves me and He's proud of me."

These were not novel concepts for Bill. However, as he personalized and internalized them in the midst of his suffering, they became the theme for his new life novel. Titling the new version of his life story *Son of Grace*, Pastor Bill was able to face the reality of his dismissal from two churches. A son of grace is not perfect, is not without failures. He is worthy, however. Even more importantly, the Worthy Groom loves him.

In the strength of his confidence in God, Pastor Bill was able to meet with the elders of both churches. He openly received their comments, integrating what seemed accurate, and sorting out what seemed unjustified. He's now thriving as a senior pastor, as a grace pastor.

The Two Competing Love Stories in Our Lives

In Genesis 3:15, God announces the theme woven throughout the rest of human history. "And I will put enmity between you and the woman, and between your offspring and hers; he will crush your head, and you will strike his heel." The Bible, in both Testaments, recounts this age-old love story and age-long battle between Christ and Satan. Two Romancers are vying for our souls—Christ our Worthy Groom and Satan the False Seducer.

What Genesis introduces, Revelation concludes. In our legitimate desire to understand the apocalyptic prophecies of Revelation, we have ignored the original audience and central theme of Revelation. The original recipients were persecuted believers hanging on by their fingertips, begging for Christ's return. The central theme, highlighted repeatedly in Revelation, teaches that our Worthy Groom is worth our wait.

Satan, the Anti-Groom, inspires the Anti-Christ to tell a different tale. He deceives many to buy the lie Job's wife believed, "Curse God and die." Then he seduces millions to sleep with the enemy, appropriately named, "the Mother of Prostitutes" (Revelation 17:5).

The central issue we face in all suffering and sin revolves around entrusting ourselves to God's good heart (His beautiful, pure, benevolent, extravagantly generous, gracious heart). "Will I or won't I? Is He or isn't He? He loves me. He loves me not. I trust Him. I trust Him not."

So how do we read our life story? Miles, in *God: A Biography*, notes that the world has stumbled upon just a few basic options to cope with the problem of evil.

♦ Yes, the innocent do suffer and the wicked prosper. The world is immoral—in effect, ruled by a fiend.

♦ No, the innocent suffer and the wicked prosper only some of the time. Sometimes the innocent prosper and the wicked suffer. The world is amoral and meaningless—in effect, ruled by nobody, or by chance.

♦ Yes, the innocent do sometimes suffer here and now, and the wicked do sometimes prosper here and now. But our world of time and space is only a part of the real world. Later, or elsewhere, the innocent will receive their just reward and the wicked their just punishment. The world, if you see it whole, is moral—in effect, ruled by a just judge.

♦ The prosperity of the wicked need imply only mercy in the world's judge. As for the suffering of the innocent, it is not simply evil (option 1) or simply meaningless (option 2) or simply to be compensated for (option 3). It may, instead of any of these be meritorious by serving as a tool by which the just judge ultimately brings justice to all. The innocent who suffer will ultimately be rewarded beyond the innocent who do not suffer. The world is moral; in effect, it is ruled by a mysteriously just judge who sometimes requires human suffering to achieve His ends.

Our Worthy Groom offers a fifth option—the biblical truth—for interpreting the meaning behind our life story.

♦ The prosperity of the wicked implies the goodness of a Father who sends His rain upon the just and the unjust (Matthew 5:45) and who withholds immediate judgment as a sign of His patient longing for all to return home (Luke 15:11-32; 2 Peter 3:3-15). When the wicked are judged in this life, God is destroying the idols of their hearts, tenaciously wooing them back to Himself (Hosea 2). As for the suffering of the innocent, it is not evil or meaningless or simply compensated for. Instead, it is the result of sin in a fallen world (Genesis 3:15-24). However, since grace superabounds beyond sin, our present sufferings will not compare with the glory that shall be revealed in us (Romans 8:17-18). The world intends suffering for evil, but our good Father uses suffering for His good purposes (Genesis 50:20). The world is both moral and loving because God is holy and loving.

When faced with suffering, we need spiritual eyes that discern both another time and another dimension. Another time reflects our awareness of eternity, of heaven, of the glory that shall be revealed in us. Another dimension reflects our acceptance of God's good heart. He is always up to something—something grand and glorious, something that offers each of us gracious opportunity after gracious opportunity to trust Him more.

Where We've Been and Where We're Heading

Biblical counselors grasp the nature of the Bible that tells us about human nature. Because it is our heroic adventure narrative, we know that biblical counseling focuses upon our role in Christ's victorious campaign. Because it is a passionate romance novel, we know that biblical counseling highlights our relationship to Christ our Worthy Groom.

The prologue complete, we're ready now for the curtains to open on Act One. Against our expectations, it does not take place in the beginning. It occurs before the beginning. The setting is not Earth, but heaven. The Actors are not Adam and Eve, but God the Father, Son, and Holy Spirit.

What kind of God tells His story by way of a romance novel that takes place in a grand adventure? The God of the Bible who has existed forever in the most exciting, intimate fellowship ever imagined.

Caring for Your Soul: Personal Applications

1. Remember your first love for Christ. Describe it. Enjoy it. Share it.

2. Do you believe in a God who blesses?

   a. In the eyes of your heart, is God a Rewarder or a Hoarder? A Blesser or a Bully? A Lover or a Tyrant? Does God have a good heart, or doesn't He?

   b. In what ways does your life evidence the conviction that God has a good heart? If you were placed on trial, charged with believing that God has a good heart, would there be enough evidence from your life to convict you? What would the evidence be?

3. Honestly respond to each of the following soul questions.

   a. Is God really telling a good story? Do you sense that He runs His universe with affectionate sovereignty?

   b. Is your life one of His great stories? Do you believe that He leads your unique life toward good ends? Are His purposes for you grand and His plans for you good? In what ways is He working all things together for good in your life?

4. Imagine that your heart was captured every second by the loveliness, love of, and love for God. How would your relationships be different—to God, family, friends, enemies, "counselees"?

5. Abraham does a little spiritual mathematics and figures that zero times God equals infinity. Describe a few times when you did some spiritual mathematics, when you believed God even though His promises seemed unbelievable, when you kept your hope even when all seemed lost.

Caring for Others: Ministry Implications

♦ **Become an Advocate for God Reality through Grace Eyes:** As a spiritual friend, you will hear stories that shake the foundation of your faith. In your soul, be vigilant to remember that where sin abounds, grace superabounds. In your biblical counseling, engage your spiritual friends in spiritual conversations that honestly explore signs of grace. God has not left Himself without witness. Where has He shown Himself full of grace, even while life has been full of sin?

♦ **Become an Advocate for Your Spiritual Friend through Grace Relationships:** Counseling involves speaking the truth in love. With our grace eyes, we help our spiritual friends see life from God's perspective. With grace relationships, we give our spiritual friends tastes of grace. The banquet is later. The feast is yet to come. However, we can offer bites of grace now. Accept your spiritual friends where they are. Love them even when they are unlovely. Forgive them when they are sinful. Weep with them when they are weeping. Hug them when they are hurting. Offer them grace to help in their time of need. Offer them yourself, as Paul offered the believers in Thessalonica the Scripture (truth) and his own soul (grace, love, relationship) (1 Thessalonians 2:8).

♦ **Share the Good News of God's Good Heart:** Think back to the last person you were helping to work through an issue of suffering or sin. How would a deep, personal awareness of God's good heart have influenced that person? What did you do to help that person sense God's goodness? What more could you have done?

♦ **Share the Bad News of Our Self-Sufficient Hearts:** Grace teaches us to say "No" to ungodly self-trust (Titus 2:11-14). Explore with your spiritual friends the fig leaves they sew to beautify themselves. Help them to acknowledge their nakedness. Point out the foolishness of their fig leaves. Point them to Christ's righteousness.

ACT ONE:
LOVE'S ETERNALITY—COMMUNITY

KNOWING THE CREATOR OF THE SOUL:
THE GREAT PHYSICIAN—TRINITY

DIRECTOR'S NOTES

When I'm browsing in a bookstore, I read the dust jacket of a book before I make a purchase. I read the author's biography. I want to know her history, her personality, what motivates her to write, and what she craves to communicate.

If there is a Book, then there must be an Author. In Act One, we read the dust jacket; we read God's autobiography. What is His history, His personality? What motivates Him to write? What does He crave to communicate through the stories He tells us and the letters He sends to us?

If there is a grand adventure, there must be a protagonist—a hero. And if there is a hero, there must be an antagonist—a fiendish enemy. The Trinity is the Hero of our theo-drama. Jesus Christ, our incarnate Worthy Groom, fleshes out the heroic Trinity. The slippery Serpent, Satan, is the despicable enemy in God's story. What is Satan, the False Seducer, like? What is his history, his personality?

If there is a great story, there must be a plot filled with tension, drama, intrigue, and conflict. The Bible's plot twists and turns around the clash between our Worthy Groom's strategy and the False Seducer's scheme. How does our Worthy Groom win our hearts back from the False Seducer with whom we are committing spiritual adultery? It is to scenes like these that we turn our gaze in Act One.

SCENE I, CHAPTER 4: OUR WORTHY GROOM'S HISTORY

SCENE II, CHAPTER 5: OUR WORTHY GROOM'S PERSONALITY

SCENE III, CHAPTER 6: THE FALSE SEDUCER'S STORY

SCENE IV, CHAPTER 7: THE BATTLE FOR OUR SOUL

As soul caregivers and spiritual directors, we can't afford a smaller story focus. Such a focus assumes that our spiritual friends fight only against flesh and blood. The smaller story focus ignores the deeper truth that our spiritual friends wrestle against "the rulers, against the authorities, against the powers of this dark world and against the spiritual forces of evil in the heavenly realms" (Ephesians 6:12). We must move beyond smaller story, solution-focused counseling.

All secular models of counseling *reduce* life to a set of principles and procedures designed to help counselees manage life better without God. All truly Christian models of counseling *expand* life to God's eternal perspective, assisting counselees to realize they cannot live by bread alone, but by every word that proceeds from the mouth of God.

CHAPTER FOUR

OUR WORTHY GROOM'S HISTORY

"God does not need the creation in order to have something to love because within himself love happens" (Frederick Buechner).

The Trinity is the original community of oneness. The god of the Muslims is one person within one being and, therefore, is a prisoner of his own limitations. Not so for the God revealed in Jesus Christ. He is three persons within oneness. He values community supremely because He experiences the dynamics and synergy of three in one. Thus, when He creates in His image, He creates community (Paraphrased from Gilbert Bilezikian, *Community 101*, pp. 16-18).

"God is unchangeably personal" (Stanley Grenz, *The Social God and the Relational Self*, p. 56).

Unanchored Souls

Sixteen-year-old Aminah McKinnie of Madison, Mississippi, confesses that she is beset by feelings of isolation mixed with longings to be connected (Sharon Begley, "A World of Their Own," *Newsweek*, May 8, 2000, pp. 54-55). Like other teens of her generation, she is isolated to an extent that has never been possible before. In the class I teach on *Counseling Adolescents*, I call teens the "Chat Room Generation." They experience fleeting, fragmented relationships epitomized by the Internet chat room where they can have one identity today, another tomorrow, and yet a third persona next week.

We live in a world of disconnected people with unanchored souls. How tragic individually and socially. But more important, it is spiritual tragedy. We bear God's image. He is not, and therefore we are not, unanchored souls. Nor is God a disconnected being. I propose that the solution to disconnected, unanchored souls is Trinitarian theology.

Before the Beginning

Think for a moment about that infinite stretch of "time" before anything was created. Let your imagination contemplate what it must have been like for the Trinity to exist together with no one and nothing else. Now try to reduce to a single word what you have imagined.

Here's my best attempt:

♦   In the Beginning God *Created*
♦   Before the Beginning God *Related*

Before they created, the Trinity related. What were the Father, Son, and Holy Spirit *doing* before they created? They were experiencing constant, uninterrupted, intimate relationship. They were together, in harmony, giving, sharing, relating—loving.

Recognizing that relationship enables us to answer an important question: "What type of person writes a romance novel within the context of a grand adventure?" Answer: A person who relates and creates, whose very essence is love in action.

Too many Christian counseling models start at the wrong place. A few begin at the beginning with Creation—God's original design, intent, and Genesis 1-2. Some start with the Fall—sin, depravity, and Genesis 3. Others begin with Redemption—salvation, sanctification, and the New Testament. But if we were to proceed truly chronologically, where would we begin? What is the first section in the Bible chronologically?

"Genesis!" you shout, hoping to win a Bible quizzing contest. Nice guess. Wrong response. A purely chronological rendering of the Bible would progress something like this:

♦   *Eternity Past*—Before the Foundations of the Earth: John 1:1-14; John 17:1-26; Ephesians 1:4-6; Colossians 1:15-17; 1 Peter 1:18-20
♦   *Creation*—The Foundations of the Earth: Genesis 1:1-2:25; Job 38:1-41:34; Psalm 8:1-9; Psalm 19:1-6
♦   *Fall*—The Rebellion in Heaven and on Earth: Genesis 3:1-24; Isaiah 14:10-20; Ezekiel 28:12-19; Romans 1:18-28; Romans 5:12-21; 1 Timothy 2:11-15
♦   *Redemption*—The Redeemer on Earth: Matthew 1-2; Luke 1-2; John 3:16; Ephesians 1:3-11

I propose that we construct a biblical counseling model that begins before the beginning. I suggest we build our model of Christian counseling on the foundation of the Triune relationship that existed before the foundations of the earth. *If we are going to learn spiritual friendship, then let's look to the ultimate Spiritual Friend and the eternal Spiritual Friendship: the Trinity.* The relationship within the Trinity models how we ought to relate. Father, Son, and Holy Spirit demonstrate how love lives.

Intimacy Beyond Our Wildest Imagination

The god of the Muslims is a monad—the Alone with the Alone. He exists in sterile oneness. Not so the Trinity. "In the beginning was the Word, and the Word was with God, and the Word was God. He was with God in the beginning" (John 1:1-2).

In *The Book of God*, Jack Miles surmises that God has no history. Before He created us, since He had no one to relate to, He had failed to develop any personality. He was a God alone and a lonely God in need of companions. Not so the Trinity. "No one has ever seen God, but God the One and Only, who is at the Father's side, has made him known" (John 1:18).

The apostle John styles his introduction to echo the Genesis account of the beginning. Then he takes us time traveling back before the beginning of time. Upon arrival, we find that the Word *was* with God in the beginning. In using the Greek word for "was," John could have chosen the aorist past tense. This would have pictured a snapshot where we travel back in time to a moment when the Son happened to be in the Father's presence. Instead, John selects the imperfect past tense picturing an ongoing video. *Whenever* we might travel back in time, at *whatever* point we would arrive, we would *always* find Father and Son (and Spirit) together. We might translate John's phrase the way his first century readers would have heard it. "The Word was continually, without interruption, with the Father always and forever."

As our story begins, we do not find our Author alone at His desk. We discover the Author of our heroic adventure narrative, of our passionate romance novel, in relationship. The everlasting, intimate connection shared within the Trinity demonstrates that relationship is the gravity that holds our universe together.

> Community finds its existence and definition deep within the very being of God. Oneness is primarily a divine mode of being that pertains to God's own existence, independently from and prior to any of His works of creation. Whatever community exists, it is only a reflection of an eternal reality that is intrinsic to the being of God. Because God is eternally One, when He created in His image, He created oneness (Paraphrased from Gilbert Bilezikian, *Community 101*, pp. 16-18).

God's Relational Community

Notice again where the Word was. "And the Word was *with* God" (John 1:1, emphasis added). The Greek preposition signifies "before, in the presence of, face-to-face with." When my children were young, we played a game called "Eye Contact." I would bellow, "Josh! Marie! Let's play 'Eye Contact!'" They'd race to me, shove their eye sockets into my eye sockets, press their eyeballs into my eyeballs, and we would make eye contact. Father and Son (and Spirit) play an eternal game of "Eye Contact," except they call it "Soul Contact." The Trinity always enjoys the sheer delight of eternal, unbroken communion, connection, and community. Theologian Carl F. H. Henry elaborates:

> God is continually engaged in inter-communion, in internal self-revelation and holy love. This activity is not an addition to His nature, it is God's essential being in tripersonal activity (Henry, *God, Revelation, and Authority*, Vol. 5: "God Who Stands and Stays," p. 15).

How intimate is their fellowship? John tells us. No; he shows us by describing where we find Jesus and God when we time warp back before the beginning. Jesus is at the Father's side; He is at the bosom of the Father. "Bosom" (*kolpon*) stresses the closest, most intimate, relaxed, and comfortable shared relationship imaginable. John uses the same word later in his Gospel to describe himself sharing a meal with Jesus, reclining on Christ's bosom. Without being disrespectful, we might say that the Trinity enjoys an eternal cuddle, an everlasting hug, an endless embrace.

They dwell together, they make their home together, and their home is the home that we all long for and dream of. Not because it is a massive mansion, but because it is a warm embrace. Spiritual director Larry Crabb captures the scene for us.

> Imagine the sheer delight of enjoying perfect relationships with two others with no fear of things turning sour, a community of three cut from the same fabric yet unmistakably distinct. Imagine three who, without a hint of competitiveness, are absolutely thrilled with the uniqueness of the other two, who will stop at nothing to give each other the opportunity to display their special glory. Imagine a community without even the shadow of evil, with nothing but perfect goodness, where every member can be fully himself without fear of promoting rivalry or releasing something bad (Crabb, *Connecting*, p. 57).

Think of your best moments of love and friendship. Perhaps your mind goes to those "glory days" at college with a roommate who knew you through and through. Maybe you think of your long-term, intimate, committed relationship with your spouse and some of the tenderest times you have ever shared. Or you might recall great moments together, parent-to-child, times of closeness, laughter, fun, and depth. Now consider this. These wonderful moments are but mere minor reflections of the love that flows ceaselessly within and among the Trinity.

We must realize something that's not easy for our modern mind or post-modern sense of self to hear. *God does not need us*. We are radically contingent. We are unnecessary to the Trinity. They were perfectly happy without us and could have gotten along fine apart from us.

Because God is not a Hoarder, He chose to share. Not a Miser, His sharing is extravagant. "The Word became flesh and made his dwelling among us" (John 1:14). Jesus left His Father's glory, moved out of His heavenly home, and built a home here with us. Why? "No one has ever seen God, but God the One and Only, who is at the Father's side, *has made him known*" (John 1:18, emphasis added). Jesus exegetes the Father. He explains, makes clear, reveals the very nature of God to us. Though God could never need us, it is within His nature to communicate Himself to us.

> It is the very nature of God to reveal Himself . . . God is not to be thought of as aloof and indifferent . . . John's *Logos* does not show us a God who is serenely detached, but a God who is passionately involved. The *Logos* speaks of God's coming where we are, taking our nature upon Himself, entering the world's struggle, and out of this agony winning men's salvation (Leon Morris, *The Gospel According to John*, pp. 74-75, 117).

This is why Jesus is called "the Word" (*logos*) (John 1:1). He is the Communicator, the Story Teller, the Singer, and the Revealer. Before God created, He related. He did create, however, and He created in order to relate with us. Not out of need, but out of love, out of grace.

Deuteronomy 7:7-8 indicates God's strong love for Israel. As with Israel, God loves us simply because He loves us. Or as Deuteronomy 10:15 teaches, "Yet the LORD set his affection on your forefathers and loved them, and he chose you, their descendents, above all the nations, as it is today." Literally: "the LORD delighted in your fathers to love them." The Hebrew word for "delight" means to love or be attached to. It is full of feeling and desire as the love of a man for a woman. It is not a word denoting dispassionate commitment. Deuteronomy 10:15 uses it with the infinitival "to love." Literally, "The LORD *loved* your fathers to *love them*." Or, "The LORD was attached to your fathers to love them." This double word for love strongly emphasizes that the motive was love rooted only in love and nothing else. The love was deep, passionate, and full of desire. God freely chose to take pleasure in loving us not because He had to, or needed to, but because He wanted to. God's love is a love of passionate commitment.

When we begin to grasp what this means, we'll come to see that we don't have to work to earn a place in God's heart. We can do nothing to make Him love us more or less. He loves us because He loves us.

Our Relational Manual

The Bible is our relational manual, written by the most relational Being in the universe, inspired by the universe's most inspiring Lover. Why is He writing His Book? What are His qualifications to write a love story? John 1 has answered both those questions. The Trinity is "qualified" to write the relational manual we use in soul care and spiritual direction because they are the epitome of healthy, intimate relationship. Why did they write? The Spirit, Messenger, inspired the Bible to communicate who God is and how we can relate to Him and one another.

How should we relate? What might spiritual friendship look like if we modeled it after the friendship of the Trinity? Certainly it would *not* follow a distant, aloof, "one-up," detached, professional therapy model. Rather, spiritual friendship modeled after the ultimate Spiritual Friends would overflow with engagement, enjoyment, playfulness, faith, hope, and love. We would delight in our spiritual friends; make eye contact and soul contact with them. We would come out from behind our desk, removing all barriers, and sit face-to-face in unashamed intimacy. We would marvel at our spiritual friends. They are, after all, image bearers—bearers, though finite and fallen, of the image of the awesome Trinity.

Admiration Beyond Our Grandest Dream

Father, Son, and Holy Spirit marvel at one another. Immediately after telling His disciples to take heart because He had overcome the world, Jesus lifted His eyes toward heaven and prayed, "Father, the time has come. Glorify your Son, that your Son may glorify you" (John 17:1). From before the foundation of the world, the Trinity has shared intimacy beyond our wildest imagination and admiration beyond our grandest dreams. "You loved me before the creation of the world" (John 17:24b). "And now, Father, glorify me in your presence with the glory I had with you before the world began" (John 17:5).

The Trinity is a mutual admiration and adoration society of shared glory. In John 1, the apostle John carries us back before time began. In John 17, Jesus is our time traveling Guide. In His prayer, He transports us to that infinite stretch before time so we can sense the unbounded esteem the Trinity shares. Five times in the first five verses, Jesus speaks of "glory" (*doxa*). The Greeks used this word to denote reputation and good standing. The Old Testament equivalent (*kābôd*) has the root sense of something weighty that gives importance and honor. In relationship to God it expresses what makes God impressive. He's a heavyweight, not a lightweight. When the Septuagint (LXX, or Greek translation of the Old Testament) uses *doxa* to translate *kābôd*, it refers to the splendor of God's majesty. Glory is the Divine nature in its invisibility or its perceptible manifestation. In the New Testament, glory embraces the Divine honor, splendor, power, and radiance, which are the essence of God's being. To glorify God means to acknowledge or extol what is already a reality. It includes praising, valuing, and honoring God for who He is.

When I was a teenager, my friends and I had a sarcastic, mocking phrase we'd use when we thought someone was showing off. If a guy in his car peeled his tires, we'd yell, "Wow, impressive!" What we did mockingly, the Trinity does delightfully. "Wow! Impressive!"

They are like Amber and her Mom. In high school our youth group took a bus trip from the flat lands of Indiana to the mountains of Pennsylvania. Amber and her Mom had never been outside of Indiana, had never seen mountains. They were amazed. When Mom would spot another one on the horizon, she would yell, "Hey, Amber, look out the window!" After a while, every time we encountered another glorious vista, the entire bus would yell, "Hey, Amber, look out the window!" To this day, when we go on a family vacation, even though none of us is named Amber, whenever we see an amazing sight, we yell, "Hey, Amber, look out the window!" That's how the Trinity relates. They never get over the thrill of delighting in the glory they see in one another.

So what did the Trinity *do* before they created? They enjoyed each other and bragged on each other. They were thrilled with each other. They shared sheer delight. The Trinity is radically other-centered, totally unselfish. "Father, you are incredible!" "Son, you are amazing!" "Spirit, you are awesome!" There never was a time when the Trinity was denied the pleasure of delighting in their mutual glory.

When Jesus came to earth, nothing changed. "I have brought you glory on earth by completing the work you gave me to do" (John 17:4). As John 1:18 and 17:6 teach, Jesus came to reveal, to unveil, and to display His Father's glorious nature. Jesus is the Father's Press Agent and Biographer. According to Hebrews 1:1-3, Jesus is the eloquence of God, the dazzling outshining, God's mirror image. He's the clean, clear, crisp imprint of God. "Anyone who has seen me has seen the Father" (John 14:9b).

As remarkable as God's glory is, Jesus thrills us when He prays, "I have given them the glory that you gave me, that they may be one as we are one" (John 17:22). What? We participate in God's glory? The goal of our salvation is our glorification. What is sown in dishonor is raised in glory. God will say of us, "Beautiful! Powerful! Graceful! Wise! Joyful!"

Remember that God could have hoarded His glory. From all eternity, the one reality that has always existed is God. However, the ever-living God has not been "alone." He has not been a solitary center of consciousness. There has always been another who has been one with God in essence and glory, and yet distinct in personhood so that they have had a personal relationship of mutual love and shared glory for all eternity.

He chose to share, but not because He had to or needed to. God acts in sovereign freedom. His acts do not spring from the need to make up deficiencies, but from a passion to express the abundance of His delight. Because He is good and generous, God delights to give us the very delight that He has in Himself. "Part of God's fullness which He communicates, is his happiness. This happiness consists in enjoying and rejoicing in himself; so does also the creature's happiness" (Jonathan Edwards, *The End for Which God Created the World*, p. 4).

No one would want to spend eternity with an unhappy God. Instead, God invites us to enjoy what is most enjoyable with unbounded energy and passion forever. "The enjoyment of God is the only happiness with which our souls can be satisfied" (Edwards, "The Christian Pilgrim," in *The Works of Jonathan Edwards*, p. 2).

Our Relational Model

The God who reveals Himself in John's Gospel as Triune community also reveals Himself in John's Epistle as love. "God is love" (1 John 4:8). God is Lover and Beloved. Father, Son, and Holy Spirit exist in reciprocal self-dedication. This corresponds to John's concept of *agapē,* which he defines as the giving of oneself for the other. We can summarize the love relationship within the Trinity:

- ♦ **Enjoying:** A constant love exchange of intimate knowing, communing, and communicating. Love continually given and received.
- ♦ **Glorying:** A mutual admiration and adoration society of shared glory. Delight continually revealed and expressed.

It's hard for us to comprehend how unique God's model of relationship is. We are accustomed to settling for so much less. Our fallen world infiltrates our minds with lesser relational models such as:

- ♦ **Shallow Relationships:** We remain aloof, distant, and comfortable. We rarely talk about vital issues, steering clear of "spiritual" topics lest we become "too personal."
- ♦ **Shaming Relationships:** We are sin-spotters who see only fallenness and evil and nothing of the image of God in one another. We confront, but we don't care. We put down, but don't build up. We discourage rather than fan into flame.
- ♦ **Secular Relationships:** Like the "rulers of the Gentiles," we "lord it over one another," always having to be the one in charge or the one focused upon. We compete against one another, rather than completing and complementing one another. We expend our energy maneuvering and jockeying for position.
- ♦ **Self-Sufficient Relationships:** We play the role of "The Lone Ranger," not asking for help, though we desperately need it.

- ◆ **Self-Protective Relationships:** Like Adam and Eve, we relate out of fear and end up hiding and covering. We clothe ourselves with so many layers that we don't even know who the real "us" is. Our thoughts constantly stray to *How am I coming across? What do others think of me?*
- ◆ **Sanctioned Relationships:** We burden one another with pharisaic rules, regulations, and rituals, and, like the Pharisees, refuse to lift even one finger to help carry the burdens. Our relationships are legal, not loving.
- ◆ **Selfish Relationships:** These are manipulative relationships where we exploit one another. Adroitly we finesse conversations and situations so our "needs" are met.
- ◆ **Spiteful Relationships:** When our "needs" are not met, we retaliate. As James tells us, "we kill and we covet." We kill with words, with cold shoulders, and with silence.

How different life would be if we followed a Trinitarian relational model. Our friendships might truly become spiritual. Discussing, "Where is God in the middle of this?" would become as natural as asking, "How do you like this weather we're havin'?" We would see sin in one another, but would always look deeper—searching for the image of God waiting to break forth. Our relationships would be filled with give-and-take where we treated each other as equals, though different. Humility and vulnerability would mark our conversations; we would honestly share our suffering and our sin, our struggles and our strengths. Grace would mark us, not law. Together we would marvel at active signs of Christ's grace breaking into our character and our circumstances. We would focus on ministering to each other in the energy of the ultimate Minister, Jesus Christ. When hurt, because hurt does enter all relationships, we would discuss our hurts, confess our wrong, repent to our God, give and receive forgiveness, and learn how to build loving relationships that last through all the storms of life.

In short, we would enjoy and delight in each other. Our relationships would be a constant love exchange of intimate knowing, communing, and communicating. Love continually given and received. Our communication would be seasoned with grace, leading to a mutual admiration society of shared delight, continually revealed and expressed.

Our Relational Model in Practice

If it sounds too good to be true, too heavenly minded to be of any earthly good, it's not. Last Saturday in the most mundane of places, God nurtured a spiritual conversation. Kyle stood in the Wal-Mart checkout line just ahead of me.

"How's it goin', Kyle?"

"I'm hangin' in there," he said in a discouraged tone.

"Hanging by both hands with a solid grip, hanging by your fingertips, hanging by a thread?" I asked.

Kyle smiled. "Fingertips."

"What's up?" I asked.

"I'm just juggling too many balls right now."

Finished with our purchases now, we walked into the parking lot, stopped, and leaned against his car. Kyle told me about the balls he was juggling with tax time for the company he owned, the legal issue his adult daughter was facing, his wife's health concern . . .

"Wow! Those aren't ping pong balls you're juggling, they're bowling balls."

"Yeah. No. It's more like I'm one of those circus jugglers, juggling with knives, swords, and flaming torches."

"Man, I had no idea you were dealing with all this. I'm committing to pray for you. How are you handling everything?"

"It comes and goes."

"It?" I asked.

"My ability to hand it over to God," Kyle responded. "My ability to keep praying to Him, seeking His help, strength, and direction. I guess, overall, although I'm kinda' feeling overwhelmed, I haven't quit doing what I think God wants me to do in each situation. And I haven't quit going to Him."

"That's impressive, Kyle. I know for me, when those bowling balls start dropping on my toes, I sometimes either give up trying or give up praying. You haven't quit on yourself or on God. How'd you develop such tenacious faith?"

Our conversation continued for another five minutes or so. It wasn't "textbook." But Kyle and I did turn a mundane setting into a spiritual encounter. God allowed two brothers in Christ to engage each other in a caring and respectful way. We enjoyed a small taste, a morsel of what Trinitarian relationships are like. You can, too.

Where We've Been and Where We're Heading

In Act One, Scene I, we've witnessed the mystery of God as Trinity—perfect sociality. We've watched as the Trinity hugged and high-fived.

As we've watched, we've learned. Reality is relational because God is communal. God is not unaffiliated, isolated, fragmented, or disconnected. Forever and ever the Trinity enjoys unity in genuine diversity, solidarity, reciprocity, cooperation, peace, shalom, harmony, community, and mutuality. Because God is radically, yet self-sufficiently social, He graces us with a passionate, sacrificial love.

As we learn, we change. We change as people and as soul caregivers and as spiritual directors. Our approach to others changes to the degree that we embody, embrace, and emulate the image of God. We become spiritual friends, not academic professionals. God's history shapes our present ministry.

Additionally, God's personality influences our maturity. In Act One, Scene II, we'll witness the majesty and beauty of God in whose image we abide. If we are going to be like Him, we need to know what He is like.

The actors set foot on the stage. Let's see how they depict God's holy love.

Caring for Your Soul: Personal Applications

1. Ponder again the isolated, disconnected world of sixteen-year-old Aminah McKinnie.

    a. Who do you know that's like Aminah—experiencing fleeting, fragmented relationships?

    b. To what degree did it shock you that Trinitarian theology is the solution to disconnected, unanchored souls?

2. Forever Friends:

    a. Think of, describe, and share your best moments of love and friendship.

    b. Now ponder this. These wonderful moments are but mere reflections of the love that flows eternally among the Trinity. Contrast and compare your best relational moments with the infinite intimacy of the Trinity.

3. Think of someone you could begin to enjoy more fully. How could that relationship more fully reflect the mutual enjoyment of the Trinity?

4. Think of someone you could admire more fully. How could that relationship more fully reflect the mutual admiration of the Trinity?

5. Tap into your longing for home. What would it be like to come home each day to Trinity's home?

6. Review the eight lesser relational models.

    a. Which one(s) do you find yourself struggling against most often?

    b. What could you do to move from that lesser model toward the Trinitarian model of enjoying and glorifying?

7. Reread the vignette about Kyle.

    a. Who is "Kyle" in your life? With what person would you like to enter into a deeper level of spiritual connection?
    b. What could you do to begin moving toward that depth?

    c. Take some time now to pray for that depth to grow.

Caring for Others: Ministry Implications

♦ **Trinitarian Counseling Principle Number One—Expand Life:** Since secular models of counseling *reduce* life and Christian models of counseling *expand* life, why do you think we sometimes still settle for solution-focused counseling? In your ministry, what will it look like to be relationship-focused and character-driven—emphasizing internal and eternal issues?

♦ **Trinitarian Counseling Principle Number Two—Enter People:** We learn spiritual friendship from our ultimate Spiritual Friend and the eternal Spiritual Friendship, the Trinity. Spiritual friendship modeled after the Trinity eschews detached professionalism. Rather, it overflows with engagement, enjoyment, playfulness, faith, hope, and love. Specifically, how could these insights strengthen your current ministry?

♦ **Trinitarian Counseling Principle Number Three—Enjoy People:** Since our spiritual friends are image bearers, we can take delight in them. How can your approach to others change as you embody, embrace, and emulate God's image by relishing intimate involvement with your spiritual friends?

♦ **Trinitarian Counseling Principle Number Four—Emphasize God:** If we follow a Trinitarian relational model, our spiritual friendships will discuss: "Where is God in the middle of this?" Spiritual friendships that reflect "Trinity Community" (Ephesians 5:1-2) are foundational to dislodging sinful passions (Ephesians 5:3-17) and stirring up godly relationships (Ephesians 5:18-6:9) because only the Creator can permanently change His creations. What does it look like for you to emphasize God in your personal ministry to others?

CHAPTER FIVE

OUR WORTHY GROOM'S PERSONALITY

"There are only two things that pierce the human heart. One is beauty. The other is affliction" (Simone Weil).

"The Christian's perception of God's holiness includes the awe that comes from our awareness that God is not subservient nor tame, and a fascination—the feeling of being allured, even entranced, by God's beauty, goodness, mercy, and love. . . . God's awesomeness and His attractiveness are always blended together in a true response to His holiness" (J. I. Packer, *Rediscovering Holiness*, pp. 131-132).

"What comes to our minds when we think about God is the most important thing about us" (A. W. Tozer, *The Knowledge of the Holy*, p. 9).

The Cosmic Beauty Contest

I grew up in the days of only three TV channels and before the glut of beauty contests. Every year our entire family settled down in front of our television set to watch *Miss America*, then, later in the year, *Miss Universe*. Even back then, before the era of political correctness, the host emphasized that the winner was selected not only based on beauty, but also on ability—talent. Which woman combined the greatest ability and beauty?

Long before those days, our universe began watching a cosmic beauty contest. This contest, too, is based both on ability and beauty. The judges ask, "Whose majesty captures me? Whose beauty captivates me?"

The contestants are two. The Trinity, dressed in the splendor of holiness and the brilliance of loveliness. The second contestant is the False Seducer, garbed as an angel of light. Masquerading with great pomp and pageantry, he buys off the judges. Worse than that, he blindfolds the judges so they cannot see the light of the glory of the Trinity. But God, who made light shine out of darkness, makes His light shine in their hearts to give them the light of the knowledge of the glory of God in the face of Christ.

Here we view our cosmic beauty contest. Whose majesty captures me, the Worthy Groom or the False Seducer? Whose beauty captivates me, God or Satan?

Obviously, we are *not* to sit in judgment upon God. That is *not* our right. God paints His own picture, writes His own autobiography. The Scriptures give us a portrait of God we would have never imagined. Our calling is not to rewrite the script, but to revel in who God is.

However, in our fallen world, there *is* a battle—a battle for our affection and attention, for our love and loyalty. In fact, Jonathan Edwards taught that the greatest battle in the universe is *the battle for our delights*.

In this battle, Satan says, "The world is ugly. God must be ugly, too. Live an ugly life." Christ says, "God alone is good. There is no evil in Him at all. He is a noble Husband wanting nothing but good for His bride. Live a beautiful, powerful life for His glory."

The battle for our minds and hearts is won or lost according to our image of God. Since we reflect what we revel in and become like what we worship; we must know God in His majesty and beauty if we are to become like Him. Edwards describes the essential relationship between our view of God and our Christian character.

> When the true beauty and attraction of the holiness found in divine things is discovered by the soul, a new world of perspectives is opened. The glory of all the perfections of God and of everything that pertains to Him is revealed. It shows the glory of all God's works both in creation and in providence. . . . The glorifying of God's moral perfections is a special end of all creation. A sense of the moral beauty of divine things enables us to understand the sufficiency of Christ as Mediator. In this way the believer is led into the knowledge of the excellency of Christ's person. The saints are then made aware of the preciousness of Christ's blood and of its sufficiency to atone for sin. . . . Thus all true experiential religion comes from this sense of spiritual beauty. For whoever does not see the beauty of holiness cannot appreciate the graces of God's Spirit. Without this there is ignorance of the whole spiritual world (Jonathan Edwards, *Religious Affections*, p. 109).

Soul caregivers and spiritual directors know God. They enlighten their spiritual friends to grasp the holy love of God. They expose Satan's deceitful veiling of God's glory and grace that invades their spiritual friends' lives. They teach that God is good even when life is bad. He is the Protagonist in our book—the good Guy.

But what do we mean when we say, "God is good"? What is the essence of God's goodness? We'll answer the question from two perspectives:

- ◆ The Holy Love of God: The Perfection of His Character
- ◆ The Personage of God: The Capacities of His Personhood

God is a Person. He is a personal being with the capacity to love, think, choose, and feel. He is a perfect personal being, infinite, and absolutely pure. Journey with me as we enter the awe-inspiring realm of the character and capacities of God.

The Holy Love of God: The Perfection of His Character

When we say "God is good" and "God has a good heart," we mean that God is a God of beauty and majesty, of holy love. A vision of God's holy love will deliver us from caricatures of Him, John Stott reminds us.

We must picture him neither as an indulgent God who compromises his holiness in order to spare and spoil us, nor as a harsh, vindictive God who suppresses his love in order to crush and destroy us (Stott, *The Cross of Christ*, p. 132).

That God is holy and loving is foundational to biblical Christianity and to biblical counseling. The Scriptures express the oneness or unity of God in terms of the complementary nature of His holiness and love, His holy love.

Stott refers his readers to ten passages (Exodus 34:6-7; Psalm 85:10; Isaiah 45:21; Micah 7:18; Habakkuk 3:2; John 1:14; Romans 11:22; Romans 3:26; Ephesians 2:3-4; and 1 John 1:9) that highlight God's holiness and love, then concludes:

Here are ten couplets, in each of which two complementary truths about God are brought together, as if to remind us that we must beware of speaking of one aspect of God's character without remembering its counterpart (Stott, *The Cross of Christ*, p. 130).

I have identified my own list of "couplets of God's holy love": Exodus 33:14-23 with Exodus 34:5-7; Psalm 26:3; Psalm 40:10-11; Psalm 62:11-12; Psalm 63:2-3; Psalm 85:10; Isaiah 40:10-11; Romans 2:4-5; and 1 Peter 1:16 with 1 John 4:8. In these passages God's love and holiness are simultaneously displayed. They are equally infinite; therefore, He maintains them in perfect harmony. The Psalmist noted this when he attempted to explain the God in whom His soul found rest. "One thing God has spoken, two things have I heard: that you, O God, are strong, and that you, O Lord, are loving" (Psalm 62:11-12). The poet divinely attests to two great summarizing truths about God. They are the two grand truths that God's revelation declares through every page: *God is holy; God is loving*. He is filled with majesty and beauty. He is King and Shepherd, full of grace and truth, our Lord and our Lover, transcendent (far above us) and yet immanent (near us), just and merciful, stern and kind, controlling and caring.

What difference does it make whether or not we see God as a God of holy love? The very fact that we have to address the question indicts post-modern Christianity and current models of Christian counseling. Soul caregivers throughout Church history led their disciples on a quest for the beatific vision of God—*visio Dei*—the soul's vision of God (see R. C. Sproul, *The Soul's Quest for God*, p. 232).

Sproul reminds us that spiritual directors of the past understood that without spiritual apprehension of God's glorious excellency (majesty, holiness) and His beauty, no one could exalt or enjoy God. It is our calling as soul caregivers and spiritual directors to enlighten our spiritual friends to perceive God in His pure, Divine essence, to behold His innermost being.

This side of heaven, our vision will always remain blurred. When we cross over, then we shall see Him as He is.

The highest joy, the greatest pleasure, the purest delight will be ours without mixture and without end. One taste of this felicity will erase all painful memories and heal each dreadful wound incurred in this vale of tears. No scar will remain. The pilgrim's progress will be complete. The body of death, the burden of sin, will vaporize the moment we behold his face (Sproul, *The Soul's Quest for God*, p. 250).

Box 5:1

Our Father's Holy Love

Holy	Love
Majesty	Beauty
Truth	Grace
Righteous	Forgiving
Separate from	Near to
Transcendent (above us)	Immanent (with us/near us)
Awesome	Attractive
Control	Care
Sovereign	Sufficient
Strong	Supportive
Powerful	Present
Just	Merciful
Wrath	Tenderness
Passion	Compassion
Sternness	Kindness
Recompense	Reward
Faithful	Loyal
Discipline	Devotion
"Yes, I Am Strong"	"Yes, I Am Loving"
Boundaries	Security
Rules	Relates
King	Shepherd
Hero	Lover
Master	Groom
Lord	Friend
Judge	Savior
Omnipotent	Omnibenevolent

Couplets of Holy Love

Exodus 33:14-23 with Exodus 34:5-7
Psalm 26:3
Psalm 40:10-11
Psalm 62:11-12
Psalm 63:2-3
Psalm 85:10
Isaiah 40:10-11
Romans 2:4-5
1 Peter 1:16 with 1 John 4:8

Today, while still pilgrims in progress, we quest for a deeper and purer vision of the goodness of God's heart. Even as the perfect heavenly vision will purify our sin and erase our suffering, so a growing vision of God now will strengthen us against sin and sustain us in our suffering.

In two "God is" passages, the Bible summarizes the vision we desire our spiritual friends to see: 1 John 4:8 and 1 Peter 1:16. "God is love." "God is holy." Soul care enables people to see that "Life is bad, but God is good (holy and loving)." In the midst of suffering, when life is ugly, we sustain our spiritual friends with the truth that God is loving: beautiful, caring, kind, generous, extravagant, comforting. We help them know that it's normal to hurt, and that God cares about their suffering. They can find healing in their suffering as they realize it's possible to hope, because God is in control. Because God is holy, sovereign, and omnipotent, nothing can thwart His purposes in their lives.

In the midst of their sinning, we help our spiritual friends to acknowledge they are sinful, but God is gracious. Such conviction requires that they perceive both God's holiness and love. Spiritual directors assist people trapped in Satan's snare by exposing how horrible it is to sin against a holy God. However, we don't leave people there. We take them to the Cross, to Christ's grace, love, and forgiveness. In reconciling, spiritual directors expose people to the truth that it's horrible to sin, but wonderful to be forgiven. In guiding, we empower our repentant, forgiven spiritual friends to know it's supernatural to mature. Why? Because God is holy, and, therefore, all-powerful and all-capable of empowering us. And God is loving, therefore, love is what He empowers us to do and to be.

Portraits of Our Sovereign Shepherd

Isaiah 40:10-11 presents a captivating couplet communicating God's holy love. Isaiah invites us to gaze upon our Sovereign Shepherd.

♦ "See, the Sovereign LORD comes with power, and his arm rules for him. See, his reward is with him, and his recompense accompanies him" (v. 10—the majesty of God's holiness).

♦ "He tends his flock like a shepherd: He gathers the lambs in his arms and carries them close to his heart; he gently leads those that have young" (v. 11—the beauty of God's love).

This couplet summarizes Israel's relationship with God. They had known Him both in His sovereignty and His sweetness, in His sternness and His kindness, in His judgment and His mercy. He was their Sovereign Shepherd.

Join me on a guided tour of two exhibit halls in Isaiah's art gallery. One is filled with grand drawings of Yahweh—the Sovereign LORD—in all His majesty. In the other hall, we marvel at tender images of God—the Good Shepherd—in all His beauty.

Box 5:2

Soul Care, Spiritual Direction, and the Holy Love of God

**Soul Care
"Life Is Bad, But God Is Good"**

Sustaining: It's Normal to Hurt
Your Loving God Cares

Healing: It's Possible to Hope
Your Holy God Controls

**Spiritual Direction
"I Am Sinful, But God Is Gracious"**

Reconciling: It's Horrible to Sin
God Is Holy
It's Wonderful to Be Forgiven
God Is Loving

Guiding: It's Supernatural to Mature
You're Empowered by God's Holy Love to be Holy
and Loving

Portraits of God's Holiness: Majesty and Glory—Our Hero

Isaiah begins his tour with the startling words, "Behold your God!" (Isaiah 40:9, KJV). His words are intended to stun. No one can behold God and live. His words are also meant to remind, to remind us that Isaiah himself saw the Lord "high and exalted, the train of his robe [filling] the temple. Above him were seraphs, each with six wings: With two wings they covered their faces, with two they covered their feet, and with two they were flying. And they were calling to one another: 'Holy, holy, holy is the LORD Almighty; the whole earth is full of his glory'" (Isaiah 6:2-3).

In the Hebrew language, if you want to emphasize the perfection or the infinite nature of something, you use the same descriptor twice in a row. Isaiah does this when he tells us that God will keep us in perfect peace (Isaiah 26:3). The Hebrew simply says *shalom, shalom*—peace, peace. Here in Isaiah 6:3, Isaiah repeats the word for holy not once, but twice. Once God is holy. Twice He is perfectly holy. Three times and Yahweh is perfect holiness squared!

By saying that God is perfectly holy, Isaiah is telling us that all of God's character is an infinite cut above. Holiness involves the perfection of all His attributes so when we say God is merciful, we are saying He is perfectly, infinitely merciful. When we say He is just, we mean He is perfectly, infinitely just.

> The Hebrew word for holy (*qadhosh*) was used by the Semites to distinguish gods from humans. . . . God's otherness (or, holiness) is fundamentally moral. The ultimate gauge of His resplendence is His moral purity, a perfection which sets Him apart from sinful humanity (David Smith, *With Willful Intent*, p. 225).

Smith merges two important concepts that help us understand what the seraphs were communicating. God is perfect in His being, and, as such, He is separate from and infinitely above all other beings. The incomparability of God is essential to His holiness.

> God is the most unique and separate being who stands apart from men. He is transcendent in his splendor and majesty, towering in his enthroned glory above the temple, the prophets, and the people. He is not like other holy ones and his holiness takes its unique quality from his own exalted character. Indeed, the other gods are idols. Such deities shall pass away, but men will flee in fear before the terror of Yahweh (Eric Rust, *Covenant and Hope*, p. 78).

Isaiah's response to God's holiness reveals a third nuance to the word holy. "'Woe to me!' I cried. 'I am ruined! For I am a man of unclean lips, and I live among a people of unclean lips, and my eyes have seen the King, the LORD Almighty'" (Isaiah 6:5). God is perfect, He is infinitely above us, and He is absolutely pure. The biblical viewpoint relates the holiness of God to His character as totally good and entirely without evil.

Isaiah's encounter with God's holiness was no boring lecture on God's attributes. Isaiah models the response that God's holiness ought to produce in each of us: awe. Throughout the Old Testament, holiness is used alongside words like splendor, glory, and majesty. Psalm 96:9 speaks of the splendor of God's holiness, while Psalm 21:5 pictures the splendor of God's majesty, and Psalm 113:4-7 emphasizes the radiance of God's glory. God's holiness inspires awe. He is weighty beyond all measurement. He is admired beyond all beings.

Our family once enjoyed a three-day canoe trip in West Virginia. I was delighted each time my daughter, Marie, expressed her amazement at the scenery. "It's won-der-ful," she'd exclaim, stretching out each syllable as long as possible. When we "see" God, our souls exclaim, "Won-der-ful! Incredible! Amazing! Cool! Awesome! Magnificent! Hey, Amber, look out the window and see God!"

God is our pristine Hero. We swell up with pride and want to brag about Him to everyone we know. "You think Peyton Manning was incredible the way he threw touchdown passes. Let me tell you about my Hero—God. He's Jesus to me, eternal Deity. Creator of heaven and earth. God of the universe."

Better yet, we could tell others the way Isaiah tells us, "Look! Sovereign Yahweh. He's coming with infinite power, His omnipotent arms ruling the universe for Him. His justice riding alongside" (author's paraphrase of Isaiah 40:10). To a discouraged people, this was grand news. The grandest! "Our holy God will right all wrongs. Though we have suffered, He has not left us. Though evil seems to reign, in reality, our good God reigns. Entrust yourself to Him. Behold your Hero. Your Rescuer. Your white Knight on His glorious steed. More powerful than Superman. More timely than the Lone Ranger. God, your sovereign Hero."

Portraits of God's Love: Beauty and Grace—Our Lover

Modern males complain that the expectations placed on them have been too high. "Boy, it used to be that it was okay if I was just tough—if I got the job done, provided for my family, protected them. But not anymore. Now I'm also supposed to be tender. Kind, loving, gentle, caring. This tough *and* tender business is hard!"

Hollywood doesn't help. Even great warriors like William Wallace in *Braveheart*, as played by Mel Gibson, are also great lovers. Wallace fights because of a lost love. Though he is a ferocious fighter, he is also the best friend his followers ever had.

What Hollywood portrays and women long for is simply a caricature of who God is: our loving Hero. Our heroic Lover. Tough and tender. Holy and loving.

Isaiah describes our tender Warrior. "He tends his flock like a shepherd: He gathers the lambs in his arms and carries them close to his heart; he gently leads those that have young" (Isaiah 40:11). He shuttles us into the second section of His spiritual art gallery. This one marked, "Portraits of God's Love: Beauty and Grace—Our Lover." Isaiah shows us pictures of our Lover smiling, taking care of His sheep. We view rustic images of a rugged, yet sensitive, Shepherd leading His flock to quench their thirsts beside still waters.

The same Hero with the huge arms from our first gallery now scoops up a baby lamb in His arms. The canvas displays a series of scenes. First the scooping, then the holding, then the carrying close to His heart. All the women on our tour "Oooohh" and "Aahhhh." "So sweet." "So cute." Then they nudge the men. "Why can't you be like that?"

In defense of males, we can't be exactly like that because only God is good. His very character defines goodness. God is good; therefore, He does good. The primary word New Testament authors use to describe God's goodness is *agathos*, which emphasizes God's relational beauty. That is, out of the goodness of God's heart overflows His generous, kind, liberal, loving way of relating to us. My Aunt Dorothy used to say, "He's such a beautiful person." She was talking about the person's soul—the way he related to others was beautiful, attractive. Likewise, God's style of relating to us is beautiful.

That is why Isaiah insists that we behold the beauty of God's shepherding love. That is why David makes it his ultimate life goal to gaze upon God's beauty. "One thing I ask of the LORD, this is what I seek: that I may dwell in the house of the LORD all the days of my life, *to gaze upon the beauty of the LORD* and to seek him in his temple" (Psalm 27:4, emphasis added). The friends of the groom in Song of Solomon 6:13 utilize the same Hebrew word for gaze when they say, "Come back, come back, O Shulammite; come back, come back, that we may gaze on you!" As men appreciate the appearance of a beautiful woman, so much more we are delighted by the splendor of God's beautiful heart. Alert to God's holiness we marvel, "God big!" Gazing at God's loveliness we marvel, "God pretty!" (See Alan Wright, *Lover of My Soul*).

Box 5:3

God Has a Good Heart!

God Is Holy: Majesty and Glory—Our Hero

He is exactly what is best.	He captivates our souls with His perfection.
He is infinitely above His creation.	He commands our attention with His glory.
He is totally without evil.	He captures our hearts with His purity.

God Is Loving: Beauty and Grace—Our Lover

He gives exactly what is best for us.	He forgives everything that is worst in us.
He creates good out of chaos.	He creates good out of evil.
He gives generously.	He forgives graciously.

Isaiah directs our gaze to an even more attractive drawing. We see a compassionate Father tenderly receiving His prodigal son back home. This is exactly what the original readers of Isaiah 40 would have seen. Isaiah begins the chapter with the words, "'Comfort, comfort my people,' says your God. 'Speak tenderly to Jerusalem, and proclaim to her that her hard service has been completed, that her sin has been paid for'" (Isaiah 40:1-2a). Israel's suffering was just suffering sent from their holy God. Now her comfort is gracious comfort delivered by her loving God.

When we say, "God has a good heart," we mean that He has a gracious heart. Grace is the cosmic ethic—God gives generously, extravagantly. Grace is not a husband loving an attractive wife. Grace is not even a husband seeing attractiveness where others might see only ugliness. Grace is the loyal love of our Divine Husband transforming our ugliness into beauty. God is the noble Husband wanting only the best for His faithless wife. He woos her. Pursues her. When she returns, He cleanses her from all her impurity. He beautifies her then compliments her on her beauty. "You are soooo beautiful!" Out of His good heart God reconciles rebels, receives prodigals, and beautifies the faithless bride. He takes joy in being beautiful to the ugly.

The Personage of God: The Capacities of His Personhood

John Calvin reminds us that, "nearly all of the wisdom we possess, that is to say, true and sound wisdom, consists of two parts: the knowledge of God and of ourselves (Calvin,

The Institutes of the Christian Religion, Vol. 1, p. 48). Modern secular psychology focuses upon knowing ourselves apart from knowing God. Much current Christian counseling focuses upon knowing ourselves through God's revelation. Our approach is to begin with an understanding of God as He has revealed Himself. Before we can understand humanity in the image of God, we must understand God.

John Laidlow summarizes the traditional Christian view of God's being by explaining that God has a personal nature with all the faculties required of personhood. "Pervading every line of Scripture, from first to last, runs the assumption that God is personal" (Laidlow, *The Bible Doctrine of Man*, p. 168).

God is a Person, not an impersonal "force." He is a personal being with the capacity to love, think, choose, and feel. He is a perfect personal being—infinite and absolutely pure in all His longings, thoughts, choices, and emotions. Who is God?

- God Is Relational: The Romancer Who Loves Passionately
- God Is Rational: The Dreamer Who Reflects Wisely
- God Is Volitional: The Creator Who Purposes Responsibly
- God Is Emotional: The Singer Who Experiences Fully

Read any text of Scripture and you will touch the personality of God. From cover to cover, God reveals His personal nature. The final prophet of the Old Testament, Malachi, is our source for a sampler of the Divine personality. Malachi begins seventy years after Israel's return from the Babylonian captivity. God is again forgotten; His grace taken for granted. "Ho hum." Business as usual. Apathy. Disloyalty. Infidelity. What kind of personal God do we encounter during this pathetic scenario?

God Is Relational: The Romancer Who Loves Passionately

Love is God's essential nature in tripartite existence. God is the Divine Romancer, the ultimate Lover in the entire universe who models the nature of true love. God loves freely, passionately, graciously, and sacrificially.

The God of Malachi is such a Being. "The word of the LORD to Israel through Malachi. 'I have loved you,' says the LORD" (Malachi 1:1-2). Israel, always playing the part of the prodigal, asks, "How have you loved us?" (v. 2). God reminds them of His free choice to love them when they were yet unborn—without any attractiveness that would compel Him to love them.

We might think, *Well, if God loves with absolute freedom, then His love is detached— nothing we do impacts Him, makes an impression on Him.* Malachi disabuses us of this notion by propping open the bedroom door so we can hear the Father "getting in the face" of His son.

"'A son honors his father, and a servant his master. If I am a father, where is the honor due me? If I am a master, where is the respect due me?' says the LORD Almighty" (Malachi 1:6). In return for His love, they offer Him dishonor. As a personal being, God responds passionately. He loves *coram anthropos/coram Deo*: face-to-face, God-to-humanity. He's not some distant human father whose son has run away and who says, "Fine. Leave. I disown you. It is as if you have never been born!" Nor is He the human father who, when the prodigal returns, acts as if nothing happened because He is too afraid to feel.

Instead, He is our heavenly Father who receives us back graciously. Despite endless infidelity, God expresses eternal fidelity. "'I the LORD do not change. So you, O descendents of Jacob, are not destroyed. Ever since the time of your forefathers you have turned away from my decrees and have not kept them. Return to me, and I will return to you,' says the LORD Almighty" (Malachi 3:6-7).

Despite all false accusations of disloyalty, God remains fiercely loyal. "'You have said harsh things against me,' says the LORD. . . . 'They will be mine,' says the LORD Almighty, 'in the day when I make up my treasured possession. I will spare them, just as in compassion a man spares his son who serves him'" (Malachi 3:13, 17). Who says the Old Testament downplays God's love? "They will be mine—my treasured possession." Who says the Old Testament downplays God's grace and forgiveness? "In compassion I will spare them."

However, *God does not wink at sin. He crucifies it.* God loves sacrificially by sacrificing His own Son to pay for the sins of His wayward sons and daughters. Malachi's entire prophecy makes clear God's disdain for the distorted sacrificial system practiced by the Jews. "If not sacrifices, then how in the world do we atone for our sins?" the Jews would inquire. "By Someone beyond the world entering into your world," God replies in Malachi 3:1-6 (the prophecy of the Refiner and Purifier yet to come), and in Malachi 4:1-6 (the prophecy of the sun/Son of righteousness who will rise with healing in His wings). With these promises God concludes volume one of His autobiography. For more than 400 years He waits to pen the sequel. Producing in the hearts of His people an ever increasing, desperate yearning for the One who will come and love them freely, passionately, graciously, and sacrificially.

God Is Rational: The Dreamer Who Reflects Wisely

In John 14:6, Jesus labels Himself "truth." Proverbs 8:22-23 personifies wisdom as an eternally existing aspect of God's essential being. God is rational. He is a Dreamer, a visionary with perfect, infinite mental capacities to reflect wisely. He remembers the past with grace, interprets the present with imagination, and envisions the future with hope.

"'Ever since the time of your forefathers you have turned away from my decrees and have not kept them. Return to me, and I will return to you,' says the LORD Almighty" (Malachi 3:7). Functioning as a perfect personal being, God graciously remembers His past with Israel and mercifully invites them to return. He remembers the past so He can be a gracious Rewarder in the future. "Then those who feared the LORD talked to each other, and the LORD listened and heard. A scroll of remembrance was written in his presence concerning those who feared the LORD and honored his name" (Malachi 3:16).

God, being infinitely rational, interprets the present with Divine imagination. God uses a unique form of question and answer in His dialogue with His wayward people (Malachi 1:2; 1:6; 1:7-8; 2:17; 3:7-8; 3:13). At times, we Christian leaders assume we've communicated when we've placed an announcement in a bulletin or shared our view in a meeting. However, this is monologue, not dialogue. Talking, not communicating. God not only correctly interprets the actions and the motives of His people, He interacts with them in the same creative, imaginative question/answer style Jesus used throughout His earthly ministry.

Mental functioning includes remembering the past, interpreting the present, and envisioning the future. God's perfect vision involves envisioning the future with hope; He anticipates the best possible future for His people. He tells His repentant children about the coming day when, "But for you who revere my name, the sun of righteousness will rise with healing in its wings. And you will go out and leap like calves released from the stall" (Malachi 4:2). Those are DVD–quality images meant to seize our attention and capture our imagination.

God Is Volitional: The Creator Who Purposes Responsibly

Doing something volitionally means doing it freely, responsibly, actively, out of one's own will. Ephesians 1:3-9 unveils God's eternal, sovereign purpose that He works according to His will. G. E. Whitlock describes God as "teleological"—God guides, directs, and determines His plans and leads His creation according to His purposes (Whitlock, "The Structure of Personality in Hebrew Psychology," *Interpretations*, p. 4). A perfect, volitional being like God is the Creator who eternally purposes to rule responsibly and to relate passionately. He acts creatively employing visionary movement that brings something into existence, then subdues and shapes it into a higher form of beauty and usefulness. In Malachi we see how God purposes with absolute sovereignty (King), purposes to create order out of chaos (Potter), and purposes to reconcile relationships (Father, Husband).

God, being infinite, is sovereign in His being volitional. That is, whatever He wills to happen does indeed occur. Notice all the verses in Malachi in which God causes, creates, purposes, and wills: 1:4, 11, 14; 2:2, 3, 9; 3:1, 5, 7, 10, 17; 4:1, 5, 6.

God could simply be big—nothing more than a Bully who attacks and destroys. However, Malachi reveals God's righteous design to create order out of chaos. Sinful Edom insists that they will continue to build cities without pity. God insists that He will demolish their strongholds of evil. Having demolished, God rebuilds. "He will sit as a refiner and purifier of silver; he will purify the Levites and refine them like gold and silver. Then the LORD will have men who will bring offerings in righteousness" (Malachi 3:3). God purposes to shape new life and to shepherd ugly into beauty.

In all His purposes, God aims to reconcile relationships between Himself and His people (Malachi 4:1-4), between husbands and wives (Malachi 2:14-16), and between parents and children (Malachi 4:5-6). Nothing is beyond God's touch. God actively works to restore every fractured relationship and to heal every broken heart.

God Is Emotional: The Singer Who Experiences Fully

Emotional beings have the capacity to respond to their internal perceptions and their external situations. God, the perfect and infinite emotional being, responds fully and deeply to His children. Christ is our sympathetic High Priest who is touched with the feelings of our infirmities (Hebrews 4:15). Kenneth Wuest interprets this passage as a description of God's capacity to experience subjectively and feel His world (Wuest, *Word Studies in the Greek New Testament*, Vol. 1, p. 98). In Malachi we witness how God experiences responsively, feels deeply, and responds properly.

Malachi presents God as experiencing responsively. "You have wearied the LORD with your words" (Malachi 2:17). "Weary" means a painful, joyless toil, a response of pain to a distressing situation or troublesome relationship. God does not become weary as a finite human being does. He does not throw up His hands in exasperation. However, He does feel. He feels pain in response to our dishonor, even as the Spirit experiences grief because of our sin (Ephesians 4:30).

God also feels deeply. "I will spare them, just as in compassion a man spares His son" (Malachi 3:17). Though used here for a father with his son, compassion is often used in the Old Testament for the feelings of a mother for the unborn child in her womb. God feels both joy and sorrow as He relates to us. He is always in sovereign control of His responses to His emotional experiences, and always responds according to His holy love; nonetheless, He truly feels.

God's emotional life is infinitely complex beyond our ability to comprehend fully. For example, who can comprehend that God hears in one moment the prayers of millions of Christians around the world and sympathizes with each one personally and individually as a caring Father, even though among those multi-million prayers, some are brokenhearted and some are bursting with joy?

Though God experiences responsively and feels deeply, we should not think He is controlled by His emotions, or that He "flies off the handle," or is "shocked and rocked" by our actions. God controls His own emotions; He manages His moods. In the perfect harmony of His pure being, His longing, thinking, choosing, and feeling function in concert, presenting a beautiful song that we listen to and say, "Wow! Now that's how we ought to live: alive, passionate, wise, courageous, sacrificial, sympathetic, and in control." God's emotionality is constructive.

Where We've Been and Where We're Heading

"I have trouble with both," Erica told me. "I seem to abuse His holiness sometimes, and His grace other times."

"How so?" I asked.

"Well, sometimes I give into my perfectionism and surrender to despair. I don't fight the temptation to make life work—perfectly—apart from God. In those demanding, self-sufficient moments, I'm diminishing God's holiness. Then, I find myself swinging the other way. I confess my sin. I repent. I sincerely work on changing or being changed. But I can't accept that God is faithful to forgive me. So I work, work, work to get in His good graces. Then I'm diminishing God's grace."

Erica demonstrated some solid self-awareness guided by scriptural insight. What was I to do? What was she to do? What would you have done next if you were her counselor or spiritual friend? Her insight was not preventing her from abusing either God's holiness or His love. Therefore, it was not enough simply to exhort Erica to stop sinning against

God's righteousness by stopping her self-sufficient perfectionism and to stop sinning against God's faithfulness by beginning to accept her acceptance.

Something else was at work in her soul distorting her longings, images, beliefs, goals, actions, reactions, and feelings. That something, or someone, enters the picture in Act One, Scene III. Stretch for a second while the scene changes. Then quickly, back to your seat. It's time to expose False Seducer's story.

Caring for Your Soul: Personal Applications

1. How does God help you become most aware of His goodness (beauty and majesty, loveliness and holiness)?

2. "There are only two things that pierce the human heart," wrote Simone Weil. "One is beauty. The other is affliction." When and how have you been impacted by beauty?

3. Concerning God's holiness and love:

   a. Which aspect of the couplet of holy love do you tend to lean toward more naturally and be aware of—God's love or his holiness? Why do you suppose that is? What impact does this "leaning" have on your walk with God?

   b. How could you develop a more integrated, biblical, holistic view of God's character?

4. Think about a time of struggle in your life. How could Isaiah 40:10-11 have affected how you handled that struggle? How can it influence you now?

5. Which aspect of God's "personage" (relational, rational, volitional, and/or emotional):

   a. Surprises you the most?

   b. Encourages you the most?

Caring for Others: Ministry Implications

♦ **Counsel with Spiritual Power:** When we know God intimately, we'll love God deeply, and be used by God powerfully. How will your power as a soul caregiver and spiritual director be energized as you apply Henry Scougal's concepts about God as the ultimate object of your love?

> Love is that powerful and prevalent passion by which all the faculties and inclinations of the soul are determined and on which both its perfection and happiness depend. The worth and excellency of a soul is to be measured by the object of its love. He who loveth mean and sordid things doth thereby become base and vile, but a noble and well-placed affection doth advance and improve the spirit into a conformity with the perfections which it loves. The image of these do frequently present themselves unto the mind, and, by a secret force and energy, insinuate into the very constitution of the soul and mold and fashion it into their own likeness. . . . The true way to improve and ennoble our souls is by fixing our love on the divine perfections that we may have them always before us and derive an impression of them on ourselves (Scougal, *The Life of God in the Soul of Man*, p. 49).

♦ **Counsel with Spiritual Taste:** Loving God's loveliness is a prerequisite for wisdom. How will your insight as a counselor and spiritual friend be heightened as you apply Jonathan Edwards' concept of sanctified taste?

> Whoever has a musical ear knows whether a sound is in true harmony; he does not need the reasonings of a mathematician to consider the proportion of the notes. Whoever has a taste for gourmet food does not need reasoning in order to know good food. . . . Likewise, if an unworthy or unholy action is suggested to the spiritually discerning, a sanctified eye sees no beauty in it nor is it pleased with it. Sanctified taste will only be nauseated by it. In this way a holy person is led by the Spirit by having a holy taste and disposition of heart (Edwards, *Religious Affections*, pp. 112-113).

> To have a sense of taste is to give things their real value and not to be dazzled with false lusters or be deceived in any way (Edwards, *Religious Affections*, p. 113).

> In judging actions by spiritual taste, true saints do not have specific recourse to definite rules in God's Word with respect to every word and action that they have to communicate. Yet their taste itself is generally subject to the rule of God's Word and is tested and tried by it (Edwards, *Religious Affections*, p. 114).

Chapter Six

The False Seducer's Story

"The early Christian community viewed the soul as a battle ground between God's own Spirit of truth-telling, and deceitful influences that tempt people to distort the truth about themselves" (Thomas Oden, *Classical Pastoral Care*, Vol. 3, p. 100).

"Everyone stands basically under the influence of either the Holy Spirit or some destructive spirit. It is not possible to avoid the one or the other, unless one imagines that one could be simultaneously controlled by opposite spirits. For the Comforter hates every lie, and the Devil hates all truth" (*Constitutions of the Holy Apostles*, Bk. VI, Sec. XX-VII, p. 462).

Party Hearty

There are more scenes before ours. John 1 and 17 transported us to the time before time. Job 38 warps us to the beginning of time.

Job challenged God. God was up to the challenge. Was Job? Could he pass a simple little exam? Question #1: "Where were you when I laid the earth's foundation?" Question #2: "Who marked off its dimensions?" Question #3: "Who stretched a measuring line across it?" Question #4: "On what were its footings set?" Question #5: "Who laid its cornerstones *while the morning stars sang together and all the angels shouted for joy?*" (Job 38:4-7, emphasis added.)

Job failed miserably. However, his failure is our gain—our glimpse into "prehistoric times." During prehistoric time we do not find roaming dinosaurs, but praising morning stars. "The morning stars sang together and all the angels shouted for joy" (Job 38:7). We do not know exactly when God spoke the angelic hosts into being, but we do know they were there in time to marvel at God's creativity.

God has not given us an account of His creation of the heavenly host. Gene Edwards imagines it like this:

The Lord swept his hand across the horizon of nothingness. There burst forth first three, then a thousand thousand beings of blazing light. All, as one, turned and faced the One who had made them. As they did, they divided into three innumerable bands. From out of the midst of one band rose a terrifying creature with a sword so immense it surely could slice eternity in two. "I am Michael, the first of the chief princes." Another creature of like terror rose from among the second group, a mighty trumpet in his hand. "I am Gabriel; the second host of messengers is my charge." Out of the third host rose one of indescribable beauty. "I am Lucifer, the angel of light, the most glorious of all whom you have fashioned." With those words, the Son of the Morning rose above the third host of angels and took his place near the throne of God (Edwards, *The Beginning,* pp. 3-4).

Those innumerable spirit beings sang together and shouted for joy as they beheld the events of Genesis 1. Theirs was no Friday evening bash. No. They began midnight Sunday and continued until the end of the day Friday. For six full days angels composed creation ballads. One-hundred-and-forty-four hours they jumped for joy. "Wow! Kewl! Incredible. Did you see that? Amazing. Beautiful. Majestic. Hey, Amber, look out the window!"

During the sixth day, their amazement peaked. Their own version of a song later penned by King David (Psalm 8) may have sounded like this:

O Yahweh, our Yahweh. How majestic is your name in all the universe!
You have displayed your glory throughout the heavens.
When we consider creation, we see the fingerprints of God.
When we reflect upon the moon and billions upon billions of stars,
We bow in awe and jump for joy.
Though heaven and earth are almost infinitely expansive,
We hadn't seen anything until we saw Adam. Eve.
How incredible they are—you deem them worthy of your constant attention.
How amazing they are—you care for them with your holy love.
We bow in awe and jump for joy.
Image Bearers. You made them in your image.
In your image! In your image!
Vice-Regents. Rulers over the works of your hands.
You put everything under their feet, giving them dominion.
We bow in awe and jump for joy.
O Yahweh, our Yahweh. How majestic is your name in all the universe!
You have displayed your glory throughout the heavens.
You have placed your glory in the Man and the Woman.
O Yahweh, our Yahweh. How majestic is your name in all the universe!
We bow in awe and jump for joy.

Party Leader: Lucifer—Morning Star

The heavenly choir singing in Job 38 has a choir director. His name is Lucifer. Before his fall, he reveled in leading all creation in praise hymns to Trinity's glory. This was his calling, his original design, his joy and passion.

I believe that Isaiah and Ezekiel teach us about Lucifer's original personality (Isaiah 14:11-15; Ezekiel 28:11-19). Both passages seem to refer to Lucifer, the prince of the fallen angels. As Isaiah describes the judgment of God on the king of Babylon (an earthly, human king), and as Ezekiel depicts God's judgment upon the prince of Tyre (an earthly, human prince), they begin to use language that seems far too strong to refer to any merely human ruler.

Before examining the nature of Lucifer's pre-fallen soul, we'll consider why Isaiah 14 and Ezekiel 28 appear to refer to Satan. Then we'll contrast Lucifer's pre-fallen soul with Satan's fallen nature. Doing so, we'll gain a better understanding of the relationship between spiritual warfare and spiritual friendship. We'll learn more about the rest of the story that lies behind Erica's story and behind our story.

Lucifer in Isaiah 14:11-15

In translating Isaiah 14:12, the Latin Vulgate employed the Latin derivative "Lucifer," meaning, "light bearer," to translate the Hebrew word *helel* which means, "shining one." The King James Version adheres to this translation. Many writers throughout church history, including Tertullian, Origen, most medieval thinkers, and John Milton's *Paradise Lost* have equated the "light bearer" with Satan (Stanley Grenz, *Theology for the Community of God*, p. 225).

Isaiah says of Lucifer:

How have you fallen from heaven, O morning star, son of the dawn! You have been cast down to the earth, you who once laid low the nations! You said in your heart, "I will ascend to heaven; I will raise my throne above the stars of God; I will sit enthroned on the mount of the assembly, on the utmost heights of the sacred mountain. I will ascend above the top of the clouds; I will make myself like the Most High." But you are brought down to the grave, to the depths of the pit (Isaiah 14:12-15).

Wayne Grudem notes:

This language of ascending to heaven and setting his throne on high and saying, "I will make myself like the Most High," strongly suggests a rebellion by an angelic creature of great power and dignity. It would not be uncommon for Hebrew prophetic speech to pass from descriptions of human events to descriptions of heavenly events that are parallel to them and that the earthly events picture in a limited way. If this is so, then the sin of Satan is described as one of pride and attempting to be equal to God in status and authority (Grudem, *Systematic Theology*, p. 413).

In the New Testament, John uses strikingly similar language to describe the war in heaven and the fall of Satan.

And there was war in heaven. Michael and his angels fought against the dragon, and the dragon and his angels fought back. But he was not strong enough, and they lost their place in heaven. *The great dragon was hurled down*—that ancient serpent called the Devil, or Satan, who leads the whole world astray. He was *hurled to the earth*, and his angels with him (Revelation 12:7-9, emphasis added).

The New Testament's descriptions of the nature of Satan's rebellion also bear remarkable similarity to the arrogant, prideful "I wills" of Isaiah 14. Paul warns Timothy against ordaining young converts because they might fall into the temptation that captured Satan—pride (1 Timothy 3:6). James summarizes the Devil's core fallen nature using terms like "bitter envy and selfish ambition" (James 3:14-16).

Peter describes the sin of the angels, of the people in Noah's day, and of the people of Sodom and Gomorrah, by telling us that they denied the sovereign Lord (2 Peter 2:1-9). Then he encapsulates the essence of their sin with the words, "this is especially true of those who follow the corrupt desire of the sinful nature and *despise authority*" (2 Peter 2:10, emphasis added).

Jude's language is equally reminiscent of Lucifer's sin in Isaiah 14. "And the angels who did not keep their positions of authority but abandoned their own home—these he has kept in darkness, bound with everlasting chains for judgment on the great Day" (Jude 6). They arrogantly refused to accept their assigned place. Pride epitomizes Satan's rebellion in Isaiah 14; 1 Timothy 3; James 3; 2 Peter 2; and Jude.

Lucifer in Ezekiel 28:11-19

Ezekiel uses even stronger language. In Ezekiel 28:1-10, he speaks of God's judgment upon the *Prince* of Tyre. Then beginning with verse 11, he shifts to God's judgment upon the *King* of Tyre. As you read his judgment, notice the descriptions of the "king"—descriptions of a being alive in Eden, perfect at "birth," residing in the very presence of God—concepts that are almost impossible to fathom unless they refer to Satan.

> The word of the LORD came to me: "Son of man, take up a lament concerning the king of Tyre and say to him: 'This is what the Sovereign LORD says: You were the model of perfection, full of wisdom and perfect in beauty. You were in Eden, the garden of God; every precious stone adorned you: ruby, topaz and emerald, chrysolite, onyx and jasper, sapphire, turquoise and beryl. Your settings and mountings were made of gold; on the day you were created they were prepared.
>
> You were anointed as a guardian cherub, for so I ordained you. You were on the holy mount of God; you walked among the fiery stones. You were blameless in your ways from the day you were created till wickedness was found in you. Through your widespread trade you were filled with violence, and you sinned.
>
> So I drove you in disgrace from the mount of God, and I expelled you, O guardian cherub, from among the fiery stones. Your heart became proud on account of your beauty, and you corrupted your wisdom because of your splendor. So I threw you to the earth; I made a spectacle of you before kings. By your many sins and dishonest trade you have desecrated your sanctuaries. So I made a fire come out from you, and it consumed you, and I reduced you to ashes on the ground in the sight of all who were watching'" (Ezekiel 28:11-18).

Thomas Ice and Robert Dean, in their excellent work *A Holy Rebellion: Strategies for Spiritual Warfare*, explain that the descriptions of the king of Tyre could not possibly apply to the human leader of Tyre.

> For example, he is said to have existed in Eden, the garden of God (verse 13) and to have been created blameless (verse 15). It seems that the person addressed in this section is the real power behind the human king of Tyre: Satan or Lucifer. Often in Scripture Satan is addressed through the creature he is influencing. For example, when Jesus foretold His crucifixion, Peter began to rebuke Him. But Jesus rebuked Peter and said, "Get behind Me, Satan!" (Matthew 16:23). In addition, when God pronounced a curse on Satan in Genesis 3:14-15, He addressed Satan indirectly through the serpent. So the "king of Tyre" mentioned here is none other than Satan himself (Ice and Dean, *A Holy Rebellion*, p. 40).

Just as with Isaiah 14, Ezekiel 28 agrees with 1 Timothy 3, James 3, 2 Peter 2, and Jude in identifying pride as the core sin of Satan/the King of Tyre. Ezekiel also concurs with Revelation 12 in describing Satan/the King of Tyre's expulsion from heaven.

We'll return to Ezekiel 28 and Isaiah 14 to explore Satan's fallen personality structure. But first we need to examine these Scriptures to see Satan's original personality structure. Who is Lucifer? Who was this being before his revolt? Understanding Satan's created capacities will help us to understand better and counteract his fallen capacities and insidious schemes.

Lucifer Was Relational:
Capable of Worshiping Joyfully and Uniting Others Harmoniously

Before he became the Damned One, Lucifer was the model of blamelessness and perfect in beauty (Ezekiel 28:15, 17). Ezekiel describes him as having the seal of perfection, which in the Hebrew language has the idea of the one who sets the standard. He was the prototype of beauty. His appearance, though finite, was nothing less than magnificent.

However, his beauty was not of himself, nor for himself. God created Lucifer for God's glory—to revel in and reveal the majesty of the ultimate Beautiful One of whom he was but a mere reflection. God covered Lucifer with a magnificent collection of beautiful stones. Whenever these stones are mentioned together in the Bible they relate to the very presence of God. These same jewels were in the breastplate worn by the high priest (Exodus 28:17-20) who entered the Holy of Holies, and seven of them are also found in the foundation stones of the walls of the New Jerusalem where God dwells with us (Revelation 21:19-20). Lucifer resided in the very presence of God in order to mirror the glory of God. "You were on the holy mount of God; you walked among the fiery stones" (Ezekiel 28:14).

As noted, his name, "Lucifer," (Isaiah 14:12, KJV) means "light bearer" which referred to the morning star, the planet Venus, which announced the coming of the sun by its reflection of the sun's light. In the same way, Lucifer appears to have been the herald of God through his reflection of God's glory. He announced the Son's glory by being a finite reflection of the Son's light.

Lucifer was God's appointed leader who originally ruled in a way that proclaimed God's unapproachable and incomparable glory. "You were anointed as a guardian cherub, for so I ordained you" (Ezekiel 28:14). Cherubs are associated with the glory and presence of God. When God instructed Moses to build the ark of the covenant, He told him to place the cherubs on the top of it looking down on the mercy seat (Exodus 37:9). Their wings were to cover the mercy seat. The same word for covering ("that covereth," KJV) is used in Ezekiel 28:13-14. Cherubs were also embroidered on the veil or screen that separated the Holy of Holies from the holy place. They were earthly symbols of God's heavenly throne room. The word for "veil" is the same word translated "covereth" (KJV) in Ezekiel. "Apparently Lucifer's position in the throne room of God involved personally covering the throne of God with his wings. He had a very exalted position indeed!" (Ice and Dean, *Holy Rebellion*, p. 43).

Lucifer led the angels in glorifying and enjoying God. Isaiah speaks of the sound of his harps (Isaiah 14:11), depicting Lucifer's musical giftedness. When the morning stars sang together and all the angels shouted for joy, Lucifer was their choir director. God created Lucifer as a relational being capable of worshiping joyfully and uniting others harmoniously. No wonder Isaiah cries out, "O, Lucifer, Morning Star, how far you have fallen!" (Isaiah 14:12, author's translation). Imagine God's heart. Not shocked nor surprised, nevertheless, wounded and enraged. Sin enters His pristine universe through the most pristine created being.

Lucifer Was Rational:
Capable of Thinking Beautifully and Understanding Wisely

Before his fall, Lucifer had a beautiful mind. Ezekiel describes him as "full of wisdom" (28:12). He was the Creator's most intelligent creature. In Hebrew thinking to be full of wisdom was not to be a walking, talking encyclopedia. Lucifer was not omniscient (all-knowing) like God. The wisdom Lucifer possessed was his God-given ability to apply skillfully what he learned. He was able to discern good from evil accurately.

No wonder he was able to inspire the Serpent with the craftiness to deceive Eve. No wonder he is able to blind unbelievers. No wonder he is now called the "Father of Lies" (John 8:44), since he was once capable of understanding and applying such truth.

Lucifer Was Volitional:
Capable of Acting Powerfully and Choosing Submissively

Before his willful revolt, Lucifer had an obedient, powerful will. He was the original "Type-A Personality." A born leader. A created leader. A natural leader. Ordained a guardian cherub (Ezekiel 28:14) and given special access to the throne room of God, he first leads others in worship, later in rebellion.

The word "anointed" (Ezekiel 28:14) means one who is set apart by God for special service. This is the same word transliterated "Messiah," and translated in English as "Christ." Lucifer is the first creature ever designated "an anointed one." In Scripture, three groups of people were anointed: prophets, priests, and kings. Prophets guide people through God's Word, priests lead people in worship of God, and kings govern people for God. "Before he sinned, Lucifer functioned as a prophet, priest, and king. He was the ruler of angels and led them in worship and praise of God" (Ice and Dean, *Holy Rebellion*, p. 42).

Once God judges Lucifer for the misuse of his power, then, and only then, do the people gloat over him, "You also have become weak, as we are; you have become like us" (Isaiah 14:10). The angels are the mighty ones (Psalm 103:20), and Lucifer had been the mightiest of them. No wonder Michael, another archangel, refused to demean the Devil's power during their dispute over the body of Moses (Jude 8-9). Lucifer was once a being of great power who used that power submissively. Now he is a powerful being, using his strength to lead the world astray as he led astray one-third of the angelic host. He now willfully shouts, "I will be like the most High!" (Isaiah 14:14).

Lucifer Was Emotional: Capable of Experiencing Deep and Sincere Feelings

Before he seared his conscience and lost all sensitivity, Lucifer's emotions were fine-tuned to God. Ezekiel informs us that it was not until after Lucifer's fall that he became filled with violence (28:16). Ezekiel uses a Hebrew word for violence that pictures a harsh spirit that speaks cruel words and chooses oppressive actions. Proverbs contrasts this word for violence with the person whose spirit is a well of life—a person who knows how to nourish others emotionally (Proverbs 10:11). Ezekiel himself juxtaposes the violent leader with the compassionate leader (Ezekiel 45:9-10).

Before his fall, Lucifer was filled with compassion. His inner being nourished by God, he nourished others. How unlike his present state: he is a murderer; hatred and rage, harm and hurt flow from his depraved emotional core. He has lost all sensitivity to God and others, yearning only to fill his spiteful soul.

Party Crasher: Diabolos

Before our human story (Creation) began, there existed a party and a party leader. Then an invader crashed the party. Uninvited. Unwanted. Wanting all. Inviting doubt. Betraying Father.

It's difficult to imagine the horror of his sedition. This was not a surprise attack by an enemy during war. It was not even a terrorist attack against an innocent nation during peace. This was mutiny, an internal insurrection, defiance of the King of Kings. *This was an evil betrayal of God's good heart by the one being in the universe who best comprehended God's goodness.* This was unspeakable evil of which we must now speak.

Exciting stories have both a protagonist and an antagonist. The protagonist is the "good guy," riding into town wearing the white hat and rescuing the near-helpless townspeople. The antagonist is the "bad guy," wearing the black hat and terrorizing the intimidated townspeople. God is the Bible's protagonist; Lucifer, the antagonist. In the story God tells, Lucifer becomes Diabolos in the same way that the heroic Anakin Skywalker morphs into Darth Vader, the diabolical ruler of the realm of the dark side in the *Star Wars* movies.

The apostle Paul informs us "we wrestle not against flesh and blood" (Ephesians 6:12, KJV). Diabolos wrestles against us. He is our antagonist who uses all his distorted power to overpower us. Grappling against us, he seeks not to pin our shoulders to the mat, but to use his murderous deceits to pin our soul, mind, will, and emotions to hell itself.

And why not? His own inner being, his own personality became hellacious. His fall was not only geographical—from heaven to hell, but also personal—from pure to putrid. Satan retains his capacities of personhood, but they became distorted and depraved. Consider how far he fell:

♦ Relational Fall: From Uniter of Worship to Adversary of God—False Seducer
♦ Rational Fall: From a Beautiful Mind to a Deceitful Liar—Great Deceiver
♦ Volitional Fall: From Choosing Submissively to Murdering Maliciously—Man Slayer
♦ Emotional Fall: From Sincere Sensitivity to Hateful Insensitivity—Desperate Hater

Diabolos Is a Relational Being: The False Seducer Who Allures Others to Divorce the Worthy Groom

How does Satan relate in fallen ways? He is now the exact opposite of his original design. Originally he joyfully led others in worship of God; now he spitefully leads others in rebellion against God. He uses his relational/governing capacities to organize and lead opposition to Worthy Groom. He is now the Anti-Groom, the great Divider who instigates the cosmic divorce. Ignatius Loyola, a spiritual director from the halls of church history, exposes the False Seducer's scheme.

> The enemy also behaves like a false lover who wishes to remain hidden and does not want to be revealed. For when this deceitful man pays court, with evil intent, to the daughter of some good father or the wife of a good husband, he wants his words and suggestions to be kept secret. He is greatly displeased if the girl reveals to her father, or the wife to her husband, his deceitful words and depraved intentions, for he then clearly sees that his plans cannot succeed. In like manner, when the enemy of our human nature tempts a just soul with his wiles and deceits, he wishes and desires that they be received and kept in secret. When they are revealed to a confessor or some other spiritual person who understands his deceits and evil designs, the enemy is greatly displeased for he knows that he cannot succeed in his evil design once his obvious deceits have been discovered (Loyola, *Spiritual Exercises*, p. 132).

In warfare—and we *are* in spiritual warfare—counter-intelligence is essential. We must expose the False Seducer's insidious schemes. What is his relational purpose? To divorce us from God. How does he go about divorcing us from God? By tearing down our spouse and magnifying the other "man." The apostle Paul is our intelligence agent. In 2 Corinthians 11:2-15, he forwards a secure e-mail meant to subvert False Seducer's subversion.

I am jealous for you with a godly jealousy. I promised you to one husband, to Christ, so that I might present you as a pure virgin to him. But I am afraid that just as Eve was deceived by the serpent's cunning, your minds may somehow be led astray from your sincere and pure devotion to Christ (2 Corinthians 11:2-3).

Notice the context: marriage, jealousy, virginity, and fidelity. Contemplate False Seducer's scheme as translated in the King James Version: "so your minds should be corrupted from the simplicity that is in Christ" (2 Cor. 11:3). "Simplicity" translates a Greek word (*aplotētos*) most often meaning generosity. Paul uses it in this way in 2 Corinthians 8:2 when he speaks about the Macedonians' richness, liberality, and generosity.

How is anyone first lured into an affair? We lose our first love for our spouse. Our sense of our spouse's wonder diminishes. Instead of "God pretty!" Satan now says, "God Bully!" False Seducer tears down our Spouse. "He is not good and generous. He's cold and clutching." As Paul reminded us in a previous e-mail, "The god of this age has blinded the minds of unbelievers, so that they cannot see the light of the gospel of the glory of Christ, who is the image of God" (2 Corinthians 4:4). The first stage in Satan's conspiracy is clear: blinding us to the glorious generosity and rich goodness of our Worthy Groom.

Once we open the window of lessened admiration for our spouse, then we become easy prey for the thief who will break in and steal our heart. Satan tears down our spouse, and then magnifies the other "man"—himself. Paul's secure e-mail warning continues, "Satan himself masquerades as an angel of light" (2 Corinthians 11:14). To "masquerade" (*metaschēmatizetai*) means to "put on an alluring disguise." He is, after all, the False Seducer. He is like the adulterous woman in Proverbs 5-7. His lips drip honey, his mouth is smoother than oil. He tempts us to drink his prohibited juices and eat his forbidden fruits. He decks himself in the attire of a harlot. With his much fair speech, flattering lips, and enticing dress, he beguiles us.

What the harlot of Proverbs illustrates, the book of Revelation clarifies. Satan, the Anti-Groom, inspires the world to worship the Anti-Christ (Revelation 13:11-18). "He exercised all the authority of the first beast on his behalf, and made the earth and its inhabitants worship the first beast, whose fatal wound had been healed" (Revelation 13:12). The Anti-Christ, in turn, uses the great Prostitute to intoxicate his foolish followers.

> One of the seven angels who had the seven bowls came and said to me, "Come, I will show you the punishment of the great Prostitute, who sits on many waters. With her the kings of the earth committed adultery and the inhabitants of the earth were intoxicated with the wine of her adulteries." . . .The woman was dressed in purple and scarlet, and was glittering with gold, precious stones and pearls. She held a golden cup in her hand, filled with abominable things and the filth of her adulteries. This title was written on her forehead: MYSTERY. BABYLON THE GREAT. THE MOTHER OF PROSTITUTES. AND OF THE ABOMINATIONS OF THE EARTH (Revelation 17:1-2 and 4-5).

The essence of Satan's relational sin is false worship—false love. Originally worshiping God, Satan now convinces himself, "I no longer need God. I no longer see God as good and gracious. I divorce myself from God. I worship myself. I love myself." In his fallen relationality, Satan is the False Seducer, the Great Divorcer. He moves from worshiper to divider, from worship leader to opposition leader.

In our fallenness, we bear Satan's image whenever we turn our backs on God, whenever we turn to anyone but God for ultimate satisfaction, whenever we worship anyone but God, whenever we choose to be self-sufficient, whenever we refuse to be needy.

Whenever I sin, I am paying a prostitute. I am choosing the False Seducer over my Worthy Groom. Whenever I sin, I am giving my neck to Dracula—the Prince of Darkness who loves to suck the life out of my soul.

Diabolos Is a Rational Being: The Great Deceiver Who Blinds Others to the Worthy Groom's Beauty and Majesty

Satan lost his beautiful mind. Once the singer of truth, he is now the father of lies. Jesus, who created Lucifer, understands him perfectly. Referring to Satan, He said to questioning Jews,

> You belong to your father, the Devil, and you want to carry out your father's desire. He was a murderer from the beginning, not holding to the truth, for there is no truth in him. When he lies, he speaks his native language, for he is a liar and the father of lies (John 8:44).

Jesus speaks of "your father's desire," or the lust of the father of lies. What does Satan lust for? What is he passionate about? His insatiable desire is to speak lies about our true Father. As we saw in 2 Corinthians 4:4 and 11:2-14, he craves convincing us that he is beautiful and majestic and that God is an ugly Bully.

The apostle John listened intently as Jesus described the Great Deceiver. In Revelation 12:9, 20:3, and 20:8, John reveals Satan's deceptive nature. "And the great dragon was cast out, that old serpent, called the Devil, and Satan, which deceives the whole world" (Revelation 12:9, KJV). To "deceive" means to seduce through delusion, to cause to wander from the right path. It comes from the Greek word *planē* that forms our word "planet." The Great Deceiver longs to pull us off course so that we no longer revolve around the Son.

Isn't this exactly the tack he took when attacking Eve in the Garden? The Great Deceiver, filled with cunning craftiness, questioned reality—God-reality: "Did God really say?" His meta-lie, his all-encompassing delusion is "God cannot be trusted!" Satan is the Great Deceiver who suppresses the truth of God's glorious nature. The essence of Satan's rational sinfulness is false belief: "I refuse to behold the beauty of God!" He stubbornly clings to a distorted image of God.

In our fallenness, we bear Satan's image whenever we choose to leave God out of the picture, whenever we choose to look at life with eyeballs only instead of looking at life with spiritual eyes—from God's perspective. The essence of our rational sin is our refusal to maintain a biblical image of God.

Diabolos Is a Volitional Being: The Man Slayer Who Condemns to Death the Sons of Adam and the Daughters of Eve

Jesus warns us that Satan was a murderer from the beginning (John 8:44). Christ's language is interesting; literally He says, "man slayer" (*anthrōpoktonos*). Satan is the slayer of Adam and Eve, the murderer of humanity.

Peter, who also heard Christ's call to vigilance, dramatically develops the warning. "Be self-controlled and alert. Your enemy the Devil prowls around like a roaring lion looking for someone to devour" (1 Peter 5:8). The ever-ravenous lion hungers to gulp us down, swallow us whole. Peter calls him our enemy or adversary (*antidikos*)—our opponent in a legal battle, our prosecutor and persecutor.

If a lion does not provoke a ferocious enough image, then perhaps a dragon might. Thirteen times John calls Satan the Dragon, denoting a monster, a large serpent with keen powers of sight (Revelation 12:3, 4, 7, 7, 9, 13, 16, 17; 13:1, 2, 4; 16:13; 20:2). The Greek is *drakōn* which is the Romanian root behind the name Dracul (Dracula in English)—the blood-sucking, impaling Prince of Darkness.

In Revelation 12:7-9, John piles on label after insidious label. Satan is the Great Serpent—the mega-Poisoner, the arch-Adversary who is a cunning, malicious, and hostile being who creates terror. He is also *Diabolos*—the Devil. The root meaning is "to separate from." Satan is the great Separator, the Great Divider. *Satanos* itself means the Adversary, the Opponent. He is the one who continually wars against God and God's people.

One description above all others portrays how Satan murders: "the accuser of our brethren" (Revelation 12:10, KJV). Satan's *modus operandi* is condemnation. A somewhat obscure but quite important Old Testament text televises Satan's character assassination.

> Then he showed me Joshua the high priest standing before the angel of the LORD, and Satan standing at his right side to accuse him. The LORD said to Satan, "The LORD rebuke you, Satan! The LORD, who has chosen Jerusalem, rebuke you! Is not this man a burning stick snatched from the fire?" Now Joshua was dressed in filthy clothes as he stood before the angel. The angel said to those who were standing before him, "Take off his filthy clothes." Then he said to Joshua, "See, I have taken away your sin, and I will put rich garments on you" (Zechariah 3:1-4).

Satan says to Joshua, "You're filthy, unworthy! God, the great Bully-in-the-Sky, insists that you clean yourself, beautify yourself. Until then, you are *persona non grata*—unacceptable! Unwanted." Satan sees himself as our prosecutor, jury, and judge.

Lucifer was once capable of acting powerfully and choosing submissively. Now he uses his power to overpower others and to empower people toward evil. The essence of his volitional sinfulness revolves around his purpose to destroy others with guilt and shame through condemnation and accusation.

In our fallenness, we bear Satan's image whenever we bite and devour one another (Galatians 5:15). We bear his image whenever our tongues bitterly attack others (James 3). Who are we destroying with our bitterness? Who are we condemning and shaming with our judgmental accusations?

Diabolos Is an Emotional Being: The Desperate Hater Who Despises Others

In *The Lord of the Rings*, J. R. R. Tolkien invented the despicable little creature, Gollum. Once a beautiful and wise being, the more he grasps, hoards, clutches, and clings to the ring of power, the more pathetic he becomes. Both body and soul shrivel up. The apostle Paul describes similar beings in Ephesians 4:19. "Having lost all sensitivity, they have given themselves over to sensuality so as to indulge in every kind of impurity, with a continual lust for more." The result of separation from God is rage and hatred, panic and fear, jealousy and envy. The result is a shriveled soul. Satan, though powerful, is an ever-shriveling being.

In Revelation 12:12 and 17, John divulges Satan's desperate despair. He has great anger, for he knows that his time is short. He is furious, enraged, in a panic, out of control. The Greek words John chooses for anger (*thumon* and *ōrgisthē*) picture great agitation, rage, and outbursts of wrath. James 2:19 adds the fact that the demons tremble and shiver at their thoughts of God. They are ticked, but intimidated. Satan is enraged, but terrified.

We sense the essence of Satan's fallen emotionality in his grasping, taking, and hoarding that leads to jealousy, panic, and hatred. He is a desperate, despicable hater who lives only for his own personal gratification.

We bear Satan's fallen image whenever we search for satisfaction in the temporal and the sensual. When we do, we enslave ourselves to constant addictive dissatisfaction that leads to a continual lust for more—endless cravings to grasp, take, hoard, and clutch. However, the more we grasp, the more we shrink.

Where We've Been and Where We're Heading

Biblical counselors who omit spiritual warfare from their understanding of people, problems, and solutions, focus only on the smaller story. No wonder they are fair game and easy prey for secular solution-focused therapy that highlights immediate change rather than internal repentance and eternal focus.

Remember Erica? We left Act One, Scene II, wondering why she abused God's holiness and love. Now we've identified Satan's role in her struggle. I'm not implying that Satan is the only culprit at work. We're attacked on three fronts: the world, the flesh, and the Devil. Nor am I suggesting that Erica has no personal culpability. God provides Erica with the resources for victory on each of these battlefields. I'm simply making transparent the biblical truth that the False Seducer is our Worthy Groom's archenemy who orchestrates attacks against the Bride of Christ. He is a major part of the larger story going on behind the curtain and in the souls of every counselee.

Satan loves it when Erica replaces her dependence upon God with self-sufficient perfectionism. He's at work behind the scenes and in her soul when she fails to grasp how majestic and beautiful her Worthy Groom is.

But how does Satan work? What is his grand design, his scheme? How do we counteract him? Act One, Scene IV, plays out the battle for our souls. Don't miss it.

Caring for Your Soul: Personal Applications

1. Satan is slander incarnate. He accuses God of evil and condemns us as evil before God.

   a. In what situations do you feel most tempted to doubt God's goodness?

   b. In what situations do you feel the greatest condemnation from Satan? When do you feel, "God could never love a mess like me!"?

2. How does our spiritual theology of life (seeing life as a battle of two loves) affect you?

   a. How will you live differently because of what you are learning?

   b. How will you relate differently?

   c. How will you minister (counseling, discipling, pastoring, befriending) differently?

3. Evaluate where you are in each of the following areas of bearing Satan's image instead of Christ's. How could you move increasingly away from Satan's image and increasingly toward Christ's image in each area?

   a. We bear Satan's image relationally when we refuse to cling to our Worthy Groom.

   b. We bear Satan's image rationally when we leave God out of the picture.
   c. We bear Satan's image volitionally when we manipulate/retaliate and bite/devour.

   d. We bear Satan's image emotionally when we search for satisfaction in the sensual.

4. Imagine the angels of heaven and the saints of old watching your life the past month. Now imagine that you are the only mirror of God that they have to reveal/reflect God's heart. Over the last thirty days, where have you been a beautiful reflection of His good (generous, gracious, lovely, loving) heart?

Caring for Others: Ministry Implications

♦ **Choose Truth: The Truth Shall Set You Free**

- Choosing the truth is your first line of defense as you take captive every thought. Don't simply dispel the darkness; turn on the light. Demons are like cockroaches that scurry away the moment the lights come on.
- Discipleship counselors turn on the light of grace by sharing the Scriptures and their own souls (1 Thessalonians 2:8).
- Share the Scriptures, God's grace perspective on life that teaches "God is good even when life is bad. God is gracious even when I am sinful."
- Share your souls: Grace relationships that portray Jesus with skin.

♦ **Listen with Both Ears: The Larger Story and the Smaller Story**

- Listening is central to what God calls soul physicians to do.
- *Dual Listening #1*: Listen to what God is saying through His Word, His Son, His creation, and providence (life events) (Acts 14:17; Acts 17:26-27; Romans 1:18-20). Listening requires "spiritual taste," time with God, meditation, silence, solitude, and falling in love with Jesus again and again.
- *Dual Listening #2*: Listen to your friends' stories of suffering and sin. Stop. Hear. Really hear. Enter their stories. Go slow. Stay with them. Settle on one area and focus with them, focus on them. Now you're ready to connect their smaller stories to God's larger story.

♦ **Look with "Cross Eyes": Remember the Cross**

- The Cross of Christ is God's final answer to the question, "Does God have a good heart?"
- See the Cross everywhere. See evidences of God's grace where others see only doubt.

CHAPTER SEVEN

THE BATTLE FOR OUR SOUL

"The Devil throws hideout thoughts into the soul—hatred of God, blasphemy and despair. When I awake at night, the Devil tarries not to seek me out. He disputes with me and makes me give birth to all kinds of strange thoughts. The Devil understands how to produce the arguments that exasperate me. Sometimes he has produced such as to make me doubt whether or not there is a God" (Martin Luther, *Table Talks*, IV, 5097).

"Attacks on the holy love of God are a staple of the Devil. This, then, is the most furious and sudden of all attacks, in which the Devil exerts to the full extent all his powers and arts, and transforms himself into the likeness of the angry and ungracious God" (A. Nebe, *Luther As Spiritual Advisor*, p. 183).

The Devil's Advocate

"I have so many names," John Milton tells his protégé, Kevin Lomax, in the movie *The Devil's Advocate*. Al Pacino plays John Milton, the Devil incarnated as the head partner in a New York City law firm, while Keneau Reeves plays Kevin Lomax, the brash, young small-town Florida lawyer recruited by Milton. Taking Kevin to the top of his fifty-story law office, Milton waves his hand across the horizon as he tells Kevin, "Life is rich with possibilities for those who are unafraid to sample them." Throughout the intense drama, Milton lures Lomax to sell his soul, tempting him with evil's best—lust, ambition, drive, pride, ego, vanity, gluttony, and power.

Indeed, the Devil has many names and offers many temptations. However, the Bible exposes the two-pronged attack in his basic scheme. The False Seducer tempts us to rebel against God, and then he condemns us for rebelling against God.

Kevin Lomax swallowed the bait from both of Satan's hooks. Dazzled by all that John Milton offers, Lomax ignores the warnings of his church-going mother, neglects his beautiful but terrified wife, and silences his conscience by defending a man he knows is guilty. He succumbs to the temptation to rebel against God and everything godly. The results, however, are not what he expected. Rather than feasting on the fruit, he faces fear and frustration. He's wracked with guilt over his neglect of his suicidal wife. He's shocked by his mother's revelation of her past relationship with Milton. And he's tormented by Milton's mockery. On every level, he experiences condemnation for his wicked ways. Kevin Lomax learns the hard way what we hope to learn the biblical way: Satan tempts us to sin and then he condemns us for sinning.

Tempted to Rebel

The False Seducer mounts his mutiny through a powerful argument: God is untrustworthy. In subtle and not-so-subtle ways, he places God's heart on trial whispering, "God is no Rewarder; He's a Hoarder." To counteract Satan's challenge to God's good heart, we need to expose his seductive strategies.

Seducing Strategy Number One: Enticement to Distrust God's Good Heart

The False Seducer's kryptonite is separation through slander. He slanders God to us and us to God. His devious design lures us away from God. The original lie reveals the nature of all his lies—Satan wants us to doubt God's generous goodness (Genesis 3:1-6).

Moses warns his readers with his opening words, "Now the serpent was more *crafty* than any of the wild animals the LORD God had made" (Genesis 3:1, emphasis added). "Crafty" suggests brilliant malevolence—a being who is clever enough to package his venomous hatred in sugar coating. He simply wants some information, right? "Did God really say?" He is only after a little conversation, right? "Did God really say?" He seeks simple clarification, right? "You must not eat from any tree in the garden"?

His question, "Did God really say?" seduces Eve to ask, "Why is God a 'Must Not God'?" Serpent is not simply saying, "Do I have it right?" He is implying, "God said *what*?"

God, of course, had said, "You are *free* to eat from *any* tree in the garden; but you must not eat from the tree of the knowledge of good and evil, for when you eat of it you will surely die" (Genesis 2:16-17, emphasis added). The Serpent ignores God's generosity and twists His one prohibition—a protective prohibition meant to teach God-dependence and to spare planet Earth and its inhabitants from the natural consequences of self-sufficiency.

Serpent is not finished. He blatantly calls God a liar: "You will not surely die" (Genesis 3:4). Then he shoots the poisoned arrow: "For God knows that when you eat of it your eyes will be opened, and you will be like God, knowing good and evil" (Genesis 3:5). "God is withholding! God is terrified that He might have to share some of His glory. God hoards His gifts, squirreling them away so He alone can enjoy them."

Satan wants us to see God as our Enemy, thus disconnecting us from God. Satan does not want us to see God as our gracious Creator who created us with a will, able either to obey or rebel. Rather, he deludes us into seeing God as a cruel Taskmaster who suppresses our freedom and demands that we grovel. The cursing narrative of "God-Against-Us" becomes the dominant lens through which our flesh interprets life. We no longer give our Lover the benefit of the doubt. We view every event as one more evidence of God's againstness.

Sin is like a computer virus that attempts to erase the memory of our trusting relationship with our trustworthy God. What if Adam and Eve had reminded each other that every good and gracious gift comes down from the Father of lights? What if they had recalled that God gives us richly everything to enjoy? Because they did not, they became susceptible to Satan's second seducing strategy.

Seducing Strategy Number Two: Enticement to Trust Our Own Hearts

Doubting God inevitably leads to trusting self. Imagine what might have happened had Adam and Eve cried to God between Genesis 3:6 and 3:7. In Genesis 3:6 they eat the forbidden fruit and their fall is complete. In Genesis 3:7 they realize their nakedness and *cover their shame on their own.* I imagine a God-dependent response might look something like this.

> Then the eyes of both of them were opened and they realized that they were naked. Standing exposed as failed and flawed male and female, naked before Him with whom they have to deal.
>
> Then the naked man and the naked woman heard the song of the LORD God as He walked in the garden in the cool of the day, as He always had for fellowship. And they stayed.
>
> Adam cried out to God, "I am unworthy to be called Your son, for I have sinned against You in my attempt at self-sufficiency. I have failed to be the courageous man You designed and called me to be. I have been a coward rather than a protector. Make me like one of Your animals, for I am soul-less."
>
> Eve cried out to God, "I am unworthy to be called Your daughter, for I have sinned against You in my self-sufficiency. I have failed to be the completing woman You designed and called me to be. I have poisoned rather than nourished. Make me like one of Your animals, for I am soul-less."
>
> Instead, the LORD God slew the precious animals He had handcrafted. He shed blood. Carefully, tenderly, with tears streaming down His face, He handcrafted robes of righteousness for His son and daughter.
>
> Then He ran to them, threw His arms around them, and kissed them repeatedly. Father said to his angelic servants, "Quick, bring the best robes that I have hand-crafted and put them on My son and My daughter. Put wedding rings on their fingers and sandals of peace on their feet. Bring the fatted calf and kill it. Let's have a feast and celebrate. For this son of Mine and this daughter of Mine were dead and they are alive again." So they began to celebrate!

Grace means never having to cover my sin. But Adam and Eve, having doubted God's goodness, do not focus on His grace. Instead of depending upon God, they depend upon self. Being naked and afraid, they hide. They turn their backs on God and run from Him. They work, sewing fig leaves together to make coverings for themselves. They attempt to make themselves acceptable by trying to beautify their ugliness.

In the flesh we use every strategy at our disposal, every scheme we can imagine, not to need God's grace. With what fig leaves do we cover our shame? What view of God does such shame and hiding suggest?

Satan conspires to trick us into viewing God as Javert. In Victor Hugo's classic work *Les Miserables*, Jean Val Jean is imprisoned for sixteen years for stealing a loaf of bread to feed his sister's starving family. Javert is his self-righteous, legalistic prison guard. Upon his release, Jean Val Jean is unable to find work. Destitute, he spends a night in the tiny home of a Catholic bishop who treats him with respect and provides him with a meal. During the night, Val Jean steals the bishop's silver candlesticks.

The next day the French police drag Val Jean back to the bishop's home. "We found this thief with your possessions!"

"Jean Val Jean, you left without taking the other gifts I had offered you," the bishop replies as he hands Jean additional valuables. Val Jean is shocked, and changed—changed by grace. He begins to live a life of grace, caring for others. Eventually he becomes the owner of a factory and then the mayor of a French town.

But Javert hunts him down. At every turn he reminds him of his past. At one point he shouts repeatedly, "24601!" the prison uniform number Jean Val Jean had worn for over a decade-and-a-half. Val Jean is less than human. A number only. Javert exposes Jean Val Jean's past to the townspeople and attempts to arrest him for parole violation. Shamed, Jean Val Jean runs. Taking matters into his own hands, he does not trust Javert, nor should he.

Satan wants us to imagine God as the spitting image of Javert. If Satan is successful, then, of course, we will run. We will take matters into our own hands. Whenever we mistrust God's good heart, we always trust our own fallen hearts.

Condemned for Rebelling

Once we succumb to Satan's suggestion, we might imagine that he would applaud us. "Atta' boy! Now you're cookin'. You're on my team now." Nothing could be further from the truth. Instead, once we bite his bait, he reels us in, fries us, and eats us alive. "You fool! You sinner! How could you have trusted me? How could you have disowned God? Now He hates you. You're ugly, filthy, weak, puny, and putrid. What a mess you're in. Run. Hide. Be ashamed. Be afraid, much afraid."

Condemning Method Number One: Accusing Us to God

First Satan tempts us to sin; then he taunts us for having sinned. Puritan writer Thomas Brooks explains how Satan presents the pleasure and profit of sin, but hides the misery that follows.

He paints sin with virtuous colors. After having tempted us to sin and to mind sin more than Christ, then he makes us believe that we are not good because we were beset by temptation and cannot enjoy God as we once did. The moment we give in to temptation, Satan immediately changes his strategy and becomes the accuser (Brooks, *Precious Remedies Against Satan's Devices*, p. 29).

Recall three passages picturing Satan's condemning narrative: Job 1-2, Zechariah 3:1-10, and Revelation 12:7-10. In Job, he accuses Job of being a fair-weather follower of God. In Zechariah, he slanders the filthily attired priest, Joshua. In Revelation 12, he is rightly labeled the "Accuser of our brothers." Satan not only accuses God to us; he accuses us to God.

And how does God respond? He looks at the Cross; He looks at His Son. "Who will bring any charge against those whom God has chosen?" (Romans 8:33). The answer, of course, is Satan brings the charges. However, the answer is much more than that. God is saying, "No one can bring charges that stick, charges that condemn." "If God is for us, who can be against us? He who did not spare his own Son, but gave him up for us all— how will he not also, along with him, graciously give us all things?" (Romans 8:31-32). Satan is always against us, but never victoriously. Since Christ died for us while we were His enemies, certainly now that we are His family, His grace covers our sin. Therefore, nothing in all creation, including the powerfully evil creature Satan, can ever separate us from the love of God that is in Jesus our Lord.

Condemning Method Number Two: Accusing Us to Ourselves

Satan fights a futile battle to persuade God to condemn us. Unfortunately, he's more successful with his attempts to convince *us* that we are contemptible. Luther experienced and overcame these demonic character assassinations.

> The Deceiver can magnify a little sin for the purpose of causing one to worry, torture, and kill oneself with it. That is why a Christian should learn not to let anyone easily create an evil conscience in him. Rather let him say, "Let this error and this failing pass away with my other imperfections and sins, which I must include in the article of faith: I believe in the forgiveness of sins, and the Fifth Petition of the Lord's Prayer: Forgive us our trespasses" (Luther, *Sermon on John 18:28, WLS* 1, # 983, pp. 333-334).

Satan seeks to fill our souls with shame that separates. Paul labels it "worldly sorrow [that] brings death" (2 Corinthians 7:10). Satanic shame involves self-contempt and self-disgust that causes me to despair of all hope that God could love a sinner *like me*. Condemning shame convinces me that God has forever justly rejected me. Godly sorrow, on the other hand, is guilt that leads me to return to God. It reminds me of my absolute dependency upon Christ's grace and invites me to come home to my forgiving Father. Shame separates; sorrow connects.

Condemning Method Number Three: Accusing Us to and through One Another

If we have faith like Luther, we can overcome Satan's second condemning method. Before we celebrate prematurely, however, we should remember False Seducer's persistence and remind ourselves of his third condemning method: he not only accuses us to God and to ourselves, he also accuses us to and through others.

James is aghast that out of the same mouth we release words that praise our Creator and words that curse those made in His image (James 3:9-10). He calls this a "restless evil, full of deadly poison" (3:8). More than that, he identifies the source of our bitter envy, selfish ambition and divisive speech—"it is earthly, unspiritual, of the Devil" (3:15).

Luther's practical eye, trained by life-long battle against Satan, helps us to see the connection between our devouring words and Satan's diabolical methodology.

> There is no person on earth so bad that he does not have something about him that is praiseworthy. Why is it, then, that we leave the good things out of sight and feast our eyes on the unclean things? It is as though we enjoyed only looking at—if you will pardon the expression—a man's behind. The Devil gets his name from doing this. He is called Diabolos, that is, a slanderer and reviler, who takes pleasure in shaming us most miserably and embittering us among ourselves, causing nothing but murder and misery and tolerating no peace or concord between brothers, between neighbors, or between husband and wife (Luther, *The Sermon on the Mount, Luther's Works*, Vol. 21, p. 42).

Imagine how marriages would change if we understood that Satan was our real enemy, not our spouse. Imagine how church disputes could be settled if we turned our spiritual weapons on Satan, rather than turning our unspiritual words on each other.

Diabolos loves division. He attempts to separate us from God through shame that tempts us to run, hide, and cover. He strives to separate us from ourselves through shame that produces self-contempt and the dis-integration of our shalom. And he toils to separate us from one another through shame that divides and conquers.

In the midst of Satan's insidious seductions and shrewd methods, we could be tempted to give up, to raise the white flag of surrender. Yet God calls us, "more than conquerors" (Romans 8:37). We are super-conquerors, superheroes! How? Let's consider Christ's victorious strategy in our spiritual warfare against the Prince of Darkness.

Our Worthy Groom's Counter-Strategy

In our chronological approach to the story of the Bible, we've explored God's pre-history as well as Satan's. Now let's more clearly see how both relate to us. God is the eternal community of selfless oneness who graciously created us to revel in and reveal His goodness. Could any script be better written? Could any lead actor or actress ever receive a better role?

What's the problem then? A great liar, *the* great Liar, attempts to rewrite the script. Satan, the Antagonist, the False Seducer, sneaks in his revisions. Paul warns us about them. "See to it that no one takes you captive through hollow and deceptive philosophy, which depends on human tradition and the basic principles of this world rather than on Christ" (Colossians 2:8).

At the end of life, each of us must answer the questions, "Whose story captured my soul? Which lover won my heart?" Our role in the story is to counter Satan's subversion. "We demolish arguments and every pretension that sets itself up against the knowledge of God, and we take captive every thought to make it obedient to Christ" (2 Corinthians 10:5).

We live our lives amidst two competing interpretations of life. In this competition, this warfare: "We do not wage war as the world does. The weapons we fight with are not the weapons of the world. On the contrary, they have divine power to demolish strongholds" (2 Corinthians 10:3b-4). So how do we wage war? What is our Worthy Groom's counter-strategy and what is our role in it?

The Battlefield Scouts: The Naked Eye Versus the Spiritual Eye

How do we interpret life? When death comes our way, when we're in the casket, the pit, the dark night of the soul, how do we perceive reality? Paul informs us how *not* to interpret our life story: "You are looking only on the surface of things" (2 Corinthians 10:7). "Surface" (*prosōpon*) literally means "according to facial expression," or what I like to call, "with eyeballs only." We see what only the flesh can see—mere external appearance, what is outward, only on the surface, skin deep.

God has given us all that we need to see life with spiritual eyes. There's plenty to see. When Paul and Barnabas heal a man lame from birth, the citizens of Lystra and Derbe shout, "The gods have come down to us in human form" (Acts 14:11). Paul and Barnabas respond with outrage and embarrassment. They plead with the mob.

> Men, why are you doing this? We too are only men, human like you. We are bringing you good news, telling you to turn from these worthless things to the living God, who made heaven and earth and sea and everything in them. In the past, he let all nations go their own way. Yet he has not left himself without testimony: He has shown kindness by giving you rain from heaven and crops in their seasons; he provides you with plenty of food and fills your hearts with joy (Acts 14:15-17).

Our God has not left us without witness. No one can look at life's gifts and doubt the goodness of the Giver. No one, that is, with spiritual eyes. When we interpret life with eyeballs only, God holds us without excuse. And justly so.

> The wrath of God is being revealed from heaven against all the godlessness and wickedness of men who suppress the truth by their wickedness, since what may be known about God is plain to them, because God has made it plain to them. For since the creation of the world God's invisible qualities—his eternal power and divine nature—have been clearly seen, being understood from what has been made, so that men are without excuse (Romans 1:18-20).

When we observe life with eyeballs only, we will not see God's goodness, especially when life is bad. Romans 1 teaches that *when life stinks, our God-perspective shrinks and when our God-perspective shrinks, our hearts stink.* But our Worthy Groom endures the stench and moves ever closer to us.

> The God who made the world and everything in it is the Lord of heaven and earth and does not live in temples built by hands. And he is not served by human hands, as if he needed anything, because he himself gives all men life and breath and everything else. From one man he made every nation of men, that they should inhabit the whole earth; and he determined the time set for them and the exact places where they should live. God did this so that men would seek him and

perhaps reach out for him and find him, though he is not far from each one of us. For in him we live and move and have our being. As some of your own poets have said, "We are his offspring."

Therefore since we are God's offspring, we should not think that the divine being is like gold or silver or stone—an image made by man's design and skill. In the past God overlooked such ignorance, but now he commands all people everywhere to repent. For he has set a day when he will judge the world with justice by the man he has appointed. He has given proof of this to all men by raising him from the dead (Acts 17:24-31).

God has not abandoned us in our evil world. With spiritual eyes, with faith eyes, we see Him and His goodness everywhere. We see the fingerprints of God. For faith is the assurance of things we can't see with eyeballs only. Without faith it is impossible to please God, because anyone who comes to Him must believe that He exists and that He rewards those who earnestly seek Him (compare Hebrews 11:1-6).

The role of spiritual friends is to create a greater God awareness. Faith is the awareness that God's name is Rewarder. Faith perceives that God is graciously good—rewarding those who deserve judgment.

The Battlefield Weapons: The Battle for Our Minds

Life, then, is a battle for our minds. How do we fight the battle? What's our strategy? When Paul explains that "we do not wage war as the world does" (2 Corinthians 10:3), he uses the word *strateia* meaning strategy. In Paul's day strategy was inseparably linked to "generalmanship"—the tactics and war plans of the highest-ranking military officer. Two generals hand us our marching orders. Which general's strategy will win our minds?

The False Seducer's grand strategy is to blind us to God's true nature. Being the father of lies, the creator of the lying narrative, he attempts to cause us to see God as the Evil Emperor, Darth Vader, or Ming the Merciless. He wants us to view God as malevolent. We've scouted his subterfuge. He tempts us to reinterpret our image of God. God is a Bully, Christ is our prison Warden, and the Holy Spirit is an impersonal Force. Satan also deludes us into reinterpreting our relationship to God—God is our Enemy.

We also now know our Worthy Groom's counter-strategy. He opens our eyes to the true nature of life: life is a love affair set amidst a grand adventure. God is our pursuing Father and we are His adult sons and daughters. Christ is our forgiving Groom and we are His virgin brides. The Holy Spirit is our inspiring Mentor and we are His best friends and disciples.

Two generals present us with two strategies—this is the battle for our minds, the battle for planet Earth. When Satan's lying salvos assault our position, what weapons do we use? "The weapons we fight with are not the weapons of this world. On the contrary, they have divine power to demolish strongholds" (2 Corinthians 10:4). Our weapons are Dad's weapons.

The word "weapons" (*hopla*) pictures a siege implement, a battering ram. These are not defensive weapons. They are offensive. The very gates—the protective walls that guard a city on a hill—of hell shall never prevail against them. The walls will fall! What sort of weapons can demolish demonic reasoning? Truth. The Word. The Truth about who Christ is and who we are in and to Christ.

In C. S. Lewis' novel *The Chronicles of Narnia*, Aslan, the great lion, is the Christ-figure. The evil White Witch captures him, binds him, and kills him. The four children, Lucy, Edmond, Susan, and Peter lose hope. Exhausted from battle and weeping, they sleep. Upon awaking they're horrified to see mice gnawing upon Aslan's dead body. But upon further, closer, inspection they realize that the mice are actually eating away the ropes that bind the great lion king. Before their eyes they see him arise. With their own ears they hear him roar. They're ecstatic, yet confused. *"How? Why? What?"* they stammer.

Aslan hushes them. He explains the evil, finite, temporal magic of the White Witch. With a twinkle in his eyes, he tells them, "But she did not know of the deeper magic from before the dawn of time." The White Witch, Satan, and all who follow them, perceive life with eyeballs only so they know only of the evil magic *in* time. We, with faith eyes, see the deeper magic from *before* the dawn of time. We perceive the eternal power and gracious goodness of God who raises the dead.

The weapon of our warfare is the Divine Gospel story, the "magic" from before the dawn of time that raised Christ from the dead. This "resurrection magic," Paul tells us in Ephesians 1:18-23, is the same magic that is at work now within us!

The Battlefield Soldiers: Spiritual Friends/Spiritual Soldiers

Our role is to remind our fellow actors and actresses of the true script. We're soldiers in a battle standing back-to-back as spiritual friends, speaking God's truth in love. We provide grace relationships of compassion and present grace narratives with discernment, using the weapon of truth to take down enemy lies and take captive enemy plans.

Our General commands us to demolish strongholds, arguments, and every pretension that sets itself up against the knowledge of God (2 Corinthians 10:4-5). The word "demolish" (*kathairesin*) means to take down by force by destroying the foundation. It pictures knocking the props out from under someone, knocking him off his feet. In high school wrestling, the best wrestlers are those with the best takedowns. As a wrestling coach, when I teach young wrestlers to do takedowns, I teach them that their opponent's arms are like a moat or a gate preventing them from reaching the castle. The castle's foundations are its legs. To take someone down, they have to take control of their opponent's legs by knocking them out from under them.

We wrestle against principalities and powers. We must take down their foundational strongholds, arguments, and pretensions. Stronghold (*ochurōmatōn*) is a military term referring to a fortress or fortified place. The word came to be used metaphorically for anything on which someone relies (Ralph Earle, *Word Meanings in the New Testament*, p. 260). In 2 Samuel 22:3, God claims the title of our Stronghold. So what is Paul saying? We must rip the foundations out from under all bastions of human reasoning that say, "I don't need God!" We must demolish every non-God story of life. Pulverize every God-is-not-good life narrative.

Consider Erica and her struggles with despair, perfectionism, and self-sufficiency. She alertly traced her battle to the deeper issue of spiritual adultery—her refusal to entrust herself to her Worthy Groom's majesty and beauty. In the fortress of her heart, she's clinging to the lie that "I need to be perfect to be whole. Oh, I know that God doesn't want me to take life into my own hands, but I feel so good when I'm in complete control of everything. Like I finally have it all together." Erica is relying on her perfectionistic self-sufficiency as her stronghold—her place to find life, her fortified safety zone.

Elyse Fitzpatrick helps us to see the connection between these strongholds and arguments or imaginations. "Our beliefs about the sources of joy (through finding a spouse or success, for instance) are frequently experienced as colorful imaginations that captivate our hearts" (Fitzpatrick, *Idols of the Heart*, p. 116).

Erica did not imagine in black in white. She imagined in living color, techno-color, big screen, jumbo-tron. Her thoughts of a perfect life, a perfect family, perfect friends, and a perfect church were incredibly attractive. This is exactly what Paul pictured with the word arguments/imaginations (*logismous*). It's the same word we discussed regarding Abraham's reasoning—his mental calculations. In her moments of despair, Erica was adding up reality. "Trusting God to fix the messes in my life does not measure up to the wonderful way I feel when I prevent any messes from ever occurring. I feel so alive. So fully safe!" In those instances, she would shut her thoughts off from God. Her deliberations were warped, out of joint. She failed to factor God into the equation of her life.

According to Paul, all such thoughts smack of arrogance. They're pretentious images that ascend like the Tower of Babel over the landscape of our minds shouting, "We have vaulted above God! We can make life work apart from Him!" Paul insists that we implode these top-most perches of audacious pride. For such pride rises above and against the knowledge of God, acting as if He is unworthy to be retained in our thoughts.

Erica began to experience lasting victory when she recognized the horrors of her sin. She loaded her conscience with holy guilt. "I'm saying that God is smaller to me, less significant in my mind, than I am. When I surrender to my controlling, demanding perfectionism, I'm chucking God's holiness, His majesty, and His beauty right out the window." Further, she was able to recognize that "When I reject His forgiveness and work to earn back His acceptance, I'm acting as if I can save myself. I'm like Eve tossing on a fig leaf thinking I can make myself presentable to God!"

As Erica and I continued to talk, I wanted to help her see with spiritual eyes who God is and who she is in Christ. This follows the passion of our Commander in Chief who orders us to take captive enemy plans (2 Corinthians 10:5). Literally, we are to make them prisoners of war without any rights or power. What do we take prisoner? "Thoughts." Paul uses the word *voēma* meaning plans, plots, and schemes. He chooses the identical word in 2 Corinthians 2:11 for Satan's schemes, designs, and plots. Satan's scheme is simple. His plot goes like this: "You don't need God. He's not so hot, anyhow. You can make it on your own." At root, all sin follows this same plot line, this same story line. When we sin we say, "God? I don't need God. He doesn't come through for me anyway. Doesn't really care, not when it counts. I'll make life work quite well on my own, thank you!"

As Erica's spiritual friend, I wanted to help her to pluck out her eyeballs-only thinking, and I wanted to do it in a creatively powerful and uniquely personal way. "Erica, here's the picture that I'm sensing. Tell me how it fits for you. You've been handed two blueprints for your life. One instructs you to build your lovely, oh-so-perfect life upon your own skillful organizational abilities, your logical mind, and your perceptive competency to scout out pending doom. From a human perspective, you've done very well. The dollhouse that is your life is immaculate. The problem is, you haven't invited God into your home. Plus, others don't feel comfortable there because they fear messing with your *Good Housekeeping* life.

"The other blueprint terrifies you, yet attracts you. When the Architect hands it to you, He does so with a calmness that has the power to quiet your agitated soul. Looking at His blueprint, you notice splashes of color here, dashes of personality there, creativity in this corner, and possibilities in that one. You also detect, horror of horrors, some clutter and some unfinished rooms. A speck of dust. Lint on the carpet. You're tempted to race for the vacuum, but then you see all the guests thoroughly enjoying themselves. They feel comfortable, not only in your home, but also with you. They feel invited, wanted, necessary. Most importantly, the Architect lives in your imperfect home, shaping it daily more and more into His desired design . . ."

"Dr. Kellemen, I don't like that first picture. Yet, there's no denying that it's me to a T. The second picture, you're right. I hate it and I love it. It does scare me to death, makes me feel naked, like I'm giving up everything I've ever depended on. Yet, I love it, I want it. At times I've tasted it. To give up being always-busy-Martha and become restful-relational-Mary . . . Wow. That's what I want. That's what my family wants. That's what God made me for . . ."

Where We've Been and Where We're Heading

The curtain closes on Act One. Time is about to begin. We've laid the foundation, the background. Behind every individual scene in our smaller story lies hidden the larger story, the really real story of the battle to capture our souls. Surely, understanding love's eternality—the community of the Holy Trinity loving us with grace love—surely this will help us say, "I do," to the right Groom.

Fickle as we are, more truth and love will help. Understanding love's conception, love's honeymoon, can keep us faithful until our wedding night.

Take a quick break. Then return to your seat for Act Two: The Romance.

Caring for Your Soul: Personal Applications

1. Which of Satan's seductive strategies seem to haunt you more often? Why? How do you respond victoriously?

    a. Seducing strategy Number One: Enticing You to Distrust God's Good Heart.

    b. Seducing strategy Number Two: Enticing You to Trust Your Own Heart.

2. Which of Satan's condemning methods seem to attack you more often? Why? How do you respond victoriously?

    a. Condemning Method Number One: Accusing You to God.

    b. Condemning Method Number Two: Accusing You to Yourself.

    c. Condemning Method Number Three: Accusing You to and through Others.

3. Christ counters Satan's slander with grace

    a. How does the picture of grace presented in Chapter 7 compare and contrast with your typical picture of God's grace?

    b. How is your relationship with God different when you *stay* with Him in dependence rather than *run away* in fearful self-sufficiency?

    c. What is it like for you to celebrate God's grace, to receive it/Him, to accept His acceptance?

4. When were you duped into believing Satan's lie that "God is your enemy"? How were you able to demolish that lie with God's truth?

Caring for Others: Ministry Implications

♦ **Shine the Light of Truth on the Invisible Battle:**

1. Expose Satan's Seducing strategy Number One: Distrust God's Heart.

   • Ask, "When were you enrolled into believing that God can't be trusted?"
   • Explore, "What does the Word say about God's heart?"

2. Expose Satan's Seducing strategy Number Two: Trust Your Own Heart.

   • Ask, "What fig leaves do you sew to cover your sin and shame?"
   • Explore, "What view of God does such shame and hiding suggest?"

3. Expose Satan's Condemning Method Number One: Accusing Us to God.

   • Ask, "How does the Cross impact your image of God when you sin?"
   • Explore Romans 5:1-11; 8:1-39; Ephesians 2:1-10; 3:14-21; 1 John 1:8-2:2.

4. Expose Satan's Condemning Method Number Two: Accusing Us to Ourselves.

   • Ask, "Whose view of you is more important, yours or God's?"
   • Explore Psalm 32; Psalm 51; 1 Corinthians 4:1-5; 2 Corinthians 7:8-16.

5. Expose Satan's Condemning Method Number Three: Accusing Us through Others.
   • Ask, "Whose view of you is more important, others' or God's?"
   • Explore Psalm 31; Psalm 68; 2 Corinthians 2:5-11.

♦ **Equip Your Spiritual Friends with Christ's Weapons:**

1. Equip Them with the Spiritual Eyes of Battlefield Scouts.

   • Explore signs of God's goodness in the world and in their lives.
   • Expose how they are interpreting life with "eyeballs" only.

2. Equip Them with the Battlefield Weapon of God's Divine Power.

   • Explore whose strength they are trusting in and how.

3. Equip Them through Their Role as Battlefield Soldiers.

   • Remind them of the script and the role God calls them to play.

ACT TWO:
LOVE'S HONEYMOON—THE ROMANCE
EXAMINING THE SPIRITUAL ANATOMY OF THE SOUL:
PEOPLE—CREATION

DIRECTOR'S NOTES

Welcome back. Sit a spell. Allow me to set the stage for Act Two. The scene shifts from heaven to Earth, from before the beginning of time to in the beginning. The plot, however, remains the same. It's still about relationships because reality is relational.

The Worthy Groom doesn't just take a bride; He makes a bride. He doesn't simply build an add-on to His parent's home; He creates a universe. He doesn't form a soulless robot or a brute beast; He fearfully and wonderfully fashions a beloved image bearer who is a Romancer, Dreamer, Creator, Singer, and Actor.

I hear some rustling in the seats. Some murmurs. Hints of discontent. What's that you say? "Whatever happened to sin?" Sin hasn't happened yet. This is God's story and when He sent the manuscript to us, He decided to start pre-Fall. He wanted us to know *the way things ought to be*. Only then can we understand that what we experience now is not the way things were meant to be.

Following His screenplay, I want us to build our model of soul care and spiritual direction by understanding Creation. Here are the scenes we'll enjoy in Act Two.

CHAPTER EIGHT

A MARRIAGE MADE IN HEAVEN

"The webbing together of God, humans, and all creation in justice, fulfillment, and delight is what the Hebrew prophets call shalom. We call it peace, but it means far more than mere peace of mind or a cease-fire between enemies. In the Bible, shalom means universal flourishing, wholeness, and delight—a rich state of affairs in which natural needs are satisfied and natural gifts fruitfully employed, a state of affairs that inspires joyful wonder as its Creator and Savior opens doors and welcomes the creatures in whom he delights" (Cornelius Plantinga, *Not the Way It's Supposed to Be*, p. 10).

Sin is the "vandalism of shalom" (Plantinga, *Not the Way It's Supposed to Be*, p. 7).

The Song of Creation

Before we fix anything that's broken, we need to understand how it was meant to function. Our present condition neither corresponds to our original state nor to God's ultimate design for us. By listening to the haunting melodies of the song of creation, we'll glimpse how things were meant to be. We'll taste shalom—the joyful, peaceful weaving together of Deity and humanity, of the Worthy Groom and His virgin bride.

Creation has so much to show us about who God is, who we are, and how we are meant to relate. In particular, by returning to time's beginning, we'll overhear our Worthy Groom, His Father, and His Best Man reminiscing about our romance. Listen in as they retell our love story, the story of the chosen bride, the bridal home, and the honeymoon suite.

The Chosen Bride: You're Always on My Mind

We are placed in Paradise. How long has God been planning this? Are we merely a whim? An afterthought? Or have we never once been absent from God's presence? Perhaps we should let our Worthy Groom tell us.

Long before he laid down earth's foundation, he had us in mind, had settled on us as the focus of his love, to be made whole and holy by his love. Long, long ago he decided to adopt us into his family through Jesus Christ. (What pleasure he took in planning this!) He wanted us to enter into the celebration of his lavish gift giving by the hand of his beloved Son (Eugene Peterson, *The Message*, p. 2126, Ephesians 1:4-6).

The Worthy Groom has had eternal designs for us—for you! "You're a gift to me. I've had my eye on you since before the world was created! I knew you were mine, and all along I've planned to center my love on you." The Worthy Groom has loved us with an eternal love—loved you!

Forasmuch as [you] know that [you] were not redeemed with corruptible things, as silver and gold, from your vain conversation received by tradition from your fathers; but with the precious blood of Christ, as a lamb without blemish and without spot: Who verily was *foreordained before the foundation of the world*, but was manifest in these last times for you (1 Peter 1:18-20, KJV, emphasis added).

Before our favored planet hung in space, we were the twinkle in God's eye. We were the focus of His love and the reason He spoke Earth into existence. How should we then live?

But we ought always to thank God for you, *brothers loved by the Lord*, because *from the beginning God chose you* to be saved through the sanctifying work of the Spirit and through belief in the truth. He called you to this through our gospel that you might share in the glory of our Lord Jesus Christ (2 Thessalonians 2:13-14, emphasis added).

Loved forever to be beautiful forever. Imagine it. Enjoy it. Tell the story.

First Love

Do you remember your first love? How it changed you? Made your steps lighter, your mood brighter? Changed how you looked at life? At yourself? At others? How you couldn't stop telling others about your special someone?

I can remember my first love for Christ. I was saved on Easter Sunday, 1974. I came alive that day. I was no longer simply a fourteen-year-old who felt out of place, unimportant, and unforgiven. I didn't fully grasp it all, still don't, but I knew this much— Christ died for my sins because He loved me. Loving me, He forgave and accepted me. That day I accepted Christ's salvation offer. He bathed me in His love with His vows. That day I said, "I do" in my salvation vow.

Will you receive Jesus to be your Savior and Lord, to live with Him after God's plan of the holy state of salvation? Will you obey Him, serve Him, love, and honor Him, and forsaking all others, keep only to Him until death brings you together with Him for all eternity? If this is your salvation vow, say, "I do."

Seven years later, when I was a twenty-one-year-old Bible college senior, Christ granted me a new depth of insight into His love for me. I was reading the King James Version of Ephesians 1:6, "Wherein he hath made us accepted in the beloved." How many times I had read that. This time I stopped. Stunned. The Worthy Groom was talking about me, talking to me. I was accepted in the beloved, by the Beloved. I was beloved by the Ever Loving One. Somehow I had bought the lie that Jesus put up with me, tolerated me, even forgave me, but He didn't like me, didn't want me, didn't enjoy me. That day Jesus crushed that stronghold. Demolished it. Took it down and pinned it. He loved me. Liked me. Delighted in me. Enjoyed me. Desired me. Wanted me. All out of grace, of course. Nonetheless, I was loved. And so are you.

Why did God create? So He could relate—to us, to you. Recall the nature of God's good heart—*generous*. He exists to share. I imagine the Father saying, "This is too wonderful not to share. Giving is marvelous. Let's give our goodness. Let's create." Or perhaps it went something like this:

> Let's create creatures with the capacity to fully enjoy us. We're absolutely happy with ourselves, of course, because who we are and how we relate is incomparably wonderful. But so far, we've created no one who can share deeply in the unique joys of an intimate relationship with us where we hold nothing back. Let's create personal beings like us to whom we can reveal the very depths of our glorious nature (Larry Crabb, *Connecting*, p. 58).

He wanted to make something, or better, someone, in His own image. Someone who could personally relate to Him.

Matchmaker, Matchmaker, Make Me a Match

How was this made-in-heaven marriage arranged? Like marriages in biblical times, it was just that, an arranged marriage. In the ancient Near East, the father's most trusted servant was sent as a *Shadkan* to woo a bride for his eldest son (Alan Wright, *Lover of My Soul*, p. 35). Genesis 24 depicts the pre-arranged union of Abraham's son Isaac to Rebekah. Abraham's *Shadkan* pleads with the Lord to lead him to the woman God has *appointed* for Isaac. When Rebekah meets all the predetermined qualifications, and she, her brother, and her father agree, the *Shadkan* pays the bride price and takes Rebekah to Isaac as a gift.

A Father named Jehovah had a son named Jesus. Jehovah sent His *Shadkan*, the Holy Spirit, to woo a bride for the Prince of Peace. When we accept the Spirit's offer, the bride price having been paid, we become the gift given by the Father to His Son.

In our modern culture, this all seems so very unromantic. However, marriage out of a pre-arranged union is the truest love of all. Romantic love often simply means, "You make me feel so wonderful. You give me chills. I'm smitten." Do you detect the self-centeredness of such romantic love? "I love you because of how lovely you make me feel." On the other hand, in a pre-arranged marriage, the love is a love of confident choice, not of fleeting feelings. Father describes His loyal love for us. "This is love: not that we loved God, but that he loved us and sent his Son as an atoning sacrifice for our sins" (1 John 4:10).

"I love you because I love you," Father tells us. "I choose to love you faithfully forever." What unconditional love, unfailing love, loyal love! Does it still include romance? Of course, we've shown that repeatedly. But it's unselfish passion, not selfish feelings—*passion plus permanence*. God treasures and adores us, just because.

Years ago I surprised Shirley with some roses—just because. No special occasion. No argument to mend. No ulterior motive. On the note I simply wrote, *Shirley, I love you. Just because*. Of all the love notes I've ever given Shirley, which one do you suppose she still keeps on the refrigerator? Yep. The "Just because" note. She longs to know, as we all do, that she is treasured just because.

Bridal Home: What a Dowry!

Notice what Abraham's *Shadkan* does once Rebekah and her family accept his proposal. "Then the servant brought out gold and silver jewelry and articles of clothing and gave them to Rebekah; he also gave costly gifts to her brother and to her mother" (Genesis 24:53). It was customary for the *Shadkan* to lavish the bride and her family with costly gifts known as the dowry or "bride price."

What costly gifts does God lavish upon us? The imagery of bride price for sinners is quite different from the imagery of the bride price for perfect image bearers. Out of goodness, God gives His perfect bride the gift of creation and the Garden. Out of grace, God gives His prodigal bride the grace-gift of the precious blood of Christ.

In the imagery that we're using, the bride price was sheer gift. It was the gift of an environment fit for a queen and king, for a beautiful bride. It was the gift of a home beyond compare: *a perfect home for perfect people in perfect relationships*. Before the beginning God relates. In the beginning God creates so that we have a place to relate.

The sequence of events follows the typical ancient Near Eastern pattern. First, the bride is chosen. When she accepts, the groom leaves to prepare a place for her (just as Christ has now left Earth to prepare a place for us). The Worthy Groom chose us from eternity past. Then He spent six days preparing the most incredible home any groom has ever constructed. Marvel at the lavish dowry given to us by our Worthy Groom: Earth—the blue planet.

"In the beginning God created the heavens and the earth" (Genesis 1:1). The words are so familiar, we stumble over them or race beyond them. Think of Genesis 1-2 as the tour that Worthy Groom offers His bride. The Old Testament saints certainly did. "For your Maker is your husband—the LORD Almighty is his name—the Holy One of Israel is your Redeemer; he is called the God of all the earth" (Isaiah 54:5).

"Close your eyes," Worthy Groom tells Adam and Eve.

"What did He build for us? What does our home look like?" they wonder.

Positioning them just right, He says, "Okay, you can look now!"

Speechless. Silent. Awestruck!

Worthy Groom gleams. "You like?"

"Do we like? You made all of this for us?"

"All of it," Worthy Groom answers. "I've spent the last six days, well, actually, the first six days," He says with a smile, "creating the heavens and the earth for you. You may not understand it yet, but this is the favored planet, the blue planet. See those billions upon billions upon billions of stars? Every one has a purpose that relates to our home.

The shape of the universe, the movement of the grand galaxies, the gravitational pull, all of it I've worked together with absolute precision so that our blue planet home can be the perfect place for life. See those other eight orbs, those additional eight planets in our solar system? They, too, are necessary for Earth to thrive. Even our own little satellite that I call "Moon" must be exactly where it is for the ebb and flow of the tides. Oh, that reminds me, the tides. Have you seen the waters! That's why I nicknamed our home the blue planet. Our world has water—oceans, seas, rivers, and streams. Our world is lush with life. Teeming. Well, I'm getting ahead of myself. You certainly can't miss, and I can't forget to mention, the Sun. Perfect distance, size, and strength to heat our world without scorching it. Care to take a walk around our home?"

"Would we ever!" they reply.

And so the tour continues. Mountains. Valleys. Trees. Plants. Flowers. Birds. Animals. "This is all yours!" Worthy Groom promises.

"All this, for us? What a home You've made. It's so very good."

Gazing at all that He has made for them, He concurs. "It is *very* good!"

Imagine the wonders of creation prepared for us. Read Genesis 1-2; Psalm 8:1-9; 19:1-6; Job 38-41; Acts 14:14-18; 17:24-31; Romans 1:18-25; and Colossians 1:15-20—each passage a Divine commentary on the glories of creation and our Creator. Think of the universe itself, the Milky Way, our solar system, our sun, the planets, and our moon. Think of Yellowstone, the Grand Canyon, the Nile, the Rain Forests, Niagara . . . think of the best you know now and multiply that because the Fall and the flood changed everything, diminished everything. As you think, realize that it was our dowry, our bride price, and our home beyond compare. All of it is a beautiful home for a beautiful bride.

The Honeymoon Suite: Paradise

Describe Paradise for *you*. Not heaven. Our ideas of heaven are too "other worldly," too much harp and clouds. For you, what would an ideal world *in this world* be like? Describe the tastes, sights, sounds, smells, and feels. What comes to mind?

What were relationships like in the Garden before the Fall? As spiritual beings, how did Adam and Eve relate to God? As social beings, how did Adam and Eve connect with each other? As self-aware beings, what sense of self did Adam have, did Eve experience? What do you picture? What would perfect, harmonious, meaningful relationships be like for you? What do you want?

What adventures did Adam and Eve experience? What heroic purposes did they pursue? What would you dream of doing if there were no weeds and thorns to hinder you? What would you attempt if time, money, and talent were not obstacles?

These three categories—pristine environment, peaceful relationships, and meaningful purpose—help us to address the question: "How were things meant to be?" How sad that humanity experienced this trinity of blessedness for such a short time. A study of what the Bible teaches about how life was meant to be can whet our appetite for the new heaven and the new earth. It can also teach us how to understand the ills we face today, and God's curing medicine.

Paradise: Our Intended Home—Garden of Delight

"Now the LORD God had planted a garden in the east, in Eden; and there he placed the man he had formed" (Genesis 2:8). Adam and Eve never pulled a weed before Genesis 3. They never pulled a muscle either. "Garden" in the Hebrew language and in Jewish thought pictures a place of safety, protection, shelter, and refuge. Whenever God makes reference to the Garden of Eden in later passages such as Isaiah 51:3; Ezekiel 31:9-18; 36:33-38; and Joel 2:3, the authors direct our focus to prosperity, fertility, and abundance—a place of lush vegetation God gifts us with.

"Eden" means a garden of delight, a place of enjoyment—Paradise. Jesus promises us a place in Paradise (Revelation 2:7), the place of endless bliss and incredible fruitfulness. The references in Isaiah, Ezekiel, and Joel portray Eden as a luxurious place of unbroken fellowship, total enjoyment, and meaningful work.

What were we meant for? We were *not* meant for weeds, exhaustion, frustration, bondage, decay, and the second law of thermodynamics. We *were* meant for roses without thorns, the Kansas plains without tornadoes, farms without pesticides, cars without flat tires, trips to work without traffic jams, business partnerships without embezzling, management jobs without downsizing, financial investments without bankruptcy, life without death, childbirth without labor pains, and so very much more.

What were we meant for? Our fine-tuned bodies in a perfect environment were *not* meant for frailty. Feeling tired, weak, feeble; being sick or disabled; death, murder, funerals, caskets—these are all intruders, invaders. They are not the way things were meant to be. That is why it's normal to hurt in a fallen world. It's why Paul tells us that the whole creation groans as in the agonies of childbirth. Why we ourselves groan inwardly as we wait eagerly for our glorification.

What *were* we meant for? We were designed for Paradise—towering forests, nourishing waters, health-giving springs, flowing streams, thick foliage, shade, beauty, majesty, splendor. We were created for home—an everlasting home. This is why Jesus invites everyone wise enough to recognize and honest enough to admit their thirst to come to Him and drink of the rivers of Paradise. Are you thirsty? Hungry? Do you long, want, desire? You ought to, and so should I, because we are east of Eden, out of the nest, away from home, vagabonds, and strangers in a strange land.

Peace: Our Intended Relationships—Shalom

Shalom is the Hebrew word that best describes God's design for our relationships. Shalom reflects the sigh of contentment, the smile of joy, the look of peace, the recline of rest. Shalom portrays walking with God in the cool of the day without a speck of doubt, a thread of guilt, or any threat of judgment. Shalom communicates working harmoniously, completing and complementing one another, rather than competing against each other. Shalom pictures such a clear conscience that you can see all of me, deep inside of me, and I still feel delighted in, accepted, wanted, and respected.

Shalom means that as *males* we feel supremely confident in our ability to enter God's world with penetrating strength that empowers others. Shalom suggests that as *females* we feel totally comfortable in our capacity to enter God's world with responsive encouragement that nourishes others. Shalom is that rare commodity we all seek—the sense that everything is right with the world, with me and God, with you and me, and within my own soul.

Spiritual shalom walks with God in the cool of the day. In an agrarian society, the cool of the day was family time—the time between a good day's work and a good night's sleep. Dinner together. Food, fun, and fellowship. Talking. Walking. Sharing. Listening. Laughing. Playing.

Spiritual shalom walks hand-in-hand, the Bride of Christ with her Worthy Groom. Spiritual shalom is God dwelling with us, living with us, up close and personal. Spiritual shalom is eye contact with God—we shall see His face! Spiritual shalom is the perfect love affair—guiltless passion.

As we saw during our creation tour, Isaiah emphasizes the intimacy involved in our relationship with God. In the context of the "New Eden," he writes, "For your Maker is your husband" (Isaiah 54:5). Such familiarity was unheard of in the other religions of the ancient Near East. We mistakenly think that only the New Testament speaks of a Husband-wife relationship between God and His people. Untrue. In Eden, our Maker is our Husband. Unimaginable intimacy is His gift to us.

No wonder we ache. No wonder the apostle Paul preferred death and presence with God to life and absence from God. This side of heaven we are like the parched deer panting for water. Our Worthy Groom is our water. In the absence of our spiritual thirst Quencher, we shrivel up. We experience spiritual depression and spiritual sickness. Spiritual hygiene requires spiritual nourishment from the umbilical cord of connection to Christ.

Isaiah beautifully describes *social* shalom. "For the LORD shall comfort Zion: he will comfort all her waste places; and he will *make her wilderness like Eden*, and her desert like the garden of the LORD; *joy* and *gladness* shall be found therein, *thanksgiving* and the *voice of melody*" (Isaiah 51:3, KJV, emphasis added). Relationships in Eden were filled with joy, gladness, thanksgiving, and the voice of melody. Not bad. Not bad at all.

Certainly Edenic joy, gladness, thanksgiving, and melody revolve around God. However, we would be grossly mistaken to think they stop there. In the context of sinless Adam in a sinless world experiencing intimacy with God, God Himself reminds us, "It is not good for the man to be alone" (Genesis 2:18). We are social beings designed by our Creator to experience connecting relationships with one another that produce reciprocal joy, gladness, thanks, and melody. God designed us for oneness—weaving our lives together into a beautiful tapestry (Genesis 2:24). Anything less is less than what God intended.

Isaiah and his fellow prophets used a Hebrew word for joy that meant to exalt, to jump for joy, to rejoice, to dance, and celebrate. As speaker and professor Tony Campolo likes to say, "the kingdom of God is a party!" Paradise was not boring. Nor will heaven be. C. S. Lewis was right when he said, "the serious business of heaven is joy." Our Worthy Groom gifts us with personal relationships arranged to energize, encourage, and empower.

Our Father also intends our social relationships to produce mutual enjoyment. "Gladness" pictures banqueting, delight, and pleasure. The kingdom of God is not only a party; it's a wedding reception.

Distance. Divorce. Disharmony. Fighting and arguing. Congregational conflicts and church splits. Parents who exasperate and children who dishonor. None of these are elements of God's original design. They are party-crashers, aliens, and interlopers.

Instead, God invites us to experience thankful relationships. Isaiah informs us that Edenic relationships are filled with thanksgiving. Certainly this includes worshipful thanks and honor given to God. But it does not preclude mutual respect and appreciation. In the Garden, high-fives were standard. As were pats on the back, "atta' boys," "way to go," "go girl," and endless manner of cheerleading. A thankless job would have been foreign to Adam and Eve.

They experienced the voice of melody, or, as the NIV translates it, "the sound of singing" (Isaiah 51:3). The prophet uses the identical phrase to express the wonderful celebration that lasts throughout the millennial kingdom. "The ransomed of the LORD will return. They will enter Zion with singing; everlasting joy will crown their heads. Gladness and joy will overtake them, and sorrow and sighing will flee away" (Isaiah 51:11). No more crying there. No pain. No sorrow. No grief.

Edenic relationships enjoy life in the major key. Isaiah repeats his refrain with a new emphasis—togetherness. "Together they shout for joy" (Isaiah 52:8). "Burst into songs of joy together" (Isaiah 52:9). When the curse is reversed, harmony prevails and collaboration is savored.

> You will go out in joy and be led forth in peace; the mountains and hills will burst into song before you, and all the trees of the field will clap their hands. Instead of the thornbush will grow the pine tree, and instead of briers the myrtle will grow (Isaiah 55:12-13).

Edenic relationships also experience *self-aware* shalom, or internal, personal peace, wholeness, contentment, and serenity. "The man and the woman were both naked, and they felt no shame" (Genesis 2:25). Total exposure with total acceptance is *social* shalom. Total openness with complete integrity is *self* shalom. By integrity, I mean wholeness, completeness, and the ability to integrate experiences, relationships, longings, thoughts, goals, actions, and emotions.

In Eden, Adam never experienced the splintering and dis-integration that we struggle with. He never said, "I'm falling apart, coming unglued. I have no clue who I am!" Eve never threw her hands up in despair, felt suicidal, or totally lost. She never wondered, "Who am I? Why am I here? Am I worth anything? Am I normal?" Adam was confident in who he was in God. Eve was comfortable with who she was in God. No identity crisis in Eden. No disgrace. No self-loathing, self-hatred, self-doubt, or self-contempt. They felt clean, pure, good, and free.

That is what we were created for. It is the promised future we long after. "Do not be afraid; you will not suffer shame. Do not fear disgrace; you will not be humiliated. You will forget the shame of your youth and remember no more the reproach of your widowhood" (Isaiah 54:4).

Sin shattered shalom. The people we counsel and disciple realize that they are naked, and they feel shame. So they cover up, putting on layer after layer after layer of self-protective camouflage. They are afraid, because they are naked, so they hide. God calls us to participate in the restoration of health—the return of shalom: courageous, open, transparent relationships.

Purpose: Our Intended Pastime—Meaning

Paradise, peace, and purpose are God's Edenic gifts. Because God is a Relater and a Creator, He made us to relate and create. He planted us in Paradise for relationship and purpose. Theologians label our purpose "the Creation Mandate."

> God blessed them and said to them, "Be fruitful and increase in number; fill the earth and subdue it. Rule over the fish of the sea and the birds of the air and over every living creature that moves on the ground" (Genesis 1:28).

Once placed in Paradise, Adam received further marching orders. "The LORD God took the man and put him in the Garden of Eden to work it and take care of it" (Genesis 2:15). Eve, too, received instructions. She would become a suitable helper. That is, a perfect complement, capably working side by side with Adam—she, out of the uniqueness of her femininity and he, out of the uniqueness of his masculinity.

God planted Adam and Eve in the Garden and said to them, "Work it. Till it. Guard it. Protect it. Further beautify it. Expand it." God intended Adam and Eve and their offspring to expand the Garden until it covered the entire planet. It was vital work. It was fun work.

That is, until sin entered. Then it became painful work, toil, trouble, blood, sweat, and tears. Thorns and thistles now block our path. Because of the curse, everything is hard, nothing easy. Every job takes twice as long as we plan and costs twice as much as we can afford. Our purposes are thwarted. Our dreams dashed. Our plans busted. No wonder the people we counsel are frustrated, discouraged, tired, and exhausted.

Where We've Been and Where We're Heading

So what do spiritually healthy people look like? *They are powerful people purposefully producing in a pristine Paradise.*

So what was life meant to be like? What is spiritual hygiene? What sort of wholeness does spiritual corruption attack? What sort of disintegration of integration has occurred? What sort of shalom has shame infiltrated? Our visit to Paradise enables us to answer these questions.

However, they are not the only questions that thoughtful biblical psychologists and trained soul physicians need to ask and answer. We do not only want to know, "What was life meant to be like?" We also need to understand, "What were we meant to look like?" The next five scenes in Act Two present the spiritual anatomy of the soul. Let's look at beloved image bearers who are Romancers, Dreamers, Creators, Singers, and Actors to view portraits that represent biblical personality theory.

Caring for Your Soul: Personal Applications

1. Write about some times when you have most deeply sensed that you were "accepted in the beloved."

2. What love sonnet is God weaving into your life?

3. Why not spend some time alone with God? If you can, do it outdoors. Read Genesis 1-2; Psalm 8; 19; Job 38-42; Isaiah 51; or Ezekiel 36. Marvel at the dowry God made as His generously good gift to you. Enjoy Him. Thank Him. Love Him.

4. Allow yourself to groan, grieve, and hurt.

    a. What were you meant for that you are not experiencing? What are the weeds and thorns in your life? Take them to Christ. He knows all about thorns.

    b. What relationships seem empty or are hurtful to you? What relationships lack shalom? Take them to Christ. He knows all about broken relationships.

5. Allow yourself to hope.

    a. Picture heaven—an earthly heaven. Reread Isaiah 51:3. Savor the thought of your future home, future joy, future gladness, future thanksgiving, and future voice of melody.

    b. What difference will your future make as you deal with your past and face your present?

Caring for Others: Ministry Implications

♦ **Emphasize Dignity:** Our models of counseling/discipleship must not highlight only depravity, they also must emphasize our dignity as image bearers. Our models must begin at the beginning, not at the Fall. When they begin at the beginning, we won't simply be "sin-spotters." We'll also be those who "draw out dignity." Your grace relationships can include:

- Fanning into flame the gift of God within your spiritual friends (2 Timothy 1:5-7).
- Stirring up love and good deeds among your spiritual friends (Hebrews 10:24-25).
- Praying for and sharing a vision of what God is doing in the lives of your spiritual friends (2 Timothy 4:1-5).
- Respecting your spiritual friends as image bearers (James 3:9-11).
- Relating to your spiritual friends with equality (Galatians 6:1-3).

♦ **Highlight Longings:** God created us for Paradise, but we now live in a desert. So we thirst (John 7:37-39), we suffer (John 16:33), and we groan for home (Romans 8:18-25). Biblical discipleship counselors keep their hearts and ears attuned to the discrepancy in the soul between what people were designed for (Paradise) and what they now experience (suffering). Soul physicians develop and practice a biblical theology of suffering.

- Teach that it's normal to hurt. Help your spiritual friends grieve, but not as those who have no hope. They grieve and groan, longing for what is not yet, but what will someday be. Touch their longings for what they were originally designed: shalom with God, with others, and within their own souls. They long for a pristine environment, peaceful relationships, and a purposeful existence.
- Enter the casket of unmet longings knowing that hope deferred makes the heart sick, but don't leave people in the casket. From that view, help people to look up to God and look out to the future. It's possible to hope because "Sunday's coming"! The resurrection is promised, and God is working out His grand and glorious plan.

CHAPTER NINE

THE BELOVED BRIDE

"Every human being is preceded by a legion of angels crying, 'Make way for the image of God!'" (Ancient Rabbinic saying).

"It is a serious thing to live in a society of possible gods and goddesses, to remember that the dullest and most uninteresting person you talk to may one day be a creature which, if you saw it now, you would be strongly tempted to worship or else a horror and a corruption such as you now met, if at all, only in a nightmare. All day long we are, in some degree, helping each other to one or the other of these destinations" (C. S. Lewis, *The Weight of Glory*, pp. 14-15).

"The nature of man is a wonderful instrument of many strings, delicately tuned to work God's will and upon which He plays with master hand" (J. Gresham Machen, *The Christian View of Man*, p. 101).

Fractured Souls and Fragmented Solutions

We are plagued with an identity problem. "Who am I?" we ask. "Where did I come from?" "Why am I here?" "How then should I live?"

Clouded past, confused present, and obscured future claw at our minds. Under such weight, our souls fracture. We say it so many different ways, but the meaning is the same. "I'm cracking up." "I'm falling apart." "Nothing makes sense." "My life's a mess." "I'm having a nervous breakdown." "I'm coming unglued."

We're also plagued with an information problem. For every question we ask, we receive countless conflicting answers. Our information/Internet age leaves us ever learning but never able to come to the knowledge of the truth. Fractured souls face fragmented solutions.

Where do we turn for answers to life's most fundamental questions? To psychology? Sociology? Philosophy? Anthropology? Evolutionary theory? The self-help shelf? Oprah?

Augustine, St. Catherine of Siena, St. Teresa of Avila, John Calvin, and our other predecessors in the faith did not accept the current cultural assumption that the proper places to inquire about the root nature of humanity and the core causes of human evil are the departments of psychology, sociology, and philosophy. They believed the good news that we find our identity in Christ.

Traveling further back, our most ancient ancestors in the faith—Adam and Eve— found their identity in Deity. "Who are we? Beloved image bearers. Worthy Groom's beautiful bride."

Q: "Where did we come from?"
A: "From Trinity."
Q: "Why are we here? What is our purpose?"
A: "To be the Great Shepherd's under-shepherds."
Q: "How should we then live?"
A: "Share Trinity's shalom."

The antithesis of fractured souls and fragmented sources, Adam and Eve were shameless souls with a singular source of identity integration. John Milton, in Book IV of *Paradise Lost*, pictures their peace. Adam, first of men, speaks to Eve, first of women. Adam's words describe our first parents' clear understanding of whose they were and who they were.

Sole partner and sole part of all these joys, dearer thyself than all; needs must the Power that made us, and for us this ample World be infinitely good, and of his good as liberal and free as infinite, that raised us from the dust and placed us here in all this happiness. Who at his hand have nothing merited, nor can perform anything whereof he has need. He who requires from us no other service than to keep this one, this easy charge, of all the Trees in Paradise that bear delicious fruit so various, not to taste that only Tree of Knowledge, planted by the Tree of Life. So near grows Death to Life, whatever Death is, some dreadful thing no doubt; for well thou knowest God has pronounced it death to taste that Tree. The only sign of our obedience left among so many signs of power and rule conferred upon us, and Dominion given over all other Creatures that possess Earth, Air, and Sea. Then let us not think hard one easy prohibition, who enjoy free leave so large to all things else, and choice unlimited of manifold delights. But let us ever praise him, and extol his bounty, following our delightful task to prune these growing Plants, and tend these Flowers, which were it toilsome, yet with thee were sweet (Milton, *Paradise Lost*, pp. 96-97).

Their life was an idyllic romantic adventure composed by Worthy Groom who created them to be His beautiful, beloved bride. If only life were so simple, so Edenic, now. Instead, confusion reigns both in our souls and in society. Clueless and restless, we ask:

♦ *Who Are We?* Our Design and Nature—Reflection
♦ *Where Did We Come From?* Our Origin and Originator—Relationship
♦ *Why Are We Here?* Our Destiny and Vocation—Rulership
♦ *How Then Should We Live?* Our Shalom and Satisfaction—Rest

Two divergent sources attempt to address our four critical concerns. One source, secular psychology, seeks to understand humanity from humanity—*knowing the creature through the creature*. The other source, biblical psychology, seeks to understand humanity from Deity—*knowing the creature through the Creator*.

Secular psychology presumes that we are bearers of the evolutionary image of animals. We are dust alone. Our physical brain is the sole source of what we call "soul." In Chapter 9, we briefly overview this thinking so we can contrast its presuppositions with biblical psychology.

Biblical psychology teaches that we are bearers of the Divine image of God. We are dust *and* divinity. God designed our physical brains and our metaphysical minds to function harmoniously. In this chapter, we present a biblical psychology that answers life's four most confounding questions. "Who am I?" "Where did I come from?" "Why am I here?" "How then should I live?" We uncover our answers through examining the Bible's teaching on the *imago Dei*—the image of God in humanity.

Secular Psychology: A Game of Hide-and-Seek Played by the Blind

Biblical theologian Stanley Grenz rightly remarks, "Our foundational identity arises from the fact that our ultimate origin lies in God" (Grenz, *Theology for the Community of God*, p. 127). Secular psychologists disagree. In particular, post-modern psychology insists that we co-create identity in society (see Gilligan, *Therapeutic Conversations*, and White, *Narrative Means to Therapeutic Ends*). The Creator is not the creator of our identity; we are.

Ray Anderson labels these attempts at self-understanding, "non-theological anthropology." They are purely human attempts to understand human nature. Because they deny, ignore, or claim agnosticism regarding God, their views are partial, at best.

> Therefore, at best, non-theological anthropology can only provide fragmented observations about man. The sum total of their analytical "findings" is not the true, whole person. The human self becomes nothing more than a cluster of molecules in search of a name! (Anderson, *On Being Human*, p. 14).

Secular psychologists fight a second losing battle. Their attempts to understand human nature are thwarted by our fallen nature. We no longer exist in our original condition. As Dallas Willard explains:

> Furthermore, secular psychology is *not* in an *"at-best"* set of circumstances. The question of who we are and what we are here for is not an easy one, of course. For those who must rely upon a strictly secular viewpoint for insight, such questions are especially tough. Why? Because we *do* in fact live in a world in ruins. We do not exist now in the element for which we were designed. So in light of that truth, it's essentially impossible to determine our nature by *observation* alone, because we are only seen in a perpetually unnatural position (Willard, *The Spirit of the Disciplines*, p. 45).

Our world is fallen, and so are we. Therefore, secular psychology is like a game of hide-and-seek played by the blind. Secular social scientists search a dark world with darkened eyes looking at darkened image bearers. The "facts" that they research do not portray life as God originally designed it. They then filter their interpretations of these "facts" through their fallen minds. Secular psychology proceeds from *anthropos* to *anthropos*—from humanity to humanity—without regard for the insight of Deity.

Biblical Psychology: Knowing the Creature through the Creator

Soul Physicians is a biblical psychology text. We are examining human nature as designed by God, marred by sin, and redeemed by grace. Though called by various names throughout church history, biblical psychology has a long and honorable history as an essential doctrine of the church. Franz Delitzsch, writing in 1861 (prior to the advent of modern secular psychology), noted, "biblical psychology is no science of yesterday. It is one of the oldest sciences of the church" (Delitzsch, *A System of Biblical Psychology*, p. 3).

Biblical psychology interprets the Scriptures to discern how human nature in God's image has been shaped by Creation/Fall/Redemption in order to sustain, heal, reconcile, and guide faith active in love. Wayne Rollins defines biblical psychology as "the study of the biblical perspective on the origin, nature, pathology, health, and destiny of the human psyche or soul" (Rollins, *Soul and Psyche*, p. 4).

Some may raise an objection to our course of study. "Why study the nature of the soul? Why study humanity at all? Study God. All we need to know is God: Father, Son, and Holy Spirit. If Christians simply understood the Godhead better, they would not have any problems. They would not need counseling!"

Calvin answers the question, insisting that we need to know God and ourselves. He explains the inseparable link between the knowledge of God and the knowledge of humanity:

> The knowledge of ourselves is not only an incitement to seek after God, but likewise a considerable assistance toward finding Him. On the other hand, it is plain that no man can arrive at the true knowledge of himself, without having first contemplated the divine character, and then descended to the consideration of his own (Calvin, *The Institutes of the Christian Religion*, Vol. 1, p. 48).

To know God and to grow in Christ, we must know ourselves as created by God, ruined by sin, and redeemed by grace.

Willard further describes the wedding of biblical psychology and salvation.

> Without an understanding of our nature and purpose, we cannot have a proper understanding of redemption. . . . What "salvation" is depends upon what is being saved. . . . It is the nature of what is being saved that determines how it can be at risk and at loss. . . . So, if we want to know what it is to save a human being, to redeem the human soul or personality, we cannot find a better way to begin than by asking: *what* did God make when he made us, and how could creatures such as we be at risk and at loss? (Willard, *The Spirit of the Disciplines*, p. 45).

Psychology is native to our faith. Not secular psychology, but biblical psychology— understanding and curing the soul designed by God, disordered by sin, and redeemed by grace.

Psychology has been fundamental to Christianity for 2,000 years. Rather than borrowing from the secular world, we need to recover our own historical legacy. All the classical theologians were intimately aware of and concerned with what we now call "psychology." We need to recover and translate that heritage for our post-modern context. (Box 9:1 outlines the basic nature of biblical psychology under its various names.)

Where do we start? In the beginning. We learn who we are from the One who made us in His image.

Cosmic Conception

If there is a Romance, there must be a Romancer. And if there is a Romancer, there must be a bride. What sort of being could be fitted for intimate relationship with God? Only a being created in the image of God, in the *imago Dei*. Our first parents entered the universe by cosmic conception marvelously fashioned to reflect God, to relate to God, to rule under God, and to rest in God.

All their descendants share a similar essence. Like father, like son.

When God created man, he made him *in the likeness of God*. He created them male and female and blessed them. And when they were created, he called them "man." When Adam had lived 130 years, he had a son *in his own likeness, in his own image* (Genesis 5:1-3, emphasis added).

What is this essence? How does it influence how we live and how we die? How does the nature of human nature shape how we preach and how we counsel? Where do we find this "essential human nature"? According to many theologians, including the late Francis Schaeffer, Genesis 1-3 provides God's prime directive for the human race.

In some ways, these chapters are the most important ones in the Bible, for they put man in his cosmic setting and show him for his peculiar uniqueness. They explain man's wonder and yet his flaw. Without a proper understanding of these chapters we have no answer to the problems of metaphysics, morals, or epistemology (Schaeffer, *Genesis in Space and Time*, p. 9).

Embedded within these beginning chapters we find the record of our first parents' creation in the image of God. Karl Barth called the *imago Dei* the *Magna Carta* of humanity because it is God's supreme declaration of our design, dignity, and destiny. A proper understanding of the *imago Dei* is crucial for healthy human relationships—how we relate to God, others, and ourselves.

God takes great care to assure that He has our attention before He announces His intention to create us in His image. The literary and theological arrangement of Genesis 1 builds to a crescendo. Day after day, the hovering Spirit nurtures from chaos a home fit for a king and a queen. Reading the creation account for the first time, we are left with the nagging question, "Who is all of this for? Who is worthy to rule this blue sphere?" Seven times in five days God says, "Let there be." Abruptly, as day six dawns, Trinity communes together, "Let us." The angelic hosts stop. Take note. Something very personal is afoot.

Box 9:1

Definitions of Terms Related to Biblical Psychology

Biblical Psychology

Biblical psychology interprets the Scriptures to discern how human nature in God's image has been shaped by Creation/Fall/Redemption in order to sustain, heal, reconcile, and guide faith active in love. It is "the study of the biblical perspective on the origin, nature, pathology, health, and destiny of the human psyche or soul" (Wayne Rollins, *Soul and Psyche*, p. 4). Biblical psychology studies academic theology (systematic, biblical, exegetical, lexical, and contextual), historical theology, spiritual theology, and pastoral theology to explain and apply God's special revelation about the inner nature of human beings (relational {spiritual/social/self-aware}, rational, volitional, and emotional beings) as created by God (anthropology), distorted by sin (hamartiology), and redeemed/renewed by grace (soteriology).

Spiritual Nosology

Spiritual nosology is a culturally relevant spiritual diagnostic system useful in identifying, classifying, and overcoming sins through a biblical study of the nature of the soul, sin, and salvation. It is a way of conceptualizing humanity based upon a system of diagnoses built upon a theological understanding.

Theological Anthropology

Theological anthropology is the exegetical and systematic study of the doctrine of Scripture concerning humanity. It probes the nature of humanity (its personal capacities, constitution, and make-up) as created by God, marred by sin, and restored by grace. "The task of theological anthropology is to set forth the Christian understanding of what it means to be human. Christian anthropology views the human person and humankind as a whole in relationship to God" (Stanley Grenz, *The Social God and the Relational Self*, p. 23).

Relational Anthropology

Relational anthropology is *coram Deo* anthropology—humanity in relationship to God. It is a study of humanity resting on the fulcrum of the God-human relationship. The Bible does not present a study of the nature of humanity as an end in itself. Rather, the Bible describes the human constitution (personhood, personality, psychology) and the human condition (innocent, fallen, restored, perfected) in light of our relationship to God. This is an attempt to know the creature through the Creator instead of knowing the creature through the creature. *The final source of reality about the human mind is not the human mind but the Divine mind revealed in Scripture.* Whereas secular psychology proceeds from *anthropos* (humanity) and excludes *theos* (God), relational anthropology explores *anthropos* in light of *theos*.

Gene Edwards fancies it something like this:

> Late in the afternoon of the sixth day it became obvious to every angel that the Lord's work of creation was drawing to an end. They had noticed that each time Trinity creates a new life form; it is higher than the one before.
> Angelic conversation comes to a screeching halt. Trinity is about to speak. "Now."
> The word was spoken with expectation and finality. Every spirit pulsed with excitement.
> "At this moment creation lacks but one thing . . . its Purpose!"
> Every angel gasped. Here was a thought they had instinctively known yet had never formed into words: Why did our Lord create? To what end is this creation?
> The Lord, eyes blazing with fires of uncreated light, turned and faced the heavenly citizenry. "Be it fully understood. All creation has been brought into being because of this one, and this one alone!"
> As Trinity shapes humanity, the Archangels converge and converse. "These creatures, fashioned out of sod and clay, will they be as beautiful as we?"
> Their discourse interrupted by Trinity, they quiet themselves. Ears straining to hear the next words.
> "You see, they will be fashioned . . . in . . . Our . . . image."
> There was a moment of stunned silence as every eye shifted toward the clay.
> During this moment of revelation, angels realized why their Lord had so often paused in his fashioning of this clay. He had been reflecting upon His own being, then sculpting the marks of His own invisible features upon visible clay (Paraphrased and summarized from Edwards, *The Beginning*, pp. 19-24).

Six times in five days God reflects on His handiwork and declares, "It is good." On the evening of day six, Trinity boasts, "It is *very* good." Angels draw near. Hushed. Listening. Hearing.

"Very good!" A shout of exultation. "My sculpture is beautiful! Wow! Kewl! Awesome. Impressive. Hey, Amber, look out the window! I'm delighted."

"Very good!" Trinity savors humanity. Spectacular. Superb. Wholeness. Harmonious. Pleasing. Right.

The angels crowd closer. Amazed for five days by the luster of material creation and physical beings, Adam and Eve leave them speechless, take their breath away. Or, as Edwards imagines it:

> Soon the angels quieted themselves so as not to miss even an instant of the final moments of this unfolding drama.
> The Lord rose and wiped the clay from his hands, then stepped back, studied the clay mound, and whispered words too soft for any ear to hear.
> "At last, my masterpiece. The chosen one."
> Angels hushed all but their breathing (Edwards, *The Beginning*, pp. 24-25).

With the last sculpting stroke, He stepped back from the moist sod, allowing the angels to have a full view of His completed work. They gasped in amazement and cried together. "His image! *Visible!*" (Edwards, *The Divine Romance*, p. 4).

What is the essence of human nature? It is very good. Dignity. The apex of creation. The *imago Dei*. But what exactly is the image of God in humanity?

The Scarlet Thread Visible: The *Imago Dei* in the Bible and the Church

Though directly discussed on only a handful of occasions after Genesis 1:26-28, the *imago Dei* is the scarlet thread visible in every scene of the drama of redemption. Sewn in Genesis 1:26-28, Moses twice more loops the thread in Genesis, both times post-Fall. He reminds us of our creation in God's image in Genesis 5:1-3, where he teaches that though marred, Adam passes the *imago Dei* to his son, Seth. Even after the wickedness that caused the epic flood, God insists that the image remains and that we must measure human worth on the scale of the Divine image (Genesis 9:5-6).

The weaving continues in Psalm 8. God's commentary on creation places humanity at the pinnacle of creation and the rulers over creation. It reminds us that size can be deceiving.

When I consider your heavens, the work of your fingers, the moon and the stars, which you have set in place, what is man that you are mindful of him, the son of man that you care for him? You made him a little lower than the heavenly beings and crowned him with glory and honor. You made him ruler over the works of your hands; you put everything under his feet (Psalm 8:3-6).

Psalm 8 "clearly constitutes an important and positive affirmation about humanity's place in the created order" (Edward M. Curtis, "Image of God/OT," in the *Anchor Bible Dictionary*, p. 3:389). There is more here than meets the eye. Though small by comparison with the heavenly bodies, humanity's soul is giant—Godlike. The inscription dedicating the Hall of Fame at New York's World of Tomorrow captures the essence of Psalm 8: *Man wonders over the restless sea, the flowing water, the sight of the sky, and forgets that of all wonders, man himself is the most wonderful.* Though small compared to the stars, human beings alone reflect the Son.

David, in Psalm 139, describes the knitting of the Master Knitter.

For you created my inmost being; you knit me together in my mother's womb. I praise you because I am fearfully and wonderfully made; your works are wonderful, I know that full well. My frame was not hidden from you when I was made in the secret place. When I was woven together in the depths of the earth, your eyes saw my unformed body. All the days ordained for me were written in your book before one of them came to be. How precious to me are your thoughts, O God! How vast is the sum of them! Were I to count them, they would outnumber the grains of sand. When I awake, I am still with you (Psalm 139:13-18).

David, the man who confesses that he was birthed in iniquity (Psalm 51:5), hurries to rehearse the truth that we are also created in dignity.

Speaking of Genesis 5:1-3; 9:5-6; Psalm 8; and Psalm 139, Claus Westermann states, "one point on which scholars are agreed is that according to the Old Testament the person's 'likeness-to-God' was not lost with the 'fall,' but remained part of humanity" (Westermann, *Genesis 1-11: A Commentary*, p. 148). Stanley Grenz concurs. "The Old Testament witness is crucial. It forms the basis for an anthropology that views the *imago Dei* as a universal reality, not only 'in the beginning,' but also within fallen humankind" (Grenz, *The Social God and the Relational Self*, p. 185).

The New Testament authors, too, return to the *imago Dei*. Paul uses the *imago* as the present tense basis for males praying without head coverings. "A man ought not to cover his head, since he *is* the image and glory of God" (1 Corinthians 11:7, emphasis added). James chastises us for blessing God while cursing one another, because we have been "made in God's likeness" (James 3:9).

What is this marvelous *imago*? The story of the soul has received various explanations over the centuries with theologians typically interpreting the *imago* in one of four ways: the *structural* view that understands the *imago Dei* as consisting of certain capacities lodged within human beings, the *social* view that sees the image of God as referring to the fundamental relationality of humanity, the *stewardship* view that believes the *imago* is our calling to have dominion over God's creation, and the *shalom* view that sees image and likeness as our glorious, righteous nature. We can picture these as:

- The Structural Self: Reflecting   Reflection   Capacities
- The Social Self: Relating   Communion   Community
- The Stewardship Self: Ruling   Dominion   Calling
- The Shalom Self: Resting   Cohesion   Coherence

Where We've Been and Where We're Heading

Which is true? Is the *imago* our capacities of personhood, our ability to relate, our calling to rule, our "rightness" and rest, or some combination of these? Who are we really?

Join me for Act Two, Scene III, Chapter 10, as we unveil the beautiful bride. As we do, we'll see how the *imago Dei* answers life's most perplexing questions: "Who am I?" "Where did I come from?" "Why am I here?" "How should I then live?"

Caring for Your Soul: Personal Applications

1. Who is the most richly loving human being you have ever known?

    a. What is it about her/him that most amazes you?

    b. What is it about her/him that most influences you?

    c. When are you most like this person?

2. How do you personally answer life's four critical concerns?

    a. Who am I? Am I a healthy or an unhealthy Romancer, Dreamer, Creator, Singer, and Actor? How well do I reflect God's image?

    b. Where did I come from? How am I to relate? How well do I reflect the relational nature of the Trinity?

    c. Why am I here? What's my purpose in life? What is my calling? My vocation?

    d. How should I then live? Where do I find rest? Peace? Shalom? Strength?

3. God bestows identity upon us. God bestows meaning upon us. Value is not what others perceive, or even what we think of ourselves, but what God ascribes to us.

    a. To what degree do you really believe these statements?

    b. How do you experience your life, yourself, and your relationships differently when you believe these statements?

Caring for Others: Ministry Implications

♦ **Engage Your Spiritual Friends in Spiritual Conversations about Life's Four Critical Concerns:** Every person you encounter has these concerns percolating just beneath the surface. If you want to go deep, go here:

- Who Are We? Our Design and Nature—Reflection
- Where Did We Come From? Our Origin and Originator—Relationship
- Why Are We Here? Our Destiny and Vocation—Rulership
- How Should We Then Live? Our Shalom and Satisfaction—Rest

♦ **Engage Your Pre-Christian Friends in Spiritual Conversations about Life's Four Critical Concerns:** Every unsaved person you encounter has these concerns percolating just beneath the surface. If you want to help him/her to explore his/her spiritual lives and eternal destinies, go here.

♦ **Engage the Scriptures Asking Relevant Questions about Life's Four Critical Concerns:** Secular counselors ask relevant questions without turning to the Word. Some Christian counselors turn to the Word, but neglect to ask relevant life questions. God's Word is profitable for today and for eternity. God has given us all we need for life and godliness. However, we still have to approach His Word with integrity—the integrity to ask hard questions. Build your model of counseling upon your reflections on how the Word of God addresses life's four critical concerns.

CHAPTER TEN

THE BEAUTIFUL BRIDE

"View every counseling contact as an interaction with an eternally valuable human being" (Robert Kellemen).

"If God would not give me a heart to love him, I would [wish] I never had a heart" (Richard Baxter, *Christian Directory*, p. 125).

Eternally Valuable Human Beings

For years God gave me a ministry of counseling victims of sexual abuse. I did not choose such a calling; God chose me for it. Having been chosen, I grew to connect deeply with sexually abused victims.

Then the Divine Pitcher threw me a curve. He sent a man to me who had sexually abused a young girl. What do you think I saw when I looked into his heart? I saw depravity, not dignity. It took God's grace to enable me to view him as an eternally valuable human being.

He was eternally valuable by gift—he was created in the image of God. Born a sinner, he was lost, but not worthless. He was also a believer. Therefore, he was eternally valuable by grace. Twice born and twice valuable. He was guilty of a sin that I found particularly hideous, but was he less worthy than I? No.

What do you see when you look inside other people? Inside yourself? Inside counselees, parishioners, and spiritual friends? Part of counseling involves seeing and surfacing the *imago Dei*. What is it? We'll examine each of the four prevailing views of the image of God, and then we'll explore the implications of a holistic view of the *imago Dei* for biblical counseling.

- The Structural Self: Reflecting   Reflection   Capacities
- The Social Self: Relating   Communion   Community
- The Stewardship Self: Ruling   Dominion   Calling
- The Shalom Self: Resting   Cohesion   Coherence

The Structural Self: *Imago* as Capacities of Personhood

According to Stanley Grenz, the structural view is the best known and the most widely held understanding of the *imago Dei* (Grenz, *The Social God and the Relational Self*, p. 142). Both ancient and modern theologians have held this view: Irenaeus, Clement, Athanasius, Gregory of Nyssa, Cyril of Jerusalem, Augustine, Thomas Aquinas, Martin Luther, John Calvin, Jonathan Edwards, Franz Delitzsch, Charles Hodge, and James Orr, among many others.

> Perhaps the most long-standing interpretation of the *imago* sees it as a structure of the human person. In this understanding, the divine image consists of the properties that constitute human beings as human with special emphasis on the capacity for rationality coupled with our moral nature (Grenz and Franke, *Beyond Foundationalism*, p. 197).

This ancient view claims that the *imago* consists of certain capacities of personhood—characteristics inherent in the structure of human nature. These characteristics resemble corresponding qualities in God, making humans structurally like God. The Divine image refers to "something within the substantial form of human nature, some faculty or capacity man possesses" (Paul Ramsey, *Basic Christian Ethics*, p. 254). Grenz summarizes the view for us:

> Because the *imago Dei* is a quality or capability within human nature, proponents theorize, it remains present whether or not a person acknowledges God. It constitutes a person as human, and therefore it cannot be lost. Insofar as this view sees the image as residing in the very structure of human nature, it may be denoted the "structuralist" understanding (Grenz, *The Social God*, p. 142).

Theologians have displayed a remarkable variety of opinions regarding the specific capacities of personhood shared by God and image bearers. In Chapter 5, I shared my conviction that God is a Romancer, Dreamer, Creator, and Singer. God and human beings share relational, rational, volitional, and emotional capacities. Both are personal beings with affection (we long), cognition (we think), volition (we choose), and emotion (we feel).

The Social Self: *Imago* as Relational Communion

Those who champion the social view of the *imago Dei* insist that a proper understanding of the image of God relies upon a proper understanding of the Trinitarian nature of God. In Chapter 4, I explained that before God created, He related. God exists in eternal community. To be created in the image of the Trinitarian God means that we are communitarian.

We were not created in the image of a hermit God. "The 'God' whose reality illumines Christian anthropology is not some generic deity, however, but the God of the Bible, whom Christians confess as the triune one" (Grenz, *The Social God*, p. 23). As God is unity in diversity, so humanity—male and female—is unity in diversity. "Male and female he created them" (Genesis 1:27). "It is not good for the man to be alone" (Genesis 2:18). Both of these verses, coming as they do in the immediate context of the *imago*, shed light on the nature of human nature. We are relational; we are communitarian as God is Trinitarian.

Bearing God's relational image, it is not good to be isolated, out of community. It is not in accord with God's Trinitarian nature or our communal *imago Dei* for humanity to be without community. Through the right outworking of the *imago*, God destined us to achieve within human relationships a dim reflection of the love life within the Trinity. We are to mirror Divine relationality. Image bearers avoid unwholesome solitude to pursue the innate yearning for bondedness, partnership, completeness, oneness, unity in diversity, mutuality, and reciprocal relationships of giving and receiving. Created in the image of the social God, we love.

> Man is made for *love*. He cannot do without that nurturing love from the outside, not without responding to that love. In his love God created this entire world. But he created man as a being who could understand that love, and enjoy and respond to it. And that not as just one characteristic among many: in this relation of receiving and giving love, man heeds his most central calling and actualizes his true essence. In love man becomes himself (Hendrikus Berkhof, *Christian Faith*, p. 183).

I relate; therefore, I am. Image bearers exist in community, one beside the other, created to live with each other. "Man was formed to be a social animal" (John Calvin, *Commentaries on the First Book of Moses Called Genesis*, p. 82).

The Stewardship Self: *Imago* as Rule and Dominion

Like the social interpretation, the stewardship view of the *imago* fastens onto the immediate context. "Then God said, 'Let us make man in our image, in our likeness, and let them rule . . .'" (Genesis 1:26). "God blessed them and said to them, 'Be fruitful and increase in number; fill the earth and subdue it. Rule over . . .'" (Genesis 1:28). Theologians label it the "representative view." God is Sovereign, King, and Ruler of the universe. We are created in His ruling image. As His stewards, we represent Him and His rule on planet Earth. We are God's vice-regents, His under-shepherds, and even His under-scientists. In the creation mandate of Genesis 1 and 2, God grants us a role (take care of My planet) and a rule (take dominion over My planet). "You made him ruler over the works of your hands; you put everything under his feet" (Psalm 8:6).

People of the ancient Near East commonly used the royal image motif. Their kings and pharaohs represented God on earth as His special ambassadors. Following this line of thinking, human rulers represented themselves and their rule using images.

> In the ancient Near East, images were viewed as representatives of the entity they designated. This was the case with physical images of monarchs. Ancient Assyrian kings, for example, erected statues of themselves in conquered territories, probably to represent their occupation of the land. The close link between the image and the king meant that reviling the former was viewed as an act of treason (Grenz, *The Social God*, p. 198).

Gerhard Von Rad combines this ancient practice with the basic meaning of the Hebrew word for image (*selem*—"plastic image") to describe the representational role of humankind, which he links to dominion.

> Just as powerful earthly kings, to indicate their claim to dominion, erect an image of themselves in the provinces of their empire where they do not personally appear, so man is placed upon earth in God's image as God's sovereign emblem. He is really only God's representative, summoned to maintain and enforce God's claim to dominion over the earth. The decisive thing about man's similarity to God, therefore, is his function in the non-human world (Von Rad, *Genesis: A Commentary*, pp. 59-60).

These extra-biblical accounts have only one image bearer—the king or the pharaoh. The biblical account expands the royal idea of the image of God.

> Whereas Egyptian writers often spoke of kings as being in God's image, they never referred to other people in this way. It appears that the OT has democratized this old idea. It affirms that not just a king, but every man and woman, bears God's image and is his representative on earth (Gordon Wenham, *Genesis 1-15*, pp. 30-31).

The Shalom Self: *Imago* as "Rightness" and Rest

A fourth view of the *imago Dei* emphasizes the righteousness inherent in original human nature. The Westminster Shorter Confession states: "God created man male and female, after his own image, in knowledge, righteousness, and holiness, with dominion over the creatures." Leslie Flynn, in *Man: Ruined and Restored*, labels this the "righteousness view." Robert Pyne, in *Humanity and Sin*, calls it the "glory view."

It has been a much-debated view, since it is clear from Genesis 3 that Adam and Eve corrupted their original righteousness, while it is equally clear from the repeated post-Fall references to the *imago Dei*, that the image has not been eradicated. Certainly God created Adam and Eve in a state of innocence and goodness. God pronounces His image bearers "very good" (Genesis 1:31). Moses announces that the first couple was shameless: "the man and his wife were both naked, and they felt no shame" (Genesis 2:25).

Unquestionably, Adam and Eve lost their innocence, "They realized they were naked" (Genesis 3:7). They twisted their capacities, designed to enable them to relate and create. However, they did not lose those capacities; in their fallenness they retained the capacities that allowed them to experience communion and dominion. Those capacities were incapacitated, not decapitated; twisted, not eradicated.

In pondering the shalom self, I highlight the *result* of our creation in God's image—we have "rightness." That is, we experience shalom—peace, wholeness, contentment, and integration. We find peace as we function the way God designed us to function. We're comfortable in our design, dignity, and destiny. We're confident about who we are, where we came from, why we are here, and how we should live. No worry. Tranquility. All is right with the world because we are right.

When they sinned, Adam and Eve ruined their shalom. They lost their sense of wholeness, peace, comfort, contentment, and "rightness" because their core capacities became corrupted. No longer able to function as designed by God, they found no peace with God.

Shame is their legacy to us. Built right, we desperately cover our "wrongness." We sew fig leaves in self-sufficient attempts to eradicate our shame. We cannot escape our essential design. Shame (our loss of rest and felt righteousness/rightness) is our constant reminder of the *imago Dei*.

Four views. Which are right? Which are wrong?

The Four Robes of Creation: The *Imago Dei*

So much of theological inquiry becomes either/or rather than both/and. Either the *imago Dei* is the structural view, *or* the social view, *or* the stewardship view, *or* the shalom view. Could it be that the *imago Dei* is the structural view, *and* the social view, *and* the stewardship view, *and* the shalom view? I believe it is. Consider the various ways we can describe the integrated, four-fold nature of the *imago Dei*.

- ◆ Through the *imago Dei*, Trinity marvelously fashioned us to reflect God, relate like God, representatively rule for God, and rest in God.
- ◆ God created us with the reflecting capacities necessary to relate and rule leading to rest.
- ◆ We reflect God's relational rule resulting in rest.
- ◆ The *imago Dei* consists of the capacities of personhood that allow us to be communitarian beings as God is a Trinitarian being, that empower us to fulfill our calling of stewardship, and enable us to rest in the calm assurance that we are fulfilling our design.
- ◆ The *imago Dei* involves the capacities of personhood that we share with God as social beings called to stewardship and gifted with shalom.
- ◆ The *imago Dei* includes reflection, communion, dominion, and cohesion.

David Smith, in *With Willful Intent*, explains how we can combine these varied concepts. He notes that the image of God refers to elements in the makeup of human beings that enable us to fulfill our destiny. The *imago Dei* is the power of personality that makes us, like God, beings capable of interacting with others, of thinking and reflecting, and of willing freely.

The *imago Dei* encompasses the capacities of personhood that allow us to relate and create as God relates and creates. When we relate and create according to His image, we experience shalom. I call these aspects of the *imago Dei* "The Four Robes of Worthy Groom's Beautiful Bride." Box 10:1 overviews elements of these robes of reflection, communion, dominion, and cohesion.

Millard Erickson, though presenting a different integration, expresses a similar view.

That human beings experience relationships and exercise stewardship over creation are not the image but arise out of it. These relationships and these functions presuppose something else. Man is most fully man when he is active in these

Box 10:1

The Four Robes of Worthy Groom's Beautiful Bride

◆ **The Robe of Reflection: Structural**
"Who Am I?"
"I Am an Image Bearer."
"I Reflect."
Capacities: Relational, Rational, Volitional, Emotional, and Physical
The Structural Self
"Image and Likeness"
My Design: Reflection—"I'm a Romancer, Dreamer, Creator, Singer, and Actor."

◆ **The Robe of Communion: Social**
"Where Did I Come From?"
"I Came from the Communitarian Image of the Trinitarian God."
"I Relate."
Community
The Social Self
"Let Us"
My Dignity: Relation

◆ **The Robe of Dominion: Stewardship**
"Why Am I Here?"
"I'm an Under-shepherd."
"I Rule."
Calling
The Stewardship Self
"Let Them Rule."
My Destiny: Vocation

◆ **The Robe of Cohesion: Shalom**
"How Should I Then Live?"
"I Share in My Creator's Wholeness."
"I Rest."
Coherence
The Shalom Self
"Very Good"
My Direction: Integration

relationships and performs this function, for he is then fulfilling his telos, God's purpose for him. But the image itself is those qualities of God which reflected in man make worship and work possible, relation and creation. If we think of God as a being with these qualities we will have no problem accepting the fact that man has such qualities as well (Erickson, *Christian Theology*, p. 513).

To be created in the image of our Triune God is to reflect the light of His holy love (dominion and communion). To reflect His affectionate sovereignty requires similar capacities of personhood.

What is the *imago Dei*? God conceived a beautiful bride for His Worthy Groom. He dressed her in four glorious robes. Not something borrowed, something blue, something old, and something new. But something reflecting, something relating, something ruling, and something resting. Adam and Eve's dignified design enabled them to fulfill their destiny as beings with capacities rightly ordered and beautifully reflecting God's holy love (His rule and relationality).

Even though fallen, human beings continue to engage in communion and dominion: relationship and rule, intimacy and impact, people and tasks, sharing and serving, connecting and creating. We reflect or deface the Divine character through our capacities of personhood that allow us to relate and create. Every counseling issue is ultimately rooted in some defection or corruption of our relational, rational, volitional, and/or emotional nature that causes a loss of shalom (wholeness) because of a failure to reflect properly God's communion (relationality) and/or dominion (rule).

Though fearfully and wonderfully made, we now act terrifyingly and horribly toward God, others, and ourselves. Created to connect with God and others, we shrink into less and less other-centered beings. We incarcerate ourselves within our own little universes. Destined to imitate Creator through our creative abilities, we misuse His good gifts, destroying, competing, and plundering the good world God made us to nourish. Rather than reflecting God's Trinitarian *agape*, we display the malice of the Evil One. We are hideously deformed, like the Phantom of the Opera. Yet, we are still image bearers, still "glorious ruins" as Francis Schaeffer and Dan Allender remind us.

> Man, as Francis Schaeffer has put it, is a "glorious ruin," a stately castle, intricately and masterfully constructed by the hand of an Artisan who designed his work with no thought of expense or practicality. A proper concern for God's own glory and majesty was his only guiding force in creating a person. The castle, however, was given a life of its own, capable of rearranging itself. When man took it on himself to be as God, he ruined everything. Crumbling walls, rotten wood, and overgrown gardens: the decay became so extensive that only one with the eyes of a craftsman could see the structural beauty that remained underneath the overgrown foliage and overthrown walls. Nevertheless, it has glory in its form and composition. Man is an amalgamation of dignity and depravity, a glorious ruin (Allender, *The Wounded Heart*, p. 42).

Biblical counseling involves identifying our original design, diagnosing how we fall short of that design, and dispensing God's grace to empower people to mature into the dignified likeness of Christ, the image of the invisible God. Box 10:2—"The Creation, Fall, and Redemption of the *Imago Dei*"—outlines a biblical psychology of the four robes of the beautiful bride designed by God, the four rags of the adulterous bride depraved by sin, and the four gowns of the virgin bride dignified by Christ.

The glorious ruin of the *imago Dei* provides our framework for interpreting reality from God's perspective. We answer the questions, "What went wrong? What is sin?" only by answering the questions, "What went right? What was meant to be?" We were meant to maintain the wholeness of God's creation by reflecting Trinity's communion and dominion. Now we fall short of the glory of our Trinitarian God. Sin is our failure to reflect righteously God's holy love. Sin always results in loss of shalom—separation, alienation, disintegration.

The original nature of the *imago Dei* offers the foundation from which we answer life's four critical concerns. The robe of reflection (the structural self) answers the question, "Who am I?" "I'm a bearer of the image of God, created to reflect Him." The robe of communion (the social self) answers the question, "Where did I come from?" "I came from the Trinitarian God of the universe, created to relate like him." The robe of dominion (the stewardship self) answers the question, "Why am I here?" "I'm here to be God's under-shepherd, created to rule for Him." The robe of cohesion (the shalom self) answers the question, "How should I then live?" "I live only by sharing in my Creator's wholeness; I'm created to rest in Him." The key to our identity is found in our creation in the image of the Trinity.

The Five Coverings of the Beloved Image Bearer

In the beginning of *Soul Physicians*, you read about "Soul Anatomy 101," learning that we are dust and divinity (Genesis 2:7). We are one holistic being with physical (body) and metaphysical (soul) capacities. God wove us together to reflect His image as we enjoy communion and dominion and spread His shalom.

Biblical psychology demonstrates that each human being has the following capacities of personhood:

- Relational Beings: Romancers—Love with Passion (Affections)
- Rational Beings: Dreamers—Think with Wisdom (Mindsets)
- Volitional Beings: Creators—Choose with Courage (Purposes)
- Emotional Beings: Singers—Experience with Depth (Mood States)
- Physical Beings: Actors—Live with Power (Habituated Tendencies)

This is the "shape of our soul." The goal of our redemption, and of redemptive counseling, is to make us more human. To be fully human is to reflect more fully the beauty and majesty of our Worthy Groom. Cornelius Plantinga, Jr., in *Not the Way It's Supposed to Be*, explains the way we are supposed to be as human beings.

A spiritually sound person fits the universal design. She functions properly: in the range of her relationships to God, others, nature, and self we can spot impressive manifestations of shalom. Or, following one line of New Testament usage, we

Box 10:2
The Creation, Fall, and Redemption of the *Imago Dei*

Creation	Fall	Redemption
The Four Robes of the Beautiful Bride	**The Four Rags of the Adulterous Bride**	**The Four Gowns of the Virgin Bride**
Robe of Reflection	**Rag of Corruption**	**Gown of Regeneration**
◆ "Who Am I?"	◆ "Who Am I?"	◆ "Who Am I?"
◆ "I'm an Image Bearer."	◆ "I'm a Fallen Image Bearer."	◆ "I'm a New Creation in Christ."
◆ "I Reflect."	◆ "I Deflect." Presence	◆ "I Display."
◆ Capacities: RRVE	◆ Temple Image: Polluted	◆ New Nature: Saint
◆ Structural Self	◆ Original Sin: Depravity	◆ New Purity: Capacities
◆ "Image and Likeness."	◆ "I Was Naked."	◆ New Propensity: RRVE
◆ Design: Reflection	◆ Disposition: Sinner	◆ New Life: Resurrection
Robe of Communion	**Rag of Chasm**	**Gown of Reconciliation**
◆ "Where Did I Come From?"	◆ "Where Did I Come From?"	◆ "Where Did I Come From?"
◆ "I Came from Trinity."	◆ "I Came from Myself."	◆ "I Came from Christ."
◆ "I Relate."	◆ "I Separate." Partition	◆ "I Reconcile."
◆ Community	◆ Home Image: Prodigal	◆ New Nurture: Welcome!
◆ Social Self	◆ Original Alienation	◆ New Parentage: Father
◆ "Let Us."	◆ "So I Hid."	◆ New Identity: Son/Bride
◆ Dignity: Relation	◆ Distance: Separated	◆ New Adoption: Child
Robe of Dominion	**Rag of Captivity**	**Gown of Redemption**
◆ "Why Am I Here?"	◆ "Why Am I Here?"	◆ "Why Am I Here?"
◆ "To Be an Under-Shepherd."	◆ "To Shepherd Only Myself."	◆ "To Shepherd in a Jungle."
◆ "I Rule."	◆ "I'm Ruled." Power	◆ "I'm Empowered."
◆ Calling	◆ Market Image: Property	◆ New Freedom: from Sin
◆ Stewardship Self	◆ Original Enslavement	◆ New Power: Holiness
◆ "Let Them Rule."	◆ "Sewed Fig Leaves."	◆ New Victory: over Sin
◆ Destiny: Vocation	◆ Dominion: Slave	◆ New Inclination: Love
Robe of Cohesion	**Rag of Condemnation**	**Gown of Justification**
◆ "How Should I Live?"	◆ "How Should I Live?"	◆ "How Should I Live?"
◆ "Share Trinity's Shalom."	◆ "Spread Seducer's Shame."	◆ "Share Savior's Salvation."
◆ "I Rest."	◆ "I Dread." Penalty	◆ "I Relax." Shalom
◆ Coherence	◆ Court Image: Prisoner	◆ New Peace: Forgiveness
◆ Shalom Self	◆ Original Guilt: Disgrace	◆ New Pardon: Guiltless
◆ "Very Good."	◆ "I Was Afraid."	◆ New Dignity: Righteous
◆ Direction: Integration	◆ Disintegration: Shameful	◆ New Boldness: Grace Confidence

might call them impressive manifestations of *hygiene*. (See Titus 1:13; 2:8. The Septuagint often uses cognates of *hygiainoo* to translate *shalom*. In general, I am using *shalom* in reference to social and cosmic wholeness, and *hygiene* in reference to personal wholeness.) (Plantinga, *Not the Way It's Supposed to Be*, p. 34.)

When we love with passion, think with wisdom, choose with courage, experience with depth, and live with power, society enjoys increasing harmony and we celebrate growing integrity.

Healthy image bearers are:

♦ *Romancers Who Long and Thirst in Certain Classic Ways*: We long for God, one another, beauty, peace, justice, communion, and community. We entrust our souls to Trinity.

♦ *Dreamers Who Think and Imagine in Certain Classic Ways*: We think God's thoughts after Him; we develop the mind of Christ; and we wisely follow the guiding of the Spirit. Our images of God are accurate—we see Him as our good, generous, and gracious Father.

♦ *Creators Who Choose, Purpose, Decide, and Act in Certain Classic Ways*: We risk and serve courageously. We pursue the goals of enjoying and exalting God while we connect with and care for one another. We become daring, faithful stewards and shepherds.

♦ *Singers Who Feel and Respond in Certain Classic Ways*: We experience spiritual shalom and joy over wholeness, and spiritual shame and depression over sinfulness. We grieve and groan, but not as those who have no hope.

♦ *Actors Who React and Act in Certain Classic Ways*: We use our bodies as servants of righteousness, disciplining ourselves as soldiers and sons, daring heroines and daughters.

Like God, we are personal beings who *relate* (spiritually, socially, and self-consciously), *think* (in images and pictures), *will* (choose and act), and *feel* (experience our inner and outer world). As bearers of God's image we have been given the creation mandate, God designed us with the capacities of relationality, rationality, volitionality, and emotionality necessary to reflect His image and to fulfill His mandate.

In Genesis 1 and 2, Trinity says to humanity: "Be passionate Romancers, imaginative Dreamers, courageous Creators, and experiencing Singers. As imaginative Dreamers, use your God-given reason to think God's thoughts after Him. As courageous Creators, use your God-given abilities as under-shepherds. As experiential Singers, use your God-given capacity to subjectively engage your world to grasp together with all the saints the nature of God's world. As passionate Romancers, do all of this through your relational capacity to worship God, to minister to one another, and to experience shalom."

Boxes 10:3 and 10:4 describe the capacities of the personality structure of image bearers. They depict the coverings of the innocent bride.

Relational Beings: Romancers Loving Passionately—Affections/Lovers

Created in the image of our loving, Trinitarian God who eternally relates in the unity and diversity of Father, Son, and Holy Spirit, we are *relational* beings. God designed us

---

Box 10:3

Soul Snapshot Number One: Dignified Image Bearers

Five Coverings of the Innocent Bride

1. **Relational: Spiritual, Social, and Self-Aware**
   Romancers: Loving Passionately—Affections/Lovers

2. **Rational: Images and Beliefs**
   Dreamers: Thinking Wisely—Mindsets

3. **Volitional: Strategies/Goals and Actions/Interactions**
   Creators: Choosing Courageously—Purposes/Pathways

4. **Emotional: Internal Responses/External Reactions**
   Singers: Experiencing Deeply—Mood States

5. **Physical: Body/Flesh**
   Actors: Living Submissively—Habituated Tendencies

Box 10:4

Soul Snapshot Number Two: Beloved Image Bearers

Four Inner Coverings of the Innocent Bride

Romancers	Dreamers	Creators	Singers
Relational	Rational	Volitional	Emotional
Affections	Mindsets	Purposes	Mood States
Lovers	Thinkers	Choosers/Doers	Feelers
Love with	Think with	Choose with	Experience
Passion	Wisdom	Courage	with Depth
Relate	Know	Do	Feel
Enjoy	Imagine	Choose/Act	Experience
Soul	Mind/Heart	Will/Spirit	Emotions
Relational	Rational	Responsible	Responsive
Relate	Narrate	Create	Appreciate

as *spiritual* beings who relate to Him, *social* beings who relate to others, and *self-aware* beings who relate to our own selves.

In Psalm 42:1-6, we see the three-fold longing of our soul (*nepesh*). Verses 1-2 highlight our *spiritual* longing. "As the deer pants for streams of water, so my soul (*nepesh*) pants for you, O God. My soul thirsts for God, for the living God. When can I go and meet with God?" David pictures a deer panting with thirst for the full and flowing stream of cool water. The word for "pant" indicates a strong, audible breathing, gasping, and panting caused by a prevailing drought. As the deer's throat thirsts for water, so David's soul thirsts for communion with God. His soul, designed by God and for God, is parched, empty, thirsty—desperate for God.

David mingles his spiritual thirst with his *social* thirst in verses 3-4. "My tears have been my food day and night, while men say to me all day long, 'Where is your God?' These things I remember as I pour out my soul (*nepesh*): how I used to go with the multitude, leading the procession to the house of God, with shouts of joy and thanksgiving among the festive throng." Where once David joined with others in worship, now others mock him. Where he once was a leader of people, now he flees from the people he led. It is not good for David to be alone. He hungers for fellowship with the festive throng. God designed us both for worship and for fellowship—to hunger for Him and for one another.

David's hunger includes a third dish. "Why are you downcast, O my soul (*nepesh*)? Why so disturbed within me? Put your hope in God, for I will yet praise him, my Savior and my God. My soul is downcast within me; therefore I will remember you from the land of the Jordan, the heights of Hermon—from Mount Mizar" (42:5-6). David has *self-aware* longings. He speaks to himself, to his soul. He is self-aware. Disturbed and downcast, he longs for inner peace—he's thirsty for his original design. Cats and dogs don't analyze themselves. Human beings are unique among God's creation in their ability to reflect upon their inner experience.

Throughout the rest of *Soul Physicians*, we will explore the counseling implications of what it means to be a relational being designed by God to be a *Romancer*. God created the human personality with an immense capacity for love—loving God through worship and communion, connecting with others through fellowship and community, and understanding self through conscious contentment (shalom), awareness, acceptance, and care (Genesis 2:25; Matthew 22:35-40; Ephesians 5:28-29).

Satan-inspired sin distorted our love capacity, turning it upside down into a jumbled mix of selfish love, self-centered relationships with others, and false love for false gods. Christ died to restore us to our original position as human beings with arms stretched up to God and outstretched toward others.

In coming chapters, you will learn how to use biblical eyeglasses with lenses that focus your attention on *affections* (lovers, longings, desires, delights, and idols of the heart). As a biblical cardiologist, you'll ask yourself as you work with people, *"What affection(s) reign(s) in my spiritual friend's soul?"* "Affections/lovers" will become a core diagnostic category guiding you in your soul physician ministry.

Rational Beings: Dreamers Thinking Wisely—Mindsets

Created in the image of our all-knowing, wise God, we are *rational* beings. We think in words (beliefs) and pictures (images) as Adam did when he gave each animal a name that expressed and portrayed that animal's unique nature. God designed us with minds that can perceive His world and advance His kingdom.

Throughout the remainder of *Soul Physicians* we'll examine the discipleship implications of what it means to be a rational creation designed by God to be a *Dreamer*. By "Dreamer" I mean that God created the human personality with the ability to remember the past, reflect on the present, and imagine the future. In their idyllic state, Adam and Eve remembered God's commands and His beautiful and majestic nature. They thought God's thoughts after Him, and they dreamed dreams that would honor Him. His vision was their vision. They had 20/20 spiritual vision to see their world, their relationships, their situations, their past, present, and future with spiritual eyes.

In our fallen state our vision is not only blurred, but blinded by Satan, the father of lies. We now consider God unworthy to retain in our minds. Foolishness replaces wisdom.

In Christ, we remember the past accurately, we reflect on the present spiritually, and we ponder the future hopefully. We become visionaries who dream big dreams for God because we know that God can do exceedingly abundantly above all we think or imagine.

In upcoming chapters, you will learn how to wear biblical eyeglasses with lenses that focus your attention on *mindsets* (characteristic ways of thinking, core convictions about where life is found, thematic and patterned images, and ideas about how to make life work). As a biblical cardiologist, you'll ask yourself as you work with people, *"What mindset(s) reign(s) in my spiritual friend's heart?"* "Mindsets" will become a central diagnostic category guiding you in your soul physician ministry.

Volitional Beings: Creators Choosing Courageously—Purposes/Pathways

Created in the image of our all-powerful God who creates out of nothing and whose purposes no one can ever thwart, we are *volitional* beings who act purposefully. God created us not as robots, but as sons and daughters with a will to choose His will. We are not animals who react on instinct, nor are we computers who act on input. We are human beings with a motivational capacity to act on the basis of our beliefs about what quenches our relational thirsts.

We'll study the spiritual friendship implications of what it means to be a volitional being designed by God to be a *creator*. Not *the* Creator, but *a* creator in the sense that we can shape our lives and our world by free choice. In Paradise, God gave mankind dominion over planet Earth. Adam and Eve were to subdue the planet, expanding the reign of Paradise until all was Edenic. They were to be faithful stewards serving their Creator by being co-creators, vice-regents, and under-shepherds.

Satan came to heist their reign, our reign. In our fallen state we declare, "My will be done! My kingdom come!" We are still willful, but stubbornly and rebelliously so. Christ came to restore us to our original state. In our redemption we can say, "Not my will, but Yours be done."

You'll learn how to use biblical eyeglasses with lenses focusing your attention on *purposes* (pathways of choosing, intentions, goals, patterns of behavior, characteristic strategies, and styles of relating). As a biblical cardiologist, you'll ask yourself as you work with people, *"What purpose(s) reign(s) in my spiritual friend's will?"* "Purposes/pathways" will become a vital diagnostic category for the soul physician.

Emotional Beings: Singers Experiencing Deeply—Mood States

Created in the image of our passionate and compassionate God who experiences deep joy and profound sadness, we are *emotional* beings who experience life deeply and internally. God created us to feel. Though the Christian world sometimes makes emotions the black sheep of the "soul family," God loves emotions. Jesus wept, and so do we. The Spirit grieves, as we do. The Father rejoices, as we do. We have the emotional capacity to respond to our outer world based upon our inner actions, choices, goals, beliefs, images, longings, and desires.

Throughout the rest of *Soul Physicians*, we will probe the soul care and spiritual direction implications of what it means to be an emotional being designed by God to be a *Singer*. We are impassioned poets and feelers, not apathetic, soulless androids. Before the Fall, Adam felt loneliness at the prospect of not sharing his life with another. Adam and Eve were thrilled to walk with God in the cool of the day; they passionately wove their lives together.

After the Fall, they experienced the dark side of emotions. Their lives became filled with shame and fear leading to hiding, covering, competing, and conquering. Jesus saved us not to eliminate our emotions, but to redeem them. Mature Christians groan. We grieve, but not as those who have no hope. We experience the full range of human moods, but we learn to manage our moods maturely by facing them, experiencing them, growing in self-awareness through them, and expressing them under the Spirit's sanctifying control.

You'll learn how to wear biblical eyeglasses with lenses that focus your attention on *mood states* (controlling emotions, governing feelings, and dominating moods). As a biblical cardiologist, you'll ask yourself as you work with people, *"What mood state(s) reign(s) in my spiritual friend's emotions?"* "Mood states" will become an effective diagnostic category guiding you in your soul physician ministry.

Physical Beings: Actors Living Fully—Habituated Tendencies

God, who is spirit, created us as embodied beings. He is infinite; we are finite. He is divinity; we are dust and divinity. He is non-contingent; we are contingent. He is needless; we are needy. He is independent; we are dependent. He is without limits; we are limited. God created us to entrust ourselves, body and soul, to His care, to enjoy embodied existence, to appreciate thankfully every good and perfect gift, and to use the members of our bodies as servants of righteousness (Romans 6:12-13). The body, the flesh, our skin and bones, are God's great gift to us.

We will dissect the soul physician implications of what it means to be *physical* beings designed by God as *Actors*. What role does the body play in human existence?

Generated by God, body and soul functioned in perfect harmony and health. Connected to the umbilical cord of God's Divine power, sickness of body and illness of soul were unthinkable, impossible.

Degenerated by sin, our body and soul are disintegrated, dying, dead. Disconnected from our life source, separated from the Author of life, we experience physical and mental sickness. The physical organ we call the brain can become diseased just like the heart, the liver, or the kidneys.

Regenerated by Christ, on this side of heaven we begin to experience the reintegration of body and soul. When we are reconnected to Christ's resurrection power through the spiritual disciplines, the Spirit controls the flesh and energizes our body and soul to serve God. On the other side, in heaven, we will receive our resurrection bodies—glorification. We'll be embodied souls, soulful bodies, that can never sin, never suffer sickness, but forever experience the health God first intended.

You will learn how to put on biblical eyeglasses with lenses that focus your attention on *habituated tendencies* (characteristic patterns of yielding the members of the body and disciplined or undisciplined habituated responses). As a biblical cardiologist, you'll learn to ask yourself as you work with people, "What habituated tendencies reign in my spiritual friend's physical body?" "Habituated tendencies" will become a key diagnostic category guiding you in your soul physician ministry.

Where We've Been and Where We're Heading

Is anything stirring in you as you read? Stop. Reflect.

Weren't you made to long? Thirst passionately? Think? Imagine wisely? Choose? Act courageously? Feel? Experience deeply?

Isn't this what the people you counsel want? How they want to live? They tell you, "I'm not myself!" and they are right. And now you know why.

I'm inviting you to journey with me. Let's see how Creation, Fall, and Redemption shape how we answer life's four core questions: "Who am I? Where did I come from? Why am I here? How should I then live?" Let's see how God designed us, what went wrong, and how grace sets us straight.

Caring for Your Soul: Personal Applications

1. Take a personal *imago Dei* inventory. Evaluate yourself using 10 as "Spiritually Mature" and 1 as "Spiritually Immature." To what degree are you:

   a. Reflecting God?

   b. Relating like God?

   c. Representatively ruling for God?

   d. Resting in God?

2. Looking over your responses, what can you do to live out the *imago Dei* more fully by:

   a. Reflecting God?

   b. Relating like God?

   c. Representatively ruling for God?

   d. Resting in God?

3. The five coverings of image bearers provide another means of personal evaluation. Evaluate yourself using 10 as "Spiritually Mature" and 1 as "Spiritually Immature." How well are you living as a:

   a. Relational Being: Romancer—Loving with Passion (Affections)?

   b. Rational Being: Dreamer—Thinking with Wisdom (Mindsets)?

   c. Volitional Being: Creator—Choosing with Courage (Purposes)?

   d. Emotional Being: Singer—Experiencing with Depth (Mood States)?

   e. Physical Being: Actor—Living with Power (Habituated Tendencies)?

Caring for Others: Ministry Implications

♦ **Communicate Redemptively:** When we understand the God-given capacities of personhood, we can identify the purpose and focus of spiritual friendship.

- Spiritual friendship is any redemptive communication that touches the depths of the soul encouraging people to be fully human so they can reflect God more fully.

- Spiritual friendship enables people to live/relate/communicate:

  ○ **As Romancers Who Love with Passion: Sacrifice**—Living for others. Alive. Loving. Giving. Sharing. Receiving. Caring.

  ○ **As Dreamers Who Think with Wisdom: Insight**—Creatively applying truth to life. Remembering the past with faith, interpreting the present with grace, and envisioning the future with hope. Dreaming since we can never out-dream the Divine Dreamer. Thinking God's thoughts after Him. Thinking "outside the box." Thinking relationally.

  ○ **As Creators Who Choose with Courage: Risk**—Choosing truth and beauty. Risking involvement. Moving toward relationship. Facing fears. Overcoming obstacles. Strength. Courage. Boldness.

  ○ **As Singers Who Feel/Experience with Fullness/Poetry: Depth**—Alive to life—the good and bad of life. Groaning. Enjoying. Feeling. Hurting. Touching. Aware. At peace during turmoil.

♦ **Relate to People as Romancers, Dreamers, Creators, Singers, and Actors:** These are maps you can use to work through the maze of the soul. We do soul work by exploring how healthy image bearers:

- **Long and Thirst in Certain Classic Ways:** We long for God (communion), one another (community), and peace (a clear conscience). We entrust our souls to Trinity.

- **Think and Imagine in Certain Classic Ways:** We think God's thoughts after Him; we develop the mind of Christ; and we wisely follow the guiding of the Spirit. Our images of God are accurate; He's our gracious Father.

- **Purpose, Choose, Decide, and Act in Certain Classic Ways:** We risk and serve courageously. We pursue the goals of enjoying and exalting God while we connect with and care for one another. We're daring shepherds.

- **Feel and Respond in Certain Classic Ways:** We experience spiritual shalom and joy over wholeness and spiritual shame and depression over sinfulness. We grieve and groan, but not as those who have no hope.

CHAPTER ELEVEN

ROMANCERS: GREAT LOVERS

"Love is fundamentally what moves us. Augustine says that all evil comes from disordered love, for it is love that moves me where I go. Love is my gravity: *Amor meus, pondus meum,* 'My love is my weight.' I go where my love moves me. That is why all persons are either going toward God and heaven or away from God and toward hell" (Peter Kreeft, *The God Who Loves You*, p. 50).

"God begins his good work in us, therefore, by arousing love and desire and zeal for righteousness in our hearts; or, to speak more correctly, by bending, forming, and directing our hearts to righteousness" (John Calvin, *The Institutes of the Christian Religion*, Vol. 2, p. 6).

"Thou movest us to delight in praising Thee; for Thou hast formed us for Thyself, and our hearts are restless until they find rest in Thee" (Augustine, *Confessions*, Book I.1.1).

Great Lovers Wanted

I've often been tempted to market the counseling program I chair with the hook, *Learn to be a great lover!* But I've always had second thoughts. Too much possibility for misinterpretation. Frequently I've been tempted to start a first counseling session with the question, *How's your love life?* I never have. Might be misinterpreted.

How's *your* love life? Are you a great lover? Want to learn to be one? Keep reading.

Post-modern Christianity careens between the two extremes of fluffy, surface experientialism and cold, aloof scholasticism. Biblical Christianity joins head and heart. We need a theology of relationality that builds upon the *imago Dei*.

Trinity marvelously fashioned us to reflect God, relate like God, representatively rule for God, and rest in God. God created us with the capacities to relate. He designed us to love Him with our entire being—worshiping Him as we enjoy and exalt Him. He designed us to love one another passionately—connecting to each other with neither self-protection nor selfishness. And He made us to be at peace with who we are—comfortable, content, and confident without arrogance or self-hatred. In our relationality, we are:

♦ *Spiritual* beings who worship, and, therefore, long to exalt, enjoy, and entrust ourselves to God.

♦ *Social* beings who connect, and, therefore, long for relational acceptance and relational respect.

♦ *Self-aware* beings who reflect, and, therefore, long for personal peace (wholeness and integration) and personal identity (uniqueness and individuality).

Romancers Loving Passionately: Relational Beings Who Long—Affections

I'm aware that words like "Romancers" and "passionately" are terms easily misinterpreted in our postmodern society. Certainly, I'm *not* suggesting that our ideal state involves flirtatious relationships, trifling attitudes, philandering behavior, or fleeting feelings. Nor am I implying that we ought to be controlled by fleshly, animal passion and lust.

I've already offered you a taste of biblical romance from our Worthy Groom. Image-bearing Romancers are skilled at pursuing love—holy love, pure love, selfless love. We long to enjoy reciprocal relationships of deep giving and receiving. We do so passionately. Passion is related to the word "paschal" and the biblical concept of the paschal lamb—the sacrificial Lamb of God who came not to be served, but to serve, not to take, but to give. Passionate love is sacrificial love, radically other-centered, risk-taking love.

A love that experiences? Yes. A love that feels? Yes. Those ideas are not incompatible with committed love. God designed our souls to love with ardor, affection, devotion, longing, and attachment all bound up in commitment to the well-being of the other person, a commitment that we refuse to break regardless of personal cost.

Relational Longings

Hunger was God's idea. He created us with a soul that thirsts for what can be quenched only by relationships. The Hebrew word for soul, *nepesh*, derives from a root that means "throat" and "gullet"—the organ through which we take in nourishment, fill our hunger, and quench our thirst (R. Laurin, *Concept of Man as Soul*, p. 131). The Hebrews used physical body parts to represent metaphysical or immaterial aspects of the human personality (Hans W. Wolff, *Anthropology of the Old Testament*, pp. 8-11). Proverbs 25:25 is one example: "Like cold water to a weary soul (*nepesh*) is good news from a distant land."

As the throat craves physical satisfaction, so the soul craves personal, relational satisfaction. We long for intimate involvement with others and are motivated by a thirst for union with fellow personal beings. Passages such as Genesis 2:18; 1 Samuel 18:1-3; Song of Solomon 1:7; and 3:1-4 describe our social longings; while passages like Psalm 42:1-2; 62:5; 63:1, 8; 107:8-9; 130:6; 143:6; Isaiah 26:8-9; 55:1-3; and Lamentations 3:24-25 emphasize our spiritual thirst for God. These longings for relationship are part of our essential being as created in God's image.

God inspired Old Testament writers to use soul (*nepesh*) with at least fourteen words for relational longing (Robert Kellemen, *A Biblical Counseling Model of Humanity*, p. 16). These various words mean to desire, wait longingly, pine after, to faint with great desire, eager want, appetite, attachment, affection, satisfaction, hunger, and thirst (see passages such as Genesis 34:8; Deuteronomy 4:29; 7:7; 10:15; 11:12; 12:20; 14:26; 2 Samuel 23:15; Psalm 10:3; 26:8; 84:2; 107:9; 145:16; Isaiah 26:8-9; 29:8; and 58:11).

As nineteenth-century theologian and biblical psychologist Franz Delitzsch noted, "That passions and affections of all kinds are declared of the soul, as subject and object, there needs absolutely no special text to prove" (Delitzsch, *A System of Biblical Psychology*, p. 241). Speaking of both the Hebrew and Greek words for soul, he also writes, "as Scripture uses it, it is altogether manifest in the character of desire, predominant over everything and pervading everything" (p. 242).

Relational Motivation

Love is to the soul what breathing is to the lungs and food is to the stomach. Without connection, we shrivel; we starve to death. With mutual, risky, giving, grace relationships we thrive. The exact center of our being is our capacity to give and receive in relationships.

What motivates your spiritual friends to do what they do? What compels them? In training counselors, I like to tell them, "go where the action is." The action is relational because image bearers are *relationally motivated. We pursue what we perceive to be pleasing.* "We have an immense void inside that craves satisfaction from powers and persons and pleasures outside ourselves. Yearning and longing and desire are the very stuff of our nature" (John Piper, *The Pleasures of God*, p. 48). As the Puritan writer Henry Scougal reminded us, "The soul of man has in it a raging and inextinguishable thirst" (Scougal, *The Life of God in the Soul of Man*, p. 108). We're motivated to quench our relational thirsts.

What was I born desiring? What were Adam and Eve born desiring? What relational thirsts do we have?

We Are Spiritual Beings Designed to Worship: The Holy of Holies of the Soul

We were born desiring worship. Of course, Romans 1 and a plethora of other passages inform us that in our fallenness we turn to anything but God to quench our spiritual thirsts. Nonetheless, in our original design and our current state, we have a fundamental nature that must worship.

When I began working toward my doctorate at Kent State University, I decided to develop relationships as a precursor to sharing my faith. Or so I thought. Two weeks into my initial semester, our professor assigned a paper on humanistic psychology. As the class discussed our viewpoints, our professor encouraged me to share my position. "Bob, you wrote an interesting paper contrasting humanistic psychology with Christian thinking." So much for my "go slow" approach. During the ensuing discussion, one student was particularly vocal against my views.

About a month later, in a course on counseling the culturally different, a Native American presented the guest lecture. Toward the end of her talk, she invited us to stand to worship the spirit of the four winds. Two students remained seated—the woman who had vocally opposed my views in the other class and me. As soon as class ended, she marched up to me to thank me for not standing. "You gave me the courage of my convictions. But to be honest, I'm not sure what I believe in. You seem so strong and sincere in your faith. Could we talk about your relationship to God?" This young woman exposed her fundamental spiritual nature. I could have said of her what Paul said of the people of Athens, "I see that in every way you are very religious" (Acts 17:22).

Our worshiping nature is so strong that in our fallen state we must actively suppress and re-divert it.

> The wrath of God is being revealed from heaven against all the godlessness and wickedness of men who suppress the truth by their wickedness . . . For although they knew God, they neither glorified him as God nor gave thanks to him . . . Although they claimed to be wise, they became fools and exchanged the glory of the immortal God for images made to look like mortal man and birds and animals and reptiles. . . . They exchanged the truth of God for a lie, and worshiped and served created things rather than the Creator . . . (Romans 1:18, 21a, 22-23, and 25a).

The word "suppress" (*katechontōn*) pictures forcefully pushing down. It's like the effort that we must expend if we're to keep an inflated beach ball submerged. The second we let up, it shoots to the sky. As fallen eyes follow its path to the sky, they choose to look away from the Son, looking toward the sun and other created realities. Martin Luther, with his simple eloquence clarifies, "The human mind is so inclined by nature that as it turns from the one, it of necessity becomes addicted to the other. He who rejects the Creator must worship the creature" (Luther, *Commentary on Galatians*, pp. 44-45).

We Are Motivated by Religious Affections

The Puritans called these spiritual longings "religious affections." By "affections" they did not mean emotions, but something deeper. Emotions are reactive; affections are directive. As Jonathan Edwards explains: "Affections are the mainspring of human actions. The Author of human nature not only gave affections to man, but he made them the basis of human actions" (Edwards, *Religious Affections*, p. 9). Earlier he wrote:

> The affections are the spring of men's actions. All activity ceases unless he is moved by some affection—take away desire and the world would be motionless and dead—there would be no such thing as activity or any earnest pursuit whatsoever. Everywhere the Scriptures place much emphasis on the affections (Edwards, *Religious Affections*, p. xxviii).

The energy behind life is relational/spiritual. Relationships are fundamentally what move us. As John Owen describes:

> Relational affections motivate the soul to cleave to and to seek relationships. The affections are in the soul as the helm is in the ship; if it be laid hold on by a skillful hand, he turneth the whole vessel which way he pleaseth (Owen, *Temptation and Sin*, p. ix).

Like God, as image bearers, we are persons-in-relationship. Spiritual relationships are the Holy of Holies of the soul because there truly is a God-shaped vacuum in the human soul.

We hunger for God while attempting to keep Him far from our spiritual diet. When I worked on a psychiatric inpatient unit, I counseled a young man diagnosed as manic-depressive (what is now called bi-polar affective disorder). He experienced intense mood swings. At times he struggled with bouts of crippling depression; at other times he suffered from incapacitating elation. During one of his elevated periods, I asked him what would happen if he slowed down. "When I slow down, when my mind takes a break, then I languish alone in a bottomless, loveless pit."

As we worked together, I encouraged him to invite God into the pit and onto the mountaintop. "Whatever you are experiencing," I shared, "God is there and wants to experience it with you."

In the ensuing days, weeks, months, and even years, he was able to face his spiritual dread. Though I believe part of his struggle was physical, I believe another part was spiritual. In his highs and lows, he escaped God, or at least tried to. All non-biological issues are relational issues, and ultimately spiritual ones. Blaise Pascal describes what occurs when we attempt to quench our spiritual thirst in non-God ways.

> What is it, then, that this desire and this inability proclaim to us, but that there once was in man a true happiness of which there now remain to him only the mark and empty trace, which he in vain tries to fill from all his surroundings, seeking from things absent the help he does not obtain in things present? But these are all inadequate, because the infinite abyss can only be filled by an infinite and immutable object, that is to say, only by God Himself (Pascal, *Pensées*, VII, Paragraph 425).

We Are In-Relationship-to-Deity-Beings

What the Puritans called "religious affections," I label *in-relationship-to-Deity-beings*. All reality is relational, thus we are beings designed to be in relationship. Henri Nouwen, though separating our relationality from our rationality more than I would, illustrates our core nature.

> Somehow during the centuries we have come to believe that what makes us human is our mind. Many people who do not know any Latin still seem to know the definition of a human being as a reasoning animal: *rationale animal est hommo* (Seneca). But what makes us human is not our mind but our heart, not our ability to think but our ability to love. It is our heart that is made in the image and likeness of God (Robert Durback, *Seed of Hope: A Henri Nouwen Reader*, p. 197).

Henry Scougal and John Piper more accurately, I think, dissect relational reality. "The worth and excellency of a soul is to be measured by the object of its love" (Scougal, *The Life of God*, p. 62).

> How else do we assess the beauty of an invisible heart than by what it loves? Someone might suggest, "By what it *thinks*." But clear and accurate thought is beautiful only in the service of right affections. The Devil himself is quite an able intellect. But he loves all the wrong things. Therefore his thinking serves evil and his soul is squalid. Or perhaps someone would suggest that we can assess the

beauty of a soul by what it *wills*. Yes, but there is half-hearted willing and whole-hearted willing. You don't judge the glory of a soul by what it wills to do with lukewarm interest, or with mere teeth-gritting determination. *To know a soul's proportions you need to know its passions. The true dimensions of a soul are seen in its delights.* Not what we dutifully will but what we passionately want reveals our excellence or evil (Piper, *The Pleasures of God*, p. 18, emphasis added).

Designed by God, we are face-to-face beings. In relationship to God, we are faith beings. Faith is the core of the original human personality. That core involves entrusting ourselves to someone who transcends us, yet draws near to us. In the innermost chamber of our soul resides a worshiping being; the ability to worship from the heart is what makes us human.

By these descriptions, there are no atheists. Everyone must put his trust in someone or something. Even Madelyn Murray O'Hair. Consider these excerpts from her diary, found by the IRS in 1999.

> A 1959 entry reveals an almost pathetic despair: "The whole idiotic hopelessness of human relations descends upon me. Tonight I cried and cried, but even then, feeling nothing."

> 1973 New Year's Wish List: A mink coat, Cadillac, cook, housekeeper. "In 1974 I will run for the governor of Texas, and in 1976, the president of the United States." Ironic that in 1976 we elected one of the most committed Christians ever to be president.

> In 1977 she wrote: "I have failed in marriage, motherhood, and as a politician."

> One poignant phrase appears again and again. In half a dozen places, O'Hair writes, "Somebody, somewhere, love me."

Reflecting on her words, Chuck Colson writes:

How telling that this hostile and abrasive person, who harbored nothing but hatred for God and his people, who believed human beings were merely the product of a cosmic accident, would nevertheless cry out to the great void for someone just to love her. What a powerful example of the fundamental truth that we are made for a relationship of love with our Creator, and that we can never fully escape from our true identity and purpose. No matter how much we may deny it intellectually, our nature still cries out for the love we were made to share. To paraphrase the famous words of St. Augustine, even the most bitter atheist is restless until she finds her rest in God (Colson, *Breakpoint,* 1999).

God is our primal relationship, whether we face it or not, whether we like Him or not. We always live oriented toward God—either with our faces or our backs oriented to Him.

We Are Worshiping Beings Who Long

"What do worshiping beings long for?" *Father.* We are faith-in-Father-beings. Our souls are a magnet polarized toward *Father*, longing for peace with our Father of holy love. The essence of our humanity centers on our loving trust in Father. This is the fundamental unifying factor in the human personality.

We are truly human only in fellowship with our Creator. Communion with the Logos is precisely the natural state of true humanity. Man is truly man only when he participates in divine life and realizes in himself the image and likeness of God, and this participation in no way diminishes his authentically human existence, human energy and will (Maximos the Confessor, quoted in Neil Anderson, *The Common Made Holy*, p. 52).

The deepest longing in the human soul is to be in relationship with Someone who absolutely delights in us ("This is my beloved . . .") and who fundamentally values us (". . . in whom I am well pleased"). God created our souls with an ardent desire, a yearning, an appetite for relating. Our prevailing and prominent desire is for Father.

Sowhen we say we long for Father, what do we mean? What do we long for when we long for Father? First, we long to *enjoy our Father*. Enjoying God is foreign to us today, yet it is a continual biblical theme. It was common to our parents in the faith, and it is our holy calling and happy privilege.

The psalmists sing, "Because your love is better than life, my lips will glorify you" (Psalm 63:3). "Whom have I in heaven but you? And earth has nothing I desire besides you" (Psalm 73:25). "I spread out my hands to you; my soul thirsts for you like a parched land" (Psalm 143:6). Our Father's unfailing love is the umbilical cord of our life (Psalm 107:9; Psalm 136:1-26; Proverbs 19:22).

Speaking of God's husband-wife relationship to His people, Walther Eichrodt writes:

In choosing her to be his wife, he is not amusing himself, but fully committing himself to put his love into effect by founding a community, within which it is his will to enter into an intimate relationship with his people, and through them with all humanity. When he disciplines, it is not a light-hearted disregard for his unheard-of graciousness, nor a chilly withdrawal, nor yet a penalty enforcing the letter of the law. But a solemn act of calling to account, carried out in a fit of blazing indignation, to bring about a realization of what a grave thing it is to put his holy will to shame, and at the same time to show *how seriously he takes his human partner* (Eichrodt, *Ezekiel: A Commentary*, p. 209, emphasis added).

Enjoying God is biblical and it is historical. Aelred summed up God and our relationship to Him when he wrote, "God is friendship." Satisfying friendship, at that. "The enjoyment of God is the only happiness with which our souls can be satisfied" (Edwards, "The Christian Pilgrim," in *The Works of Jonathan Edwards*, p. 2).

Enjoying God is biblical, historical, and wonderful. "The pleasure God has in His Son will become my pleasure, and I will not be consumed, but enthralled forever" (Piper, *The Pleasures of God*, p 28). He quenches our thirst and captivates our souls.

The suffering church militant of this present evil age is to cultivate one great impulse throbbing in her soul, *viz.* an aching longing for the Bridegroom to come to her, to take her in his arms, with nothing within herself to wrest her away, and to be held there for ever. Until such time as he is pleased to come, she is to center her life around the love of Jesus Christ, the King, Bridegroom and Husband of his church, to her his Queen, Bride, and Spouse, and of hers to him (Ray Ortlund, *Whoredom*, pp. 168-169).

When we say that we long for Father, we mean that we long to enjoy Him and also that we long to *entrust ourselves to Him* (Psalm 40:11; Psalm 62:11-12; Isaiah 6:1-8; Psalm 63:1-8). "Entrust" implies that we rely upon and place our confidence in Father's faithful strength to keep us safe and secure. The cry, "Abba, Father," represents our most basic relationship with God—a relationship of intimate trust. For believers, this means that every second we trust God, we are fulfilling our purpose. Every time we cling to God, we glorify Him while achieving our destiny.

We revel in Father when we enjoy Him; we take refuge in Father when we entrust ourselves to Him, and we respect Him when we *engage in our Father's good purposes*. We long for the applause of heaven.

Awaiting his martyrdom, the apostle Paul reminds Timothy, his protégé, that he has engaged in God's purposes, and now longs for God's high five.

You take over. I'm about to die, my life an offering on God's altar. This is the only race worth running. I've run hard right to the finish, believed all the way. All that's left now is the shouting—God's applause! Depend on it, he's an honest judge. He'll do right not only by me, but by everyone eager for his coming (Eugene Peterson, *The Message*, p. 2172, 2 Timothy 4:6-8).

Father fashioned our souls to long for His, "Well done, good and faithful servant!" His pleasure with us is our pleasure (Luke 3:22; 1 Corinthians 4:1-5; 2 Thessalonians 2:16-17).

We long to enjoy Father, entrust ourselves to Him, engage in His purposes, and we long to *emulate or reflect Him*. We want to hear Him say, "That's My boy! That's My girl!" We want people to say of us, "Like Father, like son and daughter." Our souls experience shalom when we fulfill our destiny of mirroring Father (Romans 8:28-29; 2 Corinthians 3:18; Ephesians 5:1-2).

Some may protest, "What about exalting God? Doesn't the Westminster Confession of Faith teach that our chief duty is to glorify God and love Him forever? You've got the love Him part, what about the glorify Him part?"

Totally true. We long to *exalt Father*. But, how do children exalt and honor parents? Is it not by enjoying parents, trusting parents, engaging in parents' purposes, and emulating or imitating parents? When we enjoy, entrust, engage, and emulate, then we exalt our Father. We glorify God *by* loving Him forever.

If people notice that my son wants to be with me, smiles as we talk, enjoys my presence, then they think, "Must be a pretty cool dad." As Piper reminds us, "Never forget that God is most glorified in you when you are most satisfied in him" (Piper, *The Pleasures of God*, p. 14). If people observe my daughter trusting me, depending upon me, believing in me, then they say, "Great father." If people see that my children join me in my values, living for Christ like I try to, then they comment, "Wow! Some parent." If people find my children following my lifestyle examples, reflecting something good in me, then they respond, "He must be quite a man."

People will honor our Father when we enjoy Him, entrust ourselves to Him, engage in His good purposes, and emulate His character. God will be honored and we will be at peace. Our longings satisfied. Our thirsts quenched. At least as deeply as they can be this side of heaven.

We Are Social Beings Created to Connect: The Holy Place of the Soul

If our spiritual longings are the Holy of Holies, then our social longings constitute a holy place. Too often we have separated love for God from love for one another. The apostle John, having heard Jesus equating the two, cautions us that:

If anyone says, "I love God," yet hates his brother, he is a liar. For anyone who does not love his brother, whom he has seen, cannot love God, whom he has not seen. And he has given us this command: Whoever loves God must also love his brother (1 John 4:20-21).

We are *in-relationship-to-one-another-beings*. The first "not" of history exposes this reality. "The LORD God said, 'It is *not* good for the man to be alone'" (Genesis 2:18a; emphasis added). Astounding! All seems well. Perfect. God and Adam together, no sin. Yet this arrangement was not reflective of Trinity. The unity in diversity experienced by Trinity could not be matched by Adam alone, or even by Adam with other males. True unity in diversity required a connecting gendered-community. "I will make a helper suitable for him" (Genesis 2:18b).

The earliest recorded human words were a love sonnet.

This one alone! This one at last!
Bone of my bones. Flesh of my flesh.
She shall be called *Ishah*—Feminine One,
For she was taken out of *Ish*—Masculine One.
(Author's paraphrase of Genesis 2:23).

Our destiny is to love like Trinity—mutual, reciprocal, interdependent, gift-love. To fulfill that destiny, God granted us the capacity to reflect His holy love. Because God is person-in-community, the ideal for humanity is humanity-in-community. "Mutual help is an existential part of human existence" (Claus Westermann, *Genesis 1-11*, p. 227).

Without social relationships and the quenching of our social thirsts, we experience unwholesome solitude and an aching void because we have an innate yearning for completeness. Ideally, humanity would be one great chorus of connectivity.

Luther insisted, "God created man for society and not for solitude." What was the basis for his interpretation? "This may be supported by the argument that he created two sexes, male and female. Likewise God founded the Christian Church, the communion of saints, and instituted Sacraments, preaching and consolations in the Church" (Tappert, *Luther: Letters of Spiritual Counsel*, p. 95).

Luther could become agitated when discussing this matter. The papist (as Luther labeled the Catholic Church of his day) and the Anabaptists (the "radical reformers" as church history called them) each taught versions of separatism. Both perspectives were anathema to Luther.

The papists and Anabaptists teach: If you wish to know Christ, try to be alone, don't associate with men, become a separatist. This is plainly diabolical advice that is in conflict with the first and the second table of the Decalogue. One must not flee into a corner. So the second table teaches that one must do good to one's neighbor. We ought not to isolate ourselves but enter into companionship with our neighbor. Likewise it (this notion) is in conflict with marriage, economic life, and political existence and is contrary to the life of Christ, who didn't choose solitude. Christ's life was very turbulent, for people were always moving about him. He was never alone, except when he prayed. Away with those who say, "Be glad to be alone and your heart will be pure" (Luther, *Luther's Works*, Vol. 54, pp. 140-141).

Luther had experienced the dangers of solitude, especially when battling spiritual depression. Thus he warns against it.

Solitude and melancholy are poisonous and fatal to all people. No one realizes how much harm it does a young person to avoid pleasure and cultivate solitude and sadness. Participation in proper and honorable pleasures with good and God-fearing people is pleasing to God, even if one may at times carry playfulness too far (Tappert, *Luther: Letters of Spiritual Counsel*, pp. 92-93).

R. Kolb, a Luther historian, summarizes Luther's viewpoint and mine:

God also created human beings to serve Him, not just by acknowledging His goodness, Luther insisted, but also by representing His goodness in the delivery of mutual care and concern within the human community. Fundamental to Luther's understanding of the biblical teaching of creation was his conviction that God had made human beings in and for community with one another. God had so structured human life that He made individual human beings not only to stand in relationship to Him in vertical dependence, but also to associate with other human beings in horizontal interdependence. God generally comes to meet human needs behind his chosen "masks," that is, other people who care for those in need (Kolb, *God Calling*, p. 5).

What do social beings created in the image of God long for? The Scriptures demonstrate that we have two central types of human longings that we attempt to quench in a variety of human contexts.

The "Two Sides" of Our Social Longings

God designed us for communion and dominion, love and action, relationship and purpose. In the Garden, Adam and Eve walked with God and worked for God. They loved each other through leaving, weaving, cleaving, and receiving (Genesis 2:24-25), while also working together to keep and care for Eden (Genesis 2:15-18).

We long for relational intimacy and relational respect. We want to hear, "You are my beloved," as well as, "Well done!" We thirst for a hug and a high five.

These longings existed before sin and are not, of themselves, sinful. Rather, they are pure. True, they can be distorted by sin. When we insist that our human relationships quench thirsts that only God can and should meet, we are guilty of gross idolatry. When we demand that others quench our thirsts, rather than gratefully enjoying longings met, we are guilty of selfish manipulation.

James 4 informs us that it is not our longings per se that are sinful, but what we do with them, how we direct them, and how we respond to the unmet longings of our souls.

(When we examine the spiritual dynamics of the Fall and of fallen image bearers, we'll more fully explore various ways we sinfully distort our longings.)

Social longings legitimately existed in the Garden of Eden and in the Garden of Gethsemane. Being exceedingly sorrowful and troubled, Jesus thirsted for His followers' companionship. "He began to be sorrowful and troubled. Then He said to them, 'My soul is overwhelmed with sorrow to the point of death. Stay here and keep watch with me'" (Matthew 26:37b-38). Returning to His protégés, he expressed sacred discontent and holy disappointment when they failed Him. "Could you men not keep watch with me for one hour?" (Matthew 26:40b).

In many passages, such as 1 Thessalonians 5:12-13 and Hebrews 13:17-18, Paul urges his followers to hold in highest honor those who minister to them. Honor is both thirst and obligation.

Box 11:1 contrasts and compares the "two sides of our social longings." As you read it, taste your thirsts. Enjoy those times when you have experienced thirsts quenched. Grieve over those times when you have remained hungry.

The Various Contexts of Our Social Longings

Ephesians 5:18-6:9 contains "household laws." In Paul's day, it was quite common for various religious groups and philosophical societies to develop a code of relational ethics within the home environment. Paul, under inspiration, offers us God's way of relating in the home.

As we read these household directives, we notice couplets: husband and wife, parent and child, and master and slave. (In Paul's day, master and slave were considered part of the common household arrangement.) Within each couplet, the commands God gives to one party also express the longings of the other party. What God commands us to fulfill in each other indicates the legitimate social thirsts He created within us.

God instructs husbands to love, nourish, and cherish their wives. Is there any doubt that every wife thirsts for *cherishing love* from her husband? Wives long for relational intimacy, love, closeness, to be cherished, focused upon, cared about, and communicated with. As one counselee expressed it, "I long for my husband, Steve, to have me as the number one person he expends his energy with."

What does a husband long for from his wife? Paul commands wives to respect their husbands (Ephesians 5:33). Husbands hunger for *relational respect.* I recall one counselee who, with tears in his eyes, both rejoiced and grieved when he said, "That was the first time in years that Vickie told me, 'You're a good man.'" Husbands thirst for respectful love—a love that encourages, uplifts, trusts, and believes.

What do parents long for from children? *Honoring love.* "Honor your father and mother" (Ephesians 6:2). Honor speaks of valuing and lifting up. It includes obedience, but focuses on a heart attitude that communicates, "I obey you because I think so highly of you."

What do children long for from their parents? *Holy love.* Parents offer children a small mirror, a meager taste, of God's holy love. "Fathers, do not exasperate your children, instead, bring them up in the training [nurture] and instruction [strong direction] of the Lord" (Ephesians 6:4). Children thirst to know that they are loved and protected.

Box 11:1

Our Social Longings

People	Purpose
Longing for intimacy that accepts all of me	Longing for an adventure that requires something of me
Love Affair	Grand Adventure
Communion	Dominion
Romance	Quest
Lover	Hero/Warrior
Shepherd	King
Relate	Create
Beauty	Majesty
Intimacy	Impact
Dream Person	Dream Job
Completing	Competing
Hug	High Five
Relationship	Task/Mission
Talking	Doing
Accept	Respect
Enjoy	Appreciate
Communing	Calling
Great Commandment	Great Commission
Mary	Martha
Love	Meaning
"Welcome Home!"	"Well Done!"
"This Is My Beloved"	"In Whom I Am Well Pleased"
Bride	Son

We also have longings for each other, whether single or married. We long for *mentoring love*—for a wise guide who believes in what we are becoming. A Paul or a Priscilla. We thirst for *brotherly/sisterly love*—a spiritual friend who journeys where we are going. A Barnabas, a Jonathan, or a David. We long for *protégé love*—a disciple who wants what we are offering. A Ruth or a Timothy.

What do we long for as workers? *Impacting love*. We were created to make a difference that is appreciated and appreciable.

All of these are legitimate, God-designed, human longings. They are not to be ignored; rather, they are to be tasted.

We Are Self-Aware Beings Created to Reflect Consciously: The Place of Wholeness in the Soul

There is no "Doggie Spiritual Friendship" training occurring anywhere on earth. Nor, as theologian Wayne Grudem notes, can we find any books entitled *The History of Canine Philosophy* (Grudem, *Systematic Theology*, p. 446). Grudem and I are making the same point: *only image bearers are self-aware*. We are conscious of our own existence and can reflect on it. We long for a sense of shalom—of inner wholeness, peace, and contentment.

As *spiritual* beings we long for communion with God. As *social* beings we long for connection with each other. And as *self-aware* beings we long for a conscious sense of personal peace. Many Bible passages describe and illustrate human self-awareness. Adam and Eve, pre-Fall, were naked and felt no shame (Genesis 2:25). Shamelessness indicates their natural ability to look within their own soul, reflect on what they noted, evaluate the nature of their personal existence, and rest in their sense of integration.

As we might say today, they felt "together." Unlike people struggling with a fractured sense of self, they did not feel they were "coming unglued," "falling apart," "having a nervous breakdown," "cracking up," "losing it," "spacing out," or any other imagery suggestive of dis-integration. But that is exactly the type of fallen self-awareness Adam and Eve battled in the aftermath of their sin. "Then the eyes of both of them were opened, and they realized that they were naked; so they sewed fig leaves together and made coverings for themselves" (Genesis 3:7). No one had to tell them they were naked; they came to this through self-realization. Sensing their brokenness, their lost innocence and wholeness, they were afraid, so they hid.

Our Self-Conscious Awareness

Psalm 8 pictures the universal human urge to discover one's place in the universe. Speaking representatively on behalf of us all, the psalmist wonders aloud, "What is man that you are mindful of him?" (Psalm 8:4). In a similar vein, David asks in Psalm 144:3, "O LORD, what is man that you care for him, the son of man that you think of him?" Do you hear the conscious longing to find one's place in the cosmos?

New Testament authors use "conscience" (*suneidēsis*) for our capacity to be aware of our own actions and attitudes, thoughts and intents. The Greek word for conscience literally implies to know within, or to know within oneself. Humans possess subjective self-awareness. In passages like 1 Corinthians 8 and Romans 2:14-15; conscience reflects self-awareness and meta-cognition—our ability to reflect on our own reflections, to reflect on our existence. Conscience is our knowledge about our relationships and ourselves.

In Acts 24:16, Paul brings together our spiritual, social, and self-aware being. "So I strive always to keep my conscience clear before God and man." Isn't that what you long for? To be at peace in your heart about your relationships with God and others?

The great apostle ties these three together again in 1 Corinthians 4:1-4. He notes that he cares what others think of him, but he is more concerned what his conscience tells him about himself, yet he is most moved by what God knows about him.

All these verses and many more (The New Testament uses "conscience" thirty-one times) inform us that an "I" exists. The evolutionary materialists tell us that we have a brain (a physical organ), but no mind (no inner, metaphysical soul). The narrative therapists tell us that we recreate a new "I" in each new social situation. But the Bible tells us there is an ongoing, everlasting "I." As J. Gresham Machen insists about our soul consciousness:

It means not only that man has mind or consciousness, but also that his mind or consciousness is a unity. It is not a mere stream of consciousness, but the consciousness of a person. Not merely does thinking go on within me, but it is *I* that think. It was I many years ago, and it is the same I today, and it will be the same I to all eternity. This is what the Bible means when it tells me that I have a soul (Machen, *The Christian View of Man*, p. 138).

Machen continues by discussing the terrible isolation of the individual soul and how that isolation is expressed by theologians and philosophers and by the cry of the human heart. He then paraphrases the words of the old spiritual, "It's not my father or my mother, but it's me O Lord, standin' in the need of prayer. It's not my sister or my brother, but it's me O Lord, standin' in the need of prayer." I long. *I* long. A personal being longs. That is what it means to be self-aware.

Our Thematic Identities

Self-awareness is a counseling key. We each possess a secret signature of the soul—our own soul print, if you will—unlike anyone else's in the universe. We not only reflect upon ourselves; we also summarize our reflections. We title our life story and live according to our summary title.

The night I led my first lay counseling training, two thematic identities battled in my conscience. I had meticulously selected twelve well-qualified and highly committed lay leaders from our large congregation. I prepared every detail of my lecture presentation. After a break, the second hour was to be an unstructured, informal small group time. Chairs no longer aligned in rows. Lectern no longer separating me from my students. As we began that second hour, I was overwhelmed with an image of myself as a ten-year-old boy in my father's oversized suit coat, seated in a huge chair, my feet dangling far above the floor.

What was my sense of self at that moment? How did I see myself?

I saw myself as a little boy, a fake, a phony, a fraud. I had no business leading such a group. I was immature, childish.

In that moment of self-awareness, I had a choice to make. Would I live out of this shame identity, or would I live out of my new identity in Christ? Was I Christ-sufficient, or was I Bob-insufficient?

My experience that day and my studies since have shown me that we have three potential thematic identities at work within us, identities that correspond to the three acts in the drama of redemption:

♦ Our Shalom Thematic Identity: Creation
♦ Our Shame Thematic Identity: Fall
♦ Our Sacred Thematic Identity: Redemption

Adam and Eve experienced a shalom thematic identity when they were naked yet unashamed. It included their ability to perceive themselves honestly and openly without coverings; accept themselves in contentment, confidence, and comfort without contempt; and their ability to integrate the potentially disparate aspects of their souls into one peaceful, whole sense of self.

Please stop to reread these descriptions. Don't read them clinically. Read them personally, passionately. Wouldn't that be wonderful? No hiding, no coverings, no layers, or facades, no longer playing the chameleon. The absence of self-deceit and the presence of accurate, honest self-assessment. An assessment that would not drive us to ludicrous attempts at self-beautification, but would leave us pleased, humbly so, content with who we were.

I see my shalom thematic identity as *reckless abandon*. When I was young, nothing stopped me. Nothing scared me. The highest tree with the slimmest limb was a challenge to be conquered. There was nothing that my buddy, Johnny, and I couldn't handle— nothing could stop us.

Sadly, our shalom thematic identity all too quickly fades. Seems like a mirage. Replaced by our shame thematic identity. "I was afraid." Confusion, fear of rejection, a sense of condemnation, lostness. "Because I was naked." Self-aware with self-disgust. The real me is deficient and defective. "So I hid." Layer upon layer of fake identity—chat room Christianity where we play one role today and another tomorrow. Whatever keeps us safe, concealed, out of sight. "So they sewed fig leaves together to cover themselves." Self-beautification. Foolish, silly self-sufficiency.

I see my shame thematic identity as *wrecked abandonment*—feeling ruined and rejected. When I was young and indoors, everything spooked me. Living with an alcoholic father, who might be a happy drunk one night and a violent alcoholic the next; terror, tension, and anxiety reigned in my soul. I was the lost little boy—the one trying to lead a lay counseling small group in my father's oversized suit.

Fortunately, God does not leave us with our shameful fig coat. Instead, He dresses us in a fur coat, in robes of righteousness and rightness. He graces us with our sacred sustaining identity. We can rise each morning with the sweet voice of Jesus whispering in our ears, "All is well. It's all right. I accept you. I respect you."

Jesus offers us copious choices of sacred thematic identities. We are Virgin Brides, Adult Sons, Saints, Holy Ones, Soldiers, Bond-servants, Warriors, Athletes, Farmers, Kings, Priests—the list goes on and on. I call these our "*universal* sacred thematic identities." Universal because they are true of, applicable to, and may be claimed by every believer.

In counseling and in my personal Christian walk, I've also detected what I call "*unique* sacred thematic identities." Unique because they are true for, applicable to, and may be claimed by only one person. That evening in my lay counseling small group, I claimed mine. "Coach for Christ!" *Renewed abandon*. The real me was not deficient and defective, not in Christ. The real me was empowered and equipped to empower others as their coach. I leaned back in my chair, smiled a sly smile, and said, "Let me tell you about the picture that almost captured my imagination." The next unplanned hour opened our group to naked sharing like nothing else could have. It lit a fire and fanned a flame that continued for the two years of our training together. We connected (social beings) because I communed with God (spiritual beings) about my conscious sense of self (self-aware beings).

Where We've Been and Where We're Heading

In our soul school curriculum, we're in the middle of our spiritual anatomy of the soul. We just learned that Romancers love passionately. We are relational beings who commune with Christ, connect with one another, and reflect on ourselves consciously, comfortably, and confidently.

In Act Two, Scene V, Chapter 12, we'll learn that we are Dreamers and Creators. Dreamers think wisely. We are rational beings who think in images and beliefs. What's the connection between our self-awareness, our thematic identities, and the capacity of imagination? What is the imagination? How do our images relate to our beliefs and how do our images and beliefs influence our affections?

Creators choose courageously. We are volitional beings who pursue goals through patterned actions and interactions. What influences our behavior? How do we decide how to live? What's the inner-play between our relational motivation, our rational direction, and our volitional interaction? We address and answer these questions in our next scene.

Caring for Your Soul: Personal Applications

1. What the *heart* most highly treasures as beautiful, worthy, valuable, pleasurable, beneficial, and perfect, the *soul* pursues.

    a.   What do you value?

    b.   What do you pursue?

2. Do you taste your own thirsts? When? How? What do you do with them?

3. Do you enter others' emptiness? When? How? What do you do?

4. Why are we so afraid to enter, engage, and offer? When are you less afraid? Why?

5. Receive your identity; don't build your identity.

    a.   Put on your new identity in Christ rather than trying to cover up your old identity with works. Who are you in Christ?

    b.   Remember your identity by reflecting on the intersection of your life story and God's larger story. Ask, "God, who have You made me to be? What are You up to in my life?"

Caring for Others: Ministry Implications

◆ **Our Focus in Counseling Spiritual Beings Includes:**

1. *The Core Question We All Ask*: "How can I experience peace (shalom, harmony, wholeness, oneness, communion, fullness) with God?"
   - *So,* since the deepest questions in the human soul are God-questions, the ultimate focus in your spiritual friendships is to assist others in their quest for peace with God.

2. *The Core Issue We All Face*: Relationship.
   - *So,* since the deepest issues in life are relational, the fundamental lens you use to direct your focus is relational. Relational issues become your predominant "diagnostic indicator."

3. *The Core Longing We Each Experience*: Relational.
   - *So,* since the deepest longing in life is relationship, the greatest power you have as a spiritual friend is your relationship with others.

◆ **Our Focus in Counseling Social Beings Includes:**

1. *It's Normal to Thirst*: Since isolation is not good and alienation quite bad, you need to allow and encourage your spiritual friends to thirst—to feel the pain of fractured relationships and experience the emptiness of shallow ones.

2. *Taste Others' Social Thirsts*: Since people quench their thirsts in a host of unhelpful ways, you need to taste their true thirsts. Ponder, "What is it like to be betrayed like she was betrayed?" "What would I feel if my spouse did that to me?" "How might I try to quench my thirsts in this situation?"

◆ **Our Focus in Counseling Self-Aware Beings Includes:**

1. *Listen for Your Spiritual Friend's Three Stories*: Read his/her story.
   - Shalom:What is the core shape of this person as designed by God?
   - Shame: What are this person's fears, covers, fig leaves?
   - Sacred:Who is this person in Christ? What is unique about your spiritual friend?

2. *Become a Main Character in Your Spiritual Friend's Story*: Enter his/her story

CHAPTER TWELVE

DREAMERS AND CREATORS: VISIONARY LIVING

"Our ability to think and represent things to ourselves also enables us to bring vast ranges of reality—and non-reality—before us" (Dallas Willard, *Renovation of the Heart*, p. 96).

"Hell is the greatest compliment God has ever paid to the dignity of human freedom" (commonly attributed to G. K. Chesterton).

"The West has finally achieved the rights of man . . . but man's sense of responsibility to God and society has grown dimmer and dimmer" (Alexsandr Solzhenitsyn, Harvard University Commencement Speech, June 8, 1978).

To Honk or Not to Honk

As a seminary professor who focuses upon a biblical understanding of motivation, I'm frequently asked questions like, "If God created Satan perfect, if evil did not exist, why and how did Satan sin? Why did Adam and Eve choose to sin? How could they have sinned if they were created innocent?"

To address such questions, we must probe the original motivational structure in the human personality. If we're going to examine the spiritual anatomy of the soul, it's not enough to know how the individual components function in isolation. Unlike our physical nature, our metaphysical nature can't be easily dissected. For teaching purposes, I'm separating various psychological functions for a chapter-by-chapter analysis. However, we have only one soul, a soul that functions in many complex, interconnected ways. Within the complexity of our human nature, what motivates us to do what we do, to live as we do, to decide what we decide?

Think about your own life. Two thoughts enter your mind. Two narratives compete for your soul. Which one do you choose? What captures your imagination and captivates your heart?

Let's make it even more practical, more real. A driver cuts you off on the expressway. His fault, yet he still blares his horn at you. Your physical brain records all the action.

Your body tenses for a reaction. Do you honk back? Gesture? Track him down? Run him off the road? Or do you take a deep breath, pray a prayer, forgive, and drive on? How do you respond?

To answer these questions we need to review and preview:

- Romancers: Relational Motivation—I'm motivated to quench my thirsts for relationship.
- Dreamers: Rational Direction—My thoughts direct my actions.
- Creators: Volitional Interaction—I act and interact purposefully.
- Singers: Emotional Reaction—I respond to my external situation based upon my internal condition.

We can outline how our complex capacities work together.

- I pursue (volitional interaction) what I perceive (rational direction) to be pleasing (relational motivation).
- What I believe (Dreamer) about what satisfies my longings for relationship (Romancer) provides the direction that I choose to pursue (Creator) and determines my response (Singer) to my inner and outer world.
- I do (volitional) what I determine/decide (rational) I delight in (relational).
- I tread purposeful pathways (volitional) to satisfy my affections (relational) according to my mindsets (rational).
- I choose (volitional) what I conclude (rational) my soul craves (relational).
- I pursue (volitional) what I perceive (rational) to be lovely and loving (relational).
- What I find (rational) beautiful (relational), I try to find (volitional).
- I direct myself (volitional) toward what I perceive (rational) will satisfy my longings for relationship (relational).

The Puritans understood how the soul operates. "The choice of the mind never departs from that which, at the time appears most agreeable and pleasing" (Jonathan Edwards, *Freedom of the Will*, p. 13). "The will never desires evil as evil, but as seeming good" (Richard Baxter, *A Christian Directory*, p. 85).

Eve had God, she had Adam, and she had a pleasing and good earth. Yet, she still sinned. Why? "When the woman *saw* [rational direction] that the fruit of the tree was *good* [relational motivation] for food and *pleasing* [relational motivation] to the eye, and also *desirable* [relational motivation] for gaining wisdom, she *took* [volitional action] some and *ate* [volitional action]. She also *gave* [volitional action] some to her husband, who was with her, and he *ate* [volitional action] it" (Genesis 3:6, emphasis added). Eve chose what she concluded was good, pleasing, and desirable.

What about us? That driver cuts you off on the expressway. Do you honk or do you pray? How do you respond? Biblical counselor Elyse Fitzpatrick urges us to ask some relational motivational questions in such situations. "What do I believe will make me happy? What good or happiness do I think that I am missing? What is the delight or joy that I'm trying to get by acting this way?" (Fitzpatrick, *Idols of the Heart*, p. 85).

I add a few. "How do I think my response will lead to quenching my thirsts? Which thirsts? Which response?" "What thirsts am I trying to quench through which behavior?"

"What do I think quenches my deepest thirsts in a situation like this?" "What do I believe satisfies my most ardent longings in this situation?" "What do I imagine fills the hunger of my soul?" "What do I cherish more than anything?" "What images control what I believe will satisfy my longing soul?" "What are my beliefs about my thirsts?" "What mindsets and ruts am I setting by the convictions I choose to follow?"

If the motivational structure of my heart is mature, I will purposely pursue God and what He chooses to provide (volitional interaction) because I personally perceive (rational direction) that He is good and great, holy and loving, sovereign and satisfying (relational motivation), and I experience true happiness (emotional reaction). If the motivational structure of my heart is immature, I will purposely pursue Satan (volitional interaction) because I am personally deceived into perceiving (rational direction) that God is not good and great, a Hoarder not a Rewarder, a dull Bully (relational motivation), and I experience the temporary pleasures of sin for a season (emotional reaction).

To honk or not to honk is a profoundly spiritual issue. "Whoa!" You protest. "How in the world can an instantaneous reaction reflect a deep spiritual condition?" That's the point, not only of Chapter 12, but also of *Soul Physicians*. Further, the point of this chapter and book is to teach a biblical process of sanctification (personal maturity as Romancers, Dreamers, Creators, and Singers). That process will reshape the motivational longings of our souls and its affections/lovers and reset the rational direction of the mindsets of our hearts. It will also reengage the volitional interactions of the purposes/pathways of our wills, and revive the emotional reactions of the mood states associated with our feelings.

Dreamers Thinking with Wisdom/Imagination:
Rational Beings Who Think—Mindsets

I need to clarify my choice of words like "Dreamers" and "imagination." I don't mean that our ideal mental state is daydreaming. Nor that we ought to live a Walter Mitty existence where we imagine ourselves to be what we are not: a professional ball player, an opera star, president of the United States, or a millionaire.

I chose "Dreamers" because our minds actively do something with the input that we receive from our senses. Animals process information based only upon a physical brain and act instinctively. Computers process information based only upon a physical chip and act accordingly. Humans actively, personally process information both with an incredibly complex physical brain and a beautifully intricate metaphysical mind. We shape the input that our senses receive.

Ideally, we think with 20/20 spiritual vision that sees our world, relationships, situations, our past, present, and future with spiritual eyes, not with physical eyes only. We remember the past with faith, seeing God's fingerprints everywhere. We reflect on the present with love, concluding that God is good even when life is bad. We envision the future with hope, knowing the end of the story written by the great Storyteller. We're visionaries, dreaming big dreams for God because we know that God can do exceedingly, abundantly above all that we think or imagine.

Rational Thinking: Rational Direction

Like God, we think. The Bible portrays our original rational capacities through the lives of Adam and Eve. They had the capacity to comprehend and organize what their senses perceived. Adam's naming and labeling the animals illustrates both his rational ability to conceptualize and his dominion (Genesis 2:18-20). Adam and Eve also had the ability to observe their world through images and beliefs, as when Adam noted his aloneness and called his wife, "Eve," the "mother of all life" (Genesis 2:20-23; 3:20). Further, they evidenced the capacity to organize the stories of their lives into a summary theme of shalom identity—nakedness coupled with shamelessness (Genesis 2:24-25).

The Old Testament consistently uses the word heart (*lēb* and *lēbāb*) to describe our rational nature. The heart is thought of as:

♦ The seat of knowledge and understanding: Genesis 20:5-6; Exodus 28:3; 36:1,

♦ The place of thoughts: Genesis 27:41; Deuteronomy 15:9-10; Isaiah 10:7,

♦ The domain of memory and recall: Psalm 27:8; Lamentations 3:21; Daniel 7:28,

♦ The realm of self-consciousness: 1 Samuel 24:5-6; 25:3,

♦ The sphere of reflexive consideration and internal contemplation: Genesis 8:21; 17:17; 24:45; Psalm 4:4; 77:6, and

♦ The site of planning and purposing: 1 Kings 12:33; Psalm 33:11; Proverbs 16:9.

Deuteronomy 29:4 clarifies the vital importance and central function of the human heart or mind. God speaks of a mind (*lēb*) to perceive, eyes to see, and ears to hear. As the primary function of the eyes is to see and the ears to hear, so the primary function of the heart is to perceive (*yāda*). Jack Lewis, Old Testament scholar, notes that "perceive" means experiential knowledge and spiritual perception—spiritual eyes (Lewis, *Theological Wordbook of the Old Testament*, Vol. 1, p. 366).

Isaiah 6:10 offers a second summation of our rational capacity. "Make the heart of this people fat, and make their ears heavy, and shut their eyes; lest they see with their eyes, and hear with their ears, and understand with their heart" (KJV). The primary function of the heart is "understanding" (*bēn*) which means to separate, distinguish, and discern through the faculty of insight and intelligence (Francis Brown, *Lexicon of the Old Testament*, pp. 106-107).

The Israelite understanding of the heart aids our understanding of our thought life. Heart (*lēb*) pictured the midst of the sea in Exodus 15:8 and Jonah 2:3. It was symbolic for what is deepest inside, hidden from view, the innermost parts in Exodus 28:29 and 1 Samuel 16:7. When used for our soulish makeup, it depicts our innermost being, the depths of our hearts, our inner thought life.

Taken together, these passages demonstrate that the Bible depicts the heart as our inner rational control center that determines our direction in life, based upon our perceptions of God, others, ourselves, and our world (Deuteronomy 29:4; Proverbs 4:23; 16:9; Isaiah 6:10). Our thoughts direct our actions (Romans 12:1-2). Our inner rational, mental control center determines our direction in life by setting and following fixed, deliberate purposes

(1 Kings 8:58; Job 17:11; Psalm 119:112; Proverbs 4:23; 16:9). As Proverbs 16:9 notes, "a man's heart deviseth his way" (KJV). To "devise" (*hāshab*) means to design, plan, consider, and purpose. It is in our inner rational control center that we decide what way or direction we will go, what actions we will take, and what affections we will pursue.

Thus, biblical counseling never stops with exhortations to change behavior. In fact, it doesn't even start here. Our starting point must be a renewed mind. But what is the mind? What does God mean when He says to renew it? What actually needs to change deep inside us if our insights and imaginations, our actions and interactions, are to please the Lover of our soul?

Our Imagination: Pictures of Reality

We are captured by what captures our imagination. "And God saw that the wickedness of man was great in the earth, and that every imagination [*yēser*, derived from *yāsar*—to fashion, form, and frame] of the thoughts of his heart was only evil continually" (Genesis 6:5, KJV). Notice that it is not simply the heart, nor even the thoughts of the heart, but the *imagination* of the thoughts of the heart that God identifies as the root source of wickedness (and, likewise, the root source of righteous, wise thinking).

What is this mysterious imagination (*yēser*)? In a concrete sense, *yēser* pictures the potter fashioning and shaping clay. The Bible often parallels it with *bārā*, which means to create, form, and shape. In an abstract, internal sense, *yēser* depicts how we fashion, frame, devise, and purpose in our minds, how we form a summary picture. Thus, the Bible can employ *yēser* for our mind's ability to fashion idols of the heart. However, it can also use *yēser* in a very positive sense. "You will keep in perfect peace (*shalom, shalom*) him whose mind (*yēser*) is steadfast, because he trusts in you" (Isaiah 26:3). With our imagination, we can form mental pictures of life where Yahweh is our Tower of Power, or where pieces of wood and stone are our place of safety.

Our imagination consists of summarizing pictures, images, stories, and narratives that control our convictions. A struggling Christian teen might be captured by an image such as, "Only a geek (nerd, wimp, fake) reads his Bible." Or that young man might be captivated by an image like, "A foolish teen builds his house upon the sand, but I'm going to be a wise teen by building my house upon the Rock of Ages!" Simply telling him, "Read your Bible," is right, but not enough. We would want to help him decipher which image controls his affections, cognitions, interactions, actions, and reactions.

The Puritans developed an entire biblical psychology based upon the *yēser*. Consider Timothy Keller's summary of their psychology of the imagination.

One of the earliest Puritans to define the "imagination" was Richard Sibbes (1577-1635). He wrote that imagination was a "power of the soul" which is "bordering between our senses on the one side and our understanding on the other." The office of imagination "is to minister matter to our understanding to work upon." However, sinful imagination usurps and misleads the understanding. Charnock is more specific for in a sermon he states that the imagination is the place of the "first motion or formation of thoughts." The imagination was not a power designed for thinking, but only to receive the images impressed upon the sense, and concoct them, that they might be fit matter for thoughts; and so it is the exchequer (bank account) wherein all the acquisitions of sense are deposited, and from thence received by the intellective faculty. Thought engenders opinion in the mind; thought spurs the will to consent or dissent; it is thought also which spirits the affections.

Let us pause for a moment to summarize what is being said. Modern cognitive therapists see "thinking" as fundamental to behavior and feeling. If we change the thinking, we can change the feelings and thus behavior, so goes this approach. However, the Puritans considered imagination, even more fundamentally than thinking, as the control of the behavior. Imagine two thoughts sitting on the intellect: "This sin will feel good if I do it" and "This sin will displease God if I do it." Both are facts in the mind. You believe both to be true. But which one will control your heart? That is, which one will capture your thinking, your will, and your emotions? (Keller, *Puritan Resources for Pastoral Counseling*, pp. 123-124).

The Puritans answered: the one that possesses the imagination will control the soul, mind, will, and emotions. The imagination makes a thought real or vivid. It is the faculty for appreciation and value. It conjures up pictures that create thoughts that direct our longings, illuminate our minds, move our wills to choose, and stir our emotions.

In summary, the imagination is more basic, base, and rudimentary than language. Our imagination is our ability to think in pictures—pictures that summarize our basic view of life. Originally used of the cast, mold, or form used for shaping or framing something, the imagination relates to the framing of thoughts ingrained in the heart (Thomas Boston, *Human Nature in Its Four-Fold State*, p. 62). It is parabolic thinking—representative, symbolic thinking, thinking that makes comparisons (co-pare, co-parable, to make a corresponding picture of a verbal reality).

Remember elementary school *Show and Tell*? Wasn't it one of your favorite times of the school week? You or a classmate could bring in some treasured possession, show it, describe it, touch it, feel it, and see it. You loved concrete, pictorial thinking. The *yēser* is the show and tell of our minds.

Psychologically speaking, the *yēser* produces concrete formations of basic images about how life works and our place in life. Through it we conceptualize our *version* (either God's version or Satan's sub-version) of reality by framing summarizing pictures (Boston, *Human Nature in Its Four-Fold State*, pp. 79-127). The imagination is our pictorial summary of reality.

Our minds do not simply react to sensory input instinctively like animals, nor do we store input like computer chips. We *story* input. We do something with it, we have a say in forming, shaping, molding, and organizing input. More than that, we *must* do something with it. To survive, we organize. We pattern truth. We "theme" our perceptions. In this, we are like God—in His imagining image (Psalm 139:15-18; Isaiah 46:10-11; Jeremiah 18:11-12).

The imagination is God's gift of the capacity to organize input into images that lead to interpretations and result in ideas (beliefs). We form the multitude of our life events into a comprehensive narrative by "storying" reality. We weave together a theme from the individual events of our lives in order to make sense of life and to have a sense of control/mastery over life.

We must make sense of our life experiences. We impose structure because we are meaning-seekers. There is an innate blueprint in the human personality that drives us to decode input, search for order, and create new associations.

We process information. We transform, store, and retrieve sensory input through the active internal processes of perceiving, attending, interpreting, understanding, elaborating, and remembering. We have unique and individual control over what we do with our perceptions. It is in the *yēser* that we actively organize input. We conceptualize—perceive in patterns that we turn into pictures. We impose structure, themes, and plot lines to our story. We arrange images into mental patterns—sentences that become the themes for how we view and live our life stories.

The imagination is like the *editor* of, say, a liberal newspaper. This editor edits in and out and *constructs* the final shape of the *article* of belief. This *slant filters* how I perceive reality. If it filters out God, grace, generosity, goodness, relationship, being my brother's keeper, etc., then I am competitive rather than cooperative, a hoarder rather than a sharer, self-sufficient rather than dependent on God and interdependent with others. The *mind set on the flesh* allows the fleshly brain to continue to edit my new perceptions so they fit with the current mindset of the world, the flesh, and the Devil. The *mind set on the Spirit/spirit* rejects the lies of the world (Satan's law meta-narrative, his diabolical imaginations) and is transformed by receiving the mind of Christ and the grace meta-narrative. Thus the need in biblical counseling for grace narratives presented in the context of grace relationships resulting in grace imagination: Dreamers who think creatively—wisely. (Box 12:1 summarizes the biblical teaching on the imagination.)

Our Beliefs: Rational Mindsets

We think in pictures and propositions, images and words. What enters your mind when you read the next phrase? *Pink elephant.* You picture a huge animal, trunk, tail, and tusks, gray. Or, pink. You can describe the animal with words: mammal, pachyderm. We think in pictures and words.

Impressions enter the brain. The imagination is like a bank account where we deposit these impressions. The imagination conjures up powerful pictures, themes, stories, and narratives that interpret reality. "Beliefs" lie somewhere between images and interpretations.

"Read your Bible," we tell our teens. Input. Deposited. A collision of pictures of geeks, nerds, little old ladies as well as images of Billy Graham, sand and rocks/Rock, a respected youth pastor.

Also a collision of ideas, sentences, interpretations, and beliefs. "Reading the Bible is for people who need a crutch, for kids who can't relate their way out of a paper bag." Or, "Reading the Bible is kewl! It's what my neat youth pastor does. I need the Word of God. I can't live by bread only but by the Bread of Life."

But how do we get to the place where godly ideas guide us? To answer that question we must use our minds to consider the patterns we form, what the Bible calls "mindsets." Images are "pictures that move us" and beliefs are "rules that guide us." Ideas become relational rules that govern how we live—mindsets.

Box 12:1

Principles of the Imagination

1. Imagination is Progressive:

We relate new input to current themes (thus the need to renew our minds *daily*). If I am depressed, then I will tend to put new input into my depressive theme.

2. Imagination is Patterned:

God designed us as *meaning makers*. There is an *innate blueprint* in the human soul that compels us to *make sense* of sensory experience, of life experience. God has designed our minds to search for order and create new associations. The *yēser* is the imaginative/conceptual capacity of our soul to *organize input actively and creatively*. We are Dreamers. We think with imagination.

3. Imagination is Propositional:

We do not simply store individual words, but rather propositions. We are like a *story editor* who weaves individual words into sentences and sentences into paragraphs, all of which connect to the *theme sentence(s) of our lives*. We story our information, not simply store it. We are imposers of structure.

4. Imagination is Pictorial:

What captures our imagination? Whatever is most vivid, alive, and real to us. Whatever is most intense and passionate. Contrast the boring parental lecture: "Behave yourself tonight and be a good kid," with, "Hey, the gang's going to . . . Want to join us!!??" The most powerful images formed in our minds produce major controlling themes that determine our beliefs and shape our ideas. The imagination is like an art lover or a diamond appraiser—it appreciates, it evaluates and values—making value judgments on what is most "beautiful." Sin begins in the imagination where we devalue God (Genesis 6:5; Jeremiah 2:5, 19, 31).

5. Imagination is Perceptual:

We determine our understanding of truth by giving it meaning through our perceptions, interpretations, and applications. In the godly, we call it "wisdom." In the ungodly, "foolishness."

6. Imagination is Purposeful:

We frame images for the purpose of using them in the pursuit of our affections. *Perceived perfections are pursued.*

John Murray, in his commentary on Romans, explains that mindsets are the absorbing object of our affections, thoughts, will, and emotions (Murray, *Epistle to the Romans*, pp. 284-287). Mindsets are the settled patterns, ruts, and habits of my thought life. They're the inward channels in my mind that lead to habituated ways of thinking about the source of life. "Those who live according to the sinful nature [flesh] have their *minds set* on what that nature *desires*; but those who live in accordance with the Spirit have their *minds set* on what the Spirit *desires* (Romans 8:5, emphasis added). What absorbs my thinking, captures my heart?

Ponder the connection between our thoughts (rationality) and affections (relationality). Mindsets always influence and relate to our desires. What absorbs my thinking? Images and ideas about God as a Hoarder or as a Rewarder, as a pursuing Father or a demanding Bully, Christ as a Worthy Groom or Unworthy Judge?

One set (mindset) of images and ideas allures and attracts us to God as the Spring of Living Water, the One we desire more than life itself. The other set of images and ideas repels and distracts us from God whom we find faulty, who is a Dark Desert, the Creator we desire less than created things.

The mind set on the flesh is broad. It is the path of death: foolish, selfish, arrogant blindness concerning the glorious grace and generosity of our Worthy Groom. The mind set on the Spirit is narrow. It is the path of life: wise, selfless, humble, discerning insight regarding Christ's gospel of grace.

Let's summarize. We do not simply react instinctively or mechanically to input. We uniquely and creatively form our perceptions into an organized schema through which we orient ourselves to our world. This orientation provides the direction we take in life. We organize our perceptions into images and beliefs. Over time, these chosen and learned mindsets develop a habituated way of thinking that becomes formulated into a controlling framework that directs how we approach life. This consistent frame of reference is the lens through which we filter our perceptions, the eyeglasses through which we approach life.

Romans 12:1-2 offers God's solution for putting off the mind-set of the flesh and putting on the mindset of the Spirit.

> Therefore, I urge you, brothers, in view of God's mercy to offer your bodies as living sacrifices, holy and pleasing to God—this is your spiritual act of worship. Do not conform any longer to the pattern of this world, but be transformed by the renewing of your mind. Then you will be able to test and approve what God's will is—his good, pleasing, and perfect will.

Did you notice the "therefore"? Paul is reminding us to look back on Romans 1-11. Our sinfulness, hopelessness, and helplessness. Our vile rejection of God, our wicked refusal to consider Him worthy even to think about; contrasted with His grace, kindness, patience, goodness, and forgiveness. Our sin abounds. Christ's grace superabounds. While enemies, He made us family. While we hated Him, He loved us. While we crucified Him, He died for us. "Therefore," in light of our good and gracious God, worship Him.

You also noticed the phrase, "in view of God's mercy." In light of God's passion and compassion, make a decision; choose a course of action. We will worship God to the extent and depth that we imagine God to be merciful. We will make the volitional choice of our wills to put ourselves at God's disposal (present ourselves a living sacrifice) if our minds (our reasonable service, our spiritual act) are captured by Christ's affections (our act of worship).

Paul is not naïve. Worship is a battle—the battle of two lovers. To worship our Worthy Groom we have to put off the mindset of the flesh that conforms us to the world ruled by the False Seducer. We have to put on the mindset of the Spirit by being transformed through renewing our minds, our inner rational control center of images and ideas about the source of life.

Paul tells us not to be "conformed" (*suschēmatizō*) to the world. That is, do not let your mindset be molded, shaped, and fashioned by images controlled by the world, the flesh, and the Devil. Put off the spirit of this age. Reject the subtle images and ideas of this present darkness. Repel all that floating mass of thoughts, opinions, maxims, speculations, hopes, impulses, aims, aspirations, concoctions, portraits, and pictures at any time current in the fallen world—the immoral atmosphere we inhale every moment of our lives, again inevitably to exhale.

Instead, put on the renewed mindset. Think reasonably. In light of so great a salvation, it is only reasonable that we would worship Jesus. Let your mind experience a metamorphosis. You are crucified with Christ, so reject that dead brain. You are resurrected with Christ, so accept the new mind. Live according to renewed images of Father, Son, and Holy Spirit. Live out the new you in Christ.

Do so by being transformed by the Word's interpretation of life—our passionate romance novel set in our grand adventure narrative. Having resisted being conformed and shaped by the world's impressions and images, daily renew your mind through grace narratives. Our minds have been renovated, Paul told us in Romans 6-8. Now in Romans 12 he's telling us, "live out that new renovation. Quit returning to the old mindset. Keep banking on the new mindset. Keep withdrawing deposits of new images and ideas that reflect God-reality, which see life with 20/20 spiritual vision. You're a new Dreamer! Think with imagination!"

The result? We'll be able to put God's way and will to the test and we will conclude, "His way is good, perfect, and pleasing because He is good, perfect, and pleasing. I want to go His way. I long to go His way. I will go His way. It's outrageously reasonable!" (Box 12:2 summarizes the interaction between our images and beliefs.)

Creators Who Choose Courageously:
Volitional Beings Who Purpose—Purposes/Pathways

"Courageous Creators." What a wonderful aspect of the *imago Dei*. As God entered the creation business, making beings with a will capable of rejecting Him, so He gave us the capacity to enter chaos courageously to create beauty from ashes. He alone creates *ex nihilo* (out of nothing). He is the Creator; we are under-creators, under-shepherds, and under-scientists who shape life using the raw material that He called into existence.

As God followed the eternal purposes He laid out before the foundation of the world, so we are beings who act and interact purposefully. We are not laboratory rats ruled by conditioned responses, nor are we dogs controlled by operant conditioning.

Box 12:2
Summary of Images and Beliefs

♦ Images create a reality, while beliefs reflect on reality.

♦ Images concoct an identity, while beliefs set direction based upon identity.

♦ Images organize perceptions, while beliefs organize direction.

♦ Images organize perceptions into a composite view (editorial bias or slant—what my story is), while beliefs organize specific rules, assumptions, and overlays (how I tell my story and decide to live my story).

♦ Images form impressions that represent my interpretation of events, while beliefs form words into ideas that have the power to control how I respond to my world.

♦ Images are my perceptions of life that formulate concepts about where life is found, while beliefs are my direction in life that provide illumination for the route I will take to find what I perceive to be life (mindset).

♦ Images are explanations of life—my unique way of explaining the world so that I can maintain a sense of control, while beliefs are my approaches to the life I perceive. Beliefs develop a strategy to approach life according to how I conceptualize life.

♦ Images lead to concepts—relatively fixed representations of reality, while beliefs lead to strategies—a set of relational rules by which I live in order to quench my thirsts.

♦ Images interpret and represent input—an ingrained way of interpreting my world, a convenient synopsis of life, while beliefs direct actions and apply concepts—direct my responses to the world by providing a strategy for finding life. Beliefs apply concepts by organizing the rules by which I live.

We act on our universe and interact with other personal beings. We are responsible beings choosing how we live and whom we love. The courage to choose is at the core of humanity. We act freely, responsibly, and actively out of our wills.

Volitional Purposing: Volitional Interaction

We are volitional beings. "Volition" comes from the Latin word for "will." Our actions are teleological—movement directed toward an end and shaped by a goal. We act purposefully in goal-oriented ways (pathways). We decide, choose, set goals, follow plans, and pursue characteristic behaviors and styles of relating (purposes).

God empowered us with a will free to choose according to our nature. Adam and Eve had innocent natures with the capacity to choose between good and evil, God and the Devil.

Joshua, in his stouthearted challenge to the people of his day, works from the biblical assumption that they can choose. "And if it seems evil unto you to serve the LORD, choose you this day whom you will serve" (Joshua 24:15, KJV). Joshua wisely acknowledges that they will make their volitional choice (choose you this day) about their relational motivation (whom you will serve) based upon their rational direction (if it seems evil unto you to serve the LORD).

We have the capacity to choose a direction and pursue it through our actions. Proverbs 16:1-3, 9; 19:21; 20:5, 11; 21:2; and James 4:1-4 teach that our behavior is purposeful and motivated. We pursue a path toward a purpose—volitional action. More than that, we pursue a path toward a relational purpose because our deepest purpose is to quench our thirst for relationship—volitional *inter*action.

"All a man's *ways* (*dareke*) seem innocent to him, but motives are weighed by the LORD" (Proverbs 16:2, emphasis added). "Ways" pictures a road trodden down by constant walking or pacing. It's the brown patch in the lawn, continually beaten down by everyone taking a shortcut. "Ways" portrays a course of life or mode of action in pursuit of a goal. It's the journey we choose to take, the customary way we decide to live, the manner of life that characterizes us.

The psalmist uses the same word when he speaks of standing in the way of the sinner and walking in the way of the righteous (Psalm 1). Sinners follow a characteristic *pathway* and so do saints. So important is the concept that Solomon uses the Hebrew word at least seventy-two times in Proverbs, eight times in Proverbs 16 alone.

In Ecclesiastes, Solomon bemoans the absence of a satisfying life purpose. He calls it vanity—emptiness, futility, soap bubbles, nothingness. Lacking a sense of purpose, image bearers are unfulfilled, unsatisfied, bored, and prime candidates for satanic counterfeits. We're goal-oriented people, and our goal is always, ultimately, to find relational happiness and purpose, however we may define them.

King David, deciding to forego his calling to lead his men against God's enemies (2 Samuel 11:1), sleeps the fitful sleep of boredom. Pacing the roof of his palace, he spies a beautiful woman bathing. He sleeps with her. Impregnates her. Successfully schemes to have her husband murdered. By deciding not to follow God's purpose, David left himself vulnerable to Satan's counterfeit purposes. Instead of defeating the enemies of God, David killed a servant of God.

David countered God's design for his soul, for anyone's soul. Aubrey Johnson notes that in our original design we are forceful and purposeful individuals with a will to do God's will (Johnson, *The Vitality of the Individual*, p. 33). David should have chosen to use his driving force, determination, activity, energy, vitality, and power toward God's purposes. He could have creatively directed his actions to achieve God's good goals.

John Owen, in *Sin and Temptation*, offers a biblical psychology of the energized, empowered will.

♦   The will is the power of action (p. xix).
♦   The will is designed to choose what appears to the mind to be good. It cleaves to what is perceived to be beautiful and chooses the good the mind discovers (p. xix). The will consents to nothing unless it is perceived by the mind as good (p. 65).

- The will follows the mind, which follows the imagination. "Sin begins in and with the deception of the imagination. The mind is the leading faculty of the soul. When the mind fixes upon an object or course of action, the will and affections follow suit. They are incapable of any other consideration" (p. 36).
- The will, through repeated acts, develops an inclination. A theme or pattern of willing, choosing, and acting is set. We develop a characteristic approach to life (p. 65).

Notice how Owen highlights the interaction between the will, the mind, and affections. This is why I've chosen the summarizing phrase "volitional interaction." It implies, first, that the will acts only in interaction with the mind and soul. Our chosen actions are always the result of our deeply held beliefs about the truest and most beautiful sources of life.

Second, volitional interaction also implies that our actions have a communal, interactive nature. Because we are relationally motivated, the choices that we make reflect our ideas about how we can best interact with God and others to quench our thirsts. As noted earlier, we purpose to pursue (volitional interaction) what we perceive (rational direction) to be pleasing (relational motivation) (Genesis 3:6).

Volitional Pathways: Volitional Patterning

So why do we do what we do, behave as we behave, choose what we choose? As counselors, how can we assist counselees to assess not only their actions, but also the motivations behind their actions? Discerning actions and motivations requires an understanding of volitional *pathways*—patterned intentions, goals, and purposes.

Recall what Owen said. "The will, through repeated acts, develops an inclination"—a theme, style, or pattern of willing, choosing, acting, and relating. We not only pursue a path toward a purpose, we also tread a beaten path to fulfill our purposes.

In our idyllic state, that was good. In our redeemed state, it can be wonderful. It's what New Testament writers describe as "character." Peter, for instance, first reminds us of our new nature, then urges us to make every effort to cultivate our new character through adding to our faith goodness, knowledge, self-control, perseverance, godliness, brotherly kindness, and love (2 Peter 1:5-8). First we habituate our minds (mind-set) toward the truth of God's love, then we habituate our actions and interactions (purposeful pathways) toward Christlike character that loves God and others (affections/lovers). The fruit of the Spirit depicts traits that reflect the character of Christ. Character is our approach to life based upon our assessments about life that lead to the affections we cherish in life.

New Testament writers use similar concepts like "walk," "manner of life," and "conversation." All these images describe life as a journey in which our will decides what pathways to pursue, what style of interacting with others to follow, and what purposes and intentions to set as life goals.

In the fallen state, volitional patterning is ugly. We keep doing the same foolish thing time after time. "As a dog returns to its vomit, so a fool repeats his folly" (Proverbs 26:11). That's ugly.

Peter makes it uglier. "Of them the proverbs are true: 'A dog returns to its vomit,' and, 'A sow that is washed goes back to her wallowing in the mud'" (2 Peter 2:22). Peter is referring to false teachers who exploit people with myths (2 Peter 2:3) and deny our

Lord's affectionate sovereignty (2 Peter 2:1-2). They are springs without water because they have forsaken the Spring of Living Water (2 Peter 2:17). They are slaves of depravity, slaves to whatever has mastered them (2 Peter 2:19). They progress from rational sin (denying God's affectionate sovereignty) to relational sin (forsaking the Spring of Living Water) to volitional sin (slaves of depravity). So what do they do? They keep returning to their own vomit. Their sinful mindsets produce habituated foolishness—the character of the False Seducer, the sins of the flesh, selfish pathways.

As counselors, our calling is to help our counselees, especially those entangled in besetting sins, to evaluate their actions and the root motivations behind their interactions. Solomon informs us "Even a child is known by his actions, by whether his conduct is pure and right" (Proverbs 20:11). As we counsel, we need to detect patterns. How does this person relate? What are his characteristic relational patterns? What are her typical styles of relating? What typical goals do I notice? What purposes do I discern? What volitional pathways do I detect?

Volitional Lifestyles: Volitional Ways of Relating

When we identify these purposeful pathways, we need to go deeper. "The purposes (motivational structure, volitional styles, personal agenda, purposeful actions) of a man's heart are deep waters, but a man of understanding draws them out" (Proverbs 20:5, parentheses added). We need to systematize biblical categories of characteristic pathways, and then apply them to the unique person we're counseling.

Biblical counselor David Powlison encourages counselors to cull the Scriptures for themes and patterns useful for developing diagnostic categories. "In the very generality and universality of God's revelation, the Bible invites systematic inquiry. The writers of the Bible intended to provide eyeglasses that enable all vision" (Powlison, *Questions at the Crossroads*, p. 37).

Powlison uses Galatians 5:19-21 as an example. There Paul lists fifteen representative examples of works of the flesh and closes with "and the like" indicating that his list, though representative, is not exhaustive. From Paul's list, we could develop systematic biblical diagnostic models using the works of the flesh and the fruit of the Spirit.

I've used Proverbs as an example. Solomon identifies four common foolish pathways: the sluggard, the mocker, the wicked, and the simple. In every case, Solomon exposes the unique relational, rational, volitional, and emotional lifestyle that each type of fool reflects. He reveals the recurring patterns of relating and the habituated pathways of attempting to make life work without God. Box 12:3 offers an introduction to these concepts, providing one biblical classification of foolish mindsets leading to self-centered pathways of purposing.

As I overview them, remember that these are simply *sample* sinful volitional purposes. They are not the only ways to characterize sinful patterns, yet they are helpful for counselors, pastors, spiritual friends, and soul physicians to conceptualize typical self-centered pathways.

Box 12:3

Sample Sinful Volitional Lifestyle Pathways/Purposes

- ◆ Sinful pathways are recurring patterns of fleshly, self-centered purposing.
- ◆ Sinful pathways are habituated ways we attempt to make our lives work without God—self-sufficient purposes and intentions.

The Sluggard: The Irresponsible Fool
1. Relationally: "Cater to me. Take care of me. Smother me."
2. Rationally: "I'm a baby. I'm overpowered." (Proverbs 12:24, 27)
3. Volitionally: Lazy (Proverbs 6:6-11; 15:19; 22:13; 24:30-31)
4. Emotionally: Overwhelmed (Proverbs 13:4)
5. Pull: Rescue

The Simple: The Clueless Fool
1. Relationally: "Be scared for me. Worry about me."
2. Rationally: "I'm shallow." (Proverbs 1:4, 22, 32; 14:15)
3. Volitionally: Naïve (Proverbs 7:7; 9:4, 6; 22:3)
4. Emotionally: Dense (Proverbs 9:16-17; 14:15)
5. Pull: Worry and Pity Mixed with Frustration

The Mocker: The Controlling Fool
1. Relationally: "Submit to me. I'm powerful."
2. Rationally: "I'm a rebel." (Proverbs 3:34)
3. Volitionally: Arrogant (Proverbs 3:34; 9:7-8; 14:9)
4. Emotionally: Angry (Proverbs 15:12; 22:10; 29:10)
5. Pull: Push Away/Get Angry (Proverbs 9:12; 24:9; 29:8)

The Wicked: The Retaliating Fool
1. Relationally: "Be scared of me. I'm evil and dangerous."
2. Rationally: "I'm an enemy." (Proverbs 2:22; 11:18; 12:5; 21:29; 26:24-26)
3. Volitionally: Malicious (Proverbs 2:12-15; 4:14-17; 26:26)
4. Emotionally: Cruel (Proverbs 18:3)
5. Pull: Fear, Shame, Anger, and Resentment

Solomon identifies four volitional lifestyles. First, he characterizes *the sluggard or the irresponsible fool* in Proverbs 6:6-11; 12:24, 27; 13:4; 15:19; 22:13; and 24:30-31. This person's relational style screams, "Cater to me! Take care of me! Smother me!" "Irresponsible" pictures their typical volitional pathway.

If you find yourself in a relationship with that type of person, you feel yourself pulled to rescue them. You have to fix them, make life work for them, because they seem so helpless. Everything is too hard for them. They present the image of a baby, so you feel drawn to baby them.

In their mindset, their pathway is always blocked with thorns too prickly to approach. They choose to avoid the hard work of weed whacking in a fallen world. One thing they are prepared with—excuses. "There's a lion in the way!" "I'll just die if I have to face that." They're great starters, perhaps, but horrible finishers. They may shoot their game, but never roast it. They crave a lot, but risk so little. Can you picture counselees like this? Co-workers? Bosses? Teens in your Sunday School class?

How do you help? First, don't rescue. Sluggards must face and feel the consequences of their irresponsibility. They need to taste the emptiness of unpursued purposes and the hunger of game not roasted. Second, share. Tell how you feel pulled to baby them. Paint them a picture. Third, stretch them. Explain that you see so much more in them.

Next Solomon portrays the purposeful pathway of *the simple or the clueless fool* who plays the role of the naïve innocent (Proverbs 1:4, 22, 32; 7:7; 8:5; 9:4, 13, 16; 14:15, 18; 19:25; 21:11; 22:3; 27:12). Simple fools act as if they are dumb and dumber; they act like the stereotypical dumb blond or clueless jock.

Simple fools are complacent and their complacency destroys them. Worse than that, they love playing the fool, being morally dimwitted because it provides them with an escape clause when consequences come. They put themselves in harm's way then swear they don't know how trouble swallowed them (Proverbs 22:3). Call them "Gullible Gus" and "Dense Denise."

When you interact with them, you feel scared for them. Protective of them. They pull pity and worry from you. You feel helpless because they seem so clueless. You wonder if they are "ever going to get it." At the same time, you sense yourself fighting frustration. If you release your sarcastic side, you'll hear yourself saying, "Duh! Hello. Get a clue. Join the real world. Engage brain."

In some ways it seems we're raising an entire generation named, "Shallow Hal." How do we counsel them? It's interesting to note in Proverbs 19:25 and 21:1 Solomon's observation that when we punish a mocker, the simple take notice. It appears that Solomon is saying, "Confront the simple repeatedly with concrete examples of the consequences of their simpleton style of managing life. Paint them pictures in living color that force them to face reality."

Third, Solomon introduces us to *the mocker or the controlling fool*. His style of making life work without God requires him to try to overpower others. He plays god, making others submit to him as servants.

Where the mocker travels, divisiveness follows. Strife, quarrels, and insults mark the mocker's pathway. Innocent victims lie strewn in the mocker's wake.

A mocker's arrogant anger might intimidate you; it might push you away; or it might make you angry. The mocker loves any of these results. He is always looking for a fight, always ready to brawl, and he's never prepared for peace.

How do you respond to this style of relating? Weakness will not do. Appeasement won't work. Neither will tit-for-tat anger. You will need soft but firm answers. Matter-of-fact confrontation that spells out boundaries and enforces consequences. Tough love is necessary.

Solomon's fourth volitional lifestyle is *the wicked or the retaliating fool*. The wicked seem to be an intensified form of the mocker, if that is possible. Whereas the mocker intimidates, the wicked will hurt and harm.

When relating with wicked people, you feel threatened, and the threat may be very real. The wicked sow shame and reap resentment. Their style highlights malicious cruelty and sly deception.

Solomon notes that they put up a bold front, implying that one intervention is to call their bluff, but you must do it with wise boundaries and an awareness of their propensity for doing harm. Solomon also emphasizes exposure. They may or may not respond to personal confrontation. If they don't, go public. Involve others in a group confrontation, church discipline, or even contact the authorities, if warranted.

Sluggard, simple, mocker, wicked: four sample styles of sinful volitional pathways. As we counsel, we need to identify these and other characteristic patterns of purposeful interacting and expose them in and to our counselees.

Where We've Been and Where We're Heading

Reality is relational because the Trinity is communal. Bearing God's image, relationality is our soul's holy of holies. We are relationally motivated to quench the thirst of our soul. Thoughts, of course, are vital, and actions are essential, but not just any thoughts or any actions. Our actions evidence the thoughts of our heart about the source of relational satisfaction—we pursue what we perceive to be pleasing.

We're beginning to understand something of the intricate interworking of the human personality. But how do relational motivation, rational direction, and volitional interaction relate to our emotional reactions and our physical actions? In Act Two, Scene VI, Chapter 13 of our love story/grand adventure, we'll explore Singers and Actors and how our emotions and bodies interact with our souls, minds, and wills. Why did God bestow emotions upon us and clothe us in a body? Let's find out.

Caring for Your Soul: Personal Applications

1. What captures your imagination?

    a. Who or what do you perceive to be most lovely and loving? Most pleasing and
        pleasant?

    b. How can you deepen your appreciation and apprehension of God's beauty
        and majesty?

2. Life is a battle for your mind (mindset) between the world and the Word.

    a. What mental impressions and images of life is the world attempting to squeeze
        into your brain? What fleshly mindsets do you sometimes conform to?

    b. What mental impressions and images of life from God's Word can you meditate
        upon to transform and renew your mind? What beautiful, majestic images of God
        absorb your thinking?

3. Seek to identify your characteristic patterns/pathways of purposing, choosing,
    acting, and interacting.

    a. Meditate upon the fruit of the Spirit in Galatians 5:22-23. Which of the fruit do
        you see yourself most clearly manifesting? How? Why? Which other fruit can
        you begin to cultivate further? How?

    b. Review Box 12:3 regarding sinful volitional lifestyles from Proverbs and read
        the accompanying verses. Which type of foolish pathway are you most prone to
        when you are not filled with the Spirit? Why? Develop a spiritual action plan for
        putting off this pattern/pathway/purpose.

Caring for Others: Ministry Implications

♦ **Mind Renewal Is Vital:** We do not simply aim for a change in circumstances, a change in behavior, or a change in feelings. We aim for a renewed mind. We seek to discern the controlling images and ideas that develop patterned mindsets. Then we enlighten counselees to the mindsets of the world, urging them to put them off, as we also enlighten them to the mindsets of the Spirit, helping them to put them on.

♦ **Mind Renewal Equals "Narrative Renewal":** We sustain, heal, reconcile, and guide our spiritual friends to put off the old satanic narrative of self/works/law, and put on the Christ narrative of grace/faith/love. Narrative renewal focuses upon the images and ideas, pictures and propositions, themes and plot lines that guide our perceptions of reality.

♦ **Mind Renewal Always Relates to Relational Thirsts:** We assist people to renew their narrative of where life is found—in the Father, of where love is found—in the Son, and of where purpose and power are found—in the Spirit. We help people renew their minds on the basis of the mercies of God, leading to worship of God.

♦ **Counseling, Discipleship, Teaching, Preaching, Mentoring—All Ministry— Must Be Done with Imagination:** We need passion, creativity, stories, parables, and other aids.

♦ **Biblical Counseling Counsels the Habits of the Heart and the Motivational Structure of the Will:** God's Word discerns the thoughts and intents of the heart. We expose the heart through a biblical evaluation of beliefs that lie beneath actions. Seek to determine what motivates specific behaviors and chosen relational styles. Seek to identify godly character patterns/pathways and fan them into flame. Seek to identify ungodly character patterns/pathways and put out those fires. Put them out by exposing the motivational structure behind the specific patterns/pathways of purposing. Put on Christlikeness by training the person in the process of daily sanctification. (See Act IV: The Reconciliation.)

CHAPTER THIRTEEN

SINGERS AND ACTORS: ALIVE TO LIFE

"Our emotions connect our inner world to the ups and downs of life. Sometimes the connection is more than we can bear" (Dan Allender and Tremper Longman, *The Cry of the Soul*, p. 19).

"Real life is physical. . . . There is no good trying to be more spiritual than God. God never meant man to be a purely spiritual creature. That is why He uses material things like bread and wine to put the new life into us. We may think this rather crude and unspiritual. God does not: He invented eating. He likes matter. He invented it" (C. S. Lewis, *Mere Christianity*, p. 55).

The Boys of Summer

In *The Boys of Summer*, Roger Kahn chronicles the 1950s Brooklyn Dodgers. Perhaps the most famous boy of summer was center fielder Duke Snider. Though enshrined at Cooperstown in Baseball's Hall of Fame, Snider fought inner demons of fear. Blessed with an extraordinarily gifted body, Snider battled the stress and anxiety of great expectations.

Charlie Dressen, Dodgers manager, once asked Roger Kahn, "Ever notice what Snider does after he's walked by the pitcher?"

"Nope."

"Well, watch the next time."

Kahn watched as the umpire called, "Ball Four" and Snider walked. He saw him smile and finally relax. He understood Dressen's point—Snider preferred to hold the bat on his shoulder, not risking failure, rather than swing and miss. For all his great physical talent, Duke Snider bore a greater emotional burden. The pressure to succeed crushed him emotionally.

Rather like the *Fortune 500* executive I told you about. Remember? "I just want to be invisible." Life in a fallen world has a way of beating us down, tempting us to run and hide—to hold the bat on our shoulder.

Rather like Adam: "I was afraid, because I was naked, so I hid."

If emotions are so distressing, why did God create us with feelings? Emotions often seem more a curse than a blessing. In Christian circles, emotions are frequently seen as the "black sheep" of the image bearing family. "More harm than good." "Suppress them." "Ignore them." "Don't have them."

The body fares little better, perhaps worse, in our mind's eye. "We'd be better off without it." "The flesh is evil," we repeat, not realizing that such thinking smacks of worldly philosophy, not biblical theology.

Somehow we've forgotten that when God paused to ponder His image bearers, He pointed out that they, emotions and bodies included, were "very good" (Genesis 1:31).

Not only was hunger God's idea, feelings were His, too. Not only did He give them to us, He experiences them Himself. God is an emotional being. Read that again. Don't dodge it. God is an emotional being. Father gets angry. Son weeps. Spirit grieves. The Trinity emotes.

Hunger, feelings, and bodies—all God's idea. "The LORD God formed the man from *the dust of the ground* and breathed into his nostrils the breath of life, and the man became a living being" (Genesis 2:7, emphasis added). We could hardly have been fruitful, increasing in number, filling the earth, subduing it, and ruling over it without bodies. We could hardly have worked the Garden, guarded and protected, nurtured and expanded it without bodies.

Singers Who Experience Deeply: Emotional Beings Who Feel—Mood States

The question is so typical that it has become trite, "How do you feel about that?" We even mock it, "I feel your pain." We are awash in an emotionally shallow society. Do we throw the baby out with the bathwater? Or do we recognize False Seducer's counterfeit and choose Worthy Groom's real deal, the genuine article?

The real deal is *imago Dei* emotionality. The real deal is *coram Deo* emotionality. Like our Creator, we are Singers who experience deeply. All our feelings are in-relationship-to-God feelings.

Dan Allender and Tremper Longman explain that emotions are windows to the soul. All emotions, positive or painful, open doors to the nature of reality. Emotions link our inner and outer world. But we want to escape the reality of both.

> The Scriptures reveal that this absence of feelings is often a refusal to face the sorrow of life and the hunger for heaven; it is not the mark of maturity, but rather the boast of evil (Isaiah 47:8; Revelation 18:7). Our refusal to embrace our emotions is often an attempt to escape the agony of childbirth and buttress the illusion of a safe world. It is an attempt to deal with a God who does not relieve our pain (Allender and Longman, *The Cry of the Soul*, p. 23).

Our emotions reveal our deepest questions about God. They vocalize the inner working of our souls. Listen to and ponder your emotions to discern what your heart is doing with God and others. They are a voice that can tell us how we are dealing with a fallen, hurtful world. Emotions force open the stuck window of our soul, compelling us to consider how we are facing life.

Every person lives a unique story, composed of moments of great joy and tragic pain. Each moment of pleasure and pain compels us to ask uniquely personal questions: "Why did my dad abuse me? . . . Why did my mom die before I had a chance to know her? . . . What is God's purpose in giving me my musical gift?" But every personal question reflects a far deeper, existential struggle: "What is the nature of life? And who or what is God?" Consequently, although our emotions are provoked by the various individual themes of our story, they all echo a common question: "Is God good?" (Allender and Longman, *The Cry of the Soul*, p. 42).

Emotions are God-given. They are not satanic. Adam had them before the Fall. God has them. Christ has them. In themselves, they are not sinful. They are beneficial, and yes, even beautiful.

The psalmist understood this. In Psalm 139, the classic passage describing God's utmost care in creating us, emotionality is the one aspect of our inner personality specifically referenced. "For you created my *inmost being*; you knit me together in my mother's womb" (Psalm 139:13, emphasis added). The Hebrew term translated "inmost being" is actually "kidneys." In Psalm 73:21 and Proverbs 23:16 the term indicates the place of sorrow and rejoicing, respectively. In the *Tractate Berakoth* of the *Babylonian Talmud* the kidneys prompt or urge to action by aroused emotions (p. 61). Hans W. Wolff notes that the Semitic languages used terms for kidneys, reins, stomach, bowels, and womb to describe the various states of feeling (Wolff, *Anthropology of the Old Testament*, pp. 62-63). As we experience an emotion in our physical being, so we feel an emotion in our psychological being. That's why we say things like, *"I have butterflies in my stomach."* God created your inmost being, your kidneys, your emotions.

Emotional Experiencing: Emotional Reaction

What are emotions? Emotions are our God-given capacity to experience our world and to respond subjectively to those experiences. This capacity includes the ability to react internally and experience a full-range of both positive (pleasant) and negative (painful) inner feelings.

The very root of the word "emotion" is *motere*, the Latin verb "to move," plus the prefix "e" meaning "away," thus, "to move away." This suggests that a tendency to act is implicit in every emotion. All emotions are, in essence, impulses to react, the instant plans for handling life that God has instilled in us. God designed our emotions to put us in motion. They represent a quick response that motivates action. Emotions signal the mind to go into high gear (see Daniel Goleman, *Emotional Intelligence*).

Emotions play a crucial editorial role that forces us to do a double-check, to look outward and inward. Goleman calls them our "psychological sentinel" that connects us to our inner and outer world.

Once connected, we react to our external and internal world. What we desire, think, and choose (our inner world) determines our emotional reaction to our external situation (our outer world). What we think (rational direction) satisfies our longing for relationship (relational motivation) provides the direction we choose to pursue (volitional interaction) and determines our experiential response (emotional reaction) to our world.

Consider a basic formula for understanding emotions: *E.S. + I.P. = E.R. Our External Situation plus our Internal Perception leads to our Emotional Response.* Box 13:1 pictures this equation.

Box 13:1

Understanding Our Emotional Responses

External Situation		*Internal Perception*		*Emotional Response*
◆ Negative Action	+	Biblical Belief	=	Legitimate Painful Emotion (Sorrow, Sadness, etc.)
◆ Negative Action	+	Unbiblical Belief	=	Illegitimate Painful Emotion (Hatred, Despair, etc.)
◆ Positive Action	+	Biblical Belief	=	Legitimate Positive Emotion (Joy, Peace, etc.)
◆ Positive Action	+	Unbiblical Belief	=	Illegitimate Positive Emotion (Pride, Self-Sufficiency, etc.)

Your boss says to you, "You blew it." Your emotions react to this external event *and to* your internal images and ideas. If you think, "I must have my boss's approval," you will respond with illegitimate negative emotions such as anger, depression, hopelessness, or hatred. If, on the other hand, you think, "I would like my boss's approval, but, with or without it, I know that I am accepted by God," you will respond with legitimate painful emotions such as sorrow, disappointment, or remorse (if you were truly in the wrong).

The key to our emotional reaction is our perception of the meaning behind the event. Thus, events determine whether our emotions are pleasant or painful, but longings, beliefs, and goals determine whether our emotional reaction is holy or sinful (see Larry Crabb, *Understanding People*).

Obviously, our emotions are useful, beneficial, and very good. Our emotions, however, may be hurtful, harmful, and very bad. We are to be angry, but not sinfully so. Anger can be good; it can also be evil. So it is with all emotions and moods. Designed for mood order, we experience mood disorders and can experience reordered moods.

Mood Order

As previously emphasized, human beings tend to develop rather patterned approaches to life. Relationally, we cling to our Creator or to created realities—*pure or impure affections, lovers of the soul, or idols of the heart*. We worship God, our Spring of Living Water, or we dig broken cisterns that can hold no water. We enjoy intimacy with the Worthy Groom or we weary ourselves pursuing false lovers.

Rationally, we develop *mindsets* that persist over time. Either we direct our lives according to the mindset of the spirit/Spirit or we pilot our lives off course according to the mindset of the flesh. Either we guide our lives along the narrow path of wisdom or along the broad road of foolishness.

Volitionally, we develop *purposeful pathways* of intentional interacting. We tread a path toward what we think will satisfy the hunger of our heart. We habituate ourselves either toward willing God's will or willing our own will. "Your will be done," or "My will be done."

Emotions are no exception. We not only experience instantaneous emotional responses, we also encounter ongoing *mood states*. A mood is a background feeling or emotional state that persists over time. It is less intense and longer lasting than emotions. My mood is my prevailing tone or coloring, my state or frame of mind. In a sense, it is my emotional outlook that occurs both at a particular time and also settles deep inside me over time (see Goleman, *Emotional Intelligence*).

As with emotions, moods are the intersection of our emotional/feeling responses and our rational attitude/perceptions. My mood reacts both to the external events of my life and to the internal longings, images, ideas, goals, and actions of my soul.

Created by God, moods, like emotions, were a very good thing. Father intricately fashioned His image bearers to experience a variety of positive emotional states, the most optimal moods. Our moods and emotions have a metaphysical function or they would not exist. They contain vital signals of readiness not simply for action, but for interaction, and rest from interaction. They signal when we need to interact and when we need to come apart (before we fall apart). Jesus identified within Himself moods that led Him to seek solitude (Mark 1:45; Luke 5:16) and that led Him to engage in intimate interaction (Luke 5:15; Mark 3:1-6).

Our moods guide us to mobilize our resources for wise relating. They work with our self-awareness so that we can become attentive to our emotional states as our inner person interacts with our outer world. Moods motivate, or better, moods jolt us into awareness, promote pondering, and motivate us toward appropriate interaction. Taken together, we can define mood order as:

♦ My God-given ability to feel my own feelings, to sense my own life experiences, and to become self-aware of my prevailing emotional mood state(s).
♦ My God-given thermostat that quickly gauges the relational temperature outside and my personal temperature inside.
♦ My God-given capacity to respond courageously, lovingly, and wisely to my inner and outer world. I perceive what I feel and I choose how I respond.

What was the mood process like for Adam and Eve? All order ultimately arises from connection. So when Adam felt happiness and joy in the presence of Eve, his entire being became focused on connecting, attaching. "I like being with her. I want to be with her. When we are together, I am outrageously happy."

Sinless Adam and Eve also could have experienced legitimate sadness—a sadness because of absence that impelled them to reconnect. Adam is working in one part of the Garden. Eve in another. Happy in her work, but aware of a growing sense of sadness, a developing mood of aloneness, Eve stops. She ponders. She recognizes the source—she misses her hubby. She runs to him, throws her arms around him, kisses him impetuously. "Just wanted you to know how much I missed you!" Separation, whether physical or psychological, is a basic cause of human sadness. Sadness provides a driving force to restore attachment, in the same way that hunger impels us to eat.

This ancient, biblical sense of mood corresponds to how other pre-modern people understood mood. Before AD 900 in Middle English, mood meant "spirit, courage, mind." In the Old Saxon, mood meant "courage and spirit." Mood had a very positive connotation. It was always correlated with courage, movement, spirit, aliveness, passion, and energy. So different from our modern or post-modern thinking. "He's so moody!" "She's in such a mood!" That could be a dynamic compliment, depending on the nature of the mood.

Mood Disorder

All disorder ultimately arises from a state of disconnection. Separated from the life of God, we demand one another to become like gods. When our fellow finite beings fail us, we face personal dis-integration. We're shamefully exposed as false trusters. The emotional result is disordered moods:

♦   My inability to sense accurately and experience my own inner and outer world and my failure to maintain a healthy self-awareness of my prevailing emotional mood state(s).
♦   My inability to read accurately my emotional thermostat so I inaccurately gauge the relational temperature outside and my personal temperature inside.
♦   My inability to respond to my inner and outer world courageously, lovingly, and wisely.

In mood order, we perceive unpleasant or distressful moods as messages sent from the soul to the body (from the mind to the brain). The message is communicating: "Necessary changes requested. Please reply ASAP! Thank you." The symptom (the distressed mood) is thus seen as a potential gift. It is like the warning light in our cars reminding us to "check under the hood."

In mood disorder, we misperceive our distressed mood and respond in non-God ways. We attempt to manage our misperceived moods self-sufficiently. (In Act Three, Adultery, we'll explore more about mismanaged moods.)

Mood Reorder

The False Seducer wants our moods to overwhelm and control us, to direct us away from God. Or, at least he wants us to respond to them by entering survival mode. Overwhelming moods lead to survival mode.

Jesus came to give us life, and that abundantly (*perisson*). "Abundant" means beyond what is necessary, surplus, left over, greatly enlarged. It is used of the abundance left over after the feeding of the 5,000. Spoiling! Jesus came to spoil us. Resurrection power allows us to do more than survive. We can thrive (2 Corinthians 1:3-11; Philippians 3:7-15). We can move from anger to love, from despair to hope, and from fear to faith. Resurrection power offers fresh, creative energy, and a reawakening of courage—of mood. As Paul Tournier insightfully describes it:

The person matures, develops, becomes more creative, not because of the deprivation in itself, but through his own active response to misfortune, through the struggle to come to terms with it and morally to overcome it—even if in spite of everything there is not cure . . . Events give us pain or joy, but our growth is determined by our personal response to both, by our inner attitude (Tournier, *Creative Suffering*, pp. 28-29).

In reordered, redeemed moods, intense moods lead to a thriving mode.

In Act IV, Reconciliation, we'll learn more about managing our moods. Here's my desire now: recognize how marvelous moods can be when managed in Christ and recognize how pernicious they can be when mismanaged under Satan. Appreciate your moods as God-given sources of instant insight into your inner and outer world. Enjoy the usefulness of reordered moods in a disjointed world, which include:

- My God-given ability to become aware of my moods, whether pleasant or unpleasant, and to accept that I am experiencing that mood.
- My God-given ability to face and feel whatever mood I am experiencing, allowing it to grant me insight into my inner self and my external situation.
- My God-given ability to bring rationality to my emotionality by coming to understand the sources of my moods and my resources to manage my moods (responding wisely to my inner and outer world).
- My God-given ability to bring volitionality to my emotionality by choosing how I will manage my moods instead of allowing them to manage me (responding courageously to my inner and outer world).
- My God-given ability to bring relationality to my emotionality by allowing my moods to motivate me toward deeper connection or reconnection with God, others, and myself (responding lovingly to my inner and outer world).

Emotional Beings and Physical Beings

Emotions truly are a bridge between our inner and outer worlds. Think of the word "feeling." Feeling is a tactile word suggesting something that is tangible, physical, touchable, and palpable. "I feel the keyboard as I type." "I feel the soft comfortable chair beneath me." "I feel my sore back and stiff wrists as they cry out, 'Give it a rest!'"

We also use this physical word, "feeling," to express emotions. "I feel sad." "I feel happy." "I feel joy." "I feel anger." It's no surprise that we use this one word in these two ways—physical and emotional. Our body feels physically what our emotions feel metaphysically. When I'm nervous, my stomach is upset. When I feel deep love, my chest tightens. When I'm anxious, my heart races. When I'm sad, my entire system slows.

The brain is an organ of the body and all physical organs in unglorified bodies in a fallen world can malfunction. My heart, liver, and kidneys can all become diseased, sick. So can the physical organ we call the brain.

It is important to realize that every emotion involves a complex interaction between body and soul. It is dangerous, therefore, to assume that all emotional struggles can be changed by strictly "spiritual means." For some, spirituality includes embracing physical weakness. Certain emotions, especially anxiety and depression, involve physiological components that sometimes may be treated with medication. When we ignore the importance of the body, we misunderstand what it means to trust God. It is wrong to place extra burdens on those who suffer emotionally by suggesting that all they need to make their struggles go away is to surrender to God (see Allender and Longman, *The Cry of the Soul*). (For a counter argument, see Robert Smith, *The Christian Counselor's Medical Desk Reference*.)

It would be equally wrong to suggest that medication is all someone needs. That would be like a pastor entering the cancer ward to talk with a parishioner who was just told she has cancer. "Well, take your medicine. Do chemo. You'll be fine. See ya' later." No! That pastor would support, comfort, talk with, and pray for his parishioner. Disease is always a battleground between False Seducer and Worthy Groom. So, when medicine may sometimes be indicated for certain people with certain emotional battles, spiritual friendship is always indicated. Physicians of the body (and the brain *is* an organ of the physical body) prescribe medication. Physicians of the soul (and the mind *is* an inner capacity and reality of the soul) prescribe grace.

Actors Who Live Contingently:
Physical Beings Who Act—Habituated Tendencies

Much of the world for much of recorded history has seen humanity as an angel in a slot machine, a soul incarcerated in a mass from which it hopes one day to be freed forever, a soul entombed in flesh (John Robinson, *The Body*, p. 14). Not so the biblical view. God gifted us with a physical body perfectly suited to fulfill our calling to reflect Him, relate, rule, and rest.

Body and soul are not antithetical. Psalm 63:1 links them inseparably—my soul thirsts and my body longs. In Hebraic thinking, we do not have a body, we are a body; we are animated bodies (Robinson, *The Body*, pp. 15-22). The flesh (*bāśār* in the Old Testament) is our whole life substance organized in corporal form.

Body (*bāśār* in Hebrew and *sarx* in Greek) represents humanity in a certain type of relationship to God—one of finitude, contingency, neediness, weakness, frailty, and mortality. God is infinite, we are finite. We need Him and what He provides to survive. Wolff notes that *bāśār* equals humanity in our infirmity (2 Chronicles 32:8; Psalm 56:4), always described in terms of restricted, insufficient human powers in contrast to the surpassing power of God (Wolff, *Anthropology of the Old Testament*, p. 30).

In the Garden, Adam and Eve needed the fruit to stay alive. They were perishable, natural creatures, not the Creator. By creation we are connected to the physical world, dependent. Apart from God we are without substantial power; we are impotent.

The body is purely natural, not supernatural, but that's not bad. Only in the Fall does the natural become unnatural. To "walk after the flesh" does not imply that the flesh is evil, for ten of the fifteen sins of the flesh listed in Galatians 5:19-21 have nothing to do with sins of sensuality. "Fleshly" means denying our need for God, trying to live independent from God. To act according to the flesh is to live in limited human strength.

Flesh, as neutral, is humanity living in the world. *Fleshly*, as sinful, is humanity living for the world, through the world, and as if this world is all there is, rather than living for God, through God, and in view of time *and* eternity, earth *and* heaven, the smaller *and* larger story. Fleshly living makes the belly God (Romans 16:18; Philippians

3:19); it governs the whole life by being careful only for the things of this world, not the things of God. "The mind of the flesh stands primarily for a denial of man's dependence upon God and for a trust in what is of human origin" (Robinson, *The Body*, p. 25). Living according to the flesh equals setting ourselves up in the strength of our creatureliness. It represents human self-sufficiency. Fleshly wisdom is trust in our own knowledge and experience. "Cursed is the one who trusts in man, who depends on flesh for his strength and whose heart turns away from the LORD" (Jeremiah 17:5).

Physical Empowering: Physical Action

Our bodies are works of art fashioned by Father who fearfully and wonderfully handcrafted us (Psalm 139:13-16). We are works of God's hand; made, shaped, molded, clothed with skin and flesh, and knit together with bones and sinews (Job 10:3-12). We are not to despise our physicality.

By making us physical beings, God empowered us to fulfill His Creation Mandate. Labor is part of our proper significance and destiny. Genesis 2:15 demonstrates that we are to use our embodied personalities to labor and protect, care and cultivate, guard and expand the Garden. Work transforms our inner being into tangible creations. Work connects us with others in the noble endeavor of leaving behind a better world than we found. Work on planet Earth requires a body—embodied personality.

Our bodies are made of matter (dust of the ground) and matter is energy. Animals also have physical bodies. They are able to live, move, eat, run, fight, breed, climb, chase, and so much more. They have a small reservoir of independent power resident in their bodies. So do we. But unlike animals, we are divinity as well as dust. We can connect to God's spiritual being, to God's spiritual power, which empowers our embodied personalities (see Dallas Willard, *The Spirit of the Disciplines*).

Body by God

What is the connection between our physical bodies and God's spiritual being? Willard, in his psychologically astute work *The Spirit of the Disciplines*, explains.

I believe men and women were designed by God, in the very constitution of their human personalities, to carry out his rule *by meshing* the relatively little power resident in their own bodies with the power inherent in the infinite Rule or Kingdom of God. . . . So long as men and women *remained in touch and harmony with God*, they could *tap the resources* of God's power to carry out the vast, impossible function assigned to them (Willard, *The Spirit of the Disciplines,* p. 54, emphasis added).

Willard makes the astonishingly practical point that we are transformed by contact with God. By creation we were endowed with the capacity to interact with the world around us, including the spiritual. Connection to God empowered our entire being—our embodied personalities. The small reservoir of independent power residing in our bodies was properly ordered and fulfilled through our relationship to God. Our connection to Him was our unifying principle that maintained our embodied personalities with integrity or coherent wholeness (Willard, *The Spirit of the Disciplines*, pp. 64-67).

Body by Self

In the Fall, we were separated from the life of God (Ephesians 2:1-3; 4:17-19). Willard explains the relationship between our separation from God and our depraved and deprived condition.

> But the question is, *what* is human life being cut off from to leave it in such a sad and *depleted* condition? . . . Humans are not only wrong, they are also *wrung*, twisted out of proper shape and proportion. The philosopher Jacob Needleman points out that 'there is an innate element in human nature . . . that can grow and develop through impressions of truth received in the organism like a special nourishing energy.' In other words, *robbed of a vital nutrient, the whole plant sickens.* Robbed of spiritual truth and reality—of right relationship to the spiritual Kingdom of God—the social, psychological, and even the *physical* life of humankind is disordered and, in Ruskin's strictly descriptive sense, corrupt. The evil that we do in our present condition is a reflection of a *weakness caused by spiritual starvation.* . . . As St. Augustine so clearly saw, the deranged condition of humanity is not, at bottom, a positive fact, *but a deprivation* (Willard, *The Spirit of the Disciplines*, pp. 62-63).

The biblical perspective exposes the missing ingredient in our deformed condition. It is the appropriate relation to the spiritual Kingdom of God that is the missing "nutrient" in the human system. "Without it our life is left mutilated, stunted, weakened, and deformed in various stages of disintegration and corruption" (Willard, *The Spirit of the Disciplines*, p. 65).

As a result, we live flesh-oriented and flesh-empowered lives. This is exactly what the Apostle Paul did when he was the Pharisee Saul (Philippians 3:1-15). He put all his confidence in the flesh—his human existence running only on the low battery power inherent in his physical, material body. Paul tried to tame his spirit using only his flesh—a flesh disconnected from God's Spirit. Once transformed from Saul to Paul, he recognized not only the futility of such attempts, but its arrogance (Galatians 1:6-24; 2:15-21; 3:1-14; 5:1-26).

Body Reconnected to and Reenergized by God

If we are a new creature in Christ, if our old man is dead, if our new persona has been given a new heart, why do we still sin? Our inner person, as we will see in Act IV, is born again. We live in the same old world, however, wrestle the same old Devil, and reside in the same old flesh. The flesh—the body—has the capacity for independent operation through the small repository of inherent physical power. The body includes our brain/belly/bones combination of neurons, cells, flesh, chemicals, glands, etc., which we can either offer to God as servants of righteousness or offer to sin as servants of unrighteousness. It can be the locus of ingrained righteousness or ingrained evil (Romans 6:11-23; 16:18; Philippians 3:19). When we live as if the body is all we have, and, therefore, surrender our members to unrighteousness, we are "fleshly." When we live as if this world is all there is and that our temporal time is all the time we have, we are "worldly." As Willard notes:

After conversion our will and conscious intent are for God or "the spiritual," as we've seen with Simon Peter. But the layer upon layer of life experience that is embedded in our bodies, as living organisms born and bred in a world set against or without God, doesn't directly and immediately follow the shift of our conscious will. It largely retains the tendencies in which it has so long lived (Willard, *The Spirit of the Disciplines*, p. 86).

In Romans 6-7, Paul deals with how our body and its members are to be transformed into servants of righteousness. Ingrained tendencies—habits—are to be transformed by our interaction with God, and thus by His grace. Paul outlines our part in this interactive, connective process in Romans 6:13. "Do not offer the parts of your body to sin, as instruments of wickedness, but rather offer yourselves to God, as those who have been brought from death to life; and offer the parts of your body to him as instruments of righteousness." We consciously direct our bodies (bone, brain, belly) in ways that ensure that they will consistently serve righteousness as they previously served sin habitually.

Habituate reliance upon God as we dedicate our bodies to righteous behavior and to all reasonable preparation for righteous behavior makes sin dispensable, even uninteresting and revolting—just as righteousness was revolting to us when our behavior was locked into the sin system. Our desires and delights are changed because our actions and attitudes are based upon the reality of God's Kingdom (Willard, *The Spirit of the Disciplines*, p. 118).

Relationally we pursue affections and lovers of the heart; rationally we follow mindsets; volitionally we choose pathways; emotionally we experience mood states; and physically we habituate who our flesh decides to serve. How do we train and discipline our flesh to serve God? Paul directs us to put to death the deeds of the body through the Spirit (Romans 6:13) and to our members that are upon the earth (Colossians 3:5). He is directing us to undertake the standard activities for training the natural desires toward godliness—the historical spiritual disciplines. They are activities and ways of living that train our entire embodied personalities to depend upon the risen Christ—upon His resurrection power. (We will explore the role of spiritual disciplines during Act IV when we discuss the process of growth in grace.)

Box 13:2

Beloved Image Bearer

Romancers Loving Passionately:
Relational Beings Who Long—Affections
Relational Longings Leading to Relational Motivation: Lovers

Spiritual Beings Who Worship and Commune
Enjoy God
Emulate God
Entrust Self to God
Engage in God's Purposes
Exalt God

Social Beings Who Minister and Connect
Relational Acceptance
Relational Respect

Self-Aware Beings Who Reflect and Are Consciously Aware
Personal Peace: Integrity/Wholeness
Personal Identity: Maturity/Uniqueness

Dreamers Thinking Imaginatively: Rational Beings Who Think—Mindsets
Rational Thinking Leading to Rational Direction: Perceptions
Rational Images: Pictures, Stories, Narratives, Themes
Rational Ideas: Words, Sentences, Plot Lines

Creators Choosing Courageously: Volitional Beings Who Purpose—Purposes
Volitional Choosing Leading to Volitional Interaction: Intentions
Volitional Goals/Strategies: Purposes, Choices, Schemes, Agendas
Volitional Interactions/Styles: Pathways of Living, Patterns of Relating

Singers Experiencing Deeply: Emotional Beings Who Feel—Mood States
Emotional Experiencing Leading to Emotional Reaction: Reactions
Internal Responses: Inner World of Affections/Perceptions/Interactions
External Situation: Outer World of Relationships and Events

Actors Living Contingently: Physical Beings Who Act—Habituated Tendencies
Physical Empowering Leading to Physical Action: Action
Physical Powers: Finite Energy Inherent in Our Physical Bodies
Spiritual Empowering: Infinite Power Available in Connection to Christ

Where We've Been and Where We're Heading

What does relational, rational, volitional, emotional, and physical health look like? How were things meant to be? How were image bearers meant to function? Act Two has addressed these questions, showing how God designed us, soul and body. Box 13:2 portrays God's original design for our created nature.

Knowing how we function when all is well, we can begin to diagnose what went wrong. How are we bent out of shape? In Act Three, The Adultery, we view the bride skipping out on her Worthy Groom during their honeymoon. We see the ghastly transmutation that occurred—idols of the heart, fleshly mindsets, self-centered pathways, ungoverned mood states, and flesh-habituated bodies. It's not pretty, but it's a prerequisite for understanding Act Four, The Reconciliation, where God turns the prostitute into a virgin, and the prodigal into a son. Keep viewing.

Caring for Your Soul: Personal Applications

◆ Take an Emotional Intelligence (EI) Test. What's your EQ—Emotional Quotient? Evaluate yourself using 10 as "Emotionally Mature" and 1 as "Emotionally Immature." (Developed from materials in *Emotional Intelligence* by Daniel Goleman.)

1. I'm aware of my feelings and moods as they occur.
2. I'm able to recognize and name my feelings and moods.
3. I'm able to understand the causes of my feelings and moods.
4. I maintain a sense of ongoing attention to my internal mood states.
5. I'm aware both of my mood and my thoughts about my mood.
6. I actively monitor my moods as the first step in gaining control of them.
7. I soothe my soul in God.
8. I have a sense of self-mastery—frustration tolerance and anger management.
9. I self-regulate my emotions—self-control.
10. I can harness my emotions in the service of a goal.
11. I can stifle my impulses ("passions of the flesh") and delay gratification.
12. I'm a hopeful person.
13. I turn setbacks into comebacks.
14. I'm resilient and longsuffering. I demonstrate perseverance.
15. I practice optimistic self-efficacy—"I can do all things in Christ who strengthens me." "I can meet challenges as they arise." "I'm competent in Christ."
16. I'm learning contentment in whatever state I am (external situation or internal mood).
17. I'm attuned to others, not emotionally tone-deaf. I have the ability to sense another's mood.
18. I have empathy built on self-awareness. I'm open to my own emotions and, therefore, skilled in reading the feelings of others.
19. I practice the creative ability of perceiving the subjective experiences of others.
20. I make another person's pain my own.
21. I can take on the perspective of another person.
22. I forgive.
23. I'm emotionally nourishing toward others.
24. I leave others in a good mood.
25. I'm effective in interpersonal relationships.
26. I help others to soothe their souls in God.
27. I can initiate and coordinate the efforts of a group of people—helping them to move with synchrony and harmony.
28. I can negotiate solutions—mediation, preventing or resolving conflicts.
29. I can make personal connection—ease of entry into an encounter along with the ability to recognize and respond fittingly to people's feelings/concerns.
30. I'm a good team player.
31. I'm skilled at social analysis—being able to detect and have insights into people's feelings, motives, and concerns. Ease of intimacy and rapport.

Caring for Others: Ministry Implications

◆ **Emotions Are God-Given:** Let people have their feelings. Face people's feelings, don't fear them. Since emotional maturity includes experiencing life deeply and acting on feelings wisely, help people to face their feelings. Point them out. Explore them. Think about them. Bring rationality to emotionality. Trialogue with spiritual friends about how they can respond to their emotions, about how their emotions reveal their deepest attitudes toward God.

◆ **Emotional Maturity Is Learned:** Explore where your spiritual friends learned how to handle their emotions. Trace their emotional education to its roots. Then help your spiritual friends unlearn (put off) unhealthy emotional living and learn (put on) healthy emotionality.

◆ **Spiritual Discipline Is Vital to Spiritual Health:** Become a spiritual director. Practice and teach the spiritual disciplines—like prayer, meditation, silence, solitude, simplicity, submission, etc. Help people to tune their whole person—body and soul— to be ready recipients of God's grace.

◆ **The Brain Is an Organ, Too:** Because of the complexity of our physical make-up and because we exist in finite and fallen flesh, medicine may indeed be God's means of care/cure in various instances. Just as the liver, heart, or kidneys can become diseased or damaged, so can the brain. It, too, is a physical organ in our finite, fallen bodies.

ACT THREE:
LOVE'S BETRAYAL—THE ADULTERY

DIAGNOSING THE FALLEN CONDITION OF THE SOUL:
PROBLEMS—FALL

DIRECTOR'S NOTES

Welcome back. Allow me to set the stage for Act Three. The scene has shifted from our physician's office where we've been examining the insides of the soul. The curtain is rising to reveal Paradise moments before it turns hellish.

The main characters are the same, yet totally different. At the outset of Scene I, the heroic Son, Adam, remains the Protective Provider. *Loving passionately* by sacrificing himself to care for Eve and for God's creation. *Thinking wisely* by naming himself and Eve and by envisioning God as good. *Choosing courageously* by moving toward Eve in total openness and by guarding the Garden. *Experiencing deeply* by being aware of and experiencing his loneliness without Eve and his joy with Eve. He bears the *imago Dei* of Trinity by being the Good Shepherd's under-shepherd.

By the end of Scene I, he mutates. *Lusting passionately* as he protects himself by blaming God and Eve and by covering himself with fig leaves. *Thinking foolishly* by concluding Father fails to know best and withholds His best. *Choosing compulsively* as he follows a nature enslaved to the Liar. *Experiencing shallowly* by running from his fears instead of racing to Father. He now bears the image of False Seducer.

At the outset of Scene I, the beautiful Bride, Eve, remains the Collaborative Celebrator. *Loving passionately* by sacrificing herself to complement Adam. *Thinking wisely* by seeing with spiritual eyes Father's beautiful plan. *Choosing courageously* by entrusting herself to Adam's care. *Experiencing deeply* by enjoying the fullness of life offered by God and Adam. She bears the *imago Dei* of Trinity as she gives and receives freely and nurtures what Adam plants and celebrates what they co-create.

By the end of Scene I, she transmutes. *Lusting passionately* after created things rather than her Creator. *Thinking foolishly* by imagining that her greatest pleasure could be in anything other than Father. *Choosing compulsively* to pursue what she mistakenly perceives to be most pleasing. *Experiencing shallowly* by clutching and demanding that her husband be her God. She now bears the image of False Seducer.

How in the world did all this transpire? What are the ramifications? We view the tragic answers to these vital questions in the six scenes of Act Three, The Adultery.

SCENE I, CHAPTER 14: THE SEDUCTION—PARADISE LOST

SCENE II, CHAPTER 15: THE FOUR RAGS OF THE ADULTEROUS SPOUSE

SCENE III, CHAPTER 16: THE RUNAWAY BRIDE—CISTERN DIGGING, PART I

CHAPTER FOURTEEN

THE SEDUCTION: PARADISE LOST

"Eve did not realize that her mind had played a trick on her. It had taken the apparent facts that the enemy had set before her and had justified them, so that they looked reasonable, rational. The thing to do then, of course, was to give in. After all, anything that is good for food, pleasant to the senses, and satisfying to the ego must be all right" (Ray Stedman, *Understanding Man*, p. 75).

"We have sailed too close to shore, having fallen in love with life, we have lost our thirst for the waters of life" (Sir Francis Drake).

Reprise

Broadway musicals contain a reprise—a symphonic recapitulation of the action, weaving in earlier songs and scenes that foreshadow later themes. To appreciate fully the tragedy of Paradise Lost, we need to listen again to the music of Paradise Created.

When we last left our Hero and Heroine, they frolicked in Paradise, their intended home—the Garden of delight. They enjoyed peace, their intended relationship—shalom. They experienced purpose, their intended pastime—meaning.

Almighty Father, in John Milton's *Paradise Lost*, bends down His eyes to view his works and their works at once.

About him all the sanctities of Heaven stood thick as stars, and from his sight received beatitude past utterance. On his right the radiant image of his Glory sat, his only Son. On Earth he first beheld our two first Parents, yet the only two of mankind, in the happy Garden placed, reaping immortal fruits of joy and love, uninterrupted joy, unrivalled love in blissful solitude (Milton, *Paradise Lost*, p. 62).

They have it all. Made in the shade! Paradise. Peace. Purpose. Very good. Father gifts them with all kinds of trees, trees that were pleasing to the eye and good for food, and also with the tree of life (Genesis 2:9). He gives generously to them without finding fault—happy that they are supremely happy in Him and what He provides (James 1:5). They receive every good and perfect gift from above, coming down from the Father of

217

the heavenly lights, who does not change like shifting shadows (James 1:17). He richly provides them with everything for their enjoyment (1 Timothy 6:17). Giving Himself as their greatest joy, God, the blessed and only Ruler, the King of kings and Lord of lords, who alone is immortal and who lives in unapproachable light, whom no one has seen or can see. To him be honor and might forever (1 Timothy 6:15-16). This invisible One, visible to them as He walks and talks with them in the cool of the day (Genesis 3:8). Unselfish, to them He gives each other. Man and woman. Husband and wife. Lovers. Companions. Naked. Shameless (author's paraphrase).

Purpose phenomenal. Keep. Protect. Create. Expand. Reign. Have dominion. Garden without weeds. Rose without thorn. Work without sweat. Guard the Garden!

Nature pure and innocent. *Imago Dei* sublime. Capable of reflecting Trinity, relating like Trinity, ruling for Trinity, and resting in Trinity. Endowed with reflection, communion, dominion, and cohesion. Romancers. Dreamers. Creators. Singers. Actors. Perfect in every way. Loving passionately. Thinking wisely. Choosing courageously. Experiencing deeply. Living contingently. Living in happy dependence upon and connection with Father, Worthy Groom, and Messenger. Freedom all, but one. Prohibition one. Free to eat from any tree in the Garden. Such glorious freedom. "But you must not eat from the tree of the knowledge of good and evil, for when you eat of it you will surely die" (Genesis 2:17). What protective prohibition!

Meaning clear. "Trust Me and what I choose to provide. Do not tempt Me as your children will later do. Grumbling. Carping. Murmuring. Craving what the world, Egypt, offers. Disrespecting what Father provides. Dishonoring Jehovah Jireh—Eternal Provider."

Whatever could possess them to trade their birthright for a bite of the one forbidden fruit? When we last spied earth's Villain, he was tumbling toward hell. Having lost the battle for heaven, his hostility and hate triggers a new plan. Why a second siege on heaven's gates, when earth's shores suggest easier prey? As Milton envisioned it:

> Nor will occasion want, nor shall we need with dangerous expedition to invade Heaven, whose high walls fear no assault or siege, or ambush from the Deep. What if we find some easier enterprise? There is a place (if ancient and prophetic fame in Heaven err not), another World, the happy seat of some new Race called Man, about this time to be created like to us, though less in power and excellence, but favored more of him who rules above. So was his will pronounced among the Gods, and by an oath, that shook Heaven's whole circumference, confirmed (Milton, *Paradise Lost*, pp. 39-40).

Toppling the blue planet appeared an easier enterprise than sinking heaven.

Lust for power was not False Seducer's sole incitement. Revenge, dark requital, propelled his monstrous motives. Again, in the images of Milton:

> To waste his whole Creation, or possess all as our own, and drive as we were driven, the puny habitants, or if not drive, seduce them to our Party, that their God may prove their foe, and with repenting hand abolish his own works. This would surpass common revenge, and interrupt his joy in our confusion and our joy

upraise in his disturbance; when his darling Sons hurled headlong to partake with us, shall curse their frail Original, and faded bliss, faded so soon (Milton, *Paradise Lost*, p. 40).

Surpassing common revenge, Seducer lives to spite the Author of life.

By Satan, and in part proposed: for whence, but from the Author of all ill could spring so deep a malice, to confound the race of mankind in one root, and Earth with Hell to mingle and involve, done all to spite the great Creator? (Milton, *Paradise Lost*, p. 41).

Demonic evil from hell's pit set against *imago Dei* from heaven's hands. Though the temptation was intense and true, one wonders how an innocent being, fashioned by a perfect Being could fall.

Such a question returns us to our reprise and our fourth main character—Trinity. When last we encountered Him, He was at rest. Rest from His creation of beings in his Trinitarian image.

Communitarian Trinity wanted relationship, not robotic, hypnotic enslavement. Communitarian Trinity forming His image bearers could make only personal beings— relational, rational, volitional, and emotional beings.

So whose fault was their fall? Milton, imagining Father's words to Worthy Groom, declares:

For man will hearken to his glozing lies, and easily transgress the sole Command, sole pledge of his obedience. So will fall he and his faithless Progeny. Whose fault? Whose but his own? Ingrate, he had of me all he could have; I made him just and right, sufficient to have stood, though free to fall (Milton, *Paradise Lost*, p. 63).

Well put. *Sufficient to have stood, though free to fall.* Made just and right and able to choose. Adam and Eve had all they could have from the generous hand of God, yet they transgressed the sole command, the sole pledge of loving, trustful obedience. Loving allegiance they chose to grant to non-god rather than to Father God.

What was the nature of False Seducer's seduction and of Image Bearers' sin? Learning this, we learn the nature of all seduction and all sin. We learn how False Seducer seduces us and the putrid nature of our sinful allegiance to him rather than our supreme loving obedience to Worthy Groom. From our Worthy Groom, the Second Adam, we also learn how to win the final victory over sin's seduction. Then we can delight in how grace superabounds over sin.

Serpentine Seduction to Sin

"Adam and Eve were both naked and unashamed" (Genesis 2:25, author's translation). "Now the serpent was more naked than any of the wild animals the LORD God had made" (Genesis 3:1, author's translation). You read that right. Moses chooses the same Hebrew root word (*ārōm*) that we can translate either as "naked" or as "crafty." Naked. Open. Transparent. Clear. Frank. Obvious. The Angel of Darkness clothed himself with light.

The Lying One masqueraded as integrity, openness, transparency, and genuineness. Milton saw through False Seducer's translucence. "So spake the false dissembler unperceived; for neither Man nor Angel can discern hypocrisy, the only evil that walks invisible, except to God alone" (Milton, *Paradise Lost*, p. 81).

The Serpent was more cunning, subtler, craftier than any other creature made by God. Malevolent brilliance. Hypocrisy shrewdly disguised as integrity. Fake portrayed as genuine. Counterfeit as authentic. Sly solicitude.

Walter Brueggemann explains that sly Serpent's entrance upon the scene suggests that the issues of human life are more inscrutable and ominous than we could ever imagine. "There is something large and external at work in the world that is antagonistic to human life" (Brueggemann, *Theology of the Old Testament*, p. 490). That something is someone—False Seducer. He is, indeed, at work behind the scenes of every seduction. In this scene, Moses draws back the curtains to expose his serpentine seduction.

Digging deeper into the dialogue between Diabolos and Dominion Bearers we discover the Divine diagnosis of depravity. In the beginning, Serpent speaks to *Eve*. "He said to the woman" (Genesis 3:1). Father commanded Adam, "Guard the Garden!" Serpent speaks to *Eve*. Father directly told Adam of all their freedom and of their one protective prohibition. Serpent speaks to *Eve*. He distorts God-given roles and preys on the lesser informed.

"Did God really say?" The first question in the Bible. Seeds of doubt planted. "Is it really so? Did God really say *that*?" Implying that what God says is open to human judgment.

"You must not." Actually, God had said, "You are *free* to eat from *any* tree in the garden" (Genesis 2:16). "He said *what!?* He commanded you *not* to eat from *any* tree in the garden?" Father, according to Serpent, must be a Must-Not God! A Shalt-Not God. Implying, as is the essence of all sin, that we should distrust God's character.

Eve, rather than calling on Yahweh, rather than involving Adam, who heard the first command, rather than resisting the Devil, dialogues with Serpent. Attempting to correct his glaring misrepresentations, she still gets it wrong. Father emphasized their scandalous freedom. "You are *free* to eat from *any* tree in the garden." Eve minimizes. "We *may* eat fruit from the trees in the garden."

Eve continues. "We must not eat *fruit* from the tree that is *in the middle of the garden*. And we must not *touch* it or we *will* die." She highlights the delicacy that God withholds— the fruit. She makes it a geographical rather than a moral issue—in the middle of the Garden, instead of the *tree of the knowledge of good and evil*. She adds restrictions—or *touch* it. She subtracts seriousness—you will die, instead of you will *surely* die.

Serpent hardly has to work. Eve in her blind deception is doing his work for him. Cunning. Naked hypocrisy. Speaking once again to Eve, serpent deceitfully assures her, "You will *not* surely die!" (Genesis 3:4).

Now the foul knife he drives deep. "God jealously hoards his Deity. His best gift he withholds—godlike wisdom."

Why then was this forbid? Why but to awe, why but to keep ye low and ignorant, his worshipers? He knows that in that day ye eat thereof, your eyes that seem so clear, yet are but dim, shall perfectly be then opened and cleared, and ye shall be as Gods, knowing both Good and Evil as they know. Or is it envy, and can envy dwell in heavenly breasts? These, these and many more causes import your need of this fair Fruit. Goddess humane, reach then, and freely taste (Milton, *Paradise Lost*, p. 222).

Milton followed the common biblical interpretation that when Satan tempted Eve, he accused God, intimating that God commanded His restriction out of envy because He would have none so great, so wise, and so happy as He. "God is needlessly restrictive. There's something in His character causing Him to deprive you. What is it about God that motivates Him to limit your pleasure? Is He cruel? Unkind? Lacking generosity?"

God was being generous and protective. Satan portrays Him as punitive and jealous. "Your so-called 'Worthy Groom' is selfish! He's holding back. He withholds what you need because He is jealous and insecure. God restricts you because He does not love you. God has a character flaw."

As John Murray (*Principles of Conduct*, p. 126) notes, the pivot of Satan's attack is not simply a denial of God's power. It is much more *diabolical*. Satan directly assails God's *veracity and integrity*, accusing God of deliberate falsehood and deception; accusing Him of being jealous of and selfish with His exclusive possession of the knowledge of good and evil.

Satan attempts to minimize Eve's perspective of God by claiming that God minimizes her freedom. Satan is the original author of the movie *Honey, I Shrunk Your God*!

Minimizing God, he maximizes himself, implying, "Serpent would never do that. I'm pro-freedom. God is pro-bondage. Serpent is more committed to your well-being than God."

Yet Satan is punitive. "Take the poison fruit!" Thus he poisons Eve's view of God. He e-mails a virus into her system that seduces her to see God in a punitive, rather than a protective way. He tempts Eve to see herself as sufficient rather than to trust God as her Sufficient Shepherd. "Be as gods. Goddess Eve."

Eve was innocent and uncorrupted, living in simple dependence upon and enjoyment of God. The only Being she knew had been only kind to her. The whole creation formed a symphony, singing God's goodness. Then someone else appeared suggesting that God might not be as good as she supposed. "Have you ever wondered why God won't let you at that tree? Have you asked yourself if there might be something good outside of God that you could enjoy if you had the sense to go for it?"

Seduced in the realm of *desire*, Eve is deceived in the sphere of *imagination*. Moses informs us that she saw (*rāāh*) the fruit (Genesis 3:6). *Rāāh* means not simply to see with the eyes, but to perceive with the imagination and to believe with the heart (Laird Harris, *Theological Wordbook of the Old Testament*, Vol. 2, p. 823). Eve looks intently upon and purposely at the fruit touching it with her eyes before touching it with her lips.

Her rational imagination is intricately connected to her relational motivation. She pursues what she perceives to be pleasing. She seeks what she senses is satisfying. "When the woman saw that the fruit of the tree was good for food and pleasing to the eye, and also desirable for gaining wisdom, she took some and ate it" (Genesis 3:6). Elyse Fitzpatrick quite accurately summarizes Eve's unhappy choice.

Why did Eve choose to disobey God? Look again at three words in the verse: *good, delight, desirable.* These are words that illustrate the motivation behind actions. Our choices are predicated upon what we think is "good," what we "delight in," what we find most "desirable." The truth about our choices is that we always choose what we believe to be our best good. We always choose what we believe will bring us the most delight (Fitzpatrick, *Idols of the Heart*, pp. 80-81).

There is nothing wrong with desire. God made the trees pleasing to the eye and good for food (Genesis 2:9). However, Eve was seduced *through* her desires. Temptation lurks around desire highway. She perceives that the fruit is good (*tôb*)—beneficial, favorable, pleasant, beautiful, precious, delightful, able to make one happy. She perceives that the fruit is pleasing (*hāmad*)—beautiful, strongly desirable, delightful, precious, pleasant. She perceives that the fruit is desirable (taăwâ)—fulfilling, craving, satisfying, earnest desire, strong affection, appetite, delight.

Desire was not the problem. The problem was desiring anything more than God. The Puritans called it *overmuch love.* Satan instigated a titanic tug of war in her soul. A contest. A competition. "Choose you this day whom you will love, whom you will desire. Decide who satisfies your soul most deeply. Who is altogether lovely? Who is your Beloved in whom you delight? Who and what are most dear to you? Whom do you hold supreme? Whom do you love with all your heart, soul, mind, and strength? What do you crave more than life itself?"

Eve chose the creature over the Creator. Choosing the forbidden fruit, she chose Serpent and herself. "She took some and ate it."

And what of Adam? "She also gave some to her husband who was right there with her, and he ate it" (Genesis 3:6). Eve was beguiled and deceived (Genesis 3:13; 1 Timothy 2:14); Adam was not deceived (1 Timothy 2:14). He sinned knowingly. He was undeceived by Serpent's lies about God's goodness and good intents in His one protective prohibition. Then why did he sin? How was *he* seduced?

Biblical interpreters before and after Augustine have agreed with his interpretation that:

> The first man did not yield to his wife in this transgression of God's precept, as if he thought she spoke the truth: but only compelled to it by his social love to her, for the apostle says: "Adam was not deceived but the woman was deceived" (Augustine, *The City of God*, p. 12).

Milton poetically interprets Adam's costly choice.

> How can I live without thee, how forgo thy sweet Converse and Love so dearly joined, to live again in these wild Woods forlorn? Should God create another Eve, and another Rib afford, yet loss of thee would never from my heart; no, no, I feel the Link of Nature draw me. Flesh of Flesh, Bone of my Bone thou art, and from thy state mine never shall be parted, bliss or woe (Milton, *Paradise Lost*, p. 227).

Moses, inspired by God, provides the original interpretation of the nature of Adam's sinful choice.

> To Adam he [God] said, "Because you *listened* [hearkened] *to your wife* and ate from the tree about which *I commanded* you, 'You must not eat of it,' cursed is the ground because of you; through painful toil you will eat of it all the days of your life" (Genesis 3:17, emphasis added).

"Listen" (*shāma*) means to obey loyally, listen diligently to, give heed to, pay attention to, hearken to. What was Adam's sin? *He knowingly chose Eve over God.* What was the seduction in Adam's sin? It was his desires. The reason for Adam's sin? His imagination. As Eve chose the goodness of the fruit over God's goodness, so Adam chose the goodness of the female over God's goodness (Romans 1:25). Seeing God as the great Forbidder, he chose the one who ate the forbidden fruit. More precious was she in his sight than Father. More wise his wisdom than Father's. More precious his will than Father's.

Certainly, it is no coincidence that Moses uses the same word for "hear/hearken" in Deuteronomy 6:4-5. "Hear, O Israel: The LORD our God, the LORD is one. Love the LORD your God with all your heart and with all your soul and with all your strength." In other words, "Don't be like Adam who hearkened to and loved his wife with all his heart, all his soul, and all his strength."

Living in fellowship with God is the intended natural state of humanity. The temptation was Satan's enticement to compel Adam and Eve to exercise their wills *independently* of God. "Contingent upon God? Needing God? Who says? Why?" Satan, who longed to be the point, says to Eve and Adam, "Wouldn't you like to be the point? Don't you desire something more than God has given you?"

Father designed Adam and Eve to *recoil at ugly and rejoice in beauty*. Their first sin, and every sin thereafter, includes the failure to discern good (beautiful) and evil (ugly). The tree of the knowledge of good and evil was Adam and Eve's opportunity to discern between God's goodness and False Seducer's evil. As beloved image bearers, they had the capacities necessary to recoil at the ugliness of *desiring and choosing anything or anyone more than God*. They had the capacities to rejoice in the beauty of God's good heart.

Had they recoiled, God would have confirmed them in holiness. They would permanently be like God as perfect bearers of His beautiful image. Instead, they became like Satan—his ugly image bearers. They chose the ugly of doubting God's good heart over the beauty of trusting God's generous soul. They could have known good and evil without ever having to experience evil. Instead, they and all their descendants become filled only with evil all the time (Genesis 6:5).

Box 14:1 summarizes the scenario of seduction that led to their choices and our consequences. As you read it, take note of the subtlety of satanic seduction.

Box 14:1

The Scenario of Seduction: Genesis 2:16-17 with 3:1-6

Revealed Truth	**Subtle Lie**
The LORD God commanded the **man** (2:16)	He said to the **woman** (3:1)

Distortion of God-given roles. Preying on the less informed.

You are **free** to eat from **any** tree in the garden (2:16)	You **must not** eat from **any** tree in the garden (3:1)

God is a must not God! Rigid rules—law.

You are **free** to eat from **any** tree in the garden (2:16)	We **may** eat fruit from the trees in the garden (3:2)

Minimizing God's generosity. Minimizing our freedom.

The LORD God **commanded** (2:16)	Did God really say? (3:1)

Planting seeds of doubt about God.

You must not eat from the tree of the knowledge of good and evil (2:17)	You must not eat **fruit** from the tree (3:3)

Planting seeds of doubt about God's goodness. Is God withholding some good fruit?

You must not eat from the tree **of the knowledge of good and evil** (2:17)	You must not eat fruit from the tree that is **in the middle of the garden** (3:3)

Shifting from a moral issue to a geographical (non-moral) issue.

You must not eat from the tree of the knowledge of good and evil (2:17)	You must not eat fruit from the tree that is in the middle of the garden, **and you must not touch it** (3:3)

More rules—law. Minimizes God's love.

For **when** you eat of it you will **surely die** (2:17)	Or you **will** die (3:3)

Denying consequences—license. Minimizes God's holiness.

For **when** you eat of it you will **surely die** (2:17)	You will **not** surely die (3:4)

God lied!

Divine Commentary on Seduction to Sin

So cataclysmic an event. So miniscule our information. So intricate to interpret. We could wish for help. Perhaps a divine commentary on satanic seduction to sin. Ask and you shall receive. Numerous later passages divinely decipher the tangled web of deceived desires implicit in every seduction to sin. In these Divine commentaries God exposes the dynamics of every seduction.

- ◆ Enticed in Our Affections: Impure Affections/False Lovers of Our Soul
- ◆ Deceived in Our Imagination (Irrational Images): Foolish Idols of Our Heart
- ◆ Blinded in Our Cognition (Irrational Beliefs): Suppression of Our Mindset
- ◆ Obsessed in Our Volition: Self-Centered/Contemptuous Purposes/Pathways of Our Will
- ◆ Ungoverned in Our Emotions: Fleshly Surrender of Our Mood States

Enticed in Our Affections: Impure Affections/False Lovers of Our Soul

Sin begins its enticement in our desires. "Each one is tempted when, by his own evil desire (*epithumias*), he is dragged away and enticed" (James 1:14). Unfortunately, the NIV translates *epithumias* as "evil desire." Actually, it is a neutral term. Luke 22:15 tells us that Jesus desired with great desire to eat the Passover with His disciples—using *epithumias* twice. Paul uses the word for his desire to see and be with Christ (Philippians 1:23) and for a person's desire to be an elder (1 Timothy 3:1).

What, then, is desire? The Greek root word (*thumos*) means passion, movement, motivation, vital force, and impulse. With the prefix *epi,* it means yearning, craving, boiling passion, bubbling want, and desperate desire. In general contexts it connotes pleasure, cherish, value, relish, deem, esteem, and appreciate. When used toward God it pictures supreme devotion, hunger, and thirst. Desire, remember, was God's idea. Temptation and the distortion of desire is False Seducer's province. Evil allures us to pursue God-designed desire in God-prohibited ways.

Each of us is seduced through our appetites, affections, delights, and desires. We are relational beings created with the capacity for relational motivation—designed to desire and pursue what we perceive will satisfy our soul. Satanic seduction always tempts us toward spiritual separation, toward spiritual adultery where we pursue false lovers of the soul.

Jeremiah 2, which provides a classic divine commentary on seduction, reinforces this explanation. Jehovah, the Husband of Israel, reflects on days gone by when His wife was faithful. "I remember the devotion of your youth, how as a bride you loved me and followed me through the desert, through a land not sown" (Jeremiah 2:2).

Sadly, Jehovah has other memories. "My people have committed two sins: They have forsaken me, the spring of living water, and have dug cisterns, broken cisterns that cannot hold water" (Jeremiah 2:13). Jehovah Himself summarizes the essence of seduction to sin. It is unfaithful awayness—spiritual adultery. Sin seduces us to love false lovers. "Long ago you broke off your yoke and tore off your bonds; you said, 'I will not serve you!' Indeed, on every high hill and under every spreading tree you lay down as a *prostitute*" (Jeremiah 2:20-21, emphasis added). Sin is spiritual prostitution.

Where does sin seek its entry point? In our cravings—in our legitimate relational longings for intimacy.

> You are a swift she-camel running here and there, a wild donkey accustomed to the desert, sniffing the wind in her craving—in her heat who can restrain her? Any males that pursue her need not tire themselves; at mating time they will find her. Do not run until your feet are bare and your throat is dry. But you said, "It's no use! I love foreign gods, and I must go after them" (Jeremiah 2:23b-25).

Our desire to love and be loved is core to our *imago*. Like God, we are relational, communal beings. Unlike God, we are finite beings. So we hunger and thirst for relationship. We satisfy our hungry souls either *coram Deo*—face-to-face with God or *coram Diabolos*—face-to-face with the False Seducer. We are either desperate for Worthy Groom or False Seducer. We either love the Lord our God with all our heart, or we love non-god with all our being.

But why in the world choose sin? Why desire False Seducer over Worthy Groom? Why savor the fruit Creator made over the Creator? Why prefer the female to the Father?

Deceived in Our Imagination (Irrational Images): Foolish Idols of Our Heart

Sin seduces us through our affections while it deceives us through our imagination. James informs us that we are tempted through our desires as we are dragged away and enticed (James 1:14). He uses a fishing and hunting analogy of bait and snares. The delicious worm tantalizes the hungry fish. The bloody scent mesmerizes the ravenous bear. We're allured by bait. What type of bait? Deceptive bait that blinds us to Worthy Groom's goodness.

It is while explaining the nature of satanic seduction that James shares these memorable words, "Don't be deceived, my dear brothers. Every good and perfect gift is from above, coming down from the Father of the heavenly lights, who does not change like shifting shadows" (James 1:16-17). Don't be deceived about the source of every good and every perfect gift. Father is *not* a Shalt-Not God! He is the Gift-Giving God.

To allure and ensnare us, False Seducer must deceive us by blinding us to our Worthy Groom's worth. Jehovah says exactly this when He asks and answers the age-old question concerning why we sin. "This is what the LORD says: 'What fault did your fathers find in me that they strayed so far from me?'" (Jeremiah 2:5). "Fault" (*āwel*) is a startling word. The KJV accurately translates it as "iniquity." *We turn from God when we perceive some iniquity in Him*. Specifically, "fault" means to act in a deceitful way, tricking, an insidious manner of relating, dishonest and unfair dealings, injustice, and even perverseness. It suggests a remarkable accumulation of unrighteousness—a contemptuous view of God. Sound familiar? False Seducer deceived Eve into thinking that God was deceptive and unfair.

How does Satan snare us? He captures our fancy as we interpret our situation. When Jehovah asked about the fault that they *found* (*māsā*) in Him, He chose a word that means a conclusion reached by interpreting experience. Here they are in the desert seeing God in their fancy (in their imagination) as their Beloved who provides for and protects them

(Jeremiah 2:2-3). They correctly imagine him as their Spring of Living Water. Though life is bad (living in a desert), their Lover is altogether lovely.

But then, something tragic happens. They interpret their desert experience through a new grid, the grid of blinded imagination. Notice how they view God now.

> You of this generation, consider the word of the LORD: "Have I been a desert to Israel or a land of great darkness? Why do my people say, 'We are free to roam; we will come to you no more'? Does a maiden forget her jewelry, a bride her wedding ornaments? Yet my people have forgotten me, days without number. How skilled you are at pursuing love! Even the worst of women can learn from your ways" (Jeremiah 2:31-33).

Jehovah, who had been worthy of following in a desert, they now imagine to be a desert. Jehovah, who illuminated their path, they now fancy as a land of great darkness. False Seducer captured their fancy, blinding their imagination. "Your so-called 'Husband' is the cosmic Killjoy! Take a look at all His shortcomings."

We move far from God when we think little of God. Don't take my word for it. Take God's. "'Your wickedness will punish you; your backsliding will rebuke you. Consider then and realize how evil and bitter it is for you when you forsake the LORD your God and have no awe of me,' declares the Lord, the LORD Almighty" (Jeremiah 2:19). We forsake God when we lose our awe (*pahdâ*) of Him—when we lose all respect for God. In our inner attitude we no longer detect His awesome holy love; we no longer appreciate His majestic beauty.

Adam and Eve perceived that being *like God* was more beautiful than being *with God*; as did Satan. Being free from God was more attractive to them than being dependent upon God (taken care of by God). "Get out of the womb, be on your own!" God no longer captured their imagination. They turned God's dream into their worst nightmare.

Blinded in Our Cognition (Irrational Beliefs): Suppression of Our Mindset

Satan entices us through our desires, deceives us in our imagination, and blinds us in our cognition. We discover this third aspect in yet another divine commentary on the dynamics of seduction—Romans 1:18-31. Paul introduces the process. "The wrath of God is being revealed from heaven against all the godlessness and wickedness of men who suppress the truth by their wickedness" (Romans 1:18). The essential idea of godlessness (*asebeian*) is irreverence, disregard, indifference, and insult that results in paying little attention to God and comes from suppressing the truth about God's nature (Ralph Earle, *Word Meanings in the New Testament*, p. 137).

According to Paul, God's glorious nature is as plain as the nose on our face. His invisible attributes are manifested in His visible creation. Those with eyes to see may observe God daily in the world around them (Romans 1:19-20; Psalm 19:1-3). It does not take a detective or a criminal science investigation team to detect the fingerprints of God. Through creation, we can see His eternal power and Godhead—the sum total of His divine attributes (Earle, *Word Meanings in the New Testament*, p. 138).

Adam and Eve not only saw God's goodness through creation, they walked with their Creator and experienced His goodness—His majesty and beauty. So what went wrong? How could they sin? They had to suppress (*katechontōn*) the awareness of what they saw, knew, and experienced. For sin to conceive, we must push away from our awareness all signs of God's goodness. "For although they knew God, they neither glorified him as God nor gave thanks to him, but their thinking became futile and their foolish hearts were darkened" (Romans 1:21).

Eve thinks, "Glorious? I thought so, but it doesn't seem like it now. The fruit seems more desirable than Father."

"Good?" Adam wonders. "I thought so, but Eve seems better for me than Creator."

Isn't this identical to Paul's summary? "They exchanged the truth of God for a lie, and worshiped and served created things rather than the Creator—who is forever praised. Amen" (Romans 1:25). Paul is quite careful with his Greek. They bartered *the truth* for *the lie. The* truth is that Worthy Groom is forever worthy of praise. *The* lie is that Worthy Groom is not worthy to be retained in our thinking (Romans 1:28).

Paul is quite specific, "They worshiped and served created things *rather than* the Creator." Literally, placed side-by-side—Creator and creature, Creator and fruit, Creator and the female—they *preferred* the creature, fruit, female to the Creator (A. T. Robertson, *Word Pictures in the New Testament*, p. 356). Eve and Adam worship substitute lovers, they pass by the Creator altogether because they are blinded to the truth that He is altogether lovely.

"Furthermore, since they did not think it worthwhile to retain the knowledge of God, he gave them over to a depraved mind, to do what ought not to be done" (Romans 1:28). "Think" (*edokimasan*) means test, prove, or approve. It was used of testing metals or coins to see if they were genuine. Earle explains the terrifying implication. "This gives a startling connotation to the passage under consideration. Humanity had tested Deity and disapproved of Him. Consequently man had rejected God" (Earle, *Word Meanings in the New Testament*, p. 139). More than suppression of His goodness, we implicate Him with badness; we insinuate that God falls short of our glory. Sin seduces us to play umpire with God, to sit in judgment upon His character. *The essence of sin is the belittling of God's glory.*

Adam and Eve once understood that all they needed was God and what He chose to provide. They once affirmed that God gave them all things richly to enjoy (Genesis 2:9; 1 Timothy 6:17; James 1:17). Then False Seducer weaseled in shrinking their freedom in Christ. In Galatians 1, Paul calls lies about our gospel freedom "anathema"—aversion, subversion, odious, worthy of an eternal curse. In 1 Timothy 4, he labels such lies as demonic doctrines.

I often ask my classes, "What are examples of demonic doctrines?" They reply the way you and I would reply if our minds were not focused on 1 Timothy 4. "Demonic doctrines deny the virgin birth of Christ." "They probably include denying the inspiration of Scripture." "Demonic doctrines must involve demon possession, or killing, hating, and the like."

Then we read 1 Timothy 4:1-2. "The Spirit clearly says that in later times some will abandon the faith and follow deceiving spirits and things *taught by demons*. Such teachings come through hypocritical liars, whose consciences have been seared as with a hot iron" (emphasis added). The tension mounts. We wait to read subsequent verses that we're sure will speak about satanic ritual abuse. We're sure we'll read about abandoning the faith through heretical teaching about the Trinity, or Christ's humanity and Deity. Then we're shocked to read Paul's description of demonic doctrine.

> They forbid people to marry and order them to abstain from certain foods, which God created to be received with thanksgiving by those who believe and who know *the* truth. For everything God created is good, and nothing is to be rejected if it is received with thanksgiving (1 Timothy 4:3-4, emphasis added).

What is *the* core truth that demonic doctrine denies? "Everything God created is good and thus God is good, and generous." This is *the truth* to which False Seducer wants to blind us. Satan's seduction always comes in the form of a story offering us godness, by lessening God's goodness.

Obsessed in Our Volition:
Self-Centered/Contemptuous Purposes/Pathways of Our Will

Remember the basic process of seduction. I always pursue (volitional) what I perceive (rational) to be most pleasing (relational). I always seek what I sense is most satisfying.

The essence of seduction is the temptation to prefer other things to God's grandeur. When we surrender to seduction, then we lack God's glory as the treasure of our lives. We lack it as our passion and goal, as our all-satisfying vision.

According to Jeremiah 2:13, sin is the choice between boundless joy and broken cisterns. In the wilderness lands of the ancient Near East, water was a constant problem— a life threatening issue. Two primary sources existed. One—the spring of living water, or running water—was much preferred. This is why Abraham and the other Patriarchs settled near springs. Here they had access to clean, cool, flowing underground water bubbling up like a modern-day artesian spring. The other—the cistern—was less to be preferred. If you could find no spring, or if a spring ran dry, then you had to dig a cistern. A cistern was a crude well that was fed not by underground water but by runoff water. They'd dig a hole, line it with clay, and pray that water that ran off from their roofs, from the camel-dung-filled streets, and from the sandy, dusty hills would collect in their cistern. Once this less-than-appealing combination of rainwater, dirt, and dung collected in the cistern, there it sat, stagnating. As bad as that was, cisterns often cracked, allowing this putrid, but life sustaining, water to escape.

Satan seduces us to choose broken cisterns over spring water. He lures us to forsake Jehovah, the Spring of Living Water, and dig our own self-sufficient broken cisterns that can hold no water.

False Seducer is no fool. He is, after all, more nakedly crafty than any other creature. He knows that what entices one of us may not allure another. This is why James notes that *each one* of us is tempted when we are drawn away through *our own* desire (James 1:14). *We are tempted in or through our idiosyncratic appetites.* Eve's fancy was captivated by good, pleasing, desirable fruit, capable, she imagined, of making her godlike. Sin captured Adam's imagination when he perceived that Eve was more desirable than God.

That is why we all create agreeable self-portraits of God. Rather than living in God's image, we create images of God that fit our distinctive personalities. The broken cistern of trusting money may tempt us. Our neighbor may care very little about money, rather placing her or his trust in personal beauty or a powerful physique. And all of us may change the god who captures our soul depending upon our situations.

Jehovah castigates Israel for their constant changing of their gods. "Why do you go about so much, changing your ways? You will be disappointed by Egypt as you were by Assyria" (Jeremiah 2:36). Gluttony, pride, hypocrisy, lying, power, prestige, lust, materialism, hobbies, praise, women, men, sex, pleasure, it really doesn't matter. They all can be false gods we depend upon, false lovers to whom we grant our supreme devotion.

Two motifs or themes run throughout the Bible: God's gracious rescue of His people pictured in the Passover-Exodus event and His people's ungrateful rejection of Him pictured by the waters of Marah, Elim, Massah, and Meribah where God's people craved other satisfactions (Exodus 12-17). Numbers 9-14 brings both together. In Numbers 9, Israel celebrates the Passover. In Numbers 11, they complain about God's provision.

> The rabble with them began to crave other food, and again the Israelites started wailing and said, "If only we had meat to eat! We remember the fish we ate in Egypt at no cost—also the cucumbers, melons, leeks, onions, and garlic. But now we have lost our appetite; we never see anything but this manna!" (Numbers 11:4-6).

Satanic seduction: crave the world and the food of the world and lose your appetite for God and God's food.

In seduction we face the constant interplay between demeaning God and elevating non-god. "We were better off in Egypt!" (Numbers 11:18). "Why did we ever leave Egypt?!" (Numbers 11:20). Yet we always end up loathing the things of this world because they can never satisfy no matter how much we stuff our bellies with them. "You will not eat it for just one day, or two days, or five, ten or twenty days, but for a whole month—until it comes out of your nostrils and you loathe it—because you have rejected the LORD who is among you" (Numbers 11:19-20). Loathe God. Long for the world. Loathe the things of the world.

Numbers 14 describes satanic seduction to loathe God. "How long will these people treat me with contempt? How long will they refuse to believe in me, in spite of all the miraculous signs I have performed among them?" (Numbers 14:11). To hold in contempt (*nāas*) means to belittle, despise, view with disdain, disbelieve, depreciate, and to prefer lesser things to God. It's especially used of a conscious change of perception and attitude—from honor to dishonor.

In seduction, Satan tempts us to depreciate God and to choose lesser gods of our own making—gods that better suit our unique personality and life situation. R. Kent Hughes summarizes the progression well. "The pathology of a hard heart originates in unbelief that spawns a hardened contempt" (Hughes, *Hebrews*, Vol. 1, p. 100). Rather than being caught up in the overflowing gladness of God, the only fountain of lasting joy, we turn to trivial pursuits, fleeting pleasures, petty resentments, and unsatisfying materialism.

As we turn, we enslave ourselves. The pathways we pursue to find life apart from God become our gods. The bondage of our will leaves us obsessively attempting to make life work without God.

Ungoverned in Our Emotions: Fleshly Surrender of Our Mood States

Satan seduces us to pursue what we perceive will be pleasing and pleasurable. Hebrews 11:25 informs us there is pleasure (*apolausin*) in sin for a season—for an undetermined period. Literally, the author of Hebrews speaks of "the demand that I clutch pleasure, take hold of it, cling to it, and hold onto it for dear life" (author's translation).

Pleasure is part of sin's seductiveness and addiction. Seductive because it does offer temporal pleasure *over which I have some control*. Eve not only wanted what was good, pleasing, and desirable, she wanted the godlike status of satisfying herself, of being her own self-sufficient source of pleasure.

Pleasure's temporal, finite nature leads to its addictiveness. Jeremiah 2:23-25 describes the results of giving in to seduction as becoming like an animal in heat—living as if the flesh is all there is, as if this temporal time zone is it. More than that, once we start down the path of finite pleasure, we always end up bemoaning the truth that "It's no use! I love foreign [fake, finite] gods, and I *must* go after them" (Jeremiah 2:25, emphasis added). *We feel enslaved because we attempt to fill an infinite, spiritual longing with a finite, material source.*

Ephesians 4:17-19 rehearses the entire process of seduction.

So I tell you this and insist on it in the Lord, that you must no longer live as the Gentiles do, in the futility of their thinking [deceived imagination]. They are darkened in their understanding [blinded cognition] and separated from the life of God [enticed affection] because of the ignorance that is in them [imagination and cognition] due to the hardening of their hearts [obsessed volition]. Having lost all sensitivity [ungoverned emotions], they have given themselves over [volition] to sensuality [emotion] so as to indulge in [volition and emotion] every kind of impurity, with a continual lust for more [volition and emotion] (Ephesians 4:17-19).

We hear a strong warning in this passage. Be careful what you wish for, for your wish may be granted. If you wish to seek God, He will be found (Hebrews 11:6). If you wish to seek the food of this world, you will consume it until it gushes from your nostrils (Numbers 9-14). If you wish to separate yourself from your spiritual umbilical cord to God, you will enslave yourself to endless addictive cycles of needing evermore non-god to fill your God-vacuum.

Romans 1:24, 26, and 28 offer an even more alarming warning. Keep wishing for non-god, keep surrendering yourself to non-god, and God will surrender you to your wants. He will give you up to them. In Romans 1:26, Paul cautions that God will give us up to ungoverned pathos—unbridled, uncontrolled, non-god appetites. We seek to be like God; we demand to be like God. When we do, we pursue non-god means of self-sufficiently satisfying our own longings. These non-gods become our master. Seeking to break loose from God's mastery, we enslave ourselves to Satan's sovereignty.

Box 14:2 helps us envision the entire process of the dynamics of seduction. It shows the intertwining of our relationality, rationality, volitionality, and emotionality as tempted by False Seducer and distorted by sin.

Box 14:2
The Dynamics of Seduction

Relational Separation: Spiritual Adultery
Pursuing False Lovers

Enticed in Our Affections: Impure Affections/False Lovers of Our Soul

Rational Suppression: Spiritual Arrogance
Believing the False Seducer

Deceived in Our Imagination: Foolish Idols of Our Heart
Blinded in Our Cognition: Suppression of Our Mindset

Volitional Stubbornness: Spiritual Self-Sufficiency
Digging Broken Cisterns

Obsessed in Our Volition: Contemptuous Purposes/
Self-Centered Pathways of Our Will

Emotional Sensuality: Spiritual Bondage
Yielding to Controlling Passions

Ungoverned in Our Emotions: Fleshly Surrender of Our Mood State

---

Worthy Groom's Victory Over Sin's Seduction

Seduction visited Adam and Eve. It haunts us. How should image bearers respond to serpentine seduction? Jesus shows the way.

Adam and Eve were in unfallen bodies, with innocent souls, in a perfect paradise, with their every spiritual, social, self-aware, mental, volitional, emotional, and physical longing satisfied. Jesus was in an unfallen body, in a fallen world, in a desert wilderness, alone, and starving after forty days of fasting. Adam and Eve succumbed to seduction. Jesus was victorious over seduction. How?

Victory Number One: Entrust Yourself Humbly to God's Goodness

The False Seducer came to Jesus just as he had to Adam and Eve—quoting Scripture. "If you are the Son of God, tell these stones to become bread" (Matthew 4:3). The issue here, as in all temptation, revolves around who will satisfy my appetite—God or me?

Unlike Eve who misquoted God, and Adam who remained silent, Jesus speaks God's Word to Satan. "It is written, 'Man does not live on bread alone, but on every word that comes from the mouth of God'" (Matthew 4:4). Quoting from Deuteronomy 8:1-4, Jesus selects a passage of Scripture focused upon satisfaction of hunger. Satan urged Eve, Adam, and Jesus to act from self, apart from God, to achieve self-sufficient satisfaction. Jesus quotes from Deuteronomy, reminding Satan that God promises to care for His children and that God uses hunger, thirst, desire, and appetite to draw us to humble dependence upon Him. Victory number one: entrust yourself humbly to God's goodness.

Victory Number Two: Trust God; Don't Test God

Ever vigilant, Satan strikes again. Taking Jesus to the highest point of the temple in Jerusalem, he says, "If you are the Son of God … throw yourself down" (Matthew 4:6). Then he quotes God. "For it is written: 'He will command his angels concerning you, and they will lift you up in their hands, so that you will not strike your foot against a stone'" (Matthew 4:6).

Jesus quotes His Father. "It is also written: 'Do not put the Lord your God to the test'" (Matthew 4:7). What are we to perceive from Jesus' quoting Deuteronomy 6:16? The rest of the verse enlightens us. "Do not test the LORD your God as you did at Massah." Remember Massah, as in the waters of Marah, Elim, *Massah*, and Meribah where the people craved other satisfactions?

Leaving Egyptian captivity, celebrating Jehovah's victory, the Israelites journey through the wilderness (Exodus 17:1). Camping where there's no water to drink, "They quarrel with Moses, 'Give us water to drink!'" (Exodus 17:2a). To which Moses replies, "Why do you put the LORD to the test?" (Exodus 17:2b). "But the people were thirsty for water there, and they grumbled against Moses. They said, 'Why did you bring us up out of Egypt to make us and our children and our livestock die of thirst?'" (Exodus 17:3).

Moses cries out to God, who responds and interprets the events, calling the place Massah and Meribah (testing and quarrelling) because "they tested the LORD saying, 'Is the LORD among us or not?'" (Exodus 17:7). They questioned, "Is He good? Can we trust Him? Will He do what He promised? Should we take matters into our own hands?"

We find this distrust and dissatisfaction motif recurring in Numbers 9-14; 20:1-13; Psalm 81:7-13; 95:8-11; and Hebrews 3:7-11. God promises to satisfy their every desire. They doubt Him, His promise and His character, His holiness and His goodness. They do not trust Him enough to honor Him as holy (Numbers 20:12). They suppress the truth of all the miracles they had witnessed (Psalm 95). He promises if they will but open wide their mouths and souls in childlike trust, then He will satisfy them (Psalm 81). Repeatedly, rather than trusting His good heart, they put God to the test. When confronted with apparent temporary evidence that He might not come through for them, they doubt His caring control, affectionate sovereignty, and holy love. They choose a heart of sinful unbelief that leads them to turn away from God (Hebrews 3:7-15).

Victory number two: trust God; don't test God. When tempted by Satan, we don't tempt God. Instead, we trust Him for our satisfaction, for our victory, for our very life.

Victory Number Three: Worship God, not False Seducer

Temptation number three. "Again, the Devil took him to a very high mountain and showed him all the kingdoms of the world and their *splendor*. 'All this I will give you,' he said, 'if you will bow down and worship me'" (Matthew 4:8-9, emphasis added). If Eve thought the fruit was good, pleasing, and desirable, what would she have thought about the splendor of the entire world? Temptation always allures us in the realm of our affections and our perceptions. What do we perceive to be most beautiful and beneficial, full of the greatest splendor? We always worship what we value as most magnificent.

Victory number three: worship God, not False Seducer. "Jesus said to him, 'Away from me, Satan! For it is written: Worship the Lord your God, and serve him only'" (Matthew 4:10). Jesus was not silent. Temptation always comes to us in the form of a choice regarding whom we worship: our Creator or the creation, God or some god of our own making, Jesus or ourselves? Father or False Seducer?

We experience victory over seduction to the degree that we worship Trinity as most glorious. "Do you love Me more than these?" "Have you chosen the better part?" Have we gone and sold all that we have to follow Him? Do we love Him with all our soul, heart, mind, spirit, will, strength, emotions, and body? Do we seek first His kingdom? We answer these questions by our response to serpentine seduction.

Reprising the Reprise: Grace Abounding to Seduced Sinners

Adam and Eve answered incorrectly. They sinned greatly. Yet grace abounds exceedingly. Milton understood this.

> As my Eternal purpose hath decreed: Man shall not quite be lost, but saved who will, yet not of will in him, but grace in me freely vouchsafed. Once more I will renew his lapsed powers, though forfeit and enthralled by sin to foul exorbitant desires; upheld by me. Yet once more he shall stand on even ground against his mortal foe, by me upheld, that he may know how frail his fallen condition is, and to me owe all his deliverance, and to none but me (Milton, *Paradise Lost*, p. 66).

Milton then pictures Jesus volunteering for the task of dying so we could live.

> Man can never seek, once dead in sins and lost; atonement for himself or offering meet, indebted and undone, hath none to bring. Behold me then, me for him, life for life I offer, on me let thine anger fall. Account me man; I for his sake will leave thy bosom, and this glory next to thee freely put off, and for him lastly die. Well pleased, on me let Death wreck all his rage; under his gloomy power I shall not long lie vanquished. Thou hast given me to possess Life in myself for ever, by thee I live . . . So Man, as is most just, shall satisfy for Man, be judged and die, and dying rise, and rising with him raise his Brethren, ransomed with his own dear life. So Heavenly love shall outdo Hellish hate (Milton, *Paradise Lost*, pp. 67-68, 69).

Heavenly love out duels hellish hate. Where sin abounds, there does grace much more abound.

Where We've Been and Where We're Heading

Biblical soul physicians understand the biblical theology of sin. Having seen why we sin in the strategy of seduction, now we see the fallout of sin revealed in the dynamics of sin in the fallen personality structure.

Here we expose the hideous reality of fallen image bearers. Brace yourself. The next three scenes are unpleasant. Unpleasant, but necessary.

Caring for Your Soul: Personal Applications

1. The parable of the prodigal son (Luke 15) is really the story of the forgiving Father with *two* troubled sons. The youngest son (the Prodigal) runs far from Father to the world, then feels he can never be close to Father again. He feels his only hope for relationship is to be a slave—self-hatred. The elder son (the Pharisaical) stays near home, but his heart is far from Father. He believes his only hope for relationship is works—self-righteousness.

    a. Compare and contrast yourself with the Prodigal Son.

    b. Compare and contrast yourself with the Pharisaical Son.

2. In what situations do you tend to question your Worthy Groom's good heart?

3. Think back to a time of temptation. Work your way through the subtle lies of Satan and the revealed truth of God from Genesis 2-3.

    a. What lies were you believing about God?

    b. What truth were you clinging to about God?

4. Remember a time when you caved into temptation. Trace the tracks of sin:

    a. **Enticed in Our Affections: False Lovers of Our Soul.** What delight, longing, thirst, desire, appetite were you attempting to satisfy? What does God's Word say about that longing? In what ways does God meet the legitimate aspects of that affection?

    b. **Deceived in Our Imagination: Foolish Idols of Our Heart.** What controlling images of God clouded your thinking? How did you see God?

    c. **Blinded in Our Cognition: Suppression of Our Mindset**. What truth about God would have delivered you from temptation? What do you think you did to push those truths out of your mind?

    d. **Obsessed in Our Volition: Contemptuous Purposes/Pathways of Our Will.** What cisterns were you digging when you caved into sin? What themes or patterns do you detect in those times when you chose sin over Jesus?

    e. **Ungoverned in Our Emotions: Fleshly Surrender of Our Mood State.** What momentary pleasure did you experience? What lasting shame did you experience?

Caring for Others: Ministry Implications

- **Trace the Root of Seduction:** Since we can trace the root of every seduction to affection for anything more than God (false lovers, overmuch love), discipleship counseling exposes the False Seducer by shedding light on and debunking his alluring lies. We ask our spiritual friends, "What did you hope to gain by that act?" "What were you longing for more than anything else?" "Do you love Jesus more than _____?" "What do you seek first in your life?"

- **Trace the Root of Sin:** Since every sin can be traced to an inadequate view of God, discipleship counseling roots out sin by exposing spiritual contempt. "What images of God pervade your thoughts?" "What fault do you find in God?" "How has your love for Christ grown cold?" "In what ways are you losing your awe of God?"

- **Expose Spiritual Contempt:** To expose spiritual contempt, work backwards as you trialogue with your spiritual friends:
  - **Emotional:** Why is this emotion here? What purpose does it serve? When is it worse? When is it better? What is happening in your life when it occurs?
  - **Volitional:** How do you respond to your emotions? What do you do with your feelings? What motivates your actions? What goals do you pursue? What do you seek in life?
  - **Rational:** What are you thinking about when you experience those feelings and make those choices? What images and beliefs are clamoring for control at those times?
  - **Relational:** How are you experiencing yourself? How do you see yourself? How are you seeing and relating to others? What are you doing with God? What are you thinking about God? How are you relating to God?

- **Counseling Adam and Eve:** Review Box 14:1 *The Scenario of Seduction* which contrasts Genesis 2:16-17 with 3:1-6. Ask yourself, "What would I say to Adam and Eve if I were their spiritual friend? How would I enter their life story passionately, wisely, courageously, and deeply?"

CHAPTER FIFTEEN

THE FOUR RAGS OF THE ADULTEROUS SPOUSE

"What a chimera then is man! How strange and monstrous! A chaos, a subject of contradiction, a prodigy. Judge of all things, yet a feeble earthworm; depository of truth, yet a cesspool of uncertainty and error; the glory and refuse of the universe. Who will unravel this tangle?" (Blaise Pascal, *Pensées*, Chapter X, Paragraph 1).

"What terrifies us is not the explosive force of the atomic bomb, but the power of the wickedness of the human heart" (Albert Einstein).

Deep Impact

I began my morning on my deck counseling a worship pastor who believes he has disqualified himself from ministry because of his out-of-control temper. Faced with a problem like his, one of my desires was to help him become more like Christ. What does Christlikeness look like and how do I help him grow in Christlikeness?

To answer that question, I could start with soteriology and sanctification—the doctrines of salvation and Christian growth. It makes sense to me, however, first to understand why someone needs saving. *Saving from what?* So I take a step back to hamartiology, the doctrine of seduction, sin, suffering, depravity, and Fall. But, I'm struck again by a preliminary question, *fallen from what?* My thinking must go back further. I need to start at anthropology, the doctrine of human nature and design. Now my question becomes, *Who is this fallen person?* What is this person fallen from, and what does the person need to be saved and from and to?

Surely this is deep enough and far enough back. No. Since human nature is created in the image of Divine nature, I must return to the most rudimentary question. *What is God like?* Now I'm ready to string together the issues necessary to help this struggling pastor.

- What is God like?
- What are image bearers like?
- In what ways has the Fall caused image bearers to fall short of God's glory?
- How does salvation restore what the Fall distorted?
- How do I help people to live out their renewed image in Christ?

You can see where we are in the process and how we need to connect each link. We've contemplated God's essential nature: a Trinitarian relational being of holy love. We've described image bearers: beings designed to reflect God, relate to God, rule for God, and rest in God. We've seen the process of satanic seduction to sin. Before we study salvation and sanctification, we have to focus on one more radically important issue: sin's deep impact.

Like you, I'm concerned about deep and lasting change. Because sin's deep impact wreaked havoc on our planet and our souls, there are no shortcuts. There are, thank God, pathways. Throughout the rest of our journey, we'll explore how to apply our great salvation so God's Creation, ruined by the Fall, can experience Christ's Redemption. (Box 15:1 reviews and overviews the twelve signposts on our journey.) I can summarize those signposts in one sentence: *salvation resurrects the gowns of the virgin bride by crucifying the rags of the adulterous bride that ruined the robes of the beautiful bride.*

I can also summarize those twelve signposts in four statements.

♦ Sin corrupted our capacity to reflect God by invading our being with the *presence of sin* and polluting us with a perverse nature. Salvation provides a new birth, *regenerating* our nature so we can live our new life in Christ.

♦ Sin created a chasm between us and God—the *partition of sin*—that separates us from our Worthy Groom. Salvation provides *reconciliation*, adopting us into Father's forever family.

♦ Sin chained us in captivity to the *power of sin*. Salvation provides *redemption*, offering us freedom from sin's captivity and victory over sin.

♦ Sin condemned our conscience as rightfully guilty and deserving of the *penalty of sin*. Salvation provides *justification*, declaring us not guilty by reason of substitution (Christ paid our penalty).

In Creation, Worthy Groom fashioned for His beautiful bride four robes to answer all her questions about life. "Who am I? Where did I come from? Why am I here? How should I then live?"

Reflecting on her Creation clothing, she enjoyed her settled answers. "I'm an image bearer. I came from Trinity. I live to be His under-shepherd. I share Trinity's shalom."

Through the Fall, these profoundly simple questions morphed into grave queries gnawing at the corners of adulterous spouse's consciousness. She hated the conclusions she drew whenever she stopped to look at her rags. "I'm a fallen image bearer created by self, protecting myself, while serving Seducer by spreading his shame."

Left to ourselves, choosing to be left without God, her answers are ours too. Answers caused by humanity's fall from grace. Answers that resulted when sin perverted the four robes of beautiful bride into the four rags of adulterous spouse (Box 15:2 portrays these four rags.) Let's climb into the crater created by sin's deep impact to examine each of adulterous spouse's four rags.

Box 15:1
The Creation, Fall, and Redemption of the *Imago Dei*

Creation	Fall	Redemption
The Four Robes of the Beautiful Bride	**The Four Rags of the Adulterous Bride**	**The Four Gowns of the Virgin Bride**
Robe of Reflection	**Rag of Corruption**	**Gown of Regeneration**
♦ "Who Am I?"	♦ "Who Am I?"	♦ "Who Am I?"
♦ "I'm an Image Bearer."	♦ "I'm a Fallen Image Bearer."	♦ "I'm a New Creation in Christ."
♦ "I Reflect."	♦ "I Deflect." Presence	♦ "I Display."
♦ Capacities: RRVE	♦ Temple Image: Polluted	♦ New Nature: Saint
♦ Structural Self	♦ Original Sin: Depravity	♦ New Purity: Capacities
♦ "Image and Likeness."	♦ "I Was Naked."	♦ New Propensity: RRVE
♦ Design: Reflection	♦ Disposition: Sinner	♦ New Life: Resurrection
Robe of Communion	**Rag of Chasm**	**Gown of Reconciliation**
♦ "Where Did I Come From?"	♦ "Where Did I Come From?"	♦ "Where Did I Come From?"
♦ "I Came from Trinity."	♦ "I Came from Myself."	♦ "I Came from Christ."
♦ "I Relate."	♦ "I Separate." Partition	♦ "I Reconcile."
♦ Community	♦ Home Image: Prodigal	♦ New Nurture: Welcome!
♦ Social Self	♦ Original Alienation	♦ New Parentage: Father
♦ "Let Us."	♦ "So I Hid."	♦ New Identity: Son/Bride
♦ Dignity: Relation	♦ Distance: Separated	♦ New Adoption: Child
Robe of Dominion	**Rag of Captivity**	**Gown of Redemption**
♦ "Why Am I Here?"	♦ "Why Am I Here?"	♦ "Why Am I Here?"
♦ "To Be an Under-Shepherd."	♦ "To Shepherd Only Myself."	♦ "To Shepherd in a Jungle."
♦ "I Rule."	♦ "I'm Ruled." Power	♦ "I'm Empowered."
♦ Calling	♦ Market Image: Property	♦ New Freedom: from Sin
♦ Stewardship Self	♦ Original Enslavement	♦ New Power: Holiness
♦ "Let Them Rule."	♦ "Sewed Fig Leaves."	♦ New Victory: over Sin
♦ Destiny: Vocation	♦ Dominion: Slave	♦ New Inclination: Love
Robe of Cohesion	**Rag of Condemnation**	**Gown of Justification**
♦ "How Should I Live?"	♦ "How Should I Live?"	♦ "How Should I Live?"
♦ "Share Trinity's Shalom."	♦ "Spread Seducer's Shame."	♦ "Share Savior's Salvation."
♦ "I Rest."	♦ "I Dread." Penalty	♦ "I Relax." Shalom
♦ Coherence	♦ Court Image: Prisoner	♦ New Peace: Forgiveness
♦ Shalom Self	♦ Original Guilt: Disgrace	♦ New Pardon: Guiltless
♦ "Very Good."	♦ "I Was Afraid."	♦ New Dignity: Righteous
♦ Direction: Integration	♦ Disintegration: Shameful	♦ New Boldness: Grace Confidence

Box 15:2

The Four Rags of Worthy Groom's Adulterous Spouse

♦ **The Rag of Corruption**

"Who Am I?"
"I Am a Fallen Image Bearer."
"I Deflect:" Sin's Presence
Temple Imagery: Polluted
Original Sin: Depravity
"I Was Naked."
Disposition: Sinner—"I'm an Adulterer, Fool, Destroyer, Addict,
    and Traitor."

♦ **The Rag of Chasm**

"Where Did I Come From?"
"I Came from Myself."
"I Separate:" Sin's Partition
Home Imagery: Prodigal
Original Alienation: Divide
"So I Hid."
Distance: Separated

♦ **The Rag of Captivity**

"Why Am I Here?"
"To Protect Myself."
"I'm Ruled:" Sin's Power
Marketplace Imagery: Property
Original Enslavement: Dead
"Sewed Fig Leaves."
Dominion: Slave

♦ **The Rag of Condemnation**

"How Should I Then Live?"
"Spread Seducer's Shame."
"I Dread:" Sin's Penalty
Law Court Imagery: Punished Prisoner
Original Guilt: Disgrace
"I Was Afraid."
Disintegration: Shameful

The Rag of Corruption: The Presence of Sin

The Rag of Corruption reveals the first *result* of the Fall. Created to reflect Trinity's image, Adam and Eve corrupted, polluted, and depraved the *imago Dei*. The Bible chooses *temple* imagery to portray the corrupting presence of sin. Elohim, whose glory permeates the temple Holy of Holies, is pristine, perfect, pure, righteous, sinless, good, and beautiful—absolutely holy. When Adam and Eve fell, they fell short of the glory of God. They failed to reflect the immaculateness of His being, nature, and capacities.

"Who am I?" they now asked. "We are fallen image bearers with a corrupted *imago Dei*." The image remained, but now it was desecrated: infected, soiled, defiled, stained, and perverted. Sin befouled our innocent Parents' holy garments, contaminating every spot, warping every inch.

Once seduced to sin, Adam and Eve immediately experienced the result of sinning; they became sinners. Their innocent being and God-directed capacities were defiled, creating an entirely new "species"—*homo hamartoloi*—human sinners.

Think clearly with me concerning human sinfulness. A correct understanding of sin is vital. Sin is not some substance, some being. It is not an impersonal force or power, nor is it a personal being eternally existing with God or coming into existence with Satan. Sin does not have a life of its own. Secular philosophers and pagan priests teach the duality of good and evil—two co-equal, co-eternal forces. The Bible does not.

Sin is what personal beings do. Or, more accurately, sin is what personal beings imagine, think, choose, do, and feel as they desire and love anything or anyone more than they love Worthy Groom.

"Skin of Evil" was an especially intriguing episode of *Star Trek: The Next Generation.* The premise revolved around citizens of a planet who found a way to extract and excise sin and evil from their bodies and souls. Having distilled it; they collected it, packaged it, and blasted it off into deep space, where it finally landed on an uninhabited planet. Unfortunately, the unsuspecting crew of the *Enterprise* stumbled upon evil's skin. Foul and freakish, cruel and barbaric, evil taunted and tortured them. It had a Devilish life of its own.

Though we might wish we could excise sin, and we might want to blame some personal or impersonal force for our evil, the biblical truth is plain. Only personal beings sin, because sin is the personal rejection of a personal God. Sin is spiritual adultery committed by spiritual adulterers. When Adam and Eve sinned, they became sinners.

What is a sinner? What is a fallen image bearer? What is the rag of corruption? The answer to these questions is so central to the nature of fallen human nature that we'll spend two additional chapters probing its contours, exploring the fallen nature of the runaway bride. For now we'll offer some introductory diagnoses.

As the label "Rag of Corruption" suggests, fallen image bearers are sinners with corrupted capacities. Created to reflect Trinity who loves passionately, thinks wisely, chooses courageously, and experiences deeply, we now deflect his nature. Our love is carnal, selfish, and false. Our thoughts are foolish, deluded, and twisted. Our choices and actions are cowardly and compulsive. Our emotional experiences are enslaved to fleeting pleasures.

Where we were Romancers, we are now Adulterers. Where we were Dreamers, we are now Fools. Where we were Creators, we are now Destroyers. Where we were Singers, we are now Addicts. Where we were Actors, we are now Traitors.

Adam and Eve had the same capacities of personhood after the Fall as before the Fall. What changed was the disposition, direction, or inclination of those capacities. Pre-Fall their *relational motivation* was inclined toward worshiping God and sacrificially loving each other. Post-Fall their relational motivation became bent toward self-worship, false worship, and idol worship. Pre-Fall their *rational direction* was inclined toward images and convictions about Father's goodness and Worthy Groom's worth. Post-Fall, their rational direction was poisoned with images and beliefs that insisted that since God was not good they must take care of themselves. Pre-Fall their *volitional interactions* were inclined toward purposes that pleased God and fulfilled His calling in their lives. Post-Fall, their volitional interactions became tainted with self-protective, self-serving will worship. Pre-Fall their *emotional reactions* were inclined to God, fully open and vulnerable, absolutely entrusting themselves to Him. Post-Fall, their emotional reactions became disconnected from God and compelled by the world, the flesh, and the Devil.

In the Fall, all of Adam's and Eve's capacities mutated from facing God to turning their backs to Him. After succumbing to seduction, Adam and Eve realized the significance of their corrupted capacities. "We're naked! Our covering of glory has departed." Sinful capacities then kicked into gear. *Emotional* fear, based upon *rational* lies about God, led them to the *volitional* choice to run and cover up, while they pursued the *relational* strategy of hiding (Genesis 3:7, 10).

These corrupted capacities are a basic aspect of original sin or sinfulness that our first Parents passed to all their offspring. Because of Adam and Eve, we're born dead.

> As for you, you were dead in your transgressions and sins, in which you used to live when you followed the ways of this world and of the ruler of the kingdom of the air, the spirit who is now at work in those who are disobedient [volitionally defiant and unable to obey God]. All of us also lived among them at one time, gratifying the cravings of our sinful nature [emotionally flesh-dominated] and following its desires [relationally perverted] and thoughts [rationally deluded] (Ephesians 2:1-3).

Our core being is unright, unrighteous, unhealthy, and polluted before God. If we were to enter His holy presence, He would see us as a dead carcass, a despoiled soul. In our sin-stained disposition, we refuse to seek God, turning our backs to Him (Romans 3:11-12). In our capacity-corrupted inclination, we do not understand God (Romans 3:11). We fail to do good in God's eyes (Romans 3:12), and endure dread and anxiety (Romans 3:17-18).

As we'll see in later chapters, we must grapple with ingrained tendencies of the flesh, filtered through the world, and prompted by the Devil, even when working with redeemed people. These came into play when I was counseling my worship pastor friend.

Regenerated, he had a decision. He could live as a sinner—his past identity under Satan, or he could live as a saint—his new identity in Christ. As we diagnosed his sin together (in this meeting and previous ones), we saw that when he gave in to sinful anger, it was emotionally pleasing. A quick fix. A great feeling. A release. Volitionally, it was a choice—a choice to feel powerful for the moment. Important, purposeful, a conquering champion. Rationally, it was a foolish belief—believing that intimidating others could somehow make him complete, manly. Relationally, it was a slap in the face to God. He was saying to God, "I need to be in control. My indignant anger and rage intimidates others. It allows me to get my way. I like that. Need it."

What's he to desire, think, do, and feel to be renewed? We started with his desires, longings, and thirsts in relationship to God. His God was someone to be obeyed, or else. Holy, but little else. His God was as intimidating as he was. I asked, "So when you pray to God, what's your focus?"

"I'm always praying that He'll make me holy enough that He won't have to judge me."

"What about praying to Him to exalt His holiness? Or asking that He make you holy enough to glorify His name? What about meditating on His grace, beauty, and loveliness? What about being floored by how incredibly awesome and attractive He is?" Experientially, these were foreign concepts for him.

Then we trialogued about his images of and beliefs about God. "Does He forgive you? When you confess your sin of intimidating anger, does He remind you that He laid His wrath on His Son on the Cross?"

Then we talked about choices. Not simply the choice in the moment of temptation, but choices throughout the day to focus on God. Choices to practice the spiritual disciplines that would connect him with God. It was at this point that it hit him. "I think I don't choose to get close to God because I'm terrified of surrendering fully to Him, of being that intimate with Him. I guess I've been believing that intimacy with an intimidating God is like friendship with a prison warden. I'm always one step away from solitary confinement." We wrestled with his insight for some time.

Just before he left, we talked about emotions. Peace in God or a sense of control through intimidation? Stuffed belly or satisfied soul? He said that resisting the urge to browbeat others leaves him feeling weak, puny, and incompetent. So we explored what it might be like to resist that urge and take those feelings to the God revealed in Christ.

Unless we inspect the rag of corruption, we can never help people root out the filthy fabric of sin. However, that's not all we need to dissect. Next, we look at rag two: the Rag of Chasm and the partition that sin erects between Father and His prodigal sons and daughters.

The Rag of Chasm: The Partition of Sin

Now we shift from temple imagery to *home* imagery, from sin's presence to sin's *partition*, from sinners to *separated ones*, from depravity to *division*, from original sin to original *alienation*, from nakedness to *hiding*, and from polluted capacities to *prodigal children*. It's bad enough that a holy God could not look on His polluted followers. It's worse that a loving Father is separated from His beloved, but wayward children. This is the most personal of images; we are now in our home with family and friends. Our original connection, broken by sin, leads to original alienation.

"So I hid." Sad words. Previously they had raced to Father when they heard His voice in the cool of the day. Longing for eye contact, soul contact. Now they run from Him.

Hiding from Yahweh Elohim among the trees of the Garden. What a chasm! What a great gulf Adam and Eve fixed between themselves and God when they sinned and became sinners!

As with original sin, so also our original Parents bequeathed to us original alienation. "Objects of wrath," Paul labels us in Ephesians 2:3. Our holy and just God not only can't look upon sinners; He must judge sinners. Dr. David Wells succinctly explains:

> In Pauline thought, man is alienated from God by sin and God is alienated from man by wrath. It is in the substitutionary death of Christ that sin is overcome and wrath averted, so God can look on man without displeasure and man can look on God without fear. Sin is expiated and God is propitiated (Wells, *The Search for Salvation*, p. 29).

Holy love mingled: holiness expressing wrath over sinners' sins and love taking the initiative to appease God's own righteous anger by bearing sin and judgment in our stead.

That's the good news, the gospel. Back to the bad news. What do you get when you intermingle human sin and divine holiness? Ruptured relationship. Separation. Alienation. Enmity. "Once you were alienated from God and were enemies in your minds because of your evil behavior" (Colossians 1:21). "The sinful mind is hostile to God" (Romans 8:7). As Adam and Eve ran from God, their running expressed both timid fear and arrogant anger. Dodging, ducking, looking over their shoulders, while shaking defiant fists in Father's face. No Father, however loving, can wink at such transgression.

As the psalmist recognized, "If you, O LORD, kept a record of sins, O LORD, who could stand?" (Psalm 130:3). None of us. So we hide. Our sins separate us from our Father and our Worthy Groom. Our unity we dislocate. Our harmony we fracture. Or, as Paul states it:

> Remember that at that time you were *separate* from Christ, *excluded from citizenship* in Israel and *foreigners* to the covenants of the promise, *without hope* and *without God in the world*. But now in Christ Jesus you who once were *far away* have been *brought near* through the blood of Christ. For he himself is our *peace*, who has made the two one and has *destroyed the barrier*, the *dividing wall of hostility* (Ephesians 2:12-14, emphasis added).

Double division: spiritual division from God and social division from one another, division squared.

Our ultimate hopelessness Paul describes as "without God in the world." Think about those words. "Without God in the world." How lonely. Solitary. Pessimistic. Desperate.

The author of Hebrews 10:19-23 addresses Christ's answer to our predicament of inaccessibility, restricted approach, limited entry, and denied access. Denied access is hard enough to handle if it means that your company has fired you and you can no longer access your computer files and your key no longer opens your office door. However, we're not in the business realm. We're in the living room. It's screened off. We can't get from here to there. Father is unapproachable. Unreachable. He's playing with His other children, partying with our brothers and sisters, but we're denied admittance.

Though reconciliation obliterates the barrier, when we counsel Christians we need to take into account their ingrained sense of denied access. The author of Hebrews did. "Brothers, be confident! Bold. That old barrier, Christ demolished it! He opened a new living way into the living room. So what are you waiting for? Rush on in. Draw near to God in full assurance of your acceptance. You're wanted. You're pure. Enjoy!" (Hebrews 10:19-23, author's paraphrase).

My worship pastor friend and I trialogued about these issues. He noticed how much like the returning Prodigal he is. He rehearses all the reasons he can no longer be Father's son, repeating to Father all the reasons he deserves to live in the slave quarters. All the while ignoring Father's holy hugs and kind kisses.

He detected how much he is like the Pharisaical older brother of Luke 15:25-32, also. "We're so alike," my friend said, explaining his similarities with the older brother's thought processes. "We both say, 'I slave for you. Perfectly obey all your high and holy stipulations. Yet you never party with me.' Like him, I pout. I get angry. Frustrated. No matter how many times God pursues me and pleads with me to enjoy His grace and party with my family, I refuse."

Remnants of the Fall, of the chasm. False Seducer loves it when we live out of our old life structure. When we continue to see ourselves as sinners instead of saints (from corruption to regeneration) and as separated instead of adopted (from chasm to reconciliation). He loves it when we ask, "Where did I come from?" and answer still, "I came from myself. I created a monster separated from God. So I don't dare come home. If I do, I do it in my own effort like the Prodigal son or the Pharisaical son."

The ministry of Christian counseling requires that we show believers the door. Show them that their Worthy Groom unlocked the door home. "Thirsty? Come sup with me. Lonely? Come celebrate with me."

The Rag of Captivity: The Power of Sin

Sin is horrible. *Temple* sin polluted Adam's and Eve's capacities, transforming them from innocent image bearers into depraved sinners. *Home* sin partitioned them from God's holy, loving presence, not only transporting them out of the Garden but also separating them from family life. Now, with the third rag, the Rag of Captivity, they receive the results of *marketplace* sin. The imagery here is the *slave market* where an exchange has occurred. They've been bought, purchased. They're owned. Property. Mastered. They are slaves.

Called to rule, now they are ruled. Commissioned to dominion, now they are dominated. Christened "Under-shepherds" who care for creation by guiding and guarding, now they self-protectively shepherd "only *moi*, only me, only myself alone."

Consumed with their own nakedness, they expend all their energy on leaf management. "Then the eyes of both of them were opened, and they realized they were naked; so they sewed fig leaves together and made coverings for themselves" (Genesis 3:7). Sinners separated from God and enslaved by sin inevitably live self-sufficiently and self-protectively.

Our first Parents pass on their original enslavement to their offspring. Like them, we find ourselves, apart from redemption, chained in the slave market. The emphasis of the marketplace image is "on our sorry state—indeed our captivity—in sin which made an act of Divine rescue necessary" (John Stott, *The Cross of Christ*, p. 175).

Paul opens our eyes to grim captivity in Romans 6-7. In 6:19, he uses a human analogy in order to depict a spiritual reality. Sin is *like* a master. Sin, remember, is what sinners are and do. So sin itself does not master us, but having become sinners with a sinful disposition, it is *as if* another power controls us. He uses a similar analogy in Romans 7 where he speaks of the law as a husband. The law, of course, is not a personal being, nor an impersonal force; it is not a husband. In the same way, sin is not a personal being, nor an impersonal force; it is not a slave master.

Yet, we *are* prisoners. We are mastered by our sinful capacities. We are free to live according to the inclination of our being, free to choose according to our core disposition. Adam and Eve, pre-Fall, were innocent and free to choose either God or the Devil, good or evil. Post-Fall, Adam, Eve, and their offspring inherit a sinful disposition and are free only to serve sin. "When you were slaves to sin, you were free from the control of righteousness" (Romans 6:20). Our sinful capacities reign. They rule what we desire, imagine, think, choose, do, and feel.

It is from that sorry, helpless state that Christ rescues us. He frees us from impotency to potency, from powerlessness to victory. In Romans 6:1-23, Paul trumpets, "Know this truth! Reckon on it! Base your Christian life upon it! You're now empowered to yield to God, free to choose God's way because you have a new nature!" (author's summary paraphrase).

Paul's good news is the last news False Seducer wants us to embrace. My worship pastor friend was buying the lie that sin in him was more powerful than Christ in him. He said to me, "Bob, I know I have the victory. But when the temptation comes, it feels like a monster ten times stronger than me. No matter what I do, I can't defeat it."

"You don't have to," I said quietly.

"What? What do you mean? You're not suggesting that I let sin win, are you?"

"No. I'm suggesting that sin has already lost. Christ defeated it. He's your Master now, not sin. More than that, he's your Victor now. He fought the battle, conquered sin, crucified your old nature, and implanted a new, potent nature within you. In your deepest being you now want to reject intimidating anger and you have the power to do so."

"Okay," my friend responded. "I hear you saying that I can't simply live by a 'Try Harder' mentality. So are you saying I live by a 'Let Go and Let God' philosophy?"

"Good question. Neither option accurately depicts the biblical concept. 'Know, reckon, and yield,' or 'Cooperate with Christ' better convey what Paul teaches and what I'm saying. First, you have to retrain and ingrain in your mind the actual truth—the fact that your old person with its sin-dominated capacities is dead as a doorknob. You are one new person now with the freedom to choose Christ's way and will because He implanted in you one new set of capacities (Romans 6:1-10; Galatians 2:20; Colossians 3:1-11). Second, you have to reckon on this. You need to 'count yourself dead indeed to sin, but alive to God in Christ Jesus' (Romans 6:11). You do not have to let sin reign in your mortal body so that you obey its desires."

Paraphrasing Romans 6:12-23, my friend said, "So sin is not some monster mightier than me. In Christ, I'm mightier than sin. I can stop offering my brain as an instrument of intimidating rage. Instead, I can offer my mind to God as a vessel of glory. When I intimidate, whether it feels like it or not, it's a choice that I make—a choice I make to love controlling others more than I love Jesus. If I develop my connection with Christ, if I connect to His resurrection power, then I have all the power I need to say 'No!' to anger and 'Yes!' to love." Wonderful progress, wonderful progressive sanctification. Great victory over the Rag of Captivity.

The Rag of Condemnation: The Penalty of Sin

God portrays sin's hideousness through at least four images. Through the *temple* image, He shows us that sin pollutes our nature, infecting every crevice of every capacity with depravity. Using the *home* imagery, God demonstrates that sin's presence separates us from His sinless presence. Using the *slave market* image, He teaches us that being dead in sin we become the property of sin, mastered, enslaved, and owned by it. Now, in the fourth repulsively true image, God employs *law court* imagery to depict sin's penalty. We are punished prisoners, guilty before a holy God, disgraced before a watching universe, and shamed in our own soul.

With the Rag of Condemnation, God's image shifts from holy God, Father God, and Lord God, to Just God. As we stand before His tribunal, He justly declares us "Guilty as charged!" His verdict pronounced, our liability to capital punishment produces dread.

Realizing his sinful, shameful nakedness before his Just Judge, Adam spoke for each of us when he said, "I was afraid." Every human being who ever lived shares in this dread of death—primal death, eternal death, everlasting alienation from God, unending separation from others, and perpetual dis-integration within self.

Jesus took on flesh and blood so that by His death He might destroy the Devil who holds the power of death and "free those who all their lives were held in slavery by their fear of death" (Hebrews 2:15). This is the "*anfechtungen*" or spiritual separation anxiety and spiritual depression that horrified Luther. And no wonder, without the shalom, peaceful assurance that God accepts us, we are left with condemnation—the shattering awareness that God rejects us. "Guilty! Condemned! Rejected! Unacceptable! Banished! To the gallows! To hell!"

Though we're dissecting these four rags, we need to understand that to Adam, God was at once Father *and* Judge. Think about that. It's hard enough to hear a distant judge speak the words, "Guilty as charged and sentenced to death." Adam sensed his shameful lack of acceptability before his *Father* (Genesis 3:7). So how did he respond?

Track the process with me. Adam personally and willfully sins against Father in Genesis 3:6. Recognizing that he is now "naked," he does what every sinner since has done; he attempts to make himself acceptable (Genesis 3:7). His self-beautification treatment uses the cosmetics at hand to create a covering (*hăgôrâ*) of fig leaves. Interestingly, though the Hebrew has both a masculine (*hăgôr*) and a feminine (*hăgôrâ*) word for "coverings," Moses chose the feminine. More to the point, throughout the Bible the *hhăgôrâ* is not an undergarment as the word "girdle" might suggest, but a valuable ornamented sash (Edwin Yamauchi, *Theological Wordbook of the Old Testament*, Vol. 1, p. 263).

In Isaiah 3, in the context of Yahweh's judgment upon sinful Judah, God pronounces the women of Zion haughty, illustrating their haughtiness by their ornamental jewelry, finery, necklaces, earrings, bracelets, veils, headdresses, ankle chains, sashes, linen garments, tiaras, and shawls (Isaiah 3:16-23). When they should have been repenting in sackcloth and ashes, instead they ignored their inward guilt, focusing on outward beautification. So Yahweh declares, "Instead of fragrance there will be a stench; instead of a sash (*hăgôrâ*), a rope; instead of well-dressed hair, baldness; instead of fine clothing, sackcloth; instead of beauty, branding" (Isaiah 3:24). Perfume cannot hide the stench of sin anymore than an ornamental sash can cover corrupted capacities.

Even the masculine *hăgôr* is suggestive. Young men fit for military service were designated as "all that were able to put on armour (*hăgôr*)" (2 Kings 3:21, KJV). Their military accouterment was a highly prized trophy of war (2 Samuel 18:11).

What exactly were Adam and Eve implying when they sewed together their *hăgôrâ/ hăgôr*? "I can create self-sufficient feminine beauty in order to cover my feminine nakedness and stand before my Worthy Groom," Eve was suggesting in her sinful folly. "I can create self-sufficient masculine strength in order to cover my masculine nakedness and stand before my holy Father," Adam was suggesting in his sinful folly.

What follows is fascinating. Adam hears Father's voice (*qôl*) and hides. Father draws him out. "Where are you?" Adam, from behind a tree, calls back, "I heard you [literally, I heard your voice—*qôl*] in the garden, and I was afraid because I was naked; so I hid" (Genesis 3:10). However, he wasn't naked! The naked-one had smugly covered himself. What caused Adam to recognize the insufficiency of his self-sufficient beauty treatment? Father's voice (*qôl*).

"Voice" (*qôl*) is the same Hebrew word used in Isaiah 51:3 for the song of joy, gladness, and celebration. Previously, when Adam and Eve heard Father's voice, it was in the major key, the voice of joy, gladness, and celebration. This same word, however, is frequently used for a voice or song in the minor key, the voice of lament as in Esau's wailing and weeping aloud for his lost blessing (Genesis 27:38). Imagine the shock that rocked Eve and Adam as they heard Father singing in a minor key. "What! Oh no. These garments won't fool Him. He sees right through us. He's in pain. We've hurt His heart. Back-stabbed His soul."

I believe they heard His voice of lament, but also His voice of judgment, for Moses uses *qôl* twice in Genesis 4 in a judicial context. After Cain murders his brother, Abel, Cain claims not to know where Abel is since he is not his brother's keeper (guard, guardian, protector). Yahweh responds, "Listen!" Then judicially announces, "The voice (*qôl*) of thy brother's blood crieth unto me from the ground. And now art thou cursed from the earth, which hath opened her mouth to receive thy brother's blood from thy hand" (Genesis 4:10-11, KJV). Cain hears the lamenting voice of judgment, cursing, and condemnation.

Later in the same chapter, Cain's descendant, Lamech, slays a man. Using the Hebrew word *qôl* (by now becoming a technical term in the early chapters of Genesis for a judicial proclamation), Lamech pronounces judgment on himself. "Hear my voice (*qôl*); ye wives of Lamech, hearken unto my speech [song]: 'for I have slain a man to my wounding, and a young man to my hurt.' If Cain shall be avenged sevenfold, truly Lamech seventy and sevenfold" (Genesis 4:23-24, KJV).

Hearing Father's voice of condemnation, Adam realizes the coverings he designed to accentuate his masculine soul still left his soul shamefully impotent. Eve, too, has to face the fact that the coverings she designed to accentuate her feminine soul still left her soul shamefully ugly. No wonder they "hid from the face of Yahweh" (a literal translation of Genesis 3:8). No more eye contact. No more soul contact. No more *coram Deo* intimacy. Shame reigns.

"How should I then live?" Adam and Eve asked themselves at this point. Their answer burst immediately. "Spread Seducer's shame!" When asked how he knew he was naked and if he had eaten from the tree that God commanded him not to eat, Adam blames and shames his wife and His God. "The *woman you* put here with me—she gave me some fruit from the tree, and I ate it" (Genesis 3:12, emphasis added). "It's her fault. It's your fault. Without her, I would have remained complete, instead of being this empty shell of a male image bearer."

Asked her role, Eve blames the Serpent. "The serpent deceived me, and I ate" (Genesis 3:13). Blaming and shaming.

Their Just Father cannot let them off the hook. He pronounces His judgment on them in Genesis 3:16-24. Driven from the Garden and barred from the tree of life, they will die. Capital punishment. Finally, they are silenced. In fact, before our Just Judge every mouth is silenced and the whole world held accountable and guilty (Romans 3:19).

As a result, you and I live in a world of shattered shalom. Every Christian, just like Luther and my worship pastor friend, struggles with shattered shalom. When we attempt to surmount our shalom struggle with self-sufficiency, we end up like Adam and Eve—covered, but naked still. We end up like the Old Testament saints who felt guilty continually, repeatedly, endlessly, year after year, day after day, again and again offering sacrifices for their sins (Hebrews 10:1-18). Exhausted, dis-integrated, our only hope is to confess our crime and throw ourselves on the mercy of God's court.

Shockingly, the Just Judge, our Father, sheds blood, but not our own. First, he sheds the blood of His innocent animals to fashion external coverings for Eve and Adam. Then He sheds the blood of His innocent Son, our Worthy Groom, to fashion internal Robes of Righteousness for us. Then He invites us to draw near in full assurance of faith with free access to His presence, cleansed from a guilty conscience. Amazing grace indeed.

My worship pastor friend was amazed both by God's grace and his own sin. "So what fig leaves do you wear in your attempt to dress yourself without Christ's righteousness?" I asked him.

Without hesitation, he replied. "Better corporate worship! Even my leading worship is stained with self-sufficiency, with arrogant sin. I know better than this. Much better. But I keep trying to deal with my guilt without grace. Trying to beautify myself is my ugliest sin of all."

"So what will it look like when you choose to stand stark naked before God without a shred of self-righteous clothing?" I wondered with him.

The dam burst. Tears streamed. Repentance flowed. Surrender. Rest.

Minutes later, walking down the stairs of my deck, he was experiencing godly sorrow, not worldly shame. He was on the path toward experiencing the truth that *"it's horrible to sin, but wonderful to be forgiven."* God had enabled me to dispense grace as the only medicine able to cure my friend's disgrace.

Four rags, four images of sin. As Stott notes, "These metaphors do not flatter us. They expose the magnitude of our need" (Stott, *The Cross of Christ*, p. 202). They expose the magnitude of Christ's grace.

Where We've Been and Where We're Heading

Three acts: Creation, Fall, Redemption. We're center stage in the ugliest of acts. Though I'd like to move immediately to Redemption (grace, forgiveness, gowns of the virgin bride, regeneration, reconciliation, redemption, and justification), we have more horror to endure.

To understand how to help Christians experience their victory over sin, we must more fully understand runaway bride's fallen capacities. To help our spiritual friends see the horrors of sin and appreciate the wonders of grace, we must more fully understand the fallenness of the runaway bride.

Introduced in this chapter to the Rag of Corruption, we expand upon it in the next two chapters. What exactly did sin do to the *imago Dei*? How did it affect our capacities? What occurs in the souls of Romancers, Dreamers, Creators, and Singers? In Act Three, Scenes III and IV, we view the ugly answers.

Caring for Your Soul: Personal Applications

1. Sin's Corruption: Face Your Nakedness

   a. Where do you fall short of the glorious beauty and majesty of God?

   b. In what ways do you fail to reflect Worthy Groom who is a Romancer, Dreamer, Creator, and Singer?

   c. What beautification project does God want to perform in your soul?

2. Sin's Chasm: Come Out of Hiding

   a. Long for home. Remember how good it is to dwell in peace and nearness to God.

   b. Return home. Confess sin. Be forgiven.

3. Sin's Captivity: Take Father's Clothing

   a. Identify the fig leaves that you sew. What are some personal examples?

   b. Admit the silliness of your beautification projects. What are some personal examples?

   c. Receive your cleansing and freedom from Christ. What clothing has He dressed you in?

4. Sin's Condemnation: Accept Your Acceptance in Christ

   a. Face your fears of rejection by bringing them to Christ. What specific fears do you want to hand to Him now?

   b. Exchange your disgrace for Christ's grace. What would this look and feel like in your life?

   c. Celebrate. Enjoy the embrace of God. How could you do that today?

Caring for Others: Ministry Implications

◆ **Biblical Counseling and the Rag of Corruption:** Nakedness is good. Help your spiritual friends see and admit their nakedness. Hold a mirror up to them, showing them the distorted images they now wear: Whore, Prostitute, Adulterer, Divorcee, Fool, Liar, Myth-Maker, Nightmare-Believer, Slave, Destroyer, Self-Protector, Addict, Screamer, Off-Key Singer, Traitor, etc. Then help them live out their new identity in Christ: Saint, not Sinner.

◆ **Biblical Counseling and the Rag of Chasm:** Hiding is bad. Your spiritual friends attempt to run from God and from any representative of God. They play the Prodigal. Use home imagery to assist them to see how far they have wandered. Help them come to their senses and return to Father's house. Invite them home, based on their thirst for Father and longing for Worthy Groom.

◆ **Biblical Counseling and the Rag of Captivity:** Self-protection is prominent. Expose the foolish, silly rags they are wearing. Expose their attempts to beautify themselves apart from God. Demonstrate the addictive enslavement that results. Show them the key to escape their captivity. Help them apply the "Know, Reckon, Yield" process of Romans 6.

◆ **Biblical Counseling and the Rag of Condemnation:** Fear reigns. Shame spreads. Be gentle, but firm. Bring their guilt into the open. Discuss their disgrace. Then dispense grace. Explore justification, forgiveness, and peace.

CHAPTER SIXTEEN

THE RUNAWAY BRIDE: CISTERN DIGGING, PART I

> "It is particularly important for us to contemplate Christ's perfect nature because idolatry is always an assault against the character of God. Every time our hearts turn toward the worship of false gods we're saying, God isn't really good. He's not righteous. He's not loving or holy. I have to find other gods who will satisfy me because Jesus either can't or won't" (Elyse Fitzpatrick, *Idols of the Heart*, p. 66).
>
> "Poor intricated soul! Riddling, perplexed, labyrinthical soul!" (John Donne, Sermon on January 25, 1629).

Corrupted Capacities

The media's response to crisis and corruption amazes me. In the aftermath of the September 11, 2001, terrorist attacks, everyone wanted to know why. Commentators interviewed psychologists, psychiatrists, sociologists, educators, politicians, lawyers, pundits, authors, reporters, bureaucrats, and ambassadors. I never heard a single Christian theologian interviewed.

In the aftermath of the 2002 accounting scandals that plagued big business, I listened to discussions led by accountants, CEOs, ethicists, economists, stockbrokers, and business leaders. I never heard a single Christian theologian asked to explain the source of corruption.

I am even more amazed when the church ignores theology. Visiting an adult Sunday School class, I listened as they discussed conflict causes. I wondered whether they would turn to James 4:1 to find God's answer to the question, "What causes fights and quarrels among you?" Not surprisingly, they turned to pop psychology, identifying the root source of relational conflicts as ongoing damage from childhood.

It is past time to follow a different path. In this chapter and the next, we will use theological lenses to identify the core causes of conflict, crisis, and corruption. In short, we will learn that fallen human beings sin because they are sinners.

Whereas in Chapter 14 we explored how we were seduced to sin, in Chapters 15 and 16 we present a spiritual diagnosis of the structure of sin in the fallen human personality. What does a sinner look like? How does a sinner sin? What is the basic nature of relational, rational, volitional, and emotional sinfulness? How has sin corrupted these created capacities? In psychological parlance, we are dealing with abnormal psychology and psychopathology. We are diagnosing problems and disorders—why people do what they do.

Theologian Cornelius Plantinga accurately describes how original sin corrupted our original capacities.

> Human nature itself with its vast and mysterious amalgam of capacities to think, feel, supervise, love, create, respond, and act virtuously—that is, with its capacities for imaging God—has become the main carrier and exhibit of corruption. Human nature, says the Formula of Concord, has been *despoiled* of its powers by original sin. The image suggested by this language is that of stripping—stripping a tree of its bark, an animal of its hide, or an enemy army of its arms and provisions. To do these things is to remove the skin that protects against outside invaders and keeps one's innards from spilling out. In other words, to despoil is to remove that which preserves integrity (Plantinga, *Not the Way It's Supposed to Be*, pp. 30-31).

Adam and Eve sensed their nakedness. They realized they had lost their covering of innocent glory, replacing it with despoiled dishonor.

Reformer John Calvin explains, "Original sin is humanity's inherited corruption" (Calvin, *The Institutes of the Christian Religion*, Vol. 2, p. 246). He assists our understanding further by explaining what original sin is.

> . . . the hereditary depravity and corruption of our nature, diffused into all parts of the soul, which first makes us liable to God's wrath, then also brings forth in us those works which Scripture calls "works of the flesh" (Galatians 5:19) (Calvin, *The Institutes*, Vol. 2, p. 251).

Sin pervasively corrupted our relational, rational, volitional, and emotional capacities.

To understand fallen human nature, we need to ask "Instead" questions. Instead of existing as the beautiful bride, who are we? Instead of existing as the faithful son, what are we? In our fallenness, we are runaway brides and prodigal sons.

Each human being was intended to frame a matchless individual masterpiece of God's own reflected glory. What we now have instead is an art gallery of putrid paintings. These paintings are more frightening than the ones Rod Sterling exhibited when he hosted the 1970s horror show *The Night Gallery*. Monsters we are. Ghosts of our past selves. If you're brave enough, follow me into God's Night Gallery of the Fallen Human Personality where we'll see:

- ◆ We are Romancers turning ourselves into spiritual Adulterers.
- ◆ We are Dreamers turning ourselves into arrogant Fools.
- ◆ We are Creators turning ourselves into mastered Destroyers.
- ◆ We are Singers turning ourselves into moody Addicts.
- ◆ We are Actors turning ourselves into materialistic Traitors.

Relational Corruption: Impure Affections/False Lovers
From Virgin Romancers to Spiritual Adulterers

When Adam and Eve fell, they retained their relational, rational, volitional, and emotional capacities, as well as their physical nature. These capacities still existed, but were twisted. Deprived of connection with God, their capacities degenerated. Devolution, not evolution is the rule of spiritual nature. Depraved because of disconnection from God, they became spiritually decadent. They dedicated their natural capacities away from and against God rather than *coram Deo sola gloria Dei*: face-to-face with God for God's glory alone.

As bad as this is, there's something much worse. They were dead. The moment Adam and Eve surrendered to Serpent's seduction, they died spiritually. Severing themselves from the umbilical cord of life, they shriveled up and died.

As their spiritual heirs, we inherit their corrupt nature at birth. We're depraved and dead. Fallen human nature is separated from the life of God (Ephesians 4:17-19). Tightly tie this together.

- We're relational beings created for communion with God.
- We're dead relational beings separated from connection with God.
- We're deprived and depleted: starving, hungry, thirsty relational beings.
- We're depraved and decadent: crawling anywhere but to God for relational sustenance.

What a paradox. We're dead, but alive. We're zombies in the night of the living dead.

What is a sinner? Sinners are Spiritual Adulterers who reject their Worthy Groom for the False Seducer. Sin is what sinners do in their relationships. Sin is always *awayness*. Instead of moving toward, I move away. Instead of loving God by glorifying Him (Matthew 22:35-40), I live to glorify myself (James 4:1-10). Instead of loving others by ministering to them (Matthew 22:35-40), I manipulate them to satisfy myself (James 4:1-10). Reality is relational, so sin is relational. Sinners are relationally motivated, but God-rejecting.

What is a relational sinner? Sinners are:

- Fallen spiritual beings who experience alienation from God and pursue false lovers of the soul in their desperate thirst for reunion with God.
- Fallen social beings who experience separation from one another and dig broken cisterns in their endless quest for reconnection with others.
- Fallen self-aware beings who experience disintegration within their own souls and yield to destructive habits of the will and controlling passions of the affections in their futile attempts to quiet their inner restlessness.

The next trail on our journey leads us to an exploration of how these fallen spiritual, social, and self-aware beings relate.

Relational Prodigals: From Faith in Father to Fearful Flight from Father

Like Cain, fallen human beings are terrified fugitives, wanderers, and vagabonds. The controlling passion of the fallen soul moved from faith in Father to fear of Father. The controlling image of God in the fallen soul moved from generous, gracious, and good Father, to hoarding, condemning, angry Judge. As Luther eloquently testified:

> The poets fancied that souls were terrified by the bark of Cerberus; but real terror arises when the voice of the wrathful God is heard, that is, when it is felt by the conscience. Then God, who previously was nowhere, is everywhere. Then he who earlier appeared to be asleep hears and sees everything; and his wrath burns, rages, and kills like fire (Luther, *Luther's Works*, Vol. 2, p. 22).

Luther recognized that our ultimate fear is cosmic condemnation (Romans 8:1-39). Sinners are in fearful flight from Father while still in desperate need of Him.

We are psycho-spiritual beings—souls related to God. Luther labeled us *homo spiritualis nititur fide*, meaning spiritual beings with original trust, spiritual beings living by faith. This counters Freud's hypothesis that we are psychosexual beings. He believed that the root of all issues was sexual. He identified a *symptom* of our problem as our *core* problem. True, many people turn to sex and sexuality as a false god in their frantic attempt to quench their sense of isolation. However, sexual sin is simply a symptom of spiritual sin. We need God; we fear God; we reject God; we pursue non-god substitutes.

When I'm counseling people who are struggling against sin, my mind is not focused on, "What psycho-sexual issue lies beneath their cluster of symptoms?" I'm not searching for a root problem from their poor relationship with their opposite gender parent. Instead, I'm wondering, "Where does Christ fit into their souls? Is He welcomed? Wanted? Feared? Avoided?" I'm pursuing causes of their pursuit of non-God substitutes.

Relational Adulterers: From Solely Devoted to Worthy Groom to Frantically Pursuing False Lovers of the Soul

Still existing as relational beings, albeit corrupted, we desperately search for substitutes. We seek false lovers. Calvin reacts strongly to our relational sinfulness. "God is provoked to jealousy whenever we substitute our figment in place of him, as when a lewd woman, openly parading her adulterer before her husband's very eyes, infuriates his mind all the more" (Calvin, *The Institutes*, Vol. 2, p. 816).

What is a sinner? Not simply a thief caught in a crime, but an adulterer caught in the act. Sin is a betrayal of love. Sin is not only breaking God's law, it is wounding His heart.

Our marriage covenant with God insists that we offer our devotion to no other lover, just as a man will share his wife with no other. According to Ray Ortlund, God reacts to spiritual adultery even more strongly than Calvin does.

> True religion is marital in nature. What sort of husband would look at his wayward wife and dismiss her adulteries by mumbling, "As long as she and her lovers don't shake the bed and make too much noise, as long as I can get my sleep, what's the big deal? It's only marriage!"? No one but a knave would own such a sentiment.

So how can we trivialize our covenant with God? The covenant is a marriage. It is *the* marriage (Ortlund, *Whoredom*, p. 174).

Sinners are relational Divorcees who reject the Spouse who no longer measures up to their expectations.

In Jeremiah 3, God accuses sinners of being prostitutes, whores, adulterers, and betrayers. Sinners are betrayal incarnate; betrayal *is* the fallen disposition. Cringe at Yahweh's fierce indictments that expose how fallen image bearers have a predisposition toward whoredom and a persistent bent toward adultery.

> You have lived as a prostitute with many lovers . . . Is there any place where you have not been ravished? By the roadside you sat waiting for lovers, sat like a nomad in the desert. You have defiled the land with your prostitution and wickedness . . . Have you seen what faithless Israel has done? She has gone up on every high hill and under every spreading tree and has committed adultery there . . . Because Israel's immorality mattered so little to her, she defiled the land and committed adultery with stone and wood . . . Return, faithless people, declares the LORD, for I am your husband (Jeremiah 3:1, 2, 6, 9, 14).

Fallen image bearers stake their lives on the false lovers they can win, discarding the reality of God and embracing the unreality of counterfeit gods.

Sin is always about distorted desire. Desire is not wrong—it is God-designed. But we distort our desire. More than that, we exchange our desire for God with desire for lesser gods, for false loves. Sin is always false love and idols of the heart. "The language of turning to other gods means that Israel rejects Yahweh, regards him lightly, sees little in him to desire or hope in, and instead invests those affections in others" (Jeremiah Burroughs, *Commentary on the Prophecy of Hosea*, p. 182).

Corrupt relationality perversely turns loyalty, love, energy, and desire away from God. It is a twisting of our design. False love is a pollution that divides and disintegrates by introducing a third party into the spiritual marital relationship. Divided love destroys love.

When I'm meeting with a friend who is devoured by a besetting sin, my mind constantly considers false lovers. "What is it about this sin that my friend loves more than Jesus? What distorted desire does this sin indicate? What idol of the heart needs to be exposed and rooted out? What broken cistern do I detect?"

Relational Narcissist: From Dependence upon Messenger to Self-Sufficiency

Looking for love in all the wrong places, sinners find nothing to fill their empty places. Rejecting dependence upon the Holy Spirit—the stream of living water flowing within—they're parched. As Plantinga succinctly states, "If we try to fill our hearts with anything besides the God of the universe, we find that we are overfed but undernourished" (Plantinga, *Not the Way It's Supposed to Be*, p. 122). Now what? Needy but empty, sinners' stomachs demand self-sufficient self-satisfaction.

> Our substitutes can never adequately serve as proper sources for life, but following the Deceiver who led Adam and Eve to doubt, we lie to ourselves and learn to live

with our idols. At some level of semi-consciousness, though, we recognize our lie, and therefore we live in dread, dread that the gods we have fashioned for ourselves will fall apart. That makes us defensive: Luther's term was that we are "*turned in upon ourselves*," and "*protecting ourselves*" from the evils that assault us (A. Nebe, *Luther As Spiritual Advisor*, p. 5, emphasis added).

Narcissism—living for self, loving self, caressing self, shepherding self, and feeding self. All the self-sins flow out of our rejection of God-satisfaction: self-love, self-centeredness, self-sufficiency, self-effort, selfishness, self-dependence, and self-protection. Rather than lifting up our hands in worship and reaching out our hands in ministry, we turn in upon ourselves, all wrapped up in self and wrapped around ourselves.

Ezekiel links self-sufficiency and self-beautification as he records Yahweh's allegory of love. Israel, an abandoned newborn, lies naked in her own blood. Yahweh passed by and "saw you kicking about in your blood" (Ezekiel 16:6). He rescues her, nurtures her, and recognizes her inherent, but hidden, beauty. When she comes of age, He marries her, adoring and adorning her. Through Him, she became "very beautiful and rose to be a queen." And He told her, "your fame spread among the nations on account of your beauty, because the splendor I had given you made your beauty perfect" (Ezekiel 16:13b-14).

Beautiful by birth, heinous by sin, beautified by God; we'd expect loyalty. "But *you trusted in your beauty* and used your fame to become a prostitute. You lavished your favors on anyone who passed by and your beauty became his" (Ezekiel 16:15, emphasis added). Life focused on self. Self focused on self. Self satisfying self.

Self-sufficiency is the arrogant deification of human nature. "I must satisfy and I can satisfy my soul's cravings." The fallen nature has an unbounded eagerness to trust its own resources.

Spiritual adultery entails more than religious offenses. When we do not pursue God passionately and trust Him fully, we deny the adequacy of His care and control, protection and provision, so we fend for ourselves on our own terms.

Self-sufficiency is a *de facto* denial of Christ's all-sufficiency, of our Lover's sufficient resource for all of life. It's slapping God's face. Sin is trusting in ourselves, or anyone, or anything else rather than God. In Ezekiel, as the wife ought to lie under the shadow of her husband, so God wished the Jews to be content under His protection. But when danger reared, they trembled and fled to Egypt. "They renounced God's help, since they could not rest under His protection, but were hurried hither and thither by vague impulse" (Calvin, *Commentary on Ezekiel*, p. 10).

The biblical motif of "turning to other gods" means that Israel rejects Yahweh, regards Him lightly, sees little in Him to desire or hope in (compare Romans 1:28), and instead invests those affections in others. Patrick Fairbairn's penetrating commentary captures the sinfulness of sinners.

> Instead of seeking, as is duty bound, to promote her Husband's credit and renown in the world, the unfaithful wife acts rather as if her object were to show how low a place he held in her esteem and how much she preferred others before him (Fairbairn, *Commentary on Ezekiel*, p. 169).

When I'm offering spiritual direction, my mind thinks in categories like those raised by Fairbairn and our preceding discussion. "How are they dishonoring God? How are they depending on themselves? What self-beautification projects are they expending their energy on? How are they wrapping their arms narcissistically around themselves?" Relational corruption forces us to ponder these types of questions.

Longings, thirsts, and affections provide the energy behind life, motivating the soul to satisfy a hunger for intimate involvement and union with other personal beings. Sinners change the direction they turn in order to quench their relational thirsts. As worshiping beings created to trust Father, but wrenched by a sinful nature, sinners resort to worshiping created reality. The longing for God remains, but humanity turns in other directions to meet that longing for Father/Groom/Messenger. Sinners are *moving-away-from-God-beings* who turn their backs on God. Their sinful relational capacity disrupts and distorts worship through rebellious self-centered self-sufficiency. In summary, sinners are Princesses turning themselves into ugly Whores, passionately pursuing anyone but their Worthy Groom.

Rational Corruption: Foolish Mindsets
From Imaginative Dreamers to Arrogant Fools

Relationally, sinners retreat from whole-hearted worship of God to corrupt-hearted love for false gods. *Rationally*, sinners move from Dreamers who imagine that nothing is impossible for God, to foolish lie-believers who arrogantly suppress the truth of God's holy love. We can summarize sinful *relational* capacities using the language of false love, impure affections, and spiritual adultery. We can encapsulate sinful *rational* capacities using the language of fleshly, foolish mindsets. *Relational* evil is heinous. *Rational* evil is ludicrous.

To comprehend sinful rational capacities, we need to probe the foolish imagination. Imagination is not simply "creative thinking." Imagination is the ability to perceive natural things with spiritual eyes. So the foolish imagination is the inability and refusal to look at life with spiritual eyes; it is the fallen disposition to see life with eyeballs only—choosing to leave God out of the picture.

Remember also how Genesis 6:5 and 8:21 speak of the sinfulness of our imagination (*yēser*). We shape our own picture, vision, dream, or version of reality. Instead of worshiping the Potter who forms us, we form the Potter in our own image. We weave a fabricated version of reality (Proverbs 6:18).

At bottom, fools are out of touch with God-reality; they attempt to displace the irreplaceable God. Wisdom is a reality-based phenomenon. The wise discern reality and how to live well within it. The wise live with 20/20 spiritual vision, fitting themselves into God's universe. Folly, on the other hand, is a witlessness that has no knack for fitting into the world as it is. Sinners are wrong and foolish, living with eyeballs only, refusing to adjust their lives to God-reality.

Rational Idolaters: Creating Gods in Our Image

What are rational sinners like? They are rational idolaters who create gods in their own image—*imago anthropos*. Asaph, speaking as Elohim's mouthpiece, condemns those who "thought I [Elohim] was altogether like you" (Psalm 50:21). We imagine God in our image.

We all have a golden calf (or two or three or more) before which we bow and worship. In our fallen state, we all worship ourselves and created reality (Romans 1). Both Rabbis and Reformers recognized this. Jewish Rabbis say, "In every sin there is something of the golden calf" (Quoted in Ortlund, *Whoredom*, p. 137). Calvin concurs. "The human mind is a perpetual forge of idols. Idolatry has its origin in the idea which men have that God is not present unless his presence is carnally exhibited" (Calvin, *The Institutes*, Vol. 1, p. 97).

To understand this process, we need to connect the links in the chain of faith, false love, idols, and the imagination. Faith is the core of the original human personality. God originally designed human beings as *faith-in-God-beings*, but now people are *faith-in-anything-but-God-beings*. Luther provides the insightful connection.

A god is that to which we look for all and in which we find refuge in every time of need. To have a god is nothing else than to trust and believe him with our whole heart. If your faith and trust are right, then your God is the true God (Luther, *Large Catechism*, p. 1).

By Luther's definition, every person has a god. There is no such thing as an atheist, for everyone must put trust in something, or some combination of other persons and things, or life will disappear.

The Heidelberg Catechism in the *Book of Confessions* defines idolatry as imagining or possessing something in which to place one's trust other than the one true God. Putting our ultimate trust in anything besides God is idolatry. Idolatry is misdirected worship. It is misdirected trust, faith, commitment, hope, glorification, honor, and attachment. Idolatry is misdirected love. Augustine summarizes this well, explaining that the foundation for sin is putting our ultimate faith, trust, and loving commitment in anything besides God.

But how does my heart manufacture the *specific* idol(s) I carve and worship? First, I create sub-biblical images of God—contemptuous images that have no awe of God, no sense of the attractiveness of His beauty and the awesomeness of His majesty. With God dismissed, I give birth to idols in my own image to make my life work without God. I become the most beautiful thing in the world. I think of myself as "God's gift to the world." Stephen Charnock, the brilliant Puritan theologian, connects contemptuous images of God and arrogant images of self:

> All sin is found in secret atheism. Every sin is a kind of cursing God in the heart. A man at every sin aims to set up his own will as his rule, and his own glory as the end of his actions. Every sin is an effort to turn from the worship of God to the worship of self. At root, sin is self-worship (Charnock, *The Existence and Attributes of God*, p. 171).

I start by saying, "God is not good enough for me." Then I conclude, "I am sufficient for myself."

Isaiah 44:9-23 offers further convincing evidence that we all imagine unique idols that best fit our unique hearts. The blacksmith uses his personal tools to create a personal god who best fits his own personality, talents, needs, longings, and beliefs (44:10-12). Then the carpenter comes along to measure a block of wood, shaping it into a distinct god using the particular tools he's most adept with (44:13-17). When each is done, they both proclaim, "Save *me*; you are *my* god" (44:17, emphasis added). What a clear physical picture of a spiritual reality: I form and shape the very idol of self that I worship instead of God.

Biblical counselor Elyse Fitzpatrick understands how our self-focused, idol-creating imagination works.

> Can you see how every person has a unique heart that responds in uniquely different ways? Although we all have the same sinful nature and bent to create false gods, we create them for very different reasons. We create images out of our thoughts of our highest good or happiness (Fitzpatrick, *Idols of the Heart*, p. 87).

Some of us believe that the source of our greatest good and happiness is pastoring a large church. So numbers and church growth become the idol of our heart. Some of us believe that we can find peace in pleasing people. So we play the "nice guy" or the "good girl." Our idol means never rocking the boat, never standing up for what is right. Peace at any price. Some of us believe that life is meaningful only when we're on top. So we live competitive lives, worshiping promotions and accomplishments. The examples are as endless as the infinite uniqueness God designed within each of us.

What does this imply for biblical counseling? Loosening sin at the motivational level requires detecting the characteristic roots and shape of foolish mindsets (Romans 8) and fleshly styles (Romans 1:17-28). We need biblical wisdom to perceive the specific false route(s) our counselee is pursuing to satisfy the specific longing(s) of his or her soul.

That requires entering their lives, hearing their stories, listening to their themes and plot lines. It means exploring with them what motivates them, what they believe about God, about themselves, about others, and about their world. It means engaging their souls so deeply that we can begin to sense who they are, how they relate to us, what drives them, and what they trust in to make their lives work apart from Christ.

Rational Fools: Arrogant Minds and Deluded Hearts

Courting other lovers describes our *relational* sinfulness. *Why* we court other lovers relates to our *rational* sinfulness. Isaiah 44:20 summarizes the fallen nature, "A deluded heart misleads him." Hebrews 3:12-15 labels it "an unbelieving heart"—a heart without trust in God. Such a heart turns away from, goes astray, rebels, revolts against, and stands aloof from our Worthy Groom. Numbers 14:11 describes it as "contempt" and defines it as our refusal to believe that God can/will take care of us. We place God on trial to see whether He meets our approval and measures up to our standards of excellence. Our deluded hearts deceive us into seeing Him either as a 98-pound weakling or a 398-pound bouncer.

Isaiah pictures how our spiritually dull minds mock us.

> Half of the wood he burns in the fire; over it he . . . roasts his meal and eats his fill. He also warms himself and says, "Ah! I am warm; I see the fire." From the rest he makes a god, his idol; he bows down to it and worships. He prays to it and says, "Save me; you are my god" (Isaiah 44:16-17).

How ludicrous. Outrageous. Stupid. Blind. "They know nothing, they understand nothing; their eyes are plastered over so they cannot see, and their minds closed so they cannot understand" (Isaiah 44:18). Fallen humanity is blind to its blindness. Thinking themselves wise, they became fools. Thinking themselves alive, they are dead. Working their way to heaven, hell resides within.

Foolishness is so foolish that it requires effort to perpetuate. "No one stops to think" (Isaiah 44:19). We refuse to say, "Half of this tree I used for fuel; shall I bow down to the other block of wood and worship it?" We refuse to say, "God gave me the gift of counseling, shall I bow down and worship the praise people give me when I help them?" We never stop to think, "My children are God's gift to me. Shall I bow down and worship them, cling to them, pamper them, spoil them?" We never stop to think, "God gives me all things richly to enjoy. Shall I worship the almighty dollar?"

Jeremiah joins Isaiah and Paul in their exasperation over fallen suppression. "How can you say I am not defiled?" (Jeremiah 2:23). Confronted with proof through reproof, hardened people evade self-examination. Sinners defend and deceive themselves. Jeremiah catches them in the act, shows them the video, and they still plead, "Not guilty!" They cover their ears so they can't hear the truth shouting to them, because they've corrupted their fallen minds through self-chosen deceit (Ephesians 4:22).

How does foolishness show up in daily life? John Owen proposes that sinners sin because they've lost a true sense of the beauty of God, the vileness of evil, and the wonder of grace. Those things become abstractions and people lose control over their imagination. Sinners turn away from God as their affection and appreciation for Him cools. The sinful will then consent to whatever appears as good, and sinners choose to surrender to the enticement of false gods. After time this develops into a habituate mental pattern (foolish mindsets) and an almost automatic cycle of action-reaction (habituated volitional pathways and styles of relating).

How does the fallen mind ignite this process? Luther sneaks into the mind to diagnose the connection between our image of God and fallen human reasoning.

> According to reason alone, our God is always in the wrong, no matter what he does. Either he is viewed as too severe and judgmental, or he is considered too indulgent. When a skeptic thinks about God and sees what happens in this world, he cannot do other than conclude that either God is very weak and cannot stop suffering, or he is very evil and wicked and delights in suffering (Luther, *Luther's Works*, Vol. 54, p. 105).

God provides rain for the evil, food for the birds, sun for the flowers, and they toil not (Matthew 6:25-30). They rest in and receive God's good provision. Why is it then, that in all creation, humanity alone fails to trust God alone? We work and worry, as if either will guarantee anything. We should perceive God's caring providence as evidence of His loving generosity. Given our history with our Worthy Groom, we should know full well His creative abundance, but we choose to misperceive the source of our bounty.

Ezekiel simplifies the process. He informs us that we choose a surface level perspective, a superficial awareness that rejects the loving protection of our Divine Husband. Like a naïve schoolgirl, love-struck by a cool guy, we're attracted to non-god options (Ezekiel 23:5-10).

Perhaps you've had the experience of repenting of a besetting sin and finding some measure of consistent victory. Later, when you looked back on your past sinfulness, you said, "Duh. Hello! What's wrong with this picture?" I've experienced it more times than I care to admit. "I did what? I trusted in that! What was I thinking?"

When Christians live as though the fallen nature still reigns, they are oblivious to self-discovery and impervious to self-reproach. When we counsel Christians who are living as non-Christians, we must help them come to their senses, as the Prodigal did. Not only after repenting of sin, but also when caught in the middle of sin, Christians need to come to their senses and say, "How many of my Father's servants have food to spare, and here I am starving to death! What's the matter with me? How could I believe that the world could ever satisfy my soul?"

When tempted to sin, we must obey our thirst for God and follow mindsets of the Spirit so we can say, "Not this time. No way. I'm stopping to think. God is good. Holy. Loving. God and what He chooses to provide is all I need. I worship Him."

Biblical thinking counteracts the pull of the sinful mind. Saints are Dreamers cleaving to truths like, "Man does not live by bread alone, but by every word that comes from the mouth of God" (Matthew 4:4). And, "Do not put the Lord your God to the test" (Matthew 4:7). And, "Worship the Lord your God, and serve him only" (Matthew 4:10). On the other hand, fallen sinners are imaginative Dreamers, turning themselves into arrogant Fools, fooled into thinking that the Worthy Groom is unworthy and unloving.

Where We've Been and Where We're Heading

Relational sin is ugly and rational sin is stupid. Unfortunately, there's more to say about volitional and emotional sin. Volitional sinners choose self-protective pathways instead of living according to Christ's sacrificial model. Emotional sinners experience survival modes and unmanaged mood states instead of learning how to be emotional and sin not. Additionally, fallen sinners live in a fallen world where they battle the world, the flesh, and the Devil.

In Act Three, Scene IV, we'll explore the connection between false lovers of the soul, foolish mindsets, self-protective pathways, unmanaged mood states, the world, the flesh, and the Devil. By the time we finish, we'll have God's perspective on fallen relational, rational, volitional, and emotional capacities and how they interact within a fallen world.

Caring for Your Soul: Personal Applications

1. What is your tendency when you become aware of sin in your life? Do you ignore it? Do you become overwhelmed by guilt and become discouraged? Do you confess it and find newness of life in God's gracious forgiveness?

2. Which of the following *Night Gallery* portraits of sin best mirror your struggle against sin? How? Why? How are you cooperating with God to defeat these sin issues?

    ♦   We are Romancers turning ourselves into spiritual Adulterers.
    ♦   We are Dreamers turning ourselves into arrogant Fools.
    ♦   We are Creators turning ourselves into mastered Destroyers.
    ♦   We are Singers turning ourselves into moody Addicts.
    ♦   We are Actors turning ourselves into materialistic Traitors.

3. In what situations do you find yourself fearfully fleeing Father? Why?

4. In what ways are you tempted toward self-sufficiency? How do you attempt to satisfy your soul apart from your Savior?

5. Sinners are Princesses turning themselves into ugly Whores passionately pursuing anyone but their Worthy Groom.

    a. Compare and contrast the above summary with how you have normally thought of sin and sinners.

    b. How does this relational summary impact your view of yourself when you were/are apart from God? How does it affect your view of God's grace?

6. Read Genesis 6:5; Genesis 8:21; and Isaiah 44:12-17. These passages teach that we create idols in our own image to make our life work without God. List some modern-day "idols" that *we* create. That *you* create.

7. Idolatry is misdirected worship, false love, impure affections, and misplaced trust—worshiping, loving, and trusting anything but God.

    a. Give modern-day examples of these forms of sin.

    b. As biblical counselors, how do we begin to perceive the false routes a person is pursuing to satisfy his/her longings?

8. Read Jeremiah 2:20-23; Romans 1:19-28; Hebrews 3:7-14; and Hebrews 4:12-16. Based upon our discussion of these verses, why do *we* sin? Why do *you* sin?

Caring for Others: Ministry Implications

♦ **Reconciliation Begins Relationally:** Biblical counseling deals with suffering *and* with sin. Chapter 16 highlights the sin-focus. In reconciling, help your spiritual friends understand the horrors of sin. Load their conscience with guilt, as the Puritans did. Expose the horror and guilt of sin by exposing the fact that sin is spiritual adultery.

♦ **Diagnosis Begins Relationally:** Biblical counseling diagnosis exposes:

1. Spiritual Death: How is your spiritual friend separated from the life of God?

2. Relational Alienation: How is your spiritual friend in fearful flight from Father? How is he or she betraying God by turning to false lovers? How is he or she hiding from God? How is he or she practicing self-sufficiency through self-beautification?

♦ **Reconciliation Highlights the Heart:** Behavioral sin is the external evidence of inner heart sin. Biblical counselors emphasize false lovers of the soul/impure affections, idols of the heart, foolish mindsets, fleshly images, arrogant beliefs, stubborn blindness, and selective suppression.

♦ **Diagnosis Examines the Heart Condition:** Biblical counseling diagnosis exposes:

1. Foolish Mindsets: Where is your spiritual friend looking at life with eyeballs only? Where is he or she choosing to leave God out of the picture?

2. Fleshly Images and Idols of the Heart: Where is your spiritual friend trying to make life work apart from God? What is he or she trusting in? Putting faith in?

3. Contemptuous Beliefs: Where is your spiritual friend holding God in contempt? Dethroning God? What signs do you see of an unbelieving heart?

4. Stubborn Blindness and Selective Suppression: Where is your spiritual friend denying the goodness of God? Where is he or she refusing to acknowledge sin?

CHAPTER SEVENTEEN
THE PRODIGAL BRIDE: CISTERN DIGGING, PART II

> "The will may be conditioned by tendencies. Repeated acts of the will to sin often produce a disposition and inclination toward sin. This proneness leads to easy consent" (John Owen, *Sin and Temptation*, p. 66).
>
> "You cannot have power for good without having power for evil too. Even mother's milk nourishes murderers as well as heroes" (Bernard Shaw, *Major Barbara*).

What Tangled Webs We Weave

"Master, I am in great distress! The spirits that I conjured up I cannot now get rid of" (Goethe, *The Sorcerer's Apprentice*). In our futile attempts to control life without God, our foolish imagination conjures up false lovers who consequently exercise control over our lives.

We remember Dylan Thomas, one of the best-known British poets of the mid-20th century, for his highly original, obscure poems, his amusing prose tales and plays, and his turbulent, well-publicized personal life. Listen to his existential angst over losing control while trying to find control. "I hold a beast, an angel, and a madman in me, and my enquiry is as to their working, and my problem is their subjugation and victory, downthrow and upheaval, and my effort is their self-expression." What went wrong in his life? What is the source of our life problems?

To answer these questions, we need to untangle our corrupted capacities. As fallen *relational* beings, we reject God's awesomeness, refusing to experience our Worthy Groom as enough. We transform ourselves into adulterers, loving false lovers. As fallen *rational* beings, we foolishly shun God. Without Father in our lives, we believe counterfeit stories about where we find life. Without Worthy Groom, we worship what makes our lives work either to quench perceived thirsts or to deny unmet longings. Consequently, as fallen *volitional* beings, we are swallowed whole by our gods. Not being God, but being finite, we can't pull off our goals on our own. So we either manipulate others so they meet our perceived needs and false goals, or we retaliate against them for not meeting our perceived needs and false goals. Then as fallen *emotional* beings, we face the fearful failure of our fallen schemes. Not being God, our false lovers fail to fill us. We now dread feeling anything deeply and become emotionally addicted to experiencing shallow pleasure and avoiding pain.

Box 17:1

Sin's Developmental Stages

Sin Relationally: From Romancers to Adulterers
Impure Affections/False Lovers

Rejecting God's awesomeness, refusing to experience God as sufficient, I reject Him by:

1. Relying on myself, not God.
2. Trusting in myself, not God.
3. Making myself god.
4. Worshiping false gods and loving false lovers.

Sin Rationally: From Dreamers to Fools
Foolish Mindsets

Without God in my life, my belly becomes my god. Without the Spirit, I believe counterfeit stories about where life is found. Without Christ, I worship what makes my life work to:

1. Quench my perceived thirst—gain pleasure by self-fulfillment.
2. Deny my unmet longings/groanings—avoid pain by self-protection.

Sin Volitionally: From Creators to Destroyers
Self-Centered Purposes/Pathways

Not being God, but being finite, I can't pull off my goals on my own. So I:

1. Manipulate you (use you) to meet my perceived needs and false goals (gain pleasure/avoid pain).
2. Retaliate against you (abuse you) for not meeting my perceived needs and false goals.

Sin Emotionally: From Singers to Addicts
Ungoverned Mood States

Not being God, you fail to fill me. I now dread feeling anything deeply. I become emotionally addicted to:

1. Experiencing shallow pleasure.
2. Avoiding personal pain.

Volitional Corruption: Self-Centered Purposes/Pathways
From Empowered Creators to Mastered Destroyers

Volitionality reflects a distinctive mark of the *imago*. God, who freely wills and powerfully purposes, designed us with the capacity to choose. We are goal-oriented people—neither animals controlled by instinct, nor souls controlled by lust.

How tragically far we've fallen. In our fallen state, we're unable to have dominion over our own passions, much less God's planet. "At one time we too were foolish, disobedient, deceived and enslaved by all kinds of passions and pleasures. We lived in malice and envy, being hated and hating one another" (Titus 3:3).

Notice the first link in the chain—foolishness. *Our wills obey our minds, which obey our thirsts.* If we're convinced God is our Supreme Good, we'll pursue Him with a steely will. If we're persuaded God is not good, we'll pursue non-god substitutes with an enslaved will. Ultimately, volitional sin is the choice of self as the supreme end that constitutes the antithesis of supreme love to God.

Our choice comes with a cost—enslavement. *We are only free to choose according to our nature.* If our nature is innocent, we are free to choose either good or evil. If our nature is fallen, we're free to choose only evil. "When you were slaves to sin, you were free from the control of righteousness" (Romans 6:20). The unbelieving nature is depleted and depraved. Accordingly, the will descends from choosing courageously to choosing compulsively.

Volitional Slaves: Enslaved to Our Gods

Christians debate the language of addiction. Some cringe at the word "addiction," feeling it smacks of irresponsibility: "I can't help myself. My addiction to alcohol controls me." The truth is, volitionally fallen people cannot help themselves. That much is accurate. However, they are responsible. They're without excuse for their continued rejection of Christ that results in the continued corruption of their capacities. Helpless, but responsible.

Foolishness about the greatest Lover of the soul results in ruts in the brain and routes in the mind—fleshly mindsets. Sinners develop ingrained patterns of thinking about the final source of life. These fleshly mindsets lead to habituate interactive styles—self-centered pathways. Recall Peter's haunting words about slaves to depravity. "For a man is a slave to whatever has mastered him . . . 'A dog returns to its vomit,' and 'A sow that is washed goes back to her wallowing in the mud'" (2 Peter 2:19, 22).

Biblically, the language of enslavement seems preferable to the language of addiction. We can picture the "enslavement cycle" as a natural chain of events, a logical sequence.

- ◆ We were created for relationship with the infinite God of the universe.
- ◆ Only God can satisfy our soul.
- ◆ We reject God as our source of life.
- ◆ We retain the God-shaped and God-sized vacuum in our soul.
- ◆ We seek to fill that vacuum in non-God ways and through non-God means, i.e., through finite means.

- ♦ Filling our soul's emptiness becomes our god ("whose god is their belly"). Priority one becomes indulging or feeding our soul's hunger.
- ♦ It takes an infinite amount of finite "food" to fill the infinite, God-sized vacuum in our soul.

Think about it. We're driven to quench *spiritual* thirsts with *physical* water. We attempt to fill *metaphysical* hunger with *physical* sustenance. We try to feed our *infinitely* hungry souls through *finite* morsels for our stomachs.

Picture the infinite goodness of God as a huge dotted line indicating that He is without limits, boundless, utterly immense, immeasurable, and endless. Only his illimitable Being could ever quench our thirst.

Now picture our petty substitutes as puny dots, a period at the end of a sentence, a pinprick, a speck, or a grain of sand. Pornography, lust, power, promotions, pleasure, money, an affair, acclaim, being liked—these are portions smaller than a crumb off the table. So how many crumbs will it take to fill the God-sized hunger in my soul? How many grains of sand are required to fill the ocean-sized longing of my heart?

I eat one morsel of flirtatious conversation with an also-starving co-worker. "Mmmm, good," my fallenness thinks. "Stolen water is sweet; food eaten in secret is delicious," Solomon informs us in Proverbs 9:17. I want more. Crave more. Compulsively need more. My co-worker and I have lunch together. Tell each other how wonderful we are. Swallow another morsel off False Seducer's buffet. An hour later, my stomach growls. You can imagine the ugly, compulsive steps that follow in the ever-maddening attempt to satisfy God-sized and God-shaped longings with anything but our Worthy Groom.

Trying to satisfy our soul by our own self-sufficiency, we lose all self-control. Drinking water from broken cisterns that hold no water, we entangle ourselves in an endless, vicious cycle of "more, More, MORE!" We habituate our wills toward self-indulgence. "Having foolishly separated themselves from God, they surrender themselves to horrible sensuality in order to practice every manner of impurity in which they crave personal indulgence with a continual lustful demand for more" (Ephesians 4:19, author's paraphrase).

Enslavement produces sensuality or *lasciviousness*—the ugliest word in the New Testament. Lasciviousness evokes images such as passions gone wild, self-indulgence run amok, desires out of control, living without restraint and without regard for any one but me.

Triggered by the flesh (body, bones, brain, belly), fallen humanity pursues instant flesh reactions and craves personal pleasure. Making no attempt at self-control, people live without self-discipline, surrendering only to their own greed.

In essence, Jeremiah 2:20-25 is saying, "It is hopeless. For I have loved strangers, and after them I must go." Living at the mercy of their cravings, with a sigh, they admit it. "I'm hopelessly hooked." As Ray Ortlund describes it, "What they ought to do is clearly evident. It is even in their own interests. But they are addicted" (Ortlund, *Whoredom*, p. 89).

Jeremiah 3:1-3 and the image of an easy pick-up making herself available at a truck stop may translate this into modern terms. Ezekiel 16:28-29 paints a similar picture: "You were insatiable, you played the harlot and you still were not satisfied. You multiplied your harlotry, and even with this you were not satisfied" (author's paraphrase). They have an out of control, unquenchable appetite. "Their nymphomaniacal desire was still not sated" (Ortlund, *Whoredom*, p. 111).

Calvin's commentary is just as searing.

The sum of the whole is that the Jews were seized with such furious impulse that they manifested no moderation in their wickedness. Let us learn from this passage to put the bridle on our lusts in time; for when the fire is lighted up, it is not easily extinguished, and the Devil is always supplying wood or adding oil to the furnace. Let us restrain ourselves, lest the Devil seize upon us with insane fury (Calvin, *Commentary on Ezekiel*, p. 233).

Volitional sin would be "sinful enough" if we kept it to ourselves. But we don't. We can't. Volitional slavery begins a process that must end with volitional destroyers. Recall the warning words of Titus, foolishness leads to enslavement which leads to envy and hatred (Titus 3:3).

Volitional Destroyers: Manipulation and Retaliation

Volitional slaves maintain a subtle but ruthless disregard for the rights of others, along with an unbridled concern for the satisfaction of their own impulses. Personal volitional enslavement always leads to inter-personal volitional exploitation.

James asks the age-old question, "What causes fights and quarrels among you?" (James 4:1). "Why can't we all just get along?" His answer: "Don't they come from your desires that battle within you? You want something but don't get it" (James 4:1b-2a).

Since desire itself is not evil, volitional sin involves *our sinful responses to our unmet desires*. You want your husband to cherish you. He doesn't. How do you respond?

"You kill and covet, but you cannot have what you want. You quarrel and fight" (James 4:2b). What do I do with my frustrated desires? *I covet.* I attempt to *manipulate* you into meeting my need. "Perhaps my husband will cherish me if I'm a 'submissive' wife, if I cook and clean." What drives such thinking? A servant's heart? No. The motivation is self-centered. "I *must* be cherished by my husband!" Of course she must be *if* she has separated herself from being cherished by Worthy Groom.

Wrongly motivated, empty, what happens if hubby does not comply? I *kill.* I *retaliate.* "I want what I want and I want it now! Give it to me or else!" If hubby does not meet her need, and ultimately he can never satisfy her deepest longing for Worthy Groom's cherishing love, she will retaliate. "I'll either get back at you or hold back from you." Perhaps she will be cruel. Or perhaps she will be aloof.

What's going on in her soul? "You do not have, because you do not ask God" (James 4:2c). The root cause of all human quarrels flows from a divine problem. We refuse to ask God humbly; we refuse God-sufficiency.

"When you ask, you do not receive, because you ask with wrong motives, that you may spend what you get on your pleasures" (James 4:3). God demands that our final goal be His glory. We exist to exalt and enjoy Him. Any other motivation placed above that motivation is sinful.

"You adulterous people, don't you know that friendship with the world is hatred toward God? Anyone who chooses to be a friend of the world becomes an enemy of God"

(James 4:4). Fascinating. Spiritual adultery causes every relational problem. Once we flick God away, we're doomed.

These theological truths are eminently practical, especially when we apply them specifically and individually. That is, we need to diagnose the characteristic sinful patterns of the specific individual we're counseling.

- ♦ *Fallen Romancers*: Impure Affections/False Lovers—"What are the unique false lovers of their souls?"
- ♦ *Fallen Dreamers*: Foolish Mindsets—"What are their personal foolish, fallen mindsets?"
- ♦ *Fallen Creators*: Self-Centered Purposes/Pathways—"What are their specific, self-protective patterns of relating? What are their typical interactive styles? What unique goals do they pursue to quench their personal thirsts?"

I look inside myself and wonder, "What do I really want?" My answer becomes my God or my god. I'm stirred to move everything in my life toward the pursuit of my "*want-deity*."

After repeated foolish thinking about the source of life, I develop mindsets of the flesh. I create within the pathways of my physical brain and within the depths of my metaphysical mind ingrained ways of perceiving reality. I imagine life according to a few concrete themes and story lines. My story lines fit me, or my understanding of me. "How can a person like me make life work in a world like this? Well, I'm smart, articulate, an enterprising person. I'll become a teacher and an author. I'll use what I have to get what I want. What I want more than anything is respect. Applause fills my soul like nothing else."

Since I pursue (volitional) what I perceive (rational) to be pleasing (relational), I develop a rut of relating designed to accomplish my life goals. I design my way of relating to find a way for a sinner like me to use what I have to get what I want. The pattern of my behavior is my unique way of living out the idol in my heart. "I'm not really effective 'on the spot.' I'm much better responding to questions (and, thus, impress people and win their applause) when I'm well prepared. I don't dare become spontaneous. I'm like a Boy Scout. 'Always prepared.' Yes! That's my life motto and model. Stay on the sidelines until I have all my ducks in a row. Spend my time in the study. It's safe there. Leave only when I'm well armed with my arsenal of data. Yeah. Now I'm ready to serve my god."

None of this feels like a choice. "This is just the way life is. Just the way I am. This fits me and my world, as I see it." Designed to choose free and courageous pathways of worship and ministry, now we habitually and compulsively choose ingrained pathways of self-sufficiency and self-protection. Sinners are empowered Creators turning themselves into mastered Slaves unable to have dominion over their own passions, much less over God's planet.

Emotional Corruption: Ungoverned Mood States
From Soulful Singers to Moody Addicts

Because life is a story, we develop thematic approaches to life. Romancers follow a *sole lover/affection* of the soul, loving one master at a time, either Worthy Groom or False Seducer. Dreamers develop *mindsets* that persist over time—consistent ways of viewing life characterized either by wisdom or folly. Creators tread a path toward a goal following *purposes/pathways of interacting,* habituating themselves either toward worship/ministry or self-sufficiency/self-protection. Singers feel ongoing *mood states*—prevailing tones or colorings either alive to hope or dead in despair.

Ephesians 4:17-19 offers a not-too-pretty picture of the process.

♦ Relational False Lovers/Impure Affections: Separated from the Life of God
♦ Rational Foolish Mindsets: The Futility of Their Thinking/Darkened in Their Understanding
♦ Volitional Self-Centered Purposes/Pathways: The Hardening of Their Hearts
♦ Emotional Ungoverned Mood States: Having Lost All Feelings
♦ Physical Disconnected Tendencies: Given Themselves Over to Sensuality

Once I separate myself from the life of God, believing He is not my Supreme Good, and I am good without Him, hardening my heart to live for myself, I am emotionally doomed to deadness. Once this entire "inner life process" completes itself, I am physically doomed to sensuality—living as though my body is all there is, living as though the belly is God.

In Ephesians 4:19, Paul chooses a very rare Greek word, *apēlgēkotes,* to describe how the unregenerate person is destined to emotional deadness. The word literally means "past feeling." They cease to feel and care. Tired of feeling, they shut themselves down to the messages that pain sends. Feelingless. Apathetic. A-pathos or without passion, lacking emotional intelligence, sensitivity, and awareness.

Designed to be responsive to the world, to others, and to God, they close themselves off. They are emotionally numb and thus apathetic toward God and others, and even toward themselves. It's normal to hurt, but they don't think so. They're too smart to hurt anymore. In their folly, they decide that hurt is too painful, even if reflecting on hurt enhances their relationships. They're all grieved out. Being grieved out, they're shamed out. They're insensitive to shame. They're calloused. They're obtuse to emotional messages.

So what happens? They give themselves over to sensuality. They're ungoverned. Out of control. Sensually triggered to indulge in every possible physical pleasure. They become addicted to anything that might somehow quiet the screams of emotional pain and personal shame. They give themselves up to lewdness, to work uncleanness in all greediness, with a continual lust for more.

What a grim commentary on the nature of natural humanity. A monster. A mad beast. Fleshly living resulting from a dead spirit.

What is the essence of fallen emotionality? Instead of using emotions to experience deeply the life God grants us, we misuse our emotions to forget the pain in our soul and the sin in our heart. We pursue whatever pleases us for a season. We live to survive, to make it somehow. We live as if this world is all there is. So when working with fallen Singers (emotional beings) we want to sense, "What emotional mood states characterize my spiritual friend? What survival mode is he pursuing? What unmanaged mood is she exhibiting?"

Fallen image bearers pinball between three survival modes. Sometimes they play the emotional stoic, repressing their moods. Other times they act the role of emotional sensationalists, expressing their moods. On still other occasions they take the part of emotional sensualists, anesthetizing their moods. Though they use these three distinct styles, you should note that each mood state shares *apēlgēkotes* (Ephesians 4:19)—the refusal to listen well to their emotions, the refusal to use their emotionality to evaluate where they are spiritually.

Emotional Stoics: Repressing Their Moods

Instead of being passionate Poets we become apathetic Stoics. We try to live without pathos, without passion and feeling. Mr. Spock of *Star Trek* fame was a Stoic. He tried to repress his emotions and deny them; if he could, he would eradicate them.

It's easy to understand stoicism's attraction. Hatred, despair, and terror are not attractive emotions. When they sweep over us, we flee from them like from an invading army.

We can understand Stoics by contrasting them with Poets. What should biblical Poets do with their anger, hatred, and rage? First, they should not eradicate them. Paul tells us to be angry but sin not; he does not tell us never to be angry (Ephesians 4:26). So Poets acknowledge their moods to themselves and Father.

Psalm 73 is a classic expression of a believer's struggle to comprehend and control his envy, jealousy, and hatred. Asaph is dismayed that a good God could allow bad things to happen to good people and good things happen to bad people. He faces his envy *coram Deo,* telling Father all about it. He doesn't wait to be rid of his envy before he dares enter Father's presence. He takes himself, all that he is, including his envy, to Father.

Second, Poets explore their moods with spiritual eyes. Asaph enters the presence of God to gain perspective on his perspective. "When I tried to understand all this, it was oppressive to me till I entered the sanctuary of God; then I understood their final destiny" (Psalm 73:16-17).

Third, Poets confess their sinful anger to Father. "When my heart was grieved and my spirit embittered, I was senseless and ignorant; I was a brute beast before you" (Psalm 73:21-22).

Fourth, Poets receive grace. "Yet I am always with you; you hold me by my right hand" (Psalm 73:23).

Fifth, Poets recognize that only God is enough. "Whom have I in heaven but you? And earth has nothing I desire besides you" (Psalm 73:25).

Stoics, on the other hand, try to eradicate their hatred. "If I don't think about it, it's not there. If I repress it, it will go away." When it doesn't vanish, they mull over it again and again with eyeballs only. Asaph was once trapped there, seeing only the prosperity of the wicked.

Stoics don't confess their mismanaged moods to God. They don't believe they could come to God unless they perfectly, serenely suppress their rage. So they never receive grace. Why do they need grace? They manage quite well on their own.

Why? *Facing moods forces us to face our insufficiency*. Nothing makes us feel punier than being overwhelmed by feelings. No one wants to hear the derogatory comment, "He's so moody." "She's so emotional!" When feelings overpower us we feel powerless, impotent. Fallen emotional beings would rather stuff their moods, would rather survive self-sufficiently, than admit they need help managing their moods.

Emotional Sensationalists: Expressing Their Moods

On the other hand, some people want nothing to do with managed moods. They don't deny themselves any experiences. If they feel it, they express it. They are emotional sensationalists.

Saul massaged his jealousy toward David. When the women of Israel met Saul and David with dancing and song, they sang, "Saul has slain his thousands, and David his tens of thousands" (1 Samuel 18:7). Saul was enraged. This refrain galled him. "And from that time on Saul kept a jealous eye on David" (1 Samuel 18:9).

Caressed anger leads to expressed anger. "Saul had a spear in his hand and he hurled it, saying to himself, 'I'll pin David to the wall'" (1 Samuel 18:10b-11a).

Like all unmanaged moods, Saul's resulted from a foolish internal evaluation of a difficult external situation. No doubt it would be emotionally distressing for most leaders to hear subordinates praised to the extent people praised David. Experiencing this, Saul kept thinking to himself, rather than talking to God. "'They have credited David with tens of thousands,' he thought, 'but me with only thousands. What more can he get but the kingdom?'" (1 Samuel 18:8b). He catastrophized. Imagining God to be a Hoarder, he could not imagine there was enough respect and responsibility to go around for both David and himself. This town was not big enough for both of them because God was not big enough for Saul.

Emotional sensationalists wear their emotions on their sleeves and hurl their feelings like a spear. They will not be controlled. They refuse to be inhibited. Their feelings are their god. Yet their feelings never direct them to God. They may sense their feelings, indulge their feelings, but they never engage their feelings, never use their mood states to detect their spiritual state.

Emotional Sensualists: Anesthetizing Their Moods

There's at least one additional survival strategy prevalent among fallen Singers—anesthetizing their moods. They don't really stuff their feelings; rather they stuff their stomachs. They don't really hurl their feelings at others; instead they devour anything that might make them feel good momentarily. Their bellies are their god.

In Jeremiah 2:20-25, the disgusting image of the covenant people, driven with animal cravings to be sexually satisfied by anyone, is meant to shock and offend. It's also meant to portray the consequences of natural living. Make pleasure paramount and pleasure becomes a demanding paramour, a dictatorial lover, an all-consuming passion. Yet pleasure's pleasure is fleeting. Ezekiel 23:43-45 pictures sinners worn out with adulteries—wasted, given up to debauchery, having exhausted their capacities in their adulterous binge.

When Nancy Guthrie endured the death of her two babies to Zellweger Syndrome, she was tempted to anesthetize. Listen to her testimony after the death of Hope, her second child.

> The day after we buried Hope, I understood for the first time why so many people choose to medicate their pain in so many harmful ways. That day I tried to sleep it away. And in the days that followed, I discovered that I could not sleep it

away, shop it away, eat it away, or travel it away. I just had to feel it. And it hurt. Physically. I realized I had a choice—I could try to stuff the hurt away in a closet, pretend it wasn't there, and wish it would disappear, or I could bring it out into the open, expose it to the Light, probe it, accept it head-on, trudge through it, feel its full weight, and do my best to confront my feelings of loss and hopelessness with the truth of God's Word at every turn (Guthrie, *Holding onto Hope: A Pathway Through Suffering to the Heart of God*, p. 12).

Nancy lives poetically with beauty and grace, because she believes in God's grace.

When we reach the point of dissatisfaction, the choice is clear. Either our souls starve to death, or we surrender to God's grace—giving up all effort while we rest and trust. Fallen emotional beings choose soul starvation—preferring starving to surrender. Having lost all sensitivity to the Spirit, they give themselves over more and more to the flesh (sensuality) to indulge every kind of impurity with a continual lust for more. Sinners are soulful poets turning themselves into moody survivalists existing to satisfy their deified bellies.

Physical Depletion: Habituate Tendencies
From Contingent Actors to Materialistic Traitors

Notice the difference between this heading and previous ones. With relational, rational, volitional, and emotional capacities, I chose the word "corruption." With the physical nature of human beings, I am choosing the word "depletion." The flesh is neutral. It is neither righteous nor evil. Only embodied personal beings are either righteous or evil. Thus fallen capacities are corrupted, while the flesh is depleted.

When human beings severed themselves from their umbilical cord of nutrient—God's Spirit—their souls and bodies became disconnected from God. Their bodies did not become corrupt; they became depleted. Previously they were embodied personal beings who lived and acted contingently—dependent upon God, nourished by God, connected to and empowered by God. Now they live independent of God, disconnected from Him, and empowered only by self.

To understand the nature of disconnected flesh, we need to reflect on a central truth. We are dust and divinity (Genesis 2:7). Secular psychologists tend to see us as dust only. They like to think that our physical brain explains everything about us. Some Christian thinkers write as though we are only divinity. They like to think our metaphysical mind explains everything about us. Our Creator informs us that if we want to understand the human personality—created, fallen, and redeemed—we must understand something of the intricate interaction between the physical brain and the metaphysical mind, between dust and divinity, between flesh and spirit, between body and soul.

The flesh (dust of the earth) constitutes everything mortal about us—our material side, all that is peculiar to human nature in its corporeal existence, our physicality. It is what connects us to our physical world and to one another. The flesh includes our body, bones, brain, belly, glands, and five senses. It is our vast, intricate, complex, interconnected matrix of chemicals, electronic impulses, physical senses, organs, and brain synapses. Through our five senses, our physical brain receives impressions about the world around us and perceives the relevance of those impressions for our life. We are fearfully and wonderfully made.

If we were only dust, we would be exactly what the secularists claim we are—incredibly developed physical specimens. However, Creator created us dust *and* divinity. Body *and* soul. Brain *and* mind. We are holistic beings integrating our physicality and our spirituality. *When functioning harmoniously, the mind evaluates what the brain receives and perceives.* The brain can discern a direction, but the mind provides our moral compass. Eve's ears received the sound waves of False Seducer's speech. Her brain received and interpreted the words, and then her mind went to work discerning meaning and deciding a course of beliefs and actions.

Having succumbed to sin's seduction, Adam and Eve's capacities were corrupted and their flesh depleted. As an unfortunate result, fallen personhood functions in sinful harmony. A depleted brain joined to a corrupt mind births depravity. Every offspring of Adam and Eve is born depraved and depleted.

The physical implications afflict us: sickness, illness, AIDS, viruses, smallpox, malaria, poor eyesight, blindness, poor hearing, deafness, acne, deformity, Down's syndrome, kidney dialysis, diabetes, Alzheimer's, liver disease, heart disease, and brain disease.

Though our fallen brains are incredible, compared to Adam and Eve's unfallen brains, we are kindergarten students and they were graduate students. Our brains have not evolved; they have devolved. Worse still, by birth our minds are hostile to Christ (Romans 8:7). Information enters our less-than-perfect brains, and we process it in less-than-perfect ways. We evaluate that information through anti-God presuppositions and anti-Christ perspectives.

You receive news that your mother is dying of cancer. A less-than-perfect doctor with a less-than-humane bedside manner coldly shares the diagnosis. In the ensuing days and weeks you hear conflicting reports on Mom's prognosis. You don't fully comprehend much of the medical jargon, and you sense the hospital staff is less than forthcoming. If you are unsaved, you process this information through your hostile-to-God grid. Perhaps you bargain with God, since you think He is a tit-for-tat God whom you can manipulate. Perhaps you rage against God, thinking Him to be cruel and inexplicable.

How your depleted brain and unsaved mind actually respond will depend upon the characteristic shape of your false lovers, foolish mindsets, self-centered pathways, emotional mood states, *and* ruts, roots, and routes ingrained in your physical brain since birth. If modern brain science has proven anything, it is that our brains become habituate to think, act, and feel in certain prescribed ways (Rita Carter, *Mapping the Mind*; Daniel Goleman, *Emotional Intelligence*; Joseph LeDoux, *The Emotional Brain*; Robert Thayer, *The Origin of Everyday Moods*).

Perhaps now we can make sense of Paul's idea of "flesh," "the mind of the flesh," and "fleshly." "Flesh" is Paul's neutral term for our embodied personality. "Fleshly" describes our embodied personality severed from God and living for and by self. The "mind of the flesh" suggests the harmonious symphony occurring when the depleted physical brain and the depraved metaphysical mind join in anti-god chorus. (We'll examine these concepts, highlighting more Pauline distinctions, when we explore the impact of redemption on our capacities. Then we'll place our emphasis on why we still sin, and on the battle between the flesh and the spirit/Spirit.)

It's all so different from our original major-key harmony. Then our body/brain complex was contingent upon God. All was spiritual. Now the physical is god, king, and master, turning against the Master. Sinners are contingent Actors turning themselves into materialistic Traitors living like animals in heat.

Worldly Indoctrination
From *Cosmos Deo* to *Cosmos Diabolicus*

Devolved brains joined to a corrupt mind enter a degenerate world. Unredeemed flesh—our mortal body, brain, bones, belly, glands, senses, and chemical complex—can be culturally, diabolically, and pathologically influenced. The world incessantly bombards the brain with counterfeit stories of where to find life.

Paul explains why life is so hard for fleshly beings with fallen capacities. "As for you, you were dead in your transgressions and sins . . ." (Ephesians 2:1). Not simply spiritually sick, they're spiritually dead. Then Paul adds the *coup de grace*. "In which you used to live when you followed the ways of this world and of the ruler of the kingdom of the air, the spirit who is now at work in those who are disobedient" (Ephesians 2:2). Paul props up dead folks, places them in a dark, dank cave, and introduces them to the three-headed dragon: the world, the flesh, and the Devil.

"*Cosmos*," from which we obtain our word "cosmetic," reflects the masquerading Angel of Light's attractive, organized, ravishing system of attitudes and ideas in competition with God's narrative of life. It is the *cosmos diabolicus* promoted and programmed by Satan. The world is Satan's window dressing, presenting evil as good.

False Seducer's fallen world system contains a worldview, a mindset. The fallen *cosmos* is the systematic arrangement of individual ideas into an ordered whole. It's the organization of non-biblical thinking, and the human viewpoint under the sun captive to Satan. He pervades human society with an anti-God bias. His world has a decided preference for all that is temporal, tangible, earthly, physical, and sensual.

As god of this age, Satan sets the agenda. He makes the world dance in harmony to the tune of his evil world system. This system operates similarly to the way a radio station functions. (I'm indebted to Thomas Ice and Robert Dean, *A Holy Rebellion*, for this concept.) The demons and fallen humanity produce the programming, which propagates and reinforces the agenda (false doctrine, false narrative). Fallen flesh is the receiver tuned to the radio station WORLD or WSELF with the volume turned up all the way. Fallen flesh, disconnected from God, is attracted to Satan's frequency because both are on the same wavelength. Both send and receive the same message: "I am envious of God. I do not trust God's generosity and goodness. I will not be a dependent being."

False Seducer's programming is not dull. In 1 Timothy 4:1, Paul speaks of demonic doctrine (*didaskaliais*), selecting a word that means rehearsing a drama and reciting a teaching with flare and oratorical skillfulness. Used in the plural, as in 1 Timothy 4:1 (see also Isaiah 29:13 in the Greek translation of the Old Testament), *didaskaliais* denotes human teachings that have no claim to absoluteness. In the singular it equals God's revealed narrative that relates teaching to the entire person, imparting theoretical and practical knowledge in the highest development of the pupil. It is the right ordering of right relationship with God and others. Demonic doctrine is the wrong ordering of wrong relationships presented in a dramatic fashion through an enticing narrative.

If the fallen flesh is embodied personality severed from God, then the world is organized humanity separated from God and ruled by False Seducer. He rules this dark age (*aiōna*, Ephesians 2:2), which is a period of human history with marked off eras during which Satan uses various worldly philosophies to attract the flesh away from the spirit.

In our day, postmodernity is a prominent philosophy that False Seducer is using to distance people from Christ. However, he's not too choosy. He used pre-modernity to terrify superstitious people into working their way to heaven. He used modernity to persuade "enlightened" people to believe they had no need for God. And he'll use postmodernity to convince people their personal narrative is the only true narrative. "There's no meta-narrative. No final arbiter. No theme that captures all the other minor themes. You shape your own version of reality," he says.

There are a few themes that seem to cut across all satanically inspired counter-narratives. According to Revelation 17-18, we should look to Babel/Babylon to see the great picture of the *cosmos diabolicus*. Gallery one parades the great whore, the fornicator who leads all people to worship her as their false lover and to commit spiritual fornication with her. False Seducer consistently uses the *cosmos* to intoxicate people with the wine of false lovers.

Gallery two presents the triple threat of power, prestige, and pleasure resulting in pride. The *cosmos diabolicus* lives deliciously and luxuriously, never sharing. She claims to sit as a queen who will never be widowed nor ever see sorrow. She entices the flesh to lust after fruit to satisfy the soul—dainty and good things. She struts her stuff, clothed in precious stones and beautiful garments. False Seducer entices the *cosmos* to construct the ultimate city built by humanity without God.

In gallery three hang the lie, falsehood, and deception of False Seducer. "By your magic spell all the nations were led astray" (Revelation 18:23). "Magic spell" is the Greek *pharmakeia*, meaning either medicine or poison. The ancient Near East used *pharmakeia* for the magic secret to obtaining immortality, divinity. Masquerading as medicine for a sick heart, False Seducer's magic spell poisons the fleshly mind. It is the false promise of the false lover that poisons the heart into believing the lie that False Seducer offers divinity. Two cities represent two loves, Jerusalem for the love of God, and Babel for the love of this age. False Seducer consistently uses the *cosmos* to allure people into Babel-love.

How do the flesh, the False Seducer, and the fallen world work together? Fallen flesh finds itself attracted to the allurements of the fallen world made ever so ravishing by the False Seducer. The spirit of the *cosmos diabolicus* gratifies the cravings of the flesh. The flesh is hungry and thirsty because it is separated from true nourishment, the spiritual nourishment of the umbilical cord of God.

The lust of the flesh is the impulse we have when we are disconnected from the life of God—impulses toward self, self-trust, self-fulfillment, self-sufficiency, and self-protection. Babel epitomizes the love of this world. It is the earth-bound, time-bound, natural, materialistic, demonic perspective. This perspective has one *purpose*: to unite humanity apart from God. It has one *mindset*: grasping and hoarding because God cannot be trusted. He cannot satisfy the hunger of the soul. It has one *affection*: to break Father's heart by stealing away as many of His children as possible.

Thematic Approaches to Life

I mentioned earlier how seldom the media interviews theologians when a new tragedy arises such as high school students slaughtering their peers or snipers viciously and randomly killing innocent victims. In response to such neglect, it's easy for us to say,

"Well, that's because of the media's bias against Christianity." That certainly could be, but I wonder if it also might be because of our own failure to develop *relevant theological categories* that explain why we do what we do.

"Thematic approaches to life" summarizes my attempt to provide biblical categories that help us understand people, problems, and solutions. They offer soul physicians biblical lenses so they can become expert spiritual cardiologists.

We've emphasized how image bearers undertake characteristic ways of living out their capacities. Many labels fit this concept: we have inclinations, dispositions, habituate ways of responding to life, styles of relating, patterns of living, reigning life themes, and thematic approaches to life.

We've conceptualized our inner life as designed by God in terms of the following thematic approaches: affections/lovers (relational), mindsets (rational), purposes/pathways (volitional), and mood states (emotional). Fallen image bearers career through a downward spiral in their characteristic sinful approach to life. Impure affections/false lovers (relational) following foolish mindsets (rational), choosing self-centered purposes/self-sufficient pathways (volitional), resulting in unmanaged mood states (emotional). Box 17:2 unites all these concepts, summarizing everything we've examined to this point.

When faced with the urgency of a troubled spiritual friend, we must have a framework, a format, some guide that directs our thinking. Characteristic or thematic approaches to life help the soul physician: a) to conceptualize life biblically, b) to diagnose relational, rational, volitional, and emotional life scripturally, c) to think theologically about helping people, and d) to think spiritually about psychology.

Thematic approaches to life help us ask and answer real life questions like: What causes non-biological depression? Why do serial killers and snipers go on rampages? Why does the parent I'm working with rage at his children? Why is the life of my counselee filled with anxiety? What do I need to understand and focus on to help this sexual abuse victim? What select concepts should run through my mind as I counsel this couple? What makes people tick? What causes people to be ticked off? Why do people do what they do? How do I make sense of life? How do I help people? How do people change and grow? What in the world am I supposed to do when hit with the myriad of input and information during a counseling session? What "handles" can I "hang my hat on" when I'm trying to make sense of a counseling interaction? What approach to diagnosing problems should I follow? What flow should I anticipate in counseling interactions? How do I determine what's central or core to an issue? How do I figure out what causes specific struggles? What's really going on in people's lives? What are the core soul issues God wants me to identify and counsel? What are the root causes of life's problems?

Thematic approaches to life are crucial for another reason. In the absence of a well thought-out biblical model of personality, we tend to counsel from our experience/personality, race to the secular self-help shelf, throw up our hands in exasperation, and surrender to simplistic words of advice or confrontation.

"Universal life themes" are our handles. They offer something of the "science" of biblical counseling. However, we don't stop here. We don't counsel generic image bearers. We counsel individual, unique image bearers. So we must learn to look for, sense, recognize, and label idiosyncratic (unique, particular, person-specific, distinctive, typical) characteristics of the spiritual friend who sits in front of us. Unique, individual life themes offer something of the "art" of biblical counseling.

Box 17:2

Image Bearers and Universal Life Themes

Creation: Designed by God

Image Bearing Capacities and Characteristic Approaches to Life

- Relational Romancers: Affections   Passion/Lovers
- Rational Dreamers: Mindsets   Cognition/Images
- Volitional Creators: Purposes   Volition/Pathways
- Emotional Singers: Mood States   Emotion/Moods

Original Personality/Motivational Structure and Characteristic Approaches to Life

- What I believe (mindsets) about my desires (affections/lovers) leads to my actions (purposes/pathways) and results in my emotions (mood states).
- I pursue (volitional) what I perceive (rational) to be pleasing (relational) which prompts internal reactions (emotional).
- I freely pursue (created volitionality) God as the Chief Affection of my soul (created relationality) because I perceive God to be my Spring of Living Water (created rationality) so I experience love, joy, and peace (created emotionality).

Fall: Depraved by Sin

Fallen Image Bearing Capacities and Characteristic Approaches to Life

- Fallen Romancers: Impure Affections   False Lovers/Idols of the Heart
- Fallen Dreamers: Foolish Mindsets   Fleshly Imaginations
- Fallen Creators: Self-Centered Purposes   Broken Cisterns
- Fallen Singers: Ungoverned Mood States   Survival Modes

Fallen Personality/Motivational Structure and Characteristic Approaches to Life

- I slavishly pursue broken cisterns (fallen volitionality) because I foolishly suppress perceptions of God's holy love (fallen rationality) so I sinfully worship false lovers of the soul, experiencing God as less than pleasing, not my Supreme Good (fallen relationality), which prompts internal responses in which I selfishly react with ungoverned mood states (fallen emotionality).

Box 17:3

Alexis' Story: Idiosyncratic/Unique Life Themes

♦ **False Lovers of the Soul: Her Unique Affection Set**

"What I want, what I long for more than anything else, is for Jodi never to have to experience life like I did growing up. The fights, the turmoil, the uncertainty. Is that so wrong? Jodi is all the world to me. For the first time I know that someone loves me and needs me and that I love someone with all my heart. If anything ever happened to Jodi, I couldn't go on."

We might conceptualize the *false lover of Alexis' soul* as "being in control of loving and being loved." She insists that some human being (her daughter) provide her with a guaranteed, safe love relationship. Alexis needs to *repent* of having made Jodi her "spring of living water" and having determined that God is not enough. She's turned to a false *lover and idol*. She's set her affections on things below, on herself, on her daughter, and ultimately on the things of the False Seducer.

♦ **Foolish Mindsets of the Heart: Her Unique Mindset**

"Everyone tells me I'm out of control in my desire to control and protect Jodi. But what do I do with my fear? My terror? Honestly, when I don't 'over-control,' I think I'm a horrible mom. It's my job to protect Alexis, isn't it?"

We might conceptualize the *foolish mindset/fleshly imagination of Alexis' heart* as her personal conviction that God cannot be trusted to do what is right, that Father does not know best. From her upbringing she's bought the lie that God does not take care of little children, but that she can and must. Alexis needs to *repent* of the lies she's chosen to believe, of her contemptuous images of God, and of her arrogant images of herself.

♦ **Self-Centered Purposes/Pathways of the Will: Her Unique Will Set**

"Ever since my teen years I've lived by the motto, 'God takes care of those who take care of themselves.' And now I'm taking care of someone else. That's godly, right? Unselfish service? I pour everything into protecting Jodi and all I get for it is criticism. What gives?"

We might summarize the *self-centered pathway of Alexis' will* as her habituate style of "self-protective, possessive parenting." That's core to her broken cistern, her unique way of making her life work apart from God. So natural has it become, so much a part of her fleshly nature, that she's blind to her ulterior motive. Alexis needs to *repent* of her specific, self-sufficient, self-protective, self-centered style of relating—her habituate pathway of possessive parenting designed to prevent her from experiencing hurt, to keep her in control, and to take care of life apart from God.

Box 17:3, Continued

Alexis' Story: Idiosyncratic/Unique Life Themes

♦ **Unmanaged Mood States: Her Unique Mood Set**

"For years and years my life felt out of control. Then Jodi came along. I could meet her every need. Here was something I could do well—parent, love my child. I do this so well. I could write a book on parenting. I love how Jodi makes me feel—peaceful, happy, fulfilled."

We might identify Alexis' *unmanaged mood state* as her "need to be needed, her need to feel in control of making herself feel good." She needs to *repent* of her ongoing survival mood—trying to survive emotionally apart from God by living for the immediate pleasure of sinful control.

Imagine Alexis. She's twenty-eight. Grew up in a Christian home. Graduated from a Bible college. She and her husband have a beautiful two-year-old daughter (Jodi). Under duress and at the insistence of her husband and her pastor, Alexis arranges an appointment with you. You soon learn she's tormented by fears for her daughter's safety and is obsessive about protecting Jodi from all harm, real or imagined.

Imagine that as you counsel Alexis, you engage her personally, all the while wondering about her unique or idiosyncratic life themes. You want to sense deep in your soul her characteristic ways of relating, thinking, choosing, and feeling. The unique person you are engages the unique person she is and together you develop a biblical assessment of her heart condition. Perhaps it would look something like "Alexis' Story" in Box 17:3.

Reading about Alexis, note the deep change biblical counseling identifies. Everyone talks about "root causes and root change." What are they and how do they happen? Unique life themes help us identify root problems and core solutions—from the perspective of the Divine Physician of the Soul.

Where We've Been and Where We're Heading

Other than increasing depravity, the unredeemed personality structure has changed little since Genesis 6:5. "The LORD saw how great man's wickedness on the earth had become, and that every inclination of the thoughts of his heart was only evil all the time." Depleted embodied souls—depraved relationally, rationally, volitionally, and emotionally—enter a demonically inspired world system programmed by False Seducer. Box 17:4 depicts the horrifying harmony of humanity hostile to God.

How great is our fall from grace? *Relationally*, we move from Romancers to spiritual Adulterers. Divorcing Worthy Groom, we are fearful. Instead of loving passionately, we lust carnally. *Rationally*, we shift from Dreamers to arrogant Fools. Deluded, we foolishly believe False Seducer. Instead of thinking imaginatively, we suppress truth arrogantly. *Volitionally*, we abandon our role as Creators and Shepherds, choosing to be Destroyers—Wolves who attack, or Sheep who retreat. Demandingness leads to a false fullness and a futile search for more. Instead of choosing courageously, we now choose compulsively. *Emotionally*, we change from Singers to moody Addicts. Disconnected from God, others, and ourselves, futility reigns. Instead of experiencing life deeply, we anesthetize our experiences fully.

Caution. Detour ahead. You might anticipate that the next stop on our journey would take us to our redeemed personality structure. However, before we examine our new nature, we'll explore the truth that *our world is fallen, and it often falls on us*.

Christian counseling deals not only with *the sins we commit*, but it also faces *the evils we have suffered*. Because we exist in a fallen world inhabited by fallen people, we will suffer. We'd rather ignore this truth. God does not. His Word contains a detailed *sufferology*—a theology of suffering. What happens when people created for Paradise live in a desert? How do they handle their thirsts? How can we grieve but not as those who have no hope? These are the matters we view in the next two scenes of our drama of redemption.

Box 17:4

Fallen Image Bearers

Romancers turning themselves into spiritual Adulterers,
Dreamers turning themselves into arrogant Fools,
Creators turning themselves into mastered Destroyers,
Singers turning themselves into moody Addicts, and
Actors turning themselves into materialistic Traitors, living in a
Cosmos diabolicus, attractively organized to attack God and attach to the flesh,
Enchanted by False Seducer's lies masquerading as truth.

Fallen Relational Beings: Adulterers

Sinners are passionate Romancers turning themselves into spiritual Adulterers,
passionately pursuing anyone but the Worthy Groom.

Fallen Rational Beings: Fools

Sinners are imaginative Dreamers turning themselves into arrogant Fools,
fooled into thinking that the Worthy Groom is unworthy and unloving.

Fallen Volitional Beings: Destroyers

Sinners are empowered Creators turning themselves into mastered Destroyers,
unable to have dominion over their own passions, much less over God's planet.

Fallen Emotional Beings: Addicts

Sinners are soulful Singers turning themselves into moody Addicts,
existing to satisfy their deified bellies.

Fallen Physical Beings: Traitors

Sinners are contingent Actors turning themselves into materialistic Traitors,
living like animals in heat.

Fallen World System: *Cosmos Diabolicus*

Cosmos diabolicus, attractively organized to attack God and attach itself to the flesh.

False Seducer: Angel of Darkness

The Angel of Darkness masquerades as an Angel of Light,
portraying God as evil, Christ as unworthy, and Messenger as a liar.

Caring for Your Soul: Personal Applications

1. Read Jeremiah 2:11-13, 20-25; 3:1-3; Ezekiel 16:28-29; Titus 3:3; and 2 Peter 2:19, 22.

    a. Why is it inevitable that once we forsake the Spring of Living Water, we *must* drink from broken cisterns that can hold no water?

    b. In your own life and in your ministry to others, what biblical principles have provided the power to overcome enslavement/addiction?

2. Read James 4:1-4.

    a. How do you normally respond to the unmet longings of your soul?

    b. Share examples of times when you responded with manipulation and retaliation.

3. Concerning your emotional maturity:

    a. Which pattern of emotional survivalism do you fight against the most: repression, expression, or anesthetizing?

    b. How are you cooperating with Christ to become more of an emotional Poet?

4. Growth occurs when we apply God's truth to the specific issues at war in our souls.

    a. What unique impure affections/false lovers battle for your attention?

    b. What specific foolish, fallen mindsets attempt to root themselves in your thinking?

    c. What consistent self-centered purposes/pathways are typical of your style of interacting?

    d. What representative ungoverned mood states and survival modes do you struggle against?

    e. For each of these, how are you cooperating with Christ to experience victory?

Caring for Others: Ministry Implications

♦ **Biblical Diagnosis, Treatment Planning, and Characteristic Sinful Patterns:** When counseling believers struggling with sin, we need to think idiosyncratically. That is, we need to diagnose the characteristic sinful patterns of the specific individual we're counseling.

  • Fallen Romancers/False Lovers: "What are their unique false lovers/impure affections of the soul?"
  • Fallen Dreamers/Foolish Mindsets: "What are their personal foolish, fallen mindsets?"
  • Fallen Creators/Self-Centered Purposes: "What are their specific, self-protective patterns of relating? What are their typical interactive styles and unique pathways?"
  • Fallen Singers/Unmanaged Mood States: "What are their individual styles of mishandling their moods?"

♦ **Biblical Diagnosis, Treatment Planning, and the Enslavement Cycle:** When counseling believers entangled in besetting sins, we must identify the God-substitutes they are feeding upon to satisfy the God-shaped and God-sized vacuum in their souls.

♦ **Biblical Diagnosis, Treatment Planning, and the Destructive Cycle:** When counseling believers embroiled in relational conflicts, we must identify their unbiblical responses to their unmet desires. Where are they being manipulative? Where are they being retaliatory? Where are they pursuing wrong motives? Where are they becoming spiritual adulterers?

♦ **Biblical Diagnosis, Treatment Planning, and Disordered Mood States:** When counseling believers surrendered to unmanaged moods, we must assess whether they tend toward being emotional stoics (repressing their moods), emotional sensationalists (expressing their moods), or emotional sensualists (anesthetizing their moods).

CHAPTER EIGHTEEN

THE HURTING SUFFERER: SUFFEROLOGY, PART I

"Incompetent spiritual directors know no way with souls but to hammer and batter them like a blacksmith" *(Saint John of the Cross)*.

"Clinical pastoral care has, as its introduction, the task of listening to a story of human conflict and need. To the extent that our listening uncovers a situation which borders the abyss or lies broken within it, we are nearer to the place where the Cross of Christ is the only adequate interpretative concept" (Frank Lake, *Clinical Theology*, pp. 18-19).

In a Coffin in Egypt

Consider the contrast between the first five and the last five words of Genesis. "In the beginning God created" (Genesis 1:1a). "In a coffin in Egypt" (Genesis 50:26). Creation/Fall. Paradise/Egypt. Freedom/Slavery. Life/Death. Birth/Coffin. "You will surely die," God assured Adam, and God cannot lie.

Theologians have developed well thought-through models of Creation (anthropology), Fall (hamartiology), and Redemption (soteriology). Various biblical counselors ponder our design (Creation), our depravity (Fall), and our dignity (Redemption). But, did you notice what's missing? *Sufferology*—a biblical theology of suffering. ✓

A truly theological and practical grasp of the implications of the Fall will highlight both suffering *and* sin. Suffering reveals the fallenness of our world. Sin exposes the fallenness of our soul. Suffering teaches that life is bad, although God is good. Sin shows that we are evil, but God is gracious. Soul caregivers help image bearers wrestle with the evils they have suffered. Spiritual directors assist image bearers to face the sins they have committed. Suffering and sin are intricately intertwined.

Twentieth-century British Christian psychiatrist Frank Lake notes, "the maladies of the human spirit in its *deprivation* and in its *depravity* are matters of common pastoral concern" (Lake, *Clinical Theology*, p. 37). Christ's Cross defeated our deprivations—the evils we suffer, and our depravity—the sins we commit. Lake explains Christ's victory over both.

The very powers of evil, standing in the shadows behind "the mystery of iniquity" and "the mystery of suffering," were dethroned by Christ's active, obedient submission to their onslaught. Therefore, He reconciles to God by His Cross not only sinners, but sufferers. Not only memories of culpable sin which condemn the conscience, but the deeper memories of intolerable affliction which condemn faith as a delusion, these too are confronted by the fact of Christ's Cross. These passive evils, which are not of the soul's own making, are not accessible to a pastoral care which can talk only in terms of the forgiveness of sins. Such sufferers are usually not insensitive to their status as sinners. They have sought God's forgiveness. *But, like Job, they complain of the comforters whose one-track minds have considered only the seriousness of sin, and not the gravity of grinding affliction* (Lake, *Clinical Theology*, pp. 24-25, emphasis added).

In Chapters 14 through 17 we considered the seriousness of sin—hamartiology. In Chapters 18 and 19 we examine the gravity of grinding affliction—sufferology.

Why have we lost the biblical integration of suffering and sin? Lake correctly, I believe, tracks our neglect of suffering to a shift in the locale of ministry training.

If theological training had not lost its Galilean accent on persons encountered by the roadside or on the roof tops, in favour of libraries and essays in the schools, it would be unnecessary to argue the case for pastoral listening and dialogue (Lake, *Clinical Theology*, p. 1).

Secluded in our ivory towers, far from the ghettos of grinding affliction, we lose our perspective and our sensitivity.

Pastors who are taught in such settings are trained to preach *at* sinful people. Then they enter a parish with suffering people, people like the man born blind in John 9. The religious leaders of Jesus' day were sure that someone must have been at fault, just as Job's comforters were positive he was to blame for his suffering. They queried Jesus regarding the place to plant blame—Mom and Dad or blind son? Jesus informed them and us that this man's suffering was not because of his or his parents' personal sin. Rather, his suffering occurred so God's beauty and majesty might be revealed.

Following Christ's mentality requires creative thinking and passionate engagement. Ignoring His perspective leads to shallow reasoning and professional distance. Lake describes what stereotypically occurs when pastors trained to talk *at sinners*, are forced to *face sufferers*.

The pastoral counselor, in spite of himself, finds himself tittering out his usual jocular reassuring prescriptions, minimizing the problem, and thumping in optimism or the need for further effort. He has the ingrained professional habit of filling every unforgiving minute with sixty seconds' worth of good advice (Lake, *Clinical Theology*, p. 58).

There has to be a better way, don't you think?

Toward a Theology of Suffering

In the midst of promise, Jesus guarantees we will suffer. "I have told you these things, so that in me you may have peace. In this world you will have trouble. But take heart! I have overcome the world" (John 16:33). "You're gonna' get squashed!" is a fair vernacular paraphrase. Hemmed in, harassed, and distressed. Oppressed, vexed, and afflicted. Both internal and external afflictions are in view in the word "trouble," the former covering fear, anguish, and anxiety, the latter persecution by enemies and such troubles as illness, poverty, abandonment, and the like (H. Schlier, *Theological Dictionary of the New Testament*, pp. 334-335).

The Bible repeatedly recites Jesus' not-so-wanted guarantee. Some sample books and passages from which we'll develop our sufferology include: Genesis 45:1-11; 50:20; Deuteronomy 8:1-10; Psalm 13; 42; 73; 77; 88; Job; Jeremiah; Lamentations; John 9:1-3; 16:33; Romans 5:3; 8:17-39; 1 Corinthians 11:27-32; 2 Corinthians 1:3-11; 4:1-18; 12; 2 Timothy 3:12; Hebrews 4:14-16; 10-12; James 1:2-18; 1 Peter 1:3-9 and 2:11-25. From passages like these we learn that:

- In this life, we will suffer (John 16:33).
- All suffering first passes through the hands of God (Job 1-2).
- Some suffering is because of our own sin (1 Corinthians 11:27-32).
- Some suffering is because of the sin of others against us (2 Timothy 3:12).
- In His affectionate sovereignty (Deuteronomy 8:1-10; John 9:1-3; Romans 8:28; 1 Peter 1:3-9) God redeems all suffering to glorify Himself, benefit others, and beautify us.

The Puritans labeled suffering "losses and crosses." Reformed theologian and author J. I. Packer offers a succinct definition of suffering.

There is an umbrella-word that we use to cover the countless variety of situations that have this character, namely *suffering*. Suffering . . . may conveniently be defined as *getting what you do not want while wanting what you do not get*. This definition covers all forms of loss, hurt, pain, grief, and weakness—all experiences of rejection, injustice, disappointment, discouragement, frustration, and being the butt of others' hatred, ridicule, cruelty, callousness, anger, and ill-treatment— plus all exposure to foul, sickening, and nightmarish things that make you want to scream, run, or even die. . . . *Ease is for heaven, not earth.* Life on earth is fundamentally out of shape and out of order by reason of sin. . . . So strains, pains, disappointments, traumas, and frustrations of all sorts await us in the future, just as they have overtaken us already in the past" (Packer, *Rediscovering Holiness*, pp. 249, 254, emphasis added).

I would add that suffering is getting what you do not want, wanting what you do not get, *and* getting what you want but being dissatisfied in the getting.

- *Getting What You Do Not Want*: Illness, rejection, layoff, downsizing, divorce, death, poverty, persecution, oppression, depression, etc.
- *Wanting What You Do Not Get*: Love, marriage, a raise, a promotion, a new home, children, church growth, counselees who change, students who learn, etc.

♦ *Getting What You Want but Being Dissatisfied in the Getting*: You get married, but remain lonely. You earn the raise, but still feel empty. Your congregation grows, but you want more, feel like you need more. Someone praises you, but it's never enough.

How do we deal with such losses and crosses? If sanctification teaches us how we deal with sin and grow in Christlikeness, then sufferology shows us how we respond to suffering in Christlike ways. (See Box 18:1 for a sufferology summary.)

Brilliantly the Apostle Paul summarizes his sufferology. Do not "grieve like the rest of men, who have no hope" (1 Thessalonians 4:13). Paul, who offered people the Scriptures and his soul (1 Thessalonians 2:8), skillfully ministers to sufferers. We'll follow his outline as we integrate a wide array of scriptural passages regarding:

♦ Levels of Suffering: Causes of Grief
♦ Sustaining in Suffering: Stages of Grief
♦ Healing in Suffering: Stages of Hope

Levels of Suffering

Luther, an astute student of Paul, found that we always experience suffering as a trial of faith. He conceptualized two levels of faith trials.

♦ *Level One Suffering*: What Happens *to* Us and Around Us. What we are facing. This is the external "stuff" of life to which we respond internally. I lose a job, my child is ill, I face criticism, and the like. Level one suffering involves our situation and our circumstances—what happens to us.
♦ *Level Two Suffering*: What Happens *in* Us. How we face what we are facing. Level two is the suffering of the mind that gives rise to fear and doubt as we reflect on our external suffering. It is what happens in us as we face our circumstances. Do we doubt, fear, and run away from God? Or do we trust, cling, and face our suffering by facing God *coram Deo*? How do we respond internally to our external situations?

Level One Suffering: What Happens *to* Us—Separation

Suffering is just as true a theological reality as sin. Sufferology teaches us that we live in a fallen world and it falls on us.

Much-Afraid, the lead character in Hannah Hurnard's dramatic allegory *Hinds' Feet on High Places* learns suffering's lessons. Tired of valley living, but terrified to trek the high places, Shepherd promises companions for Much-Afraid on her journey. Encouraged by his pledge, she starts alone, awaiting the arrival of her comrades. When they appear, she's horrified. Shepherd introduces them.

They are good teachers; indeed, I have few better. As for their names, I will tell you them in your own language, and later you will learn what they are called in their own tongue. "This," said he, motioning toward the first of the silent figures, "is named Sorrow. And the other is her twin sister, Suffering" (Hurnard, *Hinds' Feet on High Places*, pp. 65-66).

Box 18:1

Biblical Sufferology

Levels of Suffering

Level One Suffering: External Suffering
- Circumstances: What Happens *to* Us—Separation
- Theological Reality: Our World Is Fallen and It Falls on Us

Level Two Suffering: Internal Suffering
- Condemnation: What Happens *in* Us—Spiritual Depression
- Experiential Reality: Our World Is a Mess and It Messes with Our Minds

Sustaining in Suffering
"It's Normal to Hurt and Necessary to Grieve"

Stage	Typical Grief Response	Biblical Grief Response
Stage One	Denial/Isolation	Candor: Honest with Self
Stage Two	Anger/Resentment	Complaint: Honest to God
Stage Three	Bargaining/Works	Cry: Asking God for Help
Stage Four	Depression/Alienation	Comfort: Receiving God's Help

Healing in Suffering
"It's Possible to Hope in the Midst of Grief"

Stage	Typical Acceptance Response	Biblical Acceptance Response
Stage One	Regrouping	Waiting: Trusting with Faith
Stage Two	Deadening	Wailing: Groaning with Hope
Stage Three	Despairing/Doubting	Weaving: Perceiving with Grace
Stage Four	Digging Cisterns	Worshiping: Engaging with Love

Poor Much-Afraid! Her cheeks blanched and she trembled from head to toe.

"I can't go with them," she gasped. "I can't! I can't! I can't! O my Lord Shepherd, why do you do this to me? How can I travel in their company? It is more than I can bear . . . Couldn't you have given me Joy and Peace to go with me, to strengthen and encourage me and help me on the difficult way? I never thought you would do this to me!" And she burst into tears (Hurnard, *Hinds' Feet*, p. 66).

A strange look passed over Shepherd's face.

"Joy and Peace. Are those the companions you would choose for yourself? You remember your promise, to accept the helpers that I would give, because you believed that I would choose the very best possible guides for you. Will you still trust me, Much-Afraid?" (Hurnard, *Hinds' Feet*, p. 66).

Don't misunderstand. Fear of suffering is normal. Grief is necessary. These are authentic life responses. Shepherd's message communicates that trust is vital because suffering is inevitable.

Why is suffering so dreadful? Suffering is *death*. All suffering is the dying, separating, and severing of relationships. Eternal death is *apollumi*—to perish, to be cut off, lost, dead, flicked away, separated from God forever (John 3:16). Eternal death/separation is the paradigm of all our losses. All suffering is experienced as death. This is why Paul could say, "I die daily." Be it the little death of a flat tire, or the bigger death of a broken engagement, or the grand death that ends our earthly life, we each face daily casket experiences. These casket journeys are not the way things are supposed to be. We were not meant to end up in a coffin in Egypt. Death is an intruder.

Walter Wangerin, in his healing book *Mourning Into Dancing*, expresses more insight into death than any mortician.

Death doesn't wait till the ends of our lives to meet us and to make an end. Instead, we die a hundred times before we die; and all the little endings on the way are like a slowly growing echo of the final *Bang!* before that bang takes place (Wangerin, *Mourning Into Dancing*, p. 26).

Because reality is relational, death is separation. All deaths, all caskets are the same—the sundering of relationships.

So why would Shepherd send Suffering and Sorrow to guide us? What are they supposed to teach us? Throughout *Mourning Into Dancing*, Wangerin explains that *suffering and death are meant to teach us our need again*. Paul learned from the same lesson plan.

We do not want you to be uninformed, brothers, about the hardships we suffered in the province of Asia. We were under great pressure, far beyond our ability to endure, so that we despaired even of life. Indeed, in our hearts we felt the sentence of death. But this happened that we might not rely on ourselves but on God, who raises the dead (2 Corinthians 1:8-9).

In suffering, God is not getting back at you; He is getting you back to Him. "The actual experience of dying persuades the little god that he is finite after all" (Wangerin, *Mourning Into Dancing*, p. 76). When Paul felt the sentence of death, he understood that his only hope was the dead-raising God.

Suffering opens our hands to God. Augustine declared, "God wants to give us something, but cannot, because our hands are full—there is nowhere for him to put it." Moses taught the same truth in the passage Jesus quoted during His temptation. Why does God allow us to endure desert wanderings? According to Deuteronomy 8 and Matthew 4, it is to humble us, teaching us how desperately needy we are.

Our greatest need is eternal life and eternal life is experienced in intimacy with God (John 17:1-3). Suffering, therefore, reveals God's extraordinary love. Without suffering we forget God and our need for Him (Deuteronomy 8:6-12). Suffering is grace. It was grace that barred Adam and Eve from the tree of life, lest they live forever, immortal, immoral beings, never having to face their need for God. "Perhaps we suffer so inordinately," Peter Kreeft reminds us, "because God loves us so inordinately." God loves us too much to allow us to forget our neediness.

God makes therapeutic use of our suffering. Suffering, as Luther taught, creates in the child of God a *delicious despair*. Suffering is God's putrid-tasting medicine of choice resulting in delicious healing. Healing medicine for what? For our ultimate sickness—the arrogance that we do not need God.

Suffering causes us to groan for home and to live in hope. The author of Hebrews, surveying the landscape of Old Testament journeys, shows us the way home.

> All these people were still living by faith when they died. They did not receive the things promised; they only saw them and welcomed them from a distance. And they admitted that they were aliens and strangers on earth. People who say such things show that they are looking for a country of their own. If they had been thinking of the country they had left, they would have had opportunity to return. Instead, they were longing for a better country—a heavenly one. Therefore God is not ashamed to be called their God, for he has prepared a city for them (Hebrews 11:13-16).

God refuses to allow us to become too comfy here. Instead, He allows suffering—daily casket processionals—to blacken our sun so we cry out to His Son. Suffering reminds us that we're not home yet.

At least, that's God's intent. Satan plots an altogether different strategy. We learn about his scheme in level two suffering.

Level Two Suffering: What Happens *in* Us—Spiritual Depression

The *theological* reality of suffering teaches that our world is fallen and it often falls on us. The *experiential* reality of suffering tutors us in the truth that our world is a mess and it messes with our minds. In other words, suffering is not only what happens *to* us, it is also, and more importantly, what happens *in* us.

All suffering and mourning amount to a sense of death, divorce, aloneness, and forsakenness. The doubts that we endure while in the casket of suffering lead to a potential hemorrhage in our triune relationship to God, others, and self so that we end up feeling:

- ♦ Spiritual Abandonment: "I feel forsaken."
- ♦ Social Betrayal: "I feel betrayed."
- ♦ Self-Contempt: "I feel shame."

In spiritual abandonment, I see God as my enemy (Job 3:1-26; 6:4; 10:1-3; Psalm 13; 88; Jeremiah 20:7-18; Lamentations 3:1-20; 5:20). Luther called this aspect of level two suffering *anfechtungen* or spiritual depression. He considered it the trial of faith produced when reason unaided by faith reflects on and interprets my suffering. It includes the terrified conscience that perceives that God is against me, and the sense of ultimate terror that God may have forsaken me. *The presence of suffering can result in the absence of faith.*

I call it "spiritual separation anxiety"—the terror of a felt sense of abandonment. False Seducer incites this terror when he whispers, "Life is bad. God controls life. God must be bad. How can you trust His heart? He has left you all alone. Again."

Spiritual depression and spiritual separation anxiety are the results of our internal interpretations of external events. They are satanic temptations to doubt God, spiritual terrors, restlessness, despair, pangs, panic, desolation, and desperation. The absence of faith in God in the presence of external suffering leads to a terrified conscience which perceives God as angry and evil instead of loving and good.

Jeremiah felt and expressed such condemnation and rejection. "Why do you always forget us? Why do you forsake us so long?" (Lamentations 5:20). His language is even stronger, making us squeamish, in Jeremiah 20:7. "O LORD, you deceived me, and I was deceived; you overpowered me and prevailed." Heman, considered one of the wisest believers ever (1 Kings 4:31), pens the "Psalm of the Dark Night of the Soul" (Psalm 88) in which his concluding line sums up his spiritual struggle. "You have taken my companions and loved ones from me; the darkness is my closest friend" (Psalm 88:18).

As if excruciating spiritual abandonment is not enough, level two suffering continues with social betrayal. In social betrayal we're bombarded by paradoxical realities. "Extra! Extra! Read All About It! 'Bob learns that you can't live without trusting. Bob finds that you can't live without betrayal.'" Trust and betrayal.

Joseph faced it everywhere from everyone. Betrayed by his brothers, by slave traders, by Potiphar's wife, by Potiphar, and by the baker.

David, too, knew betrayal. He speaks for all of us when he describes the wracking torment of broken trust.

> If an enemy were insulting me, I could endure it; if a foe were raising himself against me, I could hide from him. But it is you, a man like myself, *my companion, my close friend*, with whom I once enjoyed sweet fellowship as we walked with the throng at the house of God (Psalm 55:12-14, emphasis added).

What pastor has not said similar words? What pastor's wife has not shed similar tears?

To spiritual abandonment and social betrayal we add self-contempt. "If God and others reject me," we surmise, "then I must be unworthy of their friendship. Something must be wrong with me. I am not only at fault. I am faulty."

Job loathed his very life (Job 10:1). He lost all hope for himself and his future. "My days have passed, my plans are shattered, and so are the desires of my heart" (Job 17:11). He felt stripped of honor, torn down, hope uprooted (Job 19:9-10).

What are we to do when assaulted outside and in? What next when overwhelmed by circumstances and feeling condemned by God, our friends, and our own souls?

We don't move toward healing simply by quoting, "God works all things together for good to those who love him." Before we can truly sense the depths of God's goodness, we have to admit the lowest pits of life's "badness." Joseph models acknowledging evil as well as good, "You intended to harm me, but God intended it for good" (Genesis 50:20).

Grief through groaning begins with sustaining in suffering, which says, "It's normal to hurt and necessary to grieve." Later, grief through groaning moves to healing in suffering, when we conclude, "It's possible to hope in the midst of grief." Hurt then hope.

Sustaining in Suffering: "It's Normal to Hurt and Necessary to Grieve"

Students of human grief have developed various models that track typical grief responses. Jane Bissler (*Counseling for Loss and Life Change*) uses the acronym TEAR:

- ♦ T: To accept the reality of the loss.
- ♦ E: Experience the pain of the loss.
- ♦ A: Adjust to the new environment without the lost object.
- ♦ R: Reinvest in the new reality.

Swiss-born psychiatrist Elisabeth Kubler-Ross, in her book *On Death and Dying*, popularized a five-stage model of grieving based upon her research into how terminally ill persons respond to the news of their terminal illness. Her five stages, which have since been used to describe all grief responses, are:

- ♦ *Denial*: This is the shock reaction. "It can't be true." "No, not me." We refuse to believe what happened.
- ♦ *Anger*: Resentment grows. "Why me?" "Why my child?" "This isn't fair!" We direct blame toward God, others, and ourselves. We feel agitated, moody, on edge.
- ♦ *Bargaining*: We try to make a deal, insisting that things be the way they used to be. "God, if you heal my little girl, I'll never drink again." We call a temporary truce with God.
- ♦ *Depression*: Now we say, "Yes, me." The courage to admit our loss brings sadness (which can be healthy mourning and grieving) and/or hopelessness (which is unhealthy mourning and grieving).
- ♦ *Acceptance*: Now we face our loss calmly. It is a time of silent reflection and regrouping. "Life has to go on. How? What do I do now?"

These various stages in the grief process record what *does typically occur*. They do not attempt to assess whether this is what is *best to occur*, or if it is *God's process for hurting and hoping*.

My study of biblical sufferology suggests an eight-stage process for moving hurting people to hope in Christ. The first four stages concern sustaining in suffering, which we examine in this chapter, while the second four stages relate to healing in suffering, which we explore in the next chapter. (Refer back to Box 18:1 for a summary.)

Stage One: Candor—Honest with Self Rather Than Denial and Isolation

Candor contrasts with the typical first stage of grieving—denial. When suffering first hits; when we first hear the news of the unexpected death of a loved one; when we're told that we've been fired, we respond with shock. We can't believe it. Life seems unreal.

I experienced this when I was ten years old. I was coming home from Riddle's Pond where we had been playing hockey. Billy Trapp and I were fighting. My Mom pulled up beside us in her car, rolled down the window, and said, "Get in the car. Grandpa died."

My response, "You're kidding." Like my Mom would kid about something like that. I was in shock. In denial.

Denial is a common initial grief response. I believe that initial response of denial is the grace of God, allowing our bodies and physical brains to catch up, to adjust. After the necessary period of time, however, long-term denial is counter-productive. More than that, it is counter to faith, because true faith faces all of life *coram Deo*.

I once worked with a pastor who was struggling to move past denial. His wife had died while giving birth to their second child. He denied the reality for months. He continued preaching, continued ministering. He never grieved, never wept. He put on a happy face. Under the surface, he was a mess. He constantly hallucinated that he saw and heard his deceased wife. He was near the point of a psychotic breakdown, largely because he could not move out of the stage of denial and into the stage of candor.

What exactly is biblical candor? *Candor is courageous truth telling myself about life, in which I come face-to-face with the reality of external and internal suffering*. In candor, I admit what is happening to me and I feel what is going on inside me.

I had to move from denial to candor after the death of my father on my 21st birthday. In fact, it was not until my 22nd birthday that the process truly began. I had been handling my loss like a good Bible college graduate and seminary student—I was pretending.

On my 22nd birthday, I went for a long walk around the outskirts of the seminary campus. I started facing the loss of my dad. The reality that I would never know him in an adult-to-adult relationship. The fact that my future children would never know their grandfather. As I faced some of those external loses, the tears came. Then I began to face some of the internal crosses—what was happening in me. I felt like a loner. Fatherless. Orphaned. Unprotected. On my own. The tears flowed. The process of candor began. The floodgate of emotions erupted. I was being honest with myself.

Was it a biblical process? Can candor be biblically supported?

David demonstrates candor in Psalm 42:3-5.

> My tears have been my food day and night, while men say to me all day long, 'Where is your God?' These things I remember as I pour out my soul: how I used to go with the multitude, leading the procession to the house of God, with shouts of joy and thanksgiving among the festive throng. Why are you downcast, O my soul? Why so disturbed within me?

Notice that David is honest about his external suffering. He describes his losses—the loss of fellowship, leadership, and worship. He also is candid about his internal suffering. He depicts his crosses, accurately labeling his soul as downcast and disturbed within him.

One could profitably examine the accounts of biblical character after biblical character who practiced candor—Job, Jeremiah, Solomon, Asaph, Heman (Psalm 88), Jesus, Paul, and so many more.

The apostle Paul does not tell us not to grieve. He tells us not to grieve *without hope* (1 Thessalonians 4:13). He chooses a Greek word (*lupēsthe*) meaning to feel sorrow, distress, and grief, and to experience pain, heaviness, and inner affliction. Paul is teaching that grief is the grace of recovery because mourning slows us down to face life. *No grieving, no healing. Know grieving; know healing.* The only person who can truly dare to grieve and bear grief is the person with a hope that things will eventually be better. When we trust God's good heart, we trust Him no matter what. We need not pretend. We can face and embrace the mysteries of life.

Candor or denial? The choice is a turning point. It is a line drawn in the sand, a hurdle to confront. Faith crosses the line. Trust leaps the hurdle. We face reality and embrace truth, sad as it is. If facing suffering is wrestling face-to-face with God, then candor is our decision to step on the mat.

Stage Two: Complaint—Honest to God Rather Than Anger and Resentment

Stage one seeks to diagnose and treat spiritual friends so they move from denial to candor. Stage two diagnoses and treats them so they move from destructive anger to constructive complaint.

Satan is the master masquerader (2 Corinthians 11:13-15). His counterfeit for biblical complaint is unhealthy, destructive anger. He substitutes cursing for complaint, like Job's wife counseling Job to curse God and die, "Give up on God, on yourself, and on life." Cursing God demeans Him, thinking of Him as a lightweight, as a dark desert and a land of great darkness (Jeremiah 2). Cursing separates. Complaint connects. Complaint draws us toward God; hatred and anger push us away from Him.

What then is complaint? In candor we're honest with ourselves; in complaint we're honest with God. *Complaint is vulnerable frankness to God about life, in which I express my pain and confusion over how a good God allows evil and suffering.*

We needlessly react to the word "complaint." "Christians can't complaint!" we insist. Yet, there are more Psalms of Complaint and Lament than Psalms of Praise and Thanksgiving.

Complaints are faith-based acts of persistent trust. They are one of the many moods of faith. Psalm 91's exuberant trust is one faith-mood while Psalm 88's dark despair is another. A mood of faith is simply trusting God enough to bring everything about us to Him. In complaint we hide nothing from God because we trust His good heart and because we know He knows our hearts.

In the weeks and months after my 22nd birthday, I engaged in passionate complaint. What made my struggle even more difficult was my lack of assurance that my father was a believer. I had witnessed to him, prayed for him, and he had begun to attend church with me. Yet, even on his deathbed, he made no verbal commitment of faith in Christ.

So I shared with God. I complained to God. I told God, "What's the use? Why did I pray, witness, and share? Why should I ever pray again? Why should I ever try again, trust again?" I shared my confusion and my doubt with God. "Why do other people's parents accept Christ in a glorious deathbed conversion? What's wrong with me? What's wrong with You, God? You have not kept Your promise!"

Were my expressions of complaint biblical? Can complaint be biblically supported?

Consider Psalm 62:8. "Trust in him at all times, O people; pour out your hearts to him, for God is our refuge." The biblical genre of complaint expresses frankness about the reality of life that seems incongruent with the character of God. Complaint is an act of truth-telling faith, not unfaith. Complaint is a rehearsal of the bad allowed by the Good. Complaint lives in the real world honestly, refusing to ignore what is occurring. It is radical trust in God's reliability in the midst of real life.

Psalm 73 is a prime example of complaint. Asaph begins, "Surely God is good to Israel." He then continues with a litany of apparent evidence to the contrary. However, he concludes, "But as for me, it is good to be near God" (v. 28). Asaph illustrates that in complaint we come to God with a sense of abandonment, divorce, being orphaned, forgotten, and forsaken (Isaiah 49:14; 54:7-8; Lamentations 5:20). We then exercise a courageous, yet humble, cross-examination. Not a cross-examination of God, but a cross-examination and a refuting of earth-bound reality.

That's exactly what occurred in Jeremiah 20:7; Lamentations 5:20; and Psalm 88:18. In those three passages, it appears *by reason alone* that life is bad and so is God. Yet in each of these passages, God responds positively to a believing rehearsal of life's incongruities.

In Job 3, and much of Job for that matter, Job forcefully and even violently expresses his complaint.

> What's the point of life when it doesn't make sense, when God blocks all the roads to meaning? Instead of bread I get groans for my supper, then leave the table and vomit my anguish. The worst of my fears has come true, what I've dreaded most has happened. My repose is shattered, my peace destroyed. No rest for me, ever—death has invaded life (Eugene Peterson, *The Message*, pp. 846-847, Job 3:23-26).

In Job 42:7-8, God honors Job's complaint saying that Job spoke right of life and right of God. God prizes complaint and rejects all deceiving denial and simplistic closure, preferring candid complexity.

To deny or diminish suffering is to refuse arrogantly to be humbled. It is to reject dependence upon God. We are chastised in Deuteronomy 8:1-10 for forgetting our past suffering. God wants us to remember our suffering, our need for Him in our suffering, and to rehearse our suffering (external and internal) before Him.

Stage Three: Cry—Asking God for Help Rather Than Bargaining and Works

Stage one moves from denial to candor, stage two from anger to complaint, and stage three from bargaining and works to crying out to God for help. Notice that when I evaluate the typical third stage of grief, I put works with bargaining. Kubler-Ross recognized this reality. The dying people she worked with bargained with God, believing they would be rewarded for their good behavior and they would be granted special favors.

That is exactly what Job's miserable counselors counseled him to do—behave, be good, do right and God will treat you right. Bargaining knows nothing of grace. It's all works, all self-effort, all self-sufficiency. That's why, as Christian counselors, we want to move people from works to cry.

What is cry? *Cry is a faith-based plea for mobilization in which I humbly ask God for help based upon my admission that I can't survive without Him.* Cry is reaching up with open palms and pleading eyes in the midst of darkness and doubt.

Cry is the core theme of life in a fallen world. Stop crying; stop hoping. As long as we can cry, we can hope.

Crying out is the piety of vigorous embrace in suffering. God wants us to take the initiative to call Him to action on our behalf. He will not force Himself on His lover; however, He'll never disappoint His pleading lover.

That's why the opposite of cry is arrogance. It's the tough, stoic, self-made lone ranger who needs no one, especially not God. The last thing Satan wants us to do is to cry out to God for help.

Throughout my 22nd year of life, I cried out to God for help. "God, I'm confused. I'm scared. Everything I trusted in is gone. I used to think that if I prayed hard enough and worked long enough, eventually everything I longed for would come true in this life. But now I know that's a lie. So what is true? What have You really promised? What can I count on? I can't count on myself. Father, I want to count on You. Don't let me down. Rescue me. Help me. Save me."

Did God hear my cries? Were my cries biblical? Can we find biblical support for cry as a scriptural stage of grief?

Psalm 56:8 (KJV) teaches that we pray our tears and God collects them in His bottle. Psalm 72:12 assures us, "For he will deliver the needy who cry out" ("when he crieth," KJV).

Psalm 34 reminds us, "The righteous cry out, and the LORD hears them; he delivers them from all their troubles. The LORD is close to the brokenhearted and saves those who are crushed in spirit" (Psalm 34:17-18). I learned the significance of those verses from a counselee whose husband had left her for a man. Yes, for a man. She clung to the truth and taught me the truth that God's good heart goes out, especially, to the humble needy. She practiced biblical cry—the hopeful, trusting expression that God would mobilize Himself on her behalf.

Crying out to God, lamenting, is a testimony that God is responsive, while the idols are non-responsive (1 Samuel 12:20-24). When we cry out, we entreat God to help because expressed neediness compels God's very character to act. God acts on voiced pain. He is not a deaf and dumb idol.

Crying empties us, so there is more room in us for God. David wept until he had no strength left, but then he found strength in God (1 Samuel 30:4-6). His cry, his confession of neediness, summoned God into action—supportive action.

Suffering is God's *opus alienum*—God's dominant way of destroying our self-reliance and complacency. He uses suffering to gain our attention. Suffering is a slap in the face, the shock of icy water, a bloodied nose meant to snatch our attention. Cry is our admission that God has our attention, that God has *us*.

Stage Four: Comfort—Receiving God's Help Rather Than Depression and Alienation

Stage one involves denial *or* candor, stage two anger *or* complaint, stage three bargaining/works *or* cry. Stage four involves depression because of alienation *or* finding comfort through communion. Through *candor* we choose to step on the mat with God. With *complaint*, the match begins. With *cry*, we shout, "Uncle." We say, "I'm pinned. I'm helpless. You win, God. Now I win, too." *Comfort*, then, is the crippling touch of God that plants the seed for healing. In cry, we ask for God's help. In comfort, we receive God's help. In comfort, the God we cried out to, comes.

The typical fourth stage of grief includes a type of depression that we might best describe as hopelessness. The sufferer accepts reality, but only from an earthly perspective. He can see no higher plan.

It reminds me of the chilling opening scene in *Les Miserables*. Hundreds of prisoners are chanting, "Look down, look down, don't look them in the eyes." They're filled with shame. Then one prisoner attempts to break free from his emotional prison by singing that there are people who love him and are waiting for him when he's released. The guards, and even the other prisoners, heap more shame upon him. One cries, "Sweet Jesus doesn't care." Others sing, "You'll always be a slave, you're standing in your grave." That's hopelessness. That's the fourth stage of grief without Christ.

What then is comfort? Before the definition, let's consider some history. Historically, sustaining has attempted to draw a line in the sand of retreat. Horrible things happen to us. We're charging headlong away from the life we once dreamed of. We're ready to give up and give in. Sustaining steps in to say, "Yes, you do have a wound. You will have the scar. But it is neither fatal nor final. Don't quit. You can make it. You can survive."

It's within this context of surviving scars that I'm using the word "comfort." Originally, comfort meant co-fortitude—being fortified by the strength of another. Being en-couraged—having courage poured into you from an outside source. That outside source, for Christians, is Christ and the body of Christ. In this life, your scar may not go away, but neither will Christ's. He understands. He cares. He's there.

Now we can define comfort. *Comfort experiences the presence of God in the presence of suffering—a presence that empowers me to survive scars and plants the seed of hope that I may yet thrive.* At the end of sustaining, I'm not necessarily thriving. More likely, I'm limping, but at least I'm no longer retreating.

For me, comfort reflected itself in my decision not to give up on God and not to give up on ministry. There I was—in seminary, preparing for ministry, and secretly doubting God, doubting His goodness, trustworthiness, ability, or at least His desire to protect me and care for me. As comfort came, I came face-to-face with God. We had some wild talks. We had some fierce wrestling matches.

God won. I surrendered. Still confused about the details of life, but committed to the Author of Life. More than that, surrendered to Him *and* dependent upon Him. My attitude was like Peter's when Jesus asked His disciples, "Will you, too, leave Me?" Remember Peter's reply? "To whom could we go? You alone have the words of life."

I was surviving again, surviving though scarred. I was not and never again would be that same naïve young Christian who assumed if I prayed and worked hard enough, God would grant me my every expectation. My faith was no longer a naïve faith; it was now a deeper faith—a faith that could walk in the dark.

Did my experience of comfort reflect a biblical process? Can we biblically support comfort? Jacob's wrestling match with God certainly illustrates it. Recall the context. Jacob is terrified that his brother Esau will kill him. In self-sufficiency, Jacob plans and plots ways to manipulate Esau into forgiving him.

Then, at night (isn't it always at night?) Jacob encounters God. He wrestles God throughout the night until God overpowers Jacob by dislocating his hip. In response,

"Jacob called the place Peniel, saying, 'It is because I saw God face to face, and yet my life was spared'" (Genesis 32:30). Jacob shows us that tenacious wrestling with God results in painful yet profitable comfort through communion.

Interestingly, as the sun rose, Jacob was limping. He looks up and there's Esau. Jacob limps up to Esau and, with the pain of his dislocated hip, bows down seven times. Imagine the excruciating pain. Then he receives from Esau an embrace instead of a dagger. He faced his fear, still wounded and scarred, but surviving. God humbled Jacob, weakened him, and in the process strengthened him.

What is illustrated in Jacob's life is taught in Asaph's story. According to Psalm 73:21-28, suffering is an opportunity for God to divulge more of Himself and to release more of His strength. When Asaph's heart was grieved, and his spirit embittered, God brought him to his senses. Listen to his prayer. "My flesh and my heart may fail, but God is the strength of my heart and my portion forever" (Psalm 73:26). "My flesh may be scarred, my heart may be scared, but with God I can survive—forever."

Thus faith perceives that God feels our pain, joins us in our pain, and even shares our pain. In fact, faith believes that, "in all their distress he too was distressed" (Isaiah 63:9). His sharing of our sorrow makes our sorrow endurable.

Faith does not demand the removal of suffering, but desires endurance in suffering, temptation, and persecution (1 Corinthians 10:13). Faith understands that what can't be cured, can be endured.

Faith delights in weakness, because when we are weak, then God is strong, and we are strong in Him (2 Corinthians 12:9-10).

Faith believes that every problem is an opportunity to know God better. Since our primary battle is to know God well, in suffering we ask a core soul care question. "How is your suffering influencing your relationship with God?" Suffering can either shove us far from God into the land of despair, or drag us kicking and screaming, closer to Him into the solid soil of comfort.

The Christ of the Cross is our ultimate comfort. As the hymn writer Katharina von Schlegel poetically states it:

> Be still, my soul! the Lord is on thy side;
> Bear patiently the cross of grief or pain;
> Leave to thy God to order and provide;
> In every change He faithful will remain.
> Be still, my soul! thy best, thy heavenly Friend
> Thro' thorny ways leads to a joyful end.

Comfort develops through communion with Christ and through connection to the body of Christ. The great soul caregivers of the past called human comfort *compassionate commiseration*. Think about those words. Co-passion: sharing in another's passion and pathos. Co-misery: sharing misery with another. It is because we experience suffering as separation, that shared sorrow (compassionate commiseration) is so vital.

Stage one takes the sufferer from denial to candor, stage two from anger to complaint, stage three from bargaining/works to cry, and stage four from depression to comfort. Grieving is a normal response to loss. God does not abandon us in our dark, dank casket, however. God, who is Light, shines His light of comfort into our hurting hearts.

Where We've Been and Where We're Heading

Creation, *Fall*, Redemption—we're still in the Fall of our journey. We've explored God's path through the desert of suffering. That's where we've been.

Here's where we're headed. Created for Paradise, we now live in a desert. Obviously, then, we will be thirsty. Made for fine spring water, sand will not do. Facing hurts is necessary; hurting is normal. We don't want to stay there, however. Though trapped in a wilderness outside, through Christ we can be rescued inside—healed through hope. Hope that groans for heaven later and trusts in God now.

The curtain is rising on Act Three, Scene VI: The Hoping Sufferer: Sufferology, Part II. Hope beckons. We need her healing. What are we waiting for?

Caring for Your Soul: Personal Applications

1. Spiritual depression is the absence of faith during the presence of suffering.

    a. Read Lamentations 3:1-20 to probe what it is like to feel abandoned by God. How does Jeremiah's experience compare with yours?

    b. According to Job 17:11 and Proverbs 13:12, how do dashed dreams impact us? How have they impacted you?

    c. Read Job 3:1-26; 7:1-10; and 10:1-22 to sense the despair and dread brought on by spiritual depression. Have you been there? How so? How did you respond?

2. Ponder your most recent experience of "level one suffering." Did you experience any "level two suffering"—feelings of abandonment, betrayal, doubt, and despair?

    a. If not, how did you manage to avoid such thoughts?

    b. If so, how did you manage those thoughts?

3. *Coram Deo* suffering is the biblical response to spiritual depression.

    a. It starts with *candor*—being honest with yourself. In what sense is Asaph candidly soul-aware in Psalm 73? How soul-aware and honest with yourself do you tend to be?

    b. It continues with *complaint*—being honest to God. Do you have enough courageous faith to pen a Psalm 13, 73, or 88? What would it sound like?

    c. The next stage is *cry*. Read Psalm 72:12-14. Why does God want us to cry out for help? What happens when *you* cry to Him?

    d. Then comes *comfort*—connecting with Christ and Christians. Read Isaiah 63:9. Do you believe it? Read 2 Corinthians 1:3-10. Have you experienced it?

4. Which seems to be harder for you: candor, complaint, cry, or comfort?

    a. Why do you suppose that is?

    b. How could you mature in this area?

Caring for Others: Ministry Implications

♦ **Don't Rescue:** Rescue is stealing. It steals the gift of grief. God expects us to grieve (1 Thessalonians 4:13) and to groan (Romans 8:17-28). Use grieving and groaning to help your spiritual friends grasp grace.

♦ **Follow the Trail of Trials:** Suffering is wanting what I do not get, getting what I do not want, and getting what I want and not wanting it. Be thinking: "Where has my spiritual friend wanted what he did not get?" "Where has my spiritual friend received what she did not want?" "Where are my spiritual friends realizing that what they wanted was not enough?"

♦ **Start With What Is Most Accessible:** In suffering, the emotional and relational tend to be "closest to the surface." Go there. Camp there. "What is missing in my spiritual friend's life?" "What losses and crosses is she enduring?" "How does he feel because of it?" "What level one circumstances are leading to level two condemnation?"

♦ **Hold Gently to Some Handles:** Candor, complaint, cry, and comfort are handles helping us sense where our spiritual friends are in the grief process and where they might need us to take them. However, they are handles, not straightjackets. No two people bear grief identically. Don't force a grid or model on others. Apply it where it fits, but apply it gently, carefully, and respectfully.

♦ **Expect Integrity:** Sustaining expects integrity—faith-based integrity that faces life, all of life, with honesty. If you sense denial, slowly move with your spiritual friend toward candid exploration of losses and crosses. If you sense anger that creates distance, carefully journey with your spiritual friend toward courageous complaint that is honest with God. If you sense bargaining and works, gently expose your spiritual friend's arrogant refusal to seek Divine assistance. If you sense hopelessness, despair, and depression, join it, but also join comfort to it. Feel your spiritual friend's grief while stretching him or her to God's caring comfort.

♦ **Role Play Number One:** A friend comes to you, and you assess that she is saying in her soul, "Life is not bad; God is not bad." She is in denial about the reality of her suffering. How would you attempt to move with her from denial to candor?

♦ **Role Play Number Two:** A friend comes to you, and you "assess" that he is saying in his soul, "Life is bad; God must be, too. Or at least He must be ticked with me." He is angry with God, others, and himself. How would you move with him from anger to candor, complaint, cry, and communion?

CHAPTER NINETEEN

THE HOPING SUFFERER: SUFFEROLOGY, PART II

"There is no human experience which cannot be put on the anvil of a lively relationship with God and man, and battered into a meaningful shape" (Frank Lake, *Clinical Theology,* p. 97).

"This life ought to be spent only as a journey towards heaven" (Jonathan Edwards).

"Man's happiness is God himself" (Augustine).

Creative Suffering

You may recall Terry Waite. The British hostage, released in 1991 after nearly five years of solitary confinement in Lebanon, was chained to the wall of his room for almost twenty-four hours a day. Reflecting on his circumstances he noted:

I have been determined in captivity, and still am determined, to convert this experience into something that will be useful and good for other people. I think that's the way to approach suffering. It seems to me that Christianity doesn't in any way lessen suffering. What it does is enable you to take it, to face it, to work through it and eventually convert it (Waite, *Taken on Trust*, p 11).

"Creative suffering" we might call it. God transforms suffering, composing good from evil, turning our mourning into dancing, and creating beauty from ashes.

What role do soul caregivers play in converting suffering? How do we cooperate with God to batter mangled caskets into a meaningful shape? In the introduction, we defined counseling: counseling builds upon the gospel of Christ's grace to deal both with *the evils we have suffered* and with the sins we have committed. In suffering, soul caregivers compassionately identify with people in pain and redirect them to Christ and the body of Christ to *sustain* and *heal* their faith so they experience communion with Christ and conformity to Christ even in the midst of suffering in a fallen world.

Sufferology exists because sin, death, and separation exist. Created for life in Paradise, we now reside east of Eden. Designed for the refreshing, rejuvenating waters of relational connection, now we endure the arid desert of forsakenness, betrayal, and dis-integration. Desperately thirsty, we clamor for communion and long for resurrection. During Sufferology, Part I, soul caregivers climb into the casket of daily desert deaths—*sustaining* we call it. During Sufferology, Part II, soul caregivers celebrate the resurrection that promises a day when all thirsts are quenched—*healing* we call it.

Sustaining helps faith *survive*. We fortify faith to resist retreat and to promote spiritual stability and security. Healing helps faith *thrive*. We deepen faith to move forward, promoting spiritual maturity.

In sustaining, we taste God's comfort; in healing, His goodness. In sustaining, we face the world's evil; in healing, God's goodness. In sustaining, we learn that we need something. In healing, we learn that we need Christ and Christians. In sustaining, we participate in the fellowship of Christ's suffering. In healing, we appropriate the power of Christ's resurrection. Together, sustaining and healing teach that even when life is bad, it's possible to hope, because God is good. "It's normal to hurt and possible to hope."

Toward a Theology of Healing: Thirst-Based Dependence

Consider where we last saw our suffering friend in sustaining. In a casket. Not alone, not dead, not separated. Nevertheless, in a casket. We're in the casket with her. She's invited Christ, also. Her soul gushes forth, spilling a lifetime of daily deaths. At this threshold of awareness of the fragility of her life and the frailty of human existence, a door of opportunity opens for her. Surprisingly, a door of hope.

More surprisingly, a door of eternal hope entered by way of the death of earthly hope. A rudimentary principle of spiritual existence teaches that until death crucifies our earthly hope, we refuse to surrender ourselves to resurrected heavenly hope. Remember Paul?

> We were under great pressure, far beyond our ability to endure, so that we despaired even of life. Indeed, in our hearts *we felt the sentence of death*. But this happened that we might not *rely* on ourselves but *on God, who raises the dead* (2 Corinthians 1:8-9, emphasis added).

Remember the woman at the well in John 4? "Water. Give me water!" She knew she was thirsty, but she was not yet at the end of her rope. She was consciously aware only of her physical thirst and all the self-effort it took to placate it. "I don't want to keep coming here to draw water." Hard work, but doable in human strength.

So Jesus shifted her sights from physical thirsts to relational ones. "Go get your hubby."

"Husband? I have no husband."

"That's right. The fact is, you have five husbands, and the man you now have is not even your husband."

What was Jesus up to? The same thing He's always up to in all our thirsty desert journeys—inviting us to Himself based on acknowledged relational thirsts. "If anyone is thirsty, let him come to me and drink" (John 7:37).

No matter how hard the woman at the well worked, no matter how many times she pursued her relational strategy of "having a man," it was never enough. Thirsty, with only a broken cistern to draw from, she gave up all human hope. She surrendered to heavenly hope, placing her trust in the "Savior of the world" (John 4:42).

Some thirsts are too deep to be fulfilled by works. Thank God! Hope, prompted by thirsts (John 4 and 7), watered by longings (Psalms 42-43; 63), and seeded by the groanings of life (Romans 8), grows into a contact point to embrace and be embraced by Christ.

In sustaining, we face our loss. That's good; however, secular counseling can enter here, offering solutions—secular healing. "Here, do this. Regroup. Start afresh. Grieve. Then move on. In your own strength. You can do it. Others have. You're okay. Life must go on. Don't quit."

Christian healing is soul *care* at its purest. It is not so much a *cure*, if by that we mean a definitive change in circumstances, or even a return to the previous state of being. Rather, it is *care*. We care about what is most important internally and eternally—a dependent, intimate grace relationship with Christ. We enter saying, "Here, stop doing that. Stop trying to regroup on your own. Don't even think about climbing out of that casket alone. Cry out for resurrection help. Drink from the Spring of Living Water. Entrust yourself to Jesus and streams of living water will flow from within you." Or, put in Paul's terms, "He has *delivered* us from such *deadly* peril, and he will *deliver* us. On him we have set our *hope* that he will continue to *deliver* us (2 Corinthians 1:10, emphasis added).

Healing makes what cannot be removed, creatively bearable. It is the divinely creative use of pain and loss that cannot be cured. In our weakness, He is strong; in our parched condition, He is satisfying. His strength is made perfect in our weakness. Healing blossoms in the souls of thirsty image bearers who groan for what only God can supply.

In suffering, the tempter tempts us to despair. Outwardly, life is bad. Inwardly, however, we perceive that God is good as we gain Christ's larger perspective. "So that's what God's about! You mean He takes the ugliness of this situation, and reshapes it, and me, into something glorious? He's making me spiritually beautiful? Oh, so all of this is His cosmic beauty treatment!"

Healing in Suffering: "It's Possible to Hope in the Midst of Grief"

Spiritual emergencies allow for spiritual emergence. We heal spiritual disabilities by encouraging spiritual maturity through a greater awareness of God's good heart and His good purposes even in the midst of suffering. We plant seeds that help faith thrive as people experience the benefits of faith to see the benefits of trials. Thirsty sufferers move forward with a new beginning through a new hope based upon a new perspective.

Sufferology through healing offers a four-stage process that moves sufferers toward the conviction that "it's possible to hope in the midst of grief."

- ◆ Stage One: Waiting—Trusting with Faith
- ◆ Stage Two: Wailing—Groaning with Hope
- ◆ Stage Three: Weaving—Perceiving with Grace
- ◆ Stage Four: Worshiping—Engaging with Love

When we say, "it's possible to hope," we're saying it's possible to trust God with faith, groan to God with hope, perceive suffering with grace, and engage God and others with love, even during times of suffering.

Stage One: Waiting—Trusting with Faith Rather Than Regrouping with Self-Sufficiency

You're in a casket. Finally, you've come face-to-face with death and with utter human hopelessness. Do you want to stay there? No! Frantic to escape? Yes! You cry out to God for help. What's He say? "*Wait.*" Now you're at a faith-point. "I trust Him; I trust Him not. I'll wait; I'll not wait." Which will it be? Will you wait or regroup?

John 4 illustrates the contrast between waiting and regrouping. The woman at the well was in a husband-casket. One husband left the scene, "Encore! Encore!" she'd shout, bringing the curtain down on another failed marriage. Frantically she searched time after time for a man she could have—a man she could desperately clutch and who would meet her desperate needs by desperately desiring her above all else.

We don't know what came next for her after she surrendered her thirsts to Christ. If she were to live out her new Christ-life, she would certainly have to change her pattern of regrouping by having another man. Suppose she took her longing to God in prayer. Suppose God told her to stop living with this man who was not her husband. Don't you think that on a human plane she would experience excruciating emptiness, starving hunger?

So she prays to God, "Father, I know that all I need is You and what You choose to provide. I'm cleaning up my life. Would You please send me a godly man?"

God says, "Wait. Delay your gratification. Don't get involved with a man." Everything inside her—her flesh-habituated past way of surviving, her cistern-digging style of relating—craves satisfaction *now*. If she regroups, she grasps yet another husband on the rebound. She takes matters into her own hands.

So what would "hope" look like in her immediate context? Hoping in God, she would choose delayed gratification over immediate gratification. She would accept her singleness, cling to God and trust His timing.

Hope waits. Hope is the refusal to demand heaven now.

If hope leads to waiting, what then is waiting? *Waiting is trusting God's future provision without working to provide for oneself.* Waiting is refusing to take over while refusing to give up. Waiting refuses self-rescue.

Tony Campolo preaches a message in which he repeatedly says, "It's Friday, but Sunday's comin'." He's focusing his audience on Friday-truth—the crucifixion of Christ—and on Sunday-truth—the coming resurrection of Christ. I would change the metaphor a tad because we aren't living on Friday; we're living on Saturday. Symbolically, life lived on fallen planet Earth is Saturday living—the day between the crucifixion and the resurrection. The day of waiting. The day that tests our trust.

You'll never see waiting as one of the stages in any research study because it is not natural in a fallen world. It is supernatural.

I once worked with a missionary couple (we'll call them Tim and Terri) whose mission agency refused to allow them to return to the field. In essence, they were fired without cause. Frankly, the situation appeared to be nothing more than a power struggle.

We worked through the candor, complaint, cry, and comfort process. When it came time for waiting, Tim battled. Everything in him wanted, almost desperately needed, to regroup. He was ready to join a ministry, any ministry, on the rebound. He was ready to take a job, any job, on the rebound. However, I counseled him to wait before making any long-term commitments to a new ministry position because I sensed that he was motivated by a desire for self-rescue, for regrouping, not by a desire to wait on God.

Was my counsel godly or ungodly? Wise or foolish? Too heavenly-minded to be of any earthly good? Can we find biblical support for the principle of waiting rather than regrouping?

Waiting is rooted in the Old Testament. Prophets promised Israel that a better day was coming, *later*. The New Testament writers develop the waiting motif when they urge us toward patience, perseverance, longsuffering, and remaining under. That's the message of Romans 5; James 1; 1 Peter 1-2; and Hebrews 11. In waiting, we hold on to God's rope of hope, even when we can't see it. In biblical waiting, we neither numb our longings nor fulfill them illegitimately.

The opposite of waiting is meeting my "needs" *now*, taking matters into my own hands now, and acting as though I'm my only hope. Esau embodies regrouping through immediate gratification (Hebrews 12:16). For a single meal, a bowl of soup, he sold his birthright. He refused to look ahead, to wait, to delay gratification.

What is your bowl of soup? Mine? What am I convinced I must have now that I believe is more pleasing to my deepest appetite than God and what He promises?

Moses exemplifies delayed gratification and waiting.

> By faith Moses, when he had grown up, refused to be known as the son of Pharaoh's daughter. He *chose to be mistreated* along with the people of *God rather than to enjoy the pleasures of sin for a short time*. He regarded disgrace for the sake of Christ as of greater value than the treasures of Egypt, *because he was looking ahead to his reward* (Hebrews 11:24-26, emphasis added).

No quick fix for Moses. No "Turkish Delight" from the White Witch of Narnia. No pleasures of sin for a season. Why? How could he? He chose eternal pleasure over temporal happiness. *He remembered the future.*

Faith looks *back* to the past recalling God's mighty works. Faith says, "He did it that time, He can do it now." Hope looks *ahead* remembering God's coming reward. Hope says, "I consider that our present sufferings are not worth comparing with the glory that will be revealed in us. The creation *waits* in eager expectation for the sons of God to be revealed" (Romans 8:18-19, emphasis added). Hopeful waiting gives love time to take root.

Stage Two: Wailing—Groaning with Hope Rather Than Deadening

Stage one explores waiting versus regrouping while stage two ponders wailing versus deadening. The barren Shunammite woman of 2 Kings 4 helps us to picture deadening. After years of barrenness, she bears a son who fulfills a lifetime of hopes and dreams. Tragically, he dies. Life sent her two caskets, the first her inability to conceive, the second the death of the child she finally bore.

Rather than face her groaning, she keeps repeating, "It's all right." Her heart is sick, her soul vexed, yet she keeps insisting, "It's all right. I'm all right."

However, she eventually screams at Elisha, "Did I not say to you, 'Don't deceive me? Don't get my *hopes* up'?" Deadening refuses to hope ever again, to dream ever again.

Hope deferred makes the heart sick. Hope hoped for, received, then lost, makes the heart deathly ill. Fragile. Needy. We hate being there, so we block it out. We deaden ourselves by refusing to hope, long, wail, or groan because groaning exposes us as the needy people we are.

The problem is, God made us longing, thirsting, hungering, desiring beings. So we follow a variety of strategies to deaden our desires and shut out the wail of our soul. We live as if this world is all there is. We refuse to hope for something more. Our goal is to satisfy the flesh to quench the ache in our soul.

What then is wailing? How would we define it? By wailing, I don't mean weeping as in complaining or sustained crying (though weeping often accompanies wailing). *Wailing is longing for heaven* **and** *living passionately for God and others while still on earth.*

Paul epitomizes wailing in Philippians 1:23-25.

> I am torn between the two: I desire to depart and be with Christ, which is better by far; but it is more necessary for you that I remain in the body. Convinced of this, I know that I will remain, and I will continue with all of you for your progress and joy in the faith.

Paul neither deadens his longing for heaven nor does he minimize his calling on earth.

Wailing is longing, hungering, thirsting, and wanting what is legitimate, what is promised, but what we do not have. It is grieving the "not yet."

How is wailing different from candor and complaint? Candor says, "I hate what has happened to me." Complaint says, "God, I'm confused and devastated by what has happened to me." Wailing says, "I wanna' go home. This world is so messed up. I ache for Paradise. However, I'm pulling weeds till the day I die!"

In the situation with the missionary couple, Terri knew how to groan. She told me once, "Bob, everything in me wants to tell Tim never, ever to go into the ministry again. He's so wounded, and I'm so scared for him. Everything in me wants to say, 'I'll never be a ministry wife again.'"

Then she leaned forward with a glimmer in her eyes as she said, "I watched the *Les Miserables* DVD you loaned me. Fantine sang, 'There are some storms you cannot weather,' and 'Life has killed the dream I dreamed.' By God's grace, that's not going to happen to me. I'm not going to quit feeling. I'm not going to quit living. I'm not going to quit connecting. I've experienced a taste of the fellowship of Christ's suffering and I'll never be the same. I'm more alive today than I have ever been in my life. God's given me a vision of ministering to other women, to ministry wives." Then she leaned back, engulfed in a restful, confident smile, almost a smirk. It's been two years now. God's fulfilling her dream.

Was her wailing, her groaning with hope, biblical? What biblical support is there for wailing as a stage of acceptance, as God's plan for responding to suffering? Consider Romans 8:18-25.

> I consider that our *present sufferings* are not worth comparing with the glory that will be revealed in us. The creation waits in eager expectation for the sons of God to be revealed. For the creation was subjected to *frustration*, not by its own choice, but by the will of the one who subjected it, *in hope* that the creation itself will be

liberated from its bondage to decay and brought into the glorious freedom of the children of God. We know that the whole creation has been *groaning* as in the pains of *childbirth* right up to the present time. Not only so, but we ourselves, who have the firstfruits of the Spirit, *groan inwardly as we wait eagerly* for our adoption as sons, the redemption of our bodies. For in this hope we were saved. But hope that is seen is no hope at all. Who hopes for what he already has? But if we hope for what we do not yet have, we wait for it patiently (emphasis added).

Designed for Paradise, we live in a desert. No wonder we are thirsty image bearers. No wonder we groan for heaven. We might picture the big picture like this:

♦　Paradise:　"Now!"　　Full
♦　Desert:　　"No!"　　Empty
♦　Thirst:　　"Not Yet!"　Groaning

Everything was very good and completely satisfying in Paradise. Generous Father gifted less-than-grateful Adam and Eve with all they needed and so much more. They were full. Because they refused to rest in Father's fullness, they were barricaded from the Garden, sent roaming east of Eden into the desert. Instead of the happy cry of "Now! All my needs are met now!" they now cry, "No! We are empty. Thirsty. Hungry." Created for Paradise and living in a desert, they and their offspring become thirsty. The new cry is "Not yet!" We say, "I want what I want and I want it now." God says, "I promise you that I will quench all your legitimate thirsts, *but not yet*." So we groan.

What type of groans? Paul links suffering, frustration, eager waiting, and pregnant groaning. "Frustration" suggests the ache we feel because of the emptiness and void we experience living in a fallen world. It's the same Greek word (*mataiot☐ti*) used in the Septuagint to translate Solomon's word "vanity"—meaningless, soap bubbles, unsatisfying, pointless, absurd. All this describes life south of heaven.

"Eager waiting" pictures ferocious, desperate desire. When we wail, we declare how deeply out of the nest we are, how far from home we've wandered, and how much we long for heaven.

Paul illustrates our desperate desire with the image of pregnancy. He describes a woman groaning as in labor that lasts not hours, not nine months, but a lifetime. Imagine a pregnant woman in labor for seventy years! That's groaning. Groaning not only from the pain of seemingly unending labor, but *groaning from the pain of not having the joy of the baby*.

That's our current condition. For our allotted years on this blue planet, we're pregnant with hope, groaning for Paradise, for Eden, for walking with God in the cool of the day, for being naked and unashamed, for shalom. When we groan, we admit to ourselves and express to God the pain of our unmet desires, the depth of our fervent longing for heaven's joy, and our total commitment to remain pregnant with hope— to labor for a lifetime.

And what is the result? Weak, mournful surviving? No way. The result is thriving. In Romans 8:28-39, Paul insists that even in the midst of trouble, hardship, persecution, and suffering, nothing can separate us from the love of God in Christ Jesus. He teaches that in all our suffering we are more than conquerors through Him who loved us so. "More than conquerors" comes from the Greek word *nikao* from which we gain our word "Nike"—victors, Olympic champions, winners. Wailing empowers us to long passionately for heaven and to live victoriously on earth. Wailing moves us from being victims to victors in Christ.

Stage Three: Weaving—Perceiving with Grace Rather Than Despairing and Doubting

In stage one we move from regrouping to waiting, in stage two from deadening to wailing, and in stage three from despairing and doubting to weaving—perceiving with grace. To understand doubting, track the world's typical grief and acceptance process thus far.

Suffering crashes upon us. In shock, we *deny* its reality. At some point, our emotions can no longer suppress the truth and we explode with *anger*. Anger doesn't get us what we want, so we switch tactics and try *bargaining*, behaving, and good works. No matter what we try, we can't manage our loss. *Depression* sets in, alienation.

At some point, the depression lifts a tad. We figure we have to get on with life somehow. We *regroup*. We re-enter the game, not with a new heart, but with no other choice. The game's still rough, it still hurts, so we do what we can to *deaden* and suppress the pain—perhaps workaholism, ministryaholism, or counselaholism. But like the Shunammite woman, life assaults us again, only worse. None of our strategies work. Now what? What do we do? What do we feel? How do we respond? What do we think? We *despair*. We *doubt*. We give up any hope of ever making life work, of ever figuring out the mystery of life, and of ever completing the puzzle. We trudge on in doubt, despair, and darkness. Despair is the negative of hope.

What then is weaving? *Weaving is entrusting oneself to God's larger purposes, good plans, and eternal perspective.* It's seeing life with spiritual eyes instead of eyeballs only. It's looking at suffering, not with rose-colored glasses, but with faith eyes, with Cross-eyes, with 20/20 spiritual vision.

When Terri returned for her next appointment, I asked her what made the difference in her life, what helped her turn the corner. She said, "Two things, no, two people. Joseph and the Bishop."

I had asked Terri to watch *Les Miserables*. She was struck by Jean Val Jean's response to the scene in chapter seven when the Bishop of Digne graciously refuses to press charges against Val Jean for stealing from him.

As Terri put it, "I was floored by the scene right after the police released Val Jean. The Bishop sings, 'By the witness and the martyrs, by the passion and the blood, I have bought your soul for God. Now become an honest man. See in this some higher plan.' Val Jean, amazed by grace, changed by grace, concludes the scene by singing, 'Another story must begin.'"

Terri continued, "Now in everything that happens to me, I'm looking for God's higher plan. I'm setting my thoughts on things above, always wondering what God might be up to in this. For me, another story must begin—God's story that doesn't obliterate my painful story, but that gives it meaning."

Was Terri's approach a biblical stage in the acceptance process? What biblical support can we find for weaving?

Weaving is everywhere in Scripture. We find weaving in passages like John 14; Romans 8; Ephesians 3; Colossians 3; Hebrews 11; and Revelation 19-22.

Terri had referred to Joseph. Hear his words to his fearful family in Genesis 50:19-20. "Don't be afraid. Am I in the place of God? You intended to harm me, but God intended it for good to accomplish what is now being done, the saving of many lives."

Joseph uses "intended" both for his brothers' plans and God's purposes. The Hebrew word has a very tangible sense of weaving, plaiting, interpenetrating as in the weaving together of fabric to fashion a robe, perhaps even a coat of many colors. It was also used in a negative, metaphorical sense to suggest a malicious plot, the devising of a cruel scheme. Other times the Jews used "intended" to picture symbolically the creation of some new and beautiful purpose or result through the weaving together of seemingly haphazard, miscellaneous, or malicious events.

"Life is bad," Joseph admits. "You plotted against me for *evil*. You *intended* to spoil or ruin something wonderful."

"God is good," Joseph insists. "God wove good out of evil," choosing a word for "good" that is the superlative of pleasant, beautiful. That is, God *intended* to create beauty from ashes.

Joseph discovers healing through God's grace narrative. Further, he offers tastes of grace to his blundering brothers.

> And now, do not be distressed and do not be angry with yourselves for selling me here, because it was to save lives that God sent me ahead of you. For two years now there has been famine in the land, and for the next five years there will not be plowing and reaping. But God sent me ahead of you to preserve for you a remnant on earth and to save your lives by a great deliverance. So then, it was not you who sent me here, but God. He made me father to Pharaoh, lord of his entire household and ruler of all Egypt (Genesis 45:5-8).

Amazing! I hope you caught the words. "To save lives," "to preserve," "by a great deliverance." That's a grace narrative, a salvation narrative. Had God not preserved a remnant of Abraham's descendants, Jesus would never have been born. Joseph uses his spiritual eyes to see God's great grace purposes in saving not only Israel and Egypt, but also the entire world.

I hope you also caught Joseph's repetition. "God sent me." "God sent me ahead of you." "It was not you who sent me here, but God." Joseph sees the smaller story of human scheming for ruin. However, Joseph perceives that God trumps that smaller scheme with His larger purpose by weaving beauty out of ugly.

Life hurts. Wounds penetrate. Without grace narratives, hopelessness and bitterness flourish. With a grace narrative, hope and forgiveness flow and perspective grows.

Instead of our perspective shrinking, suffering is the exact time when we must listen most closely, when we must lean over to hear the whisper of God. True, God shouts to us in our pain, but His answers, as with Elijah, often come to us in whispered still small voices amid the thunders of the world.

In weaving, our wounds are healed as we envision a future while all seems lost in the present. Through hope we remember the future. We move from Good Friday to Easter Sunday while living on Saturday. Grace narratives point the way to God's larger story, assuring us that our Worthy Groom is worth our wait.

Healing wounds requires grace narratives and grace math. Grace math teaches us that *present suffering plus God's character equals future glory*. The equation we use is the Divine perspective.

From a Divine faith perspective on life, we erect a platform to respond to suffering. *Coram Deo* faith perceives the presence of God in the presence of suffering.

How a person views life makes all the difference in life. Luther understood this. "The Holy Spirit knows that a thing only has such value and meaning to a man as he assigns it in his thoughts" (Luther, *Luther's Works*, Vol. 42, p. 124). Therefore, Luther sought to help people reshape their perspective or interpretation of their life situation. He wanted his followers to contemplate suffering from a new, divine perspective. He nurtured alternative ways to view life.

Speaking of Luther's *Letter of Fourteen Consolations*, J. E. Strohl writes:

> The whole treatise is concerned with what one sees. It presents fourteen images for contemplation, and their purpose is to renew our sight. The consolation offered by the Word is a new vision, the power of faith to see suffering and death from the perspective of the crucified and risen Lord. It turns our common human view of these matters upside down, lifting us as Luther puts it, above our evils and our blessings, making them "*res indifferentes.*" This does not eradicate the pain or the fear of our misery, but it robs it of its hopelessness (Strohl, *Luther's Fourteen Consolations*, p. 179).

Our earth-bound, non-faith human story of suffering must yield to God's narrative of life and suffering—to God's grace narrative and grace math.

> If only a man could see his God in such a light of love . . . how happy, how calm, how safe he would be! He would then truly have a God from whom he would know with certainty that all his fortunes—whatever they might be—had come to him and were still coming to him under the guidance of God's most gracious will (Luther, *Luther's Works*, Vol. 42, p. 154).

That's the perspective that prompts healing.

For Luther, and for us, the Cross forever settles all questions about God's heart for us. Without faith in God's grace through Christ's death, we are deaf to God-reality.

> He who does not believe that he is forgiven by the inexhaustible riches of Christ's righteousness is like a deaf man hearing a story. If we consider it properly and with an attentive heart, this one image—even if there were no other—would suffice to fill us with such comfort that we should not only not grieve over our evils, but should also glory in our tribulations, scarcely feeling them for the joy that we have in Christ (Luther, *Luther's Works*, Vol. 42, p. 165).

The Christ of the Cross is the only One who makes sense of life when suffering comes. Only the Cross of Christ can make sense out of the sufferings of life.

Stage Four: Worshiping—Engaging with Love Rather Than Digging Cisterns

As we progress through the stages of healing, we are transformed from regrouping to waiting, from deadening to wailing, from despair to weaving, and from digging cisterns to worshiping. In worship, we engage God and others with love.

Put yourself back into that casket. You've tried to claw your way out through immediate gratification. Your bowl of soup may be power, prestige, pleasure, pleasing people, or any of a multitude of pathways of relating. Since soup never satisfies the soul, only the stomach, you still ache. What to do with your ache? Well, if you face it, then you have to admit your insufficiency. That simply will not do. So you deaden it. You block out and suppress the reality of your hungry heart. Keep busy. Fantasize. Climb the corporate ladder. These tricks of the godless trade work no better than immediate gratification. Somewhere, deep down inside, despair brews. "Is this all there is?"

Now what? If you follow the beaten path, despair guides you to false lovers. Idols of the heart. Digging cisterns, broken cisterns that can hold no water. Something or someone who will rescue you from agony's clutches—or so you imagine.

If, on the other hand, you have been waiting in the casket, wailing out to God, weaving together in your imagination His good plans from His good heart, your path is marked "Worship." You glorify God when you rest in Him even in your casket. Rather than turning to false lovers who tame your soul, you turn to your untamed God who enraptures your soul. Then you give witness, testimony to God's glory, to His personal and universal beauty and majesty.

Now we're prepared for a biblical definition of worship in the context of suffering. Let's start with some subtle contrasts. In cry, you cry out for God's help; in worship, you cry out for God. In comfort, you receive God's strength; in worship, you experience God. In wailing, you long for heaven because you're tired of earth; in worship, you long for God because you miss Him. In weaving, you glimpse God's perspective; in worship, you glimpse the face of God.

Worship is wanting God more than wanting relief. Worship is finding God even if you don't find answers. Worship is walking with God in the dark and having Him as the light of your soul.

I received an e-mail from Terri. She began with words I'm sure she typed with a smile. "Guess what? Not everything's perfect in our new ministry." I smiled knowingly as I read her first line. She continued, "But God is. God is perfectly beautiful. Perfectly holy. Perfectly in control. Perfectly good." Terri is glimpsing the face of God. She's worshiping.

Many passages support the concept of worship in the midst of suffering and worship as the end result of suffering. Asaph, reflecting on his suffering, concludes, "Whom have I in heaven but you? And earth has nothing I desire besides you" (Psalm 73:25).

David concurs, as his suffering creates a God-thirst. "As the deer pants for streams of water, so my soul pants for you, O God. My soul thirsts for God, for the living God. When can I go and meet with God?" (Psalm 42:1-2).

Peter explains the purpose of problems, teaching that they come so our faith in God may be refined. He then concludes with these words about suffering's significance, "Though you have not seen him, you love him; and even though you do not see him now, you believe in him and are filled with an inexpressible and glorious joy" (1 Peter 1:8).

Peter's message reminds us of Paul as he looks back upon a lifetime of suffering and says, "I consider everything a loss compared to the surpassing greatness of knowing Christ Jesus my Lord, for whose sake I have lost all things. I consider them rubbish that I may gain Christ. ... I want to know Christ and the power of his resurrection and the fellowship of sharing in his sufferings, becoming like him in his death" (Philippians 3:8, 10).

Suffering's ultimate purpose is worship—intimate, loving engagement with God. Suffering's ultimate purpose is to know and worship God as our Spring of Living Water—our only satisfaction and our greatest joy.

Where We've Been and Where We're Heading

Sufferology teaches us how to respond to being sinned against, how to live when we feel like dying. Soul physicians seek to sustain and heal their hurting spiritual friends who are experiencing the groanings of living east of Eden.

Leaving sufferology, we now move to *soteriology*: our salvation from sin through Christ's grace. Soul physicians seek to reconcile and guide their redeemed spiritual friends by helping them understand and apply their new life in Christ.

We'll be probing four foundation-shaking words: regeneration, reconciliation, redemption, and justification. For most of us, unfortunately, these are intimidating theological concepts rather than profound life-changing realities. To rectify this, join me in Act Four where we'll move from diagnosis to treatment. Let's learn together how to intervene to help others to live out their new nature and new nurture in Christ.

Caring for Your Soul: Personal Applications

1. Think back to a time when God brought hope, joy, newness, and "resurrection" into your life after a casket experience.

   a. What did God use to bring about that spiritual victory for you?

   b. How did you begin to see God differently? How did you begin to experience more of His goodness? How were you able to love Him more in His romance novel?

   c. As you found His strength in your weakness, what was God able to accomplish through you? How was He able to use you as a hero/heroine in His grand adventure narrative?

2. In Psalm 73, Asaph faced internal suffering *coram Deo*.

   a. As you read the song of his heart, how do you relate to his story?

   b. What in his story would you like to add to your story as you face discouraging events and distancing relationships? How do you think you could do that?

3. Take a Thirst Quotient (TQ) Test. How's your TI—Thirst Intelligence? Evaluate yourself using 10 as "Highest TQ" and 1 as "Lowest TQ."

   a. Am I waiting patiently by avoiding self-rescue?

   b. Am I delaying gratification by refusing to sell my soul for a bowl of soup?

   c. Am I wailing by tasting my hunger for home?

   d. Am I wailing by lamenting my unmet longings and the aches in my soul?

   e. Am I weaving by meditating on God's grace narrative in my life?

   f. Am I weaving by doing some grace math and comparing my present circumstances with my future reward?

   g. Am I worshiping as a Romancer by loving God better than life?

   h. Am I worshiping as a Dreamer by renewing my perspective of God?

   i. Am I worshiping as a Creator by not simply enduring, but maturing?

   j. Am I worshiping as a Singer by resting peacefully in Christ?

Caring for Others: Ministry Implications

♦ **Move with Your Spiritual Friends from Regrouping to Waiting (Gratification Delayed):** Ponder whether they are more like Esau or Moses. Are they facing their thirsts by regrouping or by taking refuge in Christ?

♦ **Move with Your Spiritual Friends from Deadening to Wailing (Groaning):** Are they groaning? Facing their unmet thirsts? Lamenting? Are they pregnant with hope? Facing God while facing thirsts?

♦ **Move with Your Spiritual Friends from Despair to Weaving (Grace-Healed Wounds):** How is their grace narrative? Can they distinguish between what people intend and what God superintends? How is their grace math? Can they factor God and His goodness into their life equation?

♦ **Move with Your Spiritual Friends from Digging Cisterns to Worshiping (Glorifying):** Trialogue with them as Romancers, Dreamers, Creators, and Singers.

   • As *Romancers* explore: "What are you doing with God in this? What is God doing with you in this? What is God up to in this? How can you draw nearer to God in this? How is God wanting to shape your character through this?"

   • As *Dreamers* examine: "Who are you to God in this? Who is God to you in this? Whose story is capturing your imagination?"

   • As *Creators* ponder: "Who are you becoming through this? How could you grow through groaning? How are you trying to protect yourself without trusting God in this?"

   • As *Singers* wonder: "What song is your soul singing? Lament? Praise? How are you soothing your soul in God?"

ACT FOUR:
LOVE'S TENACITY—THE RECONCILIATION

PRESCRIBING GOD'S CURE FOR THE SOUL:
SOLUTIONS—REDEMPTION

DIRECTOR'S NOTES

Welcome back. Sit a spell. Allow me to set the stage for Act Four.

The scene shifts from the Garden of Eden to the Garden of Gethsemane. From East of Eden to Jerusalem and the ends of the earth. From Babel's confusion of languages to Pentecost's "translation" of languages. From broken cistern to Spring of Living Water. From law to grace.

How the characters change! From hellish to heavenly. From the first Adam to the second Adam. They're transformed from lusting passionately to loving sacrificially, from thinking foolishly to dreaming wisely, from choosing compulsively to purposing courageously, and from feeling shallowly to experiencing deeply.

Theirs is the ultimate *Prince Rescues Fallen Princess Fairy Tale*, but for one fact— their tale is true. Once a ravishing beauty, the fallen Princess lost her glory. Only one Prince can restore her. Prince Worthy Groom invades her world from beyond her planet. The supernatural realm incarnates into her natural realm. He fights and slays Dragon False Seducer, but at great cost. Mortally wounded, Worthy Groom dies a seemingly tragic death. Then magic from before the dawn of time resurrects Him.

Fallen Princess shares in His resurrection. Coming back to life, her glory and memory return. Hers is the ultimate *Rags to Riches Fairy Tale*, but for one fact—her tale is true. She receives a gown of *Regeneration* to replace her rag of Corruption, a gown of *Reconciliation* to replace her rag of Chasm, a gown of *Redemption* to replace her rag of Captivity, and a gown of *Justification* to replace her rag of Condemnation. You certainly won't want to miss a single scene in this incredible act. Settle in for eight thrilling scenes from Act Four: The Reconciliation.

SCENE I, CHAPTER 20: VIRGIN BRIDE PURSUED, WOOED, WON, AND RENEWED

SCENE II, CHAPTER 21: VIRGIN BRIDE'S FOUR GOWNS

SCENE III, CHAPTER 22: VIRGIN BRIDE'S NEW NURTURE

SCENE IV, CHAPTER 23: VIRGIN BRIDE'S NEW NATURE

SCENE V, CHAPTER 24: VIRGIN BRIDE'S REDEEMED PERSONALITY STRUCTURE

SCENE VI, CHAPTER 25: VIRGIN BRIDE GROWS IN GRACE

SCENE VII, CHAPTER 26: VIRGIN BRIDE PUTS OFF HER OLD GRAVE CLOTHES

SCENE VIII, CHAPTER 27: VIRGIN BRIDE PUTS ON HER NEW WEDDING ATTIRE

CHAPTER TWENTY

VIRGIN BRIDE PURSUED, WOOED, WON, AND RENEWED

"Do you know the price God paid to make you lovely in His eyes? The cross. He was stripped bare so you would be adorned with righteousness. The scars that made Him ugly made you beautiful. The blood that stained Him made you spotless" (Alan Wright, *Lover of My Soul*, p. 64).

"God's purpose in revelation is that we may know Him personally as He is, may avail ourselves of His gracious forgiveness and offer of new life, may escape catastrophic judgment for our sins, and venture personal fellowship with Him. 'I will be your God, and you shall be my people' (Lev. 26:12), He declares. His revelation is not some impersonal mass media commercial or routine news report of the 'state of the invisible world;' it is, rather, a personal call and command to each individual" (Carl F. H. Henry, *God and Revelation*, p. 31).

Family Feuds

Father had every right to give up on his prodigal children. They broke their vow, grieved His soul, and filled His heart with pain (Genesis 6:5-6). Grace alone prevented humanity's extermination. "So the LORD said, 'I will wipe mankind, whom I have created, from the face of the earth . . . for I am grieved that I have made them.' But Noah found favor in the eyes of the LORD" (Genesis 6:7-8).

Reading the Prophets, says Philip Yancey, is like hearing a lovers' quarrel through the apartment walls. It's also like overhearing a family feud between a father and his adolescent children. Eavesdrop on the arguments and heated exchanges to catch a glimpse of God's heart.

Heaven and earth, you're the jury. Listen to God's case: "I had children and raised them well, and they turned on me. The ox knows who's boss, the mule knows the hand that feeds him, but not Israel. My people don't know up from down. Shame! Misguided God-dropouts, staggering under their guilt-baggage. Gang of miscreants, band of vandals—My people have walked out on me, their God, turned their backs on The Holy of Israel, walked off and never looked back" (Eugene Peterson, *The Message*, page 1203, Isaiah 1:2-4).

A son honors his father, and a servant his master. If I am a father, where is the honor due me? (Malachi 1:6).

I myself said, "How gladly would I treat you like sons and give you a desirable land, the most beautiful inheritance of any nation. I thought you would call me 'Father' and not turn away from following me. But like a woman unfaithful to her husband, so you have been unfaithful to me, O house of Israel" (Jeremiah 3:19-20).

The word of the LORD came to me: "Son of man, there were two women, daughters of the same mother. They became prostitutes in Egypt, engaging in prostitution from their youth. In that land their breasts were fondled and their virgin bosoms caressed. The older was named Oholah, and her sister was Oholibah. They were mine and gave birth to sons and daughters. Oholah is Samaria, and Oholibah is Jerusalem. Oholah engaged in prostitution while she was still mine; and she lusted after her lovers, the Assyrians . . . Her sister Oholibah saw this, yet in her lust and prostitution she was more depraved than her sister. She too lusted after the Assyrians . . . Therefore, Oholibah, this is what the Sovereign LORD says: I will stir up your lovers against you, those you turned away from in disgust, and I will bring them against you from every side . . . I will direct my jealous anger against you, and they will deal with you in fury (Ezekiel 23:1-5, 11, 12a, 22, 25).

In *The Sacred Romance*, Brent Curtis and John Eldredge encourage us to ponder how God is feeling at this point in the story. As a Person *in the story*, what is *His* heart experiencing? If God were a quitter, the story might have ended. However, the Bible insists that God is love: He is forming a covenant community. As a true Lover, God never gives up on those He loves. He never jettisons His eternal project of community building. Out of the wreckage of the old community, He draws a new community.

The Old Testament story (the Old Covenant relationship) of the wreckage of Yahweh's marriage to His adulterous wife begs for completion. The New Testament (the New Covenant grace relationship) births the consummation.

Grace alone provides humanity's redemption. A model of counseling built solely upon Christ's gospel of grace grows from the soil of salvation by grace through faith. Through grace, Worthy Groom pursues us tenaciously, woos us tenderly, wins us benevolently, and renews us preciously.

Pursued Tenaciously

Worthy Groom was well within His rights to stop pursuing His wayward bride. Yet pursue He did, repeatedly. "O Jerusalem, Jerusalem, you who kill the prophets and stone those sent to you, how often I have longed to gather your children together, as a hen gathers her chicks under her wings, but you were not willing" (Matthew 23:37). Love's tenacity.

Nowhere do we find love's tenacity more tenacious than in Jesus. Pursuing. Intense. Passionate. Engaging. Honest. Tough love. Bold love. Grace love.

You see, at just the right time, when we were still powerless, Christ died for the ungodly. Very rarely will anyone die for a righteous man, though for a good man someone might possibly dare to die. But God demonstrates his own love for us in this: While we were still sinners, Christ died for us (Romans 5:6-8).

Of course, before Jesus died for His bride, He had to come for His bride. She ran. He chased. She hid. He sought.

No wonder they call Him *Immanuel*—"God with us." God pursuing us. God coming near to us. God finding us. God living where we live.

He came to seek and to save the lost, the sinner. To welcome sinners, eat with them, fellowship with them. Like a shepherd with ninety-nine sheep in the pen and one lone sheep in the wilderness, Jesus diligently hunts for His little lost sheep. Like a woman with ten silver coins who loses one, He lights a lamp, sweeps the house, and searches carefully until He finds His single lost coin (see Luke 15).

The eternal Word became flesh so He could pitch His tent among us. Hang out with us. Be like us. Be one of us (see John 1).

He laid aside His glory, making Himself nothing, taking on Himself the very nature of a servant, being made in human likeness. And being found in human appearance, He humbled Himself and became obedient to death (see Philippians 2).

Since the children have flesh and blood, He too shared in their humanity so that by His death He might destroy him who holds the power of death. For this reason He had to be made like His brothers in every way, in order that He might become a merciful and faithful High Priest and that He might make atonement for the sins of His people (see Hebrews 2).

The runaway bride could run, but she couldn't hide. "Here I am! I stand at the door and knock. If anyone hears my voice and opens the door, I will come in and eat with him, and he with me" (Revelation 3:20). "The Spirit and the Bride say, 'Come!' And let him who hears say, 'Come!' Whoever is thirsty, let him come; and whoever wishes, let him take the free gift of the water of life" (Revelation 22:17). Incarnational invitation. He came so He could invite. He pursued so He could propose.

Worthy Groom doggedly seeks us. His determination is our salvation.

Wooed Tenderly

Pursuing tenaciously, Worthy Groom woos tenderly. The nineteenth-century theologian, Soren Kierkegaard, pictures Christ wooing with love, not forcing with power.

Suppose there was a king who loved a humble maiden. The king was like no other king. Every statesman feared his wrath and dared not breathe a word of displeasure, for he had the strength to crush all opponents.

And yet this mighty king was melted by love for a humble maiden. How could he declare his love for her? In an odd sort of way, his kingliness tied his hands. If he brought her to the palace and crowned her head with jewels and clothed her body in royal robes, she would surely not resist—no one dared resist him. But would she love him?

She would say she loved him, of course, but would she truly? Or would she live with him in fear, nursing a private grief for the life she had left behind? Would she be happy at his side? How could he know? If he rode to her forest cottage in his royal carriage, with an armed escort waving bright banners, that too would overwhelm her. He did not want a cringing subject. He wanted a lover, an equal. He wanted her to forget that he was a king and she a humble maiden and to let shared love cross the gulf between them. For it is only in love that the unequal can be made equal (Kierkegaard, *Parables of Kierkegaard*, pp. 39-45).

Because the essence of Deity is holy love, God loves us with the perfect blend of tough love (holiness) and tender love (love). He knows when to confront and when to comfort. When to challenge and when to caress. He knows how to crush our false lovers, leaving us gravely empty; and He knows how to allure us romantically, leaving us desperately desirous of His filling.

First he confronts adulterous Gomer, and by implication, all his spiritually adulterous people. "Lest I strip her naked, and set her as in the day that she was born, and make her as a wilderness, and set her like a dry land, and *slay her with thirst*" (Hosea 2:3, KJV, emphasis added). Then he changes course. "Therefore, behold, I will *allure* her, and bring her into the wilderness, and speak *comfortably* unto her" (Hosea 2:14, KJV, emphasis added).

To "allure" means to persuade, to attract by tender persuasion, and to entice. It is used in other places in the Old Testament for a man seducing a woman (Exodus 22:16) and of Delilah enticing Samson (Judges 14:15-16). Used with God in a positive sense, it means wooing, courting, romantically persuading. Reflecting on how God woos us, Margaret Durham writes:

> With those spiritually glorious interviews, holy courtings, most superlative, but most sincere, commendings and cordial entertainings of each other, those mutual praisings and valuings of fellowship, those missings, lamentings and bemoanings of the want thereof, those holy impatiencies to be without it, swelling to positive and peremptory determinations not to be satisfied nor comforted in anything else, those diligent, painful and restless seekings after it, till it be found and enjoyed, importunity, and gracious grantings of it, on the other; with those high delightings, solacings, complacencies and acquiescings in, and heartsome embracings of, one another's fellowship . . . these vehement joint-longings to have the marriage consummated and the fellowship immediate, full and never any more to be interrupted (Durham, *Clavis Cantici*, pp. 13-14).

God stops at nothing to cause us to crave Him more than anything.

Won Benevolently

Romans 2:4 explains how Worthy Groom wins our hearts. "Or do you show contempt for the riches of his kindness, tolerance, and patience, not realizing that God's kindness leads you toward repentance?"

God initiates salvation—we don't. He begins the chain of love. "We love because he first loved us" (1 John 4:19). "This is love: not that we loved God, but that he loved us" (1 John 4:10).

When couples fight, someone has to be big-hearted and humble-spirited enough to restart the chain of love. When Shirley and I have a disagreement, there are times we disobey the biblical command not to let the sun go down on our wrath. Going to bed angry, we sleep back-to-back, as far apart in our bed as possible. Not daring to touch one another. Neither wanting to be the one who "gives in," or "caves." Neither wanting to start the chain of love. But the moment one of us rolls over, places a tender hand softly on the other's shoulder and says, "I'm sorry," then anger melts. The other is "won back."

How much more is this true with God, who never has to say, "I'm sorry"! He reaches a soft hand and whispers a kind word, "I forgive you." And our hearts melt.

How are our hearts won? The opposite from how they are lost. Satan dupes us into abandoning God when he tricks us into seeing Him as a Hoarder and a cruel Bully. Worthy Groom allures us back to God when He tantalizes our imagination with God's goodness. Notice the KJV translation of Romans 2:4. "Or despisest thou the riches of his *goodness* and forbearance and longsuffering; not knowing that the *goodness of God* leadeth thee to repentance?" (emphasis added).

To "despise" (*kataphroneis*) God's goodness means to look down or think down upon it. We deny His goodness; we make little of it or distort it entirely. Until our hearts surrender. Then we're melted by His goodness (*chrēstotētos*)—His "gracious kindness toward us" (Ralph Earle, *Word Meanings in the New Testament*, p. 141). God's gracious goodness leads us to repentance—to a change of mind about His character. Now we think highly of Him and His grace.

Paul develops the nature of God's goodness. It includes "forbearance/tolerance" (*anochēs*) which implies a holding back or delaying of wrath. Why do the wicked seem to prosper now? Why does God seem to be slack in His judgment? Because He is patient with us, not wanting any of us to perish, but every one of us to come to repentance (2 Peter 3:9). Were He to mete out justice the second we deserved it, none of us would be breathing now.

God's goodness wins our hearts as we're enticed by His "longsuffering/patience" (*makrothumias*). God is long-tempered, not short-fused. He demonstrates self-restraint in the face of provocation, not hastily retaliating or promptly punishing. In short, He's merciful (Earle, *Word Meanings in the New Testament*, p. 141).

This is exactly what melted Dulcinea's heart in *The Man of La Mancha*. Living the life of a prostitute, she encounters Don Quixote who sees buried beauty in her. She resists ferociously, mocking him ruthlessly.

Don Quixote refuses to relent. Treating her like a princess, he even risks death to defend her honor.

On his deathbed, she finally surrenders. Won by his persistently good heart. Her life changed now, changed by indefatigable grace. It's reminiscent of Paul's words to Titus. "For the grace of God that brings salvation has appeared to all men. It teaches us to say 'No' to ungodliness and worldly passions, and to live self-controlled, upright and godly lives in this present age" (Titus 2:11-12).

Renewed Preciously

Grace is free, but it is not cheap. In the next chapter we'll see the four-fold nature of our renewal: regeneration, reconciliation, redemption, and justification. In our current scene we're witnessing the price paid for our renewal.

Runaway bride's *corruption* required cleansing—*regeneration*. What price cleansing? What cleansing agent? Blood. Christ's blood. "He saved us through the washing of rebirth and renewal by the Holy Spirit, whom he poured out on us generously through Jesus Christ our *Savior*" (Titus 3:5-6, emphasis added). By our Savior's blood, we're renewed, washed, regenerated, cleansed from corruption.

The *chasm* between the runaway bride and her Pursuing Groom required *reconciliation* by blood.

> And through him to reconcile to himself all things, whether things on earth or things in heaven, by making peace through his blood shed on the cross. Once you were alienated from God and enemies in your minds because of your evil behavior. But now he has reconciled you by Christ's physical body through death to present you holy in his sight, without blemish and free from accusation (Colossians 1:20-22).

What price peace? Shed blood. Crucifixion. Death so we could live with God.

Runaway bride's *captivity* required that Christ pay the maximum bride price for her *redemption*—His precious blood.

> For you know that it was not with perishable things such as silver or gold that you were redeemed from the empty way of life handed down to you from your forefathers, but with the precious blood of Christ, a lamb without blemish or defect (1 Peter 1:18-19).

Another suitor claimed ownership. False Seducer said, "She's slept with me. Chosen me. Followed me. She's mine! You can't have her."

Christ shows otherwise. "You don't love her. You don't even know what love is. I'll show you love. I'll lay my life down for her" (1 John 3:16, author's paraphrase). "Greater love has no man than this, that he lay down his life for his wife. I lay down my life to renew my wife" (John 15:13, author's paraphrase).

God loves by giving. Father gives His only Son for His prodigal children. Worthy Groom gives His life, His blood, for His runaway bride. "In him we have redemption *through his blood*, the forgiveness of sins, in accordance with the riches of God's grace that he lavished on us" (Ephesians 1:7-8, emphasis added).

Runaway bride's *condemnation* required *justification* through Christ's blood. "And are justified freely by his grace through the redemption that came by Christ Jesus. God presented him as a *sacrifice of atonement*, through faith in his *blood*" (Romans 3:24-25, emphasis added). Worthy Groom's death, burial, and resurrection secured runaway bride's justification. "He was delivered over to death for our sins and was raised to life for our justification" (Romans 4:25).

Renewed Adoration: Our Lover and Our Vows

After His death, burial, and resurrection, Jesus asked Peter the question He directs to each of His renewed brides, "Do you love me more than these?" "These" include any of our idiosyncratic false gods and unique false lovers. For Peter, it seems that "these" meant his trust in his old way of life, his old vocation, his old means of self-sufficiency—fishing. For others, "these" might mean works righteousness, pride, husband, wife, child, parent, job, power, pornography—anything or anyone we place above Worthy Groom and trust in more than Faithful Father.

Worthy Groom insists that we ask ourselves, "Do I love Him with everything I am, or do other lovers clamor for my attention? Do I worship additional gods, or do I passionately give Him my undivided adoration?"

When we accept Christ as Savior, we're repenting of our false lovers and foolish idols. We are agreeing with God that He alone is holy and good. We're acknowledging the worthiness of Worthy Groom. We are saying, "I receive you, the Worthy Groom, to love and cherish, to honor and obey, to submit and respect, to desire and pursue."

Our vow is so strong because His love is so deep. Just what did our Groom do for us? "This is love: not that we loved God, but that he loved us and sent his Son as an atoning sacrifice for our sins" (1 John 4:10).

What was this death that He died for us? With the shadow of the impending cross brooding over Him, Jesus "began to be sorrowful and troubled. Then he said to them, 'My soul is overwhelmed with sorrow (*perilupos*) to the point of death'" (Matthew 26:37-38). "And being in anguish (*agōnia*), he prayed more earnestly, and his sweat was like drops of blood falling to the ground" (Luke 22:44). "He took Peter, James, and John along with him, and he began to be deeply distressed (*ekthambeisthai*) and troubled (*adēmonein*). 'My soul is overwhelmed with sorrow to the point of death,' he said to them" (Mark 14:33-34).

B. B. Warfield wrote a careful study entitled *On the Emotional Life of Our Lord*, in which he explained the terms employed in relation to Gethsemane. Luke's word *agōnia*, Warfield defines as "consternation, appalled reluctance." Matthew and Mark share two expressions. The primary idea of "troubled" (*adēmonein*) is "loathing aversion, perhaps not unmixed with despondency." While Jesus' self-description as "overwhelmed with sorrow" (*perilupos*) "expresses a sorrow or perhaps we would better say, a mental pain, a distress, which hems Him in on every side, from which there is therefore no escape." Mark uses another term, "deeply distressed" (*ekthambeisthai*), which Warfield renders "horror-stricken, a term of consternation—which more narrowly defines the distress as consternation—if not exactly dread, yet alarmed dismay" (Warfield, *Person and Work*, pp. 130-131).

John Stott summarizes our Worthy Groom's agony. "Put together, these expressive words indicate that Jesus was feeling an acute emotional pain, causing profuse sweat, as he looked with apprehension and almost terror at his future ordeal" (Stott, *The Cross of Christ*, p. 74).

Exactly what was this bitter cup that Jesus ardently prays, if possible, might be taken from Him, so He does not have to drink it? Stott explains what it was not and what it was.

In that case the cup from which he shrank was something different. It symbolized neither the physical pain of being flogged and crucified, nor the mental distress of being despised and rejected even by his own people, but rather the spiritual agony of bearing the sins of the world, in other words, of enduring the divine judgment which those sins deserved (Stott, *The Cross of Christ*, p. 76).

The perfectly sinless Worthy Groom bears the horrible sins of His runaway bride. The completely innocent Christ dies for the completely guilty sinner. The eternal member of the Triune community endures alienation from His Father, for the first and only time in all eternity. Hear again His God-forsaken cry of dereliction. "About the ninth hour Jesus cried out in a loud voice, 'Eloi, Eloi, lama sabachthani?'—which means, 'My God, my God, why have you forsaken me?'" (Matthew 27:46).

As Calvin put it, "If Christ had died only a bodily death, it would have been ineffectual . . . Unless his soul shared in the punishment, he would have been the Redeemer of bodies alone" (Calvin, *The Institutes of the Christian Religion*, Vol. 2, xvi.10). In consequence, "He paid a greater and more excellent price in suffering in his soul the terrible torments of a condemned and forsaken man" (Calvin, *The Institutes of the Christian Religion*, Vol. 2, xvi.12). So then:

> An actual and dreadful separation took place between the Father and the Son; it was voluntarily accepted by both the Father and the Son; it was due to our sins and their just reward; and Jesus expressed this horror of great darkness, this God-forsakenness, by quoting the only verse of Scripture which accurately described it, and which he had perfectly fulfilled, namely, "My God, my God, why have you forsaken me?" (Stott, *The Cross of Christ*, p. 81).

For us to be accepted by Father, Worthy Groom had to be abandoned by Father. We live for Him because He died for us. Grace changes us. "Then suddenly there dawns upon us the vast, entire endowment of God's free love and forgiveness. It is this which bowls us over, frees us, transforms us" (Paul Tournier, *Guilt and Grace*, p. 193).

Renewed Admiration: Our Hero and Our Victory

Worthy Groom is not only our Lover, He is our Hero. He has given us the victory. Rescued us from False Seducer's clutches. Carried us out of the dungeon. Climbed the tower to release us from prison. Broken down doors to free us from our kidnapper. "For he has rescued us from the dominion of darkness and brought us into the kingdom of the Son he loves" (Colossians 1:13). "To open their eyes and turn them from darkness to light, and from the power of Satan to God, so that they may receive forgiveness of sins and a place among those who are sanctified by faith in me" (Acts 26:18).

Picture the conclusion to any great fairy tale or romantic-dramatic movie. The dashing hero rescues the damsel in distress. She's smitten. Taken. Swoons. Forever grateful. Amazed. "My hero!"

Jesus is our dashing Hero. He has overcome the world (John 16:33), made us more than conquerors (Romans 8:37), disarmed our enemies (Colossians 2:15), empowered us to be overcomers because He is greater than False Seducer (1 John 4:4), and given us the victory that overcomes the world (1 John 5:4).

How should we respond? Revelation 4-5 shows us. Who is worthy to break the seal and open the scroll that begins to unfold our final victory? No one is found! Everyone weeps. Then one of the elders says, "Do not weep! See, the Lion of the tribe of Judah, the Root of David, has *triumphed*. He is able to open the scroll and its seven seals" (Revelation 5:5, emphasis added).

The slain Lamb and triumphant Lion, mingled in the crucified/resurrected Worthy Groom, receives all praise.

> You are *worthy* to take the scroll and to open its seals, because you were *slain*, and with your *blood* you purchased men for God from every tribe and language and people and nation. You have *made them to be a kingdom* and priests to serve our God, and they will *reign* on the earth (Revelation 5:9-10, emphasis added).

How does runaway bride turned virgin bride respond to her Worthy Groom? "In a loud voice they sang: 'Worthy is the Lamb, who was slain, to receive power and wealth and wisdom and strength and honor and glory and praise!'" (Revelation 5:12).

"I adore you. I admire you. You're my Lover. You're my Hero. You are good. You are worthy. You are loving. You are holy."

Where We've Been and Where We're Heading

If someone arrived late to Act Four, Scene I, having already seen the first three Acts, they would be totally dumbfounded. The last they knew, runaway bride was gallivanting around in Rags of Corruption, Chasm, Captivity, and Condemnation. All of a sudden in Act Four, Scene II, she's the virgin bride dancing about in Gowns of Regeneration, Reconciliation, Redemption, and Justification.

Act Four, Scene I—Pursued, Wooed, Won, and Renewed—offers the only explanation for this change of inner and outer clothing. Worthy Groom tenaciously pursues His runaway bride. She can run, but she can't hide. Finding her, He tenderly woos her, slaying her with thirst and alluring her with compassion. Convinced of His goodness, she's won benevolently. She surrenders to the Lover of her soul. Renewed by sacrifice, blood, and death, she renews her vows and receives her victory. Worthy Groom once more becomes her Lover-Hero.

There's power in the blood. Power to turn corrupt rags into regenerated gowns. Power to transform rags of chasm into reconciled gowns. Power to change rags of captivity into gowns of redemption. Power to alter condemning rags into gowns of justification.

If we are to counsel Christians in the power of Christ, we must apply the four Gowns of Salvation. Join me for Act Four, Scene II, where we'll witness the leading characters in our drama of redemption donning Gowns of Regeneration, Reconciliation, Redemption, and Justification.

Caring for Your Soul: Personal Applications

1. At the beginning of Chapter 20 you read paraphrases from the Prophets about prodigal children and unfaithful spouses. What did you feel as you read these words? How would you like to respond?

2. Have you ever felt allured by Christ?

    a. If so, when? What was it like? How often do you experience this? What is happening when you experience it? How do you respond?

    b. If not, why do you suppose you don't? How could you open your heart to Christ's allure?

3. In light of what Jesus paid for you, what do you want to give to Him?

4. Pen a Psalm of Adoration to your Wild Lover.

5. Pen a Psalm of Praise to your Pristine Hero.

Caring for Others: Ministry Implications

♦ **Tell the Greatest Love Story Ever Told:** Whatever else biblical counseling is, it is *not* boring! Trialogue about the greatest love story ever told. Return people to their first love. Expose them to scenes of pursuing, wooing, winning, and renewing.

♦ **Listen for the Whispered Wooings:** As you trialogue, tune into any missed signs that Jesus is afoot. Where is Jesus sending unopened love letters? How is He alluring your spiritual friend? In what ways is He speaking tenderly to your spiritual friend?

♦ **Unearth the Bridal Treasury:** Your spiritual friend is blind to the treasure trove Christ gave. Unbury it. Discover it together. Trialogue about the bridal price—blood, crucifixion, and death—and what it says about Christ's love and our responsibility.

♦ **Adore Our Lover:** Help your spiritual friends see Worthy Groom in all His kindness, goodness, graciousness, patience, longsuffering, forbearance, and mercy.

♦ **Applaud Our Hero:** Help your spiritual friends see Christ as the one who rescues them from the clutches of the Evil One. Enlighten them to their victory in and through Christ.

♦ **Call for the White Flag of Surrender:** Challenge your spiritual friends to respond. Urge them to open the door—Christ is knocking. Help them see His wonder and His worth.

CHAPTER TWENTY-ONE

VIRGIN BRIDE'S FOUR GOWNS

"Even in its ruined condition a human being is regarded by God as something immensely worth saving. Sin does not make us worthless, but only lost" (Dallas Willard, *Renovation of the Heart*, p. 46).

"So exceedingly evil and harmful is sin, both intensively and extensively, that there is no moderate therapy that can cure it, no satisfactory amendment of life can be expected from the old earth. The flood denounces the perversion of sin as a radical evil, as total depravity" (Henri Blocher, *In the Beginning*, p. 206).

Dress Up Time

From the beginning, Adam and Eve played dress up. Noticing their shameful nakedness, they did their best to beautify themselves. Hopeless.

Scour as hard as they might, their sinful rags remained scarlet, not white. Red as crimson. "All our righteous works are like filthy rags," they concluded in despair.

Father's conclusion was worse. "Your best is rubbish. Your robes are dung. Trash. Your beautification efforts add up to zero." Helpless.

Only red could make their robes white. Only washing their robes in blood could remove their stains. Blood stains removing sin's stain. Salvation by grace is paradoxical. The sinless One sacrificed for sinners. Death bringing life.

Salvation by grace is paramount. Otherwise our souls are lost and our counseling becomes works-based. *When we fail to understand and apply the four gowns of salvation by grace through faith, we end up counseling Christians as though they were non-Christians.* We end up encouraging Christians to reenter bondage, law, and works. Something Paul called "Anathema!" (Galatians 1:6-9; 3:1-5; 5:1-7).

Salvation is deliverance by death from corruption, chasm, captivity, and condemnation. Salvation is the broad term for new life through regeneration, reconciliation, redemption, and justification.

Through the Gown of *Regeneration*, we lose our Rag of Corruption. Christ instantaneously imparts new spiritual, eternal life. Through the Gown of *Reconciliation*, we abandon our Rag of Chasm. Christ restores spiritual fellowship and moral, personal harmony with Father. Through the Gown of *Redemption*, we're freed from the Rag of Captivity. Christ liberates us from bondage to sin and Satan, purchasing us from bondage and freeing us to victory. Through the Gown of *Justification*, we remove the Rag of Condemnation. Christ judicially declares the believing sinner forgiven and free from condemnation.

Our Gown of Regeneration conquers sin's *presence*. It takes us into the *Temple* where we're cleansed by blood, purified. It implants in us our new *purity*—the new capacities of our new nature. Our Gown of Reconciliation demolishes sin's *partition*, the dividing wall, the moat standing between Father and us. It takes us into the *Living Room*, takes us *Home*, where we're adopted into Father's forever family—our new *Parentage*. Our Gown of Redemption frees us from sin's *power*. It takes us into the *Slave Market* where we're bought out of slavery into the glorious freedom of the children of God. It provides our new *power* for living. Our Gown of Justification cancels our guilt and sin's *penalty*. It takes us into the *Courtroom* where we're declared, "Not guilty!" We receive our new *pardon*.

In salvation, Christ transforms us from sinner to saint, from separated to sons and daughters, from slaves to shepherds, and from shame to shalom. Our Gown of Regeneration addresses our Rag of Corruption, returning us to our Robe of Reflection. Our Gown of Reconciliation addresses our Rag of Chasm, returning us to our Robe of Communion. Our Gown of Redemption addresses our Rag of Captivity, returning us to our Robe of Dominion. Our Gown of Justification addresses our Rag of Condemnation, returning us to our Robe of Cohesion. Box 21:1 reviews the Creation, Fall, and Redemption of the *imago Dei*.

Why is this so vital? Why start with theological truths about who we are in Christ? Why not "cut to the chase," and teach *how to* practice Christian counseling? Why devote five chapters (Chapters 20-24) to our salvation before describing the process of sanctification? Christian growth in sanctification demands an understanding of Christian justification by grace through faith. Counseling Christians requires an awareness and application of who Christians are *in* Christ *by* grace. Soul physicians study the anatomy of the redeemed soul before performing spiritual surgery. We understand *solutions*. Not short-term, works-based solutions, but *eternal and internal, grace-focused solutions*.

The Apostle Paul precedes the Christian living section of his letters with content about the nature of the Christian life. First he tells us who we are in Christ (Romans 6:1-10), then he tells us, based on that awareness, to "count yourselves dead to sin but alive to God in Christ Jesus" (Romans 6:11). His approach is ours. We saturate ourselves as soul physicians with a biblical anatomy of the redeemed soul (see Box 21:2). Then we are prepared for the operating room of heart surgery that assists new creations in Christ to live growing, healthy lives for Christ.

Gown One: The Gown of Regeneration

Jesus robes us in the Gown of Regeneration while we stand in the Temple. Wearing our robe of Christ's righteousness, we shamelessly enter the Holy of Holies, standing confidently before Father, adorned with the dignity of restored Romancers, Dreamers, Creators, Singers, and Actors.

Our Regeneration Gown replaces our Corruption Gown as Christ implants within us a new nature. He exorcises our old corrupt desires, replacing them with a new covenant heart. Consider the radical change taking place the instant Jesus saves us.

Box 21:1

The Creation, Fall, and Redemption of the *Imago Dei*

Creation	Fall	Redemption
The Four Robes of the Beautiful Bride	**The Four Rags of the Adulterous Bride**	**The Four Gowns of the Virgin Bride**

Creation — The Four Robes of the Beautiful Bride

Robe of Reflection
- "Who Am I?"
- "I'm an Image Bearer."
- "I Reflect."
- Capacities: RRVE
- Structural Self
- "Image and Likeness."
- Design: Reflection

Robe of Communion
- "Where Did I Come From?"
- "I Came from Trinity."
- "I Relate."
- Community
- Social Self
- "Let Us."
- Dignity: Relation

Robe of Dominion
- "Why Am I Here?"
- "To Be an Under-Shepherd."
- "I Rule."
- Calling
- Stewardship Self
- "Let Them Rule."
- Destiny: Vocation

Robe of Cohesion
- "How Should I Live?"
- "Share Trinity's Shalom."
- "I Rest."
- Coherence
- Shalom Self
- "Very Good."
- Direction: Integration

Fall — The Four Rags of the Adulterous Bride

Rag of Corruption
- "Who Am I?"
- "I'm a Fallen Image Bearer."
- "I Deflect." Presence
- Temple Image: Polluted
- Original Sin: Depravity
- "I Was Naked."
- Disposition: Sinner

Rag of Chasm
- "Where Did I Come From?"
- "I Came from Myself."
- "I Separate." Partition
- Home Image: Prodigal
- Original Alienation
- "So I Hid."
- Distance: Separated

Rag of Captivity
- "Why Am I Here?"
- "To Shepherd Only Myself."
- "I'm Ruled." Power
- Market Image: Property
- Original Enslavement
- "Sewed Fig Leaves."
- Dominion: Slave

Rag of Condemnation
- "How Should I Live?"
- "Spread Seducer's Shame."
- "I Dread." Penalty
- Court Image: Prisoner
- Original Guilt: Disgrace
- "I Was Afraid."
- Disintegration: Shameful

Redemption — The Four Gowns of the Virgin Bride

Gown of Regeneration
- "Who Am I?"
- "I'm a New Creation in Christ."
- "I Display."
- New Nature: Saint
- New Purity: Capacities
- New Propensity: RRVE
- New Life: Resurrection

Gown of Reconciliation
- "Where Did I Come From?"
- "I Came from Christ."
- "I Reconcile."
- New Nurture: Welcome!
- New Parentage: Father
- New Identity: Son/Bride
- New Adoption: Child

Gown of Redemption
- "Why Am I Here?"
- "To Shepherd in a Jungle."
- "I'm Empowered."
- New Freedom: from Sin
- New Power: Holiness
- New Victory: over Sin
- New Inclination: Love

Gown of Justification
- "How Should I Live?"
- "Share Savior's Salvation."
- "I Relax." Shalom
- New Peace: Forgiveness
- New Pardon: Guiltless
- New Dignity: Righteous
- New Boldness: Grace Confidence

Box 21:2

The Four Gowns of Worthy Groom's Virgin Bride

♦ **The Gown of Regeneration**

"Who Am I?"
"I'm a New Creation in Christ."
"I Display:" Christlikeness
New Nature: Saint
New Purity: New Capacities
New Propensity: Restored Romancer, Dreamer, Creator, Singer, and Actor
New Life: Resurrected with Christ

♦ **The Gown of Reconciliation**

"Where Did I Come From?"
"I Came from Christ."
"I Reconcile:" Ambassador of Reconciliation
New Nurture: "Welcome Home!"
New Parentage: Member of Father's Forever Family
New Identity: Father's Son/Daughter and Worthy Groom's Virgin Bride
New Adoption: Adult Child of God

♦ **The Gown of Redemption**

"Why Am I Here?"
"To Shepherd in a Jungle."
"I'm Empowered:" Empowering Others
New Freedom: Freed from Sin to Righteousness
New Power: Holy Living
New Victory: Victory Over Sin
New Inclination: To Obey Father Lovingly

♦ **The Gown of Justification**

"How Should I Then Live?"
"Share Savior's Salvation."
"I Relax:" Shalom
New Peace: Forgiveness
New Pardon: "Not Guilty!"
New Dignity: Righteousness
New Boldness: Grace Confidence

His divine power has given us everything we need for life and godliness through our knowledge of him who called us by his own glory and goodness. Through these he has given us his very great and precious promises, so that through them you may participate in the divine nature and escape the corruption in the world caused by evil desires (2 Peter 1:3-4).

"Who Am I?" "I'm a New Creation in Christ."

Adam and Eve defined themselves by the *imago Dei*. Had they been asked, "Who are you?" they would have replied, "We are image bearers." Their fallen descendants received an entirely different "self-image." In answer to the question, "Who am I?" the honest sinner must respond, "I am a fallen image bearer."

How tragically sin corrupted the core self. Made to reflect Deity, we no longer even adequately reflect humanity. Though we were created with dignity, depravity permeates our fallen existence. The fallen human personality structure is perverted and polluted, sickened by original sin. The cracked, marred mirror that is the human psyche now deflects away from God. No one looking upon the fallen human soul could guess the glorious nature of God.

How magically salvation purifies the core self. Modeling our Regeneration Gown, we stride down the aisle showing off not our beauty, but the genius of the One who designed our gown. We display Worthy Groom's Divine nature. "The first duty of the Christian," wrote John Calvin, "is to make the invisible kingdom visible."

Dwight Edwards explains, "God's reputation has always been the whole point of human history and His foremost objective in choosing and blessing a people of His own" (Edwards, *Revolution Within*, p. 23). When people look at us, they ought to be shouting, "Hey, Amber, look out the window!" They should be yelling, "Impressive! Kewl. God pretty. God big. Spectacular!" God regenerates us to display His reputation.Some assume that God's glory and our good are mutually exclusive. Not so. When asked, "Who are you?" the Christian can respond, "I'm a new creation in Christ. Because Christ made me new, because I'm His opus. He gets the credit, the glory. Yet I reap present and eternal benefits. I'm delivered from a sinner's depraved self-image to a saint's dignified Christ-image. I gain Christ-esteem."

I'm no longer a spiritual Adulterer, arrogant Fool, mastered Destroyer, moody Addict, or materialistic Traitor. That me died. Crucified with Christ. God created the new me to be like Jesus in true righteousness and holiness (Ephesians 4:24). In Christ, I'm a virgin Bride, penetrating Sage, empowered Shepherd, soulful Poet, and connected Character. I'm the exact opposite of the person I used to be. That's good news. Gospel news! News that glorifies God and benefits me. Don't deny it. Enjoy it.

Our New Nature: Saints

Worthy Groom clothed us in a robe of righteousness, our Gown of Regeneration. "God made him who had no sin to be sin for us, so that in him we might become the righteousness of God" (2 Corinthians 5:21). Theologians call this righteous gown our new nature. Understanding our new nature is so vital to biblical counseling that we'll commit an entire chapter (Chapter 22) to its elaboration. For now we'll introduce the new nature and examine the spiritual implications of the new you.

Regeneration addresses our need not by dressing our corrupt nature, but by supplanting it with a new nature. It's not as though we're an old dirty car about to be sold on the used car lot. The owner takes us to the car wash, washes dirt, dust, and grime from our exterior, but ignores the chunks of rust, not to mention leaving the same old clunky engine under the hood. Christ replaces our "engine." He imparts new life. He re-generates us. To generate is to birth. We are re-birthed, born again. Born of the Spirit and Spirit gives birth to spirit (John 3:5-6). "He saved us through the washing of rebirth [regeneration] and renewal by the Holy Spirit" (Titus 3:5b).

Birth determines nature. Born of the flesh, we have a fleshly nature. Born of sinful parents, we have a sinful nature. Born again of the Spirit, we have a new spiritual nature. Born of God, we have implanted within us a Divine, Christlike nature. "For those God foreknew he also predestined to be conformed to the likeness of his Son, that he might be the firstborn among many brothers" (Romans 8:29).

Peter shifts the imagery from birth to seeds. You plant an apple seed, and an apple grows. Plant a peach seed, and a peach grows. Plant a fallen image bearer, and a fallen image bearer grows. Plant a regenerated image bearer, and a regenerated image bearer grows. "For you have been born again, not of perishable seed, but of imperishable, through the living and enduring word of God" (1 Peter 1:23). God deposited a new nature that is now the core of who I am. The old nature He crucified.

> We died to sin; how can we live in it any longer? Or don't you know that all of us who were baptized into Christ Jesus were baptized into his death? We were therefore buried with him through baptism into death in order that, just as Christ was raised from the dead through the glory of the Father, we too may live a new life [regeneration]. If we have been united with him like this in his death, we will certainly also be united with him in his resurrection. For we know that our *old self was crucified with him so that the body of sin might be done away with,* that we should no longer be slaves to sin—because anyone who *has died* has been freed from sin (Romans 6:2-7, emphasis added).

The old birth, old generation, old seed, old nature—they're all dead. Replaced by something new, born of God. "Now if we died with Christ, we believe that we will also live with him" (Romans 6:8).

So what? Pastor and author Tony Evans, writing in *Free At Last*, reminds us that the Devil wants sinners to think they are saints and saints to think they are sinners. He wants to confuse and confound us about our core nature. As we'll demonstrate in subsequent chapters, the essence of our core nature is *saint* not sinner. I'm a saint whom Satan wants to dupe into believing I am a sinner.

If I believe I'm a sinner, then I'll live inclined to sin. If I'm convinced I'm a saint, then I'll live like a saint. "In the same way, count yourselves dead to sin but alive to God in Christ Jesus. Therefore do not let sin reign in your mortal body so that you obey its evil desires" (Romans 6:11-12).

Evans wonders why we would want to hang out at the cemetery. We're not dead. We're alive. Risen. Our sin nature crucified—put to death. The power of sin destroyed in our lives. Christ executed the old you at the Cross. Consider, reckon, count it as true. Live based on the death of the old you and the life of the new you in Christ.

Our New Purity: New Capacities

Edwards (*Revolution Within*) describes our new purity as *a new want to* and *a new can do*. Through regeneration we gain divinely implanted new capacities of affection (Relational Romancers), cognition (Rational Dreamers), volition (Volitional Creators), and emotion (Emotional Singers). These equip us with a nature that wants to and is able to do God's will.

We remain relational, rational, volitional, and emotional beings, but now God purifies our capacities. Relationally, He renews our affections to long for and love Worthy Groom. Rationally, He enlightens our minds to perceive life with spiritual eyes. Volitionally, He empowers our wills to choose Father's will courageously. Emotionally, He releases us to experience life fully, without hiding or pretending.

God re-tunes our inner being so we inherently listen to Him, want Him, and are attracted to Him. We're now on Worthy Groom's wavelength. We'll explore our new capacity to resonate with God later in this section under the heading, "Dignity." We'll examine it in more detail in Chapter 24, "Virgin Bride's Redeemed Personality Structure." We'll learn how to help others apply their new purity in Chapters 25-27.

Our New Propensity: Restored Romancer, Dreamer, Creator, Singer, and Actor

Our new life creates new or renewed propensities and proclivities. We're restored Romancers, Dreamers, Creators, Singers, and Actors. Washed for salvation, we're renewed daily in sanctification. Consider a biblical outline of the ongoing sanctification of each of our regenerated capacities.

- Renewed in Affections—Relationally as Romancers: Ephesians 5:1; 5:21-6:9; 1 Peter 2:11; 1 John 2:15
- Renewed in Knowledge—Rationally as Dreamers: Romans 12:1-2; 2 Corinthians 10:5; Ephesians 4:20-24; Philippians 1:9; Colossians 1:10; 3:10
- Renewed in Will—Volitionally as Creators: Romans 6:17; 2 Corinthians 7:1; Ephesians 4:20-24; Philippians 2:13
- Renewed in Emotions—Emotionally as Singers: Galatians 5:13-26; Ephesians 4:19-32
- Renewed in Body—Physically as Actors: Romans 6:12; 1 Corinthians 6:13-20; 9:24-27; 1 Thessalonians 5:23; 1 Timothy 4:7-8

Remember that our capacities tend toward inclinations, patterns, propensities, and dispositions. We habituate ourselves to pursue what we perceive is pleasing. Just as our old nature treads a path toward sin, our new nature walks a road marked godliness. Notice contrasts between patterns of sinfulness and themes of godliness.

- Relationally/Romancers: From False Lovers/Impure Affections to Grace Lovers/Purified Affections

- ◆ Rationally/Dreamers: From Foolish, Fleshly Mindsets to Wise, Spiritual Mindsets
- ◆ Volitionally/Creators: From Self-Centered Purposes/Pathways to Other-Centered Purposes/Pathways
- ◆ Emotionally/Singers: From Ungoverned Mood States to Managed Mood States
- ◆ Physically/Actors: From Habituated Flesh-Controlled Tendencies to Disciplined Spirit-Controlled Tendencies

Biblical counselors reckon on and help their spiritual friends reckon on these truths. Alive to Christ, Christians no longer have to follow the path of false lovers, foolish mindsets, self-centered pathways, and ungoverned mood states. Christian counselors help Christians live their new life in Christ by putting off the old and putting on the new. "Just as you used to offer the parts of your body in slavery to impurity and to ever-increasing wickedness, so now offer them in slavery to righteousness leading to holiness" (Romans 6:19).

Our New Life: Resurrected with Christ

God resurrected the new you to new life with Christ. What is this new life? Henry Holloman outlines seven aspects of our new creation through regeneration.

- ◆ We are partakers of the Divine nature: 1 Peter 1:3; 2 Peter 1:3-4.
- ◆ We are children of God: John 3:1-17.
- ◆ We are permanently indwelt by Father, Son, and Holy Spirit: John 1:12-13; 14:20, 23; 1 Corinthians 6:19-20; Ephesians 4:6; Colossians 1:27.
- ◆ We receive a new heart—affections, cognitions, volition, and emotions: Romans 6:17; Galatians 4:6.
- ◆ We are empowered to receive spiritual things: 1 Corinthians 2:9-16; Hebrews 5:14.
- ◆ We are enabled to reorient our lifestyle toward righteousness: 1 John 2:29; 3:9-10.
- ◆ We experience the crucifixion of our old self and the resurrection of our new self: Romans 6:1-14; Ephesians 4:24; Colossians 3:1-11 (Holloman, *The Forgotten Blessing*, pp. 31-37).

What Adam and Eve attempted to do with fig leaves and what we try unsuccessfully to achieve by our good works, Christ performed through His death, burial, and resurrection. E. K. Simpson and F. F. Bruce describe how Christ raised us to new life and the results.

The resurrection of Christ is presented by Paul as the supreme manifestation of the power of God. Those who have been raised with Christ have been raised through faith in the divine power which brought Christ back from the dead, and henceforth that power energizes them and maintains the new life with them—the new life which is nothing less than Christ's resurrection life imparted to all the members of his body (Simpson and Bruce, *Commentary on the Epistles to the Ephesians and Colossians*, p. 236).

That's power. Changing power. Lasting power. Power that anchors us. Assures us. This is why theologians define regeneration as the impartation of spiritual life now and eternal life forever. We have not received new life to last a lifetime. We've received new life that lasts forever. What God begins in us at salvation, He continues in us during our lives through sanctification, and He completes in us through glorification (Romans 8:28-30).

Gown Two: The Gown of Reconciliation

Regeneration focuses on the Christian's new *nature*; reconciliation concentrates on the Christian's new *nurture*. Regeneration highlights who we are *in* Christ; reconciliation stresses who we are *to* Christ. Regeneration emphasizes our change from sinner to *saint*; reconciliation underscores our change from prodigals to *sons and daughters*. Through regeneration, Worthy Groom's virgin bride exchanges corrupt, polluted, putrid rags for beautiful, glorious, majestic gowns. Through reconciliation, Worthy Groom's virgin bride trades the prostitute's sleazy getup for bridal white.

Reconciliation builds the bridge that spans the chasm we created when we broke fellowship with Father. Without reconciliation, the Prodigal could not return home. The Adulterer would remain shacked up in some tacky motel. With reconciliation, Christ restores spiritual fellowship and moral, personal harmony with Father. He demolishes sin's partition, the dividing wall, the moat standing between Father and us. He brings us into the living room, takes us home, where we are adopted into Father's forever family. Communion commences.

"Where Did I Come From?" "I Came from Christ."

For reconciliation to occur, propitiation was necessary. "Propitiation," a common, meaningful word to Paul's audience, seems archaic and confusing to us. Propitiation means to appease anger. God's holiness requires that He separate Himself from sinners. God's justice obligates Him to express His wrath in judgment. Thus, humanity is alienated from God by sin; God is alienated from humanity by holy wrath. God can no longer look on us without displeasure and we can no longer look on God without fear. We run and hide. He finds and judges. Going home, apart from propitiation, is out of the question.

We must make some careful distinctions here. God's love for us never changes. He always loves us. However, His holy love requires that He not receive us home, given our corrupt condition. John Stott explains Father's intervention. "It is God himself who in holy wrath needs to be propitiated, God himself who in holy love undertook to do the propitiating, and God himself who in the person of his Son died for the propitiation of our sins" (Stott, *The Cross of Christ*, p. 175).

Christ propitiates God's holy wrath through His substitutionary death. Sin is overcome and wrath is averted. God took His own loving initiative to appease His holy wrath by bearing it in His Son when He took our place on the Cross.

Now when we ponder life's existential question, "Where did I come from?" we have two possible answers. "My existence as I now know it came from myself. I am a self-made man. An independent woman. I'll take care of myself."

Or, "I came from Christ. I owe my existence now and forever to Him and His propitiation. I am no longer separate. I no longer live in alienation." Why? "For Christ died for sins once for all, the righteous for the unrighteous, *to bring you to God*" (1 Peter 3:18, emphasis added).

The Gown of Reconciliation returns me to my original stance with arms reaching upward to Papa, to Abba, Daddy, and with hands stretching outward to my brothers and sisters. Reconciled to Father, I reconcile His wayward children to Him.

> All this is from God, who reconciled us to himself through Christ and gave us the ministry of reconciliation: that God was reconciling the world to himself in Christ, not counting men's sins against them. And he has committed to us the message of reconciliation. We are therefore Christ's ambassadors, as though God were making his appeal through us. We implore you on Christ's behalf: Be reconciled to God (2 Corinthians 5:18-20).

Our New Nurture: "Welcome Home!"

"Nature" speaks of the change *in* us. "Nurture" suggests the change in how Christ relates *to* us. Our holy Father can't have fellowship with people whose core nature is sinful. However, once He transforms our core natures into saints, fellowship blossoms. The new covenant, as we'll see in future chapters, opens the way to new relationship, new intimacy. "I no longer call you *servants*, because a servant does not know his master's business. Instead, I have called you *friends*, for everything that I learned from my Father I have made known to you" (John 15:15, emphasis added). Reconciliation converts us from servants to friends, from errant children to welcomed and celebrated daughters and sons.

More than any other biblical portrait, the parable of the prodigal son pictures reconciliation. Jesus begins the action with the youngest son's demand. To us the words seem innocent enough. "Father, give me my share of the estate" (Luke 15:12). To the father, the words are radical. They suggest heartless rejection.

Jesus tells it all so simply and matter-of-factly that we find it difficult to grasp how unheard of it is. It's offensive and in radical contradiction to the most venerated tradition of the times. Kenneth Bailey, in his penetrating explanation of Jesus' story, shows that the son's manner of leaving is tantamount to wishing his father dead.

> For over fifteen years I have been asking people of all walks of life from Morocco to India and from Turkey to the Sudan, about the implications of a son's request for his inheritance while the father is still living. The answer has always been emphatically the same. The conversation runs as follows: "Has anyone ever made such a request in your village?" "Impossible!" "If anyone ever did, what would happen?" "His father would beat him on the head, of course!" "Why?' "Because the request means that he wants his father to die" (Bailey, *The Cross and the Prodigal*, p. 56).

The implication underlying the son's request is simple. "Father, I cannot wait for you to die. Get out of my way, old man! Drop dead!"

Having wished his father dead, the Prodigal son wastes no time collecting his newfound wealth and traveling to a distant country. In our culture, this seems harmless enough. A recent survey of Americans found that 67 percent of us no longer live in the same state in which we were born. Not so for this young man and his father. In their day, moving away from the family home was a sign of great disrespect. This loving father now feels the same agony as the parents of a runaway teen. Such a home-leaving produces immense sorrow and shame in the heart of the father.

To understand the father's pain and the son's shame, we must place ourselves in the social context of Christ's parable. In Luke 15:1-2 we read, "Now the tax collectors and sinners were all gathering around to hear him. But the Pharisees and the teachers of the law muttered, 'this man welcomes sinners and eats with them.'" The religious leaders of the day are complaining because Jesus does not keep respectable company. "He welcomes sinners! He receives and accepts them."

In response, Jesus tells three parables, each portraying the same theme. The portrait Christ paints impresses upon our senses the truth that sin is *awayness*. The son moves away from the father. Nothing breaks the heart of God our Father more than His children moving away from Him spiritually.

Why do we all need reconciliation? All of us, like the Prodigal Son, have gone our own way. We have chosen to leave our Father and live on our own.

Like the Prodigal, we have all said, "I'm leaving you, Father!" Like him, we also have said, "Father, I don't need you!" Leaving the fullness of the father's love, the Prodigal Son embarks on a quest to find fulfillment in the world. The father's voice of unconditional love has always said, "You are safe with me. You can rest in me. You are my beloved." The son shuts his ears to this voice.

After a lifestyle of sin and a lifetime of awayness, the Prodigal comes to the end of his rope.

> When he came to his senses, he said, "How many of my father's hired men have food to spare, and here I am starving to death! I will set out and go back to my father and say to him: 'Father, I have sinned against heaven and against you. I am no longer worthy to be called your son; make me like one of your hired men.'" So he got up and went to his father (Luke 15:17-20a).

Now the crucial question arises. Will this father welcome home this Prodigal Son? Does Father really welcome sinners? Yes. Of course He does. Being welcomed home with open arms is exactly the point of Christ's parable.

Head down, guilt stricken, the Prodigal slumps home to the father. Head high, love motivated, the father sprints to his son, throws his arms around him, and kisses him repeatedly! So very different from the Middle Eastern expectation. Listen again to Bailey's interview.

> I asked them, "And what would happen if the boy came back home, penniless, hungry, and broken?" The Middle Eastern reply: "The father would certainly not run to him and receive him! The father would stay hidden for a while and make the son eat humble pie outside the gate of the village" (Bailey, *The Cross and the Prodigal*, p. 56).

This is not what occurs in Jesus' story. The father runs to his son. "Run" literally means to sprint to, to rush, and to race. He forgets his dignity. He forgets the insult and disrespect his son had shown him. He doesn't care what others might think. He doesn't care that his peers will call him, "Old fool!" He picks up his flowing robe and races to his son. Sprints to his son. In no other religion anywhere on the planet does one come to know God as the Racing One, the Pursuing One.

Through this parable, Jesus is saying, "Look, look at Father! Look at Him for the first time all over again. This is why I died. This is why I rose again. Father longed to build a bridge over which He could run to you, and throw His arms around you, embracing you, encompassing you, engulfing you with His forgiving love!"

We're stunned by forgiveness. We're shocked and confounded by new nurture. Like the Prodigal, we practice our concession speech all the way home. "I've sinned against you and I'm *unworthy to be called your son*. Make me like one of your *hired servants*." The hired servants occupied the lowest position on the relational totem pole of the day. The son is saying, "I am not only not worthy to be your son; I'm not worthy to be your slave, or even your servant. I am only worthy of being your temporary hired hand. Never again a member of your household."

So ingrained in his soul is his unworthiness, that he gives his entire speech to his father. His father has raced to him, is kissing him impetuously and celebrating over him wildly, and this guy is still droning on with his speech. "I---am----not----worthy." The father reacts! "Forget that! Quick! Bring the best robe and put it on him. Put a ring on his finger and sandals on his feet. Bring the fattened calf and kill it. Let's have a feast and celebrate. For this *son* of mine was dead and is alive again; he was lost and is found. So they began to celebrate" (Luke 15:22-24, emphasis added). The father is saying, "Let's party hearty! The guest of honor at my party is my son, not my hired servant." Father prepares a celebration reserved for His most special guests: you and me whenever we return home—as sons and daughters.

Perhaps we could learn from one envious of us. Marghanita Laski, secular humanist and novelist, said in a television interview shortly before her death in 1988, "What I envy most about you Christians is your forgiveness; I have nobody to forgive me." Whenever we return home, we have Somebody to welcome us. This is our new nurture.

Our New Parentage and Our New Adoption

Our new nurture overlaps with our new parentage and our new adoption. The *prerequisite* to reconciliation is propitiation; the *result* of reconciliation is adoption. In order to be reconciled, Father had to propitiate His holy wrath first. Having been reconciled, we are immediately and permanently placed into Father's forever family as adult sons and daughters with all the rights and privileges of sonship.

Reconciliation moves us from enmity to family. Once separated and alienated from God, far away from Christ, hostile to Him in our foolish minds, now the blood of Christ brings us near, produces peace, and establishes connection (Romans 8:1-10; Ephesians 2:11-16).

Consequently, we now have access to God (Romans 5:1-2; Ephesians 2:17-18; Hebrews 10:19-25). Previously we were barred from Father's presence. Never would we have thought of entering the holy place, much less the Holy of Holies where God's glory dwells. Adopted, we have confidence to enter boldly the Holy of Holies. We draw near to God with a sincere heart in full assurance of faith. Peace is established. Intimacy initiated. Access inaugurated.

"For you did not," Paul reminds us, "receive a spirit that makes you a slave again to fear [terror, anxiety, phobia], but you received the Spirit of sonship (adoption). And by him we cry, 'Abba, Father' ['Papa, Daddy']. The Spirit himself testifies with our spirit that we are God's children. Now if we are children, then we are heirs—heirs of God and co-heirs with Christ" (Romans 8:15-17a).

The adoptive aspect of reconciliation personalizes our salvation. Listen to theologian Wayne Grudem's careful distinctions.

> Although adoption is a privilege that comes to us at the time we become Christians, nevertheless, it is a privilege that is distinct from justification and distinct from regeneration. In regeneration we are made spiritually alive, able to relate to God in prayer and worship and able to hear his Word with receptive hearts. But it is possible that God could have creatures that are spiritually alive and yet are not members of his family—angels, for example, apparently fall into this category. Therefore, it would have been possible for God to decide to give us regeneration without the great privileges of adoption into his family.
>
> Moreover, God could have given us justification without the privileges of adoption into his family, for he could have forgiven our sins and given us right legal standing before him without making us his children. It is important to realize this because it helps us to recognize how great our privileges in adoption are. Regeneration has to do with our spiritual life within. Justification has to do with our standing before God's law. But adoption has to do with our *relationship* with God as our Father, and in adoption we are given many of the greatest blessings that we will know for all eternity (Grudem, *Systematic Theology*, pp. 738-739).

It would be sad to be made clean, but still be kept at arms' length from Father. It would be lonely to be declared, "Not guilty!" yet still be barred from God's chambers. Adoption reminds us that we are "no longer slaves, but sons" (Galatians 4:7). The Judge says, "Not guilty!" then leaps over the bench, swoops us into His arms, takes us into His private chambers, parties with us, then invites us home—permanently.

When we counsel men and women who feel unforgiven, unloved, and unwelcomed, we have truth for life. Truth that changes their lives by changing their outlook on who they are in Christ and to Christ.

Our New Identity: Father's Sons/Daughters and Worthy Groom's Virgin Brides

Our new nurture overlaps with our new identity. Our old identity: "Slaves," "Prodigals," "Adulterers," "Whores." Our new identity includes: "Father's Sons and Daughters" and "Worthy Groom's Virgin Brides."

Think about the latter designation, "Worthy Groom's Virgin Brides." In the physical realm, once we lose our virginity, there's no going back. In the spiritual realm, we commit spiritual adultery, become prostitutes and whores, lose our virginity, *but God* so cleanses our nature that we can legitimately wear white—bridal white. We are pure once again. Our spiritual identity is virginity.

Our cleansing is counter-cultural. In Jesus' time, during the betrothal period, the groom-to-be prepared the home while the bride-to-be prepared herself. Notice in Ephesians 5 how our Worthy Groom prepares us.

> Husbands, love your wives, just as Christ loved the church and gave himself up for her to make her holy, cleansing her by the washing with water through the word,

and to present her to himself as a radiant church, without stain or wrinkle or any other blemish, but holy and blameless (Ephesians 5:25-27).

Instead of the bride-to-be presenting ourselves all pretty and pure, our Worthy Groom cleanses us from our adultery so He can present us to Himself virginal.

When False Seducer whispers his haunting melodies of corruption, captivity, chasm, and condemnation, we must shout him down. "That's the old me! Father accepts the new me. Nurtures me. Worthy Groom marries the new me."

Gown Three: The Gown of Redemption

Regeneration takes place in the *temple*, reconciliation in the *home*, and redemption in the *slave market*. The Gown of Redemption frees us from the Rag of Captivity. It liberates us from the slave market of sin, from bondage to sin and Satan, setting us free to righteousness and Christ. Whereas regeneration conquers sin's *presence*, and reconciliation demolishes sin's *partition*, redemption releases us from sin's *power*. Redemption transforms us from slaves to free men and women.

Sin results in captivity. Redemption is release from slavery and captivity by the payment of a ransom price. "But thanks be to God that, though you used to be slaves to sin, you wholeheartedly obeyed the form of teaching to which you were entrusted. You have been set free from sin and have become slaves to righteousness" (Romans 6:17-18). We've already seen the precious ransom price—drops of Savior's precious, priceless blood, Worthy Groom's death.

"Why Am I Here?" "To Shepherd in a Jungle."

Originally, one glance at our Robe of Dominion told us why we were here: "To be under-shepherds." We were placed here, empowered by God, to be His stewards. To take care of His planet, to care for one another. However, wearing the Rag of Captivity, we blurred the perception of our purpose. "I'm here to protect myself."

Self-protection makes perfect sense when we think in terms of slavery and imprisonment. Slaves have no rights. Their very existence is up for grabs, at the mercy of others. So slaves in their right mind look out for number one. They're careful, cautious, self-protective. Prisoners have few rights and little safety. They look at their striped prison outfits and think, "I might as well have a bull's-eye on my chest." Prisoners live according to the law of the jungle. It's dog-eat-dog. Every man for himself. Every woman for herself.

"I'm here to protect myself" logically describes the purpose of life allotted to those whose lot in life is slave or prisoner. It is ill suited, however, to those who wear the suit of redemption. "Why am I here as a free person? I'm here as a shepherd in a jungle. I'm here empowered by God so I can empower others."

The Gown of Redemption frees us not only from sin's bondage, but it also frees us to Christ's righteousness, to His original right purposes for our existence. Freed, I'm no longer dominated by others. Freed, I no longer need to try to dominate others. Freed, I'm empowered to empower others. "Just as you used to offer the parts of your body in slavery to impurity and to ever-increasing wickedness, so now offer them in slavery to righteousness leading to holiness" (Romans 6:19).

What constitutes holy living in a fallen world? What is my purpose now? For instance, when a battered wife comes to you for counseling, what is your ultimate goal for her? Certainly, you want to help her know it's normal to hurt and possible to hope. Ultimately, however, you want her to know she's capable of mature love. She doesn't have to be dominated by her batterer. She doesn't have to cower in retreat. Nor does she need to give into tit-for-tat, an-eye-for-an-eye behavior. She doesn't have to become abusive toward her abuser, others, or herself.

We want to help the battered victim say, "I have been victimized, but I'm not a victim of my circumstances. My life is not ended. I can love. Bold love. Tough love. Forgiving love. I can shepherd."

Our New Power and Our New Inclination

We all want power. Strength. Will power. It's there in the new person in Christ. "Therefore do not let sin reign in your mortal body so that you obey its evil desires" (Romans 6:12). We do not have to obey or be mastered by sin's evil desires because we have a new inclination. A new set of desires. A new affection. The old capacities with their corrupted desires—Christ nailed them to the Cross. The new capacities with their redeemed desires—Christ raised to new life. Because of regeneration we have redemption. Because we are new in Christ, we have victory through Christ.

We no longer need to offer the parts of our body to sin, as instruments of wickedness, because we are freed from wicked inclinations. Now we can offer ourselves—body and soul, embodied personality—to God for righteousness because we have been brought from death to life. Sin shall not be our master because now we're under the power, the mastery, of transforming grace.

The battered wife reminds herself that she has not been given a spirit of timidity, but a spirit of power, love, and wisdom. By faith she claims her new power to love her husband with holy love. By faith she reckons on her new inclination to obey Father lovingly even when she's confused and terrified.

Our New Freedom from Sin and Our New Victory Over Sin

Battered wives, and all Christians, can lovingly shepherd because of their new freedom and new victory. We're not only freed *from* sin, we're freed *to* righteousness. "But now that you have been set free from sin and have become slaves to God, the benefit you reap leads to holiness, and the result is eternal life" (Romans 6:22).

In New Testament times, the Agora was the crowd, the marketplace. To buy in the market place was to *agorazō*. People used the term for bartering in the slave market where one buys (*agorazō*) a slave. In Galatians 4:5, Paul pictures sinners as slaves to sin, Satan, and the law. He notes that Christ not only bought us (*agorazō*), but He "redeemed" or "bought us back, bought us out" (*exagorasē*). To buy us from slavery would mean that we were still slaves. But Christ bought us back, bought us out of slavery. Now we are free to choose. We can enslave ourselves again to sin, or we can lovingly choose to obey a new master—Christ. The free choice is ours.

When a temptation to sin enters our mind, we must "count ourselves dead to sin but alive to God in Christ Jesus" (Romans 6:11). We have to remind ourselves, re-imagine who we are. "Whoa! Time out, False Seducer. I'm not your slave any more. Do you see me wearing Rags of Captivity? No! Christ garbs me in Gowns of Redemption. I'm free. Get behind me, Satan. I resist you. Flee from me! I'm free."

Gown Four: The Gown of Justification

With justification our address changes from the temple, home, and slave market to the *law court*—the courthouse, the courtroom. Regeneration conquers sin's *presence*; reconciliation demolishes sin's *partition*; redemption defeats sin's *power*; and justification cancels sin's *penalty*. Regeneration transforms us from sinner to saint, reconciliation from separated to sons/daughters, redemption from slaves to shepherds, and justification from guilty criminal to acquitted citizen.

Through the Gown of Justification, Christ removes our Rag of Condemnation. He judicially declares the believing sinner forgiven and free from condemnation. Our Gown of Justification cancels our guilt. It takes us into the courtroom where God, the righteous Judge, declares us, "Not guilty!"

Theologians offer this technical definition of justification: the legal act of God in which He declares our sins forgiven and Christ's righteousness as ours. God pronounces us legally righteous in His eternal court of law. We have broken His law, but we are free from any liability because His Son has borne the penalty of our law breaking. Justification is God's declaration that we belong to the new covenant community. We are no longer forced to be on the outside or in jail.

"How Should I Then Live?" "Share Savior's Salvation."

Our Gown of Justification assists us in answering life's fourth existential question: "How should I then live?" Originally, God intended that we live with the Robe of Cohesion and share Trinity's shalom. As they are one, so we were to be one. As they are at peace, we were to be at peace.

Sin mutates the Robe of Cohesion into the Rag of Condemnation. Instead of shalom, we feel shame. Sinners, like it or not, live to spread Seducer's shame. It can be as innocent as a father who makes his son feel like he'll never measure up unless he wins the championship. It can be as insidious as the uncle who exposes his niece to pornography, then blames her, telling her, "You're the reason I looked at this. If your Mom and Dad ever find out, they'll put you up for adoption." What is deepest in our souls, we spread. When condemnation, fear, and dread consume our souls, we spread shame, guilt, and disgrace.

How should the justified Christian live? Set free from sin's penalty, guilt, and shame, we live to share Savior's salvation. Relaxed in who we are in Christ and to Christ, we don't need to "keep up appearances." We no longer have to enter every conversation wondering, "How will I come across? Will they like me? Accept me? Want me?" Since the God of the universe already accepts us, we rest. Now we can fix our focus on others. We can approach every conversation with a new attitude. "I've been set free. How can I help others receive their pardon? Those people seem so uptight. Father, help me introduce them to your grace, pardon, and forgiveness."

Our New Peace: Forgiveness

For anyone to rest in forgiveness, he must first see the horrors of sin. If we assume that God forgives us only for petty crimes and misdemeanors, then we're always leery. "What about my secret sins? My felonies and other serious crimes?" Stott explains that to understand forgiveness, we must first understand the gravity of our sin and the majesty of God—the realities of who we are and who He is. "How can the holy love of God come to terms with the unholy lovelessness of man?" (Stott, *The Cross of Christ*, p. 133). *It's horrible to sin, but wonderful to be forgiven.* We magnify amazing grace when we recognize sin's gravity.

Sin constitutes anything that shatters shalom, everything that breaks oneness. Sin is relational. It is spiritual adultery. In justification, God says, "I forgive you for sleeping with the enemy. For loving false gods. For the idols of your heart. For your wicked, foolish imagination. For your doubts about My goodness. You're forgiven of the cowardly choices you've made to pursue anything and anyone but Me. I forgive you of your lasciviousness, of your carnal addictions to sensuality. I forgive you for the habituate sinfulness you demonstrated in your false lovers, foolish mindsets, self-centered pathways, and ungoverned, addictive mood states."

If we're forgiven of all that and more, we have peace. "Therefore, since we have been justified through faith, we have peace with God through our Lord Jesus Christ" (Romans 5:1). Paul connects the extent of our forgiveness to the depth of our assurance of God's love. "Since we have been justified by his blood, how much more shall we be saved from God's wrath through him! For if, when we were God's enemies, we were reconciled to him through the death of his Son, how much more, having been reconciled, shall we be saved through his life!" (Romans 5:9-10).

Father whispers, "You're forgiven—for sins past, present, and future. For sins you consider puny and those you consider gigantic. And all that happened while you were on the outs with Me, looking in from the outside. In prison. In bed with False Seducer. If I forgave you then, don't you think My forgiveness lasts? Continues? Covers all? Calvary covers it all. Your sin with its guilt and stain. Peace be with you. Shhh. Hush. Shalom. Peace. All is well. Rest. Relax."

Our New Pardon and Our New Dignity

Justification is wonderful, but is it *just*? Righteousness is incredible, but is it *right*? On what basis can God declare sinners, "Not guilty"? How can He, with integrity, declare you and me, sinners all, legally righteous? Not simply not guilty, but righteous?

God's holiness requires that He judge sin. His holy wrath is His personal revulsion to evil, vehement repulsion over sin, and vigorous opposition to unholiness. Wrath is God's holy love reacting against unholy evil, to anything that breaks oneness. How do we integrate God's holy wrath with our unholy character and end up with the justification of sinners? How can God be just and the Justifier at the same time?

Only the self-substitution of God explains the inexplicable. God satisfies His holy wrath through substitution—Divine self-satisfaction through Divine self-substitution. God wants us to remain the constant object of His holy love. Our sin precludes that. For God simply to wink at our sin is for Him to become less than He is. The only way for

God's holy love to be satisfied is for His holiness to be directed in judgment upon Christ, so His love may be directed toward us in forgiveness. The Substitute bears the penalty so we sinners may receive the pardon.

> The concept of substitution may be said, then, to lie at the heart of both sin and salvation. For the essence of sin is man substituting himself for God, while the essence of salvation is God substituting himself for man. Man asserts himself against God and puts himself where only God deserves to be; God sacrifices himself for man and puts himself where only man deserves to be. Man claims prerogatives that belong to God alone; God accepts penalties that belong to man alone (Stott, *The Cross of Christ*, p. 160).

My sin and guilt God imputes or places upon Christ. Christ's perfect righteousness and guiltlessness, Father imputes or places on us. "God made him who had no sin to be sin for us, so that in him we might become the righteousness of God" (2 Corinthians 5:21).

Justification by faith is what distinguishes Christianity from all other religions. It's what causes Christianity to be so hard for sinful humanity to swallow. Our pride and arrogance fight against grace. "Surely there must be something that *I* do!" We would rather lose ourselves than humble ourselves; we'd rather perish than repent. When we do humble ourselves, surrender, believe, and repent, we receive justification by faith through grace. Christ becomes our righteousness (1 Corinthians 1:30).

Our New Boldness: Grace Confidence

Because perfect love drives out fear (1 John 4:18), justification produces new boldness. Grace prompts confidence. Not confidence in the flesh, but confidence about our acceptance before God. "Therefore, there is now no condemnation for those who are in Christ Jesus" (Romans 8:1). Never again do we need to fear hearing, "Guilty! Condemned to eternal death, separated from God forever."

Just after linking justification and glorification, Paul asks the practical question, "So what?" In his words, "What, then, shall we say in response to this?" (Romans 8:31a). What difference does justification make in our daily existence? "If God is for us," Paul answers, "who can be against us?" (Romans 8:31b). In the subsequent context, it's obvious that Paul recognizes the Christian's many enemies (see Romans 8:32-39). His point is, "Who can *successfully* be against us? Overpower us? No one!"

Against us in what sense? "Who will bring any [legal] charge against those whom God has chosen? It is God who justifies [declares legally not guilty in a court of law]. Who is he that condemns? Christ Jesus, who died—more than that, who was raised to life—is at the right hand of God and is also interceding for us" (Romans 8:33-34). When False Seducer hisses his blasphemous slander against God's grace and God's chosen children, our role is to open the court books. Look in the legal documents. Read the stenographer's word-for-word report. "No way, False Seducer. Get thee behind me. It is written. God justified me in Christ by faith through grace."

Pastors, commentators, and theologians alike have called Romans 8 the heart of new covenant theology, and Romans 8:35-39 the core of new covenant personal assurance.

Here Paul asks, "Who shall separate us from the love of Christ?" (Romans 8:35), then provides a litany of possible culprits spanning the globe and beyond. He concludes with these words of assurance, of grace confidence.

> No, in all these things we are more than conquerors through him who loved us. For I am convinced that neither death nor life, neither angels nor demons, [including the False Seducer] neither the present nor the future, nor any powers, neither height nor depth, nor anything else in all creation, will be able to separate us from the love of God that is in Christ Jesus our Lord (Romans 8:37-39).

When False Seducer pens the end of our story, he entitles it, "Condemned: Rejected and Discarded." Don't buy his lie! The final chapter of Worthy Groom's story of your love life together reads, "Justified: Accepted and Embraced." Allow His truth to set you free from fear and free to grace confidence.

Where We've Been and Where We're Heading

The curtain is closing on Act Four, Scene II. In the first scene, we witnessed Worthy Groom's pursuing, wooing, winning, and renewing His virgin bride. In the second scene, we watched the main character stroll across the stage dressed not in a coat of many colors, but in a four-layered gown: the Gown of Regeneration, Reconciliation, Redemption, and Justification.

Now that we know the character of our main characters in their redeemed state, we want to view the details of their lives. Specifically, in Scene III we'll revisit them as they disclose more about their *new nurture—forgiving springs*. How is the believer's relationship to God impacted by their salvation in Christ? What implications does this have for new covenant counseling?

Caring for Your Soul: Personal Applications

1. Check yourself out in the mirror wearing your *Gown of Regeneration*. At weddings, brides wear something borrowed, something blue, something old, and something new. Christ's brides have nothing old, but something very new—a new nature, a new heart, a new purity.

    a. Read Ephesians 1:3-14. List and claim all the declarations made about the new you.

    b. Think of a current besetting sin. How would knowing, reckoning, and yielding based upon your new nature enable you to find victory?

2. Check yourself out in the mirror wearing your *Gown of Reconciliation*.

    a. Read Romans 5:1-11. Paraphrase these verses, personalizing them with your name.

    b. Think of a recent time when Satan taunted, shamed, and condemned you. How could the experiential awareness of your new identity in Christ defeat Satan?

3. Check yourself out in the mirror wearing your *Gown of Redemption*.

    a. Read Colossians 2:10-15. Describe your victory in Christ.

    b. How will you be living differently and loving more powerfully because of your redemption in Christ?

4. Check yourself out in the mirror wearing your *Gown of Justification*.

    a. Read Romans 8:1-39. Pen a praise to God for lifting your condemnation, for declaring you righteous.

    b. How will this new boldness, this new confidence in Christ, make a difference in your life over the next week?

Caring for Others: Ministry Implications

◆ **Counsel Based on the Gown of Regeneration:** Do not counsel Christians as though they are non-Christians. Because we are regenerated, we have a new heart, a new nature, a new purity, and new clothing. Do not urge believers to work up desire. Rather, stir up the desire that God has newly planted within. Do not teach believers to find a new mindset; inform them that they have the mindset of Christ implanted within. Do not urge believers to discover new will power; enlighten them of their new will—their new want to and can do. Do not urge believers to instill within themselves new mood states; empower them to live out the new mood states they received at salvation.

◆ **Counsel Based on the Gown of Reconciliation:** The believer's new identity is crucial to powerful living and a peaceful soul. Enlighten believers of their new identity in Christ. Help them see their *universal* identity—son, daughter, bride, soldier, etc. Additionally, help them see their *unique* identity—how has God shaped them? What are their gifts, passions, callings, talents? Seek to capture in a creative image the uniqueness of the redeemed image bearer sitting before you.

◆ **Counsel Based on the Gown of Redemption:** Believers have been transported from the domain of darkness to the kingdom of light. Father empowers us to serve Christ freely. Enlighten believers of their new victory in Christ. Teach them their freedom from sin. Guide and empower them to empower others.

◆ **Counsel Based on the Gown of Justification:** Your spiritual friends have a new peace with God. They are now ambassadors of reconciliation. Help them experience and share shalom. Enable them to rest secure in Christ's love.

◆ **Counsel Based on Salvation:** In spiritual direction, begin by helping people understand who they are in Christ and what they are capable of. By explaining what they can accomplish, you encourage the person toward virtue—living the good life out of a good heart. To call people to something they consider impossible does them no good. Hope must serve as the guide and companion if Christians are to pursue virtue; otherwise despair of success kills every effort to acquire the impossible. Bring to their full attention the power they can exercise, and clearly explain the good their new nature is capable of performing.

◆ **Guide Based on Sanctification:** Guiding says, "It's supernatural to mature." Guide people by focusing on them as Romancers capable of loving sacrificially, as Dreamers capable of perceiving with spiritual eyes, as Creators capable of choosing courageously, and as Singers capable of experiencing life fully with integrity.

CHAPTER TWENTY-TWO

VIRGIN BRIDE'S NEW NURTURE: FORGIVING SPRINGS

"The gospel is the proclamation of free love; the revelation of the boundless charity of God. Nothing less than this will suit our world; nothing else is so likely to touch the heart, to go down to the lowest depths of depraved humanity, as the assurance that the sinner has been loved; loved by God; loved with a righteous love; loved with a free love that makes no bargains as to merit, or fitness, or goodness" (Horatio Bonar, *God's Way of Holiness*, pp. 56-57).

"We are all prodigal sons, and not disinherited; we have received our portion and misspent it, not been denied it. We are God's tenants here, he, our landlord, pays us rents, not yearly, nor monthly, but hourly, and quarterly; every minute he renews his mercy" (John Donne, *Devotions*, p. 10).

Nurture Versus Nature

In parenting, psychology, and criminology, experts and interested lay people debate the relative influences of *nurture* versus *nature*. We wonder whether a child's personality is more influenced by nurture—how parents relate to and treat their children, or more influenced by nature—the genetic make-up the child is born with and basic inclinations inherited from parents.

A recent situation forced our local high school to ponder the nurture/nature question. A twenty-five-year-old female teacher had been promiscuous with ten male high school students. As expert opinions and letters to the editor appeared in our local paper, the nature/nurture divide became obvious. Some claimed that the teacher acted as she did because of nurture issues—when she was young she was distant from her aloof father and seen as unattractive by her peers. Others supposed that her promiscuity might be related to a genetic propensity toward addictive behavior and/or a hormonal imbalance. Still others argued for a third cause—personal responsibility.

In Ephesians 2:1-3, Paul explains the fallen personality structure by integrating nurture, nature, and personal responsibility. Fallen human beings *personally choose* to gratify the cravings of the flesh. Additionally, fallen human beings live in a fallen world where they're *nurtured* away from God—following the ways or nurture of the fallen world and of the ruler of the kingdom of the air (False Seducer). Fallen beings in a fallen world are also by *nature* objects of wrath—born dead in sin.

In Romans 5-8, Paul describes the redeemed personality structure by integrating nurture, nature, and personal responsibility. What a gracious new *nurture* Father provides—redeemed human beings are sons of God, adopted, crying out, "Abba, Daddy." His Spirit testifies with our spirit that we are beloved children of God. Christ's death and resurrection assure us that nothing can ever separate us from Father's loving nurture.

To our new nurture, Paul adds our new *nature*—the old me is dead, the new me is born again, raised to new life. The new me, the new you, our new nature wants to and is able to trust and obey Father.

Our new nurture and new nature still require *personal choice* and responsibility. We must count ourselves dead to the old nature and alive in our new nature. We must choose to resist the world, the flesh, and the Devil by living out our new nurture and nature. We must reckon on who we are *to* Christ—new nurture, and who we are in Christ—new nature.

When the author of Hebrews describes our redeemed personality, he emphasizes new covenant nurture and nature:

- The New *Nurture* of the New Covenant: "For I will forgive their wickedness and will remember their sins no more" (Hebrews 8:12). Our new nurture is grace nurture—reconciliation, redemption, forgiveness, freedom from condemnation, bold access to God, confident assurance of eternal adoption, personal enjoyment of sonship.
- The New *Nature* of the New Covenant: "This is the covenant I will make with the house of Israel after that time, declares the Lord. I will put my laws in their minds and write them on their hearts" (Hebrews 8:10a). Our new nature is grace nature—regeneration, justification, new creation, death to sin, new life with Christ, resurrection power to trust and obey God.

In Chapters 22 and 23, we enjoy new scenes in the drama of redemption. We delight in the forgiving springs of our new nurture and are empowered by the cleansing springs of our new nature. In these chapters we'll synthesize and apply God's teaching about our four Gowns of Redemption.

- Forgiving Springs: The New *Nurture* of the New Covenant
  - Who We are *to* Christ by Grace through Faith
  - Our New Relationship: God's Heart Toward Me—Peace with God
  - Reconciliation: Sonship
  - Justification: Forgiveness of Sin and Declaration of Righteousness

- Cleansing Springs: The New *Nature* of the New Covenant
  - Who We are *in* Christ by Grace through Faith
  - Our New Reality: A New Heart in Me—Power in Christ
  - Regeneration: Sainthood
  - Redemption: Freedom from Sin and to Righteousness

Enjoying Who I Am, Becoming Who I Am

The Christian life is the process of *enjoying* who I am *to* Christ and *becoming* who I am *in* Christ. Sanctification involves living out my Sonship (new nurture) and my Sainthood (new nature). The key to our victory is faith in our new identity. I'm convinced that everything in the Christian life revolves around how we answer the questions: "Who am I *to* Christ (new nurture)?" "Who am I *in* Christ (new nature)?"

In our current chapter, we're focusing on the first question: Who am I *to* Christ? What is God's heart toward me? What does He think of me? Does He love me? Like me? Want me? Enjoy me? Do I fit in? Have I made the grade, the cut? How can I enjoy who I am *to* Christ? How can I exalt God for His gracious love?

In our next chapter, we'll focus on the second question: Who am I *in* Christ? Am I just a forgiven sinner? Still a sinner? Or am I truly a saint? Has the "old man" actually been crucified with Christ? Am I righteous in God's eyes? How can I become who I am *in* Christ? How can I glorify God by reflecting His Son?

Some argue against any thoughts about ourselves. "Just think about Christ!" they urge. "Thinking about ourselves is humanistic, arrogant," they suggest. Paul doesn't think so. He tells us to think of ourselves with sober judgment (Romans 12:3). In context, he's saying that our renewed minds should think accurately about ourselves, about who we are *in* Christ and *to* Christ *by* Christ's grace. In fact, Paul prays that we would have renewed, enlightened minds about who we are *to* Christ.

> And I pray that you, being rooted and established in love, may have power, together with all the saints, to grasp (*katalabesthai*) how wide and long and high and deep is the love of Christ, and to know this love that surpasses knowledge—that you may be filled to the measure of all the fullness of God (Ephesians 3:17b-19).

Paul emphasizes the importance of Christians meeting together to enlighten one another to new covenant truth about our new nurture, new Sonship, new reconciliation, new relationship, new peace, new forgiveness, new acceptance, and new access. He wants us to grasp (*katalabesthai*) personally the relevance, significance, and application of our new nurture. "Grasp" means to comprehend, appropriate, possess, and make one's own. When I'm struggling with suffering, what difference does my new relationship to Christ make? When I'm struggling against sin, how does it matter that Christ's love for me is wider than east to west, longer than north to south, higher than the stars, and deeper than the galaxy?

Grasping and personalizing my reconciled relationship with Christ does not result in pride. It leads to praise. "To him be glory in the church and in Christ Jesus throughout all generations, for ever and ever! Amen" (Ephesians 3:21). Applying God's new covenant nurturing love does not result in arrogance. It results in Christ-confidence and Christ-competence. That's the glory of new covenant Christianity and the joy of new covenant ministry.

> Such confidence as this is ours through Christ before God. Not that we are competent in ourselves to claim anything for ourselves, but our competence comes from God. He has made us competent as ministers of a new covenant—not of the letter but of the Spirit; for the letter kills, but the Spirit gives life (2 Corinthians 3:4-6).

Christ wants us to enjoy who we are *to* Him so that we can glorify Him eternally and minister for Him powerfully.

Who We are *to* Christ

Who are we *to* Christ? What is God's heart toward us now? How does He feel about us? What are His thoughts toward us? Box 22:1 summarizes New Testament answers to these vital questions about who we are *to* Christ by grace.

For your Christian walk, meditate on these passages, read them, memorize them, and apply them. In your spiritual friendship ministry to people tempted by False Seducer to doubt Father's love for them, encourage your friends to meditate on, read, memorize, and apply these passages.

Luther, the master pastor, urged his people, when assailed by Devilish doubts about God's love (our new nurture), to cling to the Word.

> Therefore, whenever any one is assailed by temptation of any sort whatever, the very best that he can do in the case is either to read something in the Holy Scriptures, or think about the Word of God, and apply it to his heart. The Word of God heals and restores again health to the mind and heart of man when wounded by the arrows of the Devil (A. Nebe, *Luther As Spiritual Advisor*, p. 178).

When Luther spoke of "temptation," he used the German word we examined in our study of biblical sufferology—*anfechtungen*. These are spiritual temptations to doubt God's love for us, temptations, once succumbed to that result in spiritual depression and spiritual separation anxiety. Listen to Luther's words about the Scriptures' power to assure us of our acceptance in Christ.

> Christ heals people by means of his precious Word, as he also declares in the 50th chapter of Isaiah (verse 4): "The Lord hath given me a learned tongue, that I should know how to speak a word in season to the weary." St. Paul also teaches likewise, in Romans xv 14, that we should obtain and strengthen hope from the comfort of the Holy Scriptures, which the Devil endeavors to tear out of people's hearts in times of temptations (*anfechtungen*). Accordingly, as there is no better or more powerful remedy in temptations (*anfechtungen*) than to diligently read and heed the Word of God (Nebe, *Luther As Spiritual Advisor*, p. 179).

Wanted

Perhaps you're not moved by this left-brained, analytical defense of our new nurture. Perhaps some right-brained, imaginative descriptions might help.

Once upon a time, a gaggle of toys banded together to form a home they called "Misfit Island." As their choice of a homeland name suggests, they felt unwanted.

Box 22:1

Who I Am *To* Christ

- Matthew 6:26—I am very valuable to Christ.
- Matthew 9:2; Mark 2:5—I am Father's forgiven son/daughter.
- Matthew 9:36-38—I am the Good Shepherd's shepherded sheep.
- Matthew 10:31; Luke 12:7—I am of great worth to Father.
- Matthew 12:12—I am of much value to Christ.
- Matthew 18:10-14—I am Father's precious, protected little one.
- Mark 3:34-35—I am Christ's brother or sister.
- Luke 6:35—I am a son or daughter of the Most High God.
- Luke 12:4—I am Christ's friend.
- Luke 20:36; John 1:12; Romans 8:14-17; 1 John 3:2—I am a child of God.
- John 1:13—I am a child born of God.
- John 3:6—I am born of the Spirit.
- John 3:16—I am so loved by Father that He gave His only begotten Son to die for me so I could live with Him forever.
- John 8:35—I am Father's forever son/daughter.
- John 10:28-30—I am eternally secure in God's holy love.
- John 13:33—Father says of me, "You are my child."
- John 15:5—I am a branch abiding in Christ the Vine.
- John 15:9—Jesus says of me, "As Father has loved me, so I have loved you."
- John 15:14—Jesus says to me, "You are my friend."
- John 15:15—Jesus says to me, "I no longer call you servant, but friend."
- John 16:27—Jesus whispers to me, "The Father himself loves you."
- John 17:23—Jesus says of me, "The Father loves you as he loves me."
- Acts 10:43—My sins are forgiven.
- Acts 20:28—I am Christ's flock.
- Acts 20:28; 1 Corinthians 1:2—Together with all the saints, I am God's Church.
- Romans 1:7—I am loved by God.
- Romans 4:7-8—My transgressions are forgiven and my sins covered.
- Romans 5:1; Ephesians 2:14-17; Colossians 1:20-22—I have peace with God.
- Romans 5:2; Ephesians 2:18—I have full, free, confident, bold access to God.
- Romans 5:5—God poured out his love into my heart.
- Romans 5:6-8—God demonstrated His love for me in that while I was yet a sinner, Christ died for me.
- Romans 5:9—I am saved, delivered from wrath.
- Romans 5:10-11; Colossians 1:20—I am reconciled to God.
- Romans 8:1, 33-34—I will never be condemned because I am in Christ Jesus.
- Romans 8:14—I am among those called, "sons of God."
- Romans 8:15; Galatians 4:6—I have received the Spirit of sonship so I can cry, "Abba, Daddy."

- Romans 8:17; Galatians 4:7; Ephesians 3:6; Titus 3:7—I am an heir of God.
- Romans 8:17—I am a joint-heir with Jesus.
- Romans 8:23—I am adopted into Father's forever family.
- Romans 8:31—God is for me, never against me.
- Romans 8:37-39—Nothing, nor anyone, anywhere can ever separate me from God's love for me in Christ.
- Romans 9:25—Along with all Christians, God says of me, "You are my people."
- Romans 9:25—God says of me, "You are my loved one."
- Romans 9:26—I am a son of the living God.
- Romans 10:11—I will never be put to shame.
- Romans 11:5—I am chosen by grace.
- Romans 14:3—I am accepted by God.
- Romans 15:7—I am accepted by Christ.
- Romans 15:16—I am an offering acceptable to God, sanctified by the Holy Spirit.
- 1 Corinthians 1:9-10—I am called into intimate fellowship with the Son.
- 1 Corinthians 12:27; Ephesians 4:12; 5:23—Together with all the saints, I am the body of Christ.
- 2 Corinthians 1:22—I am sealed by the Spirit, secure in Father's forever love.
- 2 Corinthians 5:5; Ephesians 1:14—I am indwelt by the Holy Spirit, guaranteed my eternal inheritance as a member of God's family.
- 2 Corinthians 5:18-19—I am reconciled to the Father by the Son and my sins will never be counted against me.
- 2 Corinthians 6:18—Father says of me, "You will be my sons and daughters."
- 2 Corinthians 11:2—I am espoused to Worthy Groom as His pure virgin bride.
- Galatians 3:26; Galatians 4:6-7—I am an adult son/daughter of God.
- Galatians 3:27—I am baptized into Christ.
- Galatians 3:27—I am clothed with Christ.
- Galatians 3:28—Together with all believers, we are one in Christ.
- Galatians 3:29—I belong to Christ.
- Galatians 3:29—I am an heir of promise.
- Galatians 4:5—I have received the full rights of an adult son/daughter of God.
- Galatians 4:7, 31—I am no longer a slave, but a son or daughter.
- Galatians 4:28—I am a child of promise.
- Ephesians 1:4-6—I am accepted in the beloved.
- Ephesians 1:5—I was predestined to be adopted as God's son.
- Ephesians 1:7; Colossians 1:14—I am forgiven and redeemed.
- Ephesians 1:13—I have been included in Christ.
- Ephesians 1:13—I have been marked with the seal of the promised Holy Spirit.
- Ephesians 1:14—I am God's precious, treasured possession.
- Ephesians 2:10—I am God's poem, opus, epic, masterpiece.
- Ephesians 2:13—Once far away, Christ has brought me near to God.

- Ephesians 2:19—Together with all believers, I am a fellow citizen of God's kingdom.
- Ephesians 2:19—Together with all believers, I am a member of God's family.
- Ephesians 2:22—I am a dwelling in which God lives by His Spirit.
- Ephesians 3:6; 4:25; 5:30—Together with all the saints, I am a member of Christ's body.
- Ephesians 3:6—Together with all the saints, I share in the promise of Christ.
- Ephesians 3:12—I may approach God with freedom and confidence.
- Ephesians 3:18—God's love for me is wider than east and west, longer than north and south, higher than the stars, and deeper than the galaxy.
- Ephesians 3:19—I am filled with the fullness of God.
- Ephesians 4:12—Together with all God's children, I claim the title, "God's people."
- Ephesians 4:30—I am sealed by the Holy Spirit for the day of final redemption.
- Ephesians 5:1—I am a dearly loved child of God.
- Ephesians 5:2—Christ loves me.
- Ephesians 5:25—Together with all Christians, I am the church, loved so much by Christ that He died for me.
- Ephesians 5:29—Christ nourishes me.
- Ephesians 5:29—Christ cherishes me.
- Ephesians 5:31-32—Together with all the saints, I am one with Christ.
- Colossians 1:21-22—Once alienated from God, Christ has reconciled me to God.
- Colossians 1:22—I am free from accusation.
- Colossians 3:12—I am one of God's chosen people.
- Colossians 3:12—I am dearly loved by Christ.
- Colossians 3:13—I am forgiven by Christ.
- 1 Thessalonians 1:4; 2 Thessalonians 2:13—Together with all the saints, we are brothers and sisters loved by God.
- 1 Thessalonians 1:4—I am chosen by God.
- 2 Thessalonians 2:13—I was chosen to be saved.
- 2 Thessalonians 2:16—I am loved by God the Father and the Lord Jesus Christ.
- Hebrews 2:12—Together with all believers, Christ calls me, "My brothers."
- Hebrews 3:1—Together with all believers, I am a holy brother/sister.
- Hebrews 4:16—I may approach the throne of grace with confidence.
- Hebrews 7:19—I have been drawn near to God.
- Hebrews 8:12—Father has forgiven my wickedness and remembers my sin no more.
- Hebrews 9:6-14—I have a cleansed conscience: shalom.
- Hebrews 9:15—I am guaranteed an eternal inheritance in Father's family.
- Hebrews 9:26—My sins have been done away with forever.
- Hebrews 10:2—I no longer have to feel guilty because I am cleansed once for all.

- ♦ Hebrews 10:17—My sins and lawless acts God remembers no more.
- ♦ Hebrews 10:19—I have confidence to enter the most holy place of God's holy presence.
- ♦ Hebrews 10:22—I can draw near to God with a sincere heart in full assurance, having been cleansed of a guilty conscience.
- ♦ 1 Peter 2:6—I will never be put to shame.
- ♦ 1 Peter 3:18—Christ has brought me face-to-face with God.
- ♦ 1 Peter 3:21—I have a good, clear conscience before God.
- ♦ 1 John 3:1—God has lavished His love upon me.
- ♦ 1 John 3:1—How great is the love of God that He has called me, together with all Christians, "Children of God."
- ♦ 1 John 3:16—Christ loved me so much that He laid down His life for me.
- ♦ 1 John 4:9-11—Father showed His love for me by sending His Son to die for me.
- ♦ 1 John 4:17-18; 5:14—I have full confidence in approaching God's presence.
- ♦ Revelation 1:5—I am loved by Christ.
- ♦ Revelation 19:7—Together with all believers, I am the Bride of Christ.

There was the doll with the crinkled, matted, dirty blonde hair. "Ragamuffin" she named herself. Just a waif. Orphan Annie. Abandoned urchin. Homeless child.

And the plastic soldier with a missing arm, missing his weapon. "Legion," he called himself. Leprous, he saw himself. A pariah, he felt. Untouchable.

Then there was the stuffed doggie, the one with the scraggly hair and missing stuffings. "Stray" was her chosen name. Foundling. Not even wanted by Cruella Deville.

Their reluctant leader? A silly reindeer with a grotesque shining nose. "Dropout" the name he owned. Outcast he was from others. Castaway he lived. He came late to their island and seemingly by accident.

They all felt about as valuable as bumbling Gilligan. As desired as Dennis the Menace. As snotty-nosed as the Little Rascals. So they lived together as loners. In exile. Gypsies, tramps, and thieves. Hobos and derelicts. Vagabonds.

Then one day, and what a surprising day it was, they were visited. Visited by Man of Sorrows. Acquainted with their grief, he had no beauty or majesty to attract them. Nothing in his appearance that they should desire him. He, too, was despised and rejected. Like one from whom people hide their faces. Despised and esteemed not.

It was Dropout, the shining-nosed reindeer who first noticed. Perhaps his bulbous snoot enlightened him to see what others missed. He saw Man of Sorrows' wounds. He was pierced. Like a lamb led to the slaughter and as a sheep before his shearers.

Man of Sorrows had their undivided attention. "Toy Maker sent me."

They gasped. Few even remembered Toy Maker. Those who did were sure he had forgotten them. Worse yet, abandoned them. Disliked them.

"I am stricken by Toy Maker. Smitten by him. Afflicted. For you."

"What!" they responded incredulously. "How is this possible? For *us*? Who does anything *for us*?"

"The One who is *for you*," answered Man of Sorrows. He crushed me for your iniquities. The punishment that brought you peace—shalom—He placed upon Me."

"Peace? Shalom?" They wondered. "Shalom—acceptance, access, approach to Toy Maker, clear conscience, wantability, desirability—these belong not to us."

"Silence!"

For the first time Man of Sorrows showed his teeth. "Would you denigrate so great salvation? Depreciate the price I paid? By My wounds you are healed. I was cut off that you might be grafted in. Cast away that you might be rescued. Made in the fashion of misfits that I might reconcile misfits to Toy Maker."

"Sing!" He urged them. "Burst into song, shout for joy! Do not hold back. Do not be afraid. You will never suffer shame. Do not fear disgrace, you will not be humiliated. For your Maker is your Husband. The Lord Almighty is His name. The Holy One is your Redeemer. For a brief moment you were abandoned, but with deep compassion Toy Maker calls you home. He has sworn never to be angry with you again, never to rebuke you again. He has promised, 'Though the mountains be shaken and the hills be removed, yet My unfailing love *for you* will not be shaken, nor My covenant of peace ever be removed. I want you.'"

Reconciled Relationships

Why does this matter? What is the importance of knowing who we are *to* Christ, of enjoying our new reconciled relationships? Remember False Seducer's scheme. He wants *unbelievers* to think they are *acceptable* to God, and he wants *believers* to think they are *unacceptable* to God.

Satan's a liar. A murderer. The accuser of the brethren. The last thing he wants is for brethren to feel like brethren. He wants us to feel like misfits, outcasts, ragamuffins, lepers, orphans. Satan hates Christians living out who they already are *to* and *in* Christ.

The Puritans countered False Seducer's schemes. The essence of their ministry involved showing the *unsaved* they were indeed *separated* from God, and showing the *saved* they were indeed *accepted* by God. Whereas False Seducer wants us to adjust to a fake identity, the Puritans understood that Christ wants us to adjust to our new, true identity.

Satan's false theology of personal identity is the first reason that reconciled relationships are so vital. Christ's loving theology of personal identity is the second reason. Recall that we are spiritual beings, social beings, *and* self-aware beings. Father molded us to have a sense of self, an awareness of our core being. Remember also that as self-aware beings, we have three sets of core identities:

- *Shalom Identity in Creation*: Adam and Eve accurately saw themselves as acceptable to God. Eve was comfortable in her femininity; Adam was confident in his masculinity. Together they were naked and shameless.
- *Shame Identity in the Fall*: All of Adam and Eve's descendants experience shame. Recognizing our nakedness, we hide because we fear rejection. We attempt to beautify ourselves by producing fig leaf coverings.
- *Sacred Identity in Redemption*: Reconciled to Father through Worthy Groom, we have peace with God. Again we can accurately see ourselves as acceptable to God. We can experience Christ-esteem, Christ-confidence, and Christ-competence.

Now we can contrast False Seducer's deceitful theology of personal identity with Worthy Groom's truthful theology of personal identity.

- The *Unbeliever's* Identity from *Satan*. Satan *Misidentifies* Unbelievers as:
  - Free Agents: Be Accountable Only to Yourself
  - Beautiful Brides: Produce Works of Self-Righteousness
  - Masters: Dominate Others
  - Equals: Be Like God

- The *Unbeliever's* Identity from *God*. God *Identifies* Unbelievers as:
  - Fallen Image Bearers: Corrupt, Chasm, Captive, Condemned
  - Adulterous Spouses: Filthy
  - Prodigal Sons: Guilty
  - Enemies: Hostile

- The *Believer's* Identity from *Satan*. Satan *Misidentifies* Believers as:
  - Self-Sufficient Agents: Become Acceptable to Father/Worthy Groom by Self-Effort
  - Separated Spouses: About to Be Divorced Because of Impurity
  - Disrespected Slaves: Unworthy to Be Called a Son
  - Distant Enemies: God is Upset and Angry with You

- The *Believer's* Identity from *God*. God *Identifies* Believers as:
  - Redeemed Image Bearers: Made Acceptable to Father by Worthy Groom through Grace
  - Virgin Brides: Beloved by Worthy Groom
  - Delighted in Sons: Celebrated by Forgiving Father
  - Best Friends: Encouraged by Indwelling Messenger

Redeemed Image Bearer: Made Acceptable to Father by Worthy Groom

Writing my doctoral dissertation was quite an experience. Having chosen to examine Martin Luther's pastoral counseling, I needed to communicate Christian concepts to my secular audience at Kent State University. At one point, one of my advisors urged me to provide a *one-word* definition of Luther's concept of justification. My choice? *Acceptance*. Luther taught that justification is our acceptance before God through faith in Christ.

Luther taught a corollary doctrine: sanctification is *the art of accepting our acceptance*. Alister McGrath explains Luther's view of life as a constant battleground between trusting our acceptance in Christ or despairing over possible rejection by Christ.

The Christian life is characterized by the unending tension between faith and experience. For Luther, experience can only stand in contradiction to faith, in that revealed truth must be revealed under its opposite form. This dialectic between experienced perception and hidden revelation inevitably leads to radical questioning and doubt on the part of the believer, as he finds himself unable to reconcile what he believes with what he experiences (McGrath, *Luther's Theology of the Cross*, pp. 168-169).

In other words, *life is bad, but God is good.* Experience smacks us down; False Seducer instills doubts.

Under these conditions, we find it difficult to accept our acceptance. Satan stops at nothing to keep us from who we are in Christ. "This, then, is the most furious and sudden of all attacks, in which the Devil exerts to the full extent of his powers and arts, and transforms himself into the likeness of the angry and ungracious God" (Nebe, *Luther As Spiritual Advisor*, p. 183). He falsely seduces us into believing that God no longer accepts us.

Failure to accept our acceptance was the gravest temptation Luther could imagine.

> By temptation of faith is meant that the evil conscience drives out of a person his confidence in the pardoning grace of God, and leads him to imagine that God is angry . . . The conscience places Moses upon the judgment-seat, and casts down the Savior of sinners from the throne of grace. He (Satan) says, "God is the enemy of sinners, you are a sinner, therefore, God is your enemy" (Nebe, *Luther As Spiritual Advisor*, pp. 189-190).

This was no mere theological debate or philosophical quagmire for Luther, nor is it for us. Failure to accept our acceptance in Christ is spiritual suicide that can lead to physical suicide.

> I have known many such, who, when very great and sudden temptations such as these have assailed them, did not understand the art of despising and casting out these thoughts, and in consequence lost their minds and became violently insane, when their minds had become too severely strained by these startling thoughts, took their own lives (Nebe, *Luther As Spiritual Advisor*, p. 187).

Luther taught that when we discover we are eternally accepted by God and have nothing to fear from God, we can face life's lesser fears. The ultimate resolution of all fears comes not by denying lesser fears, but by first facing our greatest fear—the fear that God is not my loving Father.

As we wait for the other shoe to drop, we realize it already dropped on Christ. As we wait for the hammer to fall, we realize it already fell on Christ. We are restored, and consequently we have peace with God.

Virgin Bride: Beloved by Worthy Groom

What is Christ's heart for me? I am His beloved and He is mine. The Cross forever answers all doubts about His heart's intent. Jesus forgives us and loves us. He woos us and pursues us. He likes us and wants us.

When tempted to believe otherwise, we can counter Satan's deception with Christ's Cross.

> For the spirit and the heart of man is not able to endure the thought of the wrath of God, as the Devil represents and urges it. Therefore, whatever thoughts the Devil awakens within us in temptation we should put away from us and cast out of our minds, so that we can see and hear nothing else than the kind, comforting word of the promise of Christ, and of the gracious will of the heavenly Father, who has

given his own Son for us, as Christ, our dear Lord, declares in John iii.16: "God so loved the world that he gave his only begotten Son, that whosoever believeth on him should not perish but have everlasting life." Everything else, now, which the Devil may suggest to us beyond this, that God the Father is reconciled to us, and graciously inclined to us, and merciful and powerful for the sake of his dear Son, we should cast out of our minds as wandering and unprofitable thoughts (Nebe, *Luther As Spiritual Advisor*, pp. 184-185).

Suffering tends to cause us to doubt God's goodness. Sin—our own personal sin—tends to cause us to doubt Worthy Groom's graciousness. "How could a Groom love an impure bride like me?" When such thoughts enter our minds, Luther encourages us to mock the Devil rather than debate him.

> When the Devil casts up to us our sin, and declares us worthy of death and hell, we must say: "I confess that I am worthy of death and hell. What more have you to say?" "Then you will be lost forever!" "Not in the least: for I know One who suffered for me and made satisfaction for my sins, and his name is Jesus Christ, the Son of God. So long as he shall live, I shall live also." Therefore treat the Devil thus: Spit on him, and say: "Have I sinned? Well, then I have sinned, and I am sorry; but I will not on that account despair, for Christ has borne and taken away all my sin, yes, and the sin of the whole world, if it will only confess its sin, reform and believe on Christ. What should I do if I had committed murder or adultery, or even crucified Christ? Why, even then, I should be forgiven, as he prayed on the cross: 'Father, forgive them' (Luke xxiii.34). This I am duty bound to believe. I have been acquitted. Then away with you, Devil!" (Nebe, *Luther As Spiritual Advisor*, pp. 213-214).

We can't separate our acquittal from our acceptance. If we're forgiven, we're accepted. Moreover, if we're accepted, we're accepted in the beloved, by the Beloved.

Delighted in Son/Daughter: Celebrated by Forgiving Father

And what is Father's heart toward you? You are a respected son or daughter celebrated by Forgiving Father.

When Luther's father lay near death and struggled with assurance, Luther told him, "Herewith I commend you to Him who loves you more than you love yourself" (Luther, *Luther's Works*, Vol. 49, p. 270). Since we know we all love, nourish, and cherish ourselves (Matthew 22:35-40; Ephesians 5:25-32), then we must be deeply loved, nourished, and cherished by our Forgiving Father who loves us more than we could ever love ourselves.

In teaching about how our Forgiving Father feels toward us, Luther echoes the words of Paul in Romans 8 about God's being for us.

> True faith draws forth the following conclusion: God is God for me because He speaks to me. He forgives my sins. He is not angry with me, just as He promises: "I am the Lord your God." Now search your heart, and ask whether you believe that God is your God, Father, Savior, and Deliverer, who wants to rescue you (Luther, *Luther's Works*, Vol. 4, p. 149).

We act as though someone had to twist God's arm, forcing Him to cry, "Uncle!" before He would submit to forgiving us. But if the Cross teaches us anything, it teaches us that God loves to forgive because He loves to love.

As we saw in the previous chapter, the parable of the prodigal son shows us the joy Father takes in forgiving us so that He can enjoy celebrating with us. God enjoys you. Do you believe it? Does it make a difference in your life? "God's friendship," Luther reminds us, "is a bigger comfort than that of the whole world" (Luther, *Luther's Works*, Vol. 49, p. 306). Father celebrates with us and over us. He likes us. Desires us. Wants to have fun with us. Delights in us.

Larry Crabb tells the story of an encounter that he experienced with author Brennan Manning.

> Several years earlier, Brennan had told me of his spiritual director's curious habit. Whenever he saw Brennan after an extended absence, he jumped up and down with delight.
>
> I remember smiling. I pictured an elderly gentleman walking down a deserted beach toward an agreed upon meeting point and, spotting Brennan from a distance, hopping three or four times. The image amused me. It also drew me.
>
> A year later, my wife Rachel and I tumbled out of a crowded elevator into a hotel lobby teeming with conference participants. Across the way, I caught a glimpse of Brennan's white hair and unmistakable smile. As I leaned toward Rachel to tell her I had just seen Brennan, he turned and saw us. Immediately, he jumped up and down. I was warmed to the bottom of my heart (Crabb, *Connecting*, p. 71).

Have you *ever* pictured Father greeting you like that? Do it now. Stop. Pause. Meditate. Envision. You're the forgiven prodigal, the accepted son, the celebrated child, the delighted-in-friend—of God. He sees you across the way. Wow! What a huge smile breaks forth across His face. Now what? He's jumping up and down. Gleeful. Dancing. Skipping. Delighted to see *you*.

Best Friend: Encouraged by Indwelling Messenger

In our new nurture *to* the Trinity we are Virgin Brides, beloved by our Worthy Groom, Delighted-in Sons, celebrated by our Forgiving Father, and we are Best Friends, encouraged by our Indwelling Messenger, our Inspiring Mentor—the Holy Spirit.

Having won our hearts, our Worthy Groom now is in heaven preparing our bridal suite. But He would never leave us alone. Never! His Best Man and our Best Friend is with us always. The Holy Spirit is not some impersonal force to use. He is our Indwelling Messenger to love, enjoy, and depend upon.

I once shared this material in a one-week marathon session meeting from 8:00 a.m. to 5:00 p.m. Monday through Friday. One of my students, Fred, had not taken a class of any type in more than thirty years. A bi-vocational pastor, he shepherds a small country church and drives a semi for a living. Encouraged to take the course by his daughter, he was reluctant. The first day of class he said he felt like a "fish out of water." At the end of the final class he commented that he felt like a "sponge in the water," wanting to soak up every word. While examining John 14-16 and its teaching on the Holy Spirit as our Counselor, Comforter, and Friend, Fred excitedly shared with the class, "I would do anything just to be called God's servant. But to think that He chooses to call me 'friend,' that He chooses to be my Friend; that's amazing grace!"

It is the indwelling Holy Spirit who testifies with our Spirit about our new nurture so that we can cry out, "Abba, Daddy." So we can say, "Best Friend!" Our Indwelling Messenger enlightens us so we can depend boldly upon our new relationship with the Sacred Trinity. It is our Inspiring Mentor who points us not to Himself but to Christ, not to the Best Man but to the Worthy Groom, saying of Christ:

> He is not the one who accuses or threatens us, but he reconciles and intercedes for us by his own death and by his shed blood for us, that we may not be afraid of him, but draw near to him with all confidence (Nebe, *Luther As Spiritual Advisor*, p. 236).

The Holy Spirit exalts our Forgiving Father, countering demonic doctrine, and teaching us freeing truth.

> The conscience, spurred by the Devil, the flesh, and the fallen world; says, "God is your enemy. Give up in despair." God, in His own Fatherly love and through His Son's grace and through His Word and through the witness of His Spirit and His people; says, "I have no wrath. You are accepted in the beloved. I am not angry with you. We are reconciled!" (Luther, *Luther's Works*, Vol. 16, p. 214).

Reckoning on Our New Nurture

Your core identity is Beloved Virgin Bride, Celebrated Son, and Best Friend. You are loved and lovely because of Christ, your Worthy Groom. You are delighted in and desired by your Forgiving Father. You are more than a conqueror through the Holy Spirit, your Indwelling Mentor/Inspiring Messenger.

Accept your acceptance. Enjoy your identity. Embrace who you are *to* God. How? By *renewing* your mind to your new core, sacred identity in Christ; by *reckoning* on your new, core sacred identity in Christ; and by *re-igniting*/fanning into flame your new core, sacred identity in Christ.

Mindset *renewal* unites truth, grace, and faith. By faith we believe and live according to the truth of our new nurture, continually reminding ourselves that God's love for us is by grace, not by works. Therefore, we know nothing we do can ever cause God to love us more or love us less.

We renew our mindsets through the individual and corporate spiritual disciplines. Individually, we renew our minds by meditating on what the Word says about who we are *to* Christ. We memorize, apply, and appropriate verses such as those summarized in Box 22:1.

Remember also what Paul told us in Ephesians 3. We grasp new covenant truth *together with all the saints*. We need one another. We need spiritual friends, small group fellowship, Bible teaching, and biblical preaching that emphasize who we are *to* Christ—corporate spiritual disciplines.

We *reckon* on our new core, sacred identity by actively disputing False Seducer's lies. They come to us during suffering or when others sin against us, tempting us to doubt

Father's goodness. They come to us when we sin against God and others, tempting us to doubt Worthy Groom's graciousness.

When we find ourselves on the battlefield between faith and doubt, we must put off Satan's lies about our primary identity. We must counter his misidentification of us as self-sufficient agents, separated spouses, disrespected slaves, and distant enemies. When these sentences run through our minds and ruin our peace, we ask questions like: "Where was I recruited into this belief about who I am to God? What Scripture(s) can I ponder to counter these lies? When have I defeated these lies before? How did I cooperate with God's Spirit to defeat these lies? To whom can I go who is a wise spiritual friend who can help me counter these lies?"

Having battled to put off these lies, we have fought only half the conflict. Now we need to put on the truth through probing questions such as: "Who am I to my Worthy Groom? Who am I to my Forgiving Father? Who am I to my Indwelling Mentor? What passages can I turn to to appropriate these truths? If I believed my new nurture in Christ right now, how would I be relating, thinking, acting, and feeling differently? To whom can I go who as a wise spiritual friend can help me incorporate these truths?"

Renewal, reckoning, and *re-igniting* are the three aspects of living out our new covenant new nurture. As Paul said to Timothy, so we need to say to each other:

> I remind you to fan into flame the gift of God, which is in you through the laying on of my hands. For God did not give us a spirit of timidity, but a spirit of power, of love and of self-discipline [wisdom] (2 Timothy 1:6-7).

We have done nothing to deserve being forgiven, accepted, loved, delighted in, or befriended. It is of grace. Yet it is by faith. It's in there. Inside us. Our new nurture is a fact, a reality. Our new relationship to God is real, actual. By faith we need to stir it up. Magnify it. We do this by making personal the promises of God. Then we specifically apply those promises.

- ◆ Who am *I to* my Worthy Groom? How is He showing *me* that He loves me? When have I experienced His love? What is it like when I sense intimacy with Christ? In what ways does He nourish and cherish me? How can I cooperate with Him to stir up and live out my acceptance in the beloved? How can I magnify Christ for loving me? How can I help others to sense and stir up their acceptance in Christ?

- ◆ Who am *I to* my Forgiving Father? When has He celebrated with me? How do I sense Him delighting in me? What would it be like to see Him jumping up and down with delight to see me? When have I sensed this before? How did that happen? How did I respond? How can I cooperate with God to enjoy more of the same? How can I exalt God for enjoying me? How can I fan into flame my spiritual friends' awareness of how much Father delights in them?

- ◆ Who am *I to* my Inspiring Mentor? When has the Holy Spirit helped me apply the truth that He is my strong Best Friend? How did that happen? How did I react? How can I cooperate with my Indwelling Messenger to experience more of the same? How can I glorify the Spirit for befriending me? How can I re-ignite in others their awareness that the Spirit is their Best Friend?

Where We've Been and Where We're Heading

To the degree that I appropriate the truths of my new covenant new nurture, I will be "un-Adam-like." I will not be ashamed or fearful. I will not run, hide, and cover up.

Instead, I will approach the throne of grace confidently, boldly accepting my acceptance. I will act on my access to God and draw near to Him in full assurance of faith. I'll experience intimacy—a taste of heaven now.

That's my new *nurture*. But that's not all I receive by the new covenant. I also receive a new *nature*. I'm not only a Son (new nurture); I'm a Saint (new nature). I not only enjoy who I am *to* Christ; I become who I am *in* Christ.

So stick around for Scene IV: Cleansing Springs—Our New Nature *in* Christ. Witness new creations. Marvel at Sinners turned into Saints, and Whores transformed into Virgins. For sanctification not only means accepting our acceptance, it also includes being who we already are *in* Christ.

Caring for Your Soul: Personal Applications

1. Of the verses and images in Box 22:1, which ones "grab you" the most? Why? How?

2. *The key to your victory is your faith in your new identity.* You are no longer a sinner in the hands of an angry God. You are now and forever a saint in the palms of your loving Father. What difference will this make:

   a. In how you relate to God?

   b. In how you relate to others?

   c. In how you see yourself, think about yourself, and feel about yourself?

3. What is God's heart toward you?

   a. Describe it personally and specifically.

   b. Write a Praise Psalm to God based upon His heart for you.

4. How would your life be different if you consistently accepted your acceptance in Christ?

Caring for Others: Ministry Implications

♦ **Empower Your Counselees by Helping Them Reckon on Their New Identity in Christ:** Counter Satan's shaming narrative with the truth of who your spiritual friends are in Christ.

♦ **Enlighten Your Counselees by Helping Them Renew Their Minds to Their New Primary Identity in Christ:** Teach them to put off, to cast off, the strongholds of Satan. Teach them how to disabuse themselves of his condemning images. Then teach them how to put on Christ's new images. Make them scriptural and specific. Then trialogue about how to love others on the basis of their renewed minds. Focus on their renewed relationship to God: son, daughter, bride, soldier, athlete, ambassador. Focus on their renewed relationships to others: brother, sister, co-worker, fellow-laborer, servant, spiritual friend, encourager. Focus on their renewed relationship to themselves. They can be comfortable in their femininity. They can be confident in their masculinity. They can experience a clear conscience.

♦ **Empower Your Counselees by Helping Them Stir Up Their New Identity in Christ:** Paul informed Timothy that he had not been given the spirit of timidity, but the spirit of power, love, and wisdom. He told him to stir up, or fan into flame, these new capacities. Then he urged him to live differently, based on the new "you." Do the same with your spiritual friends. Don't settle for conceptual counseling. Move from mental change to relational change, from renewed minds to renewed affections.

CHAPTER TWENTY-THREE

VIRGIN BRIDE'S NEW NATURE: CLEANSING SPRINGS

> "So that the old man, conceived and born in sin, is there drowned, and a new man, born in grace, comes forth and rises. In this washing a person is born again and made new. Sins are drowned in baptism, and in the place of sin, righteousness comes forth" (Martin Luther, *Luther's Works*, Vol. 35, p. 30).
>
> "Our present task is to be what we are" (J. I. Packer, *Rediscovering Holiness*, p. 55).
>
> "The regenerating work of the Spirit has so changed our nature that our heart's deepest desire (the dominant passion that rules and drives us now) is a copy, faint but real, of the desire that drove our Lord Jesus" (J. I. Packer, *Rediscovering Holiness*, p. 84).

Extreme Makeover

Once upon a time there lived a beautiful Swan. Swan reflected the Creator, related lovingly, ruled humbly over Swandom, and rested contentedly.

Until Swan ate poisoned Swan food. Then everything changed. Swan's beauty corrupted, love became a chasm of distance, rule turned to captivity, and rest disintegrated into shameful condemnation.

Until the Great Swan Prince restored order. Then Swan changed again. A new creation. Re-created. Regenerated. Reconciled. Redeemed. Justified.

Only Swan still swam like an ugly duckling. Thought like an ugly duckling. Quacked like an off-key duckling.

Once, Swan saw Swan's reflection mirrored in Swan Lake. Startled, Swan was confused. The reflection seemed to reflect a titanic change—change for the good, for the best, forever.

"No. Can't be," Swan reflected. "I'm just an ugly duckling saved by grace. I'm not perfect, just forgiven. Changes are occurring, but no drastic inner change has already occurred. Must be something wrong with this water reflecting a distorted image of me. Must be something wrong with how I see myself. Too arrogant."

So Swan returned to Duckyville. Yielded again to Ugly-Duckling Theology, to Worm Theology. Living as if still corrupt.

Swan actually felt quite smug in Duckyville. "I know who I am. Sinner Swan. No arrogance in me. Forget about myself. Don't think highly of myself. Wretched Swan that I am."

Until Ambassador Swan arrived to represent Creator. "Hear ye! Hear ye! I have come to preach the good news of regeneration and redemption." Ambassador's message struck a chord with Swan. Reminded Swan of that silly second when his reflection seemed to indicate that real change had already occurred.

Preaching regeneration, Ambassador said, "You're a new creation. Created in my image. You have a new nature. A saint you are—Saint Swan. A new you exists. New purity. New capacities. New righteous gowns. New life. Restoration. New nature."

"But, but, but," sputtered Swan. "Saint? I thought I was a sinner."

"Was is right," Ambassador concurred. "But you are a saint now."

"Not only that," Ambassador continued, "you're also salt, light, wise, righteous, noble, good, holy, blameless, without spot or wrinkle or any other blemish. You are dead to sin, buried with Christ, your old Swan crucified with Christ. United with Christ, raised with Christ, and alive to Creator."

Preaching redemption, Ambassador shared, "You're free from sin. You have victory over sin. New power to live holy because you are holy. New inclination to love because you have been renewed in the image of the One who is Love."

"But, but, but," stammered Swan. "Free? I thought I was a slave."

"Was is right," Ambassador concurred. "But you are a free Swan now. Free to fly. Free to shepherd. Free to rule. Free to empower. Free to enjoy victory over sin. Freed from sin's power. Emancipated."

New Covenant Counseling

Too much Christian counseling is old covenant counseling. We counsel Christians as though they are still pre-Christians. We counsel saints as though they are still sinners. We counsel as though we are still under the old covenant of law and not the new covenant of grace through which we enjoy our new *nurture* and our new *nature*.

Too much Christian living is old covenant living. We consume ourselves with trying to *become* what we already are, while our present task, as Packer reminds us, is to *be* what we already are.

Our new covenant salvation in Christ implants within us a new nature. We are cleansed. Sanctification does not involve making ourselves saints, but living out our sainthood. As we introduced last chapter, the key to our victory is our faith in our new identity. In this chapter, we're focusing on identity questions like: "Who am I *in* Christ? Am I just a forgiven sinner? Still a sinner? Or am I truly a saint? Has the 'old man' actually been crucified with Christ? Am I righteous in God's eyes? How can I become who I am *in* Christ? How can I glorify Father by reflecting his Son?"

Box 23:1 summarizes New Testament answers to these vital questions. For your Christian walk, meditate on these passages, read them, memorize them, and apply them. In your spiritual friendship ministry to people tempted by False Seducer to doubt Christ's resurrection power within them, encourage your friends to meditate on, read, memorize, and apply the passages found on these pages.

Box 23:1

Who I Am *In* Christ

- Matthew 4:19; Mark 1:17—I am a fisher of men.
- Matthew 5:13—I am the salt of the earth.
- Matthew 5:14—I am the light of the world.
- Matthew 28:19; Luke 14:27; John 8:31; 13:35; 15:8; Acts 6:1, 7; 11:25-26, 29; 14:20-22; 16:1—I am a disciple of Christ.
- Luke 24:48; Acts 1:8—I am Christ's witness.
- John 3:16-18; 10:28-29; 17:3; Romans 5:21; 6:23; 1 John 5:11—I have eternal life in Christ.
- John 8:32, 36—I am set free from sin in Christ.
- John 10:10—I have abundant life in Christ.
- John 14:26; 16:13—I have been taught all things by the Holy Spirit.
- John 14:27; 16:33—I have peace in Christ.
- John 15:3—I am clean in Christ.
- John 15:4, 5, 8, 16; Romans 7:4—I can bear much lasting fruit in Christ.
- John 15:5—I am a branch abiding in Christ the Vine.
- John 15:11—My joy is complete in Christ.
- John 16:33—I have overcome the world in Christ.
- John 17:16—I am not of this world.
- Acts 2:44; 4:32—I am a believer.
- Acts 5:20—I have new life in Christ.
- Acts 8:3; 2 Corinthians 1:1—Together with all the saints, I am God's Church.
- Acts 11:26—I am a Christian, a little Christ.
- Acts 13:39; Romans 3:24, 26, 28, 30; 4:25; 5:1, 9, 18; 10:10; 1 Corinthians 6:11; Titus 3:7—I am justified freely and fully.
- Acts 20:32; 1 Corinthians 6:11—I am sanctified.
- Romans 1:6—I am called to belong to Christ.
- Romans 1:7; 1 Corinthians 6:1, 2; 2 Corinthians 1:1; Ephesians 1:1; Philippians 1:1; 4:21, 22; Philemon 4; Jude 3—I am a saint.
- Romans 3:24; 1 Corinthians 1:30; Ephesians 1:7; Colossians 1:14—I am redeemed in Christ.
- Romans 3:21-26; 4:3, 5, 6, 9, 22, 23, 24; 5:17, 19; 1 Corinthians 1:30; 2 Corinthians 3:9—I have been credited with Christ's righteousness.
- Romans 5:17—I am a recipient of God's abundant provision of grace.
- Romans 5:18—I have new life in Christ.
- Romans 6:2—I am dead to sin.
- Romans 6:3—I am baptized into Christ's death.
- Romans 6:4—I am buried with Christ in His death to and over sin.
- Romans 6:4—I have been raised to new life in Christ.
- Romans 6:5—I am united with Christ in His resurrection.
- Romans 6:6—My old self is crucified with Christ.

- Romans 6:6—My body of sin has been done away with.
- Romans 6:6—I am no longer sin's slave.
- Romans 6:7—I have been freed from sin in Christ.
- Romans 6:8—I died with Christ to sin.
- Romans 6:8—I live with Christ.
- Romans 6:11—I am dead to sin.
- Romans 6:11—I am alive to God.
- Romans 6:13—I have been brought from spiritual death to spiritual life.
- Romans 6:14—Sin shall not be my master.
- Romans 6:14—I am not under law, but under grace.
- Romans 6:18, 22—I have been set free from sin.
- Romans 6:19—I am a slave to righteousness, righteousness masters my being.
- Romans 6:22—I am a slave to God.
- Romans 7:4—I have died to the law.
- Romans 7:6—I serve Christ in the new way of the Spirit.
- Romans 7:22—My inner being delights in God's law—His holy standards.
- Romans 7:25—In my innermost mind, I am a slave to God's law.
- Romans 8:1—I will never suffer condemnation because I am in Christ.
- Romans 8:2—I am set free from the law of sin and death in Christ.
- Romans 8:4—I have met the righteous requirements of the law in Christ.
- Romans 8:5—My mindset is on spiritual affections and passions.
- Romans 8:9—I am not controlled by the flesh, but I am controlled by the Spirit.
- Romans 8:29—I am predestined to be conformed to the image of the Son.
- Romans 8:37—I am more than a conqueror in Christ.
- Romans 9:23—I have been prepared in advance by God to be glorious.
- Romans 10:9, 10, 13—I am saved in Christ.
- Romans 15:14—I am full of goodness in Christ.
- Romans 15:14—I am complete in knowledge in Christ.
- Romans 15:14—I am competent to disciple others in Christ.
- Romans 15:16—I am sanctified by the Holy Spirit.
- Romans 15:16—I am acceptable to God in Christ.
- 1 Corinthians 1:2—I am sanctified in Christ Jesus.
- 1 Corinthians 1:2; Ephesians 5:26; Colossians 3:12—I am holy in Christ.
- 1 Corinthians 1:8—I am blameless in Christ.
- 1 Corinthians 1:30—I am wise in Christ.
- 1 Corinthians 1:30—I am holiness to God in Christ.
- 1 Corinthians 2:16—I have the mind of Christ.
- 1 Corinthians 3:9—I am God's fellow worker.
- 1 Corinthians 3:9—I am God's field.
- 1 Corinthians 3:9—I am God's building.
- 1 Corinthians 3:16-17; 2 Corinthians 6:16—I am God's sacred temple.
- 1 Corinthians 6:11—I am washed in Christ.

- 1 Corinthians 6:19—I am the temple of the Holy Spirit.
- 1 Corinthians 6:20—I have been bought and redeemed with a price.
- 2 Corinthians 2:14—Christ always leads me in a triumphal victory march.
- 2 Corinthians 3:6—I am a competent minister of the new covenant in Christ.
- 2 Corinthians 3:10—In Christ I have surpassing, lasting glory.
- 2 Corinthians 3:18—I am a growing reflection of the Lord's glory.
- 2 Corinthians 3:18—I am increasingly being transformed into Christ's likeness.
- 2 Corinthians 4:16—I am being renewed inwardly day by day in Christ.
- 2 Corinthians 5:17—I am a new creation in Christ.
- 2 Corinthians 5:18—I am a minister of reconciliation.
- 2 Corinthians 5:20—I am Christ's ambassador.
- 2 Corinthians 5:21—I have the righteousness of God in Christ.
- 2 Corinthians 8:9—I am spiritually rich in Christ.
- 2 Corinthians 11:2—I am Christ's spiritually pure virgin.
- Galatians 1:4—I have been rescued from this present evil age.
- Galatians 2:20—I am crucified with Christ.
- Galatians 3:13-14—I am redeemed from the curse.
- Galatians 6:1—I am spiritual in Christ.
- Ephesians 1:1—I am faithful in Christ.
- Ephesians 1:4—I have been chosen to be holy in Christ.
- Ephesians 1:4—I have been chosen to be blameless in Christ.
- Ephesians 1:17-19—I have God's resurrection power actively working in me.
- Ephesians 2:5—I am alive with Christ.
- Ephesians 2:5, 8—I am saved by grace.
- Ephesians 2:6—I have been raised up with Christ.
- Ephesians 2:6—I am seated with Christ in the heavenly realms.
- Ephesians 2:10 – I am Christ's workmanship, His opus, His poem, His masterpiece.
- Ephesians 2:10—I was prepared in advance in Christ Jesus to do good works.
- Ephesians 2:15—Together with all the saints, I am a new person in Christ.
- Ephesians 2:21—Along with all the saints, I am God's holy temple.
- Ephesians 2:22—I am a dwelling in which God lives by His Spirit.
- Ephesians 3:16—I am strengthened with power through God's Spirit.
- Ephesians 3:17—Christ dwells in my heart.
- Ephesians 3:17—I am rooted and established in love.
- Ephesians 3:18—I have power to grasp God's great love for me in Christ.
- Ephesians 3:19—I am filled to the measure of all the fullness of God in Christ.
- Ephesians 3:20—Christ's immeasurable resurrection power is at work within me.
- Ephesians 4:13—I am maturing to the full measure of the fullness of Christ.
- Ephesians 4:22—My old self is put off in Christ.
- Ephesians 4:23—I have been made new in the attitude of my mind in Christ.

- Ephesians 4:24—My new self is put on in Christ.
- Ephesians 4:24—I am created to be like God in true righteousness and holiness.
- Ephesians 5:8—I am now light in the Lord.
- Ephesians 5:9—The fruit of my life is goodness, righteousness, and truth.
- Ephesians 5:26—I am cleansed in Christ
- Ephesians 5:26—I am washed in Christ.
- Ephesians 5:27—Together with the Bride of Christ, I am presentable, radiant, without stain or wrinkle or any other blemish, but holy and blameless.
- Philippians 2:1—I am united with Christ.
- Philippians 2:1—I am in fellowship with the Holy Spirit.
- Philippians 2:13—God works in me to accomplish His good purposes.
- Philippians 2:15—I am blameless and pure, a child of God without fault.
- Philippians 2:15—I shine like the stars in the universe in Christ.
- Philippians 3:9—I have a righteousness that comes from faith in Christ.
- Philippians 3:10—Christ's resurrection power conforms me to His image.
- Philippians 3:20—My citizenship is in heaven.
- Philippians 4:13—I can do all things through Christ who strengthens me.
- Philippians 4:19—God meets all my needs through His riches in Christ Jesus.
- Colossians 1:2—I am a holy and faithful brother/sister in Christ.
- Colossians 1:12—I am qualified to share in the inheritance of the saints.
- Colossians 1:13—I have been rescued from the dominion of darkness.
- Colossians 1:13—I have been transported into the kingdom of God's beloved Son.
- Colossians 1:22—I am holy in God's sight, without blemish, and free from accusation.
- Colossians 2:10—I have been given fullness in Christ.
- Colossians 2:11—My old sinful nature/man/self/person has been put off.
- Colossians 2:12—I have been buried with Christ in baptism.
- Colossians 2:12—I have been raised with Christ from the dead.
- Colossians 2:13—God made me alive with Christ.
- Colossians 2:14-15—In Christ, sin is defeated and disarmed in my life.
- Colossians 2:20—I died with Christ to the world.
- Colossians 3:1—I have been raised with Christ.
- Colossians 3:3—I died with Christ.
- Colossians 3:3—My life is now hidden with Christ in God.
- Colossians 3:9—I have taken off the old self with its practices.
- Colossians 3:10—I have put on the new self in Christ.
- Colossians 3:10—The new me in Christ is being renewed in knowledge in the image of the Creator.
- 1 Thessalonians 3:13—I am blameless and holy before God's presence.
- 1 Thessalonians 5:23—God is sanctifying me through and through.
- 1 Thessalonians 5:23—God keeps my whole spirit, soul, and body blameless.
- 2 Thessalonians 2:14—I am called to share in the glory of the Lord Jesus Christ.

- 2 Timothy 1:7—God placed within me His spirit of power, love, and wisdom.
- 2 Timothy 2:3-4—I am a good soldier in Jesus Christ.
- 2 Timothy 2:5—I am a victorious athlete in Jesus Christ.
- 2 Timothy 2:6—I am a disciplined, hard working farmer in Jesus Christ.
- Titus 3:5—I am saved, washed, re-birthed, and renewed in Christ and by the Spirit.
- Hebrews 1:3—I am purified from sin in and by Christ.
- Hebrews 2:10—I am brought to glory in and by Christ.
- Hebrews 2:11—I am made holy in and by Christ.
- Hebrews 7:25—I am saved completely.
- Hebrews 8:10; 10:16—God's law is in my mind, written on my heart.
- Hebrews 9:12—I have eternal redemption in Christ.
- Hebrews 9:14—My conscience is cleansed in Christ.
- Hebrews 9:15—I am set free from sin in Christ.
- Hebrews 9:26-27—My sins are done away with and taken away in and by Christ.
- Hebrews 10:2—I am cleansed once for all, guiltless in Christ.
- Hebrews 10:10—I have been made holy once for all by Christ's sacrifice.
- Hebrews 10:14—I have been made perfect forever in and by Christ.
- Hebrews 10:22—I am cleansed and washed in Christ.
- 1 Peter 1:3—I am born again, given new birth in Christ.
- 1 Peter 1:18-19—I am redeemed from my old empty way of life by Christ's precious blood.
- 1 Peter 1:22—I am purified by faith in Christ.
- 1 Peter 1:23—I have been born again of imperishable seed.
- 1 Peter 2:5—I am a living stone, being built into a spiritual house.
- 1 Peter 2:5—Along with all the saints, I am a holy priesthood.
- 1 Peter 2:9—Along with all the saints, I am a chosen people.
- 1 Peter 2:9—Along with all the saints, I am a member of a royal priesthood.
- 1 Peter 2:9—Along with all the saints, I am a citizen of a holy nation.
- 1 Peter 2:9-10—Along with all the saints, I am a people belonging to God.
- 1 Peter 2:9—I am called out of darkness into Christ's wonderful light.
- 2 Peter 1:3—God's Divine power has given me everything I need for life and godliness.
- 2 Peter 1:4—Through God's great and precious promises I participate in the Divine nature.
- 2 Peter 1:4—Through God's great and precious promises I have escaped the corruption in the world caused by evil desires.
- 1 John 2:20—I have an anointing from the Holy One and I know the truth.
- 1 John 4:4—I have overcome the world, the flesh, and the Devil because greater is He who is in me, than he who is in the world.
- 1 John 4:4, 6—I am from God.
- 1 John 4:7; 5:1—I am born of God.
- 1 John 5:4-5—Born of God, I overcome the world by faith in Christ.

◆ Jude 24—I stand before God's glorious presence without fault and with great joy.
◆ Revelation 1:5—I am freed from my sins by Christ's blood.
◆ Revelation 1:6—God has made me, together with all the saints, a kingdom of priests.
◆ Revelation 19:7-8, 14—Along with all the saints, I am the pure Bride of Christ, clean, white, and righteous.

False Seducer slams you with lies like, "Who are you kidding? You're not a saint!" "Who is Kellemen trying to fool? You Christians are all just a bunch of ugly duckling sinners." When so slammed, slam back. "Thus saith the Word." These passages summarize what the Word says about *you*. About who you are *in* Christ. Don't believe me. Do believe God.

Perhaps you're thinking, "But Box 23:1 might be one-sided. I could outline a longer list that shows the negative side of who Christians still are." I don't think so. I'm not teaching that the Word says we are perfect. And in chapters 25 through 27 I will show that there is a biblical process of growth in grace. Furthermore, the issue is, "Who are we *in* Christ?" According to Christ, what is the believer's basic nature? That is what Box 23:1 addresses. Though you might be able to chart a partial page of ways in which new covenant saints sin, you would not be able to chart a line about new covenant saints being sinners, fallen, under the law, powerless, ugly, or desperately wicked. Box 23:1 is what I uncovered as I read the entire New Testament asking one simple question: "According to the New Testament, who am I *in* Christ?"

Enjoy the nature of your new nature. Know, reckon, and yield based upon the new creature that you are right now in Christ.

The Vilest Offender

Imagine the vilest offender. As cruel as Hitler, as depraved as Manson, as corrupt as Jack the Ripper. Desperately wicked. Self-deceived. Anti-social. Amoral. Mr. Mass Murderer. The day his trial begins, every major news network, cable news station, news magazine, and newspaper in the country, and hundreds around the world, join the coverage.

Shocking every reporter, every spectator, every member of the jury, and even his own legal team, Mr. Mass Murderer pleads guilty. Begs forgiveness. Asks for mercy.

Imagine the worldwide outrage as the judge responds, "Not guilty!"

"What a charade! Fool! He just said he was guilty. What is wrong with you? Have you gone mad? Retrial! Ethics probe! He must pay for his crimes."

"His crimes have been paid for," the judge retorts. "By my son. I have judged my son in place of Mr. Mass Murderer. They've exchanged places. My guiltless son, charged with nothing—his good standing I now transfer to Mr. Mass Murderer who is now free to go."

"But he's still evil through and through. A man like him can never change. He's a danger to society. He must be locked up. Looked after."

"He will live with me," the judge replies. "Enjoying all the privileges my son enjoyed. I've adopted Mr. Mass Murderer into my family. He's my adult son."

"That guarantees nothing. All your good intentions, all the love in the world, all the good nurture and best environment in the world do not guarantee that Mr. Mass Murderer will not continue his rampage."

"I'm not finished. Hear me out," the judge insists. "I've consulted the best medical, psychiatric, and psychological experts on the planet. Mr. Mass Murderer will receive a heart, brain, and soul transplant along with a DNA graft infusing into him my very nature."

Momentarily silenced. Totally stunned. Then a hand shoots up. "But that means only that he has a clean start. What about all his old acquaintances, his old habits? They will still come around clamoring for his attention, demanding his loyalty and affection."

"Fair question," the judge agrees. "We've thought of everything. I've jailed all his old acquaintances. His foes are defeated. Plus, we've infused his new heart, brain, soul, and DNA complex with core power to remain free from and victorious over these past tempters."

Father's Full Provision

You've not been watching *The Twilight Zone*. Not *The Outer Limits*. Not even reality TV. But reality. Spiritual reality.

God our Judge justifies us, declaring us not guilty, forgiving our trespasses, and reckoning His Son's righteousness to our account. The amazing grace of *justification*.

God the Judge could have stopped here, forgiving us and then leaving us on our own. Left to our same old nurture we would return to our old haunts—the world, the flesh, and the Devil. We would continue our maddening quest for relationship apart from God.

But God the Judge takes off His legal robes, replacing them with relaxed family attire and comfy slippers, inviting us into His home, into His family—reconciliation. Forgiveness (justification) as great as it is, would have been hollow had we remained separated from Father. The Judge becomes our adoptive Father, granting us access to His home and all the privileges of adult children. The amazing grace of *reconciliation*.

Justification and reconciliation combine to form the first perfection of the new covenant—our new nurture. However, as the story of Mr. Mass Murderer correctly indicates, new nurture without new nature is insufficient to change us.

The Judge of the criminal and the Father of the adult son becomes the Creator, Parent, Progenitor, Begetter, Life-giver of a newborn infant—regeneration. Like Father, like son. Born again of incorruptible seed. Born from above to reflect the image of the Creator. Born with a new nature—new soul, mind, will, spirit, emotions. Born with a new heart—new capacities, disposition, inclinations, purity. The old dies. The new lives. The amazing grace of *regeneration*.

As amazing as all this is, we still need one more salvation grace—*redemption*. Freedom from the power of sin. Freedom from bondage and slavery to sin. We need victory. Resurrection power. The Judge of the criminal, the Father of the adult son, the Creator of the newborn infant, is also the Champion, Victor, Warrior, General, and King of the overcomer, of the empowered, freed, victorious soldier. Set free from the power of sin and death, united with the resurrection power of Christ. Victorious over the world, the flesh, the Devil, sin, and death. The amazing grace of *redemption*.

Neonatal Saints and *Nikao* Saints: The Essence of Our New Nature

Through the impartation of our new nature, God makes us *neonatal* saints (regeneration) and *nikao* saints (redemption). I'm indebted to historical theologian Thomas C. Oden for the captivating and correct analogy of regeneration producing neonatal saints. In the new birth, God imparts new spiritual life. Yet it is not perfectly mature, full-grown life.

> One reborn of God is not thereby immediately mature. Birth does not preempt but invites and enables the process of growth. One reborn of God is a neonate saint, awaiting a process of growth toward ever-fuller receptivity to the Spirit. Having been cleansed in new birth, one is drawn and called to express behavioral manifestation of the new life (Oden, *Life in the Spirit*, Vol. 3, p. 168).

We are neonatal saints, but saints nonetheless.

We are also *nikao* saints. *Nikao* is the English transliteration of the Greek word for victory. Think of the shoe company, *Nike*, and their motto, "*Just do it!*" Claim your victory. Live out your competitive spirit. Be the champion that you are. Redemption makes us *nikao* saints enabled to say, "No!" to sin and, "Yes!" to God. Freed from the power of sin; freed to live under the power of God. Transferred from an old mastery: sin, Satan, death, the flesh, the world; to a new mastery: righteousness, the Spirit, the new heart, the church.

Regeneration: The Spiritual Birth of Neonatal Saints—Healthy

Something real occurred at the moment of your salvation. A great change took place in you at your regeneration. Your regeneration was more than having something taken away (guilt removed through justification), more than having something added (a second nature tacked onto the first). Something new was birthed, but only after something old was crucified.

You and I needed regeneration because we were worse than critically ill; we were spiritually dead (Ephesians 2:1-3). Our spiritually dead selves were incapable of seeking God, knowing God, obeying God, or feeling inclined toward God (Romans 3:9-20). So God crucified the old dead us. "For we know that our old self was crucified with him" (Romans 6:6a).

Now what? The dead us is dead. Our old self—oriented away from God—is dead; our deadness to God is dead. But we remain, our humanness, our capacities—relationality, rationality, volitionality, emotionality. Again, now what? Rebirth. God implants new spiritual life within us, making us new creatures with a new orientation so relationally we love and long for God. Rationally, we know God and discern His will. Volitionally, we want to and can obey God. And emotionally we are sensitively alive to God and others.

Oden offers the classical theological definition of the regenerative change birthed by the Spirit:

Regeneration is the work of the Spirit by which new life in Christ is initially imparted to one dead in sin. It implies a change in the inward person by which a disposition to the holy life is originated, and in which that life begins (Oden, *Life in the Spirit*, Vol. 3, p. 156).

God implants a new disposition, inclination, proclivity, and propensity. We are now bent toward God instead of away from Him. God enables us with right affections to love Him and keep His commandments, to trust and obey. "No one who is born of God will continue to sin, because God's seed remains in him; he cannot go on sinning, because he has been born of God" (1 John 3:9). As theologian Leslie Flynn defines and describes regeneration, "the principle of the new life is implanted in us, and the governing disposition of the soul is made holy (Flynn, *Man: Ruined and Restored*, p. 126).

What did God do at salvation? He not only forgave our sins (justification), He also made us new. In making us new, He did not simply remodel, rebuild, renovate, rehabilitate, or reform us. He *re-birthed* us. Changed us. Cleansed us. Returned us to our original stance, to our original wholeness. We're healthy again, healthy newborns. "Salvation" itself comes from the Latin *salvus* meaning to securely save, to keep safe, unhurt, to make sound, whole, and healthy. We are integrated, whole, healthy image bearers again (Romans 8:29).

God made us something we never were before. We've become someone we have never been before, neonatal saints. That does not mean we are perfect, sinless, or unable to sin. Rather, we are now *able not to sin*. In our *activity* we will sin (1 John 1:8-2:2), but in our *identity* we are not sinners. This new identity is not on the flesh level, but on the spirit level. Regeneration is an act so real that it is right to say that Christians in their essential nature are saints rather than sinners. All other identities are lesser identities. Sinfulness is not my intrinsic state (see Neil Anderson, *God's Power at Work in You*). In the deepest sense of personhood, I am a saint.

The term "neonatal saints" captures this sense of a definitive change along with the need for ongoing growth in Christ. Calvin, commenting on Philippians 1:6, explains that regeneration does not imply an end to daily growth. "For the new life is intended precisely to be continually lived, not to wither and die immediately after the birth has occurred" (Calvin, *The Institutes of the Christian Religion*, Vol. 2, 18.1).

Gregory Nazianzen's ancient address to the newly baptized offers summative metaphors expressing the regenerative work of God and the maturation process that leads from neo-nativity in Christ to maturity in Christ.

Yesterday your soul was bent by sin; today you have "touched the hem of Christ and your issue has been stayed." Yesterday paralyzed with no one to put you into the pool, today you have help from "Him who is in one Person Man and God." Yesterday you lay in the tomb; today you have heard a loud voice, come forth, and "were loosed from the bonds of your graveclothes." Yesterday full of leprosy, you have "received again the Image whole." Yesterday meanness and avarice were withering your hand; today "let liberality and kindness stretch it out." "If you were deaf and dumb, let the Word sound in your ears; if blind, in God's Light see light, and in the Spirit of God be enlightened by the Son, That Threefold and Undivided Light" (Gregory Nazianzen, *Oration*, XL.34, NPNF 2 VII, p. 372).

Christ begins the work within us; it is totally of God since we cannot birth ourselves. Christ promises to continue the work He has begun until the day of our glorification. Yet He also calls us to work out our own salvation with fear and trembling. As we shall see in chapters 25 through 27, we have a role to play in cooperating with the Spirit of God so that we grow in grace.

Our New Person in Christ: The New Biography of a Saint

You are a saint, not a sinner. Your old man/self/person/nature is dead, crucified with Christ. Your new man/self/person/nature is alive with Christ. "For you died, and your life is now hidden with Christ in God" (Colossians 3:3).

> We died to sin; how can we live in it any longer? Or don't you know that all of us who were baptized into Christ Jesus were baptized into his death? We were therefore buried with him through baptism into death in order that, just as Christ was raised from the dead through the glory of the Father, we too may live a new life. If we have been united with him like this in his death, we will certainly also be united with him in his resurrection. For we know that our old self was crucified with him so that the body of sin might be done away with, that we should no longer be slaves to sin—because anyone who has died has been freed from sin (Romans 6:2-7).

Could Paul have been any plainer? Could he have stated it any more clearly? The old you is dead. The new you is alive.

Then why the debate? Why do we resist the truth? Why do we water down our radical regeneration? Why do we say things like: "I'm a sinner. That's still my identity." "I'm a sinner and a saint. There are two me's. The unsaved me and the saved me. The unredeemed me and the redeemed me. The old me and the new me." "This is positional truth—in Christ's eyes I am new, He declares me new, but I'm not actually new."

David Needham, in his classic work *Birthright: Christian, Do You Know Who You Are?*, explains that we water down this truth because we've been conditioned to believe that all truth must fall into one of two "bins." The first bin we call *positional* truth—truth like justification that describes our standing or position before God, in God's eyes, according to His declaration. The second bin is *experiential* truth—truth like progressive sanctification that describes our conscious experience of growth. Needham speaks of a third category that we must revive—*actual* truth. These are truths that are not positional and may or may not be experiential (Needham, *Birthright*, p. 65-66).

He illustrates his point with the story of a girl with a lovely voice. Needham asks us to imagine a young girl who possesses a very beautiful singing voice. Because her parents fear that she will become proud, they keep telling her she has a terrible voice and nobody would want to listen to it. Assuming her parents to be correct, she decides to muffle her voice so it rises barely above a whisper. Then one Sunday she's so caught up in worship she forgets herself. With an overflowing heart she sings out strong, clear, and beautiful. Immediately the people around her cease their singing in order to hear her lovely, haunting voice. Needham pictures the results and explains the principle.

> "My!" they exclaim after the song. "You have a wonderful voice!"
> "Oh no," she stammers, embarrassed. "I, I know I have a terrible voice. Please forgive me. I'm sorry I bothered you with it. I'll try to be more quiet."

"No! Really your voice is beautiful, even captivating. Please sing more!"

This is what I mean by actual truth. All through those songless, whispered years, this girl had a beautiful voice—that was the real truth. But it wasn't experiential. And it certainly wasn't positional (that is, a recording of someone else's voice but with her name put on the label). Many Christians assume that unless something is being experienced, it must be positional truth rather than actual truth. If I don't *feel* a given truth from Scripture, I throw it in the positional bin. All too often we don't feel like new creations, so it is easy for us to say, "Well, then, that must be a positional truth" (Needham, *Birthright*, pp. 66-67).

It is *actually* true that we are really new. Needham is simply picturing what the Scripture teaches. We are regenerated. New. New creations. Saints. Made partakers of the Divine nature.

Do I always experience myself as new, beautiful, saintly? Of course not. Do I always feel like a saint rather than a sinner? No. Do I still sin? Yes. I do sin, but I am not a sinner. I am a saint. I may have a cough, but I am not a cougher. I may sin, but I am not a sinner, as though that is my identity, my nature, the most fundamental me. I am a saint who can sin.

Cinderella was a beautiful, worthy princess. One shining moment she experienced this actual truth. Soon, however, she returned to the old lying story and went back to believing she was an ugly stepchild. Though not experiencing the truth of her beauty, it was the truth about her, nonetheless.

Believe God when He says He has truly changed you, truly and definitely crucified your old nature. "The old man has been put to death just as decisively as Christ died upon the accursed tree" (John Murray, *Principles of Conduct*, p. 212). Believe God when He says He has truly and definitely regenerated your new nature. As pastors and commentators John Murray and W. H. Griffith Thomas explain:

> Paul announces the definitive cleavage with the world of sin, which union with Christ insures. The old man is the unregenerate man; the new man is the regenerate man created in Christ Jesus unto good works. It is no more feasible to call the believer a new man and an old man, than it is to call him a regenerate man and an unregenerate. And neither is it warranted to speak of the believer as having in him the old man and the new man. This kind of terminology is without warrant and is but another method of doing prejudice to the doctrine which Paul was so jealous to establish when he said, "our old man has been crucified" (Murray, *Principles of Conduct*, p. 218).

> It is a mistake to think of the believer as both an old man and a new man or as having in him both the old man and the new man, the latter in view of regeneration and the former because of remaining corruption. That this is not Paul's concept is made apparent by the fact that the "old man" can no more be regarded as in the process of being crucified than Christ in His sphere could thus be regarded (Murray, *St. Paul's Epistle to the Romans*, pp. 219-220).

> The old man ceased to exist at our regeneration, when it was "put off." We are never exhorted to "put off the old man." An exhortation to "put off the old man"

would be tantamount to an exhortation to become regenerate (Thomas, *St. Paul's Epistle to the Romans*, p. 168).

God has already done the crucifying and resurrecting for us. The old me died and God resurrected the new me. This is a past action with ongoing, continuous results. Speaking of our co-resurrection with Christ, Calvin explains, "even now by its virtue we are raised to newness of life, that we may obey God's will by pure and holy living" (Calvin, *Catechism of the Church of Geneva*, p. 100).

Of course, these are the words of fallible, uninspired human beings. Some reminders of the inerrant, infallible, inspired Word of God should help us to understand the actual truth of our regeneration.

Therefore, if anyone is in Christ, he is a new creation; the old has gone, the new has come! (2 Corinthians 5:17).

I have been crucified with Christ and I no longer live, but Christ lives in me. The life I live in the body, I live by faith in the Son of God, who loved me and gave himself for me (Galatians 2:20).

But because of his great love for us, God, who is rich in mercy, made us alive with Christ even when we were dead in transgressions—it is by grace you have been saved. And God raised us up with Christ and seated us with him in the heavenly realms in Christ Jesus (Ephesians 2:4-7).

In him you were also circumcised, in the putting off of the sinful nature, not with a circumcision done by the hands of men but with the circumcision done by Christ, having been buried with him in baptism and raised with him through your faith in the power of God, who raised him from the dead. When you were dead in your sins and in the uncircumcision of your sinful nature, God made you alive with Christ (Colossians 2:11-13a).

Since, then, you have been raised with Christ, set your hearts on things above, where Christ is seated at the right hand of God. Set your minds on things above, not on earthly things. For you died, and your life is now hidden with Christ in God (Colossians 3:1-3).

Do not lie to each other, since you have taken off your old self with its practices and have put on the new self, which is being renewed in knowledge in the image of its Creator (Colossians 3:9-10).

At one time we too were foolish, disobedient, deceived and enslaved by all kinds of passions and pleasures. We lived in malice and envy, being hated and hating one another. But when the kindness and love of God our Savior appeared, he saved us, not because of righteous things we had done, but because of his mercy. He saved us through the washing of rebirth and renewal by the Holy Spirit (Titus 3:3-5).

Praise be to the God and Father of our Lord Jesus Christ! In his great mercy he has given us new birth into a living hope through the resurrection of Jesus Christ from the dead (1 Peter 1:3).

His divine power has given us everything we need for life and godliness through our knowledge of him who called us by his own glory and goodness. Through these he has given us his very great and precious promises, so that through them you may participate in the divine nature and escape the corruption in the world caused by evil desires (2 Peter 1:3-4).

Could God be any clearer? Once we were depraved. But now in Christ we are new creatures, new creations, new Romancers, Dreamers, Creators, and Singers. We have a new biography. "At the moment of regeneration, an individual is no longer a sinner but is a saint (1 Corinthians 1:2; 6:11)" (Stuart Odom, *Soteriology*, p. 23).

I have not always believed that my "old man" was dead. In seminary I wrote a lengthy, exegetical paper on Ephesians 4:17-24 examining whether the "old man" was dead. I had taken the position that he was not. However, halfway through the paper, I became convinced that he was. Too late to change the entire paper, I handed it in as it was with the conclusion that the "old man" was alive.

My gracious professor gave me my grade, commented on my exegetical work, and then concluded with these words. "I'm sorry that your old man is still alive. I praise God that my old man is dead!"

Which biography are you living according to? Which story of your current existence are you reading? Which interpretation of your life as a believer controls how you see yourself? With my seminary professor I say, "Praise God that our old man is dead and that our new man is alive!"

Our New Covenant through Christ: The New Cardiology of a Saint

We are alive in Christ, but what kind of life are we living? What is the heart condition of this newborn? How healthy is the heart of the neonatal saint?

First, recall the old heart that we had in our depraved state. Remember the heart disease coursing through the sick heart of the degenerate "old man" that we were. That old heart was a slave to unrighteousness. The soul was selfish. The mind foolish. The will stubborn and manipulative. The emotions fearful and angry.

Now, reflect on the new heart of the neonatal saint. The pediatrician places her stethoscope onto the new babe in Christ, smiles, and says, "A new heart! Slave to righteousness. A new soul, free to love sacrificially. A new mind, enlightened to wisdom. A new will, soft and serving. New emotions, peaceful yet deep."

God crucified our "Mr. Mass Murderer." The great Soul Physician implanted a new heart, gave us a heart transplant. In 2 Corinthians 5:17, Paul labels us "new creations." "Creation" is *ktisis*, which the Septuagint used for creation *ex nihilo*—out of nothing. God does not simply reorder the chaos of my old heart. He removes my old heart giving me a totally new heart.

What a heart it is! In our new nature we become "partakers of the divine nature" (2 Peter 1:4, KJV). As Calvin wrote, "The end of the Gospel is to render us eventually conformable to God, and if we may so speak, deify us" (Calvin, *Commentary*, XXII, p. 371). T. Goodwin concurs, "The image of God is being renewed in previously alienated humanity" (Goodwin, *Works*, VI, pp. 187-231).

This theme of a heart that images God's appears regularly in the definitions of regeneration in the Protestant evangelical tradition. Regeneration is "a work of the triune

God, which the Holy Ghost accomplishes in us by raising us up from the death of sin and making us partakers of the Divine nature and life" (*Catechism of the Evangelical Association*, Question 295). Regeneration is "a change of heart, wrought by the Holy Spirit, who quickeneth the dead in trespasses and sins, enlightening their minds spiritually and savingly to understand the Word of God, and renewing their whole nature, so that they love and practice holiness" (Baptist Abstract of Principles, VII, *CC*, p. 341). By the new birth believers become "partakers of the divine nature and a holy disposition is given, leading to the love and practice of righteousness" (Southern Baptist Convention, 1925, *CC*, p. 347).

The Bible calls this heart transplant process "the new covenant." Under the terms of the new covenant, God not only provides forgiveness for everything bad within us, but He also plants a new source of goodness within us from which we may draw. The goodness consists of an appetite for holiness, a desire to relate well—the desire to be lovely and to love.

I suspect that Old Testament saints would grab us by the collar, lift us off the ground, shake us, and say, "Do you have a clue? We longed for new covenant living. Yet you ignore it. Minimize it. What's wrong with you?"

Living under the old covenant, they looked forward to the day when, "The LORD your God will circumcise your hearts and the hearts of your descendants, so that you may love him with all your heart and with all your soul, and live" (Deuteronomy 30:6). "And live." An odd way to end a verse. They survived. They didn't really live. They didn't thrive. They could not wait until the day when circumcision was not of the outer person, not of the flesh, but of the inner person, of the heart—the day when their spiritual life would thrive, when they would truly be alive to life because they were totally alive to God.

As the centuries passed from the days of Moses to the days of the prophets, their hunger grew. How they longed for the fulfillment of the prophecy stating, "I will give them an undivided heart and put a new spirit in them; I will remove from them their heart of stone and give them a heart of flesh" (Ezekiel 11:19). They desired to experience the promised cleansing from impurity and the promised infusion of purity (Ezekiel 36:24-28). Their ears perked up every time they heard "The Promise."

> "The time is coming," declares the LORD, "when I will make a new covenant with the house of Israel and with the house of Judah. It will not be like the covenant I made with their forefathers when I took them by the hand to lead them out of Egypt, because they broke my covenant, though I was a husband to them," declares the LORD. "This is the covenant I will make with the house of Israel after that time," declares the LORD. "I will put my law in their minds and write it on their hearts. I will be their God, and they will be my people. No longer will a man teach his neighbor, or a man his brother, saying, 'Know the LORD,' because they will all know me, from the least of them to the greatest," declares the LORD. "For I will forgive their wickedness and will remember their sins no more" (Jeremiah 31:31-34).

"Open your ears!" Old Testament saints would cry to us. "What we waited for has arrived—for you!"

The author of Hebrews echoes their plea. From Hebrews 7-10, he emphasizes the superiority of the New Covenant (7:1-28; 8:1-7, 13; 9:1-28; 10:1-14, 18), repeats the promise of the New Covenant (8:8-12; 10:15-18), and explains its application to us. "For this reason Christ is the mediator of a new covenant, that those who are called may receive the promised eternal inheritance—now that he has died as a ransom to set them free from the sins committed under the first covenant" (Hebrews 9:15). What Old Testament saints longed for, we now receive in Christ.

> The Holy Spirit also testifies *to us* about this. First He says: "This is the covenant I will make with them after that time, says the Lord. I will put my laws in their hearts, and I will write them on their minds." Then he adds, "Their sins and lawless acts I will remember no more." And where these have been forgiven, there is no longer any sacrifice for sin. *Therefore, brothers, since we* have confidence to enter the Most Holy place by the blood of Jesus, by a new and living way opened *for us* through the curtain, that is, his body, and *since we* have a great priest over the house of God, *let us* draw near to God with a sincere heart in full assurance of faith, *having our hearts sprinkled to cleanse us from a guilty conscience and having our bodies washed with pure water* (Hebrews 10:15-22, emphasis added).

At salvation, I enter the New Covenant, obtaining the "two blessings," or "two perfections" of that covenant:

♦ Forgiveness: My sins are forgiven—the Forgiving Springs (New Nurture).
♦ Cleansing: My old heart of stone and flesh is crucified. My new heart is implanted—the Cleansing Springs (New Nature).

Instead of putting His laws on stone tablets, "they are placed in the very center of the believer's being, so that there is an inner impulse that both delights in knowing his law and doing his will" (R. Kent Hughes, *Hebrews*, Vol. 2, p. 25). My new heart is a holy heart. Speaking of Christ setting aside the first covenant and establishing the second or new covenant, the author of Hebrews describes our holy heart. "And by that will [covenant], we have been made holy through the sacrifice of the body of Jesus Christ once for all" (Hebrews 10:10).

The great Scottish preacher, Dr. Donald Grey Barnhouse, describes what happens when God writes His will on our hearts, terming it, "the expulsive power of a new affection" (Barnhouse, *Let Me Illustrate*, p. 97). He illustrates the power of our new heart by reminiscing about a trip he took shortly after the Armistice of WW I, when he visited the battlefields of Belgium. It was a lovely spring day, the sun was shining, and not a breath of wind was blowing. As he walked along examining the war's remains, he noticed leaves were falling from the great trees that arched along the road. He grasped a leaf as it floated down, pressed it between his fingers, and it disintegrated. Looking up curiously, he saw several other leaves falling from the trees. Remember, it was not autumn, but spring, nor was there enough wind to blow off the leaves. These leaves had outlived the winds of autumn and the frosts of winter. Yet they were falling, seemingly without reason.

Then Barnhouse realized why. The most potent force of all was causing them to fall. It was spring. The sap was beginning to run, and the buds were beginning to push from within. From down beneath the earth, roots were sending life along trunk, branch, and twig until it expelled every bit of deadness that remained from the previous year: the expulsive power of a new affection, of new life.

Commenting on Barnhouse's illustration, Pastor R. Kent Hughes notes:

This is what happens when God writes his will on our hearts. The new life within purges the deadness from our lives. Our renewed hearts pump fresh blood through us. The life of Christ in us—the same life that said, "Here I am . . . I have come to do your will, O God"—animates us! You may be saying to yourself, "I don't think I can ever live the Christian life"—and you are right! But a new heart, the expulsive inner power of new affection, will make it possible (Hughes, *Hebrews*, Vol. 2, p. 25).

In Christ you are a neonatal saint with a new heart. In chapter 24 we'll operate on the new heart, examining its four arteries—new relational, rational, volitional, and emotional capacities—the expulsive and explosive powers of healthy affections, cognitions, volitions, and emotions.

Redemption: The Spiritual Freedom of *Nikao* Saints—Holy

To the amazing grace of regeneration, God adds the amazing grace of redemption. Through our redemption in Christ we experience the spiritual freedom of *nikao* (victorious) saints. We are free from sin's power, free to live holy and loving lives.

Our New Victory in Christ: *Christus Victor*

Christus Victor—our victorious Christ—both forgives and redeems us.

When you were dead in your sins and in the uncircumcision of your sinful nature, God made you alive with Christ. He forgave us all our sins, having canceled the written code, with its regulations, that was against us and that stood opposed to us; he took it away, nailing it to the cross. And having disarmed the powers and authorities, he made a public spectacle of them, triumphing over them by the cross (Colossians 2:13-15).

Here Paul pictures the cosmic drama of redemption. Hostile, alien powers have enslaved us. Evil taskmasters (Satan and his demons) and vicious forces (sin) have captured us. Into the fray comes *Christus Victor* freeing us from our bondage to sin and our enslavement to Satan.

Christus Victor "disarms" (*apekduō*) our enemies. He strips off their clothes. More powerfully, He strips off their arms (Ralph Earle, *Word Meanings in the New Testament*, p. 356). He disarms them of the weapons they use to hold us captive.

Wanting to be sure that we grasp the message of our newfound freedom, *Christus Victor* throws a victory parade. He makes a public spectacle (*deigmatizō*) of our defeated foes. This rare Greek word pictures a victor displaying his captives as trophies in a triumphal procession. It emphasizes publishing and proclaiming the results of a decisive victory (Earle, *Word Meanings in the New Testament*, p. 356).

This is further illustrated by the last clause of the verse, "triumphing over them by the cross." "It was a familiar scene of a conqueror returning to Rome and leading the captured kings and warriors in chains in his triumphal procession" (Earle, *Word Meanings in the New Testament*, p. 356). Greek scholar A. T. Robertson connects the dots in this picture of Christ's triumph:

> The Greek verb is *thriambeuō* to celebrate a triumph. It is derived from *thriambos*, a hymn sung in a festal procession and is kin to the Latin *triumphus* (our triumph), a triumphal procession of victorious Roman generals. God has won a complete triumph over all the fallen angelic agencies (Robertson, *Word Pictures in the New Testament*, p. 498).

Through *Christus Victor* we are Saints Victorious—*Nikao* saints.

Living Victoriously in Christ

Redemption results from our co-crucifixion and co-resurrection with Christ. "For we know that our old self was crucified with him so that the body of sin might be done away with, that we should no longer be slaves to sin—because anyone who has died has been freed from sin" (Romans 6:6-7).

Having died with Christ to sin and been raised with Christ to new life, "We know that since Christ was raised from the dead, he cannot die again; death no longer has mastery over him. The death he died, he died to sin once for all; but the life he lives, he lives to God" (Romans 6:9-10).

After emphasizing our redemption in Christ, Paul exhorts us to live our lives on the basis of our new freedom.

> In the same way, count yourselves dead to sin, but alive to God in Christ Jesus. Therefore do not let sin reign in your mortal body so that you obey its evil desires. Do not offer the parts of your body to sin, as instruments of wickedness, but rather offer yourselves to God, as those who have been brought from death to life; and offer the parts of your body to him as instruments of righteousness. For sin shall not be your master, because you are not under law, but under grace (Romans 6:11-14).

"Count," or "reckon" (*logizomai*) means that we live *based on* and *consciously aware of* our victory over sin.

Does our victory mean that we can never sin? No. It means that we never *have to* sin. But Paul clearly explains that we can still (foolishly and unnecessarily) choose to sin, choose to act *as though* we are still sin's slaves, still Satan's servants.

> What then? Shall we sin because we are not under law but under grace? By no means! Don't you know that when you offer yourselves to someone to obey him as slaves, you are slaves to the one whom you obey—whether you are slaves to sin, which leads to death, or to obedience, which leads to righteousness? But thanks be to God that, though you used to be slaves to sin, you wholeheartedly obeyed the form of teaching to which you were entrusted. You have been set free from sin and have become slaves to righteousness (Romans 6:15-18).

Professor, pastor, and author Henry Holloman, reflecting on the implication of this passage to our daily Christian life, urges us to ask ourselves the practical question: "'Am I staying in my casket in relation to sin, or am I walking around like a zombie committing sin?' If the latter is true, reaffirm that you died to sin with Christ. Then by God's grace get back in the casket in relation to sin" (Holloman, *The Forgotten Blessing*, pp. 42-43).

Why in the world would we *live as though* we were still alive to sin, still captive to sin? Christian counselor Neil Anderson answers our question by comparing our "spiritual emancipation proclamation" to the Emancipation Proclamation.

> Slavery in the United States was abolished by the Thirteenth Amendment on December 18, 1865. How many slaves were there on December 19? In reality, none, but many still lived like slaves. They did because they never learned the truth. Others knew and even believed that they were free, but chose to continue living as they had always been taught (Anderson, *God's Power at Work in You*, p. 25).

The plantation owners despaired. "We're ruined! We've lost the battle to enslave our slaves."

"Not so fast," others replied. "As long as they still think they're slaves, Lincoln's Emancipation Proclamation will have no practical effect. Keep your slaves from learning the truth, and they will not challenge your control over them."

Some plantation owners still panicked. "What if their good news spreads?"

"Then we have to deceive them. Tell them they're going to be free, but they're not free just yet. It's positional truth, not actual truth."

Anderson further represents the battle of beliefs, writing:

> Years later, many slaves have still not heard the wonderful news that they have been freed, so naturally they continue to live the way they have always lived. Some slaves have heard the good news, but they evaluate it by what they are presently doing and feeling. They reason, "I'm still living in bondage, doing the same things I have always done. My experience tells me that I must not be free. I'm feeling the same way I was before the proclamation, so it must not be true" (Anderson, *God's Power at Work Within You*, p. 26).

What would it take for freed slaves to experience their freedom freely? It takes one former slave truly believing and applying the truth of the Emancipation Proclamation. That slave's life is transformed. He reckons on the truth that his old master has no authority over him and does not need to be obeyed. He gladly and freely serves the one who set him free. As Anderson pictures it:

> The gospel is the "proclamation of emancipation" for every sinner who is sold into the slavery of sin. Every person that comes into this world is born dead in his or her trespasses and sins (Ephesians 2:1), and is by nature a child of wrath (Ephesians 2:3). The good news is that we who are Christians are no longer slaves to sin. We are now alive in Christ and dead to sin (Romans 6:11). We have been set free in Christ. We are no longer sinners in the hands of an angry God. We are saints in the hands of a loving God. We are forgiven, justified, redeemed, and born again children of God. We may not feel like it, we may not act like it, and others may tell

us that we are not, but we have been sanctified in Christ and are being sanctified in Him (Anderson, *God's Power at Work Within You*, p. 27).

Christian, do you know who you are? Are you counting on, reckoning on, and living your Christian life based on your new victory in Christ? Do you see yourself as more than a conqueror through Christ? As a victor? As a spiritual champion?

Soul physicians, do you know who your Christian clients, parishioners, and spiritual friends are? Are you counseling them based on the victory over sin that Christ has already won for them? Do you see them as spiritual champions? Are you fanning into flame the gift(s) of God within them? Are you urging them to reckon on their new life in Christ? Are you enlightening them to set their new affections on Christ, to set their new minds on things above, to put off the old way since they are dead to it, and to put on the new way since they are alive to God?

Where We've Been and Where We're Heading

You've heard four amazing announcements. Words you've longed for and dare not shun.

"Not guilty!" You're *justified*, declared righteous before our Judge.

"Welcome home!" You're *reconciled*, adopted into Father's forever family.

"It's a boy! It's a girl!" You're *regenerated*, born again with a new nature.

"Champion!" You're *redeemed*, free at last to live victoriously.

There's a new you with a redeemed personality structure. Already, the image of God, marred by the Fall, has been stamped on you again. What is the essence of your new identity as a Christian? What does the new you look like? How does the new you function, operate, act? What makes you "tick"?

The answers to these questions are vital for understanding ourselves—who we are in Christ. And they're vital for understanding how to counsel Christians. Join me in Act Four, Scene V, Chapter 24, as we examine the redeemed personality structure.

Caring for Your Soul: Personal Applications

1. What lies are you believing about yourself—about the new you in Christ?

2. Where were you recruited into these lies? What is the history of these lies?

3. What would happen if you rejected these lies? How would your life be different?

4. What truth is Christ telling you about yourself—about the new you in Christ? Of the verses and images in Box 23:1, which ones "grab you" the most? Why? How?

5. Over the next week, every time a lie about your new nature enters your conscious thought life, counter that lie with Jesus' truth about the new you.

Caring for Others: Ministry Implications

♦ **Believe the Word about Yourself and Your Christian Spiritual Friends:** In the essential you, you are a saint. Your spiritual friend's sacred identity is saint. Unless you can envision in yourself and your clients this core new nature, you will be unable to do the work of biblical counseling.

♦ **Defeat Satan's Lies:** Satan wants us to adjust to a fake personal identity. He hates and fears Christians who are aware of who they are in Christ. Expose the specific lies that your counselee believes about himself/herself. Ask, "Where were you recruited into that view?" "Who brainwashed you to think that about yourself?" "Who has bewitched you?"

♦ **Counsel Christians from the Inside Out:** The center of the new you in Christ is your capacity to love. Hold yourself and other Christians accountable to love: to forgive enemies, to risk, to sacrifice, to witness, to surrender, to comfort, and to confront. Urge Christians, like Paul does in Colossians 3:1-2, to set their new affections on Christ.

♦ **Counsel Christians Based on Their New Identity:** Enlighten your spiritual friends to who they are in Christ. Teach them how to reckon on, count on, and live according to their new victory in Christ.

Chapter Twenty-Four

Virgin Bride's Redeemed Personality Structure

"When you were born again, God deposited within you a new nature that wasn't there before, a nature that is now the core of who you are. Peter called it 'the divine nature' because it is the very life of God" (Tony Evans, *Free at Last*, pp. 29-30).

"You must understand that when you accepted Jesus Christ as your Savior and became a new creation in Him, your sin nature was put to death. Christ has destroyed the power of sin in your life. The old you died at the cross" (Tony Evans, *Free at Last*, p. 43).

"Our 'sin factory' was shut down . . . We don't have the factory anymore. We are new creations in Christ; the old has gone (see 2 Corinthians 5:17). You see, this is a different problem than having a sin nature producing sin. The problem of indwelling sin is one we can handle" (Tony Evans, *Free at Last*, pp. 44-45).

Physicians of a New Soul

Picture a team of cardiologists joining a team of oncologists scrubbing down before surgery. "Have you ever seen a case like this?" asks the heart surgeon, Dr. McCrusher.

"No, and I'm glad I haven't," replies the cancer specialist, Dr. Picarro. "Cancer spreading through the lungs, the chest. That's horrible enough. Add to that heart disease, clogging every major artery. What a mess. Poor chap. He's rather hopeless."

"Well," counters Dr. McCrusher, "at least he's an old man. Lived a long life. Experienced a great deal. The sad fact is, he's set some patterns in place that will be hard to break. As a doctor, it's frustrating. Let's say that we eliminate the obstructions blocking his arteries. This joker is just going to return to his old way of life. Eating garbage. No exercise."

As McCrusher's discouraged voice trails off, Picarro interjects. "I know what you mean. He's a three-pack-a-day smoker. Nothing seems to stop him, not even his diagnosis of lung cancer. Not the patch. Nothing. The second he leaves the hospital, assuming we're successful, he'll be lighting up."

Discouragement not withstanding, scrub down complete, patient ready, the doctors usher their teams into the operating room. Crowding around the antiseptic operating table, these two crack teams work in tandem. One to unclog diseased arteries, the other to remove diseased organs. Together, hoping to give this old man a few more months, at least.

"Nurse, more light! I can't see a thing."

"Doctor McCrusher, what do you mean?" Nurse Capel asks. "Are you all right? Your eyes okay? I see everything."

"Then someone really fouled up this time!" McCrusher protests. Of course I see everything. Everything, that is, except his obstructed arteries! This can't be my patient. Nobody move. Double check his identity!"

Shock. Scurrying. Examining. Confirmation. "This is Mr. Olman. He's our patient. No mistake about it," confirms Nurse Capel.

"Well, then my work's finished," Dr. McCrusher replies. This man's heart is as good as new. Better. It's as if he's had a heart transplant. But a transplant unlike any that I've seen. Not just a better heart, but a brand new, robust heart. Every marred part, every speck of scarred tissue, obliterated. Replaced by a heart I would die for."

Inexplicable as it is, Dr. Picarro steps in. "Well, we have Olman open. Let's remove that unhealthy lung of his." Stunned. Stopping. Repeating the complaints of Dr. McCrusher. "This is impossible. His lungs are like new. Not a trace of cancer. What's going on here?"

Days later, recovered from his open-heart "surgery," Mr. Olman leaves the hospital feeling like a new man. Saying his good-byes to Drs. McCrusher and Picarro, he thanks them profusely. "Don't thank us," Picarro responds, speaking for both doctors. "Thank your lucky stars."

"I'd prefer to thank my good God," Mr. Olman replies. "He healed me. Made my heart better than new, my lungs too. More than that, He's given me a new, healthy attitude. No more junk food for me. No more 'cancer sticks.' And I'll be working out. Have my routine planned, even started already. I'm a new man. Ha! That's funny. Mr. Olman becomes a New Man. Just call me 'Mr. Newman' from now on, Docs!"

Cleansed Capacities

Soul physicians, like body physicians, must know the "patient" they're operating on. Physicians of the soul, working with Christians, are working with a new "patient," a new man, a new woman.

In chapters 24 through 27, we view portraits of our new patient, portraits that lead to principles of progressive sanctification. *Knowing who we are in Christ is the foundation for knowing how to live like Christ*. Box 24:1 offers a snapshot portrait of saints. The remainder of chapter 24 delivers a camcorder depiction of saints in action.

Remember that as image bearers we are personal beings as God is a personal being. We share with God certain basic capacities of personhood, core components that are necessary for personal existence and interaction. God, as the infinite personal being, is relational, rational, volitional, and emotional. In finite ways we reflect these capacities of personhood. We are *relational beings with affections*—having a soul with the capacity to long for communion, connection, and a clear conscience. We are *rational beings with cognitions*—having a mind with the capacity to think in images and beliefs.

Box 24:1

Our Redeemed Personality Structure

From passionate Romancers to spiritual Adulterers to virgin Brides,
From imaginative Dreamers to arrogant Fools to penetrating Sages,
From courageous Creators to mastered Destroyers to empowering Shepherds,
From alive Singers to moody Addicts to soulful Poets,
From energized Actors to materialistic Traitors to connected Characters,
Victorious over the *Cosmos Diabolicus*, the ingrained flesh, and the False Seducer.

Redeemed Relational Beings: Virgin Brides

Saints are virgin Brides returned to purity by Worthy Groom,
motivated by gratitude to love God passionately and their neighbor as themselves.

Redeemed Rational Beings: Penetrating Sages

Saints are penetrating Sages returned to sanity by Worthy Groom,
enlightened to the reality of God's larger story invading their smaller stories.

Redeemed Volitional Beings: Empowering Shepherds

Saints are empowered Shepherds returned to vitality by Worthy Groom,
freed to exercise dominion over their passions and God's planet,
freed to empower others.

Redeemed Emotional Beings: Soulful Poets

Saints are soulful Poets returned to integrity by Worthy Groom,
enlivened to experience life honestly in all its grief and hope.

Redeemed Physical Beings: Connected Characters

Saints are connected Characters returned to connectivity/activity by Worthy Groom,
called as main characters in the drama of redemption.

We are *volitional beings with intentions*—having a will with the capacity to purpose and act. And we are *emotional beings with reactions*—having a deep capacity to respond to our inner and outer world.

Sin depraved these capacities, it did not eliminate them. Sinners still have a soul, mind, will, and emotions. Salvation restores these capacities. Historical theologian Thomas C. Oden explains how regeneration works with and in our capacities of personhood.

This does not imply that in new birth the Spirit works wholly without the human will and affections, for the Spirit's distinct purpose is to begin to transform the will and affections. The Spirit works in and through the heart, affections, will, and behavior. Human faculties are not circumvented, but given a new spring of action. Rebirth does not impart completely new human faculties, but reorders and enlivens those that already exist (Oden, *Life in the Spirit*, Vol. 3, p. 165).

In salvation, God provides the recovery of what fallen humanity lost. By His wounds our capacities are healed (1 Peter 2:24). God makes us whole, healthy, and holy—saints.

So just what does a saint look like? Saints reflect the character of Christ. Relationally, Christ transformed us from spiritual Adulterers to virgin Brides. Rationally, He changed us from arrogant Fools to penetrating Sages. Volitionally, Jesus renewed us from mastered Slaves to empowering Shepherds. Emotionally, Worthy Groom recreated us as soulful Poets rather than moody Addicts.

Regeneration cleanses every capacity of our personhood. What sin depraves, salvation purifies. Relationally we return to purity, rationally we return to sanity, volitionally we return to vitality, and emotionally we return to integrity.

Christlike Capacities

Someone once asked Gutzon Borglum, the creative genius behind the presidential carvings on Mount Rushmore, "How did you ever create those faces out of that rock!?" Borglum replied, "I didn't. Those faces where already in there. Hidden. I only uncovered them."

Christian, the face of Jesus is already in there. *In you!* This is the essence of regeneration. God originates within you a new disposition toward holiness. Christlikeness is etched within. The Divine nature is embedded in the interior recesses of your soul (2 Peter 1:3-4).

In sanctification, you yield to the Holy Spirit who uncovers the Christ who dwells within. *To grow in Christ, you need to know who you are in Christ.* Once you are clear on your identity, deep in your being, you can begin to cooperate with the Divine Architect who daily transforms you more and more into the image of Christ (2 Corinthians 3:18; 4:16-18). You may not always feel it, you may not regularly experience it, but truth is truth. You are healthy, whole, and holy. In Christ.

If you don't believe it, if you fail to remind yourself of it, Jesus is displeased. Peter explains that the person who lacks the evidence of Christ's character "is nearsighted and blind, and has forgotten that he has been cleansed from his past sins" (2 Peter 1:9). You battle spiritual amnesia regarding who you are in Christ. Christian, remember who you are. To jog your memory, look beneath the surface with me as we reveal the new you, unveiling portraits and viewing videos of who you are in Christ.

Redeemed Relational Beings: Virgin Brides—Purified Affections/Grace Lovers

Chisel away the granite. Pull open your chest. Expose your new soul.

I know, you're terrified to look. You believe that the deeper down inside you look, the uglier and scarier you appear. That's a lie. *The* lie. False Seducer's lie.

The truth is in Jesus. He died for your sins once for all, the righteous for the unrighteous to bring you to God (1 Peter 3:18).

You are a saint now. Saints are virgin brides returned to purity by Worthy Groom. Motivated by gratitude for grace, saints passionately love God and their neighbor as themselves. I have just described the core you. It is true.

It is not a new truth. What we are discussing is classic evangelical doctrine regarding regeneration. "Regeneration is that new beginning offered by the Spirit by which one is rescued from the dominion of sin and enabled with right affections to love God and keep God's commandments" (*Formula of Concord* III-VI, *COC* III, pp. 114-134). God purified your affections, enabling you to love Him with all your soul. "New birth is followed by a life of reborn affections" (Oden, *Life in the Spirit*, Vol. 3, p. 175). You are a lover—a pure lover—again. "Without a rebirth of the affections from which actions spring, there is no reason to expect that anyone would manifest a life of faith or renounce idolatry or follow the way of holiness or accept salvation" (Oden, *Life in the Spirit*, Vol. 3, p. 159).

God co-crucified the idolatrous you with Christ, co-resurrecting the worshipful you with Christ. This is what happened to you when you were saved. "It amounts to a radical reversal of the direction of the will by which the selfless love of God begins to take the place of the godless love of self and of idolatrized creaturely good" (Augustine, Conf., IV, *NPNF* 1 I, pp. 69-78).

Regeneration radically renewed you. The old heart of the unsaved you was unable not to sin. The new heart of the saved you is able not to sin and able to love. The future, final heart of the glorified you will not be able to sin and unable not to love.

You are able not to sin. You are able to love. Repeat it. Believe it. Reckon on it.

Specifically, what are your new affections, your new relational capacities? What are your new grace lovers that replace your old false lovers? Answering that question requires us to return to our biblical understanding of relational beings as spiritual, social, and self-aware beings. Venture a peek into your renewed soul:

♦ Redeemed Spiritual Beings: Purified Affections/Grace Lovers Who Worship God

♦ Redeemed Social Beings: Purified Affections/Grace Lovers Who Minister to Others

♦ Redeemed Self-Aware Beings: Purified Affections/Grace Lovers Who Rest in Christ

Redeemed Spiritual Beings: Purified Affections/Grace Lovers Who Worship God

We have seen how we must trust something. We are faith-in-something-beings. We are "trusters." As Oden reminds us:

> The human condition is such that it is bound to orient itself toward some center of value—that value that appears to someone to make other values valuable. Before the history of sin, God was trusted as that center. Afterward, humanity became seduced by alternative claims to ultimacy. Eating of the forbidden fruit, they thought they would become as gods themselves (Oden, *Life in the Spirit*, Vol. 3, p. 166).

Regeneration returned us to God's original design for our lives: a daily trusting response to God. Salvation reverses the curse. Once again we place the Triune God center-stage in our hearts. In our souls, we "set apart Christ as Lord" (1 Peter 3:15a). As redeemed spiritual beings we are:

- ◆ Entrusting and Enjoying Father: From Faithless Prodigals to Clinging Sons and Daughters
- ◆ Entrusting and Enjoying Worthy Groom: From Adulterous Whores to Faithful Virgin Brides
- ◆ Entrusting and Enjoying Messenger/Mentor/Spirit: From Independent Self-Sufficiency to Dependent Spirit-Sufficiency

As a result of the events in the Garden of Eden, our souls wilted; we became prodigals, exchanging faith in Father for fearful flight from Father. Through the circumstances in the Garden of Gethsemane, our souls blossomed; we became sons and daughters, putting off the weeds of fear and putting on the flowers of trust.

Unlike Adam and Eve, Father calls us to exercise faith in Him in a *fallen* world. Living east of Eden, the Apostle Peter insists that adult sons and daughters *cling* to Father. Bombarded daily, we tenaciously cleave to God trusting that He shields us from final destruction (1 Peter 1:5-6).

Someone rips your reputation. It hurts. Stings. Feels like death. You feel as though all you have worked toward has been ruined. Your good name trashed. By faith, rather than worshiping your good name, you worship God. By faith, instead of living to please people, you live to please God. By faith, rather than self-protectively fighting to defend yourself, you surrender to God's protection.

In this, you are like Jesus. You are Christlike. "When they hurled their insults at him, he did not retaliate; when he suffered, he made no threats. Instead, *he entrusted himself to him who judges justly*" (1 Peter 2:23, emphasis added). Jesus, as the ever-obedient, ever-trusting adult Son of God, handed His soul over to His Father for safekeeping.

Clinging faith sees Father as the safety deposit box for our souls. People can kill our bodies. They can harm our souls. But they cannot kill or destroy our souls. Only God has power over our souls. Only God protects what is most central to us, the real us, the essential us.

The new you, like the eternal Christ, lives in conscious dependence upon Father. "For it is commendable if a man bears up under the pain of unjust suffering because he is *conscious of God*" (1 Peter 2:19, emphasis added). Conscious of what God, of what sort of God? Of the God who judges justly. The God who is good. Our faith rests upon the faithfulness of God. Our trust relies upon the trustworthiness of God.

The new you, with implanted new affections, clings to God, clings to the truth that God is good even when life is bad. "So then, those who suffer according to God's will," Peter explains, "should *commit themselves to their faithful Creator* and continue to do good" (1 Peter 4:19, emphasis added). Where we once had been like sheep going astray, we now return to the Shepherd of our soul (1 Peter 2:25). We had lived as fallen spiritual beings, alienated from Father, pursuing false lovers of our soul in our desperate desire for reunion. We now live as redeemed spiritual beings, reconciled to Father, pursuing Him as the sole Lover of and Love of our soul. He satisfies our desperate desire. We entrust ourselves to Father. Cling to Father. Hold onto Him for dear life, for He is dearer to us than life itself. We enjoy Father.

Our new affections incite us to trust Father so that we move from prodigals to clinging sons and daughters. Likewise, our new affections arouse us to trust Worthy Groom so that we move from adulterous whores to faithful virgin brides. We replace false lovers of our soul with sole devotion to Worthy Groom.

Of course, other lovers still entice you. Seduce. Tempt. However, the core new you has "tasted that the Lord is good" (1 Peter 2:3). Peter knew what he was talking about. Once the false love of self-preservation ruled his soul. Surrendering to her, he denied Worthy Groom three times (Mark 14:66-72). Once the false love of self-protection dominated his desires. Surrendering to her, he went back to fishing, the only livelihood he knew. Then the tender voice, the good heart, of Jesus called him back home. Home to Worthy Groom's heart. "Simon son of John, do you truly love me more than these?" (John 21:15).

Knowing the ever-present allure of false lovers, Peter urges us to "come to him, the living Stone" (1 Peter 2:4). The one known as "Rock" (Peter, *Petra*, Stone, Rock) reminds us that there is only one Stone, one Rock of Ages. "Now to you who believe, this stone is *precious*" (1 Peter 2:7, emphasis added). What an amazing, inspired choice of words. Precious (*timē*) means worthy, to deem worthy of honor, to evaluate as dear, to value as costly and of great price, to worship as supreme. Our new affections have tasted and seen that Worthy Groom is worthy, that Worthy Groom is our Chief Good. Our Chief Joy. "Though you have not seen him, *you* [the new you] *love him* . . . you believe in him and are filled with an inexpressible and glorious joy" (1 Peter 1:8, emphasis).

Did you notice how Peter links love and trust? Trust is the ultimate act of self-surrender. Nothing is more personal, more intimate.

> To trust a person is a more decisive, risk-laden act than to trust empirical evidence. Faith as trust is implied even in the etymology of the Hebrew verb *'aman* (to believe), to remain steadfast, to stay, to make the heart firm (Ps. 31:23; Neh. 7:2; Dan. 6:4). Saving faith is *personal* trust—trust in a person, Jesus Christ, the one mediator between God and humanity. The Greek terms that translate faith (*pistis, pisteuō*) imply reliance upon and trust in another who is viewed as trustworthy (root meaning: binding, putting faith in, relying upon) (Oden, *Life in the Spirit*, Vol. 3, p. 130).

Faith in Jesus equals entrusting our souls to Jesus.

Peter teaches us that we entrust ourselves to Jesus because we have quenched our thirst in His goodness, sated our hunger in His preciousness. Spiritual affections see and seek Christ-Most-Beautiful. Jesus-Most-Satisfying. When we truly love Christ's loveliness, then we can live with a benevolent detachment from the world, enjoying the friendship of Jesus so richly that the hostility of the world will be a small price to pay. Our new affections, then, involve a deeply felt personal preference for the beauty and favor of Christ, whatever the social cost. We see that to return to False Seducer and to self is to enter the brothel again. As Old Testament scholar Ray Ortlund, Jr. describes:

> More than our popular churches and institutions and movements, God wants us ourselves. He wants our hearts, our loyalty, our love for himself alone. He wants to find in us the same sense of intimate belonging to him that is appropriate to sexual union on the human level. More than our showing the world how "relevant" the church can be, God wants us to show him how much we treasure him above all else (Ortlund, *Whoredom*, p. 176).

Worthy Groom captures our new affections. Captivates our renewed souls.

Our new affections incite us to trust Father so we move from prodigals to clinging sons and daughters. They arouse us to trust Worthy Groom so we change from adulterous whores to faithful virgin brides. And they excite us to trust Mentor (Messenger, Holy Spirit) so we shift from independent self-sufficiency to dependent Spirit-sufficiency. Like Peter, as newborn babes we recognize how unbounded God's Spirit is and how contingent we are. "All men are like grass, and all their glory is like the flowers of the field; the grass withers and the flowers fall, but the word of the Lord stands forever" (1 Peter 1:24-25).

In our fallenness, we rejected God's awesomeness, refusing to experience God as "enough." We relied on ourselves, not God. Trusted in ourselves, not Christ. But our new nature is alive to reality—God reality and self-reality. We now recognize our frailty, dependence, and neediness.

Modern consciousness demands self-justification. We assume we must justify ourselves by our own effort.

> Culture-bound, stereotyped sex-role assumptions play heavily into modern forms of works-righteousness. Men commonly justify their existence by their physical or athletic ability or prowess or production or jobs or wealth; women commonly justify their existence by their beauty or nurturance. The message of justification is difficult to accept because it seems too good to be true. It says, Stop trying to justify yourself. You do not need to. There is no way to buy or deserve God's love or acceptance. You are already being offered God's love on the cross, without passing any tests. The word of the cross is not, I will love you *if* you jump this hoop, but "while we were yet helpless, at the right time, Christ died for the ungodly" (Romans 5:6-8, RSV). God who penetrates all subterfuges and masks knows already our failures and loves us anyway, just as we are (Oden, *Life in the Spirit*, Vol. 3, p. 112).

In regeneration, God crushes our stubbornly independent old soul, replacing it with a bent, a disposition, and inclination toward humble reliance. We realize we don't have to make life work on our own. We understand we have another Counselor who is our Guide, our Mentor, leading us, caring for us, coming alongside to help us (John 14-16).

Messenger, always pointing us to Christ, whispers in our ears, "Your deepest desires cannot be met anywhere except in a dependent relationship with Jesus. Your deepest needs are met in Christ. Your deepest fears are calmed in Worthy Groom. Rest. Be still. Entrust. Enjoy."

Redeemed Social Beings:
Purified Affections/Grace Lovers Who Minister to Others

As amazed as Peter is by the grace that changes our spiritual affections, he finds it equally astonishing that grace has transformed our social affections. I can hear him shouting to believers that they have been purified "so that you have sincere love for your brothers, love one another deeply, from the heart" (1 Peter 1:22). In fact, when he summarizes the implications of our new nature he emphasizes social engagement. "*Finally*, all of you, live in harmony with one another; be sympathetic, love as brothers, be compassionate and humble" (1 Peter 3:8, emphasis added).

I know, sometimes when you see how Christians "shoot their wounded," you wonder just how deeply we have been changed. I wonder, too. Several years ago I was involved in a consulting situation with a local church. After a decade of faithful ministry, their associate pastor was forced by the deacon board to resign. The pastor had not been guilty of any moral or doctrinal failure. The decision seemed ill advised. More to the point, the manner in which the deacons determined, communicated, and implemented their decision was, to say the least, atrocious, unconscionable. I've seen the secular business world handle matters more lovingly. I've seen unsaved executives treated with more honor, dignity, and respect.

So, like you, I wonder. I'm tempted to doubt. To ask, "Has a real change really taken place in our souls? Do we truly have new affections toward one another? Is it true that at the core of the redeemed soul lies a renewed heart with the capacity to love others as self?"

Yes.

Our failure to love one another speaks volumes about our refusal to reckon on our new nature. Although God has renewed our capacities, we still have the capability to return to our old way of living. When we do so, we are living like pagans, like unbelievers, living as though we were unregenerated (Ephesians 4:17-19). Fallen social beings live in separation from one another, digging broken cisterns of self-protection, manipulation, and retaliation in their endless quest for reconnection.

Paul reminds us, "You, however, did not come to know Christ that way" (Ephesians 4:20). Redeemed social beings understand their deepest social longings are fulfilled in non-demanding, mutual, reciprocal, interdependent, sacrificial, passionate relationships with others. Our new "social selves" are able to engage deeply with others. We're able to connect intimately. To minister sacrificially.

After the dismissal of the associate pastor, one of the deacons called me, troubled by his own behavior. As we worked together, he began to recognize that he had been energized by a passion to intimidate, rather than a passion to empower, serve, and love. He identified that his worldly business mindset crept into his church relationships. "I've been acting as though God is a help to my business card rather than God is my Helper and I am my brother's keeper. I've been putting myself and my ambitions above my church family." Repentant, this deacon threw himself upon God's mercy for forgiveness and for grace to help him reconcile.

Too late to return the associate pastor to his position in the congregation, the deacon knew that it was not too late to reconcile their relationship. As humbling as it was, through the power of grace relationships, we saw healing. The deacon took the courageous step of exposing his sin to his former pastor. He took the passionate step of entering empathetically into his pastor's hurting heart. Together they enjoyed tastes of grace.

How was it possible? Surrounded by all the horror stories of unhappy endings, how did this "church mess" find some healthy closure? A deacon, no, make that a redeemed social being, tapped into his core new passion to give, to care, to love, to minister. A new passion fueled by amazement at God's grace in his life.

Shift now from "Mr. Deacon" to you. To the new you. What relationships are fractured in your life? What pride do you harbor? What fears ensnare you? What core new passions are you suppressing? That last question is an odd one, isn't it? But it is the essential question. Break free from your spiritual amnesia concerning your passion for connection. Fan into flame your capacity to love your neighbor as yourself. Stir up your inclination to be your brother's keeper, your sister's protector. Be the new social being you are, the one who ministers to others. Be the new grace lover with purified affections that God created on the day He gave you spiritual birth.

Redeemed Self-Aware Beings:
Purified Affections/Grace Lovers Who Rest in Christ

Fallen self-aware beings experience dis-integration—a lack of personal health, wholeness, and holiness. They are, by nature, discontent with themselves—to the degree that they face the truth about their existence. They pursue controlling passions in their futile attempt to quiet inner restlessness.

Regeneration changes everything. We now have self shalom. We can say deep within our souls, "I am comfortable with who I am in Christ. I'm confident in who I am in Christ. I'm content with who I am in Christ."

Our sense of self is no longer dis-integrated. We are whole again. Complete in Christ. Not splintered. No longer needing to "find ourselves." We have been found by and in Christ.

Our conscience is no longer shameful. We no longer need to fear nakedness, exposure, or rejection.

Constant, life-long fear of rejection is how the unsaved exist. Jesus came to "free those who all their lives were held in slavery [enslaved, addicted, in bondage, shackled] by their fear [phobia] of death [separation, condemnation, rejection] (Hebrews 2:15).

The movie *The Ring* tells the fictional story of a terrified little girl who is hurled down a well shaft by her mother, left to die a lingering death over the course of the next seven days. This terrified girl is held captive not only in the well, but also to hopelessness and loneliness caused by rejection. Her one plea is that someone somewhere would hear her voice—not only the sound of her voice, but the cry of her soul for rescue, love, and justice.

By some (satanic) power, the girl torments others. They receive a death sentence when they unsuspectingly watch a video with clues to her murder. Exactly seven days later (the same amount of time it took her to die) she will find them and kill them. Tortured by fear, they live their remaining days in bondage to dread.

Designed to raise goose bumps the size of California, the movie should raise to consciousness the unconscious fear that every unsaved person has regarding his final destiny. It is, as we shall show in chapters 28 and 29, a destiny of alienation, separation, and dis-integration. A destiny of rejection and condemnation. A maddening destiny that lies secretly hidden like a ghostly invader underneath every thought that every unsaved person has every second of his or her life.

We are free from that!

Free from those thoughts. No longer driven by the hunger to find some solace in the few days we have left. No longer hounded by the passion to find personal peace because by *grace* we have already found personal peace.

Peter experienced regenerative peace. "Do not fear what they fear; do not be frightened" (1 Peter 3:14). Their ultimate fear? "The face of the Lord is against those who do evil" (1 Peter 3:12). The unsaved live every moment in fear of a *coram Deo* encounter with God that is terrifying because it involves falling into the hands of an angry God who must judge sin by separating Himself from unrepentant sinners.

The saved have the pledge of a good conscience before God. "... not the removal of dirt from the body but the pledge of a good conscience toward God. It saves you by the resurrection of Jesus Christ" (1 Peter 3:21b). Regeneration does not remove filth from the body. Much better, it removes all filth from the soul. Consequently, we have the pledge (*eperōtēma*) of a good conscience before God, of a conscience that is at rest, peaceful, whole, integrated. The Greeks used "pledge" in the court context of judicial examination. When the probing light of God's holiness exposes the depths of our conscience, God sees only purity. Therefore, we experience harmony with God, and by extension, within our own souls, our own conscience. If God is at peace with us, shouldn't we be at peace with ourselves?

Since I have peace in my soul—a good conscience before the God of the universe—I don't have to live every day self-consciously wondering, "How am I coming across?" "What does so and so think of me?" "Is everyone happy with me?" Instead, I am free to reach out to others, listening to their longing to be heard, responding to their desire to be accepted, answering their questions about where they can find personal peace. My reconciled and reintegrated soul empowers me to be an ambassador of reconciliation.

Jesus summarized our new affections when He summarized the entire Bible.

"'Love the Lord your God with all your heart and with all your soul and with all your mind.' This is the first and greatest commandment. And the second is like it: 'Love your neighbor as yourself.' All the Law and the Prophets hang on these two commandments" (Matthew 22:37-40).

In the core of the new you is new grace love. The core you loves God—worships Him, exalts Him by entrusting yourself to Him and enjoying Him as the crown jewel of all desiring. The core you loves others—intimately ministering to others, serving others with sacrificial engagement, connecting to others in unlayered relationship. The core you is at peace with who you are in Christ—content, confident, competent in Christ. You are a saint filled with the pure passion of God-empowered grace love.

Redeemed Rational Beings: Penetrating Sages
Wise Mindsets/Spiritual Imaginations

Saints are penetrating Sages returned to sanity by Worthy Groom. Enlightened to the reality of God's larger story invading their smaller stories, saints perceive life from God's perspective.

New controlling images and guiding beliefs about life are possible because we have been made new in the spirit of our minds—in the very core of our rational control center (Ephesians 4:23). The new spiritual mindset focuses on, values, and desires what the Spirit desires (Romans 8:5). The renewed mind is controlled by the Spirit and results in life and peace as it exists in a spirit of submission to God's truth and friendliness toward God (Romans 8:6-9).

Rather than foolishly following the ideas of this present darkness, we now wisely follow the images and ideas of Jesus who is truth (John 14:6). With penetrating sagacity, our new mind has the capacity to think God's thoughts after Him, to see life with spiritual eyes, with 20/20 spiritual vision.

More importantly, our new mindset values what God values. Most importantly, our new mindset values God as our greatest value. It sees God as our Chief Good, Supreme Good. Consider Moses.

> He chose to be mistreated along with the people of God rather than to enjoy the pleasures of sin for a short time. He regarded disgrace for the sake of Christ as of greater value than the treasures of Egypt, because he was looking ahead to his reward (Hebrews 11:25-26).

Moses *chose*. He made a volitional choice, electing God and God's people over the world. Why did he make that decision? What rational direction (mindset) guided his volitional decision? Moses' rational reflections orbited around his relational affections. Exploring the issues Moses grappled with, we perceive their connection to desires, affections, pleasures, and longings. He chose between enjoying the immediate pleasures of sin, including the treasures of Egypt, for a short time and immediate mistreatment and disgrace along with the delayed gratification of a future reward. *Pleasure and reward legitimately occupied his thinking.*

"Pleasure" (*apolausis* from *apolauō*) is a neutral word picturing the desire, pursuit, and obtainment of enjoyment. In 1 Timothy 6:17, Paul uses the word for putting our hope in God who richly provides us with everything for our enjoyment (*apolausis*). What pleasures and treasures tempted Moses? Wealth. Nobility. Honor. Fine food and fine women in the Egyptian courts.

How was he able to resist these allurements? Why was his imagination not captured by these seductions? He was looking ahead (*apoblepō*). He was looking away from all else to one thing—his future with God. As the modern phrase suggests, he "kept eternity's values in view." His focus was not on the smaller, earthly, temporal story, but upon the larger, heavenly, eternal story.

What was Moses looking ahead to? His eternal perspective focused his attention on his "reward" (*misthapodosian*). The word means wages given for work, payment of wages. Hebrews 10:35 and 11:6 use it to speak of God as the Rewarder who gives graciously, abundantly, beyond what is deserved.

Moses' mind regarded and esteemed (*hēgomai*) his future reward to be of more value than his immediate benefits. "Regard" means to lead before the mind, consider, count, account, esteem, believe, regard as, interpret, and exegete. When Moses exegeted this passage of his life story, his interpretation was clear. "God is good. God is better. God is best. God is my Supreme Good. Worthy Groom is worthy. Messenger is marvelous. The Trinity is worth the wait."

Moses *evaluated what was of greater value* and concluded that disgrace for Christ was more pleasant, pleasurable, and pleasing than the treasures of Egypt. They were greater riches (*meizona plouton*)—overflowing, full, fullness of goods, wealth. Moses valued God as his greatest value. Like Moses, when life is bad, or even when life is good, we must remind ourselves that God is not only good, God is our Supreme Good.

We base biblical counseling on this reality. A husband I counseled consistently described himself as a "Monster." When he terrorized his wife or daughter, he'd sorrowfully say, "I've been such a monster." Unfortunately, his anguish was infiltrated with worldly sorrow instigated by satanic images. "Monster" caused him to feel bad about and sorry for himself. It made him feel hopeless and helpless. True victory came only when he pictured himself the way God saw him. "I'm a rebel." Now he was talking God's talk by labeling his sin rebelliousness against God's calling on his life as a loving husband and non-exasperating father. Now his mindset and God's mindset merged.

But the battle still raged. He had to repent of his false god, the unique idol he had created to make his life work apart from God. "Verbal Terrorist" was the label he gave his false god. "I talk for a living. Convincing people of things is my forte. I've taken this pattern of relating into every arena of my life. If you disagree with me, look out! I'll blast you. Sometimes forcefully. Other times subtly. Either way, my agenda, the passion I pursue, is to dominate. I've made browbeating my god."

Putting off his ungodly images and values began a powerful change process. Perhaps better said, it began a powerful process of fanning into flame the changed person that he already was in Christ. "If I'm not 'Mr. Monster Verbal Terrorist'; if those are sinful lies that I've used to live in independence from God, then who am I? Who's the real me that I've been burying?"

In his new grace narrative of himself, his calling, and his life, he saw himself as "Mr. Encourager." "I long to use my verbal gifts to put courage, rather than terror, into my wife's heart. I want to build up my daughter, not frighten her." His new realization of God's truth (of reality from God's viewpoint) fueled his new view of himself and his new passion to minister to others.

This was a difficult struggle for him. The world, the flesh, and the Devil were his vicious foes. They worked in tandem lying to him about who he was. A paraphrase from C. S. Lewis began to give my counselee victory—we're given a revision of our script by the other players in our life who either choose us for the wrong reasons or never choose us at all. So our evaluation of our souls is drawn from a world filled with people still terribly confused about the nature of their own souls!

My counselee was able to laugh at himself—at the folly of living his life based upon what "insane" people were telling him about himself. Eventually he began to be controlled by the controlling images of who he was to Christ and in Christ.

You can be, too. Peter wrote both his letters "as reminders to stimulate you to wholesome (*eilikrinē*) thinking" (2 Peter 3:1). "Wholesome" is a compound from *heili* meaning "sunlight" and *krinō* meaning "judge, discern." As the sun enlightens things so you can see clearly, so the Son enlightens you so you can discern clearly. Peter reminds you to examine your life according to "Sonlight." Sonlight makes reality clear and transparent, purges the blinders placed upon your mind by False Seducer, allowing you to think sincerely, purely, and wholesomely.

Notice also that Peter was *not* trying to *implant* wholesome thoughts. He was stimulating, arousing, and fanning into flame the wholesome mindset *already embedded* in renewed minds.

Peter urges you to "gird up the loins of your mind" (1 Peter 1:13, KJV). When you feel as though old habituate mindsets dominate your thought life, take responsibility. Tighten your mental belt. Prepare your mind for action. When overwhelmed by worldly thinking pressing you into its temporal, materialistic mold, select the mindset that you are an alien and a stranger in this world (1 Peter 2:11). When you encounter satanic temptation, be clear minded, be mentally alert, resist the Devil and he will flee from you (1 Peter 5:8-9).

You can think imaginatively and wisely, rather than simply and foolishly. You can live according to grace narratives that teach you how to say No! to seductive sinful desires and how to value and say Yes! to pure sanctified desires. You have been restored to sanity. You're a pure Dreamer enraptured by the Worthy Groom. God has replaced arrogance with humility through your new heart and mind. With Christ and in Christ you believe the truth about where life is found. You worship God, correctly perceiving that He satisfies your affections.

Redeemed Volitional Beings: Empowering Shepherds
Other-Centered Purposes/Empowering Pathways

Saints are empowered and empowering Shepherds returned to vitality by Worthy Groom, freed to exercise dominion over their passions and God's planet, freed to empower others. The volitionally mature saint says, "I find my life by dying to myself, taking up my cross, and following Christ. I am responsible for my actions and the motivations behind them. This is my new, other-centered pathway in Christ."

Regenerating grace makes possible our new spiritual self-control because:

Regeneration illumines this vast moral darkness, renovates the moral will, empowers the will to do the good, takes away the love of sin and the despair over sin's seeming permanence. Trust in idols is displaced by trust in the mercy of God. The cacophony of idolatrous loves is refashioned into a symphony of creaturely values loved in relation to the love of God (Oden, *Life in the Spirit*, Vol. 3, p. 167).

God frees our will. Since God enlightened our rationality, we now correctly perceive what is relationally pleasing, good, and desirable; therefore, our free will is empowered to pursue God's good and perfect will. When we arm ourselves with the same attitude as Christ (rational direction), then we do not live the rest of our lives for evil human desires but rather for the will of God (relational motivation), and we reject the pagan choices (volitional interaction) we used to make (1 Peter 4:1-3).

Based on our new birth (1 Peter 1:3-12), Peter teaches that we can "be self-controlled" (1 Peter 1:13a). He identifies us as "obedient children" (1 Peter 1:14a), while Paul labeled our former selves as "those who are disobedient" (Ephesians 2:2b). So changed are we that Peter says we can and must stop conforming "to the evil desires you had when you lived in ignorance" (1 Peter 1:14b). Instead, "just as he who called you is holy, so be holy in all you do" (1 Peter 1:15).

Our new will has a new *telos*, a new purpose, goal, and reason for existence. We have been "redeemed from the empty way of life" (1 Peter 1:18b) we lived before our regeneration. "Empty" (*mataios*) carries the sense of "vain, deceptive, pointless, futile, ineffectual, and nothingness." As Solomon noted, without God all is meaningless and purposeless. Before regenerative grace, our wills were bound to our old nature. Thus our old wills pursued foolish, selfish, temporal, materialistic, and pointless pathways. Our bellies became our gods (Romans 16:18; Philippians 3:19) in that we futilely served our own finite, foolish appetites instead of God's infinite, wise will. Our destiny was destruction (Philippians 3:19).

What renewed destiny has God freed our wills to pursue? We are free to enjoy God (1 Peter 1:8) and to love one another (1 Peter 1:22). We are mature in Christ (1 Peter 2:2) and worship and serve God (1 Peter 2:5). We're free to live as a chosen people, a royal priesthood, a holy nation, and a people belonging to God (1 Peter 2:9). Free to declare the praises of God (1 Peter 2:9), live good lives that glorify God, witness to the unsaved (1 Peter 2:12), and on and on Peter continues.

Peter emphasizes our responsibility to use our freedom to serve others rather than ourselves. "Live as free men, but do not use your freedom as a cover-up for evil; live as servants of God" (1 Peter 2:16). "Each one should use whatever gift he has received to serve others, faithfully administering God's grace in its various forms" (1 Peter 4:10).

More than anything else, God has freed us to be empowering shepherds.

> Be shepherds of God's flock that is under your care, serving as overseers—not because you must, but because you are willing, as God wants you to be; not greedy for money, but eager to serve; not lording it over those entrusted to you, but being examples to the flock (1 Peter 5:2-3).

Again we are "Creators"—under-shepherds serving the Chief Shepherd. We surrender our wills to Worthy Groom. We depend upon Christ's sufficiency and not our self-sufficiency. God has re-engaged our wills so we can choose courageously, not compulsively. All that we accomplish we label "grace creations" because we recognize that any gift we have, any talent, any creativity, is from God and for God.

In our fallen volitionality, tragically we fell from Creators to Destroyers and Slaves. Not being God, but being finite, we couldn't pull off our selfish goals self-sufficiently. So we manipulated others to meet our perceived needs and false goals, and we retaliated against one another for not meeting those perceived needs and false goals. We became enslaved to the vicious cycle of always needing more and more petty substitutes to make our puny lives seem complete.

God reversed our volitional curses. He replaced our habituate self-centered pathways with spiritually disciplined, other-centered pathways. He exchanged our self-protective styles of interactions for empowering styles of interaction.

Sounds impossible? Without God all things are impossible.

A husband and father illustrates that all things, including freely and courageously living for others, is possible with God. He found himself sinking in the quicksand of cowardice. Whenever his strength was needed at home, he abdicated. Confusion terrified him.

Knowing that courage was "in there," carved into the essence of his new will, I asked him, "What would you like to be for your three ladies (his wife and two daughters)?" "What would it look like for you to face chaos courageously?" "When have you done that, even a little, through Christ?" "How were you tapping into His resurrection power at those victorious, courageous times?"

Little by little, he began to see that he was free to love, and he was capable of loving. His new rallying cry became, "I will never abdicate!" He began to practice bold love. When his wife put him down, he would say, "That's neither true nor deserved. I'm sorry

I've allowed us to relate in these childish ways in the past, but we're simply not going to relate like that anymore." When I would suggest areas of confident sacrifice for his "three ladies," he would say, "If it will help, I'm willing." His motto became, "What would trust in God look like in my relationships?"

You can also trust God to lead you confidently and courageously into the chaos points of your life. Live by "grace empowerment"—the resurrection power imbedded in your being at regeneration. Live according to other-centered pathways—the renewed will implanted in you at salvation. You can create beauty from ashes when your life purpose is fueled by the passion to empower others. You are a saint, which means you are a shepherd, which means you have what it takes to make a difference for God's glory and others' good.

Redeemed Emotional Beings: Soulful Poets
Managed Mood States/Thriving Mode

Saints are soulful Poets returned to integrity by Worthy Groom and enlivened to experience life honestly in all its grief and hope. We are not ashamed of our emotionality. We don't consider emotions the black sheep of the image bearing family. We don't hide from our feelings. We are alive to life in all its external vicissitudes and internal joys and sorrows.

What a reversal from our fallen emotionality where we are afraid to feel anything deeply, honestly, and ended up living for shallow emotional highs and avoided personal pain at all cost. We practiced emotional stoicism (repressing our moods), emotional sensationalism (expressing moods without control or concern for others), or emotional sensualism (anesthetizing our moods).

Biblical emotionality enables us to face our feelings and manage our moods. We learn candid honesty with ourselves about our feelings. Like Jeremiah, we identify our mood states, "My soul is downcast within me" (Lamentations 3:20). We learn to express our feelings courageously to Father and to soothe our soul in our Savior. "Cast all your anxiety on him because he cares for you" (1 Peter 5:7). We learn to bring rationality to our emotionality. "In your anger do not sin. Do not let the sun go down while you are still angry, and do not give the Devil a foothold" (Ephesians 4:26-27).

Emotional maturity permeates every aspect of our renewed inner being. Spiritually, we can soothe our soul in our Savior. Socially we can empathize with others, sustaining and healing them. As self-aware beings we can admit, understand, accept, and manage our moods. Rationally we can bring rationality to our emotionality by understanding with wisdom the causes and nature of our feelings and by envisioning with spiritual eyes imaginative ways to handle our moods. Volitionally we can consciously and courageously choose to respond creatively to our emotional mood states.

I find that we tend to be kindergartners when it comes to emotional maturity. We've barely learned the "ABCs" of emotional intelligence. With this in mind, I offer some emotional ABCs.

- ♦ A: How are our emotions and mood states of value to us?
- ♦ B: How are our emotions and mood states of value to others?
- ♦ C: How can we practice the hallmarks of emotional maturity?

How Are Our Emotions and Mood States of Value to Us?

How do we develop an inner attitude that leads to reordered emotions? How do we manage our moods? Emotions serve as God-given "dummy lights"—that flashing red light on our dash that says, "Hey, dummy, you'd better pop the hood 'cause something is haywire underneath." Emotions are our warning lights that say, "There's something important going on inside, pop the hood of your heart and check it out." Our emotions point to our goals, which in turn point to our beliefs. Emotions are a God-given means for discerning inner motivation and thinking.

What can we expect of our own emotions? Often we're afraid of our emotions because we do not understand what is natural. Mark 3:5 helps us because it describes the emotional life of Christ. "He looked around at them in anger and, deeply distressed at their stubborn hearts, said to the man, 'Stretch out your hand.' He stretched it out, and his hand was completely restored."

In this passage we learn that *Jesus experienced strong emotions*. He experienced anger. This particular word for anger has the sense of "strong indignation and wrath." He also experienced compassion, which is "deep distress and grief." Shouldn't image bearers expect to experience strong emotions since Christ did? Don't deny them. Don't stuff them. Experience them.

We also learn that *Jesus experienced a full range of both pleasant and painful emotions*. He felt anger and compassion simultaneously. "While being grieved he felt intense anger" (Mark 3:5, author's paraphrase). We, too, should expect to go through a full range of both pleasant and painful emotions. The lack of intense emotions has nothing to do with emotional maturity.

When we experience an emotion, what should we do with it? First, admit it. Acknowledge to yourself and God what you are feeling. Second, identify it. "I'm hurt, angry, content, nervous, etc." Third, courageously face and feel that emotion. This is not an academic exercise. It is deeply feeling what is going on inside. Fourth, always share with God what you are feeling (Hebrews 4:15-16). When you're feeling an illegitimate emotion (hatred, etc.) confess it deeply, including confessing the goals and beliefs behind the feeling (1 John 1:8-2:2). When you're feeling a legitimate emotion (joy, sorrow, etc.) share it fully (Psalm 42:5). Fifth, use that emotion to probe and to examine your goals and beliefs. An acknowledged illegitimate emotion functions as a clue to a spiritual malfunction just as an acknowledged physical symptom (i.e., a cancer warning sign) serves as a clue to a deeper physical problem.

When do we probe? Even a good thing can be misused or overused. Should we constantly probe and become compulsively introspective? No. No one (no one in their right mind at least) checks under the hood of his car before every trip to the grocery store. No, you check periodically, before long trips, and when the light comes on. The same is true with emotions. When the light of intense emotion flashes, then check your goals and beliefs. For most Christians, the problem is checking far too infrequently. We tend to be afraid of our emotions. So I encourage you to check periodically, and always to check during times of extremely strong emotions.

How Are Our Emotions and Mood States of Value to Others?

Jesus modeled a cardinal principle of emotional maturity when He purposely expressed His feelings to others in order to minister to them. The original language of Mark 3:5 is clear. "He chose to look around with angry glances, stopping at each one of them" (author's paraphrase). Jesus made a volitional choice to express His emotional reaction. On what basis did Christ do so? On what basis should we do the same? I believe we should express our feelings to others only when we can meet the following criteria:

◆ We can answer the question: "How will expressing my feelings increase the potential for the other person's growth in Christ?"
◆ We have previously established a strong relationship with the other person.
◆ We believe the person has the emotional maturity to handle and benefit from our sharing.
◆ We believe that sharing our feelings has the potential for healing the relationship.
◆ We are under control enough to think through the previous criteria. Or stated another way, we can govern the release of our emotions.

How Can We Practice the Hallmarks of Emotional Maturity?

Emotional maturity consists of our ability to be managed by the Spirit so we can manage ourselves and master the art of relating to others. The mature person has an emotional repertoire tailored to glorify God by showing God's majesty and beauty to a weak and ugly world.

God designed our emotions to put us in motion. However, living in a fallen world, inhabiting unredeemed bodies, and tempted by an unloving enemy (False Seducer), we dare not allow our emotions to manage us. God calls on us to manage, master, and govern our emotions.

The problem is not with emotionality, but with the appropriateness of emotions and their governed expression. The question is, "How can we bring spiritual maturity to our emotions?" As Aristotle said, "Anyone can become angry—that is easy. But to be angry with the right person, to the right degree, at the right time, for the right purpose, and in the right way—that is not easy."

Without the Spirit's control, we are vulnerable to what Daniel Goleman calls emotional hijackings (see Goleman, *Emotional Intelligence*). Our emotions, being designed as bridges between our outer world and our inner life, scream at us, "Act! Don't think! 911. Emergency! Emergency!"

I tell people, "Our body has a mind of its own." The physical brain transmits urgent messages to act and react. As Paul teaches in Romans 6, however, spiritual maturity includes yielding our body, including our brain, to the service of God's will. Thus we must learn to control our physical brain with our spiritual mind. We need to bring rationality to bear on our emotionality. Emotions are fast and sloppy. Our spirit/soul/mind/will/inner person is our emotional manager. We are to be our brain's emotional damper switch.

Goleman's research into brain physiology and healthy emotionality suggests that emotional maturity includes at least five emotional management skills:

- ♦ Emotional Self-Awareness:　　Soul-Awareness
- ♦ Emotional Spirit-Mastery:　　Soothing Our Soul in Our Savior
- ♦ Emotional Motivation:　　　Managing Our Moods
- ♦ Emotional Empathy:　　　　Recognizing Emotions in Others
- ♦ Emotional Savvy:　　　　　Handling Relationships

Let us examine briefly each of these emotional life skills from a biblical perspective.

My first emotional management skill is *emotional self-awareness*. Emotional maturity begins with my awareness of my feelings as they occur. Am I able to recognize and name my own moods? Able to understand the causes of my feelings?

When I am emotionally self-aware, I give ongoing attention to my internal state. I am aware both of my mood and my thoughts about my mood. "I'm feeling down right now and it is frightening me." Actively monitoring my moods helps me begin to gain control of them.

The capacity to soothe my soul in God (*emotional spirit-mastery*) is my second emotional management skill. It begins with my ability to take *everything* I am feeling to God.

It also involves my capacity for emotional self-regulation and responsibility. Thus it eschews the ventilation fallacy that teaches that catharsis—uncontrolled expression of what I am feeling and experiencing—is necessary for emotional health. Instead, what is necessary for emotional health is candor with myself about what I am feeling, candor with God about my mood states, and selective expression of my feelings toward others.

Goleman labels managing our moods (*emotional motivation*) the "master aptitude." This third emotional management skill includes harnessing my emotions in the service of a goal (emotionality in the service of volitionality). It also involves stifling my impulses (what the Bible calls "passions of the flesh") and delaying gratification (Romans 5 and 8).

Hope is a key to emotional self-motivation and delayed gratification. Hope produces resilience, perseverance, and longsuffering. It allows us to turn setbacks into comebacks. Optimistic hope in God is vital. It says, "I can do all things through Christ who strengthens me" (Philippians 4:19 paraphrase). "I can meet challenges as they arise." The result is learned contentment in whatever state I'm in (whatever external situation or internal mood).

The fourth emotional management skill is *empathy* or the ability to recognize emotions in others. Empathy builds on self-awareness. When I don't have to strain to hear my own emotional voice, I find myself hearing others with crystal clarity. That's empathy: fluency in others' emotional language. The more open I am to my own emotions, the more skilled I will be in reading the feelings of others.

How attuned are you to others? Are you emotionally tone-deaf, or do you have the ability to sense another's mood? Do you practice the artful, creative, aesthetic ability to perceive the subjective experience of another person? Can you make another person's pain your own? Are you skilled at seeing another's perspective?

Goleman labels the fifth emotional management skill—*emotional savvy*—"the social art" or the art of emotional influence. It is the capacity to be emotionally nourishing, the ability to leave others in a good mood.

Emotional savvy involves interpersonal effectiveness that includes managing emotions in others, helping others to soothe themselves in God, and becoming an emotional tool kit for others. Obviously, it is a prime quality needed by every spiritual friend, biblical counselor, and pastor.

The new you can manage your emotions, can govern your mood states. You can thrive by experiencing joy in the midst of sorrow, hope in the midst of grief, and peace in the midst of turmoil. The power comes through grace connecting. Only as we connect with God, soothing our soul in our Savior, can we courageously choose to connect with our fallen world in an emotionally mature manner.

Of all people, Christians should be Singers and Poets. We should be the most dynamic. We should be fully open to Worthy Groom. Our lives should be poetic, not stoic. God has renewed our emotional being so we can experience life deeply.

Redeemed Physical Beings: Connected Characters
Habituated Tendencies Disciplined by the Spirit

Saints are connected Characters returned to activity by Worthy Groom and called as main characters in the drama of redemption. Regenerated, we realize we need God. We know we cannot live by bread alone, but by every Word that comes from the mouth of God. At the same time, we realize we need bread. We are frail. Contingent. Finite. Needy. We have no problem admitting, "All men are like grass, and all their glory is like the flowers of the field; the grass withers and the flowers fall" (1 Peter 1:24). Nor do we have any struggle identifying our source of strength. "If anyone serves, he should do it with the strength God provides, so that in all things God may be praised through Jesus Christ" (1 Peter 4:11).

I have had counselees ask me, "Why did God give us bodies? Why couldn't He have made us like angels?" Of course, He could have made us like angels. A prime reason God gave us bodies relates to the two passages we've just quoted. God wants our bodies to be a constant reminder of our dependency, of our need to connect to His power, His resources, and His daily provision ("give us *this day* our daily bread") in order to survive and thrive.

Through the Fall, our embodied souls used our physicality in the service of unrighteousness (Romans 6:12-23). Through regeneration, our embodied, renewed souls can serve God again. "Do not offer the parts of your body [tongue to lie, hands to steal, eyes to lust, etc.] to sin, as instruments of wickedness, but rather offer yourselves [your embodied personality] . . . to him as instruments of righteousness." (Romans 6:13).

Because our bodies (our physical selves) await final glorification (Romans 8:17-25), we still battle against the ingrained tendencies embedded in our flesh (brain/body/bones/belly/glands complex). However, because of the renewal of our inner person (our soul, mind/heart, will, and emotions; our relational, rational, volitional, and emotional being), our bodies no longer have to be Traitors. We can bring spirituality to our physicality. We can tame the Traitor making him or her again a connector, a Character playing a leading role in God's drama of redemption. Again we can fulfill God's Creation Mandate for us to have dominion over our physical world. "Connected" suggests our need to rely upon and tap into Christ's resurrection power in order to discipline spiritually our embodied selves. (Box 24:2 provides a summary of the Creation, Fall, and Redemption of the human personality.)

Box 24:2

The Creation/Fall/Redemption of the Human Personality

Creation/Paradise
Our Original Personality Structure: Innocent and Connected

♦ Relational Being Who Longs for God: Pure Affection/Grace Lover—Worship
♦ Rational Being Who Thinks Like God: Insightful Mindset—Wisdom
♦ Volitional Being Who Chooses God's Will: Empowered Purpose/Willing Pathway—Surrender
♦ Emotional Being Who Feels Alive: Controlled Mood State—Shalom
♦ Physical Being Who Experiences God's Power: Empowered Habituate Tendency—Servant of Righteousness

Fall/Cisterns
Our Fallen Personality Structure: Depraved and Deprived

♦ Relational Being Who Hates God: Impure Affection/False Lover—Independence
♦ Rational Being Who Suppresses God's Truth: Foolish Mindset—Blindness
♦ Volitional Being Who Lives for Self: Self-Centered Purpose/Manipulative Retaliatory Pathway—Willfulness
♦ Emotional Being Who Feels Dis-integrated: Ungoverned Mood State—Shame/ Disintegration (Anxiety, Anger, Depression)
♦ Physical Being Who Experiences Weakness: Disconnected Habituate Tendency—Fleshly Living

Redemption/Springs
Our Redeemed Personality Structure: Reconciled and Renewed

♦ Relational Being Who Loves Passionately: Purified Affection/Grace Lover—Entrusting
♦ Rational Being Who Thinks Wisely: Renewed Mindset/Grace Narrative—Enlightened
♦ Volitional Being Who Chooses Courageously: Empowered Other-Centered Purpose/Grace Pathway—Empowering (Ministry, Death to Self)
♦ Emotional Being Who Experiences Fully: Managed Mood State/Peace—Engaged
♦ Physical Being Who Is God's Vessel: Reconnected Habituate Tendency/ Spiritually Disciplined Living—Enlivened

Where We've Been and Where We're Heading

I hope that you are asking, "How? Tell me how I connect to Christ's resurrection power?" That's the focus of the next three chapters. Now that we've seen the "new you," we want to explore how the new you grows.

We are neonatal saints who need to grow in grace. We are *nikao* saints who need to live out our victory in Christ. Knowing who we are is much of the battle. Now that we know, we need to learn what it means to "reckon" (Romans 6:11, KJV) on these amazing truths of our new nature in Christ.

Caring for Your Soul: Personal Applications

1. Reflect on the change in Peter's life from "Foot-in-Mouth-Simon" in the Gospels to "Peter-the-Rock" in Acts and the Epistles. What changed him? Be specific.

2. Reflect on the change in Paul's life from "Paul-the-Christian-Slayer" before Acts 9 to "Paul-the-Satan-Slayer" in the rest of Acts and the Epistles. What changed him? Be specific.

3. Reflect on the change in your life since your salvation. What labels identify the old you? What new descriptions capture the new you? What changed you? Be specific.

4. Take a Redeemed Personality Inventory, evaluating your current progress toward Christlikeness. Use a 10 for "Most Like Christ" and a 1 for "Least Like Christ."

    - I cling to God/run home to Father like a faithful son or daughter.
    - I enjoy my Worthy Groom more than any other joy in life.
    - I depend upon the Holy Spirit to beautify and empower me.
    - I love others deeply from the heart.
    - I rest confidently and comfortably in who I am in Christ.
    - I value what God values.
    - I see God as my Chief Good.
    - I allow the eternal story to invade my earthly story.
    - I stir up wholesome thinking in my mindsets.
    - I find my life by dying to myself, taking up my cross, and following Christ.
    - I live to empower others.
    - In my relationships I ask, "What would courageous trust in Christ look like?"
    - I practice emotional self-awareness.
    - I practice emotional spirit-mastery: soothing my soul in my Savior.
    - I practice emotional maturity: managing my moods.
    - I practice emotional empathy: recognizing emotions in others.
    - I practice emotional savvy: handling my relationships well.
    - I admit my absolute need, body and soul, for God.
    - I allow my physical frailties to remind me of my need for God.

Caring for Others: Ministry Implications

♦ **Don't Be Shocked:** When you work with Christians, don't be shocked by goodness. Expect it. Insist upon it. As soul physicians of a new soul, stir up the new person residing within your spiritual friends. Treat them as redeemed Romancers, Dreamers, Creators, Singers, and Actors. This requires, first of all, that you believe they are new, that you see them as new. Biblical counselors have to "reckon" on the newness of their Christian counselees.

♦ **Be Focused:** What is our goal? Our target? Do we simply work toward solutions? No. We work toward ever-increasing likeness to Christ. So our targets in biblical counseling include:

- Relational Purity: Entice your spiritual friends to love God passionately and their neighbors as themselves with grace love.
- Rational Sanity: Enlighten your spiritual friends to the reality that God's larger story invades their smaller story. Help them see life with spiritual eyes.
- Volitional Vitality: Empower your spiritual friends so they are freed to empower others.
- Emotional Integrity: Enliven your spiritual friends so they face life honestly in all its grief and hope.
- Physical Activity/Connectivity: Equip your spiritual friends to practice the classic spiritual disciplines so they can connect to Christ's resurrection power and yield the members of their bodies as instruments of righteousness.

♦ **Use Renewed Life Themes:** Renewed life themes become handles that help you know where to focus your attention and energy. When confused by the myriad of possible directions to go with your spiritual friends, always return to grace lovers/purified affections, wise mindsets, other-centered purposes/pathways, managed mood states, and disciplined habituate tendencies.

CHAPTER TWENTY-FIVE

VIRGIN BRIDE GROWS IN GRACE

Sanctification is "the consistent practical outworking of what it means to belong to the new creation in Christ" (Sinclair Ferguson, "The Reformed View," in *Christian Spirituality*, p. 60).

"So, in practice we should constantly be reminding ourselves who we are. We need to learn to talk to ourselves, and ask ourselves questions: 'Don't you know? Don't you know the meaning of conversion and baptism? Don't you know that you have been united to Christ in his death and resurrection? Don't you know that you have been enslaved to God and have committed yourself to His obedience? Don't you know these things? Don't you know who you are?' We must go on pressing ourselves with such questions, until we reply to ourselves, 'Yes, I do know who I am, a new person in Christ, and by the grace of God I shall live accordingly'" (John Stott, *Romans: God's Good News for the World*, p. 187).

Peter Pan with Amnesia

The apostle Peter urges us to avoid the *Spiritual Peter Pan Syndrome*: babes in Christ who refuse to grow up in Christ. "Like newborn babies, crave pure spiritual milk, so that by it you may grow up in your salvation" (1 Peter 2:2). Likewise, he exhorts us to avoid the *Spiritual Amnesia Syndrome*: victors in Christ who forget to live out our victory through Christ.

For if you possess these qualities in increasing measure, they will keep you from being ineffective and unproductive in your knowledge of our Lord Jesus Christ. But if anyone does not have them, he is nearsighted and blind, and has forgotten that he has been cleansed from his past sins (2 Peter 1:8-9).

To avoid the *Spiritual Peter Pan Syndrome*, we will explore how neonatal saints grow up in Christ. We have demonstrated that we are neonatal saints—saints for sure, but at the inception of our regeneration we are *baby* saints. How do we grow? How do we become more like Jesus?

To avoid the *Spiritual Amnesia Syndrome*, we will ponder how *nikao* saints experience victory through Christ. We have shown that we are *nikao* saints—more than conquerors in Christ, freed from sin to righteousness through Christ, but still in a battle to experience our victory in Christ. What is the nature of our battle? How do we live victorious lives in our combat against the world, the flesh, and the Devil?

Growth in Christ and victory through Christ are essential principles for soul physicians. They inform us that in working with neonatal saints we move from soul OB/GYNs to soul pediatricians helping the growing child of God to live a healthy, whole, holy life. These principles teach us that in working with *nikao* saints, we assume the role of spiritual personal trainer or coach, assisting the maturing spiritual athlete to run the race and finish the course victorious for and through Jesus.

Neonatal Saints Growing Up in Christ: Progressive Sanctification

We are moving from positional sanctification (Chapters 20 through 24) to progressive sanctification (Chapters 25 through 27). Positional sanctification teaches what Christ has already accomplished for us and who we already are in Him. Progressive sanctification demonstrates how we make real in our daily experience what is already true about us. Henry Holloman offers a succinct biblical definition of progressive sanctification.

> Through faith in Christ a person is born into God's family and becomes His spiritual child. God has planned that His spiritual infants grow to spiritual maturity, and this requires that they practice biblical principles of spiritual growth and receive spiritual nurture from other Christians. The spiritual growth of Christians is called "progressive sanctification" (Holloman, *The Forgotten Blessing*, p. 2).

God is in the holiness business. Holiness includes moving from spiritual infancy to spiritual maturity. "The divine agenda for the rest of my life on earth is my sanctification" (J. I. Packer, *Rediscovering Holiness*, p. 60).

What does sanctification look like? It looks like Jesus. It looks like you and me looking like Jesus. The plot line of the saint's life is to be like Jesus. Speaking of progressive sanctification based on positional sanctification, John Stott teaches:

> Already the image of God, marred by the fall, has been stamped on us again. The new man, which we assumed at our conversion, was "created after the likeness of God in true righteousness and holiness" (Eph. 4:24, RSV; cf. Col. 3:10). And since that day, in fulfillment of God's predestination purpose that we should be "conformed to the image of his Son" (Rom. 8:29), the Holy Spirit has been transfiguring us "into his likeness from one degree of glory to another" (2 Cor. 3:18, RSV; cf. 1 John 2:6) (Stott, *The Epistles of John*, p. 119).

The historic Westminster Confession of Faith offers a classic definition of the nature and process of progressive sanctification.

> I. They, who are once effectually called, and regenerated, having a new heart, and a new spirit created in them, are further sanctified, really and personally, through the virtue of Christ's death and resurrection, by his Word and Spirit dwelling in

them: the dominion of the whole body of sin is destroyed, and the several lusts thereof are more and more weakened and mortified; and they are more and more quickened and strengthened in all saving graces, to the practice of true holiness, without which no man shall see the Lord.

II. This sanctification is throughout, in the whole man; yet imperfect in this life, there abiding still some remnants of corruption in every part; whence ariseth a continual and irreconcilable war, the flesh lusting against the Spirit, and the Spirit against the flesh.

III. In which war, although the remaining corruption, for a time, may much prevail, yet, through the continual supply of strength from the sanctifying Spirit of Christ, the regenerate doth overcome; and so the saints grow in grace, perfecting holiness in the fear of the Lord (*The Westminster Confession of Faith*, Chapter 13, "Of Sanctification").

These definitions encapsulate hundreds of New Testament passages teaching the twin truths that *we are new in Christ,* ***yet*** *we are still to grow in Christ. We are saved by grace,* ***yet*** *we are still to grow in grace.* "But grow in the grace and knowledge of our Lord Jesus Christ" (2 Peter 3:18). We can summarize the New Testament teaching (in my studies, I have collated 192 New Testament passages that discuss growth in grace) on the nature and process of growth in grace:

♦ Positional Sanctification—We Are Already:
  • *Forgiven*: New Nurture
  • *Changed*: New Nature

♦ Progressive Sanctification—Growth in Grace Is a Daily Process Based Upon:
  • *Faith and Neonatal Saints*: Entrusting ourselves to the person and work of the Trinity by whom we are regenerate and through whom we grow in sanctification.
  • *Communion and Nikao Saints*: Abiding in a nurturing relationship with the Trinity so that the soil of our soul remains fertile, softened ground openly receptive to the grace of Christ's resurrection power.

Examining the New Testament, three additional themes capture our attention. First, *we are in a battle.* Though we are regenerate, we are not perfect. Though we are dead to sin, sin is not dead to us. Sanctification is a daily process of battling against the ingrained flesh (*sarx*), enflamed by the world (*cosmos Diabolicus*), and enticed by Satan (the False Seducer).

Second, the ultimate goal of sanctification is *Christlikeness defined as loving like Christ loves.* The New Testament emphasizes Christlike love as the epitome of maturity. Sanctification is a daily process of renewal more and more into the image of Christ who is the image of God—into the relational image of our Trinitarian God.

Third, *the responsibility in sanctification is mutual.* Christians connect with and cooperatively work, empowered by the Trinity. The New Testament weaves together our new nature in Christ and our power to live out that nature through connection with Christ. Philippians 2:12-13 clearly explains the paradox of God's work and our responsibility.

Therefore, my dear friends, as you have always obeyed—not only in my presence, but now much more in my absence—continue to work out your salvation with fear and trembling, for it is God who works in you to will and to act according to his good purpose.

We do not work for our salvation, but we do cooperatively work with God who works out our sanctification.

Sanctification passages interlace the sovereign work of God and the active responsibility of the believer. Colossians 1:28-29 crisply delineates our role and God's. "We proclaim him, admonishing and teaching everyone with all wisdom, so that we may present everyone perfect in Christ. To this end I labor, struggling with all his energy, which so powerfully works in me."

In these verses about growing in grace, Paul clarifies the goal of progressive sanctification. Perfection in Christ, or maturity in Christlikeness, involves *our inner life increasingly reflecting the inner life of Christ*. Who is responsible to obtain this goal? Both God and us. We struggle, agonize, work hard, and work out, but not with our own power. Instead, we cooperatively work with God's power that so powerfully works within us.

In Galatians 4:19, Paul provides a clear description of our role as soul physicians in the process of growth in grace. "My dear children, for whom I am again in the pains of childbirth until Christ is formed in you." We labor as we involve ourselves in the birth and growth of a neonatal saint, and we battle alongside the *nikao* saint as we engage in his or her battle against the world, the flesh, and the Devil.

In Chapters 25 through 27, we are asking what God says about the process of progressive sanctification. We are exploring: "How do we grow in grace daily (2 Peter 3:18)? How do we grow up in our salvation (1 Peter 2:2)? How do we become renewed in our inner person day by day (2 Corinthians 4:16)? How do we mature/grow up in Christ (Ephesians 4:13-15)? How do we maintain connection with Christ the Head who causes us to grow in grace (Colossians 2:19)? How do we abide in Christ (John 15)? How do we continue to be rooted and built up and strengthened in Christ (Colossians 2:6-7)? How do we agonize and struggle with all His energy that so powerfully works in us (Colossians 1:29)? How do we make every effort to add to our faith, goodness . . . (2 Peter 1:5-9)? How do we strengthen ourselves to cooperate with the grace of God? How are we to be strong in the grace that is in Jesus Christ (2 Timothy 2:1)? What role do we play as soul physicians in assisting babes in Christ to grow from infancy to maturity in Christ (Galatians 4:19)? What process do we teach and what procedures do we suggest to our spiritual friends as we guide them toward growth in grace (1 Timothy 4:7-8)?"

In summary, we are asking, "How do we remain vitally connected to Christ who is the umbilical cord of our spiritual life and the nutrient that sustains, heals, reconciles, and guides us? How are we to work cooperatively with the Trinity to become more like Jesus?"

Nikao Saints Fighting for Victory in Christ: Our New Warfare

It would be appealing to think that the justified, reconciled, regenerated, and redeemed saint has no more relationship to sin whatsoever. How wonderful it would be if our new nurture and our new nature meant the end of our battle with sin. However, even the terminology of our current chapter—neonatal saints and *nikao* saints—suggests the "ongoingness" of the Christian life. The phrase, "neonatal saint" pictures the believer's ongoing need for growth in grace, while the phrase "*nikao* saint" portrays the believer's ongoing battle against sin.

The New Testament never hints that salvation eliminates our need for growth or eradicates our battle with sin. The opposite is actually the case. (I have collated 113 New Testament passages that describe the believer's continuing battle against sin.) Let's acknowledge what the Bible acknowledges: *there is an ongoing warfare*. Let's teach what the Bible teaches: *our warfare is with the flesh* (*sarx*).

> This I say then, Walk in the Spirit, and ye shall not fulfil the lust of the flesh (*sarx*). For the flesh (*sarx*) lusteth against the Spirit, and the Spirit against the flesh (*sarx*): and these are contrary the one to the other: so that ye cannot do the things that ye would do (Galatians 5:16-17, KJV).

The New Testament consistently portrays our warfare as *a battle between the new us and our old ingrained flesh, inflamed by the world and enticed by the False Seducer.*

Virgin Bride's Battle Against Sin

We tend to miss the mark about sin in the believer's life in one of two extremes. On the one hand, we view ourselves only as "forgiven sinners" (justification), not renewed saints (regeneration). We see ourselves as saved from sin (salvation), but not victorious over sin (redemption). False Seducer craves to control us with these lies. We have aborted these lying narratives by exposing our new nature as neonatal (regeneration) and *nikao* (redemption) saints.

On the other hand, we can miss the mark about sin in our lives by viewing ourselves as "perfected sinners" or "glorified saints" (glorification). This is the false concept of the eradication of the sin nature. In the original languages, the Bible *never* uses the phrase "sin nature." Therefore, it never says that the sin nature has been eradicated. Even if by "sin nature" we mean "sin," "the flesh," "the body of sin," or "the sin principle;" eradication is inaccurate terminology. These are all legitimate phrases that accurately translate various descriptions of our ongoing battle against sin. However, the Bible never says that salvation eradicates the flesh. It never says that regeneration obliterates the body of sin. Romans 6:6 teaches that our old man (the old unregenerate me) is crucified (decisively and actually put to death) so that the body of sin (the physical body habituated to evil and used as an instrument of unrighteousness) might be rendered impotent (not dead, but a defeated foe).

So, what died at regeneration? What was crucified? Our old man, our old person, as we have demonstrated. However, sin did not cease. The flesh did not desist.

To believe that our battle against sin ceased at salvation, we have to battle against the biblical text. "If we claim to be without sin," John insists, "we deceive ourselves and the truth is not in us" (1 John 1:8).

Though we are able *not* to sin, we are still able *to* sin. "My dear children," fatherly John continues, "I write this to you so that you will not sin. But if anybody does sin, we have one who speaks to the Father in our defense—Jesus Christ the Righteous One" (1 John 2:1).

Since salvation did not end our battle against sin, Paul exhorts us saying, "Therefore do not let sin reign in your mortal body so that you obey its evil desires" (Romans 6:12). The ministry of soul care and spiritual direction is predicated on our need for one-another-help in our continual battle against sin's deceitfulness. "See to it, brothers, that none of you has a sinful, unbelieving heart that turns away from the living God. But encourage one another daily, as long as it is called Today, so that none of you may be hardened by sin's deceitfulness" (Hebrews 3:12-13). Did you notice the word "brothers"? Christians are able to sin—we can choose to have an unbelieving heart. At some level, the new me can act like the old me and turn away from the living God. Believers are at risk for being hardened by sin's subtlety. Christians are able not to sin—none of us has to be hardened by sin's deceitfulness. However, it can, and does, occur.

We don't have to live like our old man. We don't have to live according to our old way, but we can choose to return to our former manner of life. "So I tell you this, and insist on it in the Lord, that you must no longer live as the Gentiles do, in the futility of their thinking" (Ephesians 4:17). Paul lists a litany of "old man characteristics" in Ephesians 4:17-19: relational alienation, rational darkness, volitional stubbornness, and emotional addiction. He warns us not to live in these old ways, thus indicating that we have the potential to do so, to return to our dead lives. However, we don't have to do so. "You, however, did not come to know Christ that way" (Ephesians 4:20). Paul now lists what we know as believers. We have put off our former way of life, have been made new in the attitude of our minds, and have put on the new self.

We must live out our salvation on the basis of what God has placed within us. As we do, we will have to put off the sinful works of the flesh (*sarx*) that tempt us (Galatians 5:16-21; Ephesians 4:25-32), and we'll have to put on the fruit of the Spirit that truly define the new us (Galatians 5:22-26; Ephesians 4:25-32).

Christians can be "caught in a sin" (Galatians 6:1), and we can help one another find victory over sin. But we must do so humbly "or you also may be tempted" (Galatians 6:1). Christians battle against "the sin that so easily entangles" (Hebrews 12:1)—against besetting sins that seem to haunt us. Yet we have God's power in our regenerate state to "throw off" (Hebrews 12:1) these besetting sins. In our battle against sin we can and must "put aside the deeds of darkness and put on the armor of light" (Romans 13:12). We can clothe ourselves with the Lord Jesus Christ and not set our minds on how to gratify the desires of the flesh (*sarx*) (Romans 13:14).

I do not want to discourage you. I want to forewarn you by teaching what the Bible teaches. We are *nikao* saints in a vicious battle. We are more than conquerors over the world, the flesh, and the Devil; yet these enemies are tenacious.

Regeneration, as we have seen, does not glorify us; it does not make us perfect, or sinless. We live today in the future hope of our coming glorification. "Not only so, but we ourselves who have the firstfruits of the Spirit, groan inwardly as we wait eagerly for our adoption as sons, the redemption of our bodies" (Romans 8:23). As author and pastor Tony Evans reminds us, "As long as we are on earth, sin will be an issue for us because our new nature, the real us, is still housed in a body contaminated by sin" (Evans, *Free at Last*, p. 51).

"Will my battle against sin ever cease?" you plead. Yes!

Dear friends, now we are children of God, and what we will be has not yet been made known [it is a future event]. But we know that when he [Jesus] appears, we shall be like him [our final glorification] for we shall see him as he is [the beatific vision that finally, once for all, confirms us in righteousness—not able to sin].

Everyone who has this hope in him purifies himself, just as he is pure [today we purify ourselves in light of our future, final purity] (1 John 3:2-3 added).

Virgin Bride's New Warfare

Since the warfare continues, our next question is, "Where does the warfare reside?" The answer is so central to progressive sanctification and biblical counseling that we must be biblically precise in our response.

In examining the 113 New Testament passages describing our warfare, I have collated the primary biblical terms used in the context of the believer's ongoing battle. Though these passages clearly teach that the Christian has a continuing battle against sin, variously described as "flesh," "desires of the flesh," "body of sin," "law of sin," "sin principle," "sin," "sin's deceitfulness," and "outer man," in the original languages they never say that the redeemed person's battle is between two equal persons in the core of the regenerate being—one unregenerate and one regenerate. The Bible never says the battle is between the old man and the new man. It never says the Christian's battle is between the old nature and the new nature.

We could wish that the biblical writers provided a theological dictionary offering precise definitions of each term. They did not. Rather, they used various terms to explain similar concepts. Additionally, they often used a single term with various meanings and nuances depending on the context and audience, just as we do. This does not mean that we are left with a hopeless quagmire. It does suggest, however, that we should refrain from insisting that words related to the spiritual life be easily definable and consistently used. Definitions of the spiritual life, perhaps to do justice to the complexity of life in a fallen world, are complex. All this being true, it is also critical that we think carefully and define our terms as precisely (but not more precisely) as the original authors did.

First View of Virgin Bride's New Warfare: Old Man Versus New Man

Some teach that the believer's ongoing battle rages between the "old man and the new man," or between the "old nature and the new nature." I don't believe the Bible warrants that language. First, as I have just noted, not once does the Bible use that specific terminology.

Second, the "old man," as we have seen, is dead, crucified. Yes, the "new man" that I am now can choose to live as that "old man" used to live, can choose to live *as though* that "old man" were still alive. That is far different, however, from saying that our battle is between an "old me" and a "new me."

Third, thinking logically as well as theologically, to posit an "old man" and a "new man" is to teach that there are two people within the one "me." What is a personal being? What are the capacities of personhood? Personal beings are relational, rational, volitional, and emotional. The "old man" was one personal being with depraved capacities turned away from God. The "new man" is one personal being with cleansed capacities turned toward God.

In the core of my being as a regenerated, redeemed saint, I am not simultaneously and equally both an Adulterer and a Bride (two relational beings in one person). I am not simultaneously and equally both a Fool and a Sage (two rational beings in one person).

I am not simultaneously and equally both a Destroyer and a Shepherd (two volitional beings in one person). Nor am I simultaneously and equally both a Singer and an Addict (two emotional beings in one person). I do not have two souls, two minds, two wills, and two emotive centers.

More than just having two entities, if I were an "old man" and a "new man," I would have a soul that in its core hates God and a soul that in its core loves God. I would have a mind that in its core is filled with foolishness and a mind that in its core is filled with wisdom. I would have a will that cannot and will not and does not submit to God and a will that can and will and does submit to God. In the core of my emotionality I would be ungoverned, unfeeling, shameless and in the core of my emotionality I would be governed, sensitive, and receptive to God. This would be multiple personality disorder of the worst kind. This would be Jekyll and Hyde, the Incredible Hulk and David Banner.

I am one new person in Christ with one set of capacities that are fundamentally inclined toward God. Salvation has turned the disposition of my capacities Godward. That being said, because I am not yet glorified, the one new me is still capable of choosing to orient my capacities either toward God or away from God. The one new me does battle against the ingrained flesh (*sarx*), enflamed by the world and enticed by Satan.

What about the "old nature" and the "new nature"? Doesn't the Bible describe the believer as battling the "old nature" or having a "sin nature"? It is true that some translations of the Bible translate *sarx* (flesh) as "sin nature." For instance, the NIV translates Romans 8:5, "Those who live according to the sinful nature (*sarx—flesh*) have their minds set on what that nature (*sarx—flesh*) desires; but those who live in accordance with the Spirit have their minds set on what the Spirit desires." The KJV translates the same verse, "For they that are after the flesh do mind the things of the flesh; but they that are after the Spirit the things of the Spirit." As biblical counselor Jay Adams notes:

> Unfortunately, the translators of the NIV had a proclivity for settling exegetical questions in their translations, thereby becoming interpreters rather than translators. Among the most serious blunders resulting from this practice was the decision to translate the Greek word *sarx* ("flesh") by the theologically prejudicial phrase, "sinful nature." The specialized use of the word flesh refers neither to man's sinful nature (i.e., the corrupt nature with which he was born) nor to the sinful *self* (or personality) that he developed (as some others think), but to the sinful *body* (as Paul calls it in Rom. 6:6). When Paul speaks of the body as sinful, he does not conceive of the body as originally created by God as sinful (as if he were a Gnostic), but rather of the body plunged into sinful practices and habits as the result of Adam's fall. There is no ultimate mind/body (flesh) dualism here, but only a tension in believers occasioned by the regeneration of the inner man and the indwelling of the Spirit in a body habituated to do evil. This leads to an inner/outer struggle. This warfare increasingly is won by the Spirit, who renews and activates the inner man, who helps the body to put off sinful patterns and to put on new biblical responses (Adams, *More Than Redemption*, p.160).

The Bible never actually uses the language of the "old nature" or the "sin nature" to depict our ongoing battle against sin.

I'm not wanting to quibble over words, so if someone uses "old nature" to represent the basic concept that our battle continues, I have no problem. However, if someone uses "old nature" to teach that there are two essential "me's," that is not theological, lexical, nor logical. The words of David Needham and Neil Anderson reflect my thinking.

> In view of the normal meaning of the word *nature* as referring to one's essential character, one's essence, I believe it is confusing to refer to Christians as having both a sin nature and a new nature. On the other hand, as we will emphasize in chapters 4 and 5, it is fitting to describe a Christian as being a "new natured" person (their essential nature), while still possessing a most serious fleshly propensity toward sin (but not as being their essential nature). Some may choose to call that fleshly propensity one's "sin nature," yet maintain it as distinct from one's essential nature. Other than the problem of misunderstanding, I see nothing wrong with this usage (Needham, *Birthright*, p. 242).

If you want to refer to your flesh as your old nature, I won't wrangle with you over terms. But I will contend for the biblical truth that the residual effects of who I was in Adam are no longer part of my true identity in Christ (Anderson, *Victory Over the Darkness*, p. 75).

We are one new person in Christ who can turn back to the ways of the old person we once were when we surrender in our battle against the flesh, urged on and incited by the world and the Devil.

Second View of Virgin Bride's New Warfare: Spirit Versus Flesh

As you trace these truths, you are likely experiencing conflicting thoughts. On the one hand, you are excited. "Wow! I'm free. Free at last!" On the other hand, you are confused. "If I'm free from my old man, why do I keep enslaving myself again and again?" Perhaps author Kris Lundgaard's honest struggle reflects yours.

"If God has redeemed me from sin, and given me his Holy Spirit to sanctify me and give me strength against sin, why do I go on sinning?" This question has plagued me throughout my life of faith. In my lowest moments it has brought despair; it has even darkened the edges of my brightest times (Lundgaard, *The Enemy Within*, p. 13).

Why do we continue sinning? It is a haunting question. What is the source of our battle with sin if we are regenerate neonatal saints? Why does the battle still rage if we are redeemed *nikao* saints? If the battle is not fought between two equal foes within the one me (the old man and the new man), then what is my battle?

Anderson understands these tough questions and the tough answers.

> In our attempts to understand the disobedience which so often disturbs our sense of sainthood, we toss around some pretty ominous terms: old nature, old self (or old man), flesh and sin. What do these terms really mean? Are they distinct in themselves or interchangeable elements of the same problem? Are we as saints still the unwitting victims of our old nature, old self and sinful flesh? Admittedly this is a difficult theological area. Bible scholars have wrestled with these questions for centuries and I don't in any way pretend to have the final answers (Anderson, *Victory Over the Darkness*, p. 70).

What Is the "Flesh"?

Though we don't have the final answers, examining the flesh (*sarx*) exposes us to the core questions that soul physicians must consider. We need to place our mysterious flesh under the probe of God's spiritual health manual asking, "What is the flesh? What does it mean to be in the flesh? What does it mean to walk according to the flesh? What does it mean to be fleshly? What is the nature of the battle between the flesh and the Spirit/spirit?"

Richard Lovelace understands the perplexity that arises when asking, "What does the Bible mean by the flesh (*sarx*)? The flesh is always somewhat mysterious to us, particularly in its effect on our minds and in its operation in the redeemed personality" (Lovelace, *The Dynamics of Spiritual Life*, pp. 89-90).

"*Sarx*" (flesh) is the word used in the Greek translation of the Old Testament to translate the Hebrew word *bāsār*. Paul, the Jewish believer, would have had *bāsār* in mind when he used the word *sarx*. *Bāsār* is the entire body (brain, bone, belly, glands, nervous system, chemical make-up, five senses, etc.) representing the entire person (relational, rational, volitional, and emotional) as weak, needy, and frail. *Bāsār* is embodied humanity in our infirmity.

Old Testament writers used *bāsār* as physical powerlessness, representing the feebleness of our faithfulness. *Bāsār* is humanity separated from Deity—from the life and power of God—and therefore weak and insufficient in physical and spiritual power (Genesis 6:3; Isaiah 40:6). That which is typically human (Job 10:4), the antithesis of God, it stands for *trusting in human physical power* (Jeremiah 17:5-7). "*Bāsār* always describes restricted, insufficient human power in contrast to the surpassing power of God" (Hans Wolff, *Anthropology of the Old Testament*, p. 30).

In later Judaism, *sarx* signified human frailty and corruptibility. It stressed mortality and immorality, especially sinfully arrogant humanity. It was everything human and earthly. As people put trust in it, it was envisioned as a power that opposed the Spirit. The flesh represented the wrong orientation away from God that becomes a controlling power.

The Greek world used *sarx* in the concrete sense of the flesh and bones that decay at death. At death, people put off all flesh (*sarx*).

The New Testament writers, building upon the Old Testament *bāsār* and upon *sarx* in Judaism and the Greek world, used *sarx* to represent the whole person considered from the perspective of physical existence. In our embodied personality, the flesh highlights our outward physical components (brain, bone, belly, glands, and five senses) viewed in contrast to our inward metaphysical capacities (relational, rational, volitional, and emotional). Thus it came to represent humanity in our impotency and infirmity, in our distance and difference from God (Romans 2:28; 1 Corinthians 5:5; 2 Corinthians 4:16-18; 5:12; Ephesians 2:11).

To be "in the flesh" is to be in the sphere of, under the control of, and under the jurisdiction of the flesh (body, brain, bone, belly). The unregenerate are *in* the flesh. They live all their lives in natural effort, independent of God, self-sufficient, weak. They live *in* the flesh because their spirit, their inner person, is dead. They depend upon their flesh—their body, bone, brain, belly, nervous system, glands, chemical make-up, five senses, etc.—as their source of life.

Believers are not *in* the flesh, but they can walk *according to* the flesh. The regenerate person can choose to live life in the power of the flesh, for the fulfillment of the flesh, and under the direction of the flesh. Our inner person (soul, mind, will, emotion) can choose to live dependent upon body, bone, and brain.

This is equivalent to being *fleshly*. The *fleshly* believer (a contradiction in terms, but a possibility nonetheless) lives *as though* the flesh is all there is. As though their flesh is a sufficient power source and a sufficient guide for life. "To act 'according to the flesh,' is to do so simply in the fallible power of human strength and resolution" (John Robinson, *The Body*, p. 21). To live fleshly is to make the belly one's god and only care (Romans 16:18; Philippians 3:19).

The "mind of the flesh" stands primarily for the denial of our dependence upon God and for our trust in what is of human origin and effort. "The term 'flesh' is used to describe a man's natural effort, independent of God. That which is of the flesh is that which a man does by himself, without any divine assistance, without the enablement of the Holy Spirit" (Dwight Pentecost, *Designed to Be Like Him*, p. 209). The regenerate are in the Spirit, but can choose to live controlled by the flesh, according to the flesh, and dependent upon the flesh—upon our own power.

In summary:

♦ Flesh can be holistic—our embodied personality.
♦ Flesh can be neutral—our physicality, the fact that God created us out of dust as physical beings.
♦ Flesh can be representative—our physical components (body) dominating our metaphysical (soul) capacities.
♦ Flesh can be descriptive of the unregenerate—unsaved people who are disconnected from the Spirit of God and are thus "*in* the flesh."
♦ Flesh (fleshly, according to the flesh, the mind of the flesh, the mind set on the flesh) can be descriptive of the regenerate—saved people who live not in the flesh, but *according to* the flesh, i.e., in their own frail human power, disconnecting themselves from the umbilical cord of God's Spirit. It is not only the body/brain/bone/gland complex. It is that and it is also the metaphysical being choosing to try to live *as though* the body is all there is, trying to live in the power of the body (flesh) alone. Flesh is me, living according to the pattern of self-sufficiency.

What Is the Battle Between the Flesh and the Spirit?

This brings us to our final and most practical question, *"What is the nature of the battle between the flesh and the spirit/Spirit?"* Though our old man was crucified, our flesh was not eradicated. Speaking of our ingrained flesh-orientation with which we were born and lived until our salvation, Anderson explains:

You brought to your Christian commitment a fully conditioned mind-set and lifestyle developed apart from God and centered on yourself. . . . So you learned to live your life independent of God. It is this learned independence that makes the flesh hostile toward God. During the years you spent separated from God, your worldly experiences thoroughly programmed your brain with thought patterns, memory traces, responses and habits that are alien to God. . . . Your flesh remains in opposition to God as a preprogrammed propensity for sin (Anderson, *Victory Over the Darkness*, p. 80).

While Anderson uses the phrase "a preprogrammed propensity for sin," other theologians use such phrases as: sin-contaminated body, sin-contaminated flesh, sin-programmed brains, fleshly propensity, flesh-oriented, walking according to the flesh, sinful programming, wiring toward sin, prior conditioning toward sin, ingrained tendencies, habituated patterns, old roots of sin, smoldering cinders, vestiges, tendencies, the virus of sin, residual effects, remnants of disorder, strongholds of the flesh, and flesh patterns.

Jay Adams describes the flesh as "the body wrongly habituated toward sin" (Adams, *The War Within*, pp. 78-79). While Tony Evans explains:

The Bible refers to the corrupt shell we're living in as the "flesh." Before we go any further, it's important for you to realize that this is *not* the old sin nature, which has been done away with, but the sin-ravaged bodies we will inhabit until Christ comes for us (Evans, *Free at Last*, p. 51).

Evans also notes, "the old patterns of sin are still programmed into our flesh" (p. 54). "You are one totally new nature that functions in an old, sin-infested house" (p. 54).

Why do I still struggle against sin? The one new me, my inner person, battles against the flesh—against my ingrained tendency to live according to the insights of my physical brain and according to the strength of my physical body. I live fleshly, even as a Christian, when I act independently of God by responding to the patterns and habits ingrained in my flesh (body, brain, bone, belly, glands, nervous system, chemical make-up, five senses, etc.). To walk according to the flesh is to live "a way of life patterned after the thoughts, habits, and desires of our sin-contaminated flesh that we brought with us into our new life with Christ" (Evans, *Free at Last*, p. 102).

Anderson describes the battle that results when the new man squares off against sin and *sarx*.

Your death to sin ended your relationship with sin as master, but it did not terminate sin's existence. Sin is still alive, strong, and appealing, but its power and authority have been broken (Romans 8:2). Furthermore, your flesh, that part of you which was trained to live independently of God before you met Christ, did not die either. You still have memories, habits, conditioned responses, and thought patterns ingrained in your brain which prompt you to focus on your own interests. You are no longer in the flesh as your old self was; you are now in Christ. But you can still walk according to the flesh (Romans 8:12, 13) (Anderson, *Freedom from Bondage*, p. 46).

It is one thing to say the Christian faces a battle of equal forces within his personality, a personality divided in itself as regenerate and unregenerate. *That is a hopeless battle.* It is another matter to say that the Christian faces a battle between the one new person she is in the core of her being and the "flesh." This is a battle between the essential new me who is regenerate and the vestiges of ingrained tendencies (the flesh) inflamed by the world and enticed by the Devil. This is a serious battle, no doubt, but a *hopeful* one. And it is, I am convinced, the battle that you and I fight every day.

How do we fight it? Not as in Romans 7 where we watch someone using the flesh (human self-sufficiency) to attempt somehow to defeat the flesh. Here, at least the enemy was rightly identified—it's the flesh. However, the means to victory was wrongly identified—the flesh. Instead, Romans 8 and the rest of the New Testament teaches us that we win the battle against the flesh in the power of the Spirit—in God's power, in Trinitarian power, with resurrection power.

Nikao Saints Experiencing Victory In Christ: Resurrection Power Multipliers (RPMs)

Sometimes we learn best how to do something by first being shown the wrong ways to do it. The apostle Paul seems to have such a learning and teaching style. In many passages he teaches us how *not* to live the Christian life.

Do *Not* Grow in Grace by Trying Harder

Paul teaches us not to grow in grace by dependence upon our own power, our own works, our own flesh. In Galatians, he wonders who has bewitched the saints in Galatia. Having been saved by faith apart from human effort, why are they now trying to sanctify themselves by works—through the power of the flesh, through human self-sufficiency?

In Colossians, he wonders what human philosophy has taken captive and deceived the saints in Colosse. Having been saved by faith, why would they attempt to live their Christian lives based on rules, rituals, regulations, and self-righteous works?

In Philippians, Paul makes it more personal, using himself in his illustration of the wrong way to live the Christian life. Speaking to "brothers" (Philippians 3:1), that is, to believers, he warns them not to have confidence in the flesh. If anyone could have confidence in the flesh, it would be Paul. "Circumcised on the eighth day, of the people of Israel, of the tribe of Benjamin, a Hebrew of the Hebrews; in regard to the law, a Pharisee; as for zeal, persecuting the church; as for legalistic righteousness, faultless" (Philippians 3:5-6). However, Paul counts all his human effort, both for salvation and for sanctification, as loss, as rubbish, literally, as camel dung. Good for nothing. Human effort is worthless for sanctification. Human strength is helpless in our Christian warfare.

Knowing how *not* to live out our sanctification, now Paul informs us *how to* grow in grace. What is powerful enough to produce the final product envisioned in progressive sanctification? "I want to know Christ and the power of his resurrection . . . becoming like him in his death" (Philippians 3:10). To grow in grace, to become conformed to Christ's image, we need Christ's resurrection power.

Paul emphasizes the same truth in Ephesians 1:15-23. Having spoken of the Ephesians' positional sanctification in verses 1-14, Paul moves to their progressive sanctification as he prays that they might know Christ intimately and avail themselves of His infinite power. He speaks of, "His incomparably great power for us who believe. That power is like the working of his mighty strength, which he exerted in Christ when he raised him from the dead and seated him at his right hand in the heavenly realms" (Ephesians 1:19-20).

Pauline sanctification does not follow the paradigm of "Try harder!" It is not about works and human effort. It is about resurrection power.

Do *Not* Grow in Grace by Doing Nothing

That does not mean, however, that Pauline sanctification shifts to the other pole and says, *"Do nothing!"* There is a role for us to play. We do have a responsibility.

Not that I have already obtained all this, or have already been made perfect, but I press on to take hold of that for which Christ Jesus took hold of me. Brothers, I do not consider myself yet to have taken hold of it. But one thing I do: Forgetting what is behind [works-based righteousness, self-effort sanctification, "trying harder"] and straining toward what is ahead, *I press on* toward the goal to win the prize for which God has called me heavenward in Christ Jesus. All of us who are mature should take such a view of things (Philippians 3:12-15a, emphasis added).

Paul is not "letting go and letting God." He is straining, pressing on, and laboring hard to work out the salvation that God worked in him.

How do we live out our sanctification in Christ? How do we grow in grace? It is not by trying harder. Not by human effort. Nor is it by doing nothing, by "letting go and letting God." It is not freedom from responsibility. It is by communing with God, by connecting with Christ and His grace, by cooperating with Christ's resurrection power, and by developing a transforming relationship with God.

Do Grow in Grace by Communing with God

Since the power to grow in grace is itself a grace-gift from our Worthy Groom, since Paul connects that power to Christ's resurrection power, and since we have a role to play in keeping our hearts receptive to His power, we need to understand our faith-role in progressive sanctification. Our faith-role relates to, and relates us to, each member of the Trinity.

- ◆ Trust in the Father: Faith through Grace
- ◆ Abide in the Son: Union with Christ
- ◆ Be Filled with the Spirit: Empowered by the Spirit

J. I. Packer notes that for the Puritans *communion with God* was the "comprehensive reality that is central to Christian existence" (Packer, *A Quest for Godliness*, p. 201). We grow in grace only through a relationship of mutual interchange, joint participation, and fellowship—*koinōnia* with God the Father: receiving and responding to Father's grace love. My soul must be captured by my forgiving Father, and my heart enraptured by the narrative of His grace love. My will must be surrendered to His good and generous will, and my emotions fully open to His good heart. "The grace of God in Christ is the center of the Christian mental universe" (Lovelace, *Dynamics of Spiritual Life*, p. 83).

Sanctification, just as much as salvation, begins with faith (Galatians 3:1-14). Faith is our victory that overcomes the world, the flesh, and the Devil (1 John 4:4-5; 5:4-5; Romans 6:1-8:14). We entrust ourselves to the good work God has already accomplished in our heart. As Lovelace emphasizes, "the counselor who is attempting to move people further in sanctification should therefore begin with a strong emphasis on justification and reiterate this often in the course of his work" (Lovelace, *Dynamics of Spiritual Life*, p. 114). By faith, we reckon on our new nurture and new nature. In sanctification, we depend upon God's power, the power at work when He raised His Son (Ephesians 1:15-23; 3:14-21)—God's resurrection power.

Sanctification requires trust in God the Father, and it demands *abiding in God the Son*. We are delivered from the bondage of sin through the power of our union with the indwelling Christ. "As Romans 6 makes clear, the ground of sanctification is our union with Christ in his death and resurrection, in which the old nature was destroyed and a new nature created with the power to grow in newness of life" (Lovelace, *Dynamics of Spiritual Life*, p. 104).

Just as we received Christ Jesus as Lord, so we continue to live in Him, rooted and built up in Him, strengthened in the faith (Colossians 2:6-7). We are united theologically and actually in Christ's death and resurrection. We need to abide in Christ, remaining in, residing in, sharing in Him intimately, in active, practical spiritual union. Scottish Puritan pastor and author Thomas Boston describes our growth in grace using the biblical imagery of Christ as the Vine.

> This sanctifying Spirit, communicated by the Lord Jesus to His members, is the spiritual nourishment the branches have from the stock into which they are ingrafted; whereby the life of grace, given them in regeneration, is preserved, continued, and actuated. It is the nourishment whereby the new creature lives, and is nourished up towards perfection. Spiritual life needs to be fed, and must have supply of nourishment: and believers derive the same from Christ their Head, whom the Father has appointed the Head of influences to all His members (Boston, *Human Nature in Its Fourfold State*, p. 296).

Boston concludes his lengthy theological discussion of the new nature with words of counsel for growth in grace through communion.

> To you that are saints, I say, strive to obtain and keep up actual communion and fellowship with Jesus Christ; that is, to be still deriving fresh supplies of grace from the fountain thereof in Him, by faith, and making suitable returns of them, in the exercise of grace and holy obedience (Boston, *Human Nature in Its Fourfold State*, p. 316).

Sanctification also obligates us to be *filled with the Spirit*. The Holy Spirit is the resident Counselor in every believer. He's our spiritual Care Giver serving as our Source, Guide, and Enabler of new life in Christ. He operates in our affections, thoughts, wills, and emotions.

In what power, or better, in whose power do I live? The person in Romans 7 is trying to live the good life in his own power. *We need to live the good life from a good heart from the good power of the Spirit*. We need to walk according to the Spirit; we need to be filled with the Spirit. When we're told to yield to the Spirit, be led by the Spirit, keep in step with the Spirit, and be controlled by the Spirit, we're being told to appropriate actively and depend personally upon the Spirit in our daily lives. True spirituality is not achieved in our own energy.

To be filled with the Spirit means to saturate myself with the spiritual so that I am under the Spirit's influence. Filling with the Spirit requires supplanting the old influence (putting off the flesh, not being drunk with wine—that which controls the brain/body/bone complex), and being filled up with the Spirit. It is a present tense imperative: I'm commanded to be emptying myself of the flesh's influence continually and to be filled with the Spirit continually. It is a passive voice word. I must open myself to being filled. I must desire to be filled, thirst for it, and respond to the invitation to drink.

Revving Up the RPMs

Since we grow in grace through communion with Father, Son, and Holy Spirit, we need to understand how to connect with God. We must learn how to use the means of Trinitarian connecting that God has graciously put at our disposal. I have come to label these means: *RPMs—Resurrection Power Multipliers*.

Our power path to victory is humble dependence (faith) upon God to channel His power to the depths of our being. God gives grace to the humble. His strength is made perfect in weakness—in our conscious human weakness and conscious human dependence (Packer, *Rediscovering Holiness*, pp. 237-238).

As Paul repeatedly reminds us in 2 Corinthians, "But this happened that we might not rely on ourselves but on God, who raises the dead" (2 Corinthians 1:9b). "But we have this treasure in jars of clay to show that this all-surpassing power is from God and not from us" (2 Corinthians 4:7). "But he said to me, 'My grace is sufficient for you, for my power is made perfect in weakness.' Therefore I will boast all the more gladly about my weaknesses, so that Christ's power may rest on me" (2 Corinthians 12:9).

The power to grow comes from Christ, but we're to avail ourselves of it. The core progressive sanctification question asks, "What is the process by which Christ's power rests upon and works within us?"

The RPMs are the means by which we never sever our spiritual umbilical cord. The RPMs continually nourish us in our inner person as we "eat" and "exercise" right spiritually (John 4:34; 6:35-69; 7:37-39; 1 Corinthians 9:24-27; 2 Corinthians 3:17-18; 4:16-18; 1 Timothy 4:7-8). Spiritual victory demands the dependent, contingent, connected, cooperative life (John 5:30; 6:53; 15:1-5).

Paul says that we receive grace for daily living the abundant life the same way we receive grace for living the eternal life—by faith (Galatians 3-5; Colossians 2). So the question becomes: "How do we receive grace by faith in our daily life to live the abundant life?" What does it mean to do this? What would it look like? How did Jesus do it? Paul? The early Christians? Is there a pattern to follow? What does it look like in daily life to abide in Christ? To reckon myself dead indeed to sin but alive indeed to God?

What we need is deeper insight into our practical relationship with God in sanctification. We must develop a theology of the spiritual life that can guide us into constant interaction with the grace of God as a real part of our daily lives (Dallas Willard, *The Spirit of the Disciplines*).

Understanding Our Transforming Friendship with God

How do we develop a transforming friendship with God? It comes to us by grace through faith. We obtain transforming power by working out our own salvation with fear and trembling—with utmost seriousness—with grace-empowered and inspired spiritual discipline.

Spiritual victory requires transforming ingrained tendencies of attitude and action through living out our regeneration—the impartation of new life. The seed of new life has germinated, now it needs to blossom as we connect with Christ's grace by faith active in love.

Willard, in his excellent text *The Spirit of the Disciplines*, reminds us that the human body was made to be the vehicle of human personality, ruling the earth for God and through His power. We were given dominion—a small but significant area to rule lovingly. That area is our heart, our will—what we have control over.

When we fell, life became deformed from the top down. Being separated from the life of God, we are not only wrong, we are wrung—wrung out. We are both twisted and empty, twisted out of proper shape. Robbed of the vital nutrient of grace relationships—connection, we become depraved and depleted. We are deranged and deprived (deprivation). We experience spiritual weakness caused by spiritual starvation (Willard, *The Spirit of the Disciplines*).

In the Fall, we died. The small reservoir of independent power resident in the flesh continued to exist as it does in all living beings. But we exist like a plant or an animal! We died spiritually. We were the only being given the spiritual ability to relate to God. When we sinned, we said, "I do not need God." We got what we wished for—non-contingency. We hid and we hated. We broke our connection to God, became separated from the life of God (Ephesians 4:18).

In salvation, we are *reconnected* to God. We are reconciled to Him. This opens the way of access to Him. This new nurture, this new relationship, fills our previously depleted souls. Our grace relationship with God through Christ transforms us by reconnecting us to the Spirit. *We are transformed by contact with God.* Spirituality is cooperative, contingent interaction with God. We are spiritual to the extent we are integrated into God and dominated by His grace. *The RPMs bring our total being back into effective, contingent cooperation with Christ and His resurrection power, love, and wisdom.*

Experiencing Spiritual Formation through Christ and the Body of Christ

What do we need to grow in grace? We need spiritual formation that disconnects our bodies from the old flesh patterns and connects us to Christ and the body of Christ. We need the effective full enjoyment of the active love of God and humanity in all the daily rounds of normal existence.

The flesh is habituated to the entrenched ways of the past inherited from Adam and ingrained through life before Christ. It is incited by the world and enticed by the Devil to act upon the potential within the body to exist for a time and in a limited scope in the power inherent in the flesh. How do we put off these old habits? How do we put to death the old ways? *By connecting.* Connecting with grace. How do we connect with grace? Through the RPMs (see Box 25:1).

In part, the Bible calls this "reckoning": bringing the old person into mind and resolutely and consciously disassociating ourselves from him or her. Put off the law of sin, the principle of sin—those "remnants of sin ingrained" in my body (brain, belly, bones) and incited by Satan and the world.

The Bible also calls this "yielding." We submit our members to God. We consciously direct our brain and belly (thoughts and passions) to serve righteousness habitually. Romans 6:16-18 identifies this as habituate reliance upon and relationship to Christ.

Box 25:1

RPMs: Resurrection Power Multipliers

Spiritual Foundation: Change through Christ's Word

Spiritual Theology: Preaching, Teaching, Bible Study, Personal Study, Our New Identity in Christ, Our Heroic Love Story

Spiritual Formation: Communion with Christ/Conformity to Christ

Spiritual Disciplines: The Individual and Corporate Disciplines

Spiritual Friendship: Compassionate Discernment from Christ's Ministers

Spiritual Counseling: Individual Soul Care and Spiritual Direction

Spiritual Fellowship: Connection with Christ's Body

Spiritual Discipleship: Small Group Soul Care and Spiritual Direction, and Large Group Fellowship and Worship

Spiritual Filling: Control by the Holy Spirit

Spiritual Empowerment: The Filling and Fruit of the Spirit

Spiritual Fruit: Character and Competence in Christ

Spiritual Ministry/Maturity: Service, Evangelism, Discipleship, Stewardship

Spiritual Family: Completing One Another in Christ

Spiritual Homes: Godly Marriages, Shepherding Parents

Spiritual Fighting: Conquering Christ's Enemies (The World, the Flesh, and the Devil)

Spiritual Warfare/Victory: The Whole Armor of God (Our New Bridal Clothes)

Throughout Church history, saints have used terms like "the spiritual disciplines" and "spiritual formation" to explain this process of connecting with Christ and His resurrection power so that we can put off the old and put on the new. *The historical practice of the spiritual disciplines of spiritual formation move us to a spiritual responsiveness and openness that empowers our embodied personalities toward a readiness and an ability to connect with Christ's resurrection power.* They are activities of mind and body that help bring the whole self into cooperation with God and His grace so we can experience more and more of Him and His resurrection power. They empower us to actively appropriate and depend upon God's Spirit in our lives: to live by, be led by, yielded to, filled with, controlled by, walking in, and keeping in step with God's transforming, indwelling Holy Spirit.

The spiritual formation categories in Box 25:1 offer one way to classify the various means of connecting ourselves with Christ's resurrection power. As I have studied the Word, pastored churches, shepherded believers, counseled people, and taught about the spiritual life, I have developed these categories as a helpful way to conceptualize the individual and corporate disciplines of the sanctified life. Ponder each category with me.

By *spiritual foundation* I mean change through the preaching, teaching, and personal study of the Word of God. Through these we learn who we are in Christ and to Christ. We cannot grow in God's grace apart from immersion in God's Word. We connect to Him as we feed on His living and active Word that nourishes our spiritual life.

I am using *spiritual formation* both for the entire process and for one aspect of the process. Spiritual formation is the classical name given for the practice of spiritual disciplines, both individual and corporate. They include such individual disciplines as prayer, meditation, silence, solitude, fasting, frugality, and many more. They include the corporate disciplines of mutual confession, body life, fellowship, worship, and many others. We grow in our receptivity and openness to Christ's resurrection power through these historic Christian disciplines of the faith.

My third category of resurrection power multipliers is *spiritual friendship*. By this I am highlighting the ministry of soul physicians and the arts of soul care, spiritual direction, mentoring, encouraging one another, one-to-one discipleship, and biblical counseling. We connect to Christ as we connect to Christians. We grow in grace as spiritual friends help us to sustain, heal, reconcile, and guide our faith in Christ.

Before moving ahead, I want to ask you to consider something important. Though this is a book on biblical counseling, I do *not* believe that counseling is the only way or even the primary way of growing in grace. Biblical counseling is simply one means of promoting growth in grace. Effective soul physicians disciple their spiritual friends in the practice of all of the RPMs. In my pastoral ministries, I never counseled believers until they agreed to commit themselves to the full ministry of the local church—a ministry that embodied the RPMs.

Spiritual friendship is a companion to *spiritual fellowship*. Whereas spiritual friendship recognizes how connection with one other Christian prompts connection with Christ, so spiritual fellowship discerns that connection with the body of Christ in group settings also nourishes our relationship to our Savior. This can include small group ministry as well as large group fellowship and worship. Spiritual friendship and spiritual fellowship remind us that relationships are the greatest spiritual disciplines.

Spiritual filling is yet another powerful means of tapping into Christ's resurrection power. It is our responsibility to yield our human spirit to the Holy Spirit. We are to walk in step with the Spirit, be filled with the Spirit—controlled by His passions and evidencing His fruit—the character of Christ.

The category of *spiritual fruit* (not to be confused with the fruit of the Spirit) indicates that ministry for Christ is another avenue for connecting to Christ. Evangelism, teaching, serving, discipling, all motivate us to be strong in the grace of our Lord Jesus Christ. Doing ministry for Christ in a fallen world is draining. As we pour ourselves out for others, we learn how frail we are, how needy we are. So we cling to Christ to empower us. We connect with Christ to equip us.

Spiritual family recognizes that the godly relationships in our homes are another form of resurrection power multipliers. Relationship with those who love us enhances our receptivity to the love and power of our heavenly Father.

Spiritual fighting is the final category, at least in my conceptualization of the RPMs. Part of our responsibility in the sanctification process includes availing ourselves of the whole armor of God. With it we defeat the world, the flesh, and the Devil. We put off the old and put on the new.

Taken together, I intend these eight categories to represent the types of activities that Paul undertook and that we are to undertake as we press toward the mark of the prize of the high calling of Christlikeness. These eight categories of responsibility answer the questions, "How do we remain vitally connected to Christ, the umbilical cord of our spiritual life, the nutrient that sustains, heals, reconciles, and guides us? How are we to work cooperatively with the Trinity to become more like Christ?"

The dynamic of sanctification is our co-crucifixion and co-resurrection with Christ. Christ died and rose again for us, we died and rose again with Him. That is the power, the dynamic of our sanctification. We share in the abiding fact and results of His resurrection/ resurrected life.

Speaking of Romans 6:1-10, John Murray explains that Paul is not, in this context, emphasizing that Christ died and rose again for believers, but rather the fact that *believers died and rose again with Christ.*

> It is this abiding relationship to the death and resurrection of Christ, particularly, of course, to the latter, that constitutes the power, the dynamic, in virtue of which believers live the life of death to sin and of the newness of obedience. It is what we may call the virtue emanating from the death and resurrection of Christ, viewed as their death and resurrection also, that is the constant force in the sanctification of believers (Murray, *Principles of Conduct*, p. 207).

The key to growth in grace is tapping into Christ's resurrection power by means of communing with the Trinity. This has been recognized throughout Church history. The Westminster Confession of Faith reminds us:

> They, who are once effectually called, and regenerated, having a new heart, and a new spirit created in them, are further sanctified, really and personally, through the virtue of Christ's death and resurrection, by His Word and Spirit dwelling in them (*The Westminster Confession of Faith*, Chap. XIII, Section 1).

We *are further sanctified* as we tap into the power that already dwells within us.

Where We've Been and Where We're Heading

Neonatal, *nikao* saints grow up and grow strong by connecting to Christ's resurrection power. Is that it? Is the practice of the eight categories of RPMs the extent of the biblical teaching on sanctification? Is this the extent of biblical teaching on how soul physicians disciple their spiritual friends to grow in grace? Although the RPMs are crucial, and the consistent practice of them would transform modern Christianity, they do not exhaust the Bible's teaching on progressive sanctification.

Soul physicians understand the anatomy of the soul. We know that God designed us as relational (affections), rational (mindsets), volitional (purposes/pathways) and emotional beings (mood states). We know how to diagnose soul sickness as false lovers, foolish mindsets, self-centered pathways, and unmanaged mood states. We know what healthy spiritual friends look like: trusting, grace lovers; spiritual, wise mindsets; other-centered pathways; and managed mood states.

We're also not naïve. We know that healthy saints are not sinless people. We still struggle against the world, the flesh, and the Devil. *What we need is a biblical treatment plan for putting off the old and putting on the new.* Only saints empowered by the RPMs can exercise their spiritual strength to put off the old and put on the new.

But how do they do that? What does it look like? What does the Bible mean, practically speaking, when it speaks about putting off old affections, mindsets, purposes, and mood states? What are we to do in the real world to put on new affections, mindsets, purposes, and mood states? How do we overcome the world, the flesh, and the Devil as they work to seduce us to cling to old flesh patterns? We address these questions in Act Four, Scenes VII and VIII, Chapters 26 and 27.

Caring for Your Soul: Personal Applications

Take an RPMs Self-Evaluation. With 10 being "Awesome" and 1 being "Not-So-Hot," rate how well you are tapping into Christ's Resurrection Power Multipliers. Consider this your *RPM Quotient Test*.

1. **Spiritual Foundation: Change through Christ's Word**

   Spiritual Theology: Preaching, Teaching, Bible Study, Personal Study, Our New Identity in Christ

2. **Spiritual Formation: Communion with Christ/Conformity to Christ**

   Spiritual Disciplines: The Individual and Corporate Disciplines

3. **Spiritual Friendship: Compassionate Discernment from Christ's Ministers**

   Spiritual Counseling: Individual Soul Care, Spiritual Direction, and Spiritual Friendship

4. **Spiritual Fellowship: Connection with Christ's Body**

   Spiritual Discipleship: Small Group Soul Care and Spiritual Direction, and Large Group Fellowship and Worship

5. **Spiritual Filling: Control by the Holy Spirit**

   Spiritual Empowerment: The Filling and Fruit of the Spirit

6. **Spiritual Fruit: Character and Competence in Christ**

   Spiritual Ministry: Service, Evangelism, Discipleship, Stewardship

7. **Spiritual Family: Completing One Another in Christ**

   Spiritual Homes: Godly Marriages, Shepherding Parents

8. **Spiritual Fighting: Conquering Christ's Enemies (The World, Flesh, and Devil)**

   Spiritual Warfare/Victory: The Whole Armor of God

Caring for Others: Ministry Implications

♦ **Remember Your Calling as a Spiritual Friend:** You are to cooperate with God in reveling in and revealing the beauty of your spiritual friends as virgin brides who are:

- Romancers Who Love Passionately Not Carnally
- Dreamers Who Think Wisely Not Foolishly
- Creators Who Choose Courageously Not Selfishly
- Singers Who Experience Deeply Not Shallowly

   ○ Therefore, focus on drawing out and stirring up Romancers relating with purified affections; Dreamers thinking with wise, spiritual mindsets; Creators choosing to live according to other-centered purposes; and Singers experiencing managed mood states.

♦ **Remember the Importance of Grace Relationships as a Spiritual Friend:** Galatians 5 clearly shows that the greatest inhibitor of spiritual fruit is works relationships. Any spiritual friendship, counseling, or discipleship relationship engaged in from a works standpoint is doomed to ineffectiveness. Works spiritual friendship says, "I have an agenda. I must 'win' by getting you to my destination. You must cooperate with me. I need to 'succeed' as a 'counselor.' My happiness is dependent upon it. In fact, my 'sense of self' requires it." Such relationships are not passionate, wise, courageous, or deep. They are carnal, simple, compulsive, and shallow. Mostly, they are competitive.

- Why would beloved image bearers relate like this? Because we forget to remember who God is: our Worthy Groom with a good, gracious, generous heart. And we forget to remember who we are in Christ: accepted in the beloved.
- Disconnect results from our demandingness. No one enjoys being used to fulfill someone else's personal agenda. So disconnect results from the discrepancy between our goals and the goals of our spiritual friends. Our goal is not to manipulate them into moving through some "stage of maturity." Our goal is to revel in who they already are. We enter their story where they are and journey with them to where it appears to the two of us that God is taking them.
- Disconnect also results from "moving our spiritual friends too quickly" rather than "journeying at their pace."

CHAPTER TWENTY-SIX

VIRGIN BRIDE PUTS OFF HER OLD GRAVE CLOTHES

"How do we harmonize God's sovereign work in conquering sin with our responsibility to live a life of consistent holiness?" (Donald Alexander, *Christian Spirituality*, p. 9).

Speaking of Romans 6:1-11, Gerhard Forde says, "Actually, all evangelical treatments of sanctification should be little more than comment on this passage" (Gerhard Forde in Donald Alexander's, *Christian Spirituality*, p. 21).

"The whole life of the Christian is a continual repentance" (Martin Luther).

Old Marley Is Dead

Dickens' classic *A Christmas Carol* begins with a voice-over from the narrator, spoken amidst howling winds.

Marley was dead. To begin with, there is no doubt whatever about that. The register of his burial was signed by the clerk, the clergyman, the undertaker, the chief mourner. Scrooge signed it. Old Marley was dead as a doornail. Scrooge knew he was dead. Of course he did. How could it be otherwise? Scrooge and he were partners for I don't know how many years. Though Scrooge never painted out old Marley's name. There it stood years afterward above the warehouse door. "Scrooge and Marley." Sometimes people new to the business called Scrooge, "Scrooge," and sometimes, "Marley." But he answered to both names. It was all the same to him.

How like Christians. Our Old Marley, our old man, is dead. To begin with, there is no doubt whatever about that. The register of his burial was signed by the Father, the Son, and the Holy Spirit. Our Old Marley is dead as a doornail. We know that he is dead. Of course we do. How could it be otherwise?

Yet we sometimes forget when the howling winds of life blow in a fallen world lived in fallen flesh. After all, we were partners for oh so many years. And sometimes we fail to paint out Old Marley's name. There it stands years afterward in the warehouse of our flesh. "New Man and Old Marley." We answer to both names. It's all the same to us.

However, we don't *have* to answer to both names any longer. Christ crucified our old partnership. And it certainly is *not* all the same to our Worthy Groom. Having cleansed us, having paid the price to discard our old burial clothes and to attire us in our new wedding gown, He insists that we live accordingly. "Put off your old clothes and the deeds associated with them. Instead, clothe yourself with the Worthy Groom's clothing and do not even think about how to gratify the desires of the flesh!"

Our Worthy Groom knows how to make people good and how to empower good people to live the good life out of a good heart. He knows how to move us from infancy to maturity (neonatal saints) so we experience victory over our enemies (*nikao* saints).

His Best Man, the Holy Spirit He sent to live within us until Worthy Groom returns for us, knows how to make resurrection power and progressive sanctification practical in our lives as we respond to suffering and sin. As we commune with Trinity, connecting ourselves to Divine resurrection power, we're empowered to live out our new life in Christ through:

- Co-Crucifixion with Christ: Mortification—Putting Off
- Co-Resurrection with Christ: Vivification—Putting On

"Putting off" and "putting on" are used so frequently that they represent an accepted form of Christian instruction widely used in the early church. In my studies, I've located 94 New Testament passages related to the putting off/mortification and putting on/vivification process.

The apostle Paul says, "You, however, did not come to know Christ that way" (Ephesians 4:20). What way? They did not come to know Christ in such a way that they should continue to live like the old unregenerate person they used to be (Ephesians 4:17-19). Paul continues. "Surely you have heard of him and were taught in him in accordance with the truth that is in Jesus" (Ephesians 4:21). What have they surely been taught? They were taught, with regard to their former way of life, to put off everything associated with their old way of life, to be made new in the core of their minds, and to put on everything associated with their new self in Christ (Ephesians 4:22-24).

Throughout the history of sanctification, teachers, pastors, theologians, and lay people alike have used the terms "mortification" and "vivification" to describe the practical outworking of our new life in Christ. We are co-crucified with Christ and therefore dead to sin. This is our *theological* reality. Mortification is the *practical application* of our co-crucifixion in which we put off our old grave clothes. We quit living like the old dead person we once were. We make actual in our practice what is already actual in our regeneration. United with Christ in His crucifixion, we died to sin. Our old man has been crucified. Mortification is putting off the vestiges of sin (flesh patterns) so that sin no longer exercises dominion over us because we are no longer sin's slaves.

We are also co-resurrected with Christ and therefore alive to righteousness. This is our second *theological* reality. Vivification is the *practical application* of our co-resurrection in which we put on our new wedding attire. We start living like the new alive person we now are in Christ. We make actual in practice what is already actual in our regeneration. United with Christ in His resurrection, we came alive to righteousness. Our new man has been birthed. Vivification is putting on, clothing ourselves with, and living out all the aspects of our new nurture and new nature.

Speaking of Romans 6, Ephesians 4, and Colossians 3, David Needham explains the relationship between our co-crucifixion and co-resurrection with Christ and our need to put off and put on.

> It was as though Paul saw a believer standing before two wardrobes; one contained the clothing (lifestyle) of an unregenerate person. "Take them off," Paul urged. "They don't fit, they're out of style, totally unbecoming of who you are, and, if that were not enough, they don't belong to you." The other contained the clothing (lifestyle) of a regenerate person. "They're yours!" Paul exclaimed. "Wear them. Don't worry, they'll fit!" (Needham, *Birthright*, p. 299).

Needham is simply paraphrasing God. "In the same way, count yourself dead to sin but alive to God in Christ Jesus" (Romans 6:11). Putting off the old you builds upon the reality that the old you is already deceased. Putting on the new you builds upon the reality that the new you is already alive to God through your union with Christ.

Putting Off and Putting On a Manner of Life

What exactly is it that we put off and put on? The Apostle Paul uses two terms in Ephesians 4:17-24 to teach us what we put off and put on. First, we are to put off walking (*peripateō*) as we did when we were unsaved (Ephesians 4:17). "Walk" describes our typical way of life, our accustomed lifestyle, and our normal manner of conduct.

Second, we are to put off our "former way of life" (*anastrophēn*) (Ephesians 4:22). "Way of life" refers to our habitual conduct, our routine conversation or manner of life, our customary way of living.

Jay Adams explains that God gave us a marvelous capacity that we call "habit." In itself, habit is neutral. It simply reflects a way of life, a practiced way of living, a lifestyle pattern. Referring to putting off and putting on, Adams notes, "a way or manner of life is a habitual way of living" (Adams, *More Than Redemption*, p. 241). The apostle Paul is teaching us that we work out our sanctification in the power of the Spirit as we put off old sinful habits of fleshly life patterns and as we put on new godly habits of spiritual life patterns.

Throughout our time together, we have called these "life themes." We have dissected four essential life themes associated with the four capacities of personhood:

♦ Relational Romancers and the Life Theme of *Affections/Lovers*
♦ Rational Dreamers and the Life Theme of *Mindsets*
♦ Volitional Creators and the Life Theme of *Purposes/Pathways*
♦ Emotional Singers and the Life Theme of *Mood States*

Putting off and putting on relate to our lifestyle themes and patterns (affections, mindsets, purposes, and mood states) that we live out in our relationships. As regenerate people, we operate out of a new characteristic lifestyle, walk, or manner of life controlled by the Spirit. However, the ingrained (habituated) flesh incited by the fallen world and enticed by the Devil tempts us to live according to our old lifestyle themes and patterns.

Mortification is the process of putting off or dehabituating ourselves from those old flesh patterns that reflect who we once were when we were separated from the life of God. *Vivification* is the process of putting on and rehabituating ourselves to new patterns that reflect who we already are in Christ.

"Putting off and putting on" is no mere amputation of surface manifestations, but disturbing, disrupting, uprooting, and replacing the roots of inner characteristics, patterns, and life themes in our relational, rational, volitional, and emotional capacities. Your "Old Marley" returns to haunt you. God says, "Don't carry around that corpse! It's rotten. Dead. Disgusting. Put off the old habits, the old grave clothes, the rags of corruption, the old conduct that was so characteristic of the old, dead you. Instead, continually be putting on the new manner of life that is now characteristic of the new you."

Putting Off and Putting On and Our Redeemed Motivational Structure

Though I will present something of an "order of progressive sanctification," I do not want to give the impression that the process of progressive sanctification is some "nice, neat package." It is not. Though the Bible does provide us with all we need for life and godliness, it never provides an outline. In offering my own "outline," I'm simply collating and systematizing my examination of the putting off and putting on process. As I often say to my graduate students, "this is my current best attempt at organizing the biblical data into one way of looking at this process." Neil Anderson says it well, "Trying to reduce life in the Spirit to a formula is like trying to capture the wind (John 3:8)" (Anderson, *Victory Over the Darkness*, p. 89).

In my ordering of the process, I return to our motivational structure. *Why do we do what we do?* We pursue (volitional) what we perceive (rational) to be pleasing (relational) which prompts reaction (emotional). *Rational direction determines relational motivation, which decides volitional interaction, which results in emotional reaction.* If I conclude (rational direction) that God is not my Supreme Good (relational motivation), then I will follow a self-centered lifestyle (volitional interaction) and end up emotionally out of control (emotional reaction). Therefore, we can conceptualize one "order" of the putting off process as:

- ♦ Rational: Putting Off Foolish Mindsets
- ♦ Relational: Putting Off Disordered Affections
- ♦ Volitional: Putting Off Self-Centered Purposes
- ♦ Emotional: Putting Off Ungoverned Mood States

I must live based on my changed mind before anything else changes. I have to repent of my foolish beliefs about God, or I will never passionately love God, never live an other-centered life for Christ, and never govern my emotions under the Spirit's control.

My "order of putting off" is supported not only by this theology of our motivational structure, but also by the Bible's emphasis on repentance as a change of mind (rational) and by the scriptural emphasis on mind renewal. According to Ephesians 4:23, the key to the entire putting off and putting on process is our rational control center. In between Paul's words about putting off the old (4:22) and putting on the new (4:24) he tells us, "to be made new in the attitude (*pneumati*) of your minds (*noos*)" (Ephesians 4:23). The attitude or spirit of the mind is our governing rational control center, the core interior principle of our being, the center of our personhood.

The unregenerate live according to the standard of their futile minds and darkened understanding. The regenerate live according to the standard of Christ, according to their transformed mindset. Our mind (*noos*) refers to our mindset, the sum total of the images, ideas, attitudes, beliefs, and convictions that control our outlook on life. The controlling influence of our thought life must be renewed by putting off the old ways of thinking about God, self, others, and the world and by putting on new ways of thinking.

Thus, logically the first "step" in the putting off process is rational repentance. I continually make a clean mental break with the mind of the flesh, abhorring the old contemptuous images and replacing them with the beauty of God's truth. As Dallas Willard notes, "as we first turned away from God in our thoughts, so it is in our thoughts that the first movements toward the renovation of the heart occur" (Willard, *Renovation of the Heart*, p. 95).

Regarding the three relational components (spiritual, social, self-aware), I have chosen the order of God, self, and others. This is not the only possible conceptualization. However, it seems that until we are open to God we cannot open to others or self, and until our openness to God changes who we are and how we see ourselves, we cannot open our hands to others. This reflects Paul's process. First we view God correctly (Romans 1). Then we view ourselves biblically (Romans 2:1-12:8). Only then can we love others powerfully (Romans 12:8-16:27).

The "Twelve Steps" of Mortification/Vivification

Given this basic order, I have outlined "twelve steps" in the putting off (mortification) and putting on (vivification) process. Box 26:1 provides my overview.

Notice my quotation marks around the words "twelve steps." I did not develop these from the Twelve Steps of *Alcoholics Anonymous*. Instead, I formulated them from the six aspects of our basic personality structure: rational, relational/spiritual, relational/social, relational/self-aware, volitional, and emotional. In progressive sanctification we need to put off our old foolish mindsets (rational), our old spiritual disordered affections (relational), our old self-aware disordered affections (relational again), our old social disordered affections (relational for the third time), our old self-centered purposes (volitional), and our old ungoverned mood states (emotional). When you add putting on the six characteristics of the new you, you see the origin of my "twelve steps."

"Steps" is also in quotation marks. I wish life were so easy. I long for biblical counseling to be that tidy. By "steps" I'm simply referring to principles or guidelines.

I've chosen "steps" because the word coincides with Paul's word "walk" (manner of life) and links nicely with the theological concept of life as a "journey." These twelve steps are ongoing, repeatable paths we must walk to experience the victory that Christ has already won for us.

I've also purposefully chosen to use the continuous tense language of "putting off" and "putting on" as opposed to "put off" and "put on." We were saved once for all. Sanctification, however, is ongoing. We do not once for all repent of an old way of thinking, never to have to face that lie again. Instead, we must continually gird up the

Box 26:1

The Twelve Steps of Mortification/Vivification

Putting Off/Mortification

1. **Step One: Rational Mortification—Putting Off Our Old Foolish Mindsets**

   "I repent of the insane idols of my heart."
   "I break the stranglehold of strongholds."

2. **Step Two: Relational Mortification—Putting Off Our Old Spiritual Disordered/Impure Affections**

   "I divorce the adulterous false lovers of my soul."
   "I annul my attachment to alluring lovers."

3. **Step Three: Relational Mortification—Putting Off Our Old Self-Aware Disordered/Impure Affections**

   "I reject the ugliness of my self-beautification."
   "I shed my self-sufficient, defensive thematic identities."

4. **Step Four: Relational Mortification—Putting Off Our Old Social Disordered/ Impure Affections**

   "I uproot my jealous hatred of others."
   "I dislodge my narcissistic, demanding relationships toward others."

5. **Step Five: Volitional Mortification—Putting Off Our Old Self-Centered Purposes/Pathways**

   "I put to death my enslaved acts of the flesh."
   "I discard my chosen style of destructive self-gratification."

6. **Step Six: Emotional Mortification—Putting Off Our Old Ungoverned Mood States**

   "I crucify my addictive passions that seek to make my belly my god."
   "I jettison my emotional duplicity, deadening, and denial."

Box 26:1, Continued

The Twelve Steps of Mortification/Vivification

Putting On/Vivification

7. **Step Seven: Rational Vivification—Putting On Our New Wise Mindsets**

   "I consent to the truth of Worthy Groom's grace narrative."
   "I allow myself to be transformed by the renewing of my mind."

8. **Step Eight: Relational Vivification—Putting On Our New Spiritual Purified Affections**

   "I enjoy and exalt Worthy Groom as my Supreme Good."
   "I commune deeply with God my Spring of Living Water."

9. **Step Nine: Relational Vivification—Putting On Our New Self-Aware Purified Affections**

   "I reckon on the truth of who Christ is to me and who I am in and to Christ."
   "I view myself according to Christ-sufficient, sacred thematic identities."

10. **Step Ten: Relational Vivification—Putting On Our New Social Purified Affections**

    "I stir up my new connecting love for others."
    "I nourish my new sacrificial relationships toward others."

11. **Step Eleven: Volitional Vivification—Putting On Our New Other-Centered Purposes/Pathways**

    "I fan into flame my newly freed will, empowered to empower others."
    "I provoke my new chosen style of shepherding through other-centered interactions."

12. **Step Twelve: Emotional Vivification—Putting On Our New Managed Mood States**

    "I cooperate with God in enlivening my new managed mood states."
    "I collaborate with God in living according to my new emotional integrity."

---

loins of our minds, continually allow God's Spirit to transform our thinking, continually live according to the new person we are in Christ, and continually count ourselves dead indeed to sin, but alive to God. Daily, even moment by moment, we are being transformed more and more into Christ's image (2 Corinthians 4:16-18). Any model of counseling or sanctification that promises a quick fix with permanent results contradicts God's Word.

These twelve steps outline a logical and theological process for helping others change. In counseling, we must apply them idiosyncratically. Each counselee, parishioner, and spiritual friend is uniquely complex. Though these twelve categories are useful, even necessary handles to guide our interactions, they are a guide, not a straitjacket. Each individual is responsible to connect to Christ's resurrection power.

Out of Christ's empowerment, each individual is personally, individually, and idiosyncratically responsible to put off his or her old characteristic manner of living, replacing it with the new lifestyle in Christ. The consistent practice of putting off and putting on leads to new patterns so the person's characteristic affections, mindsets, purposes, and mood states are set on God and not on the world. They are more and more according to the Spirit and less and less according to the flesh.

Mortification/Putting Off

When Paul selected the phrase, "putting off" (*apothesthai*), he chose a common clothing metaphor that suggests stripping off and laying aside an old set of clothes, clothing that somehow symbolizes the old manner of life, the old set of characteristics associated with the old person. As we might say today, "the clothes make the man." Clothing represents an outward symbol of what is inside. In Paul's day, when slaves were freed, they changed their attire, no longer wearing a slave's wardrobe. In our day, when prisoners are released, they're given a new set of clothes to wear, replacing their prison garb. Thus "putting off" suggests ceasing to act in a certain way, stripping off, being done with, and terminating everything associated with the old unregenerate person.

But Paul goes further. He speaks not simply of putting off slave clothes; he speaks of putting off grave clothes—the clothing that the "old man" wore. That old man is now dead. Take off those filthy, worn-out garments and put on a new set of clothes. Paul describes the old set of clothes as "corrupt" (*phtheiromenon*) (Ephesians 4:22), indicating they are putrid, crumbling, like the rotting waste of cadavers, stinking, and ripe to be disposed of and forgotten.

In Colossians 3:1-11, Paul maintains the same imagery, yet here his language is clearer and stronger. Since you died (3:3), put to death (*nekrōsate*) (3:5) those characteristics associated with your former manner of life. *Nekrōsate* is from *nekrōs* meaning "dead" and literally means to "treat as dead" (A. T. Robertson, *Word Pictures*, p. 499). Paul is shouting, "Put to death the old dead you. Kill the carcass that Christ crucified. Count as dead your old man. Stop carrying around that stinking corpse!"

Mortification is the habitual weakening of the flesh, of those vestiges of the old dead you. It involves the ongoing crippling of your old fleshly inclinations, putting off your old dead false lovers, foolish mindsets, self-centered pathways, and ungoverned mood states.

Isn't that what you long for? It is what you were made for, what you were created for in Christ. You have a new want to and a new can do to put off the old life themes and to live according to your new life themes in Christ.

This is the battle, the warfare, the competition to which you are called. As I write, it's the beginning of a new high school wrestling season. The varsity team I help coach is ranked fourth in the state. I love the thrill of competition. But I've begun to notice something about myself (a fleshly life theme, perhaps). When I minimize life's real battle—the battle between the flesh and the Spirit/spirit—I overemphasize life's minor skirmishes. There's nothing wrong with high school wrestling and coaching athletes to compete at peak performance. But there's everything wrong with making that my core calling in life, everything wrong with making that a life or death matter.

Though it is unlikely you are a high school wrestling coach, it's possible that, like me, you fall into False Seducer's snare of focusing on the wrong campaign. Your false fight might be obtaining that promotion, winning the legal case, becoming the top salesperson, being right in that church dispute, or any of a myriad of lesser battles. Even when our lesser battles are legitimate, we skew our perspective whenever we forget life's ultimate battle—the battle to put off the old and to put on the new in order to glorify God by reflecting Christ.

We are built to compete. God gave both males and females the dominion mandate and the weaponry to subdue themselves and their planet. Let's expend God's energy, Christ's resurrection power that flows through us, fighting the good fight of the faith, running the spiritual race, and training ourselves for godliness that has ultimate value both for this life and the life to come.

Step One: Rational Mortification—Putting Off Our Old Foolish Mindsets

Stop the madness! That's what putting off foolish mindsets does. It says, "No more!" to the insanity of False Seducer's lying narrative. It repents of the "God-is-not-good" falsehood. It rejects all non-God reality, stamping out the eyeballs-only thinking that leaves God out of the picture and suppresses the reality of Worthy Groom's holy love.

What is a foolish mindset? It is the smaller story, the earthly perspective of life that says, "Curse God and die!" It clamors for our attention claiming that anything other than God is our Supreme Good. The foolish mindset is captured and captivated by fleshly imaginations that scream, "God is a land of great darkness! He's a desert. He's not your Spring of Living Water, so dig cisterns of your own making."

"I Repent of the Insane Idols of My Heart"

When I put off my old mindsets, I repent of the insane idols of my heart. I put off my old contemptuous images of God and refuse to think like the arrogant fool I used to be. I dismiss all fabricated versions and sub-versions of reality that entice me to doubt God and trust myself. I put off dethroning God. In summary, putting off foolish mindsets requires that I repent of the idols of my heart that capture my imagination.

Facing *suffering* and wondering whether God is good, I put off all images of God as a shalt-not God. I say to God, "I put off my blindness to Worthy Groom's worth. I cease finding fault with You—perceiving injustice in You. I reject all contemptuous views of You. I refuse to think little of You and to think You little. I cast off all images of You as a cosmic Killjoy. I discard my loss of awe of You—my loss of all respect for You that causes me no longer to detect Your holy love, no longer to appreciate Your majestic beauty."

Facing *sin* and wondering whether I should choose the pleasure of sin for a season or pleasing God forever, I put off fleshly summarizing pictures, images, stories, and narratives that control my convictions and direct my actions. I say to God, "I put off the satanic strongholds that captivate my imagination. I disavow the fleshly imaginations that possess my thought life. I expose the lies of the earthly, temporal stories of reality that I've been believing. I do not allow the Cosmos Diabolicus to edit my perceptions. I take off the foolish frames of reference, lenses, and eyeglasses through which I have been viewing life mistakenly."

True repentance repents not only of actions, but also of deep-seated and satanically seeded mindsets. Whether dealing with suffering *or* sin, biblical repentance sounds something like this: "Father, I put off suppression of the truth in my mindsets. I repudiate all irreverent, disregarding, indifferent attitudes toward You. I quit actively holding down my awareness of Your awesomeness. I renounce all mindsets that say, 'Anything is better than God.' I will no longer exchange the truth of God for a lie—the lie that Worthy Groom is not worthy to be retained in my thinking. The lie that says, 'I can push You out, because placed side by side, I prefer the creature over my Creator.' I put off implicating You with badness, insinuating that You fall short of my glory. I quit playing umpire with You. I put off all mindsets that offer me godness by lessening Your goodness. Gracious Father, thank You for forgiving me and cleansing me. I count myself dead indeed to these old mindsets. I reckon myself alive indeed to You in the spirit of my mind. I claim Your power to put off the old and to put on the new in Christ, in whose name I pray. Amen."

"I Break the Stranglehold of Strongholds"

Repentance of heart idolatry is the principle we follow for putting off our foolish mindset. What is the process? It involves breaking the stranglehold of strongholds by:

- Exposing Our Unique Strongholds
- Repenting of Our Sinful Mindsets
- Loading Our Consciences with Guilt
- Enlightening Our Minds to Worthy Groom's Grace and Truth

Early in our study, we examined Paul's teaching concerning casting down strongholds (2 Corinthians 10:3-7). We saw that strongholds are fleshly mindsets burned into our minds through the world, the flesh, and the Devil. They are destructive patterns of thinking and habitual false ways of looking at life without spiritual eyes. Over time they become embedded in our minds like a mental fortress suppressing the truth.

My mental stronghold sin takes a unique shape because I manufacture or carve my idol in my image—according to my non-God story of my life, according to my idiosyncratically chosen perception of reality. Each particular act of sin is a branch off the tree from which I carve my idol. The root of the tree is my imagination. The fruit of the tree is what I choose to nourish myself with—God or non-god. In the strongholds of my mind I form and shape the very idol of self that I worship instead of God (Isaiah 44:14-17). I exchange the glory of my Creator for the shame of created things—things created in my image, not in God's (Romans 1:23-25).

Personal sanctification and biblical counseling require us to *identify and expose person-specific* strongholds. They force us to ask and answer questions like, "What is *my* image of God?" "What is *my pattern* of dethroning God?" "How do *I typically* try to make life work apart from God?" "What does *my style of relating* say about *my underlying beliefs* about life?" Since strongholds involve longstanding patterns of thinking, we also need to probe questions such as, "Where was I *recruited* into this false belief about God?" "When *did I begin to acquiesce* to this lie?" "What sinful pleasure *have I taken* in this lie?"

Identification of my unique mental stronghold(s) begins the process of dehabituation. *Repentance* continues the work. Repentance or *metanoia* literally means a change of mind. I change my mindset from a fleshly one to a spiritual one. I change my mind from a stronghold ingrained in the flesh through the enticement of the world and the allurement of the Devil, to a mindset in which I take every thought captive to make it obedient to Christ. Willard explains the prominence of repentance. "The ultimate freedom we have as human beings is the power to select what we will allow or require our minds to dwell upon" (Willard, *Renovation of the Heart*, p. 95). Repentance is the choice to reject the mental set of our old mind, replacing it with a mental focus in harmony with our new mind.

Repentance and mortification walk hand-in-hand. Repentance is the daily putting off and breaking up of the whole complex of conformity to the world, the flesh, and the Devil. In mortification through repentance, I'm involved in the life-long process of detecting my characteristic fleshly mindsets and turning from them.

To repent of a mindset, I must first recognize its insanity, see its vileness, and sense its ugliness. The Puritans labeled this process, "loading the conscience with guilt." John Owen, in his classic work *The Mortification of Sin*, describes the process. "Get a clear and abiding sense upon thy mind and conscience, first, of the guilt, secondly, of the danger, thirdly, of the evil, of that sin wherewith thou art perplexed" (Owen, *The Mortification of Sin*, p. 107).

Owen pictures a Christian struggling to defeat a besetting sin. Victory is stalled. The believer is perplexed, feels trapped, senses defeat. How can this Christian uproot sin? What will motivate this believer to hate sin with a holy hatred? Owen suggests the following principles of loading the conscience with guilt.

- Consider the danger of this particular sin. See the danger of being hardened by its deceitfulness (Hebrews 3:12-13) (p. 110). See the danger of God's discipline (p. 111). See the danger of loss of peace and strength (p. 112).
- Consider the evil of it. It grieves the Holy Spirit (p. 115). The Lord Jesus is wounded afresh by it (p. 117). It will take away your usefulness in this generation (p. 117).
- Charge your conscience with the guilt of law breaking. Consider the holiness, spirituality, severity, inwardness, and absoluteness of God's holiness (pp. 119-120).
- Bring your sin to the gospel not for relief but for further conviction—look on him you have pierced and be in bitterness (p. 121). "Say to thy soul, 'What have I done? What love, what mercy, what blood, what grace, have I despised and trampled on! Is this the return I make to the Father for his love, to the Son for his blood, to the Holy Ghost for his grace?'" (pp. 121-122). "Have I defiled

the heart that Christ died to wash, which the blessed Spirit hath chosen to dwell in?" (p. 122). "What can I say to the dear Lord Jesus? How shall I hold my head with any boldness before him? Do I account communion with him of so little value, that for this vile lust's sake I have scarce left him any room in my heart?" (p. 122).

◆ Consider the infinite patience and forbearance of God toward you in particulars (specifics) (p. 123). Remind yourself of his gracious withholding of judgment (p. 123).

◆ Pray for and pursue a constant longing for deliverance (p. 124).

◆ Ponder what occasions led to your giving in, and guard against them (p. 128).

◆ Reflect on the excellencies and majesty of God and how far short you are of him in holiness (p. 131).

◆ When your heart is disquieted by sin, speak no peace to it until God speaks it. Do not grant grace before you have a distaste for your sin (p. 145).

◆ Place faith in Christ for the killing of your sin (p. 161).

These practices seem foreign to us today because we have lost the spiritual awareness Owen had. He knew the defiled imagination glazed, adorned, and dressed the objects of the flesh, making them look beautiful, causing them to seem preferable to God and God's way. He understood that fleshly imagination darkened the soul like a thick cloud intercepting the beams of God's love and favor (Owen, *The Mortification of Sin*, p. 53). Since sin prettifies sin, we must putrefy sin; we must expose sin's horrible ugliness. We must realize that every act of sin reveals a mindset surrendered and agreeable to sinfulness. We need to allow sinful actions to expose sinful imaginations and affections, and then perceive and acknowledge how horribly corrupt it is for a saint to live like a sinner, for a child of God to live like a prodigal (Owen, *The Mortification of Sin*, p. 95).

To break the stranglehold of strongholds, I must expose my unique strongholds, repent of my sinful mindsets, load my conscience with guilt, and *enlighten my mind to Worthy Groom's grace and truth*. This final "step" merges into the putting on process, yet I need to introduce it here. As important as it is to load the conscience with guilt, unless we lighten the conscience with grace, we would be terrified ever to come before our holy God. Yet we can and should come boldly into His presence, having had our conscience cleansed by Christ (Hebrews 10:19-23). Even as I load my conscience with guilt, I do so surrounded by the awareness that God is gracious even when I am sinful. I face the horror of my sin in light of the wonders of Christ's grace.

A Prayer of Rational Repentance

"Father, I've finally come to my senses. I confess as sin my foolish belief that I can make life work apart from You. I've arrogantly suppressed the truth of how perfectly well You care for me. I've denied Your fatherly love for me. I've sinned against You by believing False Seducer's smaller story, the fleshly mindset that You are not my Supreme Good. I've allowed my view of reality to become filled with contemptuous images of You. I've allowed my mind to be squeezed into the mold of this temporal world, living according to the dominant plot theme of the earthly story. I've been like a deaf man straining to hear the gospel story. I've denied the Cross. I return to You now, repenting of these idols of my heart. Though I am not worthy in myself to be called Your child, by faith I claim my adoption in Christ. Thank You for forgiving me."

Step Two: Relational Mortification—Putting Off Our Old Spiritual Disordered/Impure Affections

Remember False Seducer's strategy. He belittles Worthy Groom, then exalts himself, all in the sick hope of causing us to be unfaithful to Christ. He tries to tempt us with foolish mindsets about God so he can lure us toward false lovers of the soul. False Seducer shrinks Worthy Groom so that we end up with a Lover so small we fail to "relentlessly worship and adore him. In the renovated mind, God constantly stands as uniquely and supremely worthy" (Willard, *Renovation of the Heart*, p. 107).

"I Divorce the Adulterous False Lovers of My Soul"

Rationally, we must put off our old foolish mindsets by saying, "I repent of the insane idols of my heart." *Relationally*, we must put off our old false lovers by saying, "I divorce the adulterous false lovers of my soul." We no longer live like the ugly whores we used to be because Christ has returned us to the purity of virgin brides who are motivated by gratitude to love God passionately.

If rational mortification focuses on foolish mindsets with their fleshly imaginations, then relational mortification centers on disordered affections and false lovers with their fleshly desires. Following Jesus always means not following fleshly affections, impulses, appetites, whims, and dreams. It always means pursuing Him with desperate desire, knowing that He alone quenches our soul's deepest thirsts. Worthy Groom calls us to mortify, crucify, and put off all fleshly longings.

Affections, longings, thirsts, delights, and desires are "where the action is." Modern Christianity reduces life to the externals of behavior while the significance of motivating desire is insufficiently emphasized (see J. I. Packer, "Introduction" in John Owen's, *Sin and Temptation*, pp. xvii-xxii). Our old flesh was habituated not simply to *do evil* but also and more insidiously, to *love evil*. Our flesh is ingrained toward patterns of false lovers from its years of disconnection from God. In Christ we have put off these patterns and must daily rid ourselves of any remnants.

Our God-created, renewed appetites face the tension of battling fleshly, worldly, satanic desires. Temptation entices us, awakening the old dead lusts through the attraction, lure, bait, and pull of sin (James 1:13-15). Sin deceives us through its offer of pleasure, fulfillment, and satisfaction. Psalm 1 pictures us as living organisms searching for nourishment. Where do we drink? From the Spring of Living Water or from broken cisterns that hold no water?

When faced with *suffering*, I'm tempted first to think, "life is bad and so is God." If I surrender to this fleshly mindset, then I'm easy game for the allure of false lovers who seem to promise protection, comfort, ease, or at least enough pleasure to cause me to forget my pain temporarily. In divorcing the adulterous false lovers of my soul, I cry out to Father, "I've been a relational prodigal. I now reject my past pattern of fearful flight from Father and I put on faith in You as my Forgiving Father. I abolish my fear of cosmic condemnation, of personal and eternal rejection. I return to original trust. When life is bad, I cling to You as my Supreme Good. I say, 'My flesh and my heart may fail, but God, You are the strength of my heart and my portion forever.'"

When faced with *suffering*, I'm also tempted to think, "Worthy Groom is not worth the wait." Then I'm easy prey for the roaring Lion who disguises himself as an angel of light promising to guide me in *his* everlasting way. In divorcing myself from False Seducer, I say to Worthy Groom, "I confess as sin my pursuit of false lovers of the soul and put on sole devotion to You, my Worthy Groom. I put off my whoredom and spiritual adultery. When life is bad, I remind myself, 'Whom have I in heaven but you? And earth has nothing I desire besides you.'"

When faced with *suffering*, I'm sometimes tempted to think, "Depending on God is foolish; I had better take care of myself." Having been strangled by this stronghold, I tumble down into the pit of worshiping false gods of my own invention. In divorcing myself from these false gods, I say to the Holy Spirit, "Dear Spirit, I exterminate my distorted desires. I put off my self-sufficient self-satisfaction. I confess as sin my denial of Christ-sufficiency. My broken cisterns are filthy and useless. I've sinned by forsaking my Spring of Living Water and I now acknowledge this for what it is—spiritual adultery."

When faced with a *besetting sin* that yanks me here and there like a yo-yo and tosses me about like a rag doll in a Doberman's mouth, I must mortify my fleshly desire. I confess, "I've allowed my religious affections to grow cold, my love to become lukewarm. I've buried the *visio Dei*—the beatific vision of God. I've rejected God as my highest joy, my greatest delight. I've replaced God my Hero with false heroes. I've replaced God my Lover with false lovers. I've not related to You as a good God with a supremely good heart. I have a fundamental worshiping nature, but I've not been putting off the fleshly tendency to worship anything or anyone but God. So right now I put off trust in non-God and put on trust in God. In Christ's resurrection power I put off my false passions, my delighting in lesser gods, my sinfully misdirected longings, and my pursuit of God-designed desires in God-prohibited ways."

"I Annul My Attachment to Alluring Lovers"

Relationally divorcing the adulterous lovers of our soul is the principle we follow for putting off false lovers. What is the process? It involves annulling our attachment to our alluring lovers, or what the Puritans labeled "the mortification of our sinful affections." The process includes:

- ◆ Relational Return: Returning Home to Father
- ◆ Relational Dissatisfaction: Acknowledging Our False Lovers' Faults
- ◆ Relational Contentment: Reveling in Our True Lover's Fullness

Repentance (*metanoia*) is not only a change of mind, but also a change of love and longing. Motivated by a vision of the majesty and beauty of God, I pine after a different relationship, life, and world. In repentance, I acknowledge that God is my first love. Thus repentance removes the barriers to seeing, experiencing, and enjoying the face of God.

The Scriptures consistently portray repentance as *relational return*. I put off my old adulterer's clothes and return home. The Prodigal repented and returned home. Christ commands the lukewarm Laodiceans to repent and invites them to open the door of their soul so they can return home to sup with Him. When the floundering Ephesians left their first love, Jesus tells them to remember, repent, and return. Desperate, despairing, depressed David repents and then pleads that he could rest in the presence of his forgiving God. Repentance is *relational return in which we first turn away from our false lovers and then return to our heart's true home.*

Hosea 14 provides a classic biblical picture of relational return. Building upon the imagery of Gomer's unfaithfulness to Hosea as a symbol of Israel's spiritual unfaithfulness to Jehovah, Hosea concludes with the words, "Return (*shub*), O Israel, to the LORD your God. Your sins have been your downfall" (Hosea 14:1). Hosea uses this same word "return" sixteen times in fourteen chapters beginning with Hosea 2:7, "She will chase after her lovers but not catch them; she will look for them but not find them. Then she will say, 'I will go back (return, *shub*) to my *husband* as at first, for then I was better off than now" (emphasis added). Mortification of false lovers calls for a return to God our true Husband.

Something else in Hosea 2:7 and 14:1 may not be quite so obvious. In both cases we find a *recognition of our false lover's inability to satisfy.* Our sinful lovers are our "downfall" (*kāshal*), a word suggesting weakness, lack of strength, inability, and insufficiency. Gomer says it even more clearly when she realizes that she was better off with her true husband than with her false lovers. Relational repentance is always relational return and *relational dissatisfaction.* The Prodigal came to his senses, realizing that even his father's hired servants were better fed than he. Jehovah urged Israel to recognize the futility of her false lovers and to acknowledge that they could neither save her nor fulfill her (Jeremiah 2). Hosea counsels Israel along identical lines telling them to say to Jehovah, "Assyria cannot save us; we will not mount war-horses. We will never again say, 'Our gods' to what our hands have made" (Hosea 14:3).

We mortify our false lovers through relational repentance that includes relational return, relational dissatisfaction, and *relational contentment* in God our true Lover. Returning to Jehovah, Hosea offers words to say to him, "Forgive all our sins and receive us *graciously,* that we may offer the fruit of our lips . . . For in you the fatherless find *compassion*" (Hosea 14:2b, 3b, emphasis added). We return content and amazed by Father's grace and compassion.

Hosea's "process" counters False Seducer's strategy. False Seducer belittles Worthy Groom and magnifies the other lovers. Relational repentance belittles the other lovers and magnifies Worthy Groom.

In helping your counselees to uproot the flesh and fleshly affections, walk them through the process of relational return. Help them mortify their false lovers through relational return in which they confess to God the sin of their false lovers, acknowledge to themselves and to God their relational dissatisfaction with their false lovers, and share with God that He alone is worthy.

A Prayer of Relational Repentance: Spiritual

"Father, I come home to You. I confess as sin my false lovers. I confess as sin living like the old person I used to be. I confess as sin my spiritual adultery and whoredom. I acknowledge to You and to myself that my false lovers are horrible lovers and that my

pursuit of them is ugly and putrid. How foolish of me ever to believe that anyone but You could ever satisfy the longings of my soul. How shameful. How disrespectful. Forgive me my relational sin. I acknowledge that You alone are my Supreme Good. I acknowledge that You alone are gracious and compassionate. I return to You as my Forgiving Father. I return to Your Son as my Worthy Groom. I return to Your Holy Spirit as my Inspiring Mentor. I love You, Lord. Renew my vision of You as a totally competent and totally good God—boundless in holy love."

Step Three: Relational Mortification—Putting Off Our Old Self-Aware Disordered/Impure Affections

We follow foolish mindsets fanned into flame by False Seducer and his lying narratives about God as a shalt-not God. Believing these, we choose to love any lover other than Worthy Groom. Doubting God, while still being designed to trust someone or something, we trust ourselves (false self-aware lovers). Turning from God's love, while still being designed to receive infinite love, we crave love in all the wrong places (false social lovers).

Augustine defined abnormality as a soul caved in on itself. That perfectly describes our old self-aware false lovers. Christians live in the flesh in this area to the degree that they are ruled by internal dispositions toward radical self-centeredness, self-sufficiency, self-protection, self-hatred, selfishness, and self-beautification.

"I Reject the Ugliness of My Self-Beautification"

Luther, like Augustine, clearly understood the flesh-oriented conscience. It's an evil conscience that replaces our sacred identity in Christ with a shame identity in self. It rejects grace in favor of works. We see ourselves as shameful since we've failed to reckon on who we are in Christ because we've refused to live by grace, choosing instead to live our lives and see ourselves according to False Seducer's lying narrative of works. Our shame leads to self-hatred that we foolishly attempt to deal with through self-sufficiency.

When bombarded by *suffering* and finding ourselves crushed by a fallen world, we believe False Seducer's fairy tale. "Life is bad, so is God, and so are you." His penetrating arrows pierce our conscience. "These bad things must be happening to me because my tit-for-tat God is displeased with me. If only I could please him. The only way to please Him is by doing good works and by beautifying myself. I have to make myself pretty enough that He'll want me. I must cover my shame."

Mortification counters these lies. We say to Worthy Groom, "I reject the ugliness of my self-beautification. Every time I beautify myself, I deny You. I demean Your grace. I act as though the Cross were foolishness. I confess as sin my refusal to count myself dead indeed to sin and alive indeed to righteousness. I confess as sin my living according to False Seducer's shame narrative. I confess as sin refusing to base my sense of self on my new nurture in Christ. I put off all of False Seducer's shame identities about me. More than that, I put off all my self-sufficient attempts to feel good about me. I put on Christ-esteem, Christ-contentment, and Christ-competence."

Facing suffering without shame is hard enough. Sometimes it seems almost impossible to face our *sinfulness* honestly without capitulating to shame. We load our conscience with guilt and then load it some more and more and more. All the time we forget to lighten our conscience with grace. We remind ourselves how horrible it is to sin, but we neglect how wonderful it is to be forgiven. We believe yet another of False Seducer's myths. "You are evil and God is unforgiving." His piercing lies whisper into our tender consciences, "God hates sin. You are a sinner. God hates you. Some sins are so deep that even the love of God cannot touch them." Now we double-time it and over-time it, trying desperately to become something we already are: saints and sons/daughters.

Mortification counters these lies. We say to Forgiving Father, "I reject the ugliness of self-beautification. I've sinned against You by doubting Your graciousness and by seeing myself according to False Seducer's condemning narrative. I've hated myself and therefore attempted to beautify myself. I've begun by faith but tried to continue by works. This is anathema to You, but I am never anathema to You. I've swallowed Satan's mental cyanide, allowing myself to be implanted and imprinted with questions about Your heart toward me. I confess as sin questioning the depth of Your holy love and pardoning grace. I've dethroned Your grace, replacing it with my works. I've believed that I'm Your enemy and You're mine. What a denial of Christ's gospel of grace. I've sinfully allowed my self-awareness to be bewitched by an evil conscience led by evil fleshly eyesight."

"I Shed My Self-Sufficient, Defensive Thematic Identities"

Rejecting the ugliness of self-beautification is the principle we follow for putting off false self-aware lovers. What is the process? It involves shedding my self-sufficient defensive identities by:

- Repenting of Core Self-Beautification
- Repenting of Specific Self-Sufficient Thematic Identities

Because we live according to life themes and because we think in summarizing ideas and images, we maintain thematic identities—rather fixed ways of looking at ourselves. In Christ we have grace-based thematic identities. Some of these are "universal" identities—ways every Christian can see himself or herself: saint, son, daughter, royal priest, and hundreds of others. We also have "unique" thematic identities—particular ways that we see ourselves based upon God having fearfully, wonderfully, and uniquely framed and formed us. These, too, are grace-based thematic identities because we recognize that all the worthy, wonderful things about us are grace gifts.

When we fall under False Seducer's spell, however, we forget who we are *in* Christ and *to* Christ. We lose our universal sense of self as a saint, son or daughter. Then, like Adam and Eve, we feel naked and ashamed. We live the rest of our fleshly lives scurrying about trying to cover our sense of shame with defensive, self-protective, and self-sufficient thematic identities.

Repentance, therefore, is two-fold. First, I must repent of my *core self-beautification*. I confess to Father the bent in my heart toward taking care of myself by myself.

Second, I must identify and repent of the *specific thematic identities* that I'm using to cover up my sense of shame and nakedness. I need to ask myself penetrating questions like, "What defensive layers am I using to protect my sense of self?" "What specific covers do I put on to make others happy with me?" "What way of relating to others do I use in order to impress them?" "What fig leaves am I using to try to deal with my shame apart from Christ?" "How am I blocking the real me from coming forth?" "What am I afraid of?" "Who do I really think I am deep down inside? If I showed this person to others, what do I think would happen? How do I think God would respond?"

A Prayer of Relational Repentance: Self-Aware

"Father, I've been so like Adam and Eve. Running. Hiding. Defensive. Playing dress up. All because I don't believe You are who You say You are—Forgiving Father. What sin! I put off my shame identity. I reject my sense of abandonment, ruin, rejection, and condemnation. I put off my futile attempts to quiet my inner restlessness. Instead, I rest in You. I rest in who I am in Christ and to Christ. It's ugly of me to try to beautify myself. It's a slap in the face to Your Son, my Savior. Forgive me. Cleanse me. Enlighten me by Your Holy Spirit to grasp how much You love me and how loving You are."

Step Four: Relational Mortification—Putting Off Our Old Social Disordered/Impure Affections

Adam rejects God's sufficiency and satisfaction (foolish mindsets), follows False Seducer (spiritual false lovers), hides and covers up (self-aware false lovers), then shames and blames his wife (social false lovers). Like father, like son. Cain jealously hates his brother, refusing to be his keeper/shepherd, instead being his judge, jury, and executioner.

Our old social disordered affections epitomize the opposite of the Trinity. The Trinity is radically other-centered. Adam, Cain, and you and I, when we live according to the flesh, are radically self-centered. More than that, we are fueled by a drive that uses others for our own well-being.

"I Uproot My Jealous Hatred of Others"

In mortification, we must put off our old flesh-oriented way of relating to others. Caved in upon ourselves because we've rejected God as our Fountain of Life, we desperately crave, and therefore demand, that others fulfill longings and thirsts that only our infinite God can fill.

Finding ourselves in this hopeless state, James tells us we frenetically race between manipulation and retaliation (James 4:1-4). Battling unmet desires, we first attempt to manipulate others to meet our needs. "I want what I want and I want it now and I want it from you!" When they don't come through for us, we retaliate. "If you won't make me feel better about me, then I will make you feel worse about you!"

In *suffering*, we feel thirsty because no one seems to be coming through for us. Rather than turning to Christ, we turn on others. In times like these we must return to God saying, "Father, forgive me. I'm running on empty because I'm not turning to You. I'm discarding Your invitation to drink whenever I am thirsty. So now I'm sinfully drinking from others, demanding that they make me feel good. I put off my shaming and blaming way of relating to others. I confess as sin my manipulation of others, using them to fill me."

We respond to our suffering by causing others to suffer. We must take our *sinful* self-centeredness to Christ. "Lord Jesus, I'm using others. My jealous hatred of my brothers and sisters is a reflection of the old me and more a mirror of False Seducer than an image or reflection of You. I confess as sin my non-Trinitarian way of relating. I put off my radically self-centered orientation."

"I Dislodge My Narcissistic, Demanding Relationships to Others"

Uprooting my jealous hatred of others is the principle we follow for putting off false social lovers. What does the process look like? It involves dislodging my narcissistic demanding relationships to others and it includes:

- Identification of Specific Characteristic Styles of Sinning
- Repentance of Specific Characteristic Styles of Sinning

As with the process in previous "steps," the key is specificity. In our own lives or in working with clients, parishioners, or spiritual friends, we must repent not simply of the general concept of sin, but of our *specific, unique, and characteristic manner of sinning.*

We need to ask ourselves questions such as, "In what ways am I demanding that others come through for me, that others meet my needs?" "How do I typically go about manipulating others?" "What do I typically do to retaliate against others when they don't seem to come through for me?" "What would it be like to be in a relationship with me?" "Do I live to feed, nourish, shepherd, and care for others or do I live to get others to take care of me?"

Having identified our characteristic styles of sinning against others with specificity, we need to practice *precise repentance*. It's not enough for us to say, "Father forgive me for my sins." I need to say, "Father, forgive me for my sin of typically and specifically manipulating my wife by pouting every time she brings up another viewpoint." "Father, forgive me for my sin of characteristically and specifically blowing up in an angry rage every time one of my employees misses a deadline."

Because this is such a personal process, and because sin is so deceitful, this is an area where feedback from trusted spiritual friends is essential. One or two honest spiritual friends can share with us how they see us relating to others. An open, caring, insightful small group can provide helpful feedback about how we relate.

A Prayer of Relational Repentance: Social

"Father, I confess as sin my living for self, loving self, caressing self. I will put off shepherding myself and focus on shepherding others. I reject all the self sins: self-sufficiency, self-promotion, self-protection, selfishness, self-centeredness. I confess as sin my cruel, harsh, manipulative, demanding, shaming, blaming, maiming way of treating others. Most of all, I confess as sin how far I've moved from reflecting You and Your radically other-centered Trinitarian existence. I am putting off the flesh, the characteristic ways I used to relate and I'm putting on the Spirit, the new me created to relate like You."

Step Five: Volitional Mortification—Putting Off Our Old
Self-Centered Purposes/Pathways

Pathways are products of the will and the will is our ability to choose, to decide, and to create. "Will is the ability to originate or refrain from originating something: an act or a thing" (Willard, *Renovation of the Heart*, p. 144). Our decisions and actions flow from our will. Pathways are our patterned and purposeful behaviors, actions, and interactions as we respond to our world.

The will is not the same as "*character*, but character does develop from it, as specific willings become habitual" (Willard, *Renovation of the Heart*, p. 144). Designed by God, our wills were free to choose courageously to create good and to empower others. Depraved by sin, our wills became enslaved to compulsive, cowardly choices—destructive choices that either overpower others or are overpowered by others. Redeemed by Christ, our wills are released to choose sacrificially to shepherd others. Habitually living to empower others is the essence of Christlike character. Volitionally, we are mature to the degree that our pathways (patterns of willing) are other-centered.

Yet we can return to the old way, the old willing, the old fleshly, self-centered pathways of volitional purposing. Theologically, we label these "enslaved acts of the flesh"—characteristic ways we will to live, habitual patterns of behavior that pursue the purpose of destructive self-gratification.

"I Put to Death My Enslaved Acts of the Flesh"

When I am convinced that God is my Supreme Good and I turn to Him as the Lover of my soul, my will is free to serve others in love (Galatians 5:13). However, when I doubt God's goodness and I turn away from Him as the Lover of my soul, my will becomes enslaved to the flesh and I live to indulge my own needs, cravings, desires, and wants (Galatians 5:13-15). Because I follow spiritual false lovers, I live an empty life from an empty spiritual reservoir. In my felt emptiness, I live to protect myself from any more pain or damage. As I look to others, I try to siphon them, stealing "gasoline" from them to fuel my empty tank.

The acts of the flesh are characteristic ways I respond to life, based upon my foolish mindsets about my false lovers. They are the enslaved strategies that I follow and the ingrained purposes I pursue by my actions and through my interactions. They reflect the compulsive choices I follow to fuel myself, rather than the courageous choices I could follow to fuel others.

I can respond to *suffering* with enslaved acts of the flesh, with habituated cowardly, compulsive, destructive choices. I don't get what I want, or I get what I want and it's not enough. I feel empty. Thirsty. I might choose the pathway of the sluggard who gives up on life and never tries again. Or I might select the way of debauchery and try to drown my sorrows. Or I may journey down the path of rage, always angry at the world for letting me down. When I recognize these fleshly character patterns, then I turn to Father saying, "Dear Lord, forgive me. Instead of coming to You in my suffering, I've taken matters into my own hands. Or tried to. What a mess I've made of things. I've shamed Your name, hurt others, and disgraced myself. I put off these old self-centered pathways. I reject my cowardly choices, designed only to make me feel good."

Or totally apart from any obvious area of suffering, I might compulsively choose to follow *sinfully* any number of godless lifestyles. When I find myself entangled in such sins, I return to Christ, taking words with me. "Lord Jesus. I have no excuse. You've given me everything I need for life and godliness. I have misused my freedom to indulge my flesh. And I wouldn't have done so if I hadn't first discarded You as my source of life. And I wouldn't have done that if I had been living according to my renewed mindset. Forgive me. I put off my fleshly behavior. I reject my characteristic pattern of responding to life."

"I Discard My Chosen Style of Destructive Self-Gratification"

Putting to death my enslaved acts of the flesh is the principle we follow for putting off self-centered pathways. What does the process look like? It involves discarding my chosen style of destructive self-gratification. It includes:

- Brutal Honesty About Our Patterns: Eschewing Excuses
- Labeling Our Patterns: Taking a Personal Inventory
- Detecting the Core Issues Driving Our Patterns: Rooting Out Central Idols
- Surrendering Our Patterns: Submitting Our Will to God
- Energetic Engagement of Our Patterns: Following God's Will.

The new you is freed to exercise dominion over your passions and God's planet, freed to empower others. Yet you can enslave yourself again by choosing to follow a hard, stubborn heart, a seared conscience, and selfish purposes. When you do, your actions become destructive to God's kingdom, to others, and even to yourself.

Brutal honesty is required. When it comes to behavior patterns, we are quick to blame our actions, and even our character, on our temperament, our basic constitution, our upbringing, our mood, or our basic proneness. The Puritans used to insist that we not excuse sin based on these. True, we might be peculiarly inclined to a certain temperament, but it is simply the peculiar "breaking out" of our characteristic flesh (our fleshly character). So rather than saying, "that's just me," we should say, "that's the fleshly me breaking free again. I need to put it off. I need to watch to avoid whatever feeds this characteristic style of sinning. I must practice spiritual disciplines that reorient me to self-control."

Rather than excusing our patterns, we must recognize our patterns and *label* them accordingly and accurately. We must take time to reflect on our characteristic ways of responding to life. Journaling, praying for God to reveal secret sins, asking God to break sin's deceitfulness and hardness in our lives, and seeking feedback from others, all of these will assist us to discover sinful patterns through taking a personal inventory.

Having taken a personal inventory of our characteristic fleshly pathways, we can say, "I have the tendency to give into the sin of pride" (or anger, self-protection, self-indulgence, stealing, homosexuality, lust, playing the sluggard, etc.). Next we should *detect and root out* the reasons (not excuses) for this sinful pattern having such dominance and sway in our lifestyles. Since our interactions are guided by our characteristic idols that are created by our characteristic fleshly imagination, we should ask ourselves some pointed questions. "What lies am I believing that are leading me to surrender repeatedly to the pathway of envy? What false images of God are captivating my mind and leading me to yield to my characteristic, habitual sin of pride?" These questions orient us to the truth that I choose a style of interaction that fulfills my strategy for controlling my world without God. They expose the truth that my pattern of behavior (character) is my unique way of living out the unique idol of my heart.

We must follow recognition with *surrender*. "In the progression toward complete identification of our will with God's there are distinctions to be noted. First there is *surrender*. When we surrender our will to God we consent to his supremacy in all things" (Willard, *Renovation of the Heart*, p. 150). We will God to be God. We may still struggle to do His will, but at least we are willing to will it. That's surrender. I put off my will and I put on Christ's will. Surrender begins to break the entanglements of my fleshly will. It weakens my fleshly will's characteristic demanding, destructive, self-gratifying bent.

Engagement is the next "step" in loosening the entangled will. Though this step begins to move us into "putting on new pathways," it's important that we consider it now. To keep the old fleshly will put off; we replace it with new spiritual willing. "Beyond contentment lies intelligent, energetic *participation* in accomplishing God's will in our world. We are no longer spectators, but are caught up in a vivid and eternal drama in which we play an essential part" (Willard, *Renovation of the Heart*, p. 151). Like Jesus, we say, "Not my will, but Thine be done!" Christ's resurrection power energizes our tiny renewed will power to will the one thing, the most needful thing.

A Prayer of Volitional Repentance

"Father, I've sinned against You by walking in the way of the sinner, by following the self-centered pathway of _____. I must put off choosing compulsively and put on choosing courageously. I must put off the old enslaved pathways and put on my new free, empowering pathways. Help me to quit coddling, cuddling, pampering, and spoiling my flesh. Empower me to be fierce in ruthlessly rejecting it and nailing it to the Cross. Reveal my secret sins, show me the patterns that I'm blind to, help me to detect my fleshly pathways. I reject my fleshly inclinations, patterns, and character. I put on the new characteristic of _____. I reject my characteristic approach to life of _____ and by Christ's resurrection power I replace it with my new manner of life."

Step Six: Emotional Mortification—Putting Off Our Old Ungoverned Mood States

Feelings, as Willard reminds us, "are a primary blessing and a primary problem for human life. We cannot live without them and we can hardly live with them" (Willard, *Renovation of the Heart*, p. 117). Nonetheless, feelings were and are God's idea. Created to be alive Singers, sin transformed us into moody Addicts, while salvation restores us to soulful Poets. We are saints returned to emotional integrity by Worthy Groom, enlivened to experience life honestly in all its grief and hope.

Yet the battle continues. The flesh attempts to rule our emotionality through ungoverned mood states. "Feelings live on the front row of our lives like unruly children clamoring for attention" (Willard, *Renovation of the Heart*, p. 117). Emotions are hauntingly present, like a ghostly power possessing us. We require an emotional exorcist, not to eradicate all feelings, but to put off our old ungoverned mood states and to put on our new managed mood states.

"I Crucify My Addictive Passions that Seek to Make My Belly God"

My mood states are bound to my volitionality (pathways of the will), my rationality (mindsets of my heart), and my relationality (lovers of my soul). In the flesh, I surrender to False Seducer's lie that "God is not good," and I solicit false lovers who seem better. Then I develop characteristic strategies that I pursue to deal with my starving soul.

Given such a state of affairs, is it any wonder that emotionally I obey addictive passions that seek to make my belly god? Casting off any hope of true soul satisfaction, of course I settle for a semblance of sensual satisfaction. I deaden my pain through feeling pleasure.

When I endure *suffering*, pain screams at me. I ache. Thirst. Hurt. My flesh impels me toward emotional stoicism: "Repress your feelings, don't face them!" Or toward emotional sensationalism: "Express your feelings indiscriminately. You hurt. Let others know. Hurt them, too!" Or toward emotional sensualism: "Anesthetize your moods. Find pleasure. Drown your sorrows." To put off these fleshly emotional responses, I need to say to Father, "I've sinned against You by surrendering to ungoverned mood states. I put off stoicism, sensationalism, and sensualism. I refuse to make my belly my god. I refuse to make feeling good the idol of my heart. Instead, I take my pain to You. Teach me to soothe my soul in my Savior."

In struggling against besetting *sin*, everything within my fleshly self wants to enjoy the pleasure of sin for a season. Wants to feel good just for one moment. Feels as if I *deserve* feeling wonderful. Putting off these sinful emotional passions, I say to Christ, "I put off my addictive passions. I crucify the flesh and my demand for instant gratification. My demand that I feel good. I confess my refusal to face the sorrow of life and my hunger for heaven. I put off my ungoverned mood states. I recognize my mood disorder of lacking self-awareness of my prevailing mood state. I acknowledge my inability to sense accurately and experience fully my inner world. I admit my inability to read accurately my emotional thermostat. I confess my hate, despair, and terror. I put off my timid responses to my inner and outer world. Empower me to put on compassion, enjoyment, and rest."

"I Jettison My Emotional Duplicity, Deadening, and Denial"

Crucifying my addictive passions is the principle we follow for putting off ungoverned mood states. What does the process look like? It involves:

♦ Jettisoning Our Emotional Duplicity
♦ Jettisoning Our Emotional Deadening
♦ Jettisoning Our Emotional Denial

Recall that Paul highlights two concepts in his description of fleshly emotionality: the loss of sensitivity (*apalgēō*) and the presence of lasciviousness (*aselgeia,* sensuality) (Ephesians 4:19). Loss of sensitivity signifies ceasing to feel and being callous. Faced with excruciatingly painful feelings, we try to deaden, deny, and repress them. So, tired of feeling pain, we try to live without feelings. We become apathetic (without passion) toward God, others, and ourselves.

We end up with emotional *duplicity* rather than emotional integrity. In emotional integrity, we feel and face whatever we are currently experiencing. We then bring rationality to our emotionality by understanding why we feel what we feel. Subsequently we can bring spirituality to our emotionality by taking our feelings to God and soothing our souls in Him. Emotional duplicity is emotional hypocrisy. We fake it. Pretend. We deceive ourselves by being dishonest about what we are really feeling, by refusing to face what we feel. We live a lie, a life of emotional pretense. We are double-minded, or, if you will, we are double-emotive. We feel one thing but pretend to ourselves and others that we are feeling nothing or something entirely different.

We try to *deaden* our emotions. We can't. They seep out. Ooze out. Explode out. Lasciviousness is the explosion of ungoverned emotions we have tried to deaden. Lasciviousness is the duplicitous me sneaking out and hurting you. My stuffed passions running wild. I live without restraint, without regard for anything but my own mood states. My mood becomes my god. I must feel good or at least not feel so revolting. I become sensually triggered to indulge in every possible pleasure. That is addiction. The result is damage. Damage to God's reputation, damage that I inflict upon others during my emotional binges, and damage to my own emotional health.

Logically, I must counter emotional duplicity with integrity. I must put off my refusal to face my feelings. I need to see repression of my feelings as a sin and confess it as such. "Father, I've been denying my emotionality and in doing so I've been denying Your creativity."

Once I've faced what I am feeling, I need to bring biblical truth to bear on my emotions, rather than practicing emotional *denial*. I need to ask myself questions such as, "Is this emotion governed or ungoverned?" "Is this a sign of emotional order or disorder?" "What does my mood state reveal about my pathways, mindsets, and lovers?" This third question is vital. Emotional integrity pinpoints what I'm feeling and why. It uses mood states as a warning sign to examine the condition of the rest of my inner capacities of personhood.

As I trace my mood states back to my pathways, mindsets, and lovers, I'll see the depths of my fleshly patterns. I'll detect how my addictive, lascivious passions reveal the true state of my soul. "The addict is the one who, in one way or another, has given in to feeling of one kind or another and has placed it in the position of ultimate value in his or her life" (Willard, *Renovation of the Heart*, p. 125). God requires me to repent of having made my belly god. I need to repent of the false lovers of my soul that leave me so desperately empty that I worship feeling states.

A Prayer of Emotional Repentance

"Father, I've sinned against You by worshiping feelings instead of worshiping You. My current mood state of _____ exposes how desperately I'm trying to live without You. My failure to face my feelings exposes my distrust in Your ability to care for me. My refusal to soothe my soul in You exposes my doubts about Your goodness. I put off my emotional duplicity replacing it, in the power of Your Spirit, with emotional integrity. I will face whatever I feel and bring it to You. I put off my emotional lasciviousness. I put off indulging my fleshly passions. I confess as sin my addiction to _____ . I recognize it for what it is: a symptom of the deeper disorder within me, a spiritual, relational, mental, willful disorder. Forgive me. Empower me to manage my moods. Empower me to put on grace lovers/purified affections, wise mindsets, and other-centered pathways so that I can put on managed mood states."

Where We've Been and Where We're Heading

Where have we been? We've been to the mortuary. To the cemetery. To the haunted house. We've taken that old dead corpse with its putrid, rotting clothing and we've disowned it.

Where are we headed? Right where you want to go. Right to "putting on new life in Christ." We're leaving mortification and moving to vivification. We're leaving the cemetery and heading for the nursery where babes in Christ grow up and grow strong by putting on their new life in Christ.

Caring for Your Soul: Personal Applications

1. Step One: Rational Mortification—Putting Off Our Old Foolish Mindsets

   a. What insane idols of the heart do you need to repent of? Will you? How?

   b. How will you break the stranglehold of strongholds in your life?

2. Step Two: Relational Mortification—Putting Off Our Old Spiritual Impure Affections/False Lovers

   a. What adulterous false lovers of your soul do you need to divorce? Will you? How?

   b. How will you annul your attachment to alluring lovers?

3. Step Three: Relational Mortification—Putting Off Our Old Self-Aware Impure Affections/False Lovers

   a. What ugliness of self-beautification do you need to reject? Will you? How?

   b. How will you shed your self-sufficient defensive sustaining identities?

4. Step Four: Relational Mortification—Putting Off Our Old Social Impure Affections/False Lovers

   a. What jealous hatred of others do you need to uproot? Will you? How?

   b. How will you dislodge your narcissistic demanding relationships toward others?

5. Step Five: Volitional Mortification—Putting Off Our Old Self-Centered Purposes/Pathways

   a. What enslaved acts of the flesh do you need to put to death? Will you? How?

   b. How will you discard your chosen style of destructive self-gratification?

6. Step Six: Emotional Mortification—Putting Off Our Old Ungoverned Mood States

   a. What addictive passions that seek to make your belly god do you need to crucify? Will you? How?

   b. How will you jettison your emotional deadening, duplicity, and damage?

Caring for Others: Ministry Implications

♦ **Teach Mortification:** Our spiritual friends, parishioners, and counselees need to learn the truth of mortification of sin. They can learn it from the pulpit, from the lectern, from books, from small groups, and from you. Your teaching does not have to be "shotgun teaching," but "high-powered rifle teaching." That is, you can make your teaching and your application specific, focused precisely where it is needed.

♦ **Counsel Using the Principles/Steps of Mortification:** You do this, first, by having mortification concepts in mind, guiding all of your spiritual friendship interactions. Always be thinking about how to help your spiritual friends put off old false lovers (impure affections), foolish mindsets, self-centered purposes (pathways), and ungoverned mood states. Second, use spiritual conversations and scriptural explorations to explore and apply the principles of mortification. Identify specific areas to be mortified, then explore how God's truth relates to your spiritual friends' mortification process. Third, use the principles of mortification as homework assignments. Counseling, at best, starts the process of change. It is during the real life hours outside your meetings that spiritual friends either truly grow or really backslide. Send your spiritual friends away with an assignment to write their own prayers of repentance. Give them the assignment to identify specific false lovers (impure affections), foolish mindsets, self-centered purposes (pathways), or ungoverned mood states. Give homework assignments to explore and apply scriptural passages that empower them to put off their old manner of life.

Chapter Twenty-Seven

Virgin Bride Puts On Her New Wedding Attire

"We grow in grace by the deliberate stirring up and exercise of the new powers and inclinations which regeneration implanted within us" (J. I. Packer, *A Quest for Godliness*, p.198).

"This dichotomized scheme of sanctification as a matter of vivifying our graces and mortifying our sins . . . is conventional Puritan teaching, going back through Calvin to Romans 6 and Colossians 2:20-3:17" (J. I. Packer, *A Quest for Godliness*, p. 201).

New Furnishings

Some Christian counseling treats believers like the man Jesus spoke about in Luke 11. Under the sway of an evil spirit, he found release. The house of his heart was swept clean of the old way, but no new furnishings decorated the rooms. When the evil spirit returned, it brought seven other spirits more wicked than itself, and they took up residence in this poor man's emptied soul. As Jesus said, "And the final condition of that man is worse than the first" (Luke 11:26).

When we exhort people to put off the old (to mortify the flesh), but we fail to empower them to put on the new (to vivify the spirit), we leave them easy prey. "But no one counsels like that," you counter. Oh, but we do all the time.

A husband and father struggles with anger; we tell him to control his temper. He mortifies his angry passions, but all he puts on is a seemingly serene demeanor. All the while his passionate soul is stirring. His passions have to go somewhere. They have to do something. He either uses his renewed passion in God-honoring ways (such as empowering his children, protecting his wife, fighting injustice, hating sin, or taking up the cause of the needy), or his old passions slowly seep out, eventually seven times worse than before.

God does not want us to mortify anger. Rather, He commands us to mortify sinful anger ("in your anger do not sin"), deal with our anger in wise and loving ways ("do not let the sun go down while you are still [sinfully] angry"), and redirect our anger toward our true enemy ("do not give the devil a foothold"). We vivify our anger—energizing it with God's holiness, redirecting and realigning it with God's will.

A teenage girl, all too surrendered to her culture and her peers, swears like a sailor and uses words to shred others to pieces. We tell her to mortify her potty mouth. Stop talking like that. Quit criticizing and ripping others. She listens. She stops. But she still has a tongue. She remains a relational being, a social being. Her relationality has to go somewhere. She either uses her tongue in God-honoring ways (such as encouraging others, building others up, complimenting people, testifying for God), or her old tongue eventually slithers out, seven times more biting, more poisonous, than before. She expresses her relationality either in God-honoring ways (such as connecting with others, asking forgiveness of others, ministering to others, developing healthy relationships with others), or she slowly reverts to her former style of relating, soon seven times worse than before.

God does not want us to mortify our relationality. He doesn't want us to cut out our tongue literally, nor does He want us to become speechless mutes. Rather, He commands us to mortify the sinful use of our tongue and our sinful ways of relating ("do not let any unwholesome talk come out of your mouths"). He commands us to practice new, healthy ways of relating (speak what is "helpful for building others up according to their needs") and to put on a ministry mindset and other-centered pathways (benefiting those who listen to you). We vivify our relationality—energizing it with God's love, redirecting and realigning it with God's grace.

Christian counseling is not some modern resurrection of Stoicism that insists we eliminate passion. If all we have are unregenerate passions, which was all the unsaved Stoics had, it makes sense at least to try to exterminate them. However, we have *new* passions. We mortify *the old use* of our old passions and vivify our new passions. We put off old false lovers, foolish mindsets, self-centered pathways, and ungoverned mood states. *Then* we put on grace lovers, wise mindsets, other-centered pathways, and managed mood states. We empty the rooms of our soul of the old, *then* we allow God's Spirit to redecorate those rooms with new, beautiful furnishings. Join me as we learn how, both in our lives and in the lives of people who visit us as soul physicians.

Vivification

Sanctification has a dual aspect. Its negative side is mortification—the weakening, defeating, and killing of the flesh. Its positive side is vivification—the growing, maturing, and enlivening of the regenerate person.

Paul urges us to "put on" (*enduō*) the new self, using a common clothing metaphor. "Putting on" pictures literally wrapping a tunic around your chest. Figuratively, it speaks of taking on, acting like, and putting on in activity what is already true internally. "Take on the characteristics of the new person you already are. Clothe yourself with the virtues Christ implanted in your new nature."

In vivification, I put on what I already am. I stir up and fan into flame the new me. I count and reckon on my new nature and new nurture. I put on my gowns of Regeneration, Redemption, Reconciliation, and Justification. I'm not dressed to kill; I'm dressed to live! Now I live out my new clothing. I put on in my lifestyle, my walk, and my manner of life what is already inwardly true of me. I put on my new want to and can do. I live out my sainthood. I express my new capacities. Grace lovers/purified affections, wise mindsets, other-centered pathways, and managed mood states flow out of the new me.

Paul clearly explains the process in Colossians 3. You're already dead, so crucify the remnants of that old dead you (3:1-5). More than that, you've been raised with Christ (3:1). You have already put on the new self that is daily being renewed in knowledge in the image of Christ (3:10). "Therefore, as God's chosen people, holy and dearly loved, clothe yourselves with compassion, kindness, humility, gentleness and patience . . . And over all these virtues put on love, which binds them all together in perfect unity" (3:12, 14). Put your new position into practice through continually clothing yourself with new lovers, mindsets, pathways, and mood states so that you are increasingly transformed into the image of God in Christ.

I want it! Don't you? I'm sick and tired of the old way. Marley's old clothes are worn out rags. I want to be transformed like New Scrooge. Isn't he a welcome sight at the end of *A Christmas Carol*? Laughing. Dancing. Giving. Willing to look foolish in the eyes of people to live wisely in the eyes of God. Changed. New from the inside out. Remodeled by God. Redecorated by the Holy Spirit. Renewed by Christ. Having put off our Old Marley through the six steps of the mortification process, it's now time to learn how to put on the New Scrooge through the six steps of the vivification process.

Step Seven: Rational Vivification—Putting On Our New Wise Mindsets

If rational mortification stops the madness, then mental *vivification* returns to sanity. In light of the Cross, it is insane to doubt God's goodness. Christ's cry, "It is finished!" is our proclamation to False Seducer. "Your old lying narrative is finished! Kaput. Rejected." Paul's words become our motto. "If *God is for us*, who can be against us? He who *did not spare his own Son*, but *gave him up for us all*—how will he not also, along with him, *graciously give us all things*?" (Romans 8:31b-32, emphasis added).

What is a new mindset? It's the larger story, the eternal, heavenly perspective on life that says, "Trust God and live!" Our new mindsets come complete with new vision. Our Divine Physician performed totally successful laser surgery on our eyes so that we no longer look at life with eyeballs only, but with faith eyes. Our perspective is captivated by Worthy Groom's worth. Our mindset is captured by spiritual imaginations that declare, "Forgiving Father is your Spring of Living Water. Worthy Groom is the Lover of your soul. Inspiring Mentor is your strong Best Friend. Trust them with your heart."

"I Consent to the Truth of Worthy Groom's Grace Narrative"

When I put on my new mindset, I consent to the truth of Worthy Groom's grace narrative, which redeems my reason by faith. That is, I don't cease using my reason, but faith cleanses my reason by clearing my vision. Faith eyes renew my mind, which in turn transforms my very being into the image of God (Romans 12:1-2; 2 Corinthians 3:18).

Having put off the insane idols of my heart, I now put on God's version of my life story. I believe Christ to be the most brilliant human being who ever lived; therefore, I accept as truth His grace narrative. I filter every life event through the lens of grace, through the screen of God's goodness. The reality of God's larger story invades my smaller story, enlightening me to what is really real.

Facing *suffering coram Deo*, I put on my new mindset. If I receive a dreaded cancer report, I ache, I groan, I'm sad, but I consent to grace truth. "God is not against me. He's not my Enemy. He is not evil. God is good. He works all things together for good, even cancer, because He is good."

If I'm stricken with cancer, False Seducer's plot line reads, "Curse God and die. I told you He couldn't be trusted. He was out to get you. If He is so good, why is your health so bad?"

I can refuse to buy his lie because I have a new mindset. I receive my plot line from Worthy Groom, not False Seducer. My new spiritual imagination allows me to see life from God's perspective and I say, "Trust God and live. I don't like this cancer. In fact, I hate it. Sickness is an alien intruder onto planet Earth. However, Worthy Groom has conquered every invader, including death. How I long for the day when death will die. But even today death has lost its sting. Death cannot kill my soul, only my body. I want physical health, but what I want more is soul health. I don't simply want to survive, I want to thrive. I'm not some bit player in a cosmic tragedy. God's given me a leading role in His drama of redemption. If all the universe is my stage, then I want my audience to know, beyond a shadow of a doubt, that God is trustworthy."

In suffering, I put on Worthy Groom's narrative, full of grace and truth about God's Supreme Goodness. I put on the mindset that says, "Cancer is bad, but God is good. In fact, God is my Chief Good, my Supreme Good."

Cancer looks like a zero, a cipher; it seems to make my life null and void. But I choose to live according to my new wise spiritual mindset, believing that zero times God equals infinity. So I factor God into the equation. What God? The God who is a Rewarder, never a Hoarder. I read and follow His larger grace narrative of reality by maintaining the mindset that God is a God who always provides exactly what is best for me from His eternal vantage point. Having put off Satan-reality, I accept God-reality.

In the midst of my suffering, I often must face my *sinning*. I struggle. I doubt. False Seducer steps up to the plate. "And you call yourself a Christian? Oh yeah, when things are going good, you trust God. But the biopsy comes back and now you whine like a baby and are tempted to drown your sorrow in wine. Maybe that's why God gave you your cancer to begin with. You're doubting God and God hates doubters, so God hates you!"

How can my new mindset offer me victory over such diabolical trash talking? When I have succumbed to sin, such as doubting God, what new controlling images of God must guide all my interpretations about His relationship to me? I must put on the spiritual image of the Cross that deciphers every narrative I ponder. I must put on mercy-generated mindsets. I live according to renewed images of Father, Son, and Holy Spirit.

So, I say to God, "Father I've sinned in doubting You. But I won't pile doubt upon doubt. I know that even when I'm sinful, You're gracious. Right now, I surrender to You to renew my mind through grace narratives. I receive Your forgiveness. I accept my acceptance in Christ. I put on the mind of Christ. Like Christ, I believe that You alone satisfy the spiritual appetites of my soul. I put on Trinitarian images of You. You are the eternal community of love and admiration. You are Holy Love. I put on images of You as Impressive. Kewl. Big. Pretty. Beautiful. Radically other-centered, totally unselfish, totally non-contingent. I look at You and yell, 'Hey, Amber, look out the window!' I know You as Majesty. Beauty. Awesome. Attractive. Hero. Lover. Inspiring Mentor. Worthy Groom. Forgiving Father.'"

"I Allow Myself to Be Transformed by the Renewing of My Mind"

Consenting to the truth of Worthy Groom's grace narrative is the principle we follow for putting on our new wise mindsets. What is the process? Listen to Paul. "Be transformed by the renewing of your mind" (Romans 12:2). Paul is telling us to experience a metamorphosis. Be like the caterpillar, shedding its outer garment and displaying its true inner nature—the beautiful, free, flying butterfly. Paul's also informing us of the central source of our transformation—mind renewal. Biblical mindset renewal includes:

♦ Preparing Our New Mindsets: Girding Up the Loins of Our Minds
♦ Aiming Our New Mindsets: Setting Our Minds on Things Above
♦ Reckoning on Our New Mindsets: Calculating According to Spiritual Reality
♦ Resting in Our New Mindsets: Lightening Our Consciences with Grace

After sharing about our glorious, grace-based regeneration, Peter says, "Therefore, prepare your minds for action" (1 Peter 1:13). The King James Version says it picturesquely: "Gird up the loins of your mind." Grab your flowing robe, pull it up tight, and get ready to rumble. Take your mental belt and pull it taut. Since we have the capacity to choose what we set our minds on, the first step in the mental renewal process is taking personal responsibility for our thought life—*preparing our new mindsets.*

Paul emphasizes the same truth when he commands us to "let the peace of God rule in your hearts" (Colossians 3:15). I'm to make sure that in my thought life God's truth acts as umpire. I'm responsible for making Christ's grace narrative the final arbiter for interpreting every life event. Paul explains how. "Let the word of Christ dwell in you richly as you teach and admonish one another with all wisdom, and as you sing psalms, hymns and spiritual songs with gratitude in your hearts to God" (Colossians 3:16). Putting on my new mindset begins when I allow God's truth about life to govern my thought life. I make a mental decision to allow God's version of reality to take up residence in my mind as I feed on and meditate upon His wisdom.

My decision in place, now I must *aim my mind.* I set my mindset and direct my thinking toward things above where Christ is seated at the right hand of God, not on earthly things (Colossians 3:1-2).

What if every morning you and I arose with a clear mental picture of Christ, seated victorious at the right hand of God, ruling over every event of our lives, graciously giving us everything we need for life and godliness? I'm to fix my mind on that amazing grace image. I'm to filter every incident I encounter through the heavenly narrative of Christ my Victor. I'm to be characteristically, habitually mindful of God-reality as I perceive and interpret life.

Let's be specific. A sinful thought enters my mind. First, I put it off, rooting out every corrupt imagination. Second, I reflect on godly thoughts. I gather up all my experiences of God and call to mind God's truth. Then I ask myself, "How would Jesus view this?" "How am I to view this in light of Christ's being seated at the right hand of God?" "How can I take on the mind of Christ?" "How can I have the attitude Christ had?" "What would Jesus think? (WWJT)"

I prepare my mind, I aim my mind, and *I reckon on my new mindset in Christ* (Romans 6:11). I am to calculate life using Divine mathematics. When I'm trying to make sense of my life, trying to figure life out, I count and take into account spiritual math. I consider and evaluate my earthly life based upon heavenly reality. That's the only reason Paul could make a statement like, "I consider that our present sufferings are not worth comparing with the glory that will be revealed in us" (Romans 8:18).

Facing life face-to-face with God, I reckon on (image, see, view) life from God's perspective. Controlling images of God, my Spring of Living Water, control my mindset. I mentally reckon on my new nurture and my new nature in Christ. I live according to His new narrative that implants in me spiritual eyes to see life with faith vision.

Rational vivification also requires *resting in my new mindset*. Recall that mortification of my old mindset required *loading our consciences with guilt* by seeing how horrible it is to sin. We never want to stop there. We also need to *lighten our consciences with grace* by recognizing how wonderful it is to be forgiven. Though we'll explore this more under self-aware vivification, we need to see its connection to mental transformation.

A moment ago you read about Christ umpiring or ruling in your heart (Colossians 3:15). Specifically, it is the *peace* of Christ that is to rule in our hearts. Since False Seducer's insidious scheme emphasizes accusation of the brethren, mind renewal counters his agenda by highlighting acceptance in the beloved. We must rest serenely in our new mindset, filled with gospel truth that says, "Once you were alienated from God and were enemies in your minds because of your evil behavior. But now he has reconciled you by Christ's physical body through death to present you holy in his sight, without blemish and free from accusation" (Colossians 1:21-22). Free from accusation! Free from the Accuser of the brethren! Without blemish. Reconciled. No longer enemies, but family.

Owen, in *The Mortification of Sin*, speaks not only of loading the conscience with guilt, but also of lightening the conscience with grace. Among his suggestions are:

- ◆ Consider the infinite patience and forbearance of God toward you (p. 123).
- ◆ Fill your thoughts with thoughts of the excellency of God's mercy and majesty (p. 131).
- ◆ Reckon on Christ's victory over sin (p. 161).
- ◆ "By faith fill thy soul with a due consideration of that provision which is laid up in Jesus Christ" (p. 162).
- ◆ Focus your faith peculiarly upon the death, blood, and Cross of Christ; that is, on Christ as crucified and slain for the forgiveness of your sins (p. 170-176).

Allow images of the flowing blood of Christ to run like cleansing rivers over your tender conscience. Accept your acceptance. Rest in Christ's work.

A Prayer of Rational Renewal

"Father, I surrender my mind to You. I consent to the truth of Worthy Groom's grace narrative. I allow You to transform me by the renewing of my mindsets. Moment by moment fill my thought life with images of God-reality. Enlighten me to know You and the

power of Your resurrection and the fellowship of Your suffering. Enlighten me together with all the saints to grasp how high and deep and wide and long is Your love. I commit to being a spiritual mathematician, adding up life from Your perspective. When I face suffering, I promise to believe that though life is bad, You are my Supreme Good. When struggling against sin, I promise to believe that even when I am sinful, You are gracious. And I promise not to take Your grace for granted, for though I know that it is wonderful to be forgiven, I understand that it's horrible to sin. Empower me to gird up the loins of my mind, to aim my mind toward heavenly things, to reckon on my new mindset, and to rest in my new mindset in Christ."

Step Eight: Relational Vivification—Putting On Our New Spiritual Purified Affections

Step eight builds upon a basic premise of *Soul Physicians*. *We pursue what we perceive to be pleasing.* "Objects are actually desired in virtue of the goodness, real or illusory, which is attributed to them. One who truly appreciates God's goodness, therefore, cannot but desire him" (J. I. Packer, *A Quest for Godliness*, p. 194). Through the ongoing process of step seven, we're putting on the truth that God is our Supreme Good. It's based on this realization, this conviction, that we're drawn toward God. Made to know good with our minds, we were also created to pursue good with our souls. Recreated to know Worthy Groom's supreme worth, we put on our new spiritual purified affections. That is, we put on loving God supremely out of recognition of His Supreme Good and flowing from gratitude for His amazing grace.

"I Enjoy and Exalt Worthy Groom as My Supreme Good"

Rationally, we put on our new wise mindsets by saying, "I consent to the truth of Worthy Groom's grace narrative." *Relationally*, we put on our new spiritual purified affections by saying, "I enjoy and exalt Worthy Groom as my Supreme Good." Our chief end is to glorify God and enjoy Him forever as our Chief Good. God is most highly exalted when He is enjoyed as the most enjoyable Being in the universe.

Motivated by gratitude, we passionately love God. Enticed by beauty and majesty (holy love), we long for Christ with desperate desire.

Stop. Read the preceding paragraph again.

Do you believe that about yourself? Do you realize that the core of the new you longs for Christ with desperate desire? It's true.

When facing *suffering*, the new you faces God. Your deepest longing is not relief from suffering (as wonderful as that might be), but communion with God in the fellowship of Christ's suffering. You entrust your soul to God, handing it over to Him for safekeeping. You say to God, "I hate suffering, yet I thank You for it. Thank You for teaching me through suffering that I cannot live by bread alone, that I cannot live alone. Thank You for teaching me that I need every word that proceeds from Your mouth. That I need You. In my suffering, help me to find You, to know You, to cling to You. Like the psalmists, draw me to Yourself in my emptiness. Help me to soothe my soul in my Savior. I'm learning to enjoy You more, rather than simply enjoying the things You graciously give me."

When struggling against *sin*, you pursue God as your purest pleasure, rather than pursuing the pleasure of sin for a season. Friendship with God becomes your one holy longing, rather than friendship with the world. The deepest affection of your soul, the deepest passion of your heart, is to know God and to make Him known. So you pray to Father, "As the deer pants for the water, so my soul longs after You. You alone are my true Joy Giver and the Apple of my eye. Worthy Groom, capture my affections. Forgiving Father, captivate my passions. Orient me to You. Help me to entrust myself to You, enjoy You, and exalt You as my Spring of Living Water, as my Thirst Quencher. I cling to You as Your child. Jesus, be most precious to me. Most satisfying. I cling to You as my Spouse."

"I Commune Deeply with God My Spring of Living Water"

Enjoying and exalting Worthy Groom as my Supreme Good is the principle we follow for putting on our new grace love. The process involves communing deeply with God, my Spring of Living Water. It is the vivification of our spiritual affections—stirring up and fanning into flame the sole love that my soul has for Christ.

Spiritual renewal involves an "affection set" just as rational renewal involves a "mind set." "*Set* your hearts on things above" (Colossians 3:1, emphasis added). "Set" is from *zēteō* meaning to seek with desire, to pursue passionately, to desire desperately. It's a word of affection that especially highlights the relational aspect of our being that longs, thirsts, hungers, and desires—our affection set.

How do we vivify, fan into flame, and stir up our spiritual appetite for and adoration of God? In one sense, all of *Soul Physicians* has been answering this question. In another sense, the entire Bible addresses this quest. Hundreds of books have discussed this journey of desire. My hope is that my contribution now will simply whet your appetite. We can begin to vivify our religious affection for God, our Spring of Living Water by:

- Tasting Our Thirsts: Daring to Desire
- Gazing upon Our Groom: Fixing Our Eyes on Jesus
- Feeding Our Soul: Pursuing Spiritual Formation

Tasting your thirsts is rarer and scarier than you might ever imagine. It is rare because modern/postmodern Christianity seems to believe that holiness is the elimination of desire. However, as Packer notes, holiness is:

> The redirecting of desire so that it focuses on fellowship with the Father and the Son, and the strengthening of desire so redirected, is the real essence of holiness. All mature forms of Christian holiness teaching down the centuries have started here, seeing this as the true foundation to everything else in the Christian life, and insisting that the only truly holy people are those with a passion for God (Packer, *Rediscovering Holiness*, p. 101).

Following Jesus never means killing the new me with all my new desires, longings, loves, affections, delights, and passions. The grace of God comes to us teaching us to say, "No!" to worldly passions, but to say, "Yes!" to God and godly passions (Titus 2:11-14).

Only those who admit they are spiritually sick ever turn to the Divine Physician of the Soul (Luke 5:31). Likewise, only those who acknowledge they are thirsty ever drink from the Spring of Living Water (John 4:1-42; 6:25-71; 7:25-44; Revelation 21:6; 22:17). The invitation to dine with Jesus goes to those who are hungry. The invitation to come to Jesus is sent to those who are thirsty. Are you hungry? Thirsty?

Tasting our thirsts is scary because so few of us dare to experience the liberating power of holy pleasure. Taste your thirsts by admitting that you're thirsty. Tap into your hunger by asking yourself, "Why do I feel so empty so often? What is it that my soul craves but goes without? Why do worldly pleasures seem so enticing but offer so little and satisfy so briefly?"

Don't run from your wants. Identify them. Label them. Ask yourself, "What do I want? What do I really want? Deep down in my soul, what do I long for?"

Then redirect them. Hunger and thirst after righteousness. Pant after God.

How do we pant after God? By *gazing on our Groom*. By fixing our eyes on the Author and Finisher of our faith.

Our gaze should never be far removed from His *scars*. "Let us fix our eyes on Jesus, the author and finisher of our faith, who for the joy set before him *endured the cross*, scorning its shame, and sat down at the right hand of the throne of God" (Hebrews 12:2, emphasis added). Owen reminds us that a sense of the love of Christ in the cross lies at the bottom of all true spiritual mortification and vivification (Owen, *The Mortification of Sin*, p. 89).

Our gaze should never be far removed from His *grace*. "Therefore, brothers, since we have confidence to enter the Most Holy Place *by the blood of Jesus* . . . and since we have *a great priest* over the house of God, *let us draw near to God* with a sincere heart in full assurance of faith" (Hebrews 10:19, 21-22a, emphasis added). Calvin explains the necessity of grace gazing:

> The ground of this assurance is, that the throne of God is not arrayed in naked majesty to confound us, but is adored with a new name, even that of grace, which ought ever to be remembered whenever we shun the presence of God . . . The Apostle, then, that he might remedy our lack of confidence, and free our minds from all fear and trembling, adorns it with "grace" and gives it a name which can allure us by its sweetness, as though he had said, "Since God has affirmed to His throne as it were the banner of 'grace' and fatherly love towards us, there are no reasons why His majesty should drive us away" (Calvin, *Hebrews*, p. 181).

If we are to enjoy the beauty of God, then we must turn our eyes upon Jesus, looking full in His wonderful face. Then the passions of this earth will grow strangely dim, in the light of His glory and grace.

To vivify our spiritual affections, we taste our thirsts, gaze upon our Groom, and *feed our souls*. Feeding our souls involves pursuing spiritual formation through the practice of the spiritual disciplines. We overviewed these during our discussion of RPMs: Resurrection Power Multipliers. It's through prayer, meditation, fasting, silence, solitude, worship, fellowship, secrecy, and the like, that we connect with Christ, commune with Christ, and become conformed to the image of Christ.

A Prayer of Relational Renewal: Spiritual

"Father, I long for You more than gold or silver. Nothing else could ever satisfy. Reorient my affections toward You and what You choose to provide. May my nearness to God be my Chief Good. Allure me. Entice me. Invite me. Captivate me. Capture me. Show me Your beauty so in worshiping Your loveliness, I exalt You. Empower me to enjoy You so the universe marvels in amazement at how fulfilling You are. Silence all the clamoring of other lovers who would seek my attention. I want to love You with everything I am. With undivided adoration. Give me a heart for You. A constant longing and breathing after You. Incite within me a deep passion for You."

Step Nine: Relational Vivification—Putting On Our New Self-Aware Purified Affections

We follow wise mindsets fanned into flame by Worthy Groom's grace narrative about God as the Rewarder not a Hoarder. Convinced by Christ, we pursue our soul's sole Lover. Entrusting ourselves to our good God, we rest, knowing who we are *in* Christ and who we are *to* Christ. Therefore, our renewed self-awareness is grace-based and Christ-focused. By grace we gain Christ-esteem. Christ-shalom.

If abnormality, as Augustine reminded us, is a soul caved in upon itself, then normality is a soul covered by Christ. Spiritual health is a soul at peace with itself *in Christ*. We live spiritually in this area to the degree that we are ruled by internal dispositions toward radical Christ-sufficiency.

"I Reckon on the Truth of Who Christ Is *to* Me and Who I Am *in* and *to* Christ"

In Romans 12, Paul begins to apply all the truth he has taught in Romans 1-11 concerning our salvation in Christ. His first two points of application are about *rational renewal* (being transformed by the renewing of our minds) and *relational spiritual renewal* (offering ourselves to God in a spiritual act of worship). His third application highlights our *relational self-aware renewal*. "For by the grace given me I say to every one of you: Do not think of yourself more highly than you ought, but rather think of yourself with sober judgment, in accordance with the measure of faith God has given you" (Romans 12:3).

Paul is a realist. We are going to think about ourselves. In fact, God designed us with this very capacity. Paul also understands that we can either distort that capacity or fulfill its original function. One way we distort our capacity for self-awareness occurs when we think more highly about ourselves than we ought. "More highly" (*huperphronein*) means hyper thoughts, haughty thoughts, assuming we're superior to others, arrogant, high-minded, and over proud. Instead, we're to think of ourselves according to sober judgment. "Sober judgment" (*sōphronein*) means clear thinking, wise thinking, and accurate self-awareness. Be wise minded about yourself, be in your right mind about yourself, about who you are in Christ.

What does this look like? How are we to evaluate ourselves? Paul begins and ends the verse with the answer: "for by the grace given to me . . . in accordance with the measure of faith God has given you." My sense of self must be grace-based. "I am who I am because of the great I Am." "I am who I am by Christ's grace."

I put on my new self-awareness in the midst of *suffering* by accepting the new grace love view of myself that's in accordance with Worthy Groom's grace meta-narrative. This counters False Seducer's law/works meta-narrative that says, "You're suffering because you're bad. Job's counselors might have been wrong about Job, but they'd be right about you. If you weren't hiding some secret sin, then God wouldn't be punishing you with obvious suffering."

I eschew diabolical deception and I place my faith, hope, and love in Worthy Groom's love for me. So I say to God, "This suffering tempts me to doubt. My level one external suffering entices me to give in to level two internal suffering where I doubt You and I doubt myself. I'm not going to do that. Yes, I will search my heart to see if there is any secret sin in me because I do know that in Your holy love You do discipline me. But even that is discipline in love. More than that, I understand that not all suffering is a direct fault of mine. I live in a fallen world and right now it's falling on me. But that doesn't mean that You've fallen on me, that You want to crush me. Break me so that I depend on You more? Yes. Crush me so I give up hope? Never! By faith, I accept my acceptance in Christ. The consciousness of being loved by my Forgiving Father through Worthy Groom rules my renewed sense of self. I make it the prayer of my life to grasp how long and high and deep and wide is the love of Christ to me and to know Your love that surpasses knowledge."

Facing the reality of my own struggle with *sin*, I maintain a sober self-assessment. I realize that I am not a perfected, glorified saint. Yet I also understand that I'm not an unregenerate sinner. Even in the midst of sin, I put on and reckon on the theological reality that I am regenerated, justified, redeemed, and reconciled.

So I say to God, "Father, I've sinned against You. Thank You for forgiving me. Empower me to be victorious over this sin. Defeat False Seducer as he attempts to cause me to think that You are against me. Seeing You in all Your holy love, I see myself holy and loved. I rest happy, calm, safe in Christ. I receive my new nurture. I hear You saying to me, 'Welcome home!' I accept my new identity as Your adult child. I put on my new peace, forgiveness, and freedom from guilt. I accept my justification. I clothe myself with my new standing in Christ. I dress myself in grace-confidence."

"I View Myself According to Christ-Sufficient, Sacred Thematic Identities"

Reckoning on the truth of who Christ is to me and who I am in and to Christ is the principle I follow in putting on my new self-awareness. The process involves viewing ourselves according to Christ-sufficient, sacred thematic identities through:

- Reckoning on Our New Universal Identity
- Reckoning on Our New Unique Identity
- Reckoning on Our New Reconciled Conscience

You must begin with a firm grasp on the new you in Jesus. Remind yourself daily of who you are *to* Christ and *in* Christ. Read, ponder, probe, study, meditate on, and memorize select verses that speak of your universal thematic identity in Christ. Claim images of yourself as son, daughter, saint, more than conqueror, athlete, bride, etc.

Bring the old you into mind and resolutely and consciously disassociate yourself from him or her. Bring the new you to mind and consciously accept your acceptance in Christ. Consciously rest in the new you in Christ. Move from shame to shalom as you understand and apply God's Word to your sense of self.

Build upon your new *universal* identity by gaining insight into your new *unique* identity in Christ. Who are *you*? What is the "shape" of *your unique* soul?

- ◆ *S*piritual Gifts: What spiritual gifts do I have? What ministries am I drawn to? Successful in? Excited about? What is the most thrilling thing I've ever done for God? For others?
- ◆ *H*opes: What are my dreams? My desires? What eulogy would I want spoken at my funeral? What epitaph do I want written on my gravestone?
- ◆ *A*bilities: What talents do I have? If time, talent, and money were no issue, what would I devote my life to? What equipping do I have for God's kingdom? What experiences do I have in ministry? What education do I have for service?
- ◆ *P*ersonality: What is unique about me? What images of myself stand out to me? To others? How am I different from others? What one word summarizes what makes me, me? What one picture captures who I am?
- ◆ *E*njoyment: What am I passionate about? What do I sense God calling me to do for His kingdom? What energizes me? What do I get excited about?

You also need to *reckon on your new reconciled conscience*. False Seducer longs to leave you with an evil conscience that doubts your standing before and relationship to God. Father offers you clear scriptural principles for resting in Him. Reckon on your shalom conscience (Ephesians 3:17-19; 6:14), calm your changed conscience (Ephesians 6:15), assure your tender conscience (Romans 8:14-16), liberate your clear conscience (Galatians 5:1), accept your forgiven conscience (James 5:15-16; 2 Corinthians 2:5-11), live according to your empowered conscience (John 17:17), and enjoy your restored conscience (Romans 12:1-8).

You and I can enjoy a new relationship to self. Not one of superiority (Romans 12:3), nor of timidity (2 Timothy 1:7). Not hypocrisy, but integrity. We can rest content in who we are in and to Christ with a clear conscience before God and people.

A Prayer of Relational Renewal: Self-Aware

"Father, I choose to live according to the peace that I have with You in Christ. I recall that one of Satan's primary tools is the power of his false accusation that You are not generously accepting and, therefore, I am your enemy. The power of the gospel renews my mind to the assurance that I am your son/daughter, Christ's bride, and the Spirit's best friend! I put on wholeness, consciously reflecting on and resting in who I am in Christ. I put on my thematic sacred identity. I enjoy who I am in Christ and who I am becoming through Christ as I become like Christ. I renew my mind to my new core sacred identity in Christ. I reckon on this, and I reignite and fan it into flame. I clothe myself in my new regenerative peace. I cover myself in my new cleared, cleansed, and good conscience. I envelope myself in contentment with who I am in Christ."

Step Ten: Relational Vivification—Putting On Our New Social Purified Affections

As relational beings, we are *spiritual* beings designed to relate to God, *self-aware* beings designed to relate to our self, and *social* beings designed to relate to others. In our renewal, we love God because He first loved us. Our renewed communion with Christ allows us to experience a new contentment with who we are in and to Christ. Communing with Christ and content in Christ, now we are free to connect to others. We're energized by a godly passion to epitomize Trinitarian relationships that are radically other-centered.

Vivification is the process of putting on in our daily relationships our new capacity to experience and enjoy mutual one anothering. Our new love for others is a *grace* love. Having received grace from God, having accepted our grace-based acceptance in Christ, now we view and relate to others from a grace perspective. We love others "warts and all." We love others when they hurt us. We value others even when they feel worthless. We esteem others when the world spits on them. And the world responds by saying of us, "Despicable friend of sinners. Must be a sinner, too!"

"I Stir up My New Connecting Love for Others"

When I put on my new social grace love, I involve myself in the process of stirring up my new cooperative love for others. I fan into flame the spirit of power, *love*, and wisdom implanted in my soul at my salvation (2 Timothy 1:6-7). I love others with authenticity that flows from my new heart.

Returned to purity by Worthy Groom, I'm motivated by gratitude to love God passionately with my whole being and to love my neighbor as myself sacrificially. As Packer says of the new us, "we pursue our goal of single-minded Jesus-likeness; the increasing mastery of life that comes as we learn to give it back to God and away to others" (Packer, *Rediscovering Holiness*, p. 93).

The new you no longer has to see every relationship as a competition. Now in every relationship you can be asking, "How can I complete my husband?" "How can I cooperate with my co-workers to advance their careers?"

You say, "No way. Not me. I wish. But that's not the core me."

Yes, it is!

That's why God calls you to believe His truth about the new social you. That's why He comes alongside you to stir up your deepest social longings, knowing that they are fulfilled in non-demanding, mutual, reciprocal, interdependent relationships with others. That's why Christ calls you to fan into flame your new other-centered focus, assenting to the truth that it is not good for you to be alone. That's why the Spirit woos you to acknowledge your desire for intimacy and adventure in your social relationships, choosing to engage yourself with others in the risky journey of passionate connection. That's why the Trinity compels you to fuel your new inclination to be your brother's keeper, because you know that only in dying for others will you really live for Christ.

When *suffering* alongside a sister in Christ, you cry out to God, "Father of all compassion and God of all comfort, as I've received compassion and comfort from You, please give me the courage to join with my sister in her time of need. Everything within me wants to flee. I don't think I can take another casket experience with another suffering saint. But I don't want to run. I want to climb in. I want to connect with her and help her to connect with You. And connecting, please give us comfort; give us co-fortitude, strength together as we connect in Christ. Help me to die to self so she can experience your resurrection power."

When walking alongside a brother in Christ who has *sinned*, you cry out to God, "Father, as You have granted me grace; help me to grant my brother grace. Not cheap grace, but costly grace. Help me not to simply exhort him to stop. Help me to enter his battle. Help me to relate in a spirit of meekness. Enlighten me to enlighten my brother to see the horrors of his sin and the wonders of Your grace. But please don't let me do it as an academician. Not as an aloof professional. But as a spiritual friend. Empower me to equip him to know that he can be victorious because of You, because it's supernatural to mature. May I walk with him along his journey, up the hills of victories and down into the valleys of the shadow of defeat."

"I Nourish My New Sacrificial Relationships Toward Others"

Stirring up our new connecting love for others is the principle we follow for putting on our new social purified affections. The process involves nourishing our new sacrificial relationships toward others through:

- ♦ Remaining in Christ's Grace Love: John 15:9-17
- ♦ Imitating Christ's Grace Love: John 13:12-17; 15:13
- ♦ Engaging in Spiritual Friendship: Hebrews 3:12-15
- ♦ Engaging in Spiritual Fellowship: Hebrews 10:24-25

To love like Jesus, we must *remain in His love*. To connect to others, we must commune with Christ. Jesus doesn't leave us to guess how it's done. He tells us to follow His example of remaining in His Father's love (John 15:10). Then He shows us how through His intimate, unbroken communion (John 17:1-26). The courage to be intimate with others has a prerequisite—the choice to be intimate with God.

Filled with God's grace love, now we're empowered to *imitate Christ's grace love*. His love is not sentimental, not syrupy sweet, not sappy. Certainly *not* easy.

His love stoops to wash filthy feet. Hangs on the cursed Cross. His love is servant love. His love lays down His life for His friends. And for His enemies.

But where in the world does this relational power come from? It should not be surprising that the power to relate like Christ comes from relating to Christ and Christians. If we are to grow in our capacity to express Christ-like love, we must choose to *engage in spiritual friendship*.

We need to connect with a spiritual friend or two who knows us deeply enough to be able to encourage us daily lest we be hardened by sin's deceitfulness. The secret to becoming a spiritual friend is having one.

We also must choose to *engage in spiritual fellowship*. Hebrews 3:12-15 suggests the spiritual friendship of one other person who knows us through and through. Hebrews 10:24-25 recommends the spiritual fellowship of a small group of kindred spirits willing to provoke, prod, needle, incite, nudge, push, entice, exhort, and encourage us toward love and good deeds. The secret to becoming a spiritual friend is participating in a spiritual fellowship.

A Prayer of Relational Renewal: Social

"Father, oh to be like You. Oh to be like the Trinitarian community. Mold me and make me, scour and shape me. Though I don't feel it, I believe it—I believe that I have what it takes to love like Jesus. Wow! I can't believe I just typed those words. I'm scared. Scared because I've been scarred. Every time I try to love like Jesus, I face what You faced. Maybe that's what You mean by the 'fellowship of Christ's suffering.' Speaking of scars. Jesus, You know scars. And You did not shrink from them. Spirit, empower me not to shrink from the scars of death-to-self relating. I'll be honest (might as well, You know everything!); the pain of entering another person's pain overwhelms me. The hurt of being hurt when I try to help—that terrifies me. Through my communion with You, through my connection with my spiritual friend and with my small group—please enable me to give others a taste of grace love. More than anything in my being, I want to give. You made me, recreated me, to give. I feel strong, powerful, purposeful when I give grace. I want it. I will. Thank You!"

Step Eleven: Volitional Vivification—Putting On Our New Other-Centered Purposes/Pathways

We are purposeful beings with a will that chooses to follow certain characteristic pathways and patterns as we engage life. Our renewed wills are freed and empowered so we can courageously create good for God's glory by sacrificially empowering others.

Other-centered pathways or patterns are the supernatural outflow of our new grace-based social relationships to others. It is in our actual behaviors and interactions that we live out our new passion to connect with others. As Packer reminds us, "holiness means not only desiring God, but also loving and practicing righteousness, out of a constant exercise of conscience to discern right from wrong and an ardent purpose of doing all that one can to please God" (Packer, *Rediscovering Holiness*, p. 101).

But what does it mean, what does it look like, to move from putting off self-centered pathways to putting on new other-centered pathways? And what resources has God provided to empower us to fulfill this calling?

"I Fan into Flame My New Freed Will, Empowered to Empower Others"

Volitional maturity starts as we fan into flame a new answer to the age-old question, "Why am I here?" In Adam, we're here to *survive*. To take care of ourselves. At best, we're here to build a tower of power that boosts our ego. At worst we're here to huddle in the corner of our domicile, hoping we'll be safe from the storms of life.

In Christ, we are here to *thrive*. We're not here for ourselves. We're here for God. We're here to fulfill His Creation Mandate. Here to be our brother's keeper. Here to be a shepherd in a jungle.

Thus volitional wholeness pursues a whole new *purpose*. We put off the futility of trying to make life work on our own for ourselves. We put on the vitality of working for God through Christ. We put off dominating others and put on empowering them.

Wholeness also pursues a whole new *pattern*. We put off cowardice and put on courage. Life is terrifying when that is all there is. We are of all people most miserable if there is no resurrection of the dead. But because there is, this life does not have to overwhelm, does not have to terrorize. We can live confidently, putting on our new power for holy living, our new inclination to obey Father lovingly and serve our brothers and sisters sacrificially. With courage we live out our new *telos*, our new reason for being.

Do you feel it? Sense it? The thrill of no longer being a mastered Slave, but now being an empowering Shepherd returned to vitality by Worthy Groom and freed to exercise dominion over your passions and God's planet. Enjoy the grace-based self-respect of knowing that you've run the race, fought the fight, and henceforth there is laid up for you a victor's crown. Long for the "Well done!" The applause of heaven.

Yes, life's hard. But it's not "Life's hard and then you die." It's "Life's hard, you've fought hard, then you die, and then you really live!"

Don't settle. Don't simply survive. Fight. Battle. Stir up the embers of your wild heart. Take risks. Live. Really live.

Then you'll be able to face *suffering* saying, "Father, these defeats are hard. Devastating. I feel like quitting. Not sure how much more I can take. But I believe Your promise. You will never give me more than I can handle (though we might define that differently!). You'll always provide a way of escape. More than that, You always have Your reasons. Your plan. I don't want only the good; I want the best. I want godliness. So, Father, whatever shattered dreams You find necessary to polish me, I accept. Gulp. Be gentle. No more than necessary. In Your gentleness, make me strong. Strong for You. Strong for others."

Then you'll be able to believe that God can even use your *sin* to bring about His purposes. "Father, I hear his insidious whisper. 'Now you've done it. Blown it good. For good. You've thwarted your Master's purposes for your life. You're cast off. Adrift. Disqualified. Dishonorably discharged.' Make it stop, Father. Can it be true that where sin abounds, grace does much more abound? Please, forgive me. Please renew me. Please take this mess I've made and create beauty from ashes. Renew within me a right spirit. In my brokenness, use me."

"I Provoke My New Chosen Style of Shepherding through Other-Centered Interactions"

Fanning into flame our new freed will so that we empower others is the principle we follow for putting on our new other-centered pathway. The process involves provoking our new chosen style of shepherding through other-centered interactions by:

- Yielding to the Spirit: Romans 6-8; Ephesians 5:18-6:18
- Walking in the Spirit: Romans 6-8; Galatians 3-5
- Cultivating the Fruit of the Spirit: Galatians 5:22-25

In volitional mortification, we put off in our purposes, practices, and behavior what Christ has already crucified in our wills. In volitional vivification, we put on in our purposes, practices, and behavior what Christ has already resurrected in our wills. We find this power, paradoxically, by admitting that we are powerless. The Bible calls this *yielding to the Spirit* (and overlapping terms such as being filled with the Spirit, controlled by the Spirit, and dependent upon the Spirit). Yieldedness to the Spirit begins with my conscious conviction that without God I can do nothing, but that with God I can do all things through Christ who strengthens me. When I yield to the Spirit, I place myself in the sort of "greenhouse environment" where the soil of my soul is so soft that I become a ready recipient of the nourishing love, power, and wisdom of God. That soil is my confession of my neediness.

Various biblical terms such as "present" and "yield" come from the Greek word *parastēsai* meaning to offer, to bring, to place beside. It was used for a bride presenting herself to her groom. Picture the vulnerability. The trust. The intimacy. "I'm yours. I need you. I want you. Take me. Fill me. Nourish and cherish me. I'm responsive to you. Submitted to you. Open to you."

Paul speaks of walking in the Spirit, being led by the Spirit, and keeping in step with the Spirit. While each of these terms maintains a distinctive emphasis, the essence is the same. We are actively to appropriate the Spirit's power in our life. We are to "allow" the Spirit to guide our walk, our way, our pathway. To direct our steps and lead our interactions with others. This implies a continual conversation where we're always asking, "Spirit, what would other-centered living look like in this situation? What are You calling me to be and to do right now? How would You want me to respond? What way of relating would please You? Would help them?"

The supernatural result of yielding to the Spirit and walking in the Spirit is the *cultivation of the fruit of the Spirit*. The fruit of the Spirit are relational traits (characteristic pathways, disciplined styles of relating, interactional patterns) that evidence love for our neighbor.

Packer describes the fruit of the Spirit as the nine-fold pattern of habitual reaction to life's pressures (Packer, *Rediscovering Holiness*, p. 106). In Galatians, Paul commands us to replace the vices of the flesh with the fruit of the Spirit. Being fruit, connection to the vine is vital for volitional maturity. We must deliberately and regularly practice the spiritual disciplines that connect us to the vine, using the means of grace to promote spiritual health. "Spiritual health, like bodily health, is God's gift. And, like bodily health, it is a gift that must be carefully cherished, for careless habits can squander it" (Packer, *Rediscovering Holiness*, p. 149).

A Prayer of Volitional Renewal

"Holy Spirit, I yield to You. I consciously choose to admit that I'm a coward without You. With You, I can do all things. With You, no purpose of Yours can be thwarted. I put on choosing to depend upon You. I put on choosing to live for You. I put on seeking not only Your power to do right, but also Your guidance to know what is right. Step by step please lead me, all the days of my life. In each relational interaction, empower and enlighten me to know what other-centered living looks like. Flow through me so that the disciplined, habitual passion and energy of my soul reflects Your fruit. Show me how to connect to You, how to depend upon You, how to be nourished by You. Then let my greatest purpose be to be like You, like Jesus."

Step Twelve: Emotional Vivification—Putting On Our New Managed Mood States

How we might wish we could stop at step eleven. Feelings seem so unspiritual. Moods so unmanageable.

Take heart. Created to be alive Singers, sin transformed us into moody Addicts, yet salvation restores us to soulful Poets. We can, with integrity, face our feelings and experience life with all its joys and sorrows. God has made a way where there seems to be no way. He's given us all we need for emotional life and emotional maturity so we can put off unmanaged moods and put on new managed mood states. So we can put off emotional hypocrisy and put on emotional integrity.

"I Cooperate with God in Enlivening My New Managed Mood States"

Emotionally, Creation/Fall/Redemption have moved us from Singers to Addicts to Poets. As Poets, we can ingeniously integrate our inner experiences. As a spiritual being experiencing intense emotion, I can soothe my soul in my Savior. As a self-aware being sensing profound moods, I can admit, understand, label, and accept my mood states. As a social being sensing emotion in others, I can empathize with others, sustaining and healing them. As a rational being, I can bring rationality to my emotionality, understanding with wisdom the causes and nature of my feelings and envisioning with spiritual eyes imaginative ways to handle my moods. As a volitional being, I can consciously and courageously choose to respond to my emotional states creatively. As an emotional being, I can openly experience whatever I am feeling, being responsive to God and God's world. Thus cooperating with God, the Creator of emotions, I put on emotional integrity, harmony, and honesty.

Facing *suffering* as an emotional being, I cry out to God, "If it weren't for bad days, there wouldn't be any days at all. If it weren't for painful emotions, I wouldn't have any emotions at all. At least that's how I feel right now. Wish I didn't have emotions, but I do. Tons of them. Right now, Father, I'm feeling _____, and _____, and _____ _____. Knowing what I know, I think I'm normal. Groaning is our lot until glory. Thank You for giving me the courage to face what I feel. Now I ask for the insight to understand what my emotions are suggesting about who I am and how I am relating to You and others. And, to be honest, I ask to feel better. Peace. Joy. Happiness. Contentment. But regardless of how I feel, I ask for self-control. Help my responses to my emotions to be honoring to You."

Facing personal *sin* as an emotional being, I cry out to God, "Do You love me? Do You really love me? How 'bout this. Do You like me? Want me? Desire me? I feel horrible. Some of my feelings are godly conviction, godly sorrow. Some of my feelings are worldly shame. Help me to face both. I've grieved You. That grieves me to the core. I want to please You. Want to bring You joy. Wow! That amazes me. That I can impact You. Grieve You. Please You. What's wrong with me? Why do I keep surrendering to the same old besetting sin? I feel so filthy. Ugly. Worthless. Forgive my sin. Forgive my self-pity. Forgive my self-hatred. Help me to sort out my mingled myriad of moods. Most importantly, help me to surrender to You. Cling to You. Obey You. Accept Your forgiveness."

"I Collaborate with God in Living According to My New Emotional Integrity"

In our "final step," I'll depart from my normal practice of offering you several practical "how to" principles for implementing the point. Instead, let's revisit the traffic scenario to integrate all twelve steps we've explored. I call it, *To Honk or Not to Honk Is a Deeply Spiritual Issue.* I've even given my story a subtitle, *To Honk or Not to Honk Is a Matter of Affections, Mindsets, Purposes, and Mood States.*

"Cut off again!"

What do you do? Blare the horn at the inconsiderate driver who cut you off twice in the last two minutes? Worse yet? Cut him off?

What difference does it make? Honking or not honking is not a spiritual issue, right? Or is it?

To answer these questions in a biblical way requires a soul physician examination of the inner life of the potential honker. More importantly, to respond in a spiritual way requires enlightenment and empowerment from our great Soul Physician.

Rational mortification includes putting off our old foolish, fleshly mindsets, the depraved imagination of our flesh. Our fleshly imagination perceives life foolishly. It thinks, "Because I find fault with God, because I have no awe of Him, since He does not satisfy my deepest thirsts, because He is not a Spring of Living Water for me but a dark, empty desert; I will make life work on my own. I'll dig broken cisterns that hold no water. I'll live for today. So, pleasure in sin for a season will satisfy my soul. I'll honk! It feels good. I'll cut off that jerk! It makes me feel good. Makes me feel so alive!"

Rational vivification includes putting on our new wise, spiritual mindsets, the renewed imagination of the spirit/Spirit. Our spiritual imagination perceives life wisely, thinking, "Because I'm in awe of God, because I find no fault in Him, because I see Him in the depths of my imagination as altogether lovely, altogether holy, altogether worthy; I will fulfill the affection of the Spirit. I will live out the deepest passion of my new heart to love God and my neighbor as myself. I would not want my neighbor to cut me off or honk at me. So I will not cut off or honk at my neighbor. Because God is good, I will be good."

Relational mortification includes putting off our old spiritual disordered affections, false lovers, the idols of our heart, and the lustful desires of our flesh. Our flesh says, "I want to feel good, feel in control. I want to do what I want to do. I want to cut that driver off! I want to honk!" Since the idols of our hearts are idiosyncratic—unique to each of us, one idolatrous heart might say, "I am the idol of my own heart. I worship being first." Or, another might say, "The idol of my heart is never being used, never being slighted." Or, still another might proclaim, "Since God will not take care of me, the idol of my heart is taking care of myself, taking matters into my own godlike hands." Whatever the specific idol, the end evil passion is the same: loving myself more than God and others.

Relational vivification includes putting on our new spiritual purified affections—our soul's sole love for God and others—renewed desires and delights of the spirit/Spirit. Our spirit/Spirit says, "More than anything, I want to enjoy and exalt God. Cutting that driver off, honking, that exalts me, that feeds me, that pleasures me. I want to please God; I want to love God; I want to be like Christ. I want to seek His kingdom more than anything else. I long to fulfill the two great commandments of loving God with all my heart and loving my neighbor as myself. Worshiping God and serving others, these are the deepest affections in my soul. So I will not honk, because I love God and others."

Volitional mortification includes putting off our old self-centered purposes and pathways, our habitual, selfish patterns of volitional interaction. Our fleshly will chooses according to our fleshly mindsets and affections, deciding, "Since God's will is not my Chief Good, not my Supreme Good, I will choose my will. In fact, my will, my unique way of living life is my sovereign right. I will ingrain in my being and my behavior the pattern that I feel most comfortable with. It is both my inalienable right and my habitual plan/pattern to act according to my own best interest. Cutting that idiot off flows out of my inner being like water out of a faucet. The fleshly me chooses according to my fleshly orientation—an orientation I've habituated toward selfishness. As a peach tree bears peaches, so my sinful affections and sinful imagination bear sinful peach choices and actions. Out of my heart my mouth speaks. Out of my soul my body acts. I will cut him off! I will honk!"

Volitional vivification includes putting on our new other-centered purposes, our spiritually disciplined, renewed patterns of sacrificial volitional interaction. Our spiritual will chooses according to our spiritual mindsets and affections. It decides, "Since I have a renewed affection that exalts and enjoys God, living in light of His mercy and grace, since I have a renewed mind that discerns that God's will is good and perfect; I will choose God's will. I will spiritually discipline myself like those running a race, those competing in a match, like the athlete, like the disciplined farmer. My spiritually disciplined pathway and pattern of interaction will develop within me a style of relating where choosing what is best for others and pleasing to God becomes natural—supernatural. Cutting off that driver is wrong, sinful, selfish, ungodly, unChristlike. I've reckoned on the new me in Christ. I'm dead to those old ways of living. Freed. Victorious. The new me chooses according to my new nature—a nature rooted in love and holiness. I'm a saint. As an apple tree bears apples, so my new affections and mindsets bear godly apple choices and actions. Out of my new heart, my body acts. I will not cut him off. I will not honk. I will forgive as Christ forgave me."

Emotional mortification includes putting off our old ungoverned mood states of the flesh, the enslaved, addicted emotional reactions driven by sinful affection, imagination, and volition. They clamor for us, scream at us, crying, "Feel good! Since God is not your Supreme Good, since eternity's values are not in view, live for today, for the moment, for this second. Feel good! Do whatever makes you feel better. Live for sensual pleasure. Grasp the pleasure of sin for a season. Honk! Cut off! What are you waiting for!"

Emotional vivification includes putting on our new managed mood states of the Spirit/spirit, the newly disciplined, freed emotional responses driven by godly affection, imagination, and volition. They calm us, speaking to us, saying, "Face your feelings. Admit them. Expose them. Be candid. Examine them. Take them to God. 'Search me, O God, try my heart today. See if there be any wicked way in me.' Manage your mood."

In fact, so discipline yourself—affection, imagination, volition—that split-second emotional responses are under your control. Control that instantaneous urge to act. You feel. You manage. Honking is not destined. Cutting off is not predetermined. It is possible to control the expression of your emotions. Not only is it possible, it is best—best for God, for you, and for others. So you say to yourself, "I will not honk. I will not cut off. I will feel the sadness of a world of selfish drivers. I will soothe my soul in God. I will long for heaven when the gold-lined streets will be filled with drivers whose hearts are lined with gold—with glorified godliness. And I will feel peace, today. Content in the knowledge that God has changed me. I'm not a honker anymore! I'm not a cutter-offer anymore! I'm new. A neonatal saint—a babe in Christ growing up. A *nikao* saint—a victorious saint winning the victory through faith and grace."

Even honking or not honking, cutting off or not cutting off, are signs of my good God fulfilling His promise to complete the good work that He began in me! "Thank You, Jesus. I love You. Thank You for helping me love my neighbor the way You love my neighbor."

A Prayer of Emotional Renewal

"Father, thank You for feelings. Thank You that You have them. Thank You that I have them. Sometimes, many times, I feel like wishing them away. But then I would be such a shell of a person. A Stoic, not a Poet. I don't want that. What I want is heaven—no more cryin' there. No more tears. No more looking in the eyes of a hurting loved one and feeling more pain than I ever thought possible. But until heaven, I want to be real. Raw. Honest. I want emotional integrity. I want emotional maturity. Help me to bring spirituality, rationality, and volitionality to my emotionality. Help me not to honk, but to hug. Help me not to honk, but where called upon, to confront lovingly. Help me to be as emotional as King David, as Jeremiah, as Job, as Asaph, as Jesus, as You, as the great saints throughout church history. Help me feel life fully. Fortify me to feel the feelings of others. Deeply. Sincerely. Accurately. Help me to feel Your pain—the fellowship of Your suffering."

Where We've Been and Where We're Heading

Where have we been? We've been to the empty tomb. To the Mount of Ascension. Easter Sunday. Resurrection power. We've traded in the dead corpse of the flesh for the living, breathing new person in Christ. We've put on the new man—relationally, rationally, volitionally, and emotionally.

Where are we now? Not home yet. Close. Longing for home. For heaven. What's it going to be like? What are we going to be like? Meet you on the other side for Father's answers.

Caring for Your Soul: Personal Applications

1. Step Seven: Rational Vivification—Putting On Our New Wise Mindsets

   a. How will you put on and consent to the truth of Christ's grace narrative?

   b. How will you allow yourself to be transformed by the renewing of your mind?

2. Step Eight: Relational Vivification—Putting On Our New Spiritual Purified Affections

   a. How will you put on enjoying and exalting Worthy Groom as your Supreme Good?

   b. How will you commune deeply with God, your Spring of Living Water?

3. Step Nine: Relational Vivification—Putting On Our New Self-Aware Purified Affections

   a. How will you put on and reckon on the truth of who Christ is *to you* and who you are *in* and *to* Christ?

   b. How will you view yourself according to Christ-sufficient, sacred thematic identities?

4. Step Ten: Relational Vivification—Putting On Our New Social Purified Affections

   a. How will you put on and stir up your connecting love for others?

   b. How will you nourish your new sacrificial relationships toward others?

5. Step Eleven: Volitional Vivification—Putting On Our New Other-Centered Purposes/ Pathways

   a. How will you put on and fan into flame your new freed will, empowered to empower others?

   b. How will you provoke your new chosen style of shepherding through other-centered interactions?

6. Step Twelve: Emotional Vivification—Putting On Our New Managed Mood States

   a. How will you put on cooperation with God in enlivening your new managed mood states?

   b. How will you collaborate with God in living according to your new emotional integrity?

Caring for Others: Ministry Implications

◆ **Send Your Spiritual Friends Away on Track, Part I:** Concerning their new nature in Christ, ask them:

- As you leave here today on track toward conformity to Christ, specifically how will you be loving passionately as a Romancer?
- As you leave here today on track toward conformity to Christ, specifically how will you be thinking imaginatively as a Dreamer?
- As you leave here today on track toward conformity to Christ, specifically how will you be choosing courageously as a Creator?
- As you leave here today on track toward conformity to Christ, specifically how will you be experiencing deeply as a Singer?

◆ **Send Your Spiritual Friends Away on Track, Part II:** Concerning putting on their new person in Christ, ask them:

- As you leave here today on track, how will you be putting on and consenting to the truth of Worthy Groom's grace narrative?
- As you leave here today on track, how will you be allowing yourself to be transformed by the renewing of your mind?
- As you leave here today on track, how will you be putting on enjoying and exalting Worthy Groom as your Supreme Good?
- As you leave here today on track, how will you be communing deeply with God, your Spring of Living Water?
- As you leave here today on track, how will you be putting on and reckoning on the truth of who Christ is to you and who you are in and to Christ?
- As you leave here today on track, how will you be viewing yourself according to Christ-sufficient, sacred thematic identities?
- As you leave here today on track, how will you be putting on and stirring up your new connecting love for others?
- As you leave here today on track, how will you be nourishing your new sacrificial relationships toward others?
- As you leave here today on track, how will you be putting on and fanning into flame your new freed will, empowered to empower others?
- As you leave here today on track, how will you be provoking your new chosen style of shepherding through other-centered interactions?
- As you leave here today on track, how will you be putting on cooperation with God in enlivening your new managed mood states?
- As you leave here today on track, how will you be collaborating with God in living according to your new emotional integrity?

EPILOGUE:
LOVE'S DESTINY—THE RESTORATION

ENVISIONING THE FINAL HEALING OF THE SOUL:
HOME—GLORIFICATION

DIRECTOR'S NOTES

Welcome back. Sit a spell. Allow me to set the stage for the epilogue.

Our epilogue is a short story about the longest story ever lived. The scene shifts from the old earth to the new earth. You thought I'd say, "The scene shifts from earth to *heaven*." No. The scene shifts from the old earth to the new *earth*. From homesickness to home. From groaning to glory. From tastes of heaven to the unending feast. From glimpses of our Beloved to intimacy with our Beloved. From flashes of purpose to unique, unending meaning. From able not to sin to not able to sin. From moments of rest to work that is ever restful.

The smaller story ends. The larger story swallows it up, as it swallows death and vanquishes suffering. Our groaning hearts to groan no more.

Our singing souls satisfied, we will shout:

All tears forever over in God's eternal day.

Face to face with Christ our Savior. Face to face we shall behold him.

When we all get to heaven, what a day of rejoicing that will be. When we all get to heaven, we'll sing and shout the victory.

When all my labors and trials are over, and I am safe on that beautiful shore, just to be near the dear Lord I adore, will through the ages be glory for me.

Friends will be there I have loved long ago. Joy like a river around me will flow.

For now we sing:

O Lord Jesus, how long, how long, ere we shout the glad song, Christ returneth! Hallelujah! Hallelujah! Amen.

You certainly won't want to miss a single scene in this endless epilogue. Settle in for two everlasting scenes.

SCENE I, CHAPTER 28: VIRGIN BRIDE'S CONSUMMATE HAPPINESS

SCENE II, CHAPTER 29: VIRGIN BRIDE'S FINAL DESTINY

501

CHAPTER TWENTY-EIGHT

VIRGIN BRIDE'S CONSUMMATE HAPPINESS:
INTIMACY AND MINISTRY

"They shall have a joyful entrance into the other world. Their arrival into the region of bliss will be celebrated with rapturous praise to their glorious Redeemer. A dying day is a good day to a godly man. Yea, it is his best day; it is better to him than his birth-day, or than the most joyous day which he ever had on earth" (Thomas Boston, *Human Nature in Its Fourfold State*, p. 356).

"Now suppose both death and hell were utterly defeated. Suppose the fight was fixed. Suppose God took you on a crystal ball trip into your future and you saw with indubitable certainty that despite everything—your sin, your smallness, your stupidity—you could have free for the asking your whole crazy heart's desire: heaven, eternal joy. Would you not return fearless and singing? What can earth do to you if you are guaranteed heaven? To fear the worst earthly loss would be like a millionaire fearing the loss of a penny—less, a scratch on a penny. But this is our true state, according to God's own Word. This is the gospel, the scandalously good news: that we are guaranteed heaven by sheer gift" (Peter Kreeft, *Heaven: The Heart's Deepest Longing*, p. 183).

The Road Goes Ever On and On

"Others." One word tucked in the thicket of life's grand adventure. On one side, the victors—Abel, Enoch, Noah, Abraham, Isaac, Jacob, Joseph, Moses, Rahab, Gideon, Barak, Samson, Jepthah, David, and Samuel—who through faith conquered. Who through faith administered justice, gained what was promised, shut the mouths of lions, quenched the fury of flames, escaped the edge of the sword, whose weaknesses were turned to strength, who became powerful in battle and routed foreign armies. Women received back their dead, raised to life again (Hebrews 11:1-35, author's summary).

On the other side, the defeated and dispossessed. "Others" were tortured and refused to be released. Some faced jeers and flogging, while still others were chained and put in

503

prison. They were stoned; they were sawed in two; they were put to death by the sword. They went about in sheepskins and goatskins, destitute, persecuted, and mistreated. They wandered in deserts and mountains, and in caves and holes in the ground. None of them received what they had been promised (Hebrews 11:35b-39, author's summary).

We don't enjoy reading about these "others." We have a decided preference for people *who in this life, this side of heaven,* win the day. For those who gain what is promised. We avert our eyes and divert our attention from those *who in this life, this side of heaven,* lose. From those who do not receive what was promised.

God maintains an altered perspective. These "losers" He commends. For these defeated ones He has planned something far better. These "others" gain a better resurrection (Hebrews 11:35).

God's altered perspective altered Paul's perspective. "I consider that our present sufferings are not worth comparing with the glory that will be revealed in us" (Romans 8:18). Eternity's vision altered Paul's earthly vision.

Unfortunately, God's altered perspective seldom alters our perspective; His eternal viewpoint rarely affects our earthly outlook. Why? Because our views of heaven are too heavenly. Our views of heaven are not earthy enough.

One summer I spoke with a group of high school wrestlers. Though Christians, they held false images of heaven. "What have you heard about heaven? What's it going to be like?"

"Harps and clouds," one wrestler responded.

"Boring!" another chimed in.

I know what you're thinking. "That's just a bunch of kids. Jocks, no less. What do they know? Of course their views of heaven are skewed."

But are their views really so atypical? Are their views actually that different from yours? Mine?

What is heaven for you? What is it going to be like? What are your images of eternity? Are they compelling enough that when you lose your job, endure cancer, or suffer slander you can say, "My suffering *now* is not worth comparing with my glory in heaven *later*"?

We need God's eternal perspective on eternity. We need an enduring grace vision of the end of the story. Four scenes depict the final and enduring act in our never-ending story with Worthy Groom.

 ♦   Communion: The Consummation—Eternal Relationship (The Love Affair)
 ♦   Dominion: The Restoration—Eternal Purpose (The Grand Adventure)
 ♦   Reflection: The Glorification—Eternal Nature (The Noble Image)
 ♦   Cohesion: The Integration—Eternal Rest (The Endless Harmony)

Heaven brings the final blossoming of the four robes, gowns, or tuxedos that we all long to wear. In heaven, we'll experience intimate communion with Christ and one another, we'll rule and reign with and for Christ, we'll be brilliant reflections of Christ, and we'll experience shalom—perfect peace.

Gripped by these scenes, we can exchange hope for despair as the early disciples did. They were distraught at the thought of Messiah's crucifixion, but Jesus pointed their hearts toward home. "Do not let your hearts be troubled. Trust in God; trust also in me. In my Father's house are many rooms (mansions)" (John 14:1-2, parentheses added).

Home, that's what we long for. As Augustine wrote, "The whole life of the good Christian is a holy longing." Stimulate your longing for home, for only that longing will still your heart during your earthly sojourn. Taste and see the goodness of Father's promise of everlasting love, adventure, glorification, and peace.

Communion: The Consummation—Eternal Relationship (The Love Affair)

All of history has been moving toward this day. All of life has been heading toward the wedding of the Lamb and His bride. It is the first event on the first day of the rest of our lives. Right now, we're engaged. Our wedding is definite. However, we don't know the date our Worthy Groom has set. What are we doing to prepare for our wedding?

We've examined Jewish wedding customs and applied them to our salvation. Now we investigate Jewish wedding customs, applying them to our glorification.

Wedding History

To understand our future wedding, we must understand wedding history. In Jesus' day, fathers chose their children's future mates. From childhood to young adulthood, the selection was sure and the anticipation great.

When the time was right and the children old enough, an official betrothal ceremony ensued forever formally linking the couple. Their betrothal was a binding covenant broken only with a certificate of divorce because of the infidelity of one of the betrothed.

During the interval between the betrothal and the actual wedding, both groom and bride needed to make preparations. The groom prepared a place, a home for himself and his beloved. He established himself in a vocation, making a living so he could gather the resources to support a home.

In the meantime, the bride prepared herself. She cultivated the social graces, learning from her mother and other older women how to be a virtuous wife, how to make a house a home. She dreaded the thought of being unprepared. Her every thought focused on being ready when her beloved returned for her, on being ready to present herself to him without any blemish.

When the father of the groom deemed the preparations complete, he'd burst into his son's presence proclaiming, "The time is right!" The best man, who had been making arrangements, gathered the wedding party. It was time for the groom to receive his bride. When the assemblage neared the bride's dwelling, they cried out in shouts of joy, "The groom is coming! The groom is coming!"

The delightfully surprised bride shrieked with joy. Having thoroughly prepared herself her entire life for this day, she felt no shame. Her lifelong longing fulfilled, joy filled her soul.

All the invited guests began to arrive. They had time—seven days. For the jubilant father of the groom threw a seven-day wedding feast. Party time! On the seventh day, all in attendance celebrated the marriage supper. At the conclusion of the marriage supper, the official ceremony occurred.

Finally the time arrived for the consummation of the vows. The new husband led his veiled wife to their wedding chamber. Alone, lifting her veil, face-to-face with his new bride, they consummated their union. Having left father and mother, he united himself to his wife, and they became one flesh. The man and his wife were both naked, and they felt no shame.

The next morning, the groom led his bride to their new home. They lived happily ever after, cleaving together, two souls knit as one.

Our Future Wedding

Worthy Groom's Father chose His Son's future bride—the church, corporate and individual. Not simply from childhood, not even only from birth, but from before the foundation of the world, Father called the bride to an eternal relationship with His Son.

When the time was right, you personally accepted Worthy Groom's salvation offer. He had been standing at your door knocking. Finally, you opened to Him. He wrote down your name in glory. You were officially betrothed, forever formally connecting you to Father's forever family. Betrothal is a binding covenant, a new covenant, broken by nothing. Nothing in all creation, neither death nor life, angels nor demons, present nor future, nor height nor depth, nor anything else in all the universe is able to separate you from the love of the Father that is in the Worthy Groom.

During the interval between the betrothal and the actual wedding, both Groom and bride make preparations. The Groom prepares a place, a home for Himself and His beloved. "I am going there to prepare a place for you. And if I go and prepare a place for you, I will come back and take you to be with me that you also may be where I am" (John 14:2-3). He's erecting a mansion fit for nobility. He's building a permanent dwelling place designed with unique specifications for your unique soul.

In the meantime, the Groom prepares His bride, again, corporately and individually. He is making us holy, cleansing and washing us with water through the Word, to present us to Himself as a radiant bride, without stain or wrinkle or any other blemish, but holy and blameless. Of course, we're involved in the process; we're just not left alone. We cooperate with His beauty treatments. We grow in the grace and the knowledge of our Worthy Groom. Moment by moment we're kept in His love. Day by day we're transformed by His grace. Our lives are anything but meaningless. We constantly focus on preparing for the day when we will see our Worthy Groom face-to-face.

When the Father of the Groom deems the preparations complete, He'll proclaim to His Son, "The time is right!" The Best Man, Messenger, who has been making arrangements, gathers the wedding party. It's time for the Groom to return for His bride. When the assemblage nears the bride's dwelling, they'll cry out in shouts of joy, "The Groom is coming! The Groom is coming!" Worthy Groom Himself will come down from heaven, with a loud command, with the voice of the archangel and with the trumpet of God. "The Groom is coming! The Groom is coming!"

Delightfully surprised, we'll shout with joy. Having been thoroughly prepared and having thoroughly prepared ourselves our entire lives for this day, we feel no shame. Our lifelong longing fulfilled, joy fills our souls.

All the invited guests arrive. Jubilant Father of the Groom throws a wedding feast. Party time! All in attendance celebrate the marriage supper of the Lamb and of His bride. At the conclusion of the marriage supper, the time arrives for the consummation of the vows. Worthy Groom dwells with His bride. They experience intimate communion. Soul connection. Love. Oneness.

Worthy Groom shows His bride—shows you—your new home. Your perfect mansion nestled in along the gold-lined streets. There you live together forever in heavenly bliss and earthly delight. With no more death, or mourning, or crying, or pain, for the old way has passed away. The new way has begun, never to end.

Our Future Marriage

We hear it all the time. "Just wait 'till the honeymoon's over." "It will never last." Earthly love does seem to evaporate like boiling water.

Not so, heavenly love. Our future wedding results in our future marriage, our eternal marriage. We experience fullness of life in the presence of God forever. The great Puritan writer Thomas Boston called it *consummate happiness*. Consummate—complete, ideal, perfect, total, supreme, ultimate. Happiness—blessed, content, thrilled, enthralled, ecstasy, shalom, rapture, joy.

Coram Deo relationship with God is the union we crave. In the movie *City of Angels*, Nicholas Cage plays an angel who falls in love with Meg Ryan. He faces a choice. Love her and become mortal, or resist love and remain immortal. He chooses love, only to face his lover's death after just one night. Yet, as the movie ends, he whispers to his dying lover that one night with her was worth more than an eternity without her. *City of Angels* depicts the union that we crave. It portrays the longing in our hearts for a love that lasts. In our finiteness, we stalk love, longing for a moment that will truly satisfy.

Heaven is that one moment with that one person forever and ever! Heaven is the consummation of all our longings. Intimate, endless relationship with Trinity quenches the desperate desire that burns within our hungry hearts.

The ravishing sight of God's infinite perfections perfectly satisfies. God will, as Boston reminds us, "Pour out of His goodness eternally into their souls: then shall they have a most lively sensation, in the innermost part of their souls" (Boston, *Human Nature in Its Fourfold State*, pp. 457-458). Jesus will take our breath away.

Jesus will take our doubts away. Boston again speaks for us and to us:

> Then shall they be perfectly satisfied as to the love of God towards them, which they are now ready to question on every turn. . . . They shall look into the heart of God, and there see the love He bore to them from all eternity, and the love and goodness He will bear to them for evermore (Boston, *Human Nature in Its Fourfold State*, p. 456).

Don't you want it? Can you taste it? A foretaste at least? Grasping intuitively and experientially the height, depth, width, and breadth of the Lover of your soul's love for you. Nourished and cherished. Love with no holding back. Love with no barriers. Love without shame. Love without a doubt. Love without end. There is a grandeur to God's love that we will not see until eternity has revealed our Worthy Groom's unending faithfulness.

When Shirley and I are "connecting on all cylinders," when our relationship is sweeter than honey, when we are best friends, soul mates, and lovers, Shirley will sometimes say to me, "Don't you dare go and die on me, Bob!" She's expressing what we all fear (and know) about earthly love. It will end. Not so, heavenly love. Not so, Worthy Groom's love.

Our Future Family

So, does heaven mean that I "lose myself in God"? Do I meld and merge into the Divine being so there is no longer an "I"? No. That is monism—the heretical belief that God will one day consume and subsume all.

The "Borg" on *Star Trek the Next Generation* depict monism. Individual identity ceases to exist. All become one great mind, one collective.

Biblically, we experience union with God—intimacy, but God remains God and we remain individuals. Unity in diversity.

This truth affects not only you and your relationship to God for all eternity, but also you and others forever and ever. People wonder sometimes, "Well, does heaven mean that I will be so caught up in God that I will have no relationships with others?" The Bible declares that we will be so caught up in loving and being loved by God that our love will overflow to one another in perfect community, harmony, and family.

As theologian Stanley Grenz summarizes:

> Taken as a whole, the Scriptures assert that God's program is directed to the bringing about of a redeemed people living within a redeemed creation enjoying fellowship with their Redeemer God. Consequently, the goal of our corporate human story is the union of the one new humanity in Christ (Ephesians 2:15), the fellowship of those whom Christ purchased for God "from every tribe and language and people and nation" (Revelation 5:9) (Grenz, *Theology for the Community of God*, pp. 608-609).

God's redemptive plan is not only individual, but also corporate (John 17:21-26; Galatians 3:28; Ephesians 1:10; 2:11-22; 4:1-6; Colossians 1:20-21; Revelation 5:9-10) and cosmic (Romans 8:18-25).

This is God's ultimate purpose: when the time is ripe He will gather us all together to be with Him *and with one another* forever. Redemption and reconciliation heal the breach in community initiated by sin. Sin and separation, prejudice and racism, individualism and isolation, these are alien intruders, invaders, enemies, unnatural.

I enjoy the privilege of teaching in an institution that is not only bi-cultural, but multi-cultural. Students in our counseling labs frequently say, "This is a taste of heaven," as they experience fellowship as male and female, as Caucasian, African-American, Asian-American, Hispanic, and as citizens of Japan, Jamaica, Nigeria, China, Korea, the United States, as well as citizens of heaven. Joint citizens. What we experience as a taste, God promises as a never-ending banquet.

Hugh Ross, Christian astronomer and author, proposes that in heaven we will be multi-dimensional beings. No longer limited to three-dimensional reality, we will be able to carry on personal, individual, intimate relationship with more than one person at a time. Whether he is accurate or not, he at least begins to stretch our imaginations so we wonder at the marvel of perfect relationships with one another forever.

Imagine no juggling of schedules. Imagine time for intimacy with everyone. Imagine no divisions, no bitterness, no selfish ambition, no slander, no fighting, no competition. Imagine cooperation, intimacy, understanding, connection, commitment, support, safety, involvement, warmth, vulnerability, sharing, openness, fearlessness, and all without shame. Sounds like heaven. Wait. It *is* heaven.

Our Future Invading Our Now

In the middle of the mess that was so frequently his lot in life, King David was able to say, "My heart is glad and my tongue rejoices; my body also will rest secure" (Psalm 16:9). How? He kept eternity's values in view.

> For thou wilt not leave my soul in hell; neither wilt thou suffer thine Holy One to see corruption. Thou wilt show me the path of life: in thy presence is fullness of joy; at thy right hand there are pleasures for evermore (Psalm 16:10-11, KJV).

Life is hell when we endure abandonment and experience corruption. Eternal life is heaven because we enjoy face-to-face relationship with God that can only be described as "fullness of joy." David selects a word for "fullness" (*sōba*) that suggests total sufficiency of nourishment and complete satisfaction. In other words, "It doesn't get any better than this!" Fullness of joy (*sāmēah*) is our lot in life for eternal life—glee, mirth, gladness, merry, rejoicing. Happiness all the time, wonderful peace of mind.

At God's right hand, or in His very presence, pleasure (*naîm*) dwells. David delights in the truth that delight will be his experience forever. Eternal life will be sweet, not sour; pleasant, not painful; beautiful, not ugly; agreeable, not disagreeable; suitable, not unsuited.

David saves his best for last. His word for "evermore" (*nēsah*—in perpetuity, unceasingly, enduring unendingly) hints at how heaven invaded his daily reality. "Evermore" pictures the most distant point of view. Think about that. Point of view. Perspective. As far ahead and beyond this life as David could possibly imagine, the eyes of his heart saw pleasure. People in David's day also used "evermore" for a goal, for the bright object at a distance that they traveled toward. We might call it, "the light at the end of the tunnel." The light at the end of David's tunnel was none other than the light of the Son of God.

The oft-read bumper sticker views life from a short-term perspective. "Life is hard and then we die." The bumper sticker David glued to his royal chariot read, "Life is hard and then we die, *but then we live again forever.*" David's long-term perspective conquered his daily experience. It can for us, also. We press ahead toward the goal of the high calling of God in Christ Jesus. We race toward the light at the end of the tunnel. We live today in light of the brilliant rapture of intimacy with Jesus.

Dominion: The Restoration—Eternal Purpose (The Grand Adventure)

Some might still be only partially satisfied. Perhaps the males among us would be the first to wonder, "Hmm, so heaven sounds like a chick flick. Tons of love and romance. And that's great. We have pleasure, but do we have purpose? Where's the macho man movie about heaven?" Though such a view displays a shallow appreciation for the wonders of intimacy with God, it does display a deep appreciation for the necessity of purpose.

John Eldredge has it right. "I think the fear of being bored is an unspoken fear of many people about the life that is coming" (Eldredge, *The Journey of Desire*, p. 145). Nineteenth-century preacher Thomas Chalmers evidently was a kindred spirit of Eldredge, as he reminds us that, "One of the Grand Essentials of human happiness is having something to *do*." Both macho men and virtuous women long for a lasting purpose. Os Guinness joins the chorus reminding us of this truth. "Somehow we human beings are never happier than when we are expressing the deepest gifts that are truly us." In case we think that men alone long for the purposeful expression of unique giftedness, ponder the words of Helen Keller, "Life is either a daring adventure or nothing."

Eternal life is the continuation of our grand adventure with God. Eternal life restores the Creation Mandate, renewing the dominion given to image bearers over heaven and earth. Eternal life equals eternal purpose that vanquishes boredom.

Be honest. You wake up some days with that dreaded feeling of "the same old, same old." Waking up, you pull the covers back over your head, curl up in the familiar fetal position, and wish that life were different. The monotony drives you crazy. The tedium sucks the life right out of you. Apathy and indifference set in. You feel listless, purposeless. Pointlessness, futility, aimlessness, weariness, paleness, and boredom sweep over you. "Is this all there is?" you cry.

The thought that heaven is "the same old, same old," drives you batty. The notion that heaven is, "more of the same," fails to comfort you one iota. "This inane, idiotic life had better give way to some grand, purposeful adventure or else heaven is hellish," you rightfully conclude.

Our Future Purposeful Role

It's a rightful conclusion because it is a biblical conclusion. "And his servants will serve him" (Revelation 22:3b). Simple. Eloquent. Direct. Authoritative. What will we do for all eternity? We'll *serve* our eternal God. We'll be key players in His eternal plan. We'll take leading roles in His never-ending story.

The context suggests the type of service God has planned for us. "No longer will there be any curse" (Revelation 22:3a). Heaven reverses the curse that made work mundane and tedious. It reverses the curse that caused our original dominion (Genesis 1:26-28; 2:15) to become full of weeds, thorns, and thistles (Genesis 3:17-19).

What was the nature of our original dominion, of our original Creation Mandate? Rule. Rulership over all creation. Specifically, we were to work it and take care of it. God's Creation Mandate calls us to be under-scientists, exploring, enjoying, and expanding the glories of Paradise until they fill the heavens and the earth. Copernicus, scientist and Christian, expresses well our calling:

To know the mighty works of God; to comprehend his wisdom and majesty and power; to appreciate, in degree, the wonderful working of his laws, surely all this must be a pleasing and acceptable mode of worship to the most High, to whom ignorance cannot be more grateful than knowledge (Copernicus, in Albert Hubbard, *Little Journeys to the Homes of Great Scientists*, p. 5).

For all eternity we will love God and one another with our brains and bodies as we subdue and rule the new heaven and new earth for His glory and for our good.

Tread backwards further in the context and we find the extent of our service. "Then I saw a new heaven and a new earth" (Revelation 21:1). Our grand adventure, our eternal purpose, includes both earth and heaven. In other words, the universe is our new domain of dominion. An astronomy buff? Enjoy! An explorer at heart? Explore! Deep sea diving? Go deep!

Speaking of Revelation 21, theologian Wayne Grudem paints his portrait of heavenly purpose.

> While we may have some uncertainty about the understanding of certain details, it does not seem inconsistent with this picture to say that we will eat and drink in the new heavens and new earth, and carry on other physical activities as well. Music certainly is prominent in the descriptions of heaven in Revelation, and we might imagine that both musical and artistic activities would be done to the glory of God. Perhaps people will work at the whole range of investigation and development of the creation by technological, creative, and inventive means, thus exhibiting the full extent of their excellent creation in the image of God (Grudem, *Systematic Theology*, p. 1162).

The particular words of Revelation 22:3 disclose more details about our service. "His servants shall serve (*latreusousin*) him." We might mistakenly assume that our service is to God alone, thus excluding service to one another. However, John selects a word for service that highlights both vertical service—service to God—and horizontal service— mutual service to one another. In non-biblical Greek, "service" was used literally for bodily service, e.g., workers on the land, and figuratively for work that one cherished and experienced great personal reward in doing (H. Strathmann, *Theological Dictionary of the New Testament*, p. 503).

In the Greek translation of the Old Testament, *latreuō* translated the Hebrew word *bd,* used when human working relationships are at issue as well as with reference to divine service (Strathmann, *Theological Dictionary of the New Testament*, p. 503). In the New Testament, all work is seen as sacred. The dichotomy between sacred and secular is removed. Anything we do for the glory of God, no matter how seemingly mundane (such as eating and drinking), is our spiritual work of service (Romans 12:1-2; 1 Corinthians 10:31).

Boring? Hardly! "Each person will live out the passion of his heart, set there by the Creator from before the beginning of time" (Eldredge, *The Journey of Desire*, p. 158). What did God make you for? What will you want to do in heaven? What is your calling? Dream big. Dream of your dream job. In eternity you'll face every moment knowing and feeling, "I was made for this job!"

Like Father, like sons and daughters. "Be ye creative, as I am creative," is the unending vocation Father bequeaths to us. Work reflects the image of God. "My Father is always at his work to this very day, and I, too, am working" (John 5:17). In heaven we will work, yet we'll experience work as rest. As Boston indicates, our work *is* our rest.

> They will have an eternal rest, with an uninterrupted joy; for heaven is not a resting place, where men may sleep out an eternity; there they rest not day nor night, but

their work is their rest, and continual recreation, and toil and weariness have no place there. They rest there in God, who is the centre of their souls. Here they find the completion, or satisfaction, of all their desires, having the full enjoyment of God, and uninterrupted communion with Him (Boston, *Human Nature in Its Fourfold State*, p. 441).

Eschatology is the theological term for the study of the end times, including eternity. Theologians also speak of your *"personal eschaton"*—the consummation of God's plan for your individual existence. Your eternal life will have a unique goal, a satisfying purpose, and lasting meaning—everlasting meaning.

Our Future Powerful Rule

We tend to leave *earth* out of the new heaven and the new earth. We forget that heaven is a very earthy place. Revelation disabuses us of these silly notions. "The *nations* will walk by its light, and the *kings* of the earth will bring *their splendor* into it" (Revelation 21:24, emphasis added). Heaven will have nations, kings, and human splendor. The new heaven and the new earth have organized structures that include human government and human workplaces.

Notice what Jesus pictures when He describes the eternal existence of the righteous, "…the righteous to eternal life" (Matthew 25:46). "Then the King will say to those on his right, 'Come, you who are blessed by my Father; take your inheritance, the kingdom prepared for you since the creation of the world'" (Matthew 25:34). Your inheritance is a kingdom—the kingdom God had in mind for you since the Creation Mandate at the beginning of the world.

In His kingdom, you will rule. "Well done, good and faithful servant! You have been faithful with a few things; I will put you in charge of many things. Come and share your master's happiness!" (Matthew 25:21). Jesus will put us in charge of many things. In the discharge of our responsibilities, we will enter the joy of our Master. We'll not lord it over one another, for that is how those headed for another destiny rule. We will rule by serving. We will work cooperatively. We will enjoy our positions of servant leadership.

We fail to understand biblical joy (*chara*) and happiness (*eudaimonia*). In the New Testament, happiness does not mean feeling giddy and being filled with laughter. Instead, it pictures a sense of flourishing as God's people fulfill in society the unique purpose for which they are designed. It means the internal fulfillment experienced as we live a purposeful and meaningful existence in society (see Martha Nussbaum, *The Therapy of Desire*).

When our founding fathers wrote that all citizens have a right to "life, liberty, and the pursuit of happiness," they never intended to communicate that we all have an inalienable right to giddy laughter. Being students of ancient Greek, and of the ancient Greek philosophers, they were speaking of *eudaimonia*—the right to meaningful existence that makes a purposeful contribution to society. Heaven is happiness in this sense. We will live fulfilling lives as we make distinctive contributions to eternal society.

Revelation 21:24 hints at the type of contributions you and I will make. "The kings of the earth will bring *their splendor* (*doxa*) into it (emphasis added)." Notice that John is not talking here about God's splendor, but about human splendor. "Splendor" (*doxa*) translates the Hebrew word for glory (*kābôd*), which means to be weighty, worthy, and impressive. The New Testament uses it of the unique honor, power, and radiance that each resurrected believer experiences for all eternity (1 Corinthians 15:40-44). In 1 Corinthians 15, Paul focuses upon the imperishability of our future glory. Peter, speaking of the un-resurrected person, compares our fading splendor to the splendor of the flowers of the field (1 Peter 1:24). When flowers blossom, they display their full beauty and majesty. In heaven, we will blossom, but never fade. We will not only have a new, glorified body; we will use that body to fulfill the purpose for which God gave it—to be productive and creative.

Finally and forever you will be God's poem, His craftsmanship. Your talents will contribute to society. Your gifts will be necessary and appreciated. Your work will be lasting and fulfilling. Your leadership will be respected and honored. Your service will satisfy your soul, glorify your Savior, and benefit your society of brothers and sisters. You will thrive as you live out the grand adventure with audacious daring.

Our Future Conquering Our Now

I live an hour from where I work. On my way home, I always call home. When people ask Shirley if I like my work, she tells them, "Well, whenever Bob calls home and talks about his day at work, he's giddy!"

I'll be honest with you; I've had jobs where I have not been "giddy." And I still have days when I don't leave campus giddy.

When you're honest, you know that "giddy" does not always describe the sensations you experience at work. Work, here on earth, is filled with obstacles. For farmers, those obstacles include weeds and thorns. For sales people, those obstacles include competition for clients and last minute reneging on contracts. For secretaries, those obstacles include harsh bosses and crashing computers. For pastors, those obstacles include worldly elders and complaining parishioners. For counselors, those obstacles include obstinate counselees and cumbersome HMOs. Weeds and thorns are our lot in life as workers in fallen bodies on a fallen planet.

This reality often causes us to despair. We feel useless, or at least hardly useful. We wonder whether we are really making any difference. "Does anyone appreciate me? Notice me? Does my work matter?" Work can be maddeningly frustrating.

The apostle Paul faced obstacles that would have crushed me. Insults. Lies. Opposition. False teachers. Slander. Ministry that seemed unproductive from a human perspective. Yet he maintained his eternal perspective. His future purpose conquered his present frustrations. How? Paul saw himself as a servant with one calling—faithfulness.

So then, men ought to regard us as servants of Christ and as those entrusted with the secret things of God. Now it is required that those who have been given a trust must prove faithful. I care very little if I am judged by you or by any human court; indeed, I do not even judge myself. My conscience is clear, but that does not make me innocent. It is the Lord who judges me. Therefore judge nothing before the appointed time; wait till the Lord comes. He will bring to light what is hidden in darkness and will expose the motives of men's hearts. At that time each will receive his praise from God (1 Corinthians 4:1-5).

God does not ask that you become famous, only that you be faithful. Work today is not about our glory, or renown, or even our "success." Work is about faithfully serving God, using whatever talents and gifts He has given us, motivated to glorify Him and benefit society.

When your current work feels fruitless, when your life seems to lack meaning, remember that in heaven each will receive his praise from God. You will hear Father's, "Well done, thou good and faithful servant. Enter into the eternal satisfaction and fulfillment of your Master."

Keep pulling up those work weeds. Keep growing roses even though they have thorns. Faithfully serve as an under-scientist whether your calling is to be a domestic scientist faithfully working in your home, or a medical scientist faithfully working to find cures for cancer.

Where We've Been and Where We're Heading

Keep loving in the romantic love affair and keep working in the grand adventure. Every morning arise, reminding yourself that *your journey today brings you one day closer to home*. It's just around the river bend. In that day, you will embrace the love and purpose you long for, the relationships and meaning you were designed for. In that day, the smaller story of this life will be swept up into the larger story of the life that never ends. Heaven—the new heaven and the new earth—is that larger way. Pursue it with eager feet. I promise that it will join God's larger way.

That larger way includes the new you—glorified, sinless, spotless. It also includes your eternal rest. Join me in Scene II for the rest of the story of the rest of your life.

Caring for Your Soul: Personal Applications

1. Which of the following aspects of eternal life do you most long for? Why?

   a. Our Future Wedding

   b. Our Future Marriage

   c. Our Future Family

   d. Our Future Purposeful Role

   e. Our Future Powerful Rule

2. Read the following passages. Which aspect of our future seems most pertinent to you? Why? How will you apply it? Which of these do you most long for? Why?

   a. Purity: Revelation 19:7-8

   b. Ecstasy: Revelation 19:9

   c. Victory: Revelation 19:10-20:10

   d. Beauty: Revelation 19:7-8

   e. Harmony: Revelation 7:9-17; 21:1-7

   f. Safety: Revelation 21:9-21

   g. Vitality: Revelation 22:1-6

Caring for Others: Ministry Implications

♦   **Invite Counselees, Spiritual Friends, and Parishioners to Taste Their Thirsts for the Eternal Love Affair:** Jesus used thirsts to invite response (John 4 and 7). The Holy Spirit uses thirsts for heaven to invite surrender (Revelation 21 and 22). As people come to you suffering because of *relational wounds*, invite them to Christ. As they come to you *sinfully loving other idols*, invite them to Christ. Explore with them how their future *wedding* can affect their current *relating*.

♦   **Invite Counselees, Spiritual Friends, and Parishioners to Taste Their Thirsts for the Eternal Grand Adventure:** As people come to you suffering *because of a sense of purposelessness*, invite them to Christ. As they come to you *sinfully working for their own glory*, invite them to Christ. Explore with them how their future *ministry* can affect their current *work*.

♦   **Explore How the Larger Story Overshadows, Not Obliterates, the Smaller Story:** Paul did not deny his smaller story of suffering. In fact, he repeatedly informs us of it (Romans 8; 2 Corinthians 1; 2 Corinthians 4; 2 Timothy 4; etc.). Enter your spiritual friend's smaller story of suffering. Then explore how the larger story—heaven/eternity—influences your spiritual friend. "How might God be using these events to conform you more to the image of His Son?" "In what ways can you say, 'It will be worth it all, when I see Jesus'?" "Paul considered his current suffering unworthy of comparing to his future glory. What do you think he meant? What future glory do you long for? How could looking ahead to your future glory make a difference in how you respond to your current suffering?"

CHAPTER TWENTY-NINE

VIRGIN BRIDE'S FINAL DESTINY: PURITY AND HARMONY

"I believe that death will be overcome by life because I believe in God—the kind of God whom Jesus shows us, the God to whom we human beings matter. It is impossible to imagine this God scrapping what is most precious to him" (Stephen Travis, *I Believe in the Second Coming*, p. 168).

"We shall have the universe for our own, and be good merry children in the great house of our Father. I think then we shall be able to pass into and through each other's very souls as we please, knowing each other's thought and being, along with our own, and so being like God. When we are all just as loving and unselfish as Jesus; when, like him, our one thought of delight is that God is, and is what he is; when the fact that a being is just another person from ourselves is enough to make that being precious" (George MacDonald, *The Heart of George MacDonald*).

Existential Questions and Eternal Answers

Pastors, counselors, professors, and theologians debate whether we should address people's felt needs or their factual needs. The debate assumes that these two categories are mutually exclusive.

The factual needs proponents decry preachers who submit to the postmodern repulsion to sound doctrine. They chastise counselors who give people what their itching ears want to hear.

The felt needs proponents rebuke teachers who refuse to relate truth to human needs. They castigate professors who speak the truth, but not in loving relevance.

Believing that God knows our nature and knows what He is doing, I suspect that in His Word we have wisdom that discloses the factual needs of people and also helps us expose the felt needs that legitimately exist in the human soul. Could it be we don't have to give only the answers people want to hear? Could it be we don't have to give only answers to questions no one is asking? Perhaps, if we study the Scriptures and the soul (through the Scriptures), we might find that felt and factual needs have a meeting place after all. I'm convinced that a biblical understanding of heaven offers us a bridge between people's existential questions (their felt needs, experiential needs) and God's eternal answers (their factual, actual needs).

Our previous chapter explained that we need God's eternal perspective on eternity—an enduring grace vision of the end of the story. That chapter and this one depict the four scenes of the final act in our never-ending story with Worthy Groom.

+ Communion: The Consummation—Eternal Relationship (The Love Affair)
+ Dominion: The Restoration—Eternal Purpose (The Grand Adventure)
+ Reflection: The Glorification—Eternal Nature (The Noble Image)
+ Cohesion: The Integration—Eternal Rest (The Endless Harmony)
    Each scene answers one of the core existential questions nagging our hearts.
+ Communion: Where Did I Come From?—My Destiny Is Intimacy
+ Dominion: Why Am I Here?—My Destiny Is Ministry
+ Reflection: Who Am I?—My Destiny Is Purity
+ Cohesion: How Should I Then Live?—My Destiny Is Harmony

"Where did I come from?" Quite the legitimate felt need. It requires biblical factual answers. "I came from my Creator/my Husband (Isaiah 54:5). I came from my Worthy Groom—worthy because of His perfect holy love." Heaven melds the existential and the eternal when it teaches us: "My destiny is intimacy."

"Why am I here?" Every honest human being grapples with this legitimate felt need. It requires eternal truth. "I'm here to fulfill a unique, meaningful purpose that no other being in the entire universe has been designed to fulfill. I'm here to serve my Lover. I'm here to serve my family." Heaven melds the existential and the eternal when it teaches us: "My destiny is ministry."

"Who am I?" In our current chapter we address this third felt need, existential question, legitimate longing. It, too, requires an eternal perspective. "I'm a glorified image bearer. A Romancer who loves like Christ. A Dreamer who has the mind of Christ. A Creator who chooses Christ forever. A Singer who experiences joy forevermore. An Actor in an imperishable body." Heaven melds the existential and the eternal, the felt and factual, when it teaches us: "My destiny is purity."

"How should I then live?" This fourth relevant question requires revelatory truth. "For all eternity I live in eternal rest. Endless harmony. Shalom. Peace. Unity. Blessedness and bliss." Heaven melds the felt and the factual when it teaches us: "My destiny is harmony."

My destiny is intimacy, ministry, purity, and harmony. If those eternal truths are not enough to motivate us today, what possibly could? If these heavenly realities are not clear enough answers for earthly questions, what are? In reality, there's no such thing as being "so heavenly minded as to be of no earthly good." When we mind the things of heaven, we bring forth truth that transforms now and answers that address felt needs with factual truth.

Reflection: The Glorification—Eternal Nature (The Noble Image)

"Who am I? How should I view myself? What is my basic nature? What is my final destiny?"

Responding to these felt need questions, evolutionists like to speak of human beings as "noble savages." Descended, so they wrongly inform us, from savage beasts, and ultimately from soulless amoebas, we have evolved to the point of nobility. In and of ourselves we have royal blood.

Our Creator, who was there and deserves a voice in explaining our origins, tells us we were Image Bearers, became Glorious Ruins, can be transformed into Christlikeness, and will one day embody either the Noble Image of our Worthy Groom or the Ignoble Image of the False Seducer.

Fairy Tales and Tales of Heaven

I've always suspected that fairy tales tell the tale of our deepest longings. The ugly duckling becoming the great white swan. The clumsy frog turned into the handsome prince. The mistreated, shabbily dressed, forgotten stepsister transformed into the belle of the ball. The beast tamed by beauty.

You detect the common theme, don't you? Metamorphosis. The change of the slimy, creeping caterpillar into the splendid, soaring butterfly.

In those rare moments of self-aware honesty, even the unredeemed are discontent with who they are. The ranting, rage-filled husband, at some level, wants to change, longs to change. Hates the way he treats his wife and kids. The insecure, embittered wife, at some level, wants to change, longs to changes. Hates the way she relates to those she wants to love. The moody, inconsiderate, selfish teen, at some level, wants to change, longs to change. Hates the way he or she mishandles life and mistreats peers and family members.

In our hopefully less rare periods of self-aware integrity, believers are discontent with who we are. The impatient, bossy boss knows better, wants to be better. Hates the way he loses his testimony for Christ in the workplace. The rigid, compulsive, self-protective teacher in a public school knows she could be a more attractive portrait of the grace of Christ. Up and down, inconsistent Christian young people want to be more passionately consistent examples of Jesus Christ.

Transformation and Glorification

Saved and unsaved. Male and female. Young and old. We all recognize, at times, our felt and factual need for transformation. The process has begun for believers. We await the final transformation, what the Bible describes as *glorification*. Unbelievers find themselves still in the cocoon. Still crawling, trying to fly, but wingless. If they fail to place faith in Father, then they face a hopeless destiny that the Bible describes as *damnation*.

Boxes 29:1 and 29:2 condense all that you've read to this point. *"The Five States of Human Existence"* summarizes the nature of human nature in Creation, Fall, Redemption, Glorification, and Damnation. *"Humanity in Our Five-Fold State"* examines the concepts of relational, rational, volitional, emotional, and physical beings as designed by God, depraved by sin, dignified by redemption, and either destined for glorification or damnation.

Box 29:1

The Five States of Human Existence

The State of Design: Creation

God created us in His image with all the capacities necessary
to enjoy perfect relationships with Him, others, and ourselves
with a totally satisfying purpose in a lush paradise.

The State of Depravity: Fall

We have forsaken "God the Spring of Living Water"
and dug our own cisterns, broken cisterns that can hold no water.
In so doing we have marred His image within us, not eliminating our soul capacities,
but changing the direction of those capacities so
now we live with our backs to God rather than our faces toward God.
Our capacities being depraved, all our inclinations move away from God.

The State of Dignity: Redemption

Through our faith in Christ's grace
displayed by His death, burial and resurrection,
God both counts us righteous (justification) and makes us righteous (regeneration)
so our soul capacities are renewed.
The inclinations at the depth of our being are all turned back to God
so we can love Him and others.

The State of Destiny: Glorification

At death the righteous believing are confirmed in holiness.
The inclination of their soul capacities will remain the same for all eternity,
the righteous forever with their faces facing God.

The State of Decadence: Damnation

At death the unrighteous unbelieving are confirmed in wickedness.
The inclination of their soul capacities will remain the same for all eternity,
the wicked forever with their faces turned away from God.

Box 29:2

Humanity In Our Five-Fold State

The State of Design: Creation—Innocent and Connected

- Romancers: Relational Beings Who Long for God—Affections and Worship
- Dreamers: Rational Beings Who Perceive God-Reality—Mindsets and Wisdom
- Creators: Volitional Beings Who Choose God's Will—Purposes and Surrender
- Singers: Emotional Beings Who Feel Integrated—Mood States and Shalom
- Actors: Physical Beings Who Receive God's Power—Connected Habituated Tendencies and Growth

The State of Depravity: Fall—Depraved and Deprived

- Adulterers: Relational Beings Who Reject God—Disordered Affections and Independence
- Fools: Rational Beings Who Suppress God-Reality—Foolish Mindsets and Blindness
- Destroyers: Volitional Beings Who Choose for Self—Self-Centered Purposes and Stubbornness
- Addicts: Emotional Beings Who Feel Dis-integrated—Ungoverned Mood States and Shame
- Traitors: Physical Beings Who Face Weakness—Disconnected Habituated Tendencies and Decay

The State of Dignity: Redemption—Reconciled and Renewed

- Romancers: Relational Beings Who Love Passionately—Purified Affections and Purity
- Dreamers: Rational Beings Who Think Imaginatively—Wise Mindsets and Sanity
- Creators: Volitional Beings Who Choose Courageously—Other-Centered Purposes and Vitality
- Singers: Emotional Beings Who Experience Life Fully—Managed Mood States and Integrity
- Actors: Physical Beings Who Serve God Capably—Disciplined Embedded Tendencies and Activity

Box 29:2, Continued

Humanity In Our Five-Fold State

The State of Destiny: Glorification—Glorified and Connected

- ♦ Romancers: Relational Beings Who Love Like Christ—Worship and Ministry
- ♦ Dreamers: Rational Beings Who Have the Mind of Christ—Creativity and Spirituality
- ♦ Creators: Volitional Beings Who Choose God Forever—Freedom and Purpose
- ♦ Singers: Emotional Beings Who Experience Happiness Eternally—Integrity and Celebration
- ♦ Actors: Physical Beings Who Are Empowered by God's Nourishing—Healed and Healthy

The State of Decadence: Damnation—Condemned and Alienated

- ♦ Haters: Relational Beings Who Hate Like Satan—Alienated and Violated Souls
- ♦ Liars: Rational Beings Who Have the Mind of Satan—Reprobate and Untrusting Minds
- ♦ Murderers: Volitional Beings Who Choose Their Own Will—Stubborn and Cowardly Wills
- ♦ Agonizers: Emotional Beings Who Experience Pain Endlessly—Angry, Anxious, and Guilty Moods
- ♦ Prisoners: Physical Beings Who Endure Just Torment—Tortured and Suffering Bodies

Since our present focus is on eternity, let's turn our attention to the final two stages: glorification or damnation. We'll be answering the question, "Who will I be for all eternity?" The unsaved will remain ugly ducklings; clumsy frogs; mistreated, shabbily dressed, forgotten stepsisters; beasts; slimy, creeping caterpillars; and much worse, ever worsening. The saved will forever exist as great white swans; handsome princes and beautiful princesses; belles of the ball; beasts transformed into royalty; splendid, soaring butterflies; and so much more.

Virgin Bride's Glorified Personality Structure

The apostle John hints at the difference between a redeemed image bearer and a glorified image bearer. "Dear friends, now we are children of God, and what we will be has not yet been made known. But we know that when he appears, we shall be like him, for we shall see him as he is" (1 John 3:2).

Now we are God's children—neonatal saints, growing daily in our reflection of Christlikeness. But in that day, *we shall be like Him*. When we see him face-to-face, He will complete our transformation. In heaven, the veil will be removed and we will be the soul that God had in mind all along.

Theologians call it "glorification." Paul speaks of it when he writes, "For those God foreknew he also predestined to be conformed to the likeness of his Son" (Romans 8:29). We reach the final goal of our salvation when we obtain the image of Christ. "We ourselves, who have the first fruits of the Spirit, groan inwardly as we wait eagerly for our adoption as sons, the redemption of our bodies" (Romans 8:23).

In Creation, we had the ability not to sin. Once Adam and Eve sinned, they took on a fallen nature. In the Fall, our fallen nature was unable not to sin. However, that nature could be redeemed. In Redemption, we again have the ability not to sin. Unlike when Adam and Eve sinned, when believers sin, we do not take on a sin nature. We maintain our redeemed nature; we maintain our ability not to sin. In heaven, in our glorified state, we are unable to sin, and we are never able to lose our glorified nature. In hell, unbelievers are not only unable not to sin; they are also unable to be redeemed. Theologians label it "confirmation in holiness" (glorification) (Revelation 7:14-17; 19:7-8; 21:1-7; 22:1-5, 14) and "confirmation in corruption" (damnation) (Daniel 12:10; Hebrews 9:27; Revelation 20:11-15; 21:8, 27; 22:11, 15). Picture it like this:

- ♦ Creation: Able Not to Sin—Sinning Leads to a Sin Nature
- ♦ Fall: Unable Not to Sin—Able to Be Redeemed
- ♦ Redemption: Able Not to Sin—Sinning Does Not Lead to a Sin Nature
- ♦ Glorification: Not Able to Sin—Never Able to Lose the Glorified Nature
- ♦ Damnation: Unable Not to Sin—Unable to Be Redeemed

Boston eloquently describes virgin bride's glorified state.

Their nature shall be altogether pure and sinless. There shall be no darkness in their minds, but the understanding of every saint, when he is come to his kingdom, will be as a globe of pure and unmixed light. There shall not be the least aversion to good, nor the least inclination to evil, in their wills, but they will be brought to a perfect conformity to the will of God; blessed with angelic purity, and fixed therein. Their affections shall not be liable to the least disorder or irregularity; it will cost no trouble to keep them right: they will get such a fixed habit of purity, as they can never lose. They will be so refined from all earthly dross, as never to savour more of any thing but of heaven. Were it possible for them to be set again amidst the ensnaring objects of an evil world, they would walk among them without the least defilement (Boston, *Human Nature in Its Fourfold State*, p. 438).

Romancers: Relational Beings Who Love Like Christ—Worship and Ministry

Let the truth of your future glorification penetrate. Imagine all susceptibility to sin rooted out. Never again tempted. Never again temptable. No misdirected love. No false lovers. No idols of the heart. No lusts. No bitterness. No divisiveness. No hypocrisy. No guilt. No shame.

Imagine, instead, being totally pure in all your longings and affections. Desiring only what God desires. Loving God with your entire being—soul, mind, heart, will, and emotions. Loving God with totally pure motives. Enjoying Him and exalting Him forever. Worship.

Loving your neighbor as yourself. Cooperative, never competitive. Giving, sharing, generous. Mutuality. Sincerity. Sacrifice. Selflessness. Ministry.

Just think. You'll never have to "fake loving" again. Never wonder if your motives are pure. Never doubt the motives or the love of another person again, ever.

No wonder theologian Stanley Grenz labels heaven the eternal comedy—forever and ever the good guys win because only the good guys reside there. Forever and ever all turns out right in the end. In fact, all is right from beginning, to middle, to end. Every scene of every act displays good's victory.

Because you are internally, extensively, and eternally purified, you will long only for and experience the Chief Good. No more longing to play in the mud puddles when God offers a week at the ocean. You'll long for, know, choose, and enjoy only what is good as God defines and embodies goodness.

Listen to Boston's amazing description of your eternal sainthood.

> The saints shall have kingly power and authority given them. Our Lord gives not empty titles to His favourites; He makes them kings indeed. The dominion of the saints will be a dominion far exceeding that of the greatest monarch who ever was on earth. They will be absolute masters over sin, which had the dominion over them. They will have complete rule over their own spirits; an entire management of all their affections and inclinations, which now create them so much molestation: the turbulent root of corrupt affections shall be forever expelled out of that kingdom, and never be able any more to give them the least disturbance (Boston, *Human Nature in Its Fourfold State*, p. 434).

Never to lust again. Never to desire selfishly. Always to want only what you should want. Every passion, every pleasure, pure.

The white garments we will wear in heaven (Revelation 7:13; 19:8) are indicative of our glorious freedom from sin. In Roman times, when they set their bond-servants free, they gave them a white garment as a badge of freedom. From the day we receive our white robes, we will experience complete freedom; we will be fully free from temptation and sin. And we will be free from all the effects of sin: "There shall be no more death, neither sorrow, nor crying, neither shall there be any more pain" (Revelation 21:4, KJV). White raiment was also a token of purity.

> The saints shall then put on the robes of perfect purity, and shine in spotless holiness, like the sun in its strength, without the least cloud to intercept its light. Absolute innocence shall then be restored, and every appearance of sin banished far from this kingdom (Boston, *Human Nature in Its Fourfold State*, p. 437).

We will experience not only right longings, but also pure relationships. Eternal life means no separation, but only "withness." In heaven we'll again walk with God in the cool of the day. So shall we ever be with the Lord (1 Thessalonians 4:17) in face-to-face (Revelation 22:4) fellowship and worship (Revelation 21:2-3). We'll dwell with God and He with us. Seeing Him, knowing Him, being loved by Him and loving Him, our souls will be totally satisfied (Psalm 16:11).

Not only will worship be perfect, but also fellowship will be exquisite. Heaven is a corporate, not an individual, experience. God will live with *them*, and *they* will be His *people* (Revelation 21:3). We'll dwell together in a city (Revelation 21:14) without drive-by shootings, with no "other side of the tracks," with multi-ethnic diversity (Revelation 5:9), and perfect harmony (Revelation 21:24-27).

"Who am I?" My destiny is purity. Forever and ever I will be a pure, passionate Romancer. What difference does my pure destiny make now? "But we know that when he appears, we shall be like him, for we shall see him as he is. Everyone who has this hope in him purifies himself, just as he is pure" (1 John 3:2b-3). Since we'll worship forever, let's start now! Since we'll love our brothers and sisters endlessly, let's do so now!

Dreamers: Rational Beings Who Have the Mind of Christ—Creativity and Spirituality

Though our brains/minds will not be infinite (only God is), no unwise, impure, foolish, stupid, ungodly thought will ever enter our heads. We will perceive all reality accurately. Truth will embed itself within us, setting us free and guiding us wisely.

Because God is infinite, for all eternity we will be learning and enjoying more and more and more about Him. Because His universe is immense, we will never complete our encyclopedic cataloging of God's creation. We will explore and invent. Not only will the kings bring their glory into the New Jerusalem, but "the glory and honor of the nations [and by implication of all the citizens of those nations] will be brought into it" (Revelation 21:26). This requires creativity.

You think that Galileo, Copernicus, and Einstein were brilliant? Wait until you encounter a glorified scientist. You think that Browning, Poe, and Longfellow composed beautiful poems? Wait until you encounter a glorified poet. You think that Shakespeare, Dickens, and Twain were great authors? Wait until you encounter a glorified Pulitzer Prize winning author. You think that Augustine, Luther, and Calvin were theological giants? Wait until you encounter a glorified theologian. You think that Da Vinci, Edison, and Curie were inventive? Wait until you encounter a glorified inventor? And guess what? You will be one of those glorified thinkers!

Since your mind will function creatively for all eternity, how then should you now live? Could it be that a heavenly focus might impact Christian couch potatoes? Would it be so wrong if the deepest thinkers on planet Earth were believers? Perhaps we should begin loving God with our brains. Stretching ourselves to think deeply—in whatever field or area of interest we find ourselves.

God gifts our glorified minds with creativity and spirituality. Nothing impure will ever enter the new heaven and the new earth, nor will anyone who does what is shameful or deceitful, because there will be no deceit on our lips, or in our minds. The father of lies is banished. Even were he not, we would easily expose his lies. We will all understand the goodness of God's holy love and seek after Him. We will know that He is a Rewarder, not a Hoarder. We will comprehend, in our own finite but glorified ways that Father is forgiving, Worthy Groom is worthy, and Messenger is inspired. Spiritual eyes, faith eyes, will enable our minds to perceive God-reality without taint or error.

Imagine never having to fight off another impure thought. Never having to deal with lies about who God is and who you are to Him. Never having to counter deceit, lies, distorted thinking, mischaracterizations, and caricatures. Truth will be your native tongue.

Imagine no more mental illness. No Alzheimer's. No schizophrenia. No brain trauma. No mental disability or incapacitation.

Since your mind will function purely for all eternity, how then should you now live? "Set your minds on things above, not on earthly things" (Colossians 3:2). That is, put to death impure thoughts, lusts, idolatry, filthy language, lies (Colossians 3:3-9), and think on whatever is true, noble, right, pure, lovely, admirable, and excellent (Philippians 4:8). Look at life now with heaven's spiritual eyes.

Creators: Volitional Beings Who Choose God Forever—Freedom and Purpose

Since we pursue what we perceive to be pleasing and since our perceptions are rightly attuned to how infinitely pleasing God is, in heaven we will freely choose to pursue Him and what He chooses to provide. We will be free to choose according to our glorified nature.

In the final scene of *Braveheart*, William Wallace is tortured mercilessly. His insides skewered, even his friends beg him to relent, to recant, to confess, and to plead for mercy. His lips tremble. His tormentor assumes that Wallace is ready to submit. Putting his ear to Wallace's mouth, he and the entire crowd hear the last words Wallace would ever speak. No. The last words Wallace would ever shout.

"Freedom!"

We will shout, "Freedom!" for all eternity. Free to choose God. Free to love one another. Free always to do what is right, good, and best. Free from sin. Not able to sin. Free from temptation. Free from lust. Free from hurtful actions and behavior. Free to choose. Free to purpose what God Himself would purpose. Free to follow the inclinations of our hearts, for they will be only godly continually.

Do you struggle with a besetting sin? Do compulsions seem to sweep over you? Do you battle addictive, enslaving behavior? Take heart. The battle will end. Victory will be yours. What's more, even now you are able not to sin. Therefore, yield your will to God. Resist Satan. He is a defeated foe. You are more than a conqueror.

To be volitional means that you have a will to choose, to set goals, to plan and follow pathways, to act with a purpose. Christian philosophers speak of this as "personal teleology"—your ability to follow and fulfill the unique purpose for which you were designed.

Earlier I mentioned my own search for self-awareness and meaning. What is unique about me? What is my calling, my purpose, my function? One word has captured my attention, captures who I am: *Coach*. Wherever I've been, whatever I've done, "coach" summarizes my approach to life, my purpose in life. I never experience more contentment then when I observe someone I've "coached" succeeding, growing, serving. My eternal teleology—to be a coach.

What is yours? What is your personal teleology now? What makes you you? What is the unique purpose for which God designed you? What is your calling? Not your job, but who you are and how you function in whatever job, whatever relationship, whatever situation you find yourself. What brings you the greatest sense of contentment, satisfaction, peace? Reflect on it, interact with others who know you. Find your personal purpose. Live it now. Get used to it. You'll enjoy it forever.

Singers: Emotional Beings Who Experience Happiness Eternally—Integrity and Celebration

Since our emotions "follow" our affections, cognitions, and volitions; since we pursue (volitional) what we perceive (rational) to be pleasing (relational) and pleasant (emotional); since our feelings respond to our inner world (which will be totally pure) and to our outer world (which will be totally safe), we will experience consummate happiness forever. Integration and celebration capture the core aspects of our consummate happiness.

We have seen that sin leads to personal dis-integration where we feel as though we are falling apart, coming unglued, splintering, going crazy, losing it. Glorified emotional beings will experience the absence of these painful experiences and negative, hurtful, ungodly emotions. "He will wipe away *every* tear from their eyes. There will be *no more* death or *mourning* or *crying* or *pain*, for the old order of things has passed away" (Revelation 21:4, emphasis added).

No more depression. No anxiety. No phobia. No manic-depressive disorder. No bitterness. No rage.

The absence of all these suggests the presence of their polar opposites. Rather than personal dis-integration, we'll enjoy personal integrity where we experience wholeness, soundness, contentment, fulfillment, and happiness. "I'm feeling with it." "I feel so together today." "All is right with the world, with my world." "Nothing's troubling me." These will be our endless experiences.

So what? Live today in hope. On your journey toward the New Jerusalem, you will undergo up and down experiences of integration/dis-integration. Don't despair. One day all will be well. One day you will wake whole to each new day. Until that day, manage your moods. Be angry, but sin not. Admit discouragement, but don't despair. Live today honestly, with personal integrity. Until that final day, know your moods, admit your moods—be self-aware.

Eternal integration leads to everlasting celebration. We'll celebrate Jesus. What thrill we'll enjoy as we proclaim our Worthy Groom "Worthy!"

We'll also celebrate one another. The word of our testimony will delight us.

We'll celebrate ourselves. Not arrogantly, but contentedly. "So this is who I was meant to be. All right! I like. I'm comfortable with me!"

Further, we'll celebrate life. Finally, life will make sense. Existence will have meaning. Being alive will be delightful. Confusion banished, reality will make sense. "So that's how life was meant to be. This is what it looks like when reality is utterly relational. I like life!"

Since celebration is our eternal destiny, how then should we now live? The Christian never has to despair. Groan and grieve? Of course. Despair and give up hope? Of course not. Sad, sour, hopeless, despairing believers are poor advertisers for belief in Jesus. We can soothe our souls in our Savior. We can party hearty now, because the kingdom of God will be one endless party, the father of all all-nighters.

Actors: Physical Beings Who Are Empowered by God's Nourishing—Healed and Healthy

"On each side of the river stood the tree of life, bearing twelve crops of fruit, yielding its fruit every month. And the leaves of the tree are for the healing (*therapeian*) of the nations" (Revelation 22:2). This verse baffles some, troubles others. "Healing? Why would I need healing once I'm in heaven?"

In heaven we will have imperishable, contingent bodies (1 Corinthians 15:42-55). Imperishable—our bodies will never die. Christ's resurrection removed the stinger from Death. However, we are not "gods," not infinite, not independent, not non-contingent. We will still *need* God. We will remain contingent beings dependent upon God. Only our continuous connection to Christ will keep our contingent bodies healthy. The tree of life is our therapy, the medicine that keeps us continually healthy, the nourishment that maintains our bodies at perfect peak performance.

In our glorified state, Christ has forever destroyed that alien intruder—Death. Our susceptibility to suffering and sickness is rooted out. Our incorruptible bodies will have no defects or deformities. They will be strong and remain powerful because of the ongoing infusion of God's infinite health-sustaining power. God will heal our earthly bodies.

> Whatever defects or deformities the bodies of saints had when laid in the grave, occasioned by accidents in life, or arising from secret causes in their formation, they shall rise out of the grave free of all these. . . . Surely Isaac's eyes shall not then be dim, nor will Jacob halt: Leah shall not be tender-eyed, nor Mephibosheth lame of his legs (Boston, *Human Nature in Its Fourfold State*, p. 388).

Our earthly bodies will be healthy.

> They shall be glorious bodies, not only beautiful, comely, and well proportioned, but full of splendor and brightness. The most beautiful face, and best proportioned body, that now appears in the world, is not to be named in comparison with the body of the meanest saint at the resurrection; for "then shall the righteous shine forth as the sun" (Matthew 13:43, KJV) (Boston, *Human Nature in Its Fourfold State*, p. 388).

People often wonder what "age" they will be in heaven. Boston believes, based upon Daniel 12:3; Matthew 17:1-13; John 5:28-29; Romans 8:19-25; 1 Corinthians 15:35-58; and Revelation 21-22, that our bodies will be perfectly proportioned and at their exact maturation point. In other words, our bodies will have the strength of our youth, while our minds will have the wisdom of our mature years.

How then should we now live? None of us feels perfectly content with our bodies. Yet the psalmist assures us that God fearfully and wonderfully made us (Psalm 139:13-18). He handcrafted us so that even our weaknesses cause us to trust in and magnify His strength (2 Corinthians 12:3-10). Accept your contingency and your frailty as reminders of your need for God's strength. And when stalked by Death and its weaker cousins, Sickness and Suffering, remind yourself, "There will be no more death or mourning or crying or pain" (Revelation 21:4). Grieve, but never as those who have no hope.

Adulterous Spouse's Debauched Personality Structure

As much as we might prefer ignoring hell, its dark realities warrant a voice. The historic *Westminster Confession* paints the stark contrast between heaven and hell.

> The bodies of men, after death, return to dust, and see corruption: but their souls, which neither die nor sleep, having an immortal subsistence, immediately return to God who gave them: the souls of the righteous, being then made perfect in holiness, are received into the highest heavens, where they behold the face of God, in light and glory, waiting for the full redemption of their bodies. And the souls of the wicked are cast into hell, where they remain in torments and utter darkness, reserved to the judgment of the great day (*The Westminster Confession*, Chapter 32, "The State of Men After Death, And of the Resurrection of the Dead".)

What the *Westminster Confession* summarizes, John 5:28-29 describes. "Do not be amazed at this, for a time is coming when all who are in their graves will hear his voice and come out—those who have done good will rise to live, and those who have done evil will rise to be condemned."

If heaven is eternal comedy, then hell is eternal tragedy. There the story line forever regresses, matters going from bad to worse forever and ever and ever. Hell encompasses absolute and unending hopelessness. It is the place where those who rejected Father in this life, where those who chose to wed the False Seducer, where those who believed the lie, exist in isolation, estrangement, loneliness, and meaninglessness. Specifically, it is the state of damnation in which personal beings experience a personal hell of condemnation and alienation. At death the unrighteous unbelieving are confirmed in wickedness. The inclination of their soul capacities remaining the same for all eternity—their faces turned away from God.

Haters: Relational Beings Who Hate Like Satan—Alienated and Violated Souls

Damned sinners, instead of being Romancers, are Haters. "Having lived enemies to God, they die in a state of enmity to Him" (Boston, *Human Nature in Its Fourfold State*, p. 345). They have disenfranchised themselves from Father's face. As a result, they are eternally alienated from God. Their abject misery, Boston hauntingly characterizes.

> They shall never more taste of His goodness and bounty, nor have the least glimpse of hope from Him. They will see His heart to be absolutely alienated from them, and that it cannot be towards them; that they are the party against whom the Lord will have indignation for ever. They shall be deprived of the glorious presence and enjoyment of God: they shall have no part in the beatific vision; nor see any thing in God towards them, but one wave of wrath rolling after another. This will bring upon them overwhelming floods of sorrow for evermore. They shall never taste of the rivers of pleasures which the saints in heaven enjoy; but shall have an

everlasting winter and a perpetual night, because the Sun of Righteousness has departed from them, and so they are left in utter darkness. So great as heaven's happiness is, so great will their loss be: for they can have none of it forever (Boston, *Human Nature in Its Fourfold State*, p. 477).

As Matthew 25:41 depicts: "Then shall he say also unto them on the left hand, 'Depart from me, ye cursed, into everlasting fire, prepared for the devil and his angels'" (KJV).

The aged apostle John calls them "idolaters" (Revelation 21:8). They've sold their souls to the False Seducer. False lovers consume and doom them. To their depraved minds, the Worthy Groom is altogether unworthy. Having divorced Him in this life, they remain spiritual adulterers throughout their eternal death.

Sinners seem to imagine that though they will spend eternity separated from God, they will enjoy one another's sinful companionship: hell's fraternity, evil's brotherhood, an unholy camaraderie. Billy Joel, in his suggestive song *Only the Good Die Young*, sings about and to Virginia (a symbolic name for a virgin Catholic teenage girl), attempting to seduce her into surrendering her virginity and purity. Mocking her moral perspective, he tells her that he'd rather laugh with the sinners than cry with the saints, because sinners are much more fun.

His message is clear. In this life and the life to come, purity never pays. In the life to come, sinners will join together in a grand party of debauchery, laughing and having a ball, while the saints up in heaven cry, dying of boredom.

We find the same message in ACDC's *Highway to Hell*. Again we hear lyrics glorifying the life of "livin' easy, lovin' freely." On the Highway to Hell, "my friends are gonna' be there too," so we're informed.

According to the song, sinners whose dues are paid by Satan, party forever together in a promised land. Meanwhile, up in heaven, saints, their dues perhaps paid by Christ, are bored forever, bereft of all laughter and fun. All this a satanic lie from the pit of hell.

The truth hurts. Haters of God, damned sinners, are "without love, unforgiving, slanderous, without self-control, brutal, not lovers of good, treacherous" (2 Timothy 3:3-4a). Hell is filled with "the cowardly, the unbelieving, the vile, the murderers, the sexually immoral, those who practice magic arts, the idolaters, and all liars" (Revelation 21:8). Outside heaven "are the dogs, those who practice magic arts, the sexually immoral, the murderers, the idolaters and everyone who loves and practices falsehood" (Revelation 22:15). Though we might picture sinners in hell jailed in a sort of solitary confinement, these verses seem to indicate that hellish sinners forever violate one another. Tormented personally, they torment one another eternally. Certainly, it will *not* be a party.

Liars: Rational Beings Who Have the Mind of Satan—Reprobate and Untrusting Minds

"Depraved nature," Boston explains, "acts in the regions of horror undisguised" (Boston, *Human Nature in Its Fourfold State*, p. 345). In hell, evil is squared, corruption cubed. "So their lusts grow up more and more towards perfection, if I may so speak. As in heaven grace comes to its perfection, so in hell sin arrives at its highest pitch" (Boston, *Human Nature in Its Fourfold State*, p. 474). Forever and ever, God gives them up to their own vile affections and reprobate minds (Romans 1:24, 26, 28), never improving, continuously worsening.

Hell is the abode of the "unbelieving" (Revelation 21:8). Forever they shake their fists at God. Endlessly they see Him as evil, denying their own wickedness. Eternally they cling to the lie that they do not need God, are not accountable to God, and are not culpable before God. Rather than existing as Dreamers, they subsist as Liars, believing and living the nightmarish lie that God is a shalt-not-God. Dark night after dark night they are the *apistois*—the unbelieving, the untrusting, the ones refusing to entrust their souls to Father's forgiveness, to Worthy Groom's love, to Messenger's comfort. The Lie shall hold them prisoner. Captivated by False Seducer, they are captive to his bewitchment.

Murderers: Volitional Beings Who Choose Their Own Will—Stubborn and Cowardly Wills

Rather than Creators, damned sinners are Murderers—heinous monsters and hideous beasts. Revelation 21:8 calls them vile, murderers, immoral. "Vile" (*bdelugma*) means to stink and brings to mind the stench of willfully chosen abominations. "Immoral" is *pornois* from which we glean our word "pornography."

In hell, Ephesians 4:19 becomes an incessant reality. "Having lost all sensitivity, they have given themselves over to sensuality so as to indulge in every kind of impurity, with a continual lust for more." The will can choose only according to its nature. The damned, corrupt nature stubbornly chooses perversion. As Revelation 22:11 explains, concerning their confirmation in corruption, "The one doing wrong, let him still do wrong; and the filthy one, let him still be filthy" (translation by Ralph Earle, *Word Meanings in the New Testament*, p. 473). "The wicked will continue to be wicked" (Daniel 12:10), in fact, their wickedness will grow more and more debased.

Interestingly, "cowardly" (*deilois*) heads the list of damned sinners' sin (Revelation 21:8). The adjective *deilois* means "fearful." In Matthew 8:26 and Mark 4:40, Jesus rebukes His fearful disciples, saying, "You of little faith, why are you so afraid?" (Matthew 8:26). "Why are you so afraid? Do you still have no faith?" (Mark 4:40). In 2 Timothy 1:7, Paul contrasts sincere faith with a spirit of timidity and being ashamed of the gospel.

Glorified saints are overcomers (Revelation 21:7). They are Creators who choose courageously, taking risks for God because they entrust themselves to God. Damned sinners are cowards (Revelation 21:8). They are Murderers and Destroyers who refuse to take risks for God because they do not entrust themselves to God. Their personal teleology revolves around self-protection, rather than ministry. Damned sinners become increasingly self-centered, increasingly dis-integrated, increasingly terrified, timid, faithless, untrusting, and ashamed. Throughout their incessant night of the living dead, their one goal is to avoid all harm. Yet in the meaninglessness and futility of hell, their one purpose is thwarted in perpetuity.

Agonizers: Emotional Beings Who Experience Pain Endlessly—Angry, Anxious, and Guilty Moods

Torment stalks every aspect of the inner being of the damned. Boston delineates first the overall agony of the damned, then the individual agony of each capacity.

As the soul was chief in sinning, it will be chief in suffering too, being filled quite full of the wrath of a sin-avenging God. The damned shall be ever under the deepest impressions of God's vindictive justice against them: and this fire will melt their souls within them, like wax (Boston, *Human Nature in Its Fourfold State*, p. 487).

Next he highlights their rational agony. "Their minds shall be filled with a terrible apprehension of God's implacable wrath: and whatever they can think upon, past, present, or to come, will aggravate their torment and anguish" (Boston, *Human Nature in Its Fourfold State*, pp. 487-488).

Then he exposes their corrupt will.

> Their will shall be crossed in all things for evermore; as their will was ever contrary to the will of God's precepts, so God, in His dealing with them in the other world, shall have war with their will for ever. . . . What they would have, they shall not in the least obtain: but what they would not, shall be bound upon them without remedy (Boston, *Human Nature in Its Fourfold State*, p. 488).

Their affections (soul, longings, passions, thirsts) also experience eternal agony.

> Hence, no pleasant affection shall ever spring up in their hearts any more; their love of complacency, joy, and delight, in any object whatever, shall be plucked up by the root, and they will be filled with hatred, fury, and rage against God, themselves, and their fellow-creatures, whether happy in heaven, or miserable in hell, as they themselves are (Boston, *Human Nature in Its Fourfold State*, p. 488).

Finally, their emotions are disordered.

> They will be sunk in sorrow, racked with anxiety, filled with horror, galled to the heart with fretting, and continually darted with despair: which will make them weep, gnash their teeth, and blaspheme for ever. . . . Conscience will be a worm to gnaw and prey upon them; remorse for their sins shall seize them and torment them for ever, and they shall not be able to shake it off, as once they did; for "in hell their worm dieth not" (Mark 9:44, 46). Their memory will serve but to aggravate their torment, and every new reflection will bring another pang of anguish (Luke 16:25) (Boston, *Human Nature in Its Fourfold State*, p. 488).

Damned sinners are emotional beings. Unlike glorified saints who are Singers, damned sinners are Agonizers. Ever tossed by anger, tormented by anxiety, and racked with guilt.

Prisoners: Physical Beings Who Endure Just Torment—Tortured and Suffering Bodies

During those rare moments when we dare think of hell, our minds tend to focus on the body—the physical torments of hell. We've just seen that the hellishness of hell involves soul torment. Nonetheless, we are also biblically accurate when we picture physical beings imprisoned in a real hell of physical punishment.

"The damned shall be punished in hell with the punishment of sense; they must depart from God into everlasting fire" (Boston, *Human Nature in Its Fourfold State*, p. 484). Whereas God represents to us heaven's happiness under the various notions of a treasure, a paradise, a feast, and a rest; hell's torments he describes for us as the second death

(Revelation 20:6), ever dying in the wine press of the wrath of God (Revelation 14:19), trampled in the Lord's fury, pressed, broken, and bruised without end (Isaiah 63:3), where the worm dies not, perpetually gnawing at them (Mark 9:44), a lake of fire burning with brimstone (Revelation 19:20; 20:10). Agony beyond imagining, Boston dares describe the fiery torments of hell.

> They will be in universal torments, every part of the creature being tormented in that flame. When one is cast into a fiery furnace, the fire makes its way into the very heart, and leaves no member untouched: what part, then, can have ease, when the damned swim in a lake of fire, burning with brimstone? There will their bodies be tormented and scorched for ever. And as they sinned, so shall they be tormented, in all parts thereof, that they shall have no sound side to turn them to; for what soundness or ease can be to any part of that body, which being separated from God, and all refreshment from Him, is still in the pangs of the second death, ever dying, but never dead? (Boston, *Human Nature in Its Fourfold State*, p. 487).

Ever dying, but never dead. I shudder at the thought. Hell is a prison from which damned sinners can never escape. A lake of fire where they will ever be drowning and burning. A pit where they will never find bottom. A darkness filled with blackness unimaginable. "They shall taste nothing but the sharpness of God's wrath, the dregs of the cup of His fury. The stench of the burning lake of brimstone will be the smell there; and they shall feel extreme pains for evermore" (Boston, *Human Nature in Its Fourfold State*, p. 489). No wonder hell is the place of weeping, wailing, and gnashing of teeth (Matthew 13:42; 22:13).

"Why tell us all of this? This is a book about soul care and spiritual direction, isn't it? We're maturing as soul physicians, right?" Physicians of the body must know the hideousness of lung cancer, if they are to warn passionately their patients to stop smoking. The misery and suffering of hell ought to embolden us to tell the truth to our *un*spiritual friends. Their coming damnation is just, yet avoidable, if they will repent and believe. Since all our psychological problems are ultimately spiritual problems, then soul physicians speak the truth in love to *fallen* image bearers.

"Here's my *diagnosis*. You're separated from God. You think of Him as unloving and unjust. You refuse to surrender to Him. Your guilt eats away at your soul. If you continue along this path, your soul will be eaten away non-stop."

"Here's my *treatment plan*. Return home to Father's heart. Repent and believe that He is altogether lovely, altogether holy, altogether worthy. Surrender to Him. He will cleanse your guilty conscience. Then your soul will be satisfied now. Then your soul will one day be satisfied forever."

The message of hell has implications for the heaven-bound, also. Just after rehearsing the future day of judgment and destruction of the ungodly (2 Peter 3:3-10), Peter speaks to his believing brothers and sisters. "Since everything will be destroyed in this way, what kind of people ought you to be?" (2 Peter 3:11a). He answers his rhetorical question for us. "You ought to live holy and godly lives" (2 Peter 3:11b). Since you will be citizens of heaven forever, live like it now.

Peter's discussion of the destiny of sinners causes him to ponder also the destiny of saints. "But in keeping with his promise we are looking forward to a new heaven and a new earth, the home of righteousness" (2 Peter 3:13). Heaven is our haven, our home. What difference should this make now? "So then, dear friends, since you are looking forward to this, make every effort to be found spotless, blameless and at peace with him" (2 Peter 3:14). The virgin bride wants to be prepared when she sees her groom. The returning prodigal son wants to be presentable when he sees his father. Heaven and hell are incitements toward holy living and loving relationships now.

Cohesion: The Integration—Eternal Rest (The Endless Harmony)

Every day we entice people either toward everlasting happiness or everlasting misery. "The wicked is driven away in his wickedness; but the righteous hath hope in his death" (Proverbs 14:32, KJV). God's children long for their eternal rest. God's enemies dread their eternal disquietude. Worthy Groom's bride longs for her consummate happiness. False Seducer's adulterous spouse fears perfect melancholy. Those who receive Inspired Messenger's inspired words will hear, "Come, ye blessed of my Father, inherit the kingdom prepared for you from the foundation of the world" (Matthew 25:34, KJV). Those who believe the lie of the father of lies will hear, "Depart from me, you who are cursed, into the eternal fire prepared for the devil and his angels" (Matthew 25:41).

The Saints' Everlasting Rest

"How should I then live?" This fourth relevant question requires revelatory truth. The believer answers this question confidently. "For all eternity I live in eternal rest. Endless harmony. Shalom. Peace. Unity. My destiny is harmony."

We'll rest forever *spiritually* in our relationship with Trinity. "Now this is eternal life: that they may know you, the only true God, and Jesus Christ" (John 17:3).

Various words describe our final spiritual destiny: bliss, satisfaction, rest, integration, cohesion, harmony, blessedness. For R. C. Sproul, blessedness is the biblical word that captures and crystallizes our final state. Blessedness "includes a wholistic satisfaction that touches the soul, the mind, the will, indeed the entire inner person. Beatitude is what we seek" (Sproul, *The Soul's Quest for God*, pp. 230-231). According to Sproul, the chief aspect of our final blessedness is the "beatific vision of the soul. The theological term for it is the *visio Dei*, the soul's vision of God" (Sproul, *The Soul's Quest for God*, p. 232).

David introduces us to this beatific vision. "And I—in righteousness I will see your face; when I awake, I will be satisfied with seeing your likeness" (Psalm 17:15). Christ promises it to us. "Blessed are the pure in heart: for they shall see God" (Matthew 5:8, KJV). John offers us the sure hope of this satisfying vision. "When he shall appear, we shall be like him; for we shall see him as he is" (1 John 3:2, KJV). Of this verse, Sproul explains:

> The church has customarily seen in this text a promise of the vision of the very essence of God. John says that we shall see him *as he is*. To see God as he is, is to perceive him in his pure, divine essence. The Vulgate translates this text, *in se est*. That is, we will behold the innermost *being* of God (Sproul, *The Soul's Quest for God*, p. 243).

Jonathan Edwards describes the sweetness of this majestic vision. "But to see God is this. It is to have an immediate, sensible, and certain understanding of God's glorious excellency and love" (Edwards, *The Works of Jonathan Edwards*, pp. 905-906). We will see Trinity's holy love, Trinity's goodness. "The understanding shall behold the glory and love of God, as a man beholds the countenance of a friend" (Edwards, *The Works of Jonathan Edwards*, p. 907).

Sproul portrays the eternal impact of face-to-face relationship with Trinity.

In the enjoyment of the beatific vision the soul finally reaches the goal of its supreme quest. At last we enter into that haven where we find our peace and rest. The end of restlessness is reached; the warfare between flesh and spirit ends. Peace that transcends anything in this world fills the heart. We reach the heights of excellency and sweetness only dreamed of in this mortal flesh. . . . The highest joy, the greatest pleasure, the purest delight will be ours without mixture and without end. One taste of this felicity will erase all painful memories and heal each dreadful wound incurred in this vale of tears. No scar will remain. The pilgrim's progress will be complete. The body of death, the burden of sin, will vaporize the moment we behold his face (Sproul, *The Soul's Quest for God*, p. 250).

Bliss without mixture and without end. Pure pleasure is our destiny.

"Heaven is a paradise for pleasure and delight" (Boston, *Human Nature in Its Fourfold State*, p. 444). Imagine it. Thirst for it. Hope patiently for it. Live in light of it.

We'll also rest forever *socially* in our mutual relationships. Community is our destiny. "The society of saints, among themselves, will be no small part of heaven's happiness" (Boston, *Human Nature in Its Fourfold State*, p. 446). One of the chief parts of heaven's happiness lies in the loving community we'll share with one another.

To the brothers and sisters at Thessalonica, who were scared to death of death, Paul said, "Therefore encourage one another with these words" (1 Thessalonians 4:18). We comfort each other with the truth that we will be caught up *together* in the clouds to meet the Lord in the air. And so we will *all* be with the Lord forever enjoying everlasting happiness *together*. Savoring our communal destiny.

And we'll rest forever as *self-aware* beings in our sense of self. Harmony is our destiny. Shalom. Peace. Cohesion. Integration. Wholeness. Personal tranquility. Being glorified, being like Him, we awake with His likeness, the perfection of God's image, and we are totally satisfied.

In our sense of self, complete happiness is our destiny. In heaven we find our completion, our satisfaction, our everlasting rest. Naked without shame. Complete. Comfortable. Confident. Content.

Finally, in our relationship to all of *creation*, we'll experience cohesion. Father reverses the curse, creates a new Eden, and frees creation itself from futility, decay, weeds, thorns, and thistles (Revelation 22:1-3; Romans 8:18-25). God perfects the physical universe, bringing it into glorious liberty and harmonious purpose.

In C. S. Lewis' *Chronicles of Narnia*, when Narnia was under the evil spell of the cruel White Witch, it was always winter, but never Christmas. In the new heaven and earth, it will always be Christmas and always Easter.

Our personal eschaton (goal, purpose, *telos* toward which we are moving) blends with the cosmic eschaton where God brings all things together in Christ, who is the integration point, and by whom all things cohere—find their unity and stability (Colossians 1:15-20). All creation participates in the unity and fullness of community.

The Sinners' Everlasting Misery

Boston's doctrine of hell says it succinctly. "The wicked shall be shut up under the curse of God, in everlasting misery, with the devils in hell" (Boston, *Human Nature in Its Fourfold State*, p. 472). Despair reigns because death makes the state of the wicked absolutely hopeless forever, for matters cannot be retrieved or amended after death. We are destined to die once, and then face judgment (Hebrews 9:27).

Dying in hopelessness, the damned awake to shame and everlasting contempt (Daniel 12:2). They will be naked and ashamed, filled with self-contempt, loathsome to one another, and filthy before the God with whom they have to deal. Totally imperfect, disgrace fills their soul, especially when they recall their refusal to receive Christ's grace. Hearing those dreaded words, "Depart, you cursed," they realize God cannot endure to look on them.

As a result, they sink to the depths of anguish. "As the saints in heaven are advanced to the highest pitch of happiness, so the damned in hell arrive at the height of misery" (Boston, *Human Nature in Its Fourfold State*, p. 476). Their greatest misery consists in experiencing God only in His just wrath.

> They cannot indeed be locally separated from God, they cannot be in a place where He is not; since He is, and will be present every where: "If I make my bed in hell," says the psalmist, "behold thou art there" (Psalm 139:8). But they shall be miserable beyond expression, in a relative separation from God. Though He will be present in the very centre of their souls, if I may so express it, while they are wrapped up in fiery flames, in utter darkness, it shall only be to feed them with the vinegar of His wrath, and to punish them with the emanations of His revenging justice (Boston, *Human Nature in Its Fourfold State*, pp. 476-477).

To understand fully the misery of the damned, we need to remind ourselves that God is the Chief Good. Therefore, to be separated from Him, must be the chief evil. God's being the Chief Good, and no good being comparable to Him, there can be no loss so great as the loss of God. The full enjoyment of Christ is the highest pinnacle of happiness we are capable of obtaining. So to be separated from Him fully is the lowest rung of misery to which we could be reduced. To be cast off by good men is distressing. What must it be then to be rejected by our good God? God is the Fountain of all goodness, from which all goodness flows to us. Separated from Him, whatever good or comfortable thing we could imagine is withdrawn from us: peace of mind, sweetness, rest, pleasure, delight, love, peace, hope, gentleness.

> Thus, in their separation from God, all peace is removed far away from them, and pain in body and anguish of soul, succeed to it: all joy goes, and unmixed sorrow settles in them: all quiet and rest separate from them, and they are filled with horror and rage: hope flies away, and despair seizes them (Boston, *Human Nature in Its Fourfold State*, p. 479).

We naturally desire the pursuit of happiness. Created to enjoy God, we find no true happiness apart from Him. This unmet longing of the soul will create an unspeakable anguish in the damned as they live under an eternal gnawing hunger for happiness. Boston believes (based upon Lazarus in Abraham's bosom and the rich man in hell) that the damned will know some are perfectly happy in God. This exquisite awareness of the happiness of the saints in heaven will aggravate the sense of their loss in hell. What torment for a hungry person to see others feasting! What agony to bring music and dancing before a person chained and tortured!

Now add to all this misery the realization that their loss is irrecoverable, irrevocable. If the damned, after millions of ages in hell, could regain what they had lost, it would be grounds for hope. But their fate is settled and never can be recovered. "And the smoke of their torments ascendeth up for ever and ever" (Revelation 14:11, KJV). The damned shall be eternal beings. Their well-being is eternally destroyed, but their being never destroyed. No intermission. No end. No hope. Total misery.

The Father's Infinite Mercy

To end here would be unfair to God. Even hell's horrors remind us of God's amazing grace. All that the damned experience, Christ experienced. "About the ninth hour Jesus cried out in a loud voice, '*Eloi, Eloi, lama sabachthani*?'—which means, 'My God, my God, why have you forsaken me?'" (Matthew 27:46). God so loved the world that He abandoned His only Son that whoever believes in Him should enjoy eternal life. Jesus so loved us that He became sin for us, that we might be the righteousness of God in and through Him. Jesus paid it all. All to Him we owe.

The Sojourner's Intimate Questions

Throughout our journey together, I've spoken of life as two versions of one story. As we've neared the end of our journey, Worthy Groom has painted portraits of the final chapter of our story. As Jonathan Edwards taught, "this life ought to be spent by us only as a journey towards heaven." Heaven is the larger way. Heaven is the final chapter—for believers—in Christ's larger story.

Based on how His bride's story ends, there are numerous questions that we need to be asking our counselees and ourselves. "Where is your story leading? To which end are you heading? Which final chapter are you building toward? What difference is the end of your story making in how you are living the beginning and middle of your story? Are you admitting that you are a stranger and alien on earth? Are you longing for a better home—your heavenly home? Are you living for earthly treasures, or are you looking ahead to eternal treasures—to God's rich rewards? What difference does the glory of heaven make when you face suffering today? What difference does the glory of heaven make when you combat sin now? How is your destiny of intimacy, ministry, purity, and harmony impacting your present life?"

Heaven is beyond comprehension, but heaven's implications are simple. We need to be so heavenly minded that we're of great earthly good. The end of our story must dictate how we progress through our story.

Where We've Been and Where We're Heading

Where have we been as we've journeyed together? We've been there and back again. We've time-traveled back before the beginning, eavesdropping on Trinity's community. We've journeyed back to Creation—Paradise. Then to Fall—Paradise lost. Then to Redemption—Paradise regained. And just now we've teleported into the future, viewing eternity through the eyes of the glorified and the damned.

Where are we headed? Where are *you* headed? Now it's time to journey. It's time to take academic, spiritual, historical, and practical theology and relate them to the lives of your spiritual friends. My prayer for you with *Soul Physicians* has been that you would know your way around the soul. My intention has been to provide relevant biblical categories for thinking about how to relate God's truth to people's lives. If you're sitting at the table over coffee with a spiritual friend and your mind starts thinking about how you can lovingly apply themes like affections, mindsets, purposes, and mood states, God has answered my prayer.

Journey on. Journey with the Divine Counselor who has made His home with you, in you (John 14:16-20). Journey knowing that *God is good.*

Caring for Your Soul: Personal Applications

1. In your final state of destiny, you will be a *Romancer*: A relational being who loves like Christ through worship and ministry.

    a. How far are you along this path? Where are you finding victory? Where do you need further growth?

    a. What are you doing now to cooperate with God's transformational process that will ultimately lead to your relational destiny?

2. In your final state of destiny, you will be a *Dreamer*: A rational being who has the mind of Christ—thinking creatively and purely.

    a. How far are you along this path? Where are you finding victory? Where do you need further growth?

    b. What are you doing now to cooperate with God's transformational process that will ultimately lead to your rational destiny?

3. In your final state of destiny, you will be a *Creator*: A volitional being who chooses God forever with freedom and purpose.

    a. How far are you along this path? Where are you finding victory? Where do you need further growth?

    b. What are you doing now to cooperate with God's transformational process that will ultimately lead to your volitional destiny?

4. In your final state of destiny, you will be a *Singer*: An emotional being who experiences happiness eternally with integration and celebration.

    a. How far are you along this path? Where are you finding victory? Where do you need further growth?

    b. What are you doing now to cooperate with God's transformational process that will ultimately lead to your emotional destiny?

Caring for Others: Ministry Implications

♦ **Explore Life's Deepest Questions with Your Spiritual Friends Using an Eternal Perspective:**

- Ask them the Communion Question: "Where Did You Come From?" Explore how their destiny of intimacy is influencing them today.

- Ask them the Dominion Question: "Why Are You Here?" Explore how their destiny of ministry is affecting them today.

- Ask them the Reflection Question: "Who Are You?" Explore how their destiny of purity is affecting them today.

- Ask them the Cohesion Question: "How Should You Then Live?" Explore how their destiny of harmony is influencing them today.

♦ **Explore Your Spiritual Friend's Current Maturity in Light of His or Her Future Relational, Rational, Volitional, and Emotional Destiny:**

- In your final state of destiny you will be a *Romancer*: A relational being who loves like Christ through worship and ministry. How far are you along this path? Where are you finding victory? Where do you need further growth? What are you doing now to cooperate with God's transformational process that will ultimately lead to your relational destiny?

- In your final state of destiny you will be a *Dreamer*: A rational being who has the mind of Christ—thinking creatively and purely. How far are you along this path? Where are you finding victory? Where do you need further growth? What are you doing now to cooperate with God's transformational process that will ultimately lead to your rational destiny?

- In your final state of destiny you will be a *Creator*: A volitional being who chooses God forever with freedom and purpose. How far are you along this path? Where are you finding victory? Where do you need further growth? What are you doing now to cooperate with God's transformational process that will ultimately lead to your volitional destiny?

- In your final state of destiny you will be a *Singer*: An emotional being who experiences happiness eternally with integration and celebration. How far are you along this path? Where are you finding victory? Where do you need further growth? What are you doing now to cooperate with God's transformational process that will ultimately lead to your emotional destiny?

BIBLIOGRAPHY

WORKS CITED AND CONSULTED

Adams, Jay. *The Christian Counselor's Manual*. Grand Rapids: Zondervan, 1973.

——. *Competent to Counsel*. Phillipsburg, NJ: Presbyterian & Reformed Publishing, 1970.

——. *How to Help People Change: The Four-Step Biblical Process*. Grand Rapids: Zondervan, 1988.

——. *More Than Redemption: A Theology of Christian Counseling*. Grand Rapids: Zondervan, 1979.

——. *Ready to Restore: The Layman's Guide to Christian Counseling*. Grand Rapids: Baker, 1981.

——. *The War Within: A Biblical Strategy for Spiritual Warfare*. Eugene, Ore.: Harvest House, 1989.

Aden, L. "Comfort/Sustaining." Pages 193-195 in *The Dictionary of Pastoral Care and Counseling*. Edited by R. J. Hunter. Nashville: Abingdon Press, 1990.

Akita, M. "A Study on Greek and Hebrew Thinking About Man." *Christianity and Culture* 1 (1964): 7-26.

Alexander, Donald, ed. *Christian Spirituality: Five Views of Sanctification*. Downers Grove, Ill.: InterVarsity, 1998.

Allen, Diogenes. *Philosophy for Understanding Theology*. Atlanta: John Knox Press, 1985.

——. *Spiritual Theology: The Theology of Yesterday for Spiritual Help Today*. Boston: Cowley, 1997.

Allender, Dan. *Bold Love*. Colorado Springs: NavPress, 1992.

——. *The Healing Path*. Colorado Springs: WaterBrook Press, 1999.

——. *The Wounded Heart: Hope for Adult Victims of Childhood Sexual Abuse*. Second edition. Colorado Springs: NavPress, 1996.

Allender, Dan, and Tremper Longman. *Bold Purpose*. Wheaton: Tyndale House, 1999.

——. *The Cry of the Soul: How Our Emotions Reveal Our Deepest Questions About God*. Colorado Springs: NavPress, 1994.

Almy, Gary. *How Christian Is Christian Counseling?* Wheaton: Crossway Books, 2000.

Alter, R. *The Art of Biblical Poetry*. London: Allan & Unwin, 1981.

Alter, R., and F. Kermode, eds. *The Literary Guide to the Bible*. London: Collins, 1987.

Althaus, Peter. *The Theology of Martin Luther*. Philadelphia: Fortress Press, 1966.

Amy, William, and James Recob. *Human Nature in the Christian Tradition*. Washington, D.C.: University Press of America, 1982.

Anderson, Neil. *The Bondage Breaker*. Eugene, Ore.: Harvest House, 1990.

———. *Freedom from Bondage*. Eugene, Ore.: Harvest House, 1990.

———. *Victory Over the Darkness: Realizing the Power of Your Identity in Christ*. Ventura, Calif.: Regal, 1990.

Anderson, Neil, and Robert Saucy. *God's Power at Work in You*. Revised edition of *The Common Made Holy*. Eugene, Ore.: Harvest House, 2001.

———. *The Common Made Holy*. Eugene, Ore.: Harvest House, 1997.

Anderson, Neil, Julianne Zuehlke, and Terry Zuehlke. *Christ-Centered Therapy: The Practical Integration of Theology and Psychology*. Grand Rapids: Zondervan, 2000.

Anderson, Ray. *On Being Human*. Grand Rapids: Eerdmans, 1982.

Anderson, William, and Richard Diesslin. *A Journey through Christian Theology: With Texts from the First to the Twenty-First Century*. Minneapolis: Fortress Press, 2000.

Arichea, Daniel. "Translating Breath and Spirit." *Bible Translator* 34, no. 2 (April 1983): 209-213.

Augustine. *The City of God*. New York: Modern Library, 2000.

———. *Confession*. Vol. 7 of *A Select Library of the Nicene and Post-Nicene Fathers of the Christian Church*. Second Series. Edited by H. Wace. New York: Christian Press, 1887.

Bailey, Kenneth. *The Cross and the Prodigal*. St. Louis: Concordia, 1973.

Bainton, Rolland. *Here I Stand: A Life of Martin Luther*. New York: Abingdon & Cokesbury Press, 1960.

Baker, Howard. *Soul Keeping: Ancient Paths of Spiritual Direction*. Colorado Springs: NavPress, 1998.

Baker, William. *In the Image of God: A Biblical View of Humanity*. Chicago: Moody Press, 1991.

Baptist Abstract of Principles. In *Creeds of the Churches*. Edited by John Leith. Richmond, Va.: John Knox Press, 1979.

Barnhouse, Donald. *Let Me Illustrate*. Old Tappan, N.J.: Revell, 1967.

Barry, W., and W. Connolly. *The Practice of Spiritual Direction*. New York: Seabury Press, 1982.

Bauer, Walter. *A Greek-English Lexicon of the New Testament and Other Early Christian Literature*. Second edition revised and augmented by F. Gingrich and F. Danker. Chicago: University of Chicago Press, 1979.

Baxter, Richard. *A Christian Directory*. Philadelphia: Soli Deo Gloria Publications, 1997.

———. *The Reformed Pastor*. Carlisle, Pa.: Banner of Truth Trust, 1999.

Becker, A. H. "Luther as *Seelsorger*: The Unexamined Role." Pages 136-150 in *Interpreting Luther's Legacy*. Edited by F. W. Meuser and S. D. Schneider. Minneapolis: Augsburg, 1969.

Beers, Mark, ed. *The Merck Manual of Diagnosis and Therapy*. 17th edition. Chicago: Merck, 2003.

Begalke, M. V. "An Introduction to Luther's Theology of Pastoral Care." Ph.D. Dissertation, University of Ottawa, 1980.

———. "Luther's *Anfechtungen*: An Important Clue to His Pastoral Theology." *Consensus* 8 (1982): 3-17.

Begley, Sharon. "A World of Their Own." *Newsweek* (May 8, 2000): 52-56.

Bilezikian, Gilbert. *Christianity 101: Your Guide to Eight Basic Christian Doctrines*. Grand Rapids: Zondervan, 1993.

———. *Community 101: Reclaiming the Local Church as Community of Oneness*. Grand Rapids: Zondervan, 1997.

Benjamin, Alfred. *The Helping Interview*. Third edition. Dallas: Houghton Mifflin, 1981.

Benner, David, ed. *Baker Encyclopedia of Psychology*. Grand Rapids: Baker, 1985.

———. *Care of Souls: Revisioning Christian Nurture and Counsel*. Grand Rapids: Baker, 1998.

———. *Psychotherapy and the Spiritual Quest*. Grand Rapids: Baker, 1988.

Berkhof, Hendrikus. *Christian Faith*. Grand Rapids: Eerdmans, 2002.

Berkouwer, G. C. *Man: The Image of God*. Grand Rapids: Eerdmans, 1962.

———. *Sin*. Translated by Philip Holtrop. Grand Rapids: Eerdmans, 1971.

Berman, J. S., and N. C. Norton. "Does Professional Training Make a Therapist More Effective?" *Psychology Bulletin* 98, no. 2 (1985): 401-407.

Bissler, Jane. "Counseling for Loss and Life Changes." www.counselingforloss.com. (Accessed March 1, 2006).

Blackaby, Henry, and Claude King. *Experiencing God*. Nashville: Broadman & Holman, 1994.

Blocher, Henri. *In the Beginning*. Translated by David Preston. Downers Grove, Ill.: InterVarsity, 1984.

———. *Original Sin: Illuminating the Riddle*. Grand Rapids: Eerdmans, 1997.

Bobgan, D. and M. Bobgan. *Prophets of Psychoheresy I*. Santa Barbara: Eastgate Publishing, 1989.

Boisen, A. *The Exploration of the Inner World*. San Francisco: Harper, 1937.

Bonar, Horatius. *God's Way of Holiness*. Ross-Shire, Scotland: Christian Focus Publications, 1996.

Boston, Thomas. *Human Nature in Its Four-Fold State*. Carlisle, Pa.: Banner of Truth Trust, 1720/1997.

Bratcher, Robert. "Biblical Words Describing Man: Breath, Life, Spirit." *Bible Translator* 34, no. 2 (April 1983): 201-209.

Briggs, C. A. "The Use of *npsh* in the Old Testament." *Journal of Biblical Literature* 16 (1900): 17-30.

Broger, John. *Self-Confrontation: A Manual for In-Depth Discipleship*. Nashville: Thomas Nelson, 1994.

Bromiley, Geoffrey, ed. *Theological Dictionary of the New Testament*. Abridged edition. Grand Rapids: Eerdmans, 1992.

Brooks, Thomas. *Precious Remedies Against Satan's Devices*. Carlisle, Pa.: Banner of Truth Trust, 1652/1997.

Brown, Francis, S. Driver, and C. Briggs. *The New Brown, Driver, and Briggs Hebrew and English Lexicon of the Old Testament*. Lafayette, Ind.: Associated Publishers, 1981.

Brueggemann, Walter. *Theology of the Old Testament*. Minneapolis: Fortress Press, 1997.

Brunner, Emil. *Man in Revolt: A Christian Anthropology*. Translated by Olive Wyon. Philadelphia: Westminster Press, 1947.

———. *The Mediator*. Translated by Olive Wyon. London: Westminster Press, 1947.

Bubek, Mark. *The Adversary: The Christian Versus Demon Activity*. Chicago: Moody Press, 1975.

———. *Overcoming the Adversary: Warfare Praying Against Demon Activity*. Chicago: Moody Press, 1984.

———. *The Satanic Revival*. San Bernardino, Calif.: Here's Life Publishers, 1991.

Bucer, Martin. *On the True Cure of Souls*. Translated by R. Johnson. Grand Rapids: Baker, 1538/1950.

Buechner, Frederick. *The Hungering Dark*. New York: Seabury Press, 1981.

———. *The Magnificent Defeat*. San Francisco: Harper, 1966.

———. *The Sacred Journey*. San Francisco: Harper, 1982.

———. *Telling the Truth: The Gospel as Tragedy, Comedy, and Fairy Tale*. San Francisco: Harper, 1977.

Bulkey, Ed. *Why Christians Can't Trust Psychology*. Eugene, Ore.: Harvest House, 1993.

Bunyan, John. *Grace Abounding to the Chief of Sinners*. Philadelphia: Bradley & Garretson, 1666/1872.

Burck, J. R. "Reconciliation." Pages 1047-1048 in *The Dictionary of Pastoral Care and Counseling*. Edited by R. J. Hunter. Nashville: Abingdon Press, 1990.

Burck, J. R., and R. J. Hunter. "Pastoral Theology: Protestant." Pages 867-872 in *The Dictionary of Pastoral Care and Counseling*. Edited by R. J. Hunter. Nashville: Abingdon Press, 1990.

Burke, Mary, and Judith Miranti, eds. *Counseling: The Spiritual Dimension*. Alexandria, Va.: American Counseling Association, 1995.

Burns, J. Patout, ed. *Theological Anthropology*. Philadelphia: Fortress Press, 1981.

Burroughs, Jeremiah. *Commentary on the Prophecy of Hosea*. Philadelphia: Soli Deo Gloria Publications, 1989.

Burton, Ernest De Witt. *Spirit, Soul, and Flesh*. Chicago: University of Chicago Press, 1918.

Burton, Robert. *The Anatomy of Melancholy*. Mineola, N.Y.: Dover Publications, 2002.

Butman, R. "Where's the Beef?: Evaluating Counseling Trends." *Christian Counseling Today* (October 1993): 20-24.

Calvin, John. *Catechism of the Church of Geneva*. Translated by Henry Beveridge. Ross-Shire, Scotland: Christian Focus Publications, 2003.

———. *Calvin's Commentaries*. 22 Vols. Grand Rapids: Eerdmans, 1981.

———. *Commentary on Ezekiel*. Grand Rapids: Eerdmans, 1994.

———. *Commentary on the First Book of Moses Called Genesis*. Wheaton: Crossway Books, 2001.

———. *Commentary on Hebrews*. Grand Rapids: Eerdmans, 1994.

———. *The Institutes of the Christian Religion*. Vols. 20-21 of *The Library of Christian Classics*. Edited by John T. McNeil. Translated by Ford Lewis Battles. London: Westminster Press, 1559/1960.

Carkhuff, Robert. *The Art of Helping*. Eighth edition. Np: Human Resource Development Press, 2001.

Carson, David. *How Long, O Lord? Reflections on Suffering and Evil*. Leicester, U.K.: InterVarsity, 1990.

Carter, Rita. *Mapping the Mind*. Berkeley, Calif.: University of California Press, 1999.

Catechism of the Evangelical Association, Question 295. In *Creeds of the Churches*. Edited by John Leith. Richmond, Va.: John Knox Press, 1979.

Chafer, Lewis. *He That Is Spiritual*. Grand Rapids: Zondervan, 1918.

Chambers, Oswald. *Biblical Psychology*. London: S. W. Partridge & Co., 1920.

———. *My Utmost for His Highest*. Grand Rapids: Discovery House, 1995.

Chan, Simon. *Spiritual Theology: A Systematic Study of the Christian Life*. Downers Grove, Ill.: InterVarsity, 1998.

Chandler, C. K., J. M. Holden, and C. A. Kolander. "Counseling for Spiritual Wellness: Theory and Practice." *Journal of Counseling and Development* 71 (1992): 168-175.

Charnock, Stephen. *The Existence and Attributes of God*. Grand Rapids: Baker, 1996.

Chesterton, G. K. *The Collected Works of G. K. Chesterton: The Everlasting Man*. Vol. 2 of *The Collected Works of G. K. Chesterton*. Ft. Collins, Colo.: Ignatius Press, 1986.

Ciarrocchi, Joseph. *The Doubting Disease: Help for Scrupulosity and Religious Compulsions*. New York: Paulist Press, 1995.

———. *A Minister's Handbook of Mental Disorders*. New York: Paulist Press, 1993.

Clebsch, William, and Charles Jaekle. *Pastoral Care in Historical Perspective*. New York: Harper, 1964.

Clines, D. *Job 1-20*. Dallas: Word Publishing, 1989.

Clinton, Timothy, and George Ohlschlager, eds. *Competent Christian Counseling*. Vol. 1 of *Foundations and Practice of Compassionate Soul Care*. Colorado Springs: WaterBrook Press, 2002.

Cloud, Henry, and John Townsend. *How People Grow: What the Bible Says About Personal Growth*. Grand Rapids: Zondervan, 2001.

Collins, Gary. *The Biblical Basis of Christian Counseling for People Helpers*. Colorado Springs: NavPress, 1993.

———. *Christian Counseling: A Comprehensive Guide*. Revised edition. Dallas: Word Publishing, 1998.

———. "Evangelical Pastoral Care." Pages 372-374 in *The Dictionary of Pastoral Care and Counseling*. Edited by R. J. Hunter. Nashville: Abingdon Press, 1990.

———. *How to Be a People Helper*. Revised edition. Wheaton: Tyndale House, 1995.

———. *The Soul Search: A Spiritual Journey to Authentic Intimacy with God*. Nashville: Thomas Nelson, 1998.

Collins, Gary, and Craig Ellison, eds. *From Stress to Well-Being: Contemporary Christian Counseling*. Eugene, Ore.: Wipf & Stock Publishers, 2003.

Colson, Charles. "The Atheist's God: The Real Madalyn Murray O'Hair." *Breakpoint*, June 17, 1999. www.pfmonline.net/transcripts.

———. *The Body: Being Light in Darkness*. Dallas: Word Publishing, 1992.

———. *Kingdoms in Conflict*. Grand Rapids: Zondervan, 1987.

Cooper, John. *Body and Soul and Life Everlasting: Biblical Anthropology and the Monism-Dualism Debate*. Grand Rapids: Eerdmans, 1989.

Crabb, Larry. *Connecting*. Nashville: Word Publishing, 1997.

———. *Finding God*. Grand Rapids: Zondervan, 1993.

———. *Inside Out*. Colorado Springs: NavPress, 1988.

————. *The Safest Place on Earth*. Nashville: Word Publishing, 1999.

————. *Shattered Dreams: God's Unexpected Pathway to Joy*. Colorado Springs: WaterBrook Press, 2001.

————. *Understanding People: Deep Longings for Relationships*. Grand Rapids: Zondervan, 1987.

Crabb, Larry, and Dan Allender. *Encouragement: The Key to Caring*. Grand Rapids: Zondervan, 1984.

Crenshaw, J. L. *A Whirlpool of Torment: Israelite Traditions of God as an Oppressive Presence*. Philadelphia: Fortress Press, 1984.

Crockett, William, J. Hayes, Clark Pinnock, and John Walvoord. *Four Views on Hell*. Grand Rapids: Zondervan, 1992.

Curtis, Brent, and John Eldredge. *The Sacred Romance*. Nashville: Thomas Nelson, 1997.

Curtis, Edward. "Image of God/OT." Pages 389-391 in *The Anchor Bible Dictionary*. New York: Doubleday, 1992.

Cusick, Michael. "A Conversation with Eugene Peterson." *Mars Hill Review* 3 (Fall 1995): 73-90.

Davies, Gaius. *Genius, Grief, and Grace*. Ross-Shire, Scotland: Christian Focus Publications, 1992.

Davison, R. *The Courage to Doubt: Exploring an Old Testament Theme*. London: SCM Press, 1983.

Day, P. L. *An Adversary in Heaven: Satan in the Hebrew*. Harvard Semitic Monographs 43, Cambridge, Mass.: Harvard University Press, 1988.

Delitzsch, Franz. *A System of Biblical Psychology*. Second edition. Translated by Robert Wallis. Eugene, Ore.: Wipf & Stock Publishers, 1861/2003.

Dever, Mark. *Richard Sibbes*. Macon, Ga.: Mercer University Press, 2000.

Dickason, Fred. *Angels: Elect and Evil*. Chicago: Moody Press, 1975.

Dickens, Charles. *A Christmas Carol*. New York: Bantam, 1986.

Dickson, William. *St. Paul's Use of the Terms Flesh and Spirit*. Glasgow: James MacLehose & Sons, 1883.

Didascalia Apostolorum. Translated by M. N. Dunlop. London: Cambridge University Press, c. 225/1903.

Donne, John. *Devotions*. New York: Vintage Books, 1999.

Durback, Robert. *Seeds of Hope: A Henri Nouwen Reader*. New York: Doubleday, 1997.

Durham, James. *Clavis Cantici*. Aberdeen: Robert King, 1840.

Durlak, J. "Comparative Effectiveness of Paraprofessional and Professional Helpers." *Psychological Bulletin* 86, no. 1 (1979); 80-92.

Earle, Ralph. *Word Meanings in the New Testament*. Peabody, Mass.: Hendricksen, 2000.

Edwards, Dwight. *Revolution Within*. Colorado Springs: WaterBrook Press, 2001.

Edwards, Gene. *The Beginning: The Chronicles of the Door*. Wheaton: Tyndale House, 1992.

————. *The Divine Romance*. Wheaton: Tyndale House, 1992.

Edwards, Jonathan. "The Christian Pilgrim." In *The Works of Jonathan Edwards*. 2 vols.

Revised by Edward Hackman. Peabody, Mass.: Hendricksen Publishing, 1998.

———. "The End for Which God Created the World." In *The Works of Jonathan Edwards*. 2 vols. Revised by Edward Hackman. Peabody, Mass.: Hendricksen Publishing, 1998.

———. *Freedom of the Will*. Philadelphia: Soli Deo Gloria Publications, 1998.

———. *Religious Affections: How Man's Will Affects His Character before God*. Portland, Ore.: Multnomah, 1984.

———. *The Works of Jonathan Edwards*. 2 vols. Revised by Edward Hackman. Peabody, Mass.: Hendricksen Publishing, 1998.

Edwards, Tilden. *Spiritual Friend: Reclaiming the Gift of Spiritual Direction*. New York: Paulist Press, 1980.

Egan, Gerald. *The Skilled Helper: A Problem Management Approach to Helping*. Sixth edition. Pacific Grove, Calif.: Brooks & Cole, 1998.

Eichrodt, Walther. *Ezekiel: A Commentary*. Louisville: Westminster John Knox Press, 1996.

Eldredge, John. *Dare to Desire: An Invitation to Fulfill Your Deepest Dreams*. Nashville: Thomas Nelson, 2002.

———. *The Journey of Desire: Searching for the Life We've Only Dreamed Of*. Nashville: Thomas Nelson, 2000.

———. *Wild at Heart: Discovering the Secret of a Man's Soul*. Nashville: Thomas Nelson, 2001.

Engles, Dennis, and Joseph Dameron, eds. *The Professional Counselor: Competencies, Performance Guidelines, and Assessment*. Alexandria, Va.: American Counseling Association, 1993.

Erickson, Millard. *Christian Theology*. Grand Rapids: Baker, 1998.

———. *Man's Need and God's Gift: Readings in Christian Theology*. Grand Rapids: Baker, 1975.

Evans, Tony. *Free at Last*. Chicago: Moody Press, 2001.

Eyrich, Howard, and William Hines. *Curing the Heart: A Model for Biblical Counseling*. Ross-Shire, Scotland: Christian Focus Publications, 2002.

Fairbairn, Patrick. *A Commentary on Ezekiel*. Harrisburg, Pa.: Sovereign Grace Truth Trust, 2001.

Ferguson, Sinclair. "The Reformed View." In *Christian Spirituality*. Edited by Donald L. Alexander. Downers Grove, Ill.: InterVarsity, 1998.

Fichtner, Joseph. *Theological Anthropology*. South Bend, Ind.: University of Notre Dame Press, 1963.

Fitzpatrick, Elyse. *Idols of the Heart: Learning to Long for God Alone*. Phillipsburg, N.J.: Presbyterian & Reformed Publishing, 2001.

Flathers, Douglas. *The Resource Guide for Christian Counselors*. Grand Rapids: Baker, 1995.

Flynn, Leslie. *Man: Ruined and Restored*. Wheaton: Victor Books, 1978.

Ford, Leighton. *The Power of Story*. Colorado Springs: NavPress, 1994.

Forde, Gerhard. "The Lutheran View." In *Christian Spirituality*. Edited by Donald Alexander. Downers Grove, Ill.: InterVarsity, 1988.

Formula of Concord, III-VI. In *Creeds of Christendom*. Vol. 3. Edited by Phillip Schaff. New York: Harper, 1919.

Forsyth, P. T. *The Cruciality of the Cross*. London: Hodder and Stoughton, 1918.

Foster, Richard. *Celebration of Discipline: The Path to Spiritual Growth*. Revised edition. San Francisco: Harper, 1998.

———. *The Challenge of the Disciplined Life*. San Francisco: Harper, 1985.

———. *Streams of Living Water: Celebrating the Great Traditions of the Christian Faith*. San Francisco: Harper, 1998.

Foster, Richard, and Emile Griffin, eds. *Spiritual Classics*. San Francisco: Harper, 2000.

Foster, Richard, and James Smith, eds. *Devotional Classics*. San Francisco: Harper, 1993.

Frame, M. W., and C. B. Williams. "Counseling African-Americans: Integrating Spirituality in Therapy." *Counseling and Values* 41, no. 1 (1991): 27-45.

Fyall, Robert. *Now My Eyes Have Seen You: Images of Creation and Evil in the Book of Job*. Downers Grove, Ill.: InterVarsity, 2002.

Gaebelein, A. C. *The Angels of God*. Grand Rapids: Baker, 1969.

Ganz, Richard. *PsychoBabble: The Failure of Modern Psychology and the Biblical Alternative*. Wheaton: Crossway Books, 1993.

Gardner, Howard. *Intelligence Reframed: Multiple Intelligences for the 21st Century*. New York: Basic Books, 1999.

George, Timothy. *Is the Father of Jesus the God of Muhammad?* Grand Rapids: Zondervan, 2002.

———. *Theology of the Reformers*. Nashville: Broadman & Holman, 1988.

Gerstner, John. *The Rational Biblical Theology of Jonathan Edwards*. Orlando: Ligonier Ministries, 1992.

Gibson, J. C. "The Book of Job and the Cure of Souls." *Scottish Journal of Theology* 42 (1990): 303-317.

Gilbert, Marvin, and Raymond Brock, eds. *Principles and Practices*. Vol. 2 of *The Holy Spirit and Counseling*. Peabody, Mass.: Hendricksen, 1988.

———. *Theology and Theory*. Vol. 1 of *The Holy Spirit and Counseling*. Peabody, Mass.: Hendricksen, 1985.

Gilligan, S., and R. Reese, eds. *Therapeutic Conversations*. New York: W. W. Norton, 1993.

Gire, Ken. *Reflections on the Movies: Hearing God in the Unlikeliest of Places*. Colorado Springs: Victor Books, 2000.

———. *Windows of the Soul*. Grand Rapids: Zondervan, 1996.

Goleman, Daniel. *Emotional Intelligence*. New York: Bantam, 1997.

———. *Vital Lies: The Psychology of Self-Deception*. New York: Simon & Schuster, 1985.

———. *Working with Emotional Intelligence*. New York: Bantam, 1998.

Goleman, Daniel, Richard Boyatzis, and Annie McKee. *Primal Leadership: Realizing the Power of Emotional Intelligence*. Boston: Harvard Business School Press, 2002.

Goodwin, Thomas. *Works*. Philadelphia: Sovereign Grace Truth Trust, 2000.

Graham, L. K. "Healing." Pages 497-501 in *The Dictionary of Pastoral Care and Counseling*. Edited by R. J. Hunter. Nashville: Abingdon Press, 1990.

Grant, Reginald. *Dallas Theological Seminary Newsletter*. July, 1999.

Grenz, Stanley. *A Primer on Postmodernism*. Grand Rapids: Eerdmans, 1996.

———. *The Social God and the Relational Self: A Trinitarian Theology of the Imago Dei.* Louisville: John Knox Press, 2001.

———. *Theology for the Community of God.* Grand Rapids: Eerdmans, 1994.

Grenz, Stanley, and John Franke. *Beyond Foundationalism.* Louisville: John Knox Press, 2001.

Grudem, Wayne. *Systematic Theology: An Introduction to Biblical Doctrine.* Grand Rapids: Zondervan, 1994.

Guenther, Margaret. *Holy Listening: The Art of Spiritual Direction.* Boston: Cowley, 1992.

Gurnall, William. *The Christian in Complete Armour.* 3 vols. Carlisle, PA: Banner of Truth Trust, 1655/1996.

Guthrie, Nancy. *Holding onto Hope: A Pathway Through Suffering to the Heart of God.* Wheaton: Tyndale House, 2002.

Habermas, G. R. "A House Divided?" *Christian Counseling Today* (October 1993): 32-35.

Hackney, Harold, ed. *Changing Context for Counselor Preparation in the 1990s.* Alexandria, Va.: American Counseling Association, 1990.

Harris, Laird. *Man: God's Eternal Creation.* Chicago: Moody Press, 1971.

Harris, Laird, Gleason Archer, and Bruce Waltke, eds. *Theological Wordbook of the Old Testament.* 2 vols. Chicago: Moody Press, 1981.

Hart, Archibald. *The Anxiety Cure: You Can Find Emotional Tranquility and Wholeness.* Nashville: Word Publishing, 1999.

Hart, Archibald, Gary Gulbranson, and Jim Smith, eds. *Mastering Pastoral Counseling.* Portland, Ore.: Multnomah, 1992.

Hartley, J. E. *The Book of Job.* Grand Rapids: Eerdmans, 1988.

Hattie, J. A., H. J. Rogers, and C. F. Sharpley. "Comparative Effectiveness of Professional and Paraprofessional Helpers." *Psychological Bulletin* 95, no. 3 (1984): 534-541.

Hays, Daniel. *From Every People and Nation: A Biblical Theology of Race.* Downers Grove, Ill.: InterVarsity, 2003.

Heeren, Fred. *Show Me God: What the Message from Space Is Telling Us About God.* Olathe, Kan.: Day Star Productions, 1997.

Hein, Rolland. *The Heart of George MacDonald.* Colorado Springs: Shaw Books, 2000.

Hendricks, Howard, and William Hendricks. *Living by the Book.* Chicago: Moody Press, 1991.

Henry, Carl. *God, Revelation, and Authority.* 5 vols. Waco, Texas: Word Publishing, 1983.

———. *God Who Stands and Stays.* Vol. 5 of *God, Revelation and Authority.* Waco, Texas: Word Publishing, 1983.

Herman, Keith. "Reassessing Predictors of Therapist Competence." *Journal of Counseling and Development* 72 (September/October 1993): 29-32.

Hiltner, Seward. *Preface to Pastoral Theology.* New York: Abingdon Press, 1954.

Hindson, Edward, ed. *Introduction to Puritan Theology.* Grand Rapids: Baker, 1991.

Hindson, Edward, and Howard Eyrich. *Totally Sufficient.* Grand Rapids: Baker, 1997.

Hodge, Charles. *Systematic Theology.* 3 vols. Grand Rapids: Hendrickson, 2003.

———. *The Way of Life.* Ann Arbor, Mich.: Banner of Truth Trust, 1996.

Hoekema, Anthony. *Created in God's Image*. Grand Rapids: Eerdmans, 1994.

Holifield, E. Brooks. *A History of Pastoral Care in America: From Salvation to Self-Realization*. Nashville: Abingdon Press, 1983.

Holloman, Henry. *The Forgotten Blessing*. Nashville: Word Publishing, 1999.

Hubbard, Albert. *Little Journeys to the Homes of Great Scientists*. Np: Kissinger Publishing, 1998.

Huggins, Kevin. *Friendship Counseling*. Colorado Springs: NavPress, 2003.

Hughes, Philip. *The True Image: The Origin and Destiny of Man in Christ*. Grand Rapids: Eerdmans, 1989.

Hughes, R. Kent. *Hebrews*. 2 vols. Wheaton: Crossway Books, 1992.

Hulme, William. *Pastoral Care and Counseling: Using the Unique Resources of the Christian Tradition*. Minneapolis: Augsburg, 1981.

Hunter, Rodney, ed. *The Dictionary of Pastoral Care and Counseling*. Nashville: Abingdon Press, 1990.

Hurnard, Hannah. *Hinds' Feet on High Places*. Wheaton: Tyndale House, 1975.

Ice, Thomas, and Robert Dean. *A Holy Rebellion: Strategies for Spiritual Warfare*. Eugene, Ore.: Wipf & Stock Publishers, 1999.

Ivarsson, H. "The Principles of Pastoral Care According to Martin Luther." *Pastoral Psychology* 13 (February 1962): 19-25.

Jackson, Stanley. *Melancholia and Depression: From Hippocratic Times to Modern Times*. New York: Yale University Press, 1990.

Jamison, K. *Touched with Fire: Manic Depressive Illness and the Artistic Temperament*. New York: Free Press, 1993.

————. *An Unquiet Mind: A Memoir of Moods and Madness*. London: Picador, 1995.

Jeeves, Malcolm. *Human Nature at the Millennium*. Grand Rapids: Baker, 1997.

Jeffrey, Grant. *Prince of Darkness*. Toronto: Frontier Research Publications, 1994.

Jewett, Robert. *Paul's Anthropological Terms: A Study of Their Use in Conflict Settings*. Louisville: John Knox Press, 1979.

John of the Cross. *Dark Night of the Soul*. Edited and translated by Allison Peers. New York: Doubleday, 1990.

Johnson, Aubrey R. *The Vitality of the Individual in the Thought of Ancient Israel*. Cardiff: University of Wales Press, 1964.

Johnson, Eric, and Stanton Jones, eds. *Psychology and Christianity: Four Views*. Downers Grove, Ill.: InterVarsity, 2000.

Johnson, Samuel Lewis. "A Survey of Biblical Psychology in the Epistle to the Romans." Th.D. Dissertation, Dallas Theological Seminary, 1945.

Jones, Alan. *Exploring Spiritual Direction: Essay on Christian Friendship*. San Francisco: Harper, 1982.

————. "Spiritual Direction and Pastoral Care." Pages 1213-1215 in *The Dictionary of Pastoral Care and Counseling*. Edited by R. J. Hunter. Nashville: Abingdon Press, 1990.

Jones, Cheslyn, ed. *The Study of Spirituality*. New York: Oxford University Press, 1986.

Jones, Stanton, and Richard Butman, eds. *Modern Psychotherapies: A Comprehensive Christian Appraisal*. Downers Grove, IL: InterVarsity, 1991.

Kahn, Roger. *The Boys of Summer*. San Francisco: Harper, 1971.

Kaiser, Walter. *Toward an Exegetical Theology*. Grand Rapids: Baker, 1981.

Kaiser, Walter, and Moises Silva. *An Introduction to Biblical Hermeneutics*. Grand Rapids: Zondervan, 1994.

Kellemen, Robert. "Hebrew Anthropological Terms as a Foundation for a Biblical Counseling Model of Humanity." Master's Thesis, Grace Theological Seminary, 1985.

———. "Our Forgiving Father's Heartbeat." In *A Century to Remember*. Edited by Homer A. Heater. Victoria, B.C.: Trafford, 2004.

———. "Spiritual Care in Historical Perspective: Martin Luther as a Case Study in Christian Sustaining, Healing, Reconciling, and Guiding." Ph.D. Dissertation, Kent State University, 1997.

———. *Spiritual Friends: A Methodology of Soul Care and Spiritual Direction*. Reprint Edition. Winona Lake, Ind.: BMH Books, 2007.

Keller, Timothy. "Puritan Resources for Pastoral Counseling." *Journal of Pastoral Practice* 9, no. 3 (1988): 11-44.

Kelly, Eugene W. *Spirituality and Religion in Counseling and Psychotherapy*. Alexandria, Va.: American Counseling Association, 1995.

Kemp, Charles. *Physicians of the Soul*. New York: MacMillan, 1947.

Kierkegaard, Soren. *Parables of Kierkegaard*. Edited by Thomas Oden. Reprint edition. Princeton: Princeton University Press, 1989.

Kolb, R. "God Calling: 'Take Care of My People': Luther's Concept of Vocation in the Augsburg Confession and Its Apology." *Concordia Journal* 8 (1982): 4-11.

———. "Luther: The Master Pastor." *Concordia Journal* 9 (1983): 179-187.

———. "Luther as *Seelsorger*." *Concordia Journal* 11 (1985): 2-9.

Kottler, Jeffrey. *The Complete Therapist*. San Francisco: Jossey Bass, 1991.

———. *On Being a Therapist*. San Francisco: Jossey Bass, 1993.

Kraus, G. "Luther as *Seelsorger*." *Concordia Theological Journal* 98 (1984): 153-163.

Kreeft, Peter. *The God Who Loves You*. Ann Arbor, Mich.: Servant Publications, 1992.

———. *Heaven: The Heart's Deepest Longing*. Baltimore: Ignatius Press, 1989.

———. *Love Is Stronger Than Death*. San Francisco: Harper, 1979.

Kubler-Ross, Elisabeth. *On Death and Dying*. Reprint edition. San Francisco: Scribner, 1997.

Laidlow, John. *The Bible Doctrine of Man*. Edinburgh: T&T Clark, 1985.

Lake, Frank. *Clinical Theology*. London: Darton, Longman & Todd, 1966.

Lane, G. *Christian Spirituality: An Historical Sketch*. Chicago: Loyola University Press, 1984.

Langberg, Diane. *On the Threshold of Hope*. Wheaton, IL: Tyndale House, 1999.

Laurin, R. "Concept of Man as Soul." *Expository Times* 72 (February 1961): 131-134.

LeDoux, J. *The Emotional Brain: The Mysterious Underpinnings of Emotional Life*. London: Weidenfeld & Nicolson, 1998.

Leech, Kenneth. *Experiencing God: Theology as Spirituality*. San Francisco: Harper, 1985.

———. *Soul Friend: The Practice of Christian Spirituality*. San Francisco: Harper, 1977.

Levicoff, Steve. *Christian Counseling and the Law*. Chicago: Moody Press, 1991.

Lewis, C. S. *The Chronicles of Narnia*. New York: Collier Books, 1956.

———. *The Four Loves*. New York: Harcourt, Brace & Co., 1960.

———. *The Great Divorce*. Nashville: Broadman & Holman, 1946.

———. *Mere Christianity*. New York: MacMillan, 1943.

———. *The Problem of Pain*. New York: Simon & Schuster, 1962.

———. *The Screwtape Letters*. San Francisco: Harper, 2001.

———. *The Weight of Glory*. San Francisco: Harper, 2001.

Lewis, Jack. "*yāda*." Pages 366-368 in vol. 1 of *Theological Wordbook of the Old Testament*. Edited by Laird Harris, Gleason Archer, and Bruce Waltke. 2 vols. Chicago: Moody Press, 1981.

Lloyd-Jones, D. Martin. *Spiritual Depression: Its Causes and Cures*. Grand Rapids: Eerdmans, 1965.

Lovelace, Richard F. *Dynamics of Spiritual Life*. Downers Grove, IL: InterVarsity, 1979.

Loyola, Ignatius. *Spiritual Exercises*. Translated by A. Mottola. New York: Doubleday, 1964.

Lundgaard, Kris. *The Enemy Within*. Phillipsburg, N.J.: Presbyterian & Reformed Publishing, 1998.

Luther, Martin. *The Bondage of the Will*. Translated by O. R. Johnston and J. I. Packer. Grand Rapids: Revell, 1525/1957.

———. *Career of the Reformer I*. Vol. 31 of *Luther's Works*. Edited and translated by H. T. Lehmann. Philadelphia: Fortress Press, 1957.

———. *Career of the Reformer II*. Vol. 32 of *Luther's Works*. Edited and translated by G. W. Forell. Philadelphia: Fortress Press, 1958.

———. *Commentary on Galatians*. Translated by P. S. Watson. Grand Rapids: Revell, 1535/1988.

———. *Commentary on Romans*. Translated by J. T. Mueller. Grand Rapids: Kregel, 1516/1947.

———. *Devotional Writings I*. Vol. 42 of *Luther's Works*. Edited and translated by M. O. Deitrich. Philadelphia: Fortress Press, 1969.

———. *Devotional Writings II*. Vol. 43 of *Luther's Works*. Edited and translated by G. Wiencke. Philadelphia: Fortress Press, 1968.

———. *The Holy and Blessed Sacrament of Baptism*. Vol. 35 of *Luther's Works*. Edited by A. Wents. Translated by A. Steinhauser. Philadelphia: Fortress Press, 1959.

———. *Large Catechism*. Translated by Robert Fischer. Philadelphia: Fortress Press, 1981.

———. *Lectures on Genesis Chapters 6-14*. Vol. 2 of *Luther's Works*. Edited by J. Pelikan. Translated by V. Schick. Saint Louis: Concordia, 1960.

———. *Lectures on Genesis: Chapters 21-25*. Vol. 4 of *Luther's Works*. Edited by J. Pelikan and W. Hansen. Translated by G. Schick. Saint Louis: Concordia, 1964.

———. *Lectures on Isaiah: Chapters 1-39*. Vol. 16 of *Luther's Works*. Edited by J. Pelikan and H. Oswald. Translated by H. Bouman. Saint Louis: Concordia, 1970.

———. *Letters I*. Vol. 48 of *Luther's Works*. Edited and translated by G. G. Krodel. Philadelphia: Fortress Press, 1963.

———. *Letters II*. Vol. 49 of *Luther's Works*. Edited and translated by G. Krodel. Philadelphia: Fortress Press, 1972.

———. *Letters III*. Vol. 50 of *Luther's Works*. Edited and translated by G. Krodel. Philadelphia: Fortress Press, 1975.

———. "Sermon on John 18:28." In *What Luther Says*. 3 vols. Edited by E. Plass. St. Louis: Concordia, 1959.

———. *The Sermon on the Mount*. Vol. 21 of *Luther's Works*. St. Louis: Concordia, 1953.

———. *Table Talks*. Vol. 54 of *Luther's Works*. Edited and translated by G. Tappert. Philadelphia: Fortress Press, 1967.

MacArthur, John, and Wayne Mack, eds. *Introduction to Biblical Counseling: A Basic Guide to the Principles and Practice of Counseling*. Dallas: Word Publishing, 1994.

Machen, J. Gresham. *The Christian View of Man*. Grand Rapids: Eerdmans, 1947.

Manchester, William. *A World Lit Only by Fire*. New York: Little, Brown & Co., 1993.

Manning, Brennan. *A Glimpse of Jesus: Stranger to Self-Hatred*. San Francisco: Harper, 2003.

———. *Lion and the Lamb: The Relentless Tenderness of Jesus*. Grand Rapids: Baker, 1986.

———. *The Ragamuffin Gospel: Embracing the Unconditional Love of God*. Sisters, Ore.: Multnomah, 1990.

———. *Ruthless Trust: The Ragamuffin's Path to God*. San Francisco: Harper, 2000.

———. *The Wisdom of Tenderness*. San Francisco: Harper, 2002.

Marius, Richard. *Martin Luther: The Christian Between God and the Devil*. Cambridge: Harvard University Press, 1999.

Marshall, I. H. *The Work of Christ*. Oxford: Paternoster Press, 1969.

Matzat, Don. *Christ Esteem: Where the Search for Self-Esteem Ends*. Eugene, Ore.: Harvest House, 1990.

Mayhue, Richard. *Unmasking Satan*. Wheaton: Victor Books, 1988.

McClain, Alva. *The Greatness of the Kingdom*. Winona Lake, IN: BMH Books, 2005.

McGrath, Alister. *Christian Spirituality*. Malden, Mass.: Blackwell, 1999.

———. *Christian Theology: An Introduction*. London: Blackwell, 2000.

———. *Historical Theology: An Introduction to the History of Christian Thought*. London: Blackwell, 1998.

———. *The Journey: A Pilgrim in the Lands of the Spirit*. New York: Doubleday, 2000.

———. *Luther's Theology of the Cross*. Grand Rapids: Baker, 1990.

McMinn, Mark. *Psychology, Theology, and Spirituality in Christian Counseling*. Wheaton: Tyndale House, 1996.

McMinn, Mark, and Timothy Phillips. *Care for the Soul: Exploring the Intersection of Psychology and Theology*. Downers Grove, Ill.: InterVarsity, 2001.

McNeil, John. *A History of the Cure of Souls*. New York: Harper, 1951.

Medical Economics Staff, eds. *The Physician's Desk Reference*. Boston: Medical Economics, 2002.

Meiburg, A. "Care of Souls." Page 122 in *The Dictionary of Pastoral Care and Counseling*. Edited by R. J. Hunter. Nashville: Abingdon Press, 1990.

Meyers, Jan. *The Allure of Hope*. Colorado Springs: NavPress, 2001.

Miles, Jack. *God: A Biography*. New York: Vintage Books, 1995.

Miller, Calvin. *Disarming the Darkness: A Guide to Spiritual Warfare*. Grand Rapids: Zondervan, 1998.

———. *Into the Depths of God*. Minneapolis: Bethany House, 2000.

Mills, L. "Pastoral Care: History." Pages 836-844 in *The Dictionary of Pastoral Care and Counseling*. Edited by R. J. Hunter. Nashville: Abingdon Press, 1990.

Milton, John. *Paradise Lost*. Edited by Merritt Hughes. New York: Odyssey Press, 1674/1962.

Moltmann, Jurgen. *The Crucified God*. Minneapolis: Fortress Press, 1993.

Moon, Gary. "Spiritual Directors and Christian Counselors: Where Do They Overlap?" *Christian Counseling Today*. (Winter 1994): 29-33.

Moon, Gary, and David Benner. *Spiritual Direction and the Care of Souls*. Downers Grove, Ill.: InterVarsity, 2004.

Morris, Leon. *The Atonement: Its Meaning and Significance*. Downers Grove, Ill.: InterVarsity, 1983.

———. *The Epistle to the Romans*. Grand Rapids: Eerdmans, 1988.

Morris, John. *The Gospel According to John*. Grand Rapids: Eerdmans, 1964.

Muller, R. "Soul." Pages 1201-1203 in *The Dictionary of Pastoral Care and Counseling*. Edited by R. J. Hunter. Nashville: Abingdon Press, 1990.

Murray, Andrew. *The Two Covenants*. Fort Washington, Pa.: Christian Literature Crusade, 1898.

Murray, John. *Epistle to the Romans*. Grand Rapids: Eerdmans, 1980.

———. "Glorification." In *Redemption Accomplished and Applied*. Grand Rapids: Eerdmans, 1961.

———. *Principles of Conduct*. Grand Rapids: Eerdmans, 1957.

Nazianzen, Gregory. *Oration*. In *A Select Library of the Nicene and Post-Nicene Fathers*. Edited by Philip Schaff. Grand Rapids: Eerdmans, 1989.

Nebe, A. *Luther as Spiritual Advisor*. Translated by C. H. Hays and C. E. Hays. Philadelphia: Lutheran Publication Society, 1894.

Needham, David. *Birthright: Christian, Do You Know Who You Are?* Sisters, Ore.: Multnomah, 1979.

———. *Birthright: Christian, Do You Know Who You Are?* Revised edition. Sisters, Ore.: Multnomah, 1999.

Nouwen, Henri. *The Return of the Prodigal: A Story of Homecoming*. New York: Doubleday, 1992.

———. *The Wounded Healer*. New York: Doubleday, 1972.

Nussbaum, Martha. *The Therapy of Desire: Theory and Practice in Hellenistic Ethics*. Princeton: Princeton University Press, 1994.

Oates, Wayne. *The Presence of God in Pastoral Counseling*. Waco, TX: Word Publishing, 1986.

———. *Protestant Pastoral Care*. Louisville: Westminster John Knox Press, 1982.

Oberman, Heiko. *Luther: Man Between God and the Devil*. New York: Doubleday, 1992.

Oden, Thomas C. *Care of Souls in the Classic Tradition*. Philadelphia: Fortress Press, 1983.

———. *Classical Pastoral Care*. 4 Vols. Grand Rapids: Baker, 1987.

———. *Life in the Spirit*. Vol. 3 of *Systematic Theology*. San Francisco: Harper, 2001.

———. *The Living God*. Vol. 1 of *Systematic Theology*. San Francisco: Harper, 2001.

———. *Pastoral Theology*. San Francisco: Harper, 1983.

———. "Whatever Happened to History?" *Good News* (January-February 1993): 8-10.

———. *The Word of Life*. Vol. 2 of *Systematic Theology*. San Francisco: Harper, 2001.

Odom, Stuart. "Soteriology." Class Notes, Capital Bible Seminary, Lanham, Md., 2003.

O'Hanlon, William, and Michele Weiner-Davis. *In Search of Solutions: A New Direction in Psychotherapy*. New York: W. W. Norton, 1989.

Olson, Roger. *The Story of Christian Theology*. Downers Grove, Ill.: InterVarsity, 1999.

Ortlund, Raymond C., Jr. *Whoredom: God's Unfaithful Wife in Biblical Theology*. Grand Rapids: Eerdmans, 1996.

Osborne, Grant. *The Hermeneutical Spiral: A Comprehensive Introduction to Biblical Interpretation*. Downers Grove, Ill.: InterVarsity, 1991.

Oswalt, John. "*kun*." Pages 432-434 in vol. 1 of *Theological Wordbook of the Old Testament*. Edited by Laird Harris, Gleason Archer, and Bruce Waltke. 2 vols. Chicago: Moody Press, 1981.

Owen, John. *The Death of Death*. London: Banner of Truth Trust, 1963.

———. *The Mortification of Sin*. Ross-Shire, Scotland: Christian Focus Publications, 1656/1996.

———. *Sin and Temptation*. Minneapolis: Bethany House, 1658/1996.

———. *Temptation and Sin*. Evansville, Ind.: Sovereign Book Club, 1658/1958.

Packer, J. I. *A Grief Sanctified*. Ann Arbor, Mich.: Servant Publications, 1997.

———. *A Quest for Godliness: The Puritan Vision of the Christian Life*. Wheaton: Crossway Books, 1990.

———. *Rediscovering Holiness*. Ann Arbor, Mich.: Servant Publications, 1992.

Pannenberg, Wolfhart. *Christian Spirituality*. Philadelphia: Westminster Press, 1989.

Pascal, Blaise. *Pensées*. New York: Penguin, 1995.

Pentecost, Dwight J. *Designed to Be Like Him*. Chicago: Moody Press, 1966.

Peters, Ted. *Sin: Radical Evil in Soul and Society*. Grand Rapids: Eerdmans, 1994.

Peterson, Eugene. *The Contemplative Pastor: Returning to the Art of Spiritual Direction*. Grand Rapids: Eerdmans, 1989.

———. *Five Smooth Stones for Pastoral Work*. Grand Rapids: Eerdmans, 1980.

———. *A Long Obedience in the Same Direction: Discipleship in an Instant Society*. Downers Grove, Ill.: InterVarsity, 1980.

———. *The Message: The Bible in Contemporary Language*. Colorado Springs: NavPress, 2002.

———. *Subversive Spirituality*. Grand Rapids: Eerdmans, 1997.

———. *The Wisdom of Each Other: A Conversation Between Spiritual Friends*. Grand Rapids: Zondervan, 1998.

Piper, John. *Counted Righteous in Christ*. Wheaton: Crossway Books, 2002.

———. *Desiring God: Meditations of a Christian Hedonist*. Revised and expanded edition. Sisters, Ore.: Multnomah, 2003.

———. *The Legacy of Sovereign Joy*. Wheaton: Crossway Books, 2000.

———. *The Pleasures of God: Meditations on God's Delight in Being God*. Revised and expanded edition. Sisters, Ore.: Multnomah, 2000.

Piper, John, Justin Taylor, and Paul Helseth, eds. *Beyond the Bounds: Open Theism and the Undermining of Biblical Christianity*. Wheaton: Crossway Books, 2003.

Plantinga, Cornelius. *Not the Way It's Supposed to Be: A Breviary of Sin*. Grand Rapids: Eerdmans, 1995.

Powlison, David. "Crucial Issues in Contemporary Biblical Counseling." *Journal of Pastoral Practice* 9, no. 3 (1988): 53-78.

———. "Needs and Idols." *Christianity Today* (May 1994): 21.

———. "Questions at the Crossroads: The Care of Souls and Modern Psychotherapies." Pages 23-61 in *Care for the Soul*. Edited by Mark McMinn and Timothy Phillips. Downers Grove, Ill.: InterVarsity, 2001.

———. *Seeing with New Eyes: Counseling and the Human Condition Through the Lens of Scripture*. Phillipsburg, N.J.: Presbyterian & Reformed Publishing, 2003.

Preisker, H. "*misthapodotēs*." Pages 599-605 in *Theological Dictionary of the New Testament*. Abridged edition. Grand Rapids: Eerdmans, 1992.

Pyne, Robert. *Humanity and Sin: The Creation, Fall, and Redemption of Humanity*. Nashville: Word Publishing, 1999.

Ramsey, Paul. *Basic Christian Ethics*. Louisville: John Knox Press, 1993.

Roberts, Robert, and Mark Talbot, eds. *Limning the Psyche: Explorations in Christian Psychology*. Grand Rapids: Eerdmans, 1997.

Robertson, A. T. *Word Pictures in the New Testament*. Concise edition. Nashville: Holman, 2000.

Robinson, John A. T. *The Body: A Study in Pauline Theology*. London: SCM Press, 1952.

Robinson, H. Wheeler. *The Christian Doctrine of Man*. Edinburg: T&T Clark, 1911.

———. *Corporate Personality in Ancient Israel*. Philadelphia: Fortress Press, 1964.

———. "Hebrew Psychology." In *The People and the Book*. Edited by Arthur Peake. Oxford: Clarendon Press, 1925.

———. "Hebrew Psychology in Relation to Pauline Anthropology." In *Mansfield College Essays*. London: Hodder & Stoughton, 1909.

Rolheiser, Ronald. *The Holy Longing*. New York: Doubleday, 1999.

Rollins, Wayne. *Soul and Psyche: The Bible in Psychological Perspective*. Minneapolis: Fortress Press, 1999.

Ross, Hugh. *Beyond the Cosmos*. Colorado Springs: NavPress, 1996.

———. *Creation and Time*. Colorado Springs: NavPress, 1994.

———. *The Creator and the Cosmos*. Colorado Springs: NavPress, 1993.

Ruffing, Janet. *Spiritual Direction: Beyond the Beginnings*. New York: Paulist Press, 2000.

Russell, Bertrand. *Why I Am Not a Christian: And Other Essays on Religion and Related Subjects*. New York: Simon & Schuster, 1957.

Rust, Eric. *Covenant and Hope*. Waco, Texaso: Word Publishing, 1972.

Ryken, Leland. *How to Read the Bible as Literature*. Grand Rapids: Zondervan, 1984.

———. *The Literature of the Bible*. Grand Rapids: Zondervan, 1974.

———. *Words of Life: A Literary Introduction to the New Testament*. Grand Rapids: Baker, 1987.

———. *Worldly Saints: The Puritans as They Really Were*. Grand Rapids: Zondervan, 1986.

Sawyer, Joy. *The Art of the Soul: Meditations for the Christian Spirit*. Nashville: Broadman & Holman, 2000.

———. *Dancing to the Heartbeat of Redemption: The Creative Process of Spiritual Growth*. Downers Grove, Ill.: InterVarsity, 2000.

Sayers, Dorothy. *The Mind of the Maker*. San Francisco: Harper, 1987.

Scaer, D. "The Concept of *Anfechtungen* in Luther's Thought." *Concordia Theological Quarterly* 47 (1983): 15-30.

———. "Sanctification in Lutheran Theology." *Concordia Theological Quarterly* 49, no. 2 (1985): 15-30.

Schaeffer, Francis. *Genesis in Space and Time*. Downers Grove, Ill.: InterVarsity, 1972.

———. *How Shall We Then Live?* Old Tappan, N.J.: Revell, 1976.

———. *True Spirituality*. Wheaton, Ill.: Tyndale House, 1971.

Schaumburg, Harry. *False Intimacy: Understanding the Struggle of Sexual Addiction*. Colorado Springs: NavPress, 1992.

Scheldrake, Philip. *Spirituality and History*. New York: Orbis Books, 1995.

Schieler, C. *Theory and Practice of the Confessional*. Second edition. New York: Benziger Brothers, 1905.

Schleiner, W. "Renaissance Exampla of Schizophrenia: The Cure by Charity in Luther and Cervantes." *Renaissance and Reformation* 9, no. 3 (1985): 157-176.

Schneider, Bernard. *The World of Unseen Spirits*. Winona Lake, Ind.: BMH Books, 1975.

Schnelle, Udo. *The Human Condition*. Minneapolis: Fortress Press, 1991.

Schon, David. *The Reflective Practitioner: How Professionals Think in Action*. New York: SCM Press, 1974.

Scougal, Henry. *The Life of God in the Soul of Man*. Ross-Shire, Scotland: Christian Focus Publications, 1948.

Shaw, Luci. *Polishing the Petoskey Stone*. Wheaton: Harold Shaw, 1990.

———. *Water My Soul: Cultivating the Interior Life*. Grand Rapids: Zondervan, 1998.

Shields, Harry, and Gary Bredfeldt. *Caring for Souls: Counseling Under the Authority of Scripture*. Chicago: Moody Press, 2001.

Shive, David. *Night Shift: God Works in the Dark Hours of Life*. Lincoln, Neb.: Back to the Bible Publishing, 2001.

Shuster, Marguerite. *Power, Pathology, and Paradox: The Dynamics of Good and Evil*. Grand Rapids: Zondervan, 1987.

Silva, Moises. *Biblical Words and Their Meanings: An Introduction to Lexical Semantics*. Grand Rapids: Zondervan, 1983.

Simpson, E. K., and F. F. Bruce. *Commentary on the Epistles to the Ephesians and Colossians*. In *The New International Commentary on the New Testament*. Grand Rapids: Eerdmans, 1957.

Smith, David. *With Willful Intent: A Theology of Sin*. Wheaton: Victor Books, 1994.

Smith, P., ed. *The Life and Letters of Martin Luther*. New York: Barnes & Noble, 1911.

Smith, P., and C. Jacobs, eds. *Luther's Correspondence and Other Contemporary Letters*. 2 vols. Philadelphia: Lutheran Publication Society, 1918.

Smith, Paul. *Enjoying God Forever: The Westminster Confession*. Chicago: Moody Press, 1998.

Smith, Robert. *The Christian Counselor's Medical Desk Reference*. Stanley, N.C.: Timeless Texts, 2000.

Southard, Samuel. *Theology and Therapy: The Wisdom of God in the Context of Friendship*. Dallas: Word Publishing, 1989.

Southern Baptist Convention. In *Creeds of the Churches*. Edited by John Leith. Richmond, Va.: John Knox Press, 1979.

Sproul, R. C. *The Soul's Quest for God: Satisfying the Hunger for Spiritual Communion with God*. Wheaton: Tyndale House, 1992.

Stafford, Tim. "The Therapeutic Revolution: How Christian Counseling Is Changing the Church." *Christianity Today* (May 13, 1993): 24-32.

Steinmetz, David. *Luther in Context*. Grand Rapids: Baker, 1995.

Stott, John. *The Cross of Christ*. Downers Grove, Ill.: InterVarsity, 1986.

———. *Romans: God's Good News for the World*. Downers Grove, Ill.: InterVarsity, 1985.

———. *The Epistles of John*. London: Tyndale House, 1964.

Strathmann, H. "*latreuō*." Pages 503-504 in *Theological Dictionary of the New Testament*. Abridged edition. Grand Rapids: Eerdmans, 1992.

Strohl, J. E. "Luther's Fourteen Consolations." *Lutheran Quarterly* 3 (1989): 169-182.

Stroup, George. *The Promise of Narrative Theology*. Eugene, Ore.: Wipf & Stock Publishers, 1997.

Styron, W. *Darkness Visible*. London: Picador, 1991.

Tan, Siang-Yang. *Lay Counseling: Equipping Christians for a Helping Ministry*. Grand Rapids: Zondervan, 1991.

Tan, Siang-Yang, and John Ortberg. *Understanding Depression: A Short-Term Structured Model*. Grand Rapids: Baker, 1995.

Tappert, G. *Luther: Letters of Spiritual Counsel*. Vol. 18 in *The Library of Christian Classics*. Edited by J. Baillie, J. McNeil, and H. van Dusen. Philadelphia: Westminster Press, 1955.

Thayer, Robert. *The Origin of Everyday Moods*. New York: Oxford University Press, 1996.

Thomas, Gary. *The Glorious Pursuit: Embracing the Virtues of Christ*. Colorado Springs: NavPress, 1998.

Thomas, W. H. Griffith. *St. Paul's Epistle to the Romans*. Grand Rapids: Kregel, 1996.

Tiessen, Terrance. *Providence and Prayer: How Does God Work in the World?* Downers Grove, Ill.: InterVarsity, 2000.

Tolkien, J. R. R. *The Hobbit*. New York: Ballantine Books, 1977.

———. *The Silmarillion*. New York: Ballantine Books, 1985.

Torrance, Thomas. *Calvin's Doctrine of Man*. Grand Rapids: Eerdmans, 1977.

Tournier, Paul. *Creative Suffering*. San Francisco: Harper, 1981.

———. *Guilt and Grace*. Translated by Arthur Heathcote. San Francisco: Harper, 1983.

Tozer, A. W. *The Knowledge of the Holy*. San Francisco: Harper, 1961.

———. *The Pursuit of God*. Wheaton: Tyndale House, 1971.

Travis, Stephen. *I Believe in the Second Coming*. Grand Rapids: Eerdmans, 1982.

Treasmontant, Claude. *A Study of Hebrew Thought*. Translated by M. F. Gibson. New York: Desclee, 1960.

Tripp, David. *Instruments in the Redeemer's Hands*. Phillipsburg, N.J.: Presbyterian & Reformed Publishing, 2002.

Tugwell, Simon. *Prayer: Living with God*. Philadelphia: Temple University Press, 1980.

Unger, Merrill. *Demons in the World Today*. Wheaton: Tyndale House, 1971.

Verduin, Leonard. *Somewhat Less Than God: The Biblical View of Man*. Grand Rapids: Eerdmans, 1970.

Von Rad, Gerhard. *Genesis: A Commentary*. Louisville: John Knox Press, 1995.

Vos, Geerhardus. *Biblical Theology: Old and New Testaments*. Grand Rapids: Eerdmans, 1948.

Waite, Terry. *Taken on Trust*. Chicago: Quill, 1995.

Wakefield, Gordon S., ed. *The Westminster Dictionary of Christian Spirituality*. Philadelphia: Westminster Press, 1983.

Walter, John, and Jane Peller. *Becoming Solution-Focused in Brief Therapy*. New York: Brunner/Mazel Publishers, 1992.

Walvoord, John. *The Blessed Hope and the Tribulation*. Grand Rapids: Zondervan, 1969.

Wangerin, Walter. *The Book of God: The Bible as a Novel*. Grand Rapids: Zondervan, 1996.

———. *Mourning into Dancing*. Grand Rapids: Zondervan, 1992.

Warfield, B. B. *The Person and Work of Christ*. Philadelphia: Presbyterian & Reformed Publishing, 1950.

Watson, Jeffrey. *Biblical Counseling for Today: A Handbook for Those Who Counsel from Scripture*. Nashville: Word Publishing, 2000.

Weisinger, Hendrie. *Emotional Intelligence at Work*. San Francisco: Jossey Bass, 1998.

Welch, Ed. *Blame It on the Brain?: Distinguishing Chemical Imbalances, Brain Disorders, and Disobedience*. Phillipsburg, N.J.: Presbyterian & Reformed Publishing, 1998.

———. *When People Are Big and God Is Small*. Phillipsburg, N.J.: Presbyterian & Reformed Publishing, 1997.

Wells, David. *The Search for Salvation*. Downers Grove, Ill.: InterVarsity, 1972.

Wenham, Gordon. *Genesis 1-15*. Waco, Texas: Word Publishing, 1987.

Westberg, Granger. *Good Grief*. Philadelphia: Fortress Press, 1971.

Westermann, Claus. *Genesis 1-11*. Minneapolis: Fortress Press, 1994.

White, M., and D. Epston. *Narrative Means to Therapeutic Ends*. New York: W. W. Norton, 1990.

Whitlock, Glenn. "The Structure of Personality in Hebrew Psychology." *Interpretations* 14 (January 1960): 3-13.

Whitney, Donald. *Spiritual Disciplines for the Christian Life*. Colorado Springs: NavPress, 1991.

Wicks, Robert, and Richard Parsons. *Clinical Handbook of Pastoral Counseling*. 2 vols. New York: Paulist Press, 1993.

Wicks, Robert, and Thomas Rodgerson. *Companions in Hope: The Art of Christian Caring*. New York: Paulist Press, 1998.

Wiersbe, Warren. *Preaching and Teaching with Imagination*. Wheaton: Victor Books, 1994.

Wilkins, Michael. *In His Image*. Colorado Springs: NavPress, 1998.

Willard, Dallas. *The Divine Conspiracy: Rediscovering Our Hidden Life in God*. San Francisco: Harper, 1998.

———. *Renovation of the Heart: Putting on the Character of Christ.* Colorado Springs: NavPress, 2002.

———. *The Spirit of the Disciplines: Understanding How God Changes Lives.* San Francisco: Harper, 1991.

Wolff, Hans. *Anthropology of the Old Testament.* Translated by Margaret Kohl. London: SCM Press, 1974.

Wolpert, Lewis. *Malignant Sadness: The Anatomy of Depression.* New York: The Free Press, 1999.

Wolterstorff, Nicholas. *Lament for a Son.* Grand Rapids: Eerdmans, 2002.

Wright, Alan D. *Lover of My Soul: Delighting in God's Passionate Love.* Sisters, Ore.: Multnomah, 1998.

Wuest, Kenneth. *Word Studies from the Greek New Testament.* 3 Vols. Grand Rapids: Eerdmans, 1973.

Yamauchi, Edwin. "*hāgar.*" Page 263 in vol. 1 of *Theological Wordbook of the Old Testament.* Edited by Laird Harris, Gleason Archer, and Bruce Waltke. 2 vols. Chicago: Moody Press, 1981.

Yancey, Philip. *The Bible Jesus Read.* Grand Rapids: Zondervan, 1999.

———. *Disappointment with God.* New York: Harper, 1992.

———. *The Jesus I Never Knew.* Grand Rapids: Zondervan, 1995.

———. *Rumors of Another World.* Grand Rapids: Zondervan, 2003.

———. *Where Is God When It Hurts?* New York: Harper, 1990.

Zemek, George. *A Biblical Theology of the Doctrines of Sovereign Grace: Exegetical Considerations of Key Anthropological, Hamartiological, and Soteriological Terms and Motifs.* Little Rock: BTDSG, 2002.

Zuck, Roy, ed. *A Biblical Theology of the New Testament.* Chicago: Moody Press, 1994.

Author and Subject Index

Scripture Index

Scriptures in Boxes throughout *Soul Physicians* are not indexed.

**You've Learned from the *Theology* of *Soul Physicians*
Now Grow through the *Methodology* of *Spiritual Friends***

Spiritual Friends:
A Methodology of Soul Care and Spiritual Direction

You love people and you love God's Word. How do you relate your two loves? *Spiritual Friends* provides a biblically relevant **training manual** and a relationally practical **workbook** for relating God's truth to human relationships. Whether you're a loving layperson, a caring pastor, a competent professional Christian counselor, or a student-in-training, *Spiritual Friends* will equip you to master the personal ministry of the Word. Enrich your spiritual friendships with thousands of illustrative interactions and hundreds of skill-building exercises that teach you how to:

- ◆ **Sustain** people so they know that *it's normal to hurt.*
- ◆ **Heal** people so they know that *it's possible to hope.*
- ◆ **Reconcile** people so they know that *it's horrible to sin, but wonderful to be forgiven.*
- ◆ **Guide** people so they know that *it's supernatural to mature.*

To order *Spiritual Friends*, visit us at: www.bmhbooks.com.

About RPM Ministries

Robert W. Kellemen, Ph.D., founded *RPM Ministries* in 2000. *RPM* is Bob's acronym for *Resurrection Power Multipliers* which takes its name from Paul's longing in Philippians 3:10 to know the power of Christ's resurrection.

RPM Ministries exists to empower Christians toward Christlikeness by relating God's truth to human relationships. Through *RPM Ministries*, Bob and others offer conferences and seminars on Spiritual Friendship, Soul Care and Spiritual Direction, African American Church History, Marriage, and Parenting.

To learn more about *RPM Ministries*, visit us at: www.rpmministries.org.

To discuss scheduling a conference, e-mail us at: bookings@rpmministries.org.